Lawfully Using Autonomous Weapon Technologies

Jonathan Kwik

Lawfully Using Autonomous Weapon Technologies

ASSER PRESS

Springer

Jonathan Kwik
TMC Asser Instituut
The Hague, The Netherlands

ISBN 978-94-6265-630-7 ISBN 978-94-6265-631-4 (eBook)
https://doi.org/10.1007/978-94-6265-631-4

Published by T.M.C. ASSER PRESS, The Hague, The Netherlands www.asserpress.nl
Produced and distributed for T.M.C. ASSER PRESS by Springer-Verlag Berlin Heidelberg

This T.M.C. ASSER PRESS imprint is published by the registered company Springer-Verlag GmbH, DE, part of Springer Nature.
The registered company address is: Heidelberger Platz 3, 14197 Berlin, Germany

Contents

Abbreviations

3D	Three-dimensional
AADA	Acquisition, Analysis, Decision, Action
AC	Accountability (*MHC Facet*)
AGI	Artificial General Intelligence
AI	Artificial Intelligence
AIV	Adviesraad Internationale Vraagstukken (Netherlands)
APC	Armoured Personnel Carrier
API	Additional Protocol I to the Geneva Conventions
AS	Attack Scope
AV	Autonomous Vehicle
AW	Awareness (*MHC Facet*)
AWA	Assessment Awareness (*MHC Facet*)
AW_C	Contextual Awareness (*MHC Facet*)
AW_I	Interaction Awareness (*MHC Facet*)
AWS	Autonomous Weapon System
AW_T	Technical Awareness (*MHC Facet*)
BCC	Broader Chain Candidate for liability
CC	Context Control
CC_L	Linked Control (*MHC Facet*)
CCo	Operational Control (*MHC Facet*)
CC_S	System Control (*MHC Facet*)
CCW	Convention on Certain Conventional Weapons
CCW-I	First Protocol to the Convention on Certain Conventional Weapons
CCW-II	Second Protocol to the Convention on Certain Conventional Weapons
CCW-IV	Fourth Protocol to the Convention on Certain Conventional Weapons
CDE	Collateral Damage Estimation
CDEM	Collateral Damage Estimation Methodology
CEP	Circular Error Probable
CIV	Civilian
CIWS	Close-In Weapon System
CPU	Central Processing Unit

C-RAM	Counter Rocket, Artillery, Mortar
D	Accused
DARPA	Defense Advanced Research Projects Agency (US)
DDD	Dirty, Dull, Dangerous
DMZ	Demilitarised Zone
DoD	Department of Defense (US)
DPH	Direct Participation in Hostilities
EU	European Union
GAN	Generative Adversarial Network
GARD	Guaranteeing AI Robustness Against Deception (DARPA agency)
GGE	Group of Governmental Experts (CCW Conference Geneva)
GPS	Global Positioning System
GPU	Graphics Processing Unit
HAF	Haftar Armed Forces (Libya)
HARM	High-speed Anti-Radiation Missile
HFACS	Human Factors Analysis and Classification System (US DoD)
HIV	Human Immunodeficiency Virus
HLEG	High-Level Expert Group (EU)
HMI	Human-Machine Interface
HPCR	Humanitarian Policy and Conflict Research
HQ	Headquarters
IAC	International Armed Conflict
ICC	International Criminal Court
ICJ	International Court of Justice
ICL	International Criminal Law
ICRC	International Committee of the Red Cross
ICTY	International Criminal Tribunal for the Former Yugoslavia
IH	Incidental Harm (collateral damage)
IHL	International Humanitarian Law
IOE	Intended Operational Environment
ISR	Intelligence, Surveillance, Reconnaissance
JCE	Joint Criminal Enterprise
LAR	Lethal Autonomous Robot
LAWS	Lethal Autonomous Weapon System
LC	Linked Control
LOAC	Law of Armed Conflict
MA	Military Advantage
MHC	Meaningful Human Control
ML	Machine Learning
MOD	Ministry of Defence (UK)
MoP	Measure of Performance
NASA	National Aeronautics and Space Administration (US)
NATO	North Atlantic Treaty Organisation
NGO	Non-Governmental Organisation
NIAC	Non-International Armed Conflict

NLP	Natural Language Processing
OOD	Out-of-distribution
OODA	Observe, Orient, Decide, Act
$\mathbb{P}$	Probability
PGM	Precision-Guided Munition
POW	Prisoner of War
PR	Predictability (*MHC Facet*)
RGB	Red Green Blue
ROC	Receiver Operating Characteristic
ROE	Rules of Engagement
RSK	Republic of Serbian Krajina
TEV&V	Test, Evaluation, Verification and Validation
TTP	Tactics, Techniques, and Procedures
UAV	Unmanned Aerial Vehicle
UK	United Kingdom
UN	United Nations
US	United States
USAF	United States Air Force
V	Victim
Wp	Weapon
WS	Weapon Selection (*MHC Facet*)
XAI	eXplainable AI

Part I
Framing the Study

Chapter 1
Introduction

Contents

Abstract Artificial intelligence (AI) has seen a surge in relevance. In the early 2020s alone, so-called autonomous weapon systems (AWS) have seen use in Libya, Ukraine and Gaza, and their relevance will only continue to increase. AWS have been subject to significant academic, diplomatic and policy discussion, but a majority of these works focus on high-level concerns, such as whether international humanitarian law (IHL) can be programmed into AWS, or how States should fulfil their weapon review obligations when AWS are involved. In contrast, the perspective of the commander—the end-user ultimately making the decision to employ AWS—is underappreciated. Their role is nevertheless crucial: commanders, due to their proximity to the battlefield, are the best positioned to ensure that weapon systems remain under control, play a decisive part in ensuring that IHL obligations remain upheld, and bear primary legal responsibility for weapons release. This chapter introduces the main question explored in this book—*how commanders should navigate the technological particularities of AI to discharge their targeting obligations when using AI*—and the analytical steps that must be taken to explore this matter. It also introduces both the technology under consideration and the different actors involved. Finally, it clarifies a crucial approach taken in this book, namely the presumption of goodwill: instead of focusing on malicious actors using the technology badly, this book prefers the constructive focus of empowering good-faith actors to *use the*

J. Kwik, *Lawfully Using Autonomous Weapon Technologies*,
https://doi.org/10.1007/978-94-6265-631-4_1

technology better. The chapter ends with a roadmap that outlines the future chapters of the book.

Keywords Autonomous weapon system · Artificial intelligence · Machine learning · Commander · Targeting · International humanitarian law · Conduct of hostilities · Goodwill · Weapon review · Control · Predictability · Military operations · Use-of-force

1.1 Aim of This Book

Artificial intelligence (AI) has taken off. What only fifteen years ago seemed to be a futuristic and niche technology now pervades daily life. Algorithms analyse and predict the preferences of millions of users of online services. Generative AI trained on thousands of works of art produce images that look remarkably human and authentic. Publicly-available large language models like Chat-GPT are assisting professors in creating exam questions, helping students write essays, and even bamboozling lawyers with fake case-law.[1] Border checkpoints and law enforcement avail themselves of facial recognition to identify persons of interest and threats. Media awareness classes warn of not being fooled by deepfakes, while social media companies struggle to manage AI-generated disinformation on their platforms. AI has rapidly embedded itself into most aspects of life, and frequently, legal and ethical frameworks struggle to keep up. Who owns the copyright to AI-generated works?[2] What are the privacy implications of using biometric facial recognition?[3] To what extent are online platforms responsible for removing synthetic disinformation?[4]

AI in the military domain has traced a very similar timeline in terms of both relevancy and public scrutiny. AI is everywhere. States readily emphasise the importance of AI for strategic and tactical success,[5] and invest significantly into research and development.[6] In the early 2020s alone, many high-profile uses have been reported. AI has been used in the Russo-Ukrainian war as a key tool for data analysis[7] and possibly even for autonomous targeting using loitering drones.[8] The Israel-Gaza conflict featured the Israeli army leveraging AI to calculate missile interception

---

[1] See Novak 2023.

[2] See Andrini 2018.

[3] Sometimes, conflicts between two competing legal frameworks even arise. See e.g. West 2022, discussing the desirability of the use of biometrics from the perspective of privacy (human rights law) and accurate targeting (international humanitarian law).

[4] See The Parliamentarian 2023.

[5] E.g. Defense Science Board 2012, p. 1 (US); Associated Press et al. 2017 (Russia); Gao 2017 (China); Ministère des Armées 2019, p. 9 (France); Boulanin et al. 2020, p. 1 (EU).

[6] Wilson 2020, p. 125; Hofman 2020.

[7] Bendett 2023.

[8] See Kallenborn 2022.

trajectories using the Iron Dome, while simultaneously relying on programs such as the Gospel to exponentially increase the production of targets in Gaza.[9] Against retreating HAF troops in Libya in 2020, the Kargu-22 was deployed, which was "programmed to attack targets without requiring data connectivity between the operator and the munition".[10] As in the civil domain, AI has firmly lodged itself into the domain of military operations, and like with civil AI, the legal and ethical ramifications of such technologies being used have raised concern.

Of all military AI applications, so-called autonomous weapon systems (AWS) have drawn the most academic and policy attention. The incorporation of modern AI techniques, such as machine learning, deep neural networks and large language models, into weapon systems is purported to bring many military advantages,[11] but also introduces a vast array of challenges unique to the technology. As such, AWS have drawn the interest of the United Nations,[12] the International Committee of the Red Cross (ICRC),[13] States[14] and non-governmental organisations (NGOs).[15] AWS have been scrutinised from a broad range of perspectives, including the fields of computer engineering,[16] disarmament,[17] ethics[18] and diplomatic and strategic

---

[9] See Davies et al. 2023.

[10] United Nations 2021.

[11] For an extended list of purported advantages the technology can provide, see Sect. 10.2.

[12] E.g. Heyns 2013; Group of Governmental Experts on Lethal Autonomous Weapons Systems (GGE on LAWS) 2023.

[13] E.g. ICRC 2013, 2018.

[14] E.g. UK House of Lords 2018, p. 104; Ministère des Armées 2019, p. 9; Li and Xie 2019; High-Level Expert Group On Artificial Intelligence 2019b; Adviesraad Internationale Vraagstukken and Commissie van Advies inzake Volkenrechtelijke Vraagstukken 2015.

[15] E.g. Article 36 2013; Human Rights Watch 2012; Garcia 2014.

[16] See e.g. Arkin 2009.

[17] Significant debate is still ongoing as to whether AWS as a technology should be banned through a regulatory or prohibitory treaty. Prohibitory calls first gained traction in 2012 by the initiative of arms control movements and some NGOs. E.g. Asaro 2012, p. 688; Human Rights Watch 2012. See more generally van den Boogaard and Roorda 2021, p. 423. At the time of writing, the desirability of internationally regulating AWS technology is still discussed annually at the Group of Governmental Experts working under the Convention for Certain Conventional Weapons in Geneva. See Group of Governmental Experts on Lethal Autonomous Weapons Systems (GGE on LAWS) 2023.

[18] For a summary of popular ethical arguments, see: Tamburrini 2016; ICRC 2018; Santoni de Sio and van den Hoven 2018, p. 2; Eklund 2020, pp. 32–34.

policy.[19] Within legal literature, AWS[20] have been discussed in the context of international humanitarian law (IHL),[21] the weapon review obligation,[22] *ius ad bellum*,[23] human rights law,[24] State responsibility, tort liability and international criminal law,[25] amongst others.

Of all legal issues regarding AWS, the following three concerns are arguably among the most frequently raised:

- How can AWS be adequately controlled on the battlefield?[26]
- How can core IHL principles related to the conduct of hostilities (e.g. distinction, proportionality, precautions) be respected when AWS are involved?[27]
- Who can be held criminally responsible for war crimes involving AWS?[28]

One commonality shared by a majority of legal research on AWS, including the sources referenced above, is that their primary addressees are relatively removed from the actual battlefield. The works are generally addressed at high-level entities (States, international organisations, diplomats and corporations[29]), parties involved in development or adoption (manufacturers, programmers and weapons reviewers) or post-hoc adjudicators (tribunals, prosecutors and judges).

---

[19] E.g. Moyes 2019, p. 2; Fornasier 2021, pp. 80–83.

[20] An editorial choice is to abbreviate both ‘autonomous weapon system’ (singular) and ‘autonomous weapon systems’ (plural) identically as ‘AWS’, since the grammatical number is almost always evident from the context. Additionally, ‘AWSs’ is cumbersome to pronounce in abbreviated form (ey-doubleyou-*esses*).

[21] ‘International humanitarian law’ (IHL) is used in this book instead of ‘law of armed conflict’ (LOAC) as a simple matter of preference.

[22] See e.g. Meier 2019, pp. 309–315; Defense Science Board 2012, p. 62; Holland Michel 2021, p. 21. The review obligation requires that States conduct a review for each weapon prior to adoption to ensure it can be used in accordance with IHL. It is generally considered as Customary IHL. See Schmitt M N (ed) 2017, Tallinn Manual 2.0 on the International Law Applicable to Cyber Warfare. 2nd edn. Cambridge University Press, Cambridge (Tallinn Manual 2.0), p. 465; Parks 2005, p. 57. The obligation is codified in Protocol Additional to the Geneva Conventions of 12 August 1949, and relating to the Protection of Victims of International Armed Conflicts, adopted 8 June 1977, entered into force 7 December 1978, 1125 UNTS 3 (API), Article 36, although there is disagreement as to whether this reflects the customary rule. Cf. Jevglevskaja 2018. The US DoD even adopted a specific directive for reviewing AWS, which is good practice more States are advised to emulate. See US Department of Defense 2023.

[23] E.g. Deeks 2021; Henderson et al. 2017, pp. 366–367; Heyns 2013, paras 57–62.

[24] See e.g. Eklund 2020, pp. 32–46; Heyns 2013, para 31.

[25] See Sect. 11.2.

[26] E.g. Article 36 2013, p. 3; ICRC 2016, pp. 79–83; UK 2020, para 1.

[27] E.g. Kalmanovitz 2016, pp. 145–148; Herbach 2012, p. 18; ICRC 2018, para 21.

[28] This is more commonly discussed under the heading of the ‘responsibility gap’. E.g. ICRC 2018, para 22; Bo 2021, p. 276; Jain 2021, p. 298.

[29] *Ius ad bellum*, disarmament and human rights law all have the State as the primary subject; AWS-specific regulatory or disarmament treaties would involve States, international organisations, diplomats and NGOs amongst others; and civil liability would involve the military organisation and corporations as the primary tortfeasors.

One perspective remains relatively underappreciated: that of the military commander ultimately in charge of ordering the deployment of AWS at the operational level. The role of these persons is nevertheless crucial. Due to their proximity to the battlefield, operational commanders are the best positioned to ensure that weapon systems remain under control, play a decisive part in ensuring that IHL obligations remain upheld,[30] and are likely also the first target for criminal liability if any harm indeed does result from AWS use.[31] Although it is true that IHL as a branch of international law has the State as its main addressee, actual operational commanders in the field play a major role in ensuring that these obligations remain upheld.[32] As the Commentary to the Additional Protocols also submits,

> the role of commanders is decisive … [T]he necessary measures for the proper application of the Conventions and the Protocol *must be taken at the level of the troops*, so that a fatal gap between the undertakings entered into by Parties to the conflict and the conduct of individuals is avoided. At this level, *everything depends on commanders*, and without their conscientious supervision, general legal requirements are unlikely to be effective.[33]

While some works have explored operational-level IHL rules (e.g. those related to distinction, proportionality, precautions and warnings) and their application to AWS, many focus on the question of whether and how the *systems* can properly be designed to perform these IHL tests.[34] However, IHL "impose[s] obligations on persons. These rules do not impose obligations on the weapons themselves".[35] Under this view—one taken by many States and authoritative commentators,[36] and the one also adopted in this book[37]—machines cannot be considered as 'implementing' IHL: they are only the means through which human commanders can do so. Irrespective of

---

[30] See US Office of General Counsel of the Department of Defense 2015, Law of War Manual, Updated December 2016. US Department of Defense, Washington D.C. (US Law of War Manual), sct 5.10.2; Australia 2006, Law of Armed Conflict. Defence Publishing Service, Canberra, Australian Defence Doctrine Publication 06.4 (Australian Law of Armed Conflict Manual), para 5.61; Schmitt 2011, p. 41.

[31] The commander ordering an attack is usually considered as the first candidate for criminal liability if this act is suspected to constitute a war crime. See Thurnher 2014, p. 226; Grut 2013, p. 19.

[32] Gill and Fleck 2010, sct 1.02.3; Bothe et al. 2013, pp. 598–599.

[33] Sandoz et al. 1987, para 3550 (emphasis added).

[34] For example, extensive debate has formed around the question of whether and how AWS can properly verify targets (e.g. Kastan 2013, pp. 59–61; Henderson et al. 2017, pp. 345–347), minimise risk to the civilian population (e.g. Boothby 2018, p. 149; Winter 2020, pp. 265–271); and perform proportionality calculations (e.g. Winter 2020, pp. 259–265; Kurosaki 2020, pp. 415–418; Arkin 2009).

[35] US Law of War Manual, above n. 30, sct 6.5.9.3.

[36] There is broad consensus that this should be the starting point for any debate involving AWS. See Group of Governmental Experts on Lethal Autonomous Weapons Systems (GGE on LAWS) 2019, Annex IV Principle (b); Sassòli 2014, p. 323; ICRC 2018, para 32; Scharre 2018, p. 269; Roorda 2015, p. 163; Cherry and Johnson 2020, pp. 17–19; UK 2020, para 10.

[37] This book takes the the position that machines cannot be considered as 'implementing' IHL; they are only the means through which human commanders can do so. Alternative views exist that propose to impart some legal or moral agency to AWS. These works are discussed in this book as opposing perspectives.

whether the systems can *perform functions consistent with* rules such as distinction and proportionality, therefore, "the commander, not the weapon system, makes legal determinations".[38]

However, there is a danger in merely *asserting* that an AWS "always remain[s] a weapons system that the commander ordered into action and for which the commander remains ultimately responsible".[39] To the prospective AWS user, using this technology responsibly does not come without difficulties. As AI becomes increasingly reliable and versatile, the systems in which they are embedded simultaneously become less predictable, less controllable and less comprehensible for the human user. These technical complexities, in combination with the already demanding working environment of military operations,[40] can lead commanders to one of two undesirable situations: military inefficiency due to hesitance in employing AWS where their use would be advantageous and appropriate, or violating rules of IHL.[41]

Despite these difficulties (and unlike what some may assert), AWS are not necessarily uncontrollable.[42] As with any other weapon technology, their behaviour can be understood, their effects limited, and the accompanying risks to the civilian population mitigated. The relative novelty of the technology at the time of writing, however, presents some practical obstacles. It is likely that:

- many of the unique technical aspects of AI are not well-understood by its prospective users (i.e. military commanders);
- minimal guidance is available to help commanders determine how to interpret existing IHL rules related to the conduct of hostilities in light of AWS technology;
- little if any practice can be drawn from as to how the targeting process should be conducted when AWS are involved; and
- no clear and practical policy has been developed that provides the commander with a consistent methodology which ensures all important factors are taken into consideration when making legal and operational analyses involving AWS.

These limitations may bring even good-faith commanders to use AWS in ways not entirely compliant with targeting rules, to the detriment of the civilian population.

---

[38] Sleesman and Huntley 2019, p. 34.

[39] Toscano 2015, p. 220.

[40] See Sect. 3.4.2.

[41] This is a practical translation of phenomena called undertrust and overtrust respectively. Undertrust occurs when a human user's "trust is less than what is appropriate given the reliability and capabilities of the technology", and leads to inefficiencies because a societally-beneficial technology is not used to its optimal extent. Fallon and Blaha 2018, p. 245. Overtrust is the "unwarranted over-reliance on automation", and can lead to societal harm because an autonomous agent is given more trust than it deserves given its capabilities. Hawley 2007, p. 4.

[42] This idea of AWS being inherently uncontrollable is prevalent in the popular debate; see Scharre 2018, pp. 241, 264. An observation by Kroes and Verbeek seems fitting to cite here in response: "It is rather curious (and telling!) that in stories that stress the positive role of technology there appears to be a tendency to praise humans for their wise use of technology, whereas in stories that stress its negative role technology often takes the blame by depicting it in some form of a bad and uncontrollable demon as in the story about the Golem." Kroes and Verbeek 2014, p. 3.

This book argues that the position that commanders ultimately remain "responsible for everything their command does or fails to do", including the use of AWS,[43] must be substantiated by solutions to abovementioned difficulties and legal indeterminacies that are both theoretically sound and actionable in practice: an exercise that few have undertaken.

To address this gap, this book centres its discussion on the military commander ultimately in charge of ordering the release of AWS at the operational level. This person, let us call them ***Deployer***,[44] is the 'protagonist' of this book. Throughout this work, we shall explore the particularities of AWS technology from their eyes, and try to answer how, at the operational level when guns are already blazing, Deployer should navigate both the novel technical aspects of AI and interpret IHL rules related to the conduct of hostilities.[45]

This Deployer-centric perspective reframes the three common questions listed above in a new light that is less commonly seen in literature and discourse:

- How can Deployer effectively control AWS on the battlefield?
- How can Deployer ensure their use of AWS remains compliant with IHL rules related to the conduct of hostilities?
- Under what conditions is Deployer criminally liable for war crimes involving AWS?

Answering these questions carries evident practical benefits: it provides both theoretical and practical clarification with regard to how the law regulates attacks involving AWS at the operational level. However, Deployers are by no means this book's only beneficiaries. The military institution, States and policymakers can equally draw benefit from understanding the difficulties and challenges their commanders may face with regard to AWS, and thereby provide appropriate guidance, training and policy to facilitate operational decision-making. Finally, this book intends to advance the theoretical discussion by decrypting and systematising many difficult questions related to AWS and IHL, and by demystifying many false or over-sensationalised conceptions related to the technology which are often found in the popular debate, thereby recentring the academic and policy debate on those issues which truly matter in the near future.

With the main focus of this book now established, the remainder of this chapter provides some further clarification as to what is actually meant by 'AWS' (Sect. 1.2)

---

[43] US Department of the Army 2020, sct 2.1.b. See also Li and Xie 2019; Dinstein 2018, para 23; Beard 2014, p. 654.

[44] See Sect. 1.3.1 for a complete definition.

[45] Outside of the use of AWS in the context of the conduct of hostilities, other applications of AWS could be envisaged, such as using AWS for guarding prisoners-of-war, counterinsurgency operations, occupation, etc. This book does not focus on these situations. The basic principle nevertheless remains the same, i.e. that the AWS-user must apply an existing framework to a challenging new technology that may require complex legal analysis or interpretation. Similar studies as the one conducted in this book may be desirable to provide legal clarity to the AWS-user in those situations, as well.

and the main actors involved in its use (Sect. 1.3). It also addresses a possible counterpoint readers may raise, namely that instead of asking how AWS should be employed *correctly* by good-faith users, we should instead concern ourselves with the threat of the technology being used *incorrectly* by malicious ones (Sect. 1.4). Finally, it explains the structure of the book and provides a preview of the themes to be explored in upcoming chapters (Sect. 1.5).

1.2 The Technology Under Consideration

Much ink has been spilled in literature on how to define AWS[46] and what constitutes an 'autonomous' system.[47] It is thus necessary to clarify early and unambiguously what type of technology this book scrutinises: these are *systems that use data-driven AI*.

AI at the operational level can be utilised in one of two general ways: as decision support[48] or embedded in weapon systems. As the title of this book suggests, we only analyse the latter, specifically the employment of AI for use-of-force functions.[49] However, AI is not a monolith, and has existed in many forms and iterations across the past fifty years.[50] What makes AWS so different from older uses of AI in military use-of-force contexts, that justifies dedicating an entire book to exploring them? The answer is reliance on data.

Data-driven machine learning is what truly separates contemporary AI[51] from older systems that exhibit automatic functionalities.[52] Machine learning "develops in

---

[46] Blank 2019, pp. 328–329; Scharre 2018, pp. 347–349. For a sample of different definitions, see e.g. Scharre and Horowitz 2015, Annex A.

[47] Some authors have developed sensible frameworks that summarise the different approaches used in literature. See, in particular, Scharre 2015; Boulanin 2016; Williams 2015. For a useful taxonomy of levels of autonomy from an engineering perspective, see Parasuraman et al. 2000, p. 287; Cummings 2004, pp. 3–5.

[48] One can think of the use of AI for data collection, sorting and analysing intelligence, logistics support, etc. See e.g. Simon-Michel 2014, para 35; Adviesraad Internationale Vraagstukken and Commissie van Advies inzake Volkenrechtelijke Vraagstukken 2015, p. 13; Defense Science Board 2016, pp. 45–75.

[49] The DoD Defense Science Board refers to this as 'autonomy in force application'. Defense Science Board 2016, p. 60. AI can also be used in weapon systems for non-use-of-force functions, e.g. navigation and mobility, interoperability, and health management. For a framework of different utilities of AI in weapon systems, see Boulanin 2016, pp. 7–8.

[50] For an extended technical explanation of the history of AI, the differences between knowledge-based and data-driven AI, a list of elements unique to modern AI, and how AI 'make' decisions, see Sect. 3.2.

[51] While 'AI' technically can also refer to older, purely symbolic systems, machine learning has become so ubiquitous that 'AI' (when referred to neutrally) usually references machine learning. See UK House of Lords 2018, p. 16. If mentioned without any clarifier, 'AI' as used in this book also refers to modern data-driven AI.

[52] I.e., systems that relied on more symbolic, knowledge-based approaches. See Russell and Norvig 2010, pp. 22–24.

absence of symbolic rules, and involves learning—meaning the extraction of information, and problem solving based on structured or unstructured perceived data … adaptation and reaction to changes, behavioural prediction, etc."[53] Data-driven AI excels in performance,[54] flexibility[55] and the ability to function in complex and difficult-to-model environments,[56] and enabled the use of AI for tasks and environments that were previously too complex to program 'manually'.[57] Yet it is simultaneously the unique properties of these data-driven models which generate the most challenges for future Deployers. While carrying many benefits, data-driven AI is also less predictable,[58] can fail unintuitively,[59] can be brittle,[60] may have its behaviour obscured by the black box phenomenon,[61] and can be vulnerable to very different kinds of enemy countermeasures.[62] Together, these factors must be properly understood and navigated by Deployer.

When speaking of 'AWS' in this book, therefore, these refer to weapon systems *utilising (partial[63]) data-driven AI models* for their use-of-force functions. To differentiate these from other weapons that may also exhibit some independently-functioning properties (note a landmine also detonates autonomously![64]), all these other weapons are referred to together as *legacy systems*.[65]

---

[53] AI Watch Joint Research Centre 2020, p. 11. For a sample of definitions from literature, see Tzimas 2021, p. 45. For an extended explanation, see Sect. 3.2.

[54] Szegedy et al. 2014, 1; Yampolskiy 2019, p. 2.

[55] High-Level Expert Group On Artificial Intelligence 2019a, p. 4; Knight 2017.

[56] US Air Force Office of the Chief Scientist 2015, p. 22; High-Level Expert Group On Artificial Intelligence 2019a, p. 3; Horkoff 2019, p. 386.

[57] Russell and Norvig 2010, p. 693.

[58] Deng 2015, p. 25; ICRC 2019, p. 10; Boulanin 2016, p. 24.

[59] See Chap. 5.

[60] See Sect. 5.6.

[61] See Sect. 4.5.

[62] See Chap. 6.

[63] Many systems pair data-driven approaches with symbolic AI, and military organisations will likely do the same for weapon systems. See Holland Michel 2021, p. 25; Flournoy et al. 2020, p. 5. Because these hybrid systems still contain a machine learning element, they still fall within the notion of 'AWS' as used in this book.

[64] Commentators have used the landmine to demonstrate why many conceptions of AWS (definitions such as "[weapon systems which] can perform a function entirely on their own with humans unable to intervene") in literature are overinclusive. E.g. Scharre and Horowitz 2015, p. 6. This is one additional reason why the definition of AWS used in this book does not depend on the scale of 'autonomy' the system exhibits.

[65] Both AWS and legacy systems are important for our analysis: many insights can be gained from exploring how IHL has responded to older weapons which, while not empowered with AI, exhibit autonomous properties. These older weapons are therefore also worth exploring, particularly as a contrast to AWS technology, as they provide indications on how Deployers would need to employ their AWS.

1.3 Dramatis Personae

This study's central figure, as noted above, is Deployer. However, more goes into the use of AWS than just the end-user. It is thus useful to briefly introduce the other actors and parties who also play important roles in the analyses to come.

1.3.1 Deployer

Deployer refers to the person who ultimately makes the decision to deploy the AWS. In standard operations, this will usually be the person(s) authorised to determine capability assignment, i.e. weapon selection and tuning.[66] It does not refer to any military rank in particular, as long as the person is acting at the operational or tactical level and bears ultimate responsibility for weapons release.

A deliberate choice is made to adopt this broader conception of who qualifies as Deployer, instead of naming specific ranks or unit sizes.[67] This purpose-based approach is consistent with IHL, which is applicable to "all those persons who ha[ve] command responsibility from commanders at the highest level to leaders with only a few men".[68] Including both the operational and tactical levels is important for inclusivity, since an AWS user can in practice also be a platoon commander or an insurgent leader. Note however that the strategic level is excluded from this current analysis: as mentioned in Sect. 1.1, this level has already received much attention in current literature, and the added contribution of the current book is precisely its shift in focus toward the 'lower' levels of war.

1.3.2 Operator

In some situations, a degree of more direct human monitoring or supervision over the AWS can be maintained. Deployer could discharge this function themselves,[69] but they could also appoint an ***Operator*** to do so. An Operator should be a subordinate to Deployer, and be responsible to them. In this configuration, Deployer would act

---

66 See NATO 2016, para 0207 (NATO); Curtis E. Lemay Center 2019, p. 11 (US).

67 This kind of purpose-based conception of what levels of war are being considered is often viewed as more useful than rigid limitations based on unit sizes: there are often no finite boundaries between the strategic, operational and tactical, and so the latter approach can lead to unnecessary confusion and entanglement during analysis. Harvey 2021, p. 76.

68 Bothe et al. 2013, p. 599. See also Sandoz et al. 1987, para 3553; ICC (PTC), *Prosecutor v. Jean-Pierre Bemba Gombo*, Decision pursuant to Article 61(7)(a) and (b) of the Rome Statute on the charges of the prosecutor against Jean-Pierre Bemba Gombo, 5 June 2009, ICC-01/05-01/08, para 408. The person's official rank or title is legally irrelevant; see Schmitt 2011, p. 41.

69 In which case Deployer fulfils the dual role of both being the commander who authorised the AWS's release and that of the system's operator while the operation is underway.

as a field commander (the person who authorises the system's deployment) and the Operator as the supervising 'field soldier'.[70] To contrast an Operator's role to that of Deployer in this case, Jain describes the latter as the person who "deploys the AWS" but who is not necessarily "equipped to direct, predict or second-guess the decision-making operation carried out by the AWS in real time".[71] As we will see in later chapters,[72] it is important to separate the two roles conceptually, since certain tasks and obligations may be reasonable to demand of an Operator who is directly supervising an AWS, but not of a Deployer who merely authorised its activation.

1.3.3 Providing Entity

Deployer is the AWS's end-user, meaning that a vast process of design, programming, testing,review, procurement, adoption, policymaking and distribution preceded the moment that the system finally came under their possession in the battlefield. How each phase contributes toward ensuring that AWS use remains lawful has been extensively explored in literature,[73] and each phase involves individuals responsible for properly executing these tasks. Ultimately, the technology Deployer has at their disposal and the conditions in which they may use this technology are shaped by these prior influences, and the discussion to follow thus cannot be complete without considering their roles in the process.

Given this book's focus on Deployer's perspective, the choice is nevertheless made to refer to this array of agencies and individuals with a higher level of abstraction, designating them collectively as the ***Providing Entity***.[74] This generally refers to the organisation[75] to which Deployer is subordinated and from which Deployer receives their weapon systems, in addition to other necessary elements such as product specifications, technical training, legal advice, policy, rules of engagement, etc.

---

[70] Jain 2016, p. 314.

[71] Ibid.

[72] See Sects. 2.4.3 and 8.7.1.

[73] For proposals related to test and evaluation of AWS, see e.g. Flournoy et al. 2020; Lohn 2020; Haughet al. 2018. For proposals and discussions related to reviewing AWS, see e.g. US Department of Defense 2023; Schuller 2019, pp. 107–108; Holland Michel 2021, p. 21. For a discussion on how policy and rules of engagement may be used to regulate AWS, see e.g. Boddens Hosang 2021.

[74] This neutral designation avoids unnecessary legal discussion on whether the Providing Entity is a State in public international law terms, as non-universally recognised entities (such as certain States or administrations) may also ultimately be the entity responsible for AWS development, procurement and adoption.

[75] 'Organisation' is used, instead of e.g. 'State' or 'ministry of defence', since Deployer could be a commander in an insurgent group with responsible hierarchical command. For a discussion on the particular dynamics of the use of AWS in non-State armed groups, see Kwik 2022.

This abstraction has the benefit of binarily demarcating responsibilities primarily incumbent upon *Deployer* and those which are *not*.[76] Many important tasks or obligations are out of Deployer's control: for example, a commander on the battlefield has little influence over how accurate or explainable[77] their systems are—they can only work with what they are given.[78] It is clear that such matters must be resolved at a 'higher' level, but *which* agency or individual must execute these tasks is left out of the debate. In many cases, it is nevertheless obvious: for example, if a recommendation is issued[79] that a clear delimitation must be provided at the review stage related to the environment in which the AWS may be employed, then this clearly must be carried out by the Providing Entity's reviewing authority. Thus, whenever the Providing Entity is referenced in coming chapters, this is primarily done in terms of what this institution must prepare or provide *in advance* in order for Deployer to be able to make informed legal decisions.

1.4 Goodwill

One important basic assumption taken throughout most[80] of this book is that its *actors are acting in good faith* and are receptive to considering and implementing the recommendations issued within. It presumes that Deployer is a good-faith reasonable commander who is committed to implementing targeting rules in force to the best of their abilities. Similarly, it presumes that the Providing Entity is an institution prepared to take the necessary effort to ensure that the AWS it is developing, purchasing, adopting are IHL-compliant, and that these are used in IHL-compliant ways.

One could criticise this methodological choice by arguing that AWS technology poses particular danger because it could be abused by bad-faith actors. As one commentator noted, "[h]uman wickedness in warfare has accustomed us to the worst atrocities. Therefore, it is far from implausible that human agents wilfully use AWS to commit international crimes".[81] The possibility of AWS being used to deliberately execute unlawful attacks certainly cannot be precluded, but unduly focalising our

[76] Section 14.2.2 collects and systematises all recommendations issued throughout this book and clearly assigns them as responsibilities primarily of either Deployer or the Providing Entity, thereby preventing role confusion.

[77] Explainability in particular is a property that can only be achieved by design or through the development of a specific explanation tool. Evidently, this is out of Deployer's hands. See Sect. 4. 5.

[78] See Sect. 3.1.

[79] See Sect. 3.5.

[80] Part V features a few exceptions where we also analyse bad-faith actors.

[81] Amoroso 2020, pp. 131–132. As an example of how this concern has penetrated the public imagination, one famous YouTube clip called *Slaughterbots* told the story of swarms of autonomous assassin drones equipped with facial recognition that are eventually hacked and used to enact political and ethnic killings. See Stop Autonomous Weapons 2017.

attention on these worst-case scenarios, while ignoring the many good-faith actors, is unwise. While (deliberate) misuse of weapons has occurred in the past, "[s]uch misuse is not … a common scenario for most types of military engagements."[82] Instead, it is argued[83] that the vast majority of problems related to AWS will instead emerge from *good-faith actors using the technology poorly*.[84] Against this backdrop, this book prefers the constructive approach of empowering these good-faith actors to *use the technology better*.

Additionally, even if one adopts a pessimistic view (and disregards the many military commanders and organisations who do sincerely care about the law), there is still value in earnestly exploring how AWS should be used in conformity with IHL. An AWS user does not necessarily need to 'believe'[85] in IHL to want to implement it. Deployer and their military organisation may see the value in using AWS in compliance with IHL for reputational reasons, to win hearts and minds, to avoid media scrutiny, or to avoid political or diplomatic repercussions.[86] In any of these cases, Deployer has an interest in understanding how they can employ their AWS in ways consistent with targeting laws—which is the main value that this book provides.

Nevertheless, we shall also not be naïve. If ambiguities or lacunae exist in the law that bad-faith actors can exploit to use AWS in a non-compliant manner without facing meaningful repercussions, they will do so. As such, legal indeterminacies which are particularly liable to being exploited will be highlighted[87] to encourage further academic discussion into possible ways to remedy these vulnerabilities in the law.

1.5 A Roadmap

The central question posed in this book, as indicated in Sect. 1.1, is: *How does an operational commander conduct attacks using AWS in accordance with IHL?*

This is not an easy problem to solve. Conducting any attack comes with a range of obligations in IHL concerning the selection and validation of targets, precautions and protections of the civilian population, and rules prohibiting certain means or methods of warfare such as those which are indiscriminate or uncontrollable.[88] That

[82] Beard 2014, p. 662.

[83] For an extended argument related to this point, see also Sect. 13.4.2.

[84] This will occur for reasons mentioned in prior sections: a lack of technical understanding, uncertainties related to the interpretation of IHL provisions, and lacking or unadjusted policies.

[85] In the sense of being morally convinced of its virtue as a normative regime.

[86] Many works are dedicated to explaining why even States or armed groups who may not necessarily care for IHL nevertheless tend to maintain compliance when conducting military operations. See Schmitt 1999, pp. 174–180; Ayres and Thurnher 2019; Geiß 2006, pp. 770–777.

[87] See e.g. Sect. 13.5.3. See also Kwik 2024, pp. 17–21.

[88] Schmitt 2012, p. 284; Turns 2013, p. 227.

these obligations apply to AWS-users is not in doubt.[89] What is less clear is how commanders can determine whether their use of AWS is IHL-compliant, what factors they need to consider to make this assessment, and under what conditions failure to do so may constitute a breach sufficiently grave so as to lead to criminal liability.

This book is, at its core, a legal analysis with a focus on IHL rules governing the conduct of hostilities. However, said analysis cannot be comprehensive without a detailed assessment of AWS from other points-of-view. As highlighted above, one problem that emerges from AWS is that the underlying technology—AI, particularly data-driven models—comes with particularities that are novel, unintuitive or require specific training to comprehend and manage, particularly for individuals with purely legal or operational backgrounds. It is therefore necessary to introduce into this work an interdisciplinary element, in the form of a technical analysis of AWS. In addition, the question related to criminal liability of Deployers necessitates an intradisciplinary element: it requires not only an examination of IHL targeting rules, but also how these rules are enforced through (international) criminal law.

To manage this challenging inter- and intradisciplinary endeavour, this book separates its analysis of AWS into three major parts: a technical prong (Part III), a legal-operational prong (Part IV), and finally a prong on criminal liability (Part V). This structure and ordering of themes is founded upon an overarching theory of control over AWS (Part II), which is necessary to introduce first.

1.5.1 Controlling AWS

Part II, the first substantive part of this book, asks the question of *what steps go into effectuating an AWS attack*. An attack is more than just the moment force is applied: a wide range of processes and preparatory acts precede and succeed it. Basing itself on an extensive review of how the notion of control is conceptualised in the AWS debate, this part advances a novel framework that identifies the key actions a commander must undertake within the targeting process to retain overall control over an AWS-attack, even if some decision-making authority is delegated to AI. Three components in particular are found to be crucial:

(1) Deployer's sufficient understanding of AI-specific properties that impact legal analysis;
(2) Deployer's legal and operational analysis of *whether* and *how* to use AWS; and
(3) Post-deployment accountability.

Each of these action-points, however, requires a distinct type of analysis. The first demands a technical exploration of the underlying technology; the second a thorough examination of operational-level IHL rules and a proper awareness of realistic

[89] Schmitt argues that there is "universal consensus" that these rules also apply to AWS, a statement that is unlikely to find many detractors. Schmitt and Thurnher 2013, p. 243. See also US Department of Defense 2023, 4; Group of Governmental Experts on Lethal Autonomous Weapons Systems (GGE on LAWS) 2021, para 12; Meier 2019, pp. 296–297.

battlefield conditions; and the third a proper understanding of the conditions that lead to responsibility for the effects of attacks. Each of these elements are found to be sufficiently complex to warrant closer inspection, which informs the next three parts of this book. The components also feed into each other and cannot be performed out of order.[90] For this reason, Part III, Part IV and Part V are discussed in this sequence.

1.5.2 Technical Analysis

Part III, the technical branch of the analysis, delves deeply into the technical aspects of AWS technology, and provides the foundation needed to make realistic and informed interpretations of legal rules in force. This part focuses on the preparatory phase preceding an attack where Deployer must analyse the systems under their possession, the attack's desired effects, and the operational environment. The information obtained from this analysis is necessary for Deployer to make reasoned decisions during weapon selection and tuning. However, some characteristics of AI make AWS fundamentally different from legacy systems, which necessitates a new set of cognitive tools to evaluate. The main question explored in this part is: *How does Deployer analyse the performance and risk of AWS in light of the unique properties of modern AI?*

This question is explored in greater depth from four different perspectives:

- The fundamental properties, advantages and weaknesses of modern AI, as well as how these interact with the often cluttered and chaotic battlefield (Chap. 3);
- General measures of AI performance, such as accuracy, reliability and understandability (Chap. 4);
- Specific causes of AI failure (Chap. 5); and
- Enemy anti-AI countermeasures (Chap. 6).

1.5.3 Legal-Operational Analysis

Part IV explores how Deployer would use the information obtained from the previous step for legal and operational analysis in a practical setting. A commander's legal obligations in attack are well-established, but Deployer may encounter difficulties in interpreting these obligations when AWS are involved. This step is crucial, since Deployer must not only be confident that an AWS attack would be lawful under targeting rules, but also must make the operational decision as to whether the purported advantages of using an AWS outweigh the precautions that must be taken to ensure lawful use. As such, this part asks *how Deployer must determine whether the use of AWS is legally and operationally justifiable.*

---

[90] See Sect. 2.5. For example, making informed legal and operational decisions (Point 2) requires a sufficient comprehension of the unique technical properties of modern AI (Point 1).

This matter is analysed through the following prompts:

- What properties of a given AWS render Deployer more or less capable of using it in accordance with IHL targeting rules? (Chap. 8)
- How must rules related to distinction, proportionality and precautions be interpreted if AWS are used? (Chap. 9)
- When is the use of AWS *operationally* justifiable? (Chap. 10).

1.5.4 Criminal Liability

Much discussion has emerged about the possibility of AWS causing harm and the inability of the law to hold persons accountable for these results. Of all forms of legal responsibility, criminal liability is closely connected to IHL due to the API Article 86(1) obligation to repress any serious breaches. Part V consequently explores *what conditions unique to AWS technology potentially present obstacles to holding Deployers criminally liable for harm caused by their utilisation.* Answering this question demands a systemic analysis of criminal liability for war crimes, which involves the following inquiries:

- What are the necessary conditions for criminal liability, and to what extent do AWS-specific properties make fulfilling these elements more difficult? (Chap. 12).

From this analysis, it is found that *mens rea* is the element most likely to present challenges, but that the problem is not uniform across all mental states. Thus, a follow-up question is posed:

- What mental states present the most obstacles to establishing mens rea? (Chap. 13).

1.5.5 Synthesis and Recommendations

Part VI reviews all conclusions and recommendations from prior parts and offers a dual output. The first is academic, and summarises the most important insights for each subject matter and identifies areas where future research is strongly encouraged.[91] The second is more applied, and reframes the study's findings and recommendations in the form of practical flowcharts that can be adopted by military organisations or policymakers. These are intended to aid future Deployers in reducing the chance that particular factors or steps that are necessary to ensure IHL-compliant use of AWS are overlooked.

---

[91] See Sects. 14.2 and 14.4.

References

Adviesraad Internationale Vraagstukken and Commissie van Advies inzake Volkenrechtelijke Vraagstukken (2015) Autonome Wapensystemen: De Noodzaak van Betekenisvolle Menselijke Controle. AIV

AI Watch Joint Research Centre (2020) Defining Artificial Intelligence: Towards an Operational Definition and Taxonomy of Artificial Intelligence. European Union, Luxembourg

Amoroso D (2020) Autonomous Weapons Systems and International Law: A Study on Human-Machine Interactions in Ethically and Legally Sensitive Domains. Nomos Verlagsgesellschaft, Baden

Andrini L (2018) Redesigning Indonesia Copyright Act to Accommodate Autonomous Intelligent System: Status Quo and Room for Improvement. Asian Journal of Law and Economics 9(3): 20180013. DOI: https://doi.org/10.1515/ajle-2018-0013

Arkin R C (2009) Governing Lethal Behavior in Autonomous Robots. CRC Press, Boca Raton

Article 36 (2013) Structuring Debate on Autonomous Weapons Systems. In: Memorandum for delegates to the Convention on Certain Conventional Weapons (CCW), Geneva, 14–15 November 2013

Asaro P (2012) On Banning Autonomous Weapon Systems: Human Rights, Automation, and the Dehumanization of Lethal Decision-Making. International Review of the Red Cross 94(886):687–709

Associated Press, Reuters, Macdonald C (2017) Vladimir Putin Warns Whoever Cracks Artificial Intelligence Will "Rule the World". Dailymail. https://www.dailymail.co.uk/sciencetech/article-4844322/Putin-Leader-artificial-intelligence-rule-world.html. Accessed 31 July 2023

Ayres T E, Thurnher J S (2019) Legitimacy. In: Williams W S, Ford C M (eds) Complex Battlespaces: The Law of Armed Conflict and the Dynamics of Modern Warfare. Oxford University Press, Oxford, pp 223–258. DOI: https://doi.org/10.1093/oso/9780190915360.003.0008

Beard J M (2014) Autonomous Weapons and Human Responsibilities. Georgetown Journal of International Law 45:617–681

Bendett S (2023) Roles and Implications of AI in the Russian-Ukrainian Conflict, 20/7/2023. Center for a New American Security. https://www.cnas.org/publications/commentary/roles-and-implications-of-ai-in-the-russian-ukrainian-conflict. Accessed 04 March 2024

Blank L (2019) New Technologies and the Interplay between Certainty and Reasonableness. In: Williams W S, Ford C M (eds) Complex Battlespaces: The Law of Armed Conflict and the Dynamics of Modern Warfare. Oxford University Press, Oxford, pp 317–344. DOI: https://doi.org/10.1093/oso/9780190915360.003.0011

Bo M (2021) Autonomous Weapons and the Responsibility Gap in Light of the Mens Rea of the War Crime of Attacking Civilians in the ICC Statute. Journal of International Criminal Justice 19(2):275–299. DOI: https://doi.org/10.1093/jicj/mqab005

Boddens Hosang J F R (2021) Control Through ROE in Military Operations: Autonomous Weapons and Cyber Operations as Reasons to Change the Classic ROE Concept?. In: Bartels R et al. (eds) Military Operations and the Notion of Control Under International Law. TMC Asser Press, The Hague, pp 393–420. DOI: https://doi.org/10.1007/978-94-6265-395-5_19

Boothby W H (2018) Highly Automated and Autonomous Technologies. In: Boothby W H (ed) New Technologies and the Law in War and Peace. Cambridge University Press, Cambridge, pp 137–181. DOI: https://doi.org/10.1017/9781108609388.007

Bothe M, Partsch K J, Solf W A (eds) (2013) New Rules for Victims of Armed Conflict: Commentary on the Two 1977 Protocols Additional to the Geneva Conventions of 1949. 2nd edn. Martinus Nijhoff, Leiden

Boulanin V (2016) Mapping the Development of Autonomy in Weapon Systems: A Primer on Autonomy. Stockholm International Peace Research Institute, Stockholm

Boulanin V et al. (2020) Responsible Military Use of Artificial Intelligence: Can the European Union Lead the Way in Developing Best Practice. SIPRI, Stockholm

Cherry J, Johnson D (2020) Maintaining Command and Control (C2) of Lethal Autonomous Weapon Systems: Legal And Policy Considerations. Southwestern Journal of International Law 27:1–27

Cummings M L (2004) Automation Bias in Intelligent Time Critical Decision Support Systems. In: AIAA 1st Intelligent Systems Technical Conference. American Institute of Aeronautics and Astronautics. DOI: https://doi.org/10.2514/6.2004-6313

Curtis E. Lemay Center (2019) Air Force Doctrine Publication 3-60 – Targeting. Curtis E Lemay Center. www.doctrine.af.mil/Doctrine-Publications/AFDP-3-60-Targeting. Accessed 05 July 2021

Davies H, McKernan B, Sabbagh D (2023) 'The Gospel': how Israel uses AI to select bombing targets in Gaza. The Guardian, 1 Dec 2023. https://www.theguardian.com/world/2023/dec/01/the-gospel-how-israel-uses-ai-to-select-bombing-targets. Accessed 04 March 2024

Deeks A (2021) Will Cyber Autonomy Undercut Democratic Accountability?. In: Liivoja R, Väljataga A (eds) Autonomous Cyber Capabilities under International Law. NATO CCDCOE Publications, Tallinn, pp 67–105

Defense Science Board (2012) The Role Of Autonomy in DoD Systems. US Department of Defense, Washington D.C.

Defense Science Board (2016) Report of the Defense Science Board Summer Study on Autonomy. Secretary of Defense for Acquisition, Technology and Logistics

Deng B (2015) The Robot's Dilemma: Working out How to Build Ethical Robots Is One of the Thorniest Challenges in Artificial Intelligence. Nature 523:25–27

Dinstein Y (2018) Autonomous Weapons and International Humanitarian Law. In: von Heinegg W H, Frau R, Singer T (eds) Dehumanization of Warfare. Springer International Publishing, Cham, pp 15–20

Eklund A M (2020) Meaningful Human Control of Autonomous Weapon Systems: Definitions and Key Elements in the Light of International Humanitarian Law and International Human Rights Law. Totalförsvarets forskningsinstitut, Stockholm

Fallon C K, Blaha L M (2018) Improving Automation Transparency: Addressing Some of Machine Learning's Unique Challenges. In: Schmorrow D, Fidopiastis C (eds) Augmented Cognition: Intelligent Technologies. Springer, Cham, pp 245–254. DOI: https://doi.org/10.1007/978-3-319-91470-1_21

Flournoy M A, Haines A, Chefitz G (2020) Building Trust through Testing: Adapting DOD's Test & Evaluation, Validation & Verification (TEVV) Enterprise for Machine Learning Systems, Including Deep Learning Systems. WestExec Advisors, Washington D.C.

Fornasier M D O (2021) The Regulation of the Use of Artificial Intelligence (AI) in Warfare: Between International Humanitarian Law (IHL) and Meaningful Human Control. Revista Jurídica da Presidência 23(129):67. DOI: https://doi.org/10.20499/2236-3645.RJP2021v23e129-2229

Gao C (2017) China Vows to Become an Artificial Intelligence World Leader. The Diplomat. https://thediplomat.com/2017/07/china-vows-to-become-an-artificial-intelligence-world-leader. Accessed 25 October 2020

Garcia D (2014) ICRAC Statement on Technical Issues to the 2014 UN CCW Expert Meeting. International Committee for Robot Arms Control 2014 UN CCW Expert Meeting. www.icrac.net/icrac-statement-on-technical-issues-to-the-2014-un-ccw-expert-meeting. Accessed 30 May 2021

Geiß R (2006) Asymmetric Conflict Structures. International Review of the Red Cross 88(864):757–777

Gill T D, Fleck D (eds) (2010) The Handbook of the International Law of Military Operations. Oxford University Press, Oxford

Group of Governmental Experts on Lethal Autonomous Weapons Systems (GGE on LAWS) (2019) Report of the 2019 Session of the Group of Governmental Experts on Emerging Technologies in the Area of Lethal Autonomous Weapons Systems. UN Doc CCW/GGE1/2019/3, 25 September 2019

Group of Governmental Experts on Lethal Autonomous Weapons Systems (GGE on LAWS) (2021) Draft Report of the 2021 Session of the Group of Governmental Experts on Emerging Technologies in the Area of Lethal Autonomous Weapons Systems. CCW/GGE1/2021/CRP1

Group of Governmental Experts on Lethal Autonomous Weapons Systems (GGE on LAWS) (2023) Report of the 2023 Session of the Group of Governmental Experts on Emerging Technologies in the Area of Lethal Autonomous Weapons Systems. CCW/GGE1/2023/CRP2

Grut C (2013) The Challenge of Autonomous Lethal Robotics to International Humanitarian Law. Journal of Conflict and Security Law 18(1):5–23. DOI: https://doi.org/10.1093/jcsl/krt002

Harvey A S (2021) The Levels of War as Levels of Analysis. Military Review 2021:75–81. www.armyupress.army.mil/Journals/Military-Review/English-Edition-Archives/November-December-2021/Harvey-Levels-of-War. Accessed 23 August 2018

Haugh B A, Sparrow D A, Tate D M (2018) The Status of Test, Evaluation, Verification, and Validation (TEV&V) of Autonomous Systems. Institute for Defense Analyses, Alexandria

Hawley J K (2007) Looking Back At 20 Years Of MANPRINT On Patriot: Observations And Lessons. Army Research Laboratory

Henderson I S, Keane P, Liddy J (2017) Remote and Autonomous Warfare Systems: Precautions in Attack and Individual Accountability. In: Ohlin J D (ed) Research Handbook on Remote Warfare. Edward Elgar, Cheltenham, pp 335–370. DOI: https://doi.org/10.4337/9781784716998.00022

Herbach J (2012) Into the Caves of Steel: Precaution, Cognition and Robotic Weapon Systems Under the International Law of Armed Conflict. 4 Amsterdam Law Forum 4(3):3–20

Heyns C (2013) Report of the Special Rapporteur on Extrajudicial, Summary or Arbitrary Executions, A/HRC/23/47

High-Level Expert Group On Artificial Intelligence (2019a) A Definition of AI: Main Capabilities and Disciplines. European Commission, Brussels

High-Level Expert Group On Artificial Intelligence (2019b) Ethics Guidelines for Trustworthy AI. European Commission, Brussels

Hofman L (2020) De Nieuwste Wapenwedloop Gaat Niet Om Bommen, Maar Om Algoritmes (En Hoe Die Te Foppen). De Correspondent, 19 August 2020. https://decorrespondent.nl/11511/de-nieuwste-wapenwedloop-gaat-niet-om-bommen-maar-om-algoritmes-en-hoe-die-te-foppen/80252bb0-a43e-06da-0cf6-5468281fcfef. Accessed 2 August 2023

Holland Michel A (2021) Known Unknowns: Data Issues and Military Autonomous Systems. UNIDIR, Geneva. https://unidir.org/publication/known-unknowns. Accessed 2 August 2023

Horkoff J (2019) Non-Functional Requirements for Machine Learning: Challenges and New Directions. In: 2019 IEEE 27th International Requirements Engineering Conference (RE). IEEE, pp 386–391. DOI: https://doi.org/10.1109/RE.2019.00050

Human Rights Watch (2012) Losing Humanity: The Case against Killer Robots. Human Rights Watch

ICRC (2013) Autonomous Weapons: States Must Address Major Humanitarian, Ethical Challenges. https://reliefweb.int/report/world/autonomous-weapons-states-must-address-major-humanitarian-ethical-challenges. Accessed 18 October 2014

ICRC (2016) Background Paper Prepared by the International Committee of the Red Cross. In: ICRC (ed) Autonomous Weapon Systems: Implications of Increasing Autonomy in the Critical Functions of Weapons. ICRC, Versoix, pp 69–85

ICRC (2018) Ethics and Autonomous Weapon Systems: An Ethical Basis for Human Control?. Group of Governmental Experts of the High Contracting Parties to the Convention on Prohibitions or Restrictions on the Use of Certain Conventional Weapons Which May Be Deemed to Be Excessively Injurious or to Have Indiscriminate Effects, CCW/GGE1/2018/WP

ICRC (2019) Artificial Intelligence and Machine Learning in Armed Conflict: A Human-Centred Approach. ICRC, Geneva

Jain N (2016) Autonomous Weapons Systems: New Frameworks for Individual Responsibility. In: Bhuta N et al. (eds) Autonomous Weapons Systems: Law, Ethics, Policy. Cambridge University Press, Cambridge, pp 303–324. DOI: https://doi.org/10.1017/CBO9781316597873

Jain A G (2021) Autonomous Cyber Capabilities and Individual Criminal Responsibility for War Crimes. In: Liivoja R, Väljataga A (eds) Autonomous Cyber Capabilities under International Law. NATO CCDCOE Publications, pp 291–320

Jevglevskaja N (2018) Weapons Review Obligation under Customary International Law. International Law Studies 94:186–221

Kallenborn Z (2022) Russia may have used a killer robot in Ukraine. Now what?. Bulletin of the Atomic Scientists, 15 March 2022. https://thebulletin.org/2022/03/russia-may-have-used-a-killer-robot-in-ukraine-now-what/. Accessed 20 April 2023

Kalmanovitz P (2016) Judgment, Liability and the Risks of Riskless Warfare. In: Bhuta N et al. (eds) Autonomous Weapons Systems. Cambridge University Press, Cambridge, pp 145–163. DOI: https://doi.org/10.1017/CBO9781316597873.007

Kastan B (2013) Autonomous Weapons Systems: A Coming Legal "Singularity"?. Journal of Law, Technology and Policy 2013(1):45–82

Knight W (2017) The Dark Secret at the Heart of AI. Technology Review. www.technologyreview.com/2017/04/11/5113/the-dark-secret-at-the-heart-of-ai. Accessed 2 July 2020

Kroes P, Verbeek P-P (2014) Introduction: The Moral Status of Technical Artefacts. In: Kroes P, Verbeek P-P (eds) The Moral Status of Technical Artefacts. Springer Netherlands, Dordrecht, pp 1–9. DOI: https://doi.org/10.1007/978-94-007-7914-3_1

Kurosaki M (2020) Toward the Special Computer Law of Targeting. In: Kreß C, Lawless R (eds) Necessity and Proportionality in International Peace and Security Law. Oxford University Press, Oxford, pp 409–436. DOI: https://doi.org/10.1093/oso/9780197537374.001.0001/oso-9780197537374-chapter-14

Kwik J (2022) Mitigating the Risk of Autonomous Weapon Misuse by Insurgent Groups. Laws 12(1):5. DOI: https://doi.org/10.3390/laws12010005

Kwik J (2024) The Conceptual Roots of the Criminal Responsibility Gap in Autonomous Weapon Systems. Melbourne Journal of International Law 24(1):1–26. https://law.unimelb.edu.au/__data/assets/pdf_file/0008/4816367/Kwik.pdf

Li Q, Xie D (2019) Legal Regulation of AI Weapons under International Humanitarian Law: A Chinese Perspective. Humanitarian Law & Policy. https://blogs.icrc.org/law-and-policy/2019/05/02/ai-weapon-ihl-legal-regulation-chinese-perspective/. Accessed 26 May 2021

Lohn A J (2020) Estimating the Brittleness of AI: Safety Integrity Levels and the Need for Testing Out-Of-Distribution Performance. http://arxiv.org/abs/2009.00802

Meier M W (2019) Lethal Autonomous Weapons Systems. In: Williams W S, Ford C M (eds) Complex Battlespaces: The Law of Armed Conflict and the Dynamics of Modern Warfare. Oxford University Press, Oxford, pp 289–316

Ministère des Armées (2019) L'intelligence Artificielle Au Service de La Défense. Ministère des Armées, Paris

Moyes R (2019) Target Profiles: An Initial Consideration of "Target Profiles" as a Basis for Rule-Making in the Context of Discussions on Autonomy in Weapons Systems. Article 36, Article 36 Discussion Paper

NATO (2016) Allied Joint Doctrine for Joint Targeting. AJP-39, Edition A Version 1 (April 2016)

Novak M (2023) Lawyer Uses ChatGPT In Federal Court And It Goes Horribly Wrong. Forbes, 27 May 2023. https://www.forbes.com/sites/mattnovak/2023/05/27/lawyer-uses-chatgpt-in-federal-court-and-it-goes-horribly-wrong/. Accessed 04 March 2024

Parasuraman R, Sheridan T B, Wickens C (2000) A Model for Types and Levels of Human Interaction with Automation. IEEE Transactions on Systems, Man, and Cybernetics 30(3):286–297

Parks W H (2005) Conventional Weapons and Weapons Reviews. Yearbook of International Humanitarian Law 8:55–142

Roorda M (2015) NATO's Targeting Process: Ensuring Human Control Over (and Lawful Use of) 'Autonomous' Weapons. In: Williams A P, Scharre P D (eds) Autonomous Systems: Issues for Defence Policymakers. NATO, The Hague, pp 152–168

Russell S J, Norvig P (2010) Artificial Intelligence: A Modern Approach. 3rd edn. Pearson, New Jersey

Sandoz Y, Swinarski C, Zimmerman B (1987) Commentary on the Additional Protocols of 8 June 1977 to the Geneva Conventions of 12 August 1949. Martinus Nijhoff, Geneva

Santoni de Sio F, van den Hoven J (2018) Meaningful Human Control over Autonomous Systems: A Philosophical Account. Frontiers in Robotics and AI 5:1–14. DOI: https://doi.org/10.3389/frobt.2018.00015/full

Sassòli M (2014) Autonomous Weapons and International Humanitarian Law: Advantages, Open Technical Questions and Legal Issues to Be Clarified. International Law Studies 90:308–340

Scharre P D (2015) The Opportunity and Challenge of Autonomous Systems. In: Williams A P, Scharre P D (eds) Autonomous Systems: Issues for Defence Policymakers. NATO, The Hague, pp 3–26

Scharre P D (2018) Army of None: Autonomous Weapons and the Future of War. WW Norton & Co, New York

Scharre P D, Horowitz M C (2015) An Introduction to Autonomy in Weapon Systems. Center for a New American Security, Working Paper, Feb 2015

Schmitt M N (1999) The Principle of Discrimination in 21st Century Warfare. Yale Human Rights and Development Law Journal 2(1):143–182

Schmitt M N (2011) Investigating Violations of International Law in Armed Conflict. Harvard National Security Journal 2:31–84

Schmitt M N (2012) "Attack" as a Term of Art in International Law: The Cyber Operations Context. In: Czosseck C, Ottis R, Ziolkowski K (eds) 4th International Conference on Cyber Conflict. NATO CCD COE Publications, Tallinn

Schmitt M N, Thurnher J S (2013) "Out of the Loop": Autonomous Weapon Systems and the Law of Armed Conflict. Harvard Law School National Security Journal 4:231–281

Schuller A L (2019) Artificial Intelligence Effecting Human Decisions to Kill: The Challenge of Linking Numerically Quantifiable Goals to IHL Compliance. Journal of Law and Policy for the Information Society 15:105–122

Simon-Michel J-H (2014) Report of the 2014 Informal Meeting of Experts on Lethal Autonomous Weapons Systems (LAWS). UN Office Geneva

Sleesman R J, Huntley T C (2019) Lethal Autonomous Weapon Systems: An Overview. Army Lawyer 1:32–35

Stop Autonomous Weapons (2017) Slaughterbots. http://www.youtube.com/watch?v=9CO6M2HsoIA. Accessed 31 July 2023

Szegedy C et al. (2014) Intriguing Properties of Neural Networks. http://arxiv.org/abs/1312.6199

Tamburrini G (2016) On Banning Autonomous Weapons Systems: From Deontological to Wide Consequentialist Reasons. In: Bhuta N et al. (eds) Autonomous Weapons Systems. Cambridge University Press, Cambridge, pp 122–142. DOI: https://doi.org/10.1017/CBO9781316597873.006

The Parliamentarian, *Parliamentary Handbook on Disinformation, AI and Synthetic Media* (Commonwealth Parliamentary Association, 2023, London).

Thurnher J S (2014) Examining Autonomous Weapon Systems from a Law of Armed Conflict Perspective. In: Nasu H, McLaughlin R (eds) New Technologies and the Law of Armed Conflict. TMC Asser Press, The Hague, pp 213–228. DOI: https://doi.org/10.1007/978-90-6704-933-7_13

Toscano C P (2015) "Friend of Humans": An Argument for Developing Autonomous Weapons Systems. Journal of National Security Law & Policy 8(1):189–246

Turns D (2013) Cyber War and the Concept of "Attack" in International Humanitarian Law. In: Saxon D (ed) International Humanitarian Law and the Changing Technology of War. Brill-Nijhoff, Leiden, pp 207–227. DOI: https://doi.org/10.1163/9789004229495_011

Tzimas T (2021) Legal and Ethical Challenges of Artificial Intelligence from an International Law Perspective. vol 46. Springer, Cham. DOI: https://doi.org/10.1007/978-3-030-78585-7

UK (2020) Expert Paper: The Human Role in Autonomous Warfare, Group of Governmental Experts on Emerging Technologies in the Area of Lethal Autonomous Weapons System Geneva, 21–25 September 2020 and 2–6 November 2020, Agenda Item 5. CCW/GGE1/2020/WP6

UK House of Lords (2018) Select Committee on Artificial Intelligence, Report of Session 2017–19, AI in the UK: Ready, Willing, and Able?. HL Paper 100, 16 April 2018

United Nations (2021) Panel of Experts Established pursuant to Security Council Resolution 1973. Letter dated 8 March 2021 from the Panel of Experts on Libya Established pursuant to Resolution 1973 (2011) addressed to the President of the Security Council. S_2021_229

US Air Force Office of the Chief Scientist (2015) Autonomous Horizons: System Autonomy in the Air Force— A Path to the Future, Volume I: Human-Autonomy Teaming. AF/ST TR 15-01

US Department of Defense (2023) Autonomy in Weapon Systems. US DoD Directive 3000.09

US Department of the Army (2020) Army Command Policy. Army Regulation 600–20

van den Boogaard J C, Roorda M P (2021) "Autonomous" Weapons and Human Control. In: Bartels R (eds) Military Operations and the Notion of Control Under International Law. TMC Asser Press, The Hague, pp 421–437. DOI: https://doi.org/10.1007/978-94-6265-395-5_20

West L (2022) Face Value: Precaution versus Privacy in Armed Conflict. In: Buchan R, Lubin A (Eds.) The Rights to Privacy and Data Protection in Times of Armed Conflict. NATO CCDCOE Publications, Tallinn, pp 132–156

Williams A P (2015) Defining Autonomy in Systems: Challenges and Solutions. In: Williams A P, Scharre P D (eds) Autonomous Systems: Issues for Defence Policymakers. NATO, The Hague, pp 27–64

Wilson C (2020) Artificial Intelligence and Warfare. In: Martellini M, Trapp R (eds) 21st Century Prometheus. Springer International Publishing, Cham, pp 125–140. DOI: https://doi.org/10.1007/978-3-030-28285-1_7

Winter E (2020) The Compatibility of the Use of Autonomous Weapons with the Principle of Precaution in the Law of Armed Conflict. The Military Law and the Law of War Review 58(2):240–273. DOI: https://doi.org/10.4337/mllwr.2020.02.18

Yampolskiy R V (2019) Unexplainability and Incomprehensibility of Artificial Intelligence. http://arxiv.org/abs/1907.03869

Part II
Controlling AWS

Chapter 2
Controlling AWS: A Cyclical Process

Contents

Abstract The ability to control weapons is an essential component of targeting. For autonomous weapon systems (AWS), the notion of meaningful human control (MHC) has frequently been advanced as a framing device for policy and legal discussions, but the concept is functionally void due to lack of precision as to what it entails. This chapter presents the results of an empiric study on the different ways MHC has been conceptualised in literature and discourse. Focal points of influence throughout the targeting process are identified during which commanders can exercise significant influence over their AWS, in the form of Awareness, Weapon Selection, Context Controls, Prediction, and Accountability. In addition, forward processes are identified between these points that suggest a forward progression: for example, Accountability is only possible if the user knows of the risks (Awareness) and makes an informed choice to deploy an AWS in particular way (Weapon Selection and Context Controls). These findings are distilled into an MHC Framework, which outlines the practical steps a commander must take in order to maintain control over their AWS when ordering (iterative) attacks, even if some use-of-force elements are delegated to the AI. The theory is validated by superimposing the MHC Framework's elements over

J. Kwik, *Lawfully Using Autonomous Weapon Technologies*,
https://doi.org/10.1007/978-94-6265-631-4_2

the NATO Targeting Cycle, which shows that the focal elements correspond well with the steps in the cycle, demonstrating the MHC Framework's viability as a workable guideline that can be implemented during real military operations.

Keywords Control · Meaningful human control · Targeting · Targeting cycle · Attack · Autonomous weapon system · Artificial intelligence · NATO · Weaponeering · Prediction · Accountability · Responsibility · Military operation · Review · Training

2.1 Introduction

Control is a crucial component of the use of any apparatus, but particularly so for safety-critical AI systems such as vehicles and weapons platforms.[1] For AWS, the significance of control is simple: it ensures that the weapon can be wielded effectively and as intended by its user.[2] Control has been important for even the most primitive of weapons: a blade so cumbersome and unwieldy that it runs the risk of accidents is not a militarily desirable asset.[3]

In the context of AWS, control has emerged as a central theme in the form of the term 'meaningful human control' (MHC). This concept, first proposed in 2013 by the British NGO Article 36,[4] developed into a talking point that dominated international discussions,[5] including those at the intergovernmental conferences of the Convention on Certain Conventional Weapons (CCW).[6] MHC rapidly became a point of convergence between stakeholders with vastly different political perspectives.[7] After only a few years of discussions, a broad agreement had emerged between States, NGOs, international organisations and commentators that meaningful control should be retained over AWS.[8] One commentator was convinced that "[w]hatever the terms ultimately become, there is consensus that no one wants weapons that operate out of human control."[9]

This apparent consensus, however, is somewhat misleading. Closer inspection of the statements reveals that stakeholders are in agreement only that MHC is important, but not what this entails. In practice, every stakeholder has their own list of criteria

---

[1] Russell et al. 2015, p. 109.

[2] Horowitz and Scharre 2015, p. 4.

[3] Ibid.

[4] Article 36 2013.

[5] UNIDIR 2014, p. 2; ICRC 2016a, sct 5.

[6] Moyes 2016, p. 46; UK 2020, para 1.

[7] Roff and Moyes 2016, p. 1.

[8] Chengeta 2016, pp. 836–837; Ekelhof 2019, p. 343.

[9] Roff 2016, p. 2.

of what constitutes meaningful human control.[10] MHC was undefined at conception and remains undefined now,[11] both as a policy concept and as a legal term.[12]

This lack of concretisation makes MHC very difficult to use in practice: "[P]olicy-makers and technical designers lack a detailed theory of what "meaningful human control" exactly means; and therefore they don't know which specific legal regulations and design guidelines should be derived from this principle."[13] Horowitz and Scharre correctly point out that without a more tangible formulation, MHC risks becoming an empty platitude or, worse, could generate flawed policy choices.[14] Until a more specific MHC requirement is agreed upon, therefore, one could be justified in ignoring it altogether for legal analyses on AWS.

The current author advances a different position, namely that MHC can be useful as a framing concept to structure legal analyses,[15] such as the one presented in this book. To determine the focal points where legal analysis is particularly needed, it is useful to first identify the crucial moments where Deployer's influence over the AWS in their possession are the greatest. Even as a simple framing device, however, the current conception of MHC in literature and discourse is still too disorganised to utilise. It is thus important first to convert MHC into a more concrete state.

What follows below is a framework which was constructed by integrating the various positions on MHC from the broader academic debate into a workable scheme of facets and processes:

- *Facets* refer to requirements which contribute toward establishing human control over weapons. They represent Deployer's 'focal points of influence'.
- *Processes* refer to mechanisms which link different facets together. They indicate causal relationships between these points of influence, and how Deployer's ability to exert control over one component may be dependent on having correctly implemented prior actions.

From this discussion, we discover that this scheme of facets and processes provides a robust overarching picture of how a Deployer at the operational level should proceed when considering the use of AWS for a particular mission. As previously indicated in Sect. 1.5, the main steps identified in this scheme inform the general structure of the coming chapters in this book, and are explored in greater depth in each.

The discussion presented in this chapter is a summary of an extensive empiric study that was published as *A practicable operationalisation of meaningful human*

---

[10] See Eklund 2020; Kwik 2022.

[11] Horowitz and Scharre 2015, p. 5; Eklund 2020, p. 27. Article 36 deliberately omitted listing specific criteria for MHC during its initial proposal to leave space for discussion and negotiation. Moyes 2016, pp. 46–47. Unfortunately, years of discussion up to the time of writing have not yielded a more concrete conception of MHC.

[12] Chengeta 2016, p. 837; Marauhn 2018, p. 211.

[13] Santoni de Sio and van den Hoven 2018, p. 3.

[14] Horowitz and Scharre 2015, p. 5.

[15] This was also one of the reasons why MHC became popular in the first place: It was "taken up by civil society and some States as a useful framing concept for discussions on autonomy in weapon systems". UNIDIR 2014, p. 2.

control by the same author.[16] For an in-depth explanation of this study and a full list of specific references which were used to define and elaborate each component described below, the reader may consult abovementioned article, which also goes into greater detail with respect to the methodology used to analyse the datapoints. In the current chapter, we instead focus on how this scheme aids the framing of the broader study on AWS as featured in this book.

2.2 Background, Data Collection, Methodology

The research process that lead to the construction of the MHC Framework drew inspiration from a comparable project by Eklund in 2020.[17] Her work, similarly motivated by the lack of clarity on what MHC entails,[18] collected different State and NGO positions on MHC and systematised and compared them, with the goal of identifying what she terms "key elements of meaningful human control".[19] Eklund found seven key elements which ranged significantly from cognitive demands (understanding of the system and interactions), system demands (reliability, predictability), restrictions on how the system is to be used (restricting the operational contexts, maintaining a data link with the platform), to guarantees of accountability.[20] One interesting observation made by Eklund was that some key elements appeared to be 'resultant states' of other elements. For example, with regard to predictability, she noted that it could be considered as

> expressing a more overarching "goal-element" which the other key elements strive to achieve. For example, by using "context-control" the predictability increase [*sic*], by "understanding the weapon" the use of it will be more predictable and by "understanding the environment" the autonomous weapon system's interaction with it will be more predictable.[21]

This remark seemed to indicate some entanglement between the elements, and led to the author hypothesising that a system of cause-and-effect could be derived. Establishing such a connection would have two benefits: First, it would allow us to elaborate not only on the elements themselves but also the mechanisms which connect them, creating an even more concrete conception of how MHC can be attained. Second, cause-and-effect implies a temporal component, which would enable us to chronologically re-arrange the different elements to conform to actual decision-making processes in the field. This, in turn, allows us to better extrapolate the resulting framework unto actual military procedures.

As an example, the block quote from Eklund above can be represented graphically as in Fig. 2.1, clearly demonstrating a causal dependency between facets.

---

[16] See Kwik 2022.

[17] Eklund 2020.

[18] Ibid., p. 27.

[19] Ibid., p. 28.

[20] See Ibid., pp. 28–31.

[21] Ibid., p. 30.

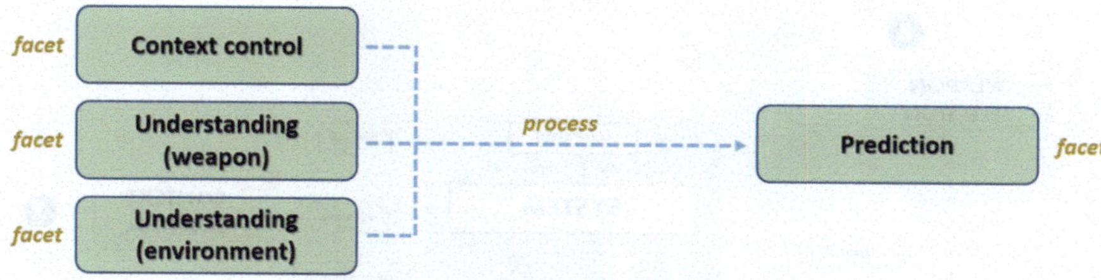

Fig. 2.1 Example of facets causally linked by processes

Departing from this hypothesis, an independent literature study was conducted of statements from States, NGOs, international organisations and commentators from the timeframe of 2013–2021. The data was qualitatively analysed and systematised twice based on different paradigms—facets and processes—respectively representing key elements of MHC (as done in Eklund's study) on the one hand, and the hypothesised linking mechanisms on the other.

Both paradigms yielded concrete and detailed results. For the facets, four major categories were found: Awareness; Weapon Selection and Context Control; Predictability; and Accountability. For the processes, an expansive substructure of interlinking mechanisms was found which connects all facets in robust ways, displaying a clear chronological forward process consistent with the overall practice of military decision-making.

2.3 Results: Integrated MHC Framework

Figure 2.2 shows the result of this analysis in schematic form.

Placed centrally in this framework are the *System* and *Environment*, which constitute the core of any weapon use. The System and Environment mutually exert influence on each other.[22] An AI system obtains percepts[23] from its Environment during Acquisition, which form the basis of its subsequent Analysis, Decision and Action.[24] This is represented graphically by the *Influence* arrow. Conversely, the system's resultant *Action*, represented by the downward arrow, interacts with the Environment and produces an *Impact*. Ideally, from a military perspective, this Impact would overlap with the desired effects of that operation, or the commander's "desired end state",[25] although this is not necessarily the case.

[22] This mutually interacting nature is what defines an 'agent' in many views. See Sect. 3.3.

[23] A percept is any input an (AI) agent receives from the environment at any given instant, based on which it can construct a world model and make decisions. See Sect. 3.3.2.

[24] Acquisition, Analysis, Decision and Action are the four steps that go into the decision-making process of any agent, including AI systems. See Sect. 3.3 for an extended discussion.

[25] Curtis E. Lemay Center 2019, p. 3.

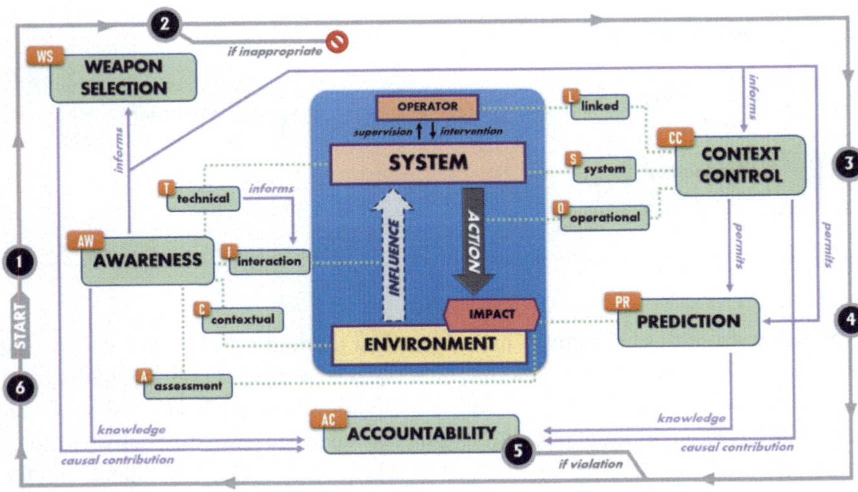

Fig. 2.2 MHC framework

Facets are labelled in this scheme with orange icons. Awareness (*AW*) and Context Control (*CC*) are also divided into more detailed sub-facets for further accuracy, noted with lower-case letters (e.g. AW_C). Processes, represented by blue dotted lines, are noted by a right arrow connecting two (sub-)facets. Abbreviations can be used to quickly indicate process pairs: for example, $AW_C \rightarrow WS$ refers to the process 'Contextual Awareness informs Weapon Selection'.

Finally, with regard to human players, *Deployer* is accorded a central role in ensuring that meaningful control is retained. The choice to place the focal point of control on Deployer has support in policy and literature: the figure who releases the weapon is almost universally designated as being primarily responsible for its usage.[26] The 2019 NATO Allied Joint Doctrine states this in no uncertain terms: "The commander is ultimately responsible for accepting risk."[27] Similarly, the US finds that "[i]n all cases, the commander is accountable and has the responsibility for authorizing weapon release in accordance with IHL".[28] This validates the choice made in this book to focus on Deployer as the central point-of-view.

As was noted in Sect. 1.3, this does not imply that Deployer is the *sole* relevant actor. There are many instances where other parties (e.g. designers, policymakers, subordinates) are also determinant as to the extent control is exercised over an AWS, sometimes more so than Deployer themselves.[29] As will be shown below, however, the influence exerted by Deployer is so significant that it is justifiable to place them in

[26] Schmitt and Thurnher 2013, p. 277; Horowitz and Scharre 2015, p. 14; Roff and Moyes 2016, p. 3; United States 2017; UK 2020, para 10.

[27] NATO 2019, para 1.75.a.

[28] United States 2017.

[29] The role of these actors and the division of their responsibilities vis-à-vis those of Deployer is highlighted particularly in Part III.

a leading role in the framework, even though we must remain vigilant in identifying circumstances where this is not the case.[30]

Astute observers may have noticed that Deployer is not featured in the framework itself. This is because the entire framework is seen from Deployer's perspective. Figuratively, the Framework is akin to a blueprint on Deployer's table that systematically informs them of the sub-tasks to carry out when considering the use of AWS.

Having briefly explained the framework's layout, we now turn to discussing the various facets and processes in more detail.

2.4 Facets

Facets, as noted above, are focal points of influence for Deployer. By properly fulfilling the tasks associated with each facet, Deployer can exert enough overall influence over AWS so as to remain 'in control', even if Deployer eventually allows AI to perform some actions autonomously related to use-of-force.

2.4.1 Awareness

Awareness is built on the philosophy that "[h]uman control in the use of a technology is … based upon those planning and deciding upon an attack having certain information."[31] The ultimate goal of this facet is to empower Deployer with the ability to make informed, conscious choices about the use of a weapon.[32] As elegantly stated in a 1991 NASA design guideline:

> To command effectively, the human operator must be involved … To be involved, the human operator must be informed.[33]

Awareness is a holistic concept and requires an understanding of the comprehensive system-environment-interaction triad.[34] Missing just one results in an incomplete picture.[35] For example, Van den Boogaard and Roorda assert that any decision to deploy AWS should be informed by "the capacity to understand the functioning of

[30] See Sect. 3.1.

[31] Article 36 2016, p. 4.

[32] Horowitz and Scharre 2015, p. 12; Boardman and Butcher 2019, p. 8.

[33] Billings 1996.

[34] See the central box in Fig. 2.2.

[35] Eklund 2020, p. 30; ICRC 2016a, sct 5.

a system and the environment in which it will operate [and] the capacity to understand the possible effects that a system will generate considering the system's functioning and the environment".[36] As such, Awareness is further developed into 3 subfacets: Technical Awareness (AW_T), Contextual Awareness (AW_C) and Interaction Awareness (AW_I).

Technical Awareness refers to an understanding of the system being considered for deployment. 'Understanding' a system means being aware of not only its capabilities and technical specifications, but also its limitations and weaknesses.[37] Many aspects can fall under this umbrella, such as properly understanding the intended functionality of the system,[38] the operational context for which it was designed,[39] and the system's safety, security, and reliability.[40] More AI-specific matters would include properly understanding the AI's performance indicators, how decisions are made by the AI and on the basis of what variables, and the AI's robustness against non-test instances.[41]

Some circumstances may preclude the possibility of Deployer attaining adequate Technical Awareness, such as situations where the AWS is too opaque[42] or where Deployer has not been provided the requisite training to properly understand the system's more technical properties.[43] These limitations can only be resolved in coordination with the Providing Entity,[44] whether this be Deployer's immediate superiors, central command, or the organisation's review and adoption agencies.

Contextual Awareness refers to an understanding of the environment in which the system will operate. The main rationale is that a "human commander cannot meet her obligations if she lacks sufficient information about context".[45] Militaries understand this very well, and place large emphasis on (continuous) intelligence, surveillance and reconnaissance (ISR) so decisions can be based on the most current information in the field.[46] Contextual Awareness is prescient as AWS will not work well outside of their intended operational parameters.[47] For instance, if an AWS is not designed to make classifications between civilian persons and combatants, it is necessary for Deployer to know if civilians will be present in the field.[48]

---

36 van den Boogaard and Roorda 2021, p. 433.

37 Santoni de Sio and van den Hoven 2018, p. 10; ICRC 2019, p. 3.

38 ICRC 2016b, p. 84.

39 Roff and Moyes 2016, p. 2.

40 Leslie 2019, p. 30.

41 Moyes 2016, p. 50; Geiß and Lahmann 2017, p. 402; ICRC 2018, para 26.

42 See Sect. 4.5.

43 Horowitz and Scharre 2015, p. 12; ICRC 2016b, p. 84; Geiß and Lahmann 2017, p. 402; Boardman and Butcher 2019, p. 11.

44 See Sect. 1.3.3.

45 Roff 2016, p. 4.

46 Roorda 2015, p. 157; Chengeta 2016, pp. 883–884; ICRC 2018, para 39; Curtis E. Lemay Center 2019, p. 11.

47 See Sect. 3.4.3. See also Sect. 9.3.2.

48 Geiß and Lahmann 2017, p. 402.

Interaction Awareness is a more advanced form of Technical Awareness where not only the system itself is understood, but also how it would react to external stimuli (i.e., the *Influence* arrow[49] in the MHC Framework). It is an essential component of control for all weapons: an artillery officer who is unable to account for the effect of wind on the ballistic trajectory of their mortars is a bad commander. As such, "military commanders and staff should be familiar, to a reasonable standard, with how a particular weapon would respond to potential situations".[50]

Influence can be either of a *natural* or *adversarial* character. Weather, as in the artillery scenario above, is an example of natural influence on the system, as would be the movement of civilians across a road or a pothole in the street. Adversarials,[51] on the other hand, are deliberate countermeasures by the enemy intended to degrade and interfere with the system's proper functioning, and perhaps even take over control of the system altogether.[52] Deployers must inform themselves of both types of foreseeable influence on their system to ultimately exercise and retain control.[53]

2.4.2 *Weapon Selection*

Having considered all relevant information during the Awareness step, Deployer now engages in the most comprehensive form of control they have over any possible type of weapon: the *decision of whether or not to use it at all.* As Van den Boogaard and Roorda submit, Weapon Selection constitutes the ultimate form of human control:

> The military commander's decision to employ a certain a weapon in a certain context is the ultimate failsafe; a lack of capacity to understand the possible effects of the use of a system, may be fully compensated by a full capacity to decide on its use.[54]

As with any weapon, Deployer will engage in the "process of determining the specific means required to create a desired effect on a given target",[55] and at this point, Deployer can opt out from using an AWS if they deem it unable to fulfil IHL requirements or unfit to achieve mission goals.[56]

---

[49] See Fig. 2.2.

[50] Roorda 2015, p. n41.

[51] See Chap. 6.

[52] Boothby 2018, p. 153.

[53] Boothby 2021, p. 386.

[54] van den Boogaard and Roorda 2021, p. 43.

[55] Office of the Chairman of the Joint Chiefs of Staff 2020, p. 229.

[56] Moyes 2016, p. 51.

2.4.3 Context Controls

If Deployer chooses to assign the weapon to the mission, they can still set advanced forms of Context Control, divided in the MHC Framework into the following sub-facets: System Control (CC_S), Operational Control (CC_O), and Linked Control (CC_L).

System Control refers to manipulating the system's internal parameters. Deployer can restrict the tasks that the system will perform, impose limits on the targets it may engage, the way it engages such targets, and, in the case where the system carries more than one type of munition, prohibit the use of certain ones.[57] Deployer can also consider whether they wish to enable online learning,[58] which can improve overall performance and adaptability but could reduce the system's predictability.[59] Imposing specific restrictions, such as '*engage only when shot upon*' or '*whatever you do, do not do X*',[60] would also fall under this category. In the end, Deployer must apply a value judgment by balancing the envisaged advantages of a specific setting with foreseeable risks.

Operational Control refers to limiting the Actions the System can inflict upon the Environment (and thereby its Impact)[61] by regulating the scope of the mission or the operational context. Imposing operational controls is particularly useful to reduce the risk of unknown or unforeseen variables which could divert the system away from what was intended by Deployer.[62] There are a few common ways to do this. *Spatial Control* refers to restricting the system's reach to a certain geographical area, e.g. by imposing boundary coordinates.[63] *Temporal Control* limits the time in which the system operates,[64] based on the reasoning that the probability of failures or unintended interactions increase proportionally with the temporal dimension.[65] Finally, Operational Control can also be achieved by manipulating the operating environment itself, for example by establishing a perimeter or closing off a section of airspace or terrain to civilian aircraft or vehicles.[66]

Linked Control is a magnified form of control that assigns a human to exercise direct or supervisory control over the AWS's activities. In Fig. 2.2, this human is represented by the box *Operator* (as noted in Sect. 1.3, this may be Deployer themselves, or

---

57 ICRC 2019, p. 4; UK 2020, para 17.

58 This refers to allowing the system to continue learning and improving after activation. See Sect. 5.6.

59 Schuller 2017, p. 397.

60 Thurnher 2012, p. 80; Sassòli 2014, p. 335; Schuller 2017, p. 423.

61 See Fig. 2.2.

62 ICRC 2019, p. 4.

63 Ekelhof 2016, p. 56; Schuller 2017, note 81.

64 UNIDIR 2014, p. 5.

65 Ibid. For more on the temporal variable, see Sects. 8.3.1 and 9.2.1.

66 Roorda 2015, p. 162; Boddens Hosang 2021, p. 405.

someone who has been delegated the task). The term 'Linked' is used to reflect the fact that this configuration requires a persistent two-way link between the System and Operator. The Operator and System must be continuously 'linked' to allow the System and Operator to communicate. The System must send data to the Operator to enable the latter to make informed choices, and the Operator must be able to communicate their choice (e.g. to authorise or veto a proposed action) to the System.[67] This is represented by the arrows *Supervision* and *Intervention* in Fig. 2.2.

The legal ramifications of each of these Context Controls, and whether some or all of them are obligatory under IHL, is discussed in Part IV.

2.4.4 Predictability

While very frequently cited as a component of MHC,[68] predictability can perhaps be viewed more accurately as a resultant state, and not as a criterion or requirement that can be fulfilled in itself. This was already remarked in passing by Eklund in her own study, where she noted that it expressed "a more overarching "goal-element" which the other key elements strive to achieve".[69] As its nature as a 'goal-element' is better captured in terms of processes rather than static facets, we defer to Sect. 2.5.2 for a better explanation of how this fits into the MHC Framework.

2.4.5 Accountability

It is frequently posited that control "requires structures of accountability"[70] or that control "concerns responsibility for the consequences of their deployment".[71] Very similarly to Prediction however, Accountability can better be construed as a goal-state rather than a criterion in itself. The reason for this is simple: responsibility is not a state that can be imposed without establishing prior legal and policy structures, lest the attribution of accountability become arbitrary, inequitable, or unjust. Indeed, this is one of the main critiques advanced in the 'responsibility gap' argument,[72] namely that it would become impossible to attribute responsibility in a 'fair' way.[73] Like with Prediction, we postpone this discussion until Sect. 2.5.3.

---

[67] Boothby 2018, p. 137.

[68] UNIDIR 2014, p. 5; ICRC 2016a, sct 5; Moyes 2016, p. 50.

[69] Eklund 2020, p. 30.

[70] Article 36 2016, p. 4.

[71] Santoni de Sio and van den Hoven 2018, p. 1.

[72] See Sect. 11.4.

[73] Gaeta 2016, p. 44; Szpak 2020, p. 126.

2.4.6 Assessment Awareness

Assessment Awareness is rarely mentioned in sources but was added to the Framework based on logical inference. It is important in terms of Awareness that Deployer is aware of *previous iterations* of the weapon's use to make adjustments to future deployment decisions. The targeting process—or, in fact, any good decision-making process[74]—places large emphasis on post-execution assessments as part of a feedback loop to determine whether objectives have been fulfilled, problems require addressing, and lessons can be learnt.[75] Any new information can then be fed back into the pre-deployment analysis to enable continuous improvement.[76] In chronological terms, Assessment Awareness is found at the very end of the decision-making process, hence its placement at Step 6 in the Framework.[77] If applicable, it loops back to Step 1 and a new deployment decision.

2.5 Processes

Processes link the previously-explored facets together, transforming the static nodes into steps which impact and influence one another. As an introduction to the concept, observe the $AW_T \rightarrow AW_I$ process arrow (between Technical Awareness and Interaction Awareness) in Fig. 2.2: To understand how a system will operate in and react to the operational environment, one must have a reasonable understanding of the system itself.[78]

2.5.1 Awareness Informs Weapon Selection and Context Control

It is evident that proper Weapon Selection and Context Control cannot be conducted in ignorance of any of the three sub-facets of Awareness. For a commander to make a proper deployment decision, they "must be fully informed as to [their] tactical options, as well as the anticipated consequences of implementing these precautions".[79] This involves understanding the weapon's abilities, parameters and limitations, how it will perform concretely in these conditions, and the situation on

[74] See e.g. Boer and van Engers 2013, 403.

[75] NATO 2016, para 0209; US Department of the Army 2019, para 5-1.

[76] NATO 2019, para E.2.

[77] See the black outer ring in Fig. 2.2.

[78] Roff 2016, p. 3.

[79] Corn 2015, p. 438.

the ground based on collected ISR.[80] Similarly, adjustments cannot be made to the system or operational circumstances without a solid understanding of how these would impact the system's behaviour and performance.[81]

A remark by Roorda provides one interesting example of how Awareness can directly impact the extent of Weapon Selection and Context Control. He postulates that if a commander has great difficulty with Technical Awareness (say, it uses a very advanced or extremely opaque AI that is difficult to comprehend), this commander would be more "inclined to restrict its use due to a lack of understanding of how the system would respond to circumstances (predictable or not) and what effects it would generate".[82] In other words, to retain control, deficiencies in Awareness can be compensated by greatly intensifying care with respect to Weapon Selection and Context Control.

2.5.2 Awareness and Context Control Permit Prediction

The link between Awareness and Prediction is perhaps the connection which is mentioned the most often.[83] Understanding the technology and the context in which it operates enables Deployer to foresee and assess likely outcomes.[84] Roorda's scenario above demonstrates how poor Awareness makes it difficult to predict the system's responses. Opaque AI[85] in particular has been linked with a reduced capability to predict.[86]

One of the main functions associated with Context Controls is to suppress unpredictability during operations.[87] For example, it is argued that the active time of a system is inversely correlated with predictability: the longer the system remains active, the higher the chance that unforeseeable or unintended variables introduce themselves into the environment.[88] Predictability is also improved by limiting the options available to a system.[89] Finally, assigning an Operator theoretically removes the variable of uncertainty attached to the system making errors, since the Operator can act as an additional human fail-safe.[90] Thus, these observations confirm our earlier statement that Predictability is more of a 'goal-state': its fulfilment is a function of Awareness and Context Control.

---

[80] Curtis E. Lemay Center 2019, pp. 11, 71; UNIDIR 2014, p. 5.

[81] UK 2020, para 16.

[82] Roorda 2015, p. 165.

[83] UNIDIR 2014, p. 6; Scharre 2016, p. 8; Roff and Moyes 2016, p. 2.

[84] Moyes 2016, pp. 50–51.

[85] See Sect. 4.5.

[86] Goussac 2019.

[87] UNIDIR 2014, pp. 5–6; Moyes 2016, p. 50; Schuller 2017, p. 416.

[88] Crootof 2015, pp. 1878–1879. See also Sect. 8.3.1.

[89] Stürchler and Siegrist 2017.

[90] Parasuraman et al. 2000, p. 293.

2.5.3 All Previous Facets Contribute to Accountability

As also noted in Sect. 2.4.5, accountability cannot be imposed *ad hoc*: certain elements such as causality or fault are necessary for many forms of moral and legal responsibility.[91] The popular 'responsibility gap' argument has as principal critique that AWS will make fulfilling criteria required for legal or moral responsibility (causality, fault, etc.) very difficult or impossible.[92] The MHC Framework takes a different position: if all prior facets are properly fulfilled by Deployer, then responsibility will come naturally. This is represented by the two main types of process arrows leading into Accountability seen in Fig. 2.2.

- *Awareness → Accountability* and *Prediction → Accountability* contribute toward the cognitive element. Awareness and Predictability are ultimately states of knowledge. As such, they connect Deployer's intent and knowledge with the eventual outcome,[93] eliminating many possible excuses a Deployer could make to claim ignorance or an inability to know.
- *Weapon Selection → Accountability* and *Context Control → Accountability* cover the causal element. We have already seen that Context Control involves a series of active choices (or omissions) which directly impact the operational and technical scope of a deployed weapon. By rejecting a system outright, Weapon Selection can straightforwardly deny any possibility of the undesired result ever taking place. Thus, if after obtaining full Awareness, Deployer still makes a reckless decision and releases a weapon that is badly paired with the operational context, or fails to enact the proper precautions[94] that would be expected of a reasonable officer in their position,[95] they 'caused' the undesired result to occur.[96]

These process arrows form the basis of one of the main arguments in Part V that difficulties in establishing criminal liability are less grave than sometimes is asserted in discussions.[97] We also explore negations of this hypothesis, namely that liability is *more* difficult to establish when Deployers do not operate in good-faith and fail to implement the MHC Framework to the best of their abilities.

[91] See also Sect. 11.2.

[92] E.g. Marauhn 2018, pp. 214–216; Brazil 2019, p. 1. See Sect. 11.4.

[93] ICRC 2018, para 34.

[94] In Sect. 9.6.1, it is argued that all Context Controls constitute precautionary measures in the sense of Protocol Additional to the Geneva Conventions of 12 August 1949, and relating to the Protection of Victims of International Armed Conflicts, adopted 8 June 1977, entered into force 7 December 1978, 1125 UNTS 3 (API), Article 57(2)(a)(ii).

[95] Ibid, Article 57(2).

[96] This argument is expanded upon in Sect. 12.2.

[97] See particularly Sect. 12.1.2.

2.6 MHC Outside of the Operational Level

It was noted above that the Framework zooms in on the operational level, i.e. the situation where Deployer already has an operation planned and has (several) AWS available. However, the study also made apparent that *ensuring* that Deployer can perform all the tasks associated with MHC (e.g. technical empowerment, having non-opaque systems available[98]) may be dependent on prior efforts, in particular those of the Providing Entity.[99] Despite this study's emphasis on Deployer and operational decision-making, therefore, any discussion on MHC remains incomplete without some additional notes on the elements that contribute toward Deployer's meaningful control over AWS, but which cannot be represented within the boundaries of our MHC Framework.

Many sources support the notion that ensuring Deployer's effective control over weapons requires *préparatifs*. The UK has consistently argued that one must consider the "multiple phases throughout a weapon lifecycle where control measures can and must be implemented", including via political direction, research and development, testing and evaluation, and personnel training.[100] Similar positions have also been vocalised by other States,[101] such as the US,[102] the Netherlands,[103] and Israel.[104] Many commentators share this opinion, such as Boothby[105] and Van den Boogaard and Roorda[106] who argue that control can also be exercised prior to 'any particular use' of such weapons. Roff and Moyes place particular importance on what they term the 'antebellum' phase, arguing that MHC "cannot be fully addressed without consideration of the processes of design and development that precede it (and that it draws upon)".[107] Further concretising this position, Boardman and Butcher have placed milestones throughout the weapon life-cycle representing crucial points when meaningful human control can be applied, and elaborate further on the specific measures, activities and the stakeholders involved in each phase.[108]

Expanding our understanding of MHC beyond the boundaries of Fig. 2.2 can help overcome some intractable limitations we had encountered. For example, our problem of $AW_T \rightarrow AC$[109] being frustrated by the supply of fully opaque systems (potentially giving Deployer the excuse that it is technically impossible to understand the system) could be solved by implementing a development policy requiring

98 As alluded to in Sect. 2.4.1.

99 As hypothesised in Sect. 1.3.3.

100 UK 2020, para 17. See also UK Mission Geneva 2019.

101 See Jensen 2020, p. 41.

102 Ibid., 42.

103 De Jonogh 2019.

104 Israel 2016.

105 Boothby 2021, pp. 387–388.

106 van den Boogaard and Roorda 2021, pp. 433–434.

107 Roff and Moyes 2016, p. 3.

108 Boardman and Butcher 2019, pp. 8–10.

109 I.e., 'Technical Awareness implies knowledge, which is required for Accountability'.

a minimum level of AI transparency for all AWS. Such a solution, however, would be entirely outside of Deployer's ability to enforce, and requires prior intervention, e.g. by the Providing Entity.[110] Similarly, many potentially important 'facet-enablers', such as designing a useful user interface,[111] incorporating an autonomy slider,[112] issuing conducive Rules of Engagement[113] and implementing the obligation to suppress and repress,[114] can only be enacted at the higher levels of design, adoption and policy.

It would seem, therefore, that proponents of this 'broader school' make strong points: implementing measures during prior phases is also a *necessary* component of MHC. However, it is also important not to take this line of argumentation to its extreme, i.e., that exercising control in the prior phases is *sufficient*. For example, one may ask:

> Would it be sufficient, for example, to rely on superior programming and strict reliability testing to make an autonomous weapon system predictably compliant with IHL for its intended operational parameters?[115]

Clearly, the answer is 'no': measures taken during prior phases *lead into* the different facets in the Framework. Ultimately, we still need Deployer to execute their tasks associated with each MHC facet to ensure control is retained at the operational level. As one example, designing for transparency can improve Technical Awareness, but transparent AI itself cannot inherently ensure the end-user always remains 'in control'.

The best way to visualise these prior measures would therefore be as 'external' process arrows (i.e., from outside the graph's boundaries) leading toward different facets. The fact that we acknowledge that such prior measures must not be disregarded (and may even play crucial roles in enabling the tasks to be fulfilled) does not detract from the choice to centre the MHC Framework at the operational level, as long as we remain conscientious of the fact that some processes stretch beyond the walls of the Framework. Thus, while Deployer remains the main actor on whom this study focuses, we must also remain aware of the presence of the multitude of other actors who played various roles throughout the weapon's lifecycle, and draw our attention to them when the need so arises. We highlight the necessary roles of these 'prior' actors in Part III in particular.

[110] See Sect. 1.2.1.

[111] See Lyons and Havig 2014, p. 185; Saariluoma 2015, p. 232.

[112] Boothby 2021, p. 386.

[113] See Boddens Hosang 2021.

[114] Geneva Convention for the Amelioration of the Condition of the Wounded and Sick in Armed Forces in the Field, adopted 12 August 1949, entered into force 21 October 1950, 75 UNTS 31 (Geneva Convention I), Article 49; API, above n. 94, Article 86(1).

[115] Stürchler and Siegrist 2017. Note that the authors cited do not imply that they would ascribe to such an interpretation. They do not argue that measures in the prior phases would be sufficient to exercise control over weapons, but merely that we should not disregard their role.

2.7 Discussion

Compiling and qualitatively analysing the vast array of opinions from the AWS debate allowed for the construction of a compact MHC Framework that is more workable than the (often abstract) conceptions found in literature and diplomatic discussions.[116] While MHC as a concept certainly has no legal binding force,[117] the Framework proposed in this chapter represents academic consensus on the crucial moments within the operational decision-making process where Deployer's actions and interventions are the most crucial (*facets*). This helps focalise discussions and academic research to those points, knowing that their effective implementation is crucial for human commanders to retain control over their weapons, even if these weapons exhibit some degree of autonomy.

At the same time, the MHC Framework is not idealistic in the slightest. Indeed, the forward progression of Deployer's 'tasks' agrees nicely with common targeting cycles such as the one applied by NATO.[118] The NATO cycle consists of six phases,[119] and the facets of the MHC Framework can easily be associated with particular phases in this cycle:

- *Contextual Awareness* includes analysing the targets and the operational environment (corresponds with NATO Phase 2).
- *Technical and Interaction Awareness* includes analysing the weapon system and how it will perform in the intended environment (corresponds with NATO Phase 3).
- *Weapon Selection* involves assigning a particular weapon to an operation while rejecting alternatives which are deemed inappropriate (corresponds with NATO Phases 3–4).
- *Context Controls* have Deployer prescribing specific ways the assigned weapon should be used (corresponds with NATO Phases 3–4).
- *Assessment Awareness* involves determining the impact a particular AWS deployment had on the environment, before the cycle repeats (corresponds with NATO Phase 6).

The forward progression of the targeting cycle is also present in the MHC Framework as represented by the outermost ring,[120] which indicates the order in which the facets must be accomplished. This compatibility of the MHC Framework with

[116] Eklund 2020, pp. 9–10; Santoni de Sio and van den Hoven 2018, p. 3.

[117] Many States involved in the international discussion also emphasise that their support for MHC is not meant to signal support for its adoption as a binding norm. Jensen 2020, p. 40.

[118] The NATO targeting cycle is chosen as a prototype for the purposes of this demonstration, since it is in use by the largest military alliance in the world at the time of writing.

[119] These phases are: (1) Commander's intent, objectives and targeting guidance; (2) Target development; (3) Capabilities analysis; (4) Commander's decision, force planning and assignment; (5) Force execution; (6) Assessment. For more details on the NATO cycle, see NATO 2021, pp. 1–14; Curtis E. Lemay Center 2019, p. 10.

[120] See the black outer ring with numbered 'steps' in Fig. 2.2.

existing targeting cycles allows the basic lessons and conclusions of this chapter to be easily applied in real life whenever militaries foresee the use of AWS.

Having now discussed the epistemological origins of the MHC Framework, how it generally aligns with actual targeting procedures as practiced by modern militaries, and the underlying logic of each facet and process, we can determine that Awareness, Weapon Selection and Context Control are the most crucial facets in a preventive sense: they each involve multiple sub-facets and are a precondition for the controlled use of AWS. As such, *Awareness* is discussed further in **Part III** and while *Weapon Selection and Context Control* are discussed in greater detail in **Part IV**. Finally, one of the major findings of the MHC Framework were the process arrows leading into *Accountability*. Taking the Framework at face value, it would seem to indicate that both knowledge and causality can be demonstrated if Deployer properly implements all prior facets, but this is an oversimplification. As such, the conditions permitting (criminal) responsibility for AWS use are discussed in greater detail in **Part V**.

References

Article 36 (2013) Structuring Debate on Autonomous Weapons Systems. In: Memorandum for delegates to the Convention on Certain Conventional Weapons (CCW), Geneva, 14–15 November 2013

Article 36 (2016) Key Elements of Meaningful Human Control, Background Paper to Comments Prepared by Richard Moyes, Managing Partner, Article 36. In: Convention on Certain Conventional Weapons (CCW) Meeting of Experts on Lethal Autonomous Weapons Systems (LAWS), Geneva, 11–15 April 2016

Billings C E (1996) Human-Centered Aviation Automation: Principles and Guidelines. NASA Technical Memorandum 110381

Boardman M, Butcher F (2019) An Exploration of Maintaining Human Control in AI Enabled Systems and the Challenges of Achieving It. In: Workshop on Big Data Challenge-Situation Awareness and Decision Support. Brussels: North Atlantic Treaty Organization Science and Technology Organization. Dstl Porton Down

Boddens Hosang J F R (2021) Control Through ROE in Military Operations: Autonomous Weapons and Cyber Operations as Reasons to Change the Classic ROE Concept?. In: Bartels R et al. (eds) Military Operations and the Notion of Control Under International Law. TMC Asser Press, The Hague, pp 393–420. DOI: https://doi.org/10.1007/978-94-6265-395-5_19

Boer A, Van Engers T (2013) Agile: A Problem-Based Model of Regulatory Policy Making. Artificial Intelligence and Law 21(4):399–423

Boothby W H (2018) Highly Automated and Autonomous Technologies. In: Boothby W H (ed) New Technologies and the Law in War and Peace. Cambridge University Press, Cambridge, pp 137–181. DOI: https://doi.org/10.1017/9781108609388.007

Boothby W H (2021) Control in Weapons Law. In: Bartels R et al. (eds) Military Operations and the Notion of Control Under International Law. TMC Asser Press, The Hague, pp 369–392. DOI: https://doi.org/10.1007/978-94-6265-395-5_18

Brazil (2019) Statement by Brazil. 2019 Group of Governmental Experts on Lethal Autonomous Weapons Systems (LAWS), 25–29 March 2019, Item 5a

Chengeta T (2016) Defining the Emerging Notion of "Meaningful Human Control" in Autonomous Weapon Systems. International Law and Politics 49:833–890

Corn G S (2015) War, Law, and the Oft Overlooked Value of Process as a Precautionary Measure. Pepperdine Law Review 42(3):419–466

Crootof R (2015) The Killer Robots Are Here: Legal and Policy Implications. Cardozo Law Review 36:1837–1915

Curtis E. Lemay Center (2019) Air Force Doctrine Publication 3-60 – Targeting. Curtis E Lemay Center. www.doctrine.af.mil/Doctrine-Publications/AFDP-3-60-Targeting. Accessed 05 July 2021

de Jonogh S (2019) Statement of the Netherlands Delivered at the Group of Experts on LAWS, 26 April 2019

Ekelhof M (2016) Human Control in the Targeting Process. In: Autonomous Weapon Systems: Implications of Increasing Autonomy in the Critical Functions of Weapons. ICRC, Versoix, pp 53–56

Ekelhof M (2019) Moving Beyond Semantics on Autonomous Weapons: Meaningful Human Control in Operation. Global Policy 10(3):343–348

Eklund A M (2020) Meaningful Human Control of Autonomous Weapon Systems: Definitions and Key Elements in the Light of International Humanitarian Law and International Human Rights Law. Totalförsvarets forskningsinstitut, Stockholm

Gaeta P (2016) Autonomous Weapon Systems and the Alleged Responsibility Gap. In: Autonomous Weapon Systems: Implications of Increasing Autonomy in the Critical Functions of Weapons. Expert meeting, Versoix, Switzerland, 15–16 March 2016. ICRC, Versoix, pp 44–45

Geiß R, Lahmann H (2017) Autonomous Weapons Systems: A Paradigm Shift for the Law of Armed Conflict?. In: Ohlin J D (ed) Research Handbook on Remote Warfare. Edward Elgar, Cheltenham, pp 371–404

Goussac N (2019) Safety Net or Tangled Web: Legal Reviews of AI in Weapons and War-Fighting. Humanitarian Law & Policy. https://blogs.icrc.org/law-and-policy/2019/04/18/safety-net-tangled-web-legal-reviews-ai-weapons-war-fighting/. Accessed 26 May 2021

Horowitz M C, Scharre P (2015) Meaningful Human Control in Weapon Systems: A Primer. Center for a New American Security, Working Paper No 031315

ICRC (2016a) Views of the ICRC on Autonomous Weapon Systems. Paper of the ICRC prepared for the Meeting of Experts on Lethal Autonomous Weapons Systems, held in Geneva from 11–16 April

ICRC (2016b) Background Paper Prepared by the International Committee of the Red Cross. In: ICRC (ed) Autonomous Weapon Systems: Implications of Increasing Autonomy in the Critical Functions of Weapons. ICRC, Versoix, pp 69–85

ICRC (2018) Ethics and Autonomous Weapon Systems: An Ethical Basis for Human Control?. Group of Governmental Experts of the High Contracting Parties to the Convention on Prohibitions or Restrictions on the Use of Certain Conventional Weapons Which May Be Deemed to Be Excessively Injurious or to Have Indiscriminate Effects, CCW/GGE1/2018/WP

ICRC (2019) 'Statement of the International Committee of the Red Cross (ICRC) under Agenda Item 5(B)'. Convention on Certain Conventional Weapons (CCW), Group of Governmental Experts on Lethal Autonomous Weapons Systems (Geneva, 25–29 March 2019)

Israel (2016) "Statement on Lethal Autonomous Weapons Systems" Delivered by Ms. Maya Yaron. Group of Experts Meeting on Lethal Autonomous Weapons Systems (LAWS) 11–15 April 2016

Jensen E T (2020) The (Erroneous) Requirement for Human Judgment (and Error) in the Law of Armed Conflict. SSRN Electronic Journal 96:26–57. DOI: https://doi.org/10.2139/ssrn.3548314

Kwik J (2022) A Practicable Operationalisation of Meaningful Human Control. Laws 11(3):43

Leslie D (2019) Understanding Artificial Intelligence Ethics and Safety: A Guide for the Responsible Design and Implementation of AI Systems in the Public Sector. The Alan Turing Institute, London

Lyons J B, Havig P R (2014) Transparency in a Human-Machine Context: Approaches for Fostering Shared Awareness/Intent. In: Shumaker R, Lackey S (eds) Virtual, Augmented and Mixed Reality: Designing and Developing Augmented and Virtual Environments, 6th International Conference, VAMR 2014, Lecture No. Springer, Cham, pp 181–190. DOI: https://doi.org/10.1007/978-3-319-07458-0_18

Marauhn T (2018) Meaningful Human Control – and the Politics of International Law. In: von Heinegg W H, Frau R, Singer T (eds) Dehumanization of Warfare. Springer International Publishing, Cham, pp 207–218. DOI: https://doi.org/10.1007/978-3-319-67266-3_11

Moyes R (2016) Meaningful Human Control over Individual Attacks. In: ICRC (ed) Autonomous Weapon Systems: Implications of Increasing Autonomy in the Critical Functions of Weapons. ICRC, Versoix, pp 46–52

NATO (2016) Allied Joint Doctrine for Joint Targeting. AJP-39, Edition A Version 1 (April 2016)

NATO (2019) Allied Joint Doctrine for the Conduct Of Operations. NATO Standard, AJP-3, Edition C Version 1, February 2019

NATO (2021) Allied Joint Doctrine for Joint Targeting. Edition B Version 1 (November 2021) AJP-39, NATO Standardization Office (NSO)

Office of the Chairman of the Joint Chiefs of Staff (2020) DOD Dictionary of Military and Associated Terms, as Amended. The Joint Staff, Washington, D.C

Parasuraman R, Sheridan T B, Wickens C (2000) A Model for Types and Levels of Human Interaction with Automation. IEEE Transactions on Systems, Man, and Cybernetics 30(3):286–297

Roff H M (2016) Meaningful Human Control or Appropriate Human Judgment? The Necessary Limits on Autonomous Weapons. Briefing Paper for the Delegates at the Review Conference on the Convention on Certain Conventional Weapons, Geneva, 12–16 December 2016

Roff H M, Moyes R (2016) Meaningful Human Control, Artificial Intelligence and Autonomous Weapons. Briefing Paper for the Delegates at the Convention on Certain Conventional Weapons Informal Meeting of Experts on Lethal Autonomous Weapons Systems

Roorda M (2015) NATO's Targeting Process: Ensuring Human Control Over (and Lawful Use of) 'Autonomous' Weapons. In: Williams A P, Scharre P D (eds) Autonomous Systems: Issues for Defence Policymakers. NATO, The Hague, pp 152–168

Russell S, Dewey D, Tegmark M (2015) Research Priorities for Robust and Beneficial Artificial Intelligence. Future of Life Institute. https://futureoflife.org/ai-open-letter/. Accessed 2 February 2021

Saariluoma P (2015) Four Challenges in Structuring Human-Autonomous Systems Interaction Design Processes. In: Williams A P, Scharre P D (eds) Autonomous Systems: Issues for Defence Policymakers. NATO, The Hague, pp 226–248

Santoni de Sio F, van den Hoven J (2018) Meaningful Human Control over Autonomous Systems: A Philosophical Account. Frontiers in Robotics and AI 5:1–14. DOI: https://doi.org/10.3389/frobt.2018.00015/full

Sassòli M (2014) Autonomous Weapons and International Humanitarian Law: Advantages, Open Technical Questions and Legal Issues to Be Clarified. International Law Studies 90:308–340

Scharre P D (2016) Autonomous Weapons and Operational Risk. Center for a New American Security, Washington, D.C

Schmitt M N, Thurnher J S (2013) "Out of the Loop": Autonomous Weapon Systems and the Law of Armed Conflict. Harvard Law School National Security Journal 4:231–281

Schuller A L (2017) At the Crossroads of Control: The Intersection of Artificial Intelligence in Autonomous Weapon Systems with International Humanitarian Law. Harvard National Security Journal 8:379

Stürchler N, Siegrist M (2017) A "Compliance-Based" Approach to Autonomous Weapon Systems. EJIL Talk. www.ejiltalk.org/a-compliance-based-approach-to-autonomous-weapon-systems. Accessed 7 June 2021

Szpak A (2020) Legality of Use and Challenges of New Technologies in Warfare – the Use of Autonomous Weapons in Contemporary or Future Wars. European Review 28(1):118–131. DOI: https://doi.org/10.1017/S1062798719000310

Thurnher J S (2012) No One at the Controls: Legal Implications of Fully Autonomous Targeting. Joint Force Quarterly 67:77–84

UK (2020) Expert Paper: The Human Role in Autonomous Warfare, Group of Governmental Experts on Emerging Technologies in the Area of Lethal Autonomous Weapons System Geneva, 21–25 September 2020 and 2–6 November 2020, Agenda Item 5. CCW/GGE1/2020/WP6

UK Mission Geneva (2019) Statement at Meeting of Group of Governmental Experts on Emerging Technologies in the Area of Lethal Autonomous Weapons Systems, Mar. 25–29, 2019. File 20190318-5(d)

UNIDIR (2014) The Weaponization of Increasingly Autonomous Technologies: Considering How Meaningful Human Control Might Move the Discussion Forward. UNIDIR Resources, No 2

United States (2017) Convention on Certain Conventional Weapons (CCW), Group of Governmental Experts (GGE) on Lethal Autonomous Weapons Systems (LAWS). Intervention on Appropriate Levels of Human Judgment over the Use of Force delivered by John Cherry, Geneva, 15 November 2017

US Department of the Army (2019) The Operations Process. ADP 5-0 (replacing ADP 5-0, dated 17 May 2012, and ADRP 5-0, dated 17 May 2012)

van den Boogaard J C, Roorda M P (2021) "Autonomous" Weapons and Human Control. In: Bartels R (eds) Military Operations and the Notion of Control Under International Law. TMC Asser Press, The Hague, pp 421–437. DOI: https://doi.org/10.1007/978-94-6265-395-5_20

Part III
Understanding AWS

Chapter 3
AI Fundamentals and the Military Environment

Contents

Abstract Awareness is an essential prerequisite for using autonomous weapon systems (AWS) lawfully and in an informed way, and comes in three main forms: knowledge of the system (Technical Awareness), of the environment (Contextual Awareness) and how the latter impacts the former (Interaction Awareness). This chapter introduces the concept of Awareness as it pertains to AWS use. First, it looks at the underlying technology of AWS: artificial intelligence (AI). Modern AI differs from old AI systems in major ways due to its reliance on data and machine learning. These techniques offer many benefits indispensable for military systems, but also come with disadvantages that must be understood. The chapter then looks at how military AI agents such as AWS make decisions on the battlefield, by dissecting the acquisition-analysis-decision-action model. Both these discussions show that an AWS's behaviour and performance depends as much on its technical properties as those of the environment in which it is used. Consequently, the military environment is explored, in particular its common properties (complex, cluttered, dynamic and adversarial) and why continuous monitoring of the environment through military intelligence-gathering is crucial. Finally, to address concerns regarding the complexity and dynamicity of military environments and modern AI's vulnerability to such variance, this chapter argues for the establishment of an Intended Operational

J. Kwik, *Lawfully Using Autonomous Weapon Technologies*,
https://doi.org/10.1007/978-94-6265-631-4_3

Environment (IOE). This refers to a fixed and concrete description of the context in which an AWS may be used, which must be maintained from the moment of design, to testing and validation, through operational-level use.

Keywords Autonomous weapon system · Artificial intelligence · Machine learning · Data-driven AI · Military environment · Agent-based modelling · OODA · Military intelligence · Dynamic environment · Narrow AI · Weapon review · Testing and validation · Intended Operational Environment

3.1 Part III: Stage-Setting

The discussion on meaningful human control (MHC) in Chap. 2 identified *Awareness* as a central prerequisite of Deployer's ability to exercise control over weapon systems. To recall, its importance can be summarised by the following quotes:

> To command effectively, the human operator must be involved. ... To be involved, the human operator must be informed.[1]
>
> Control is first and foremost based on knowledge of the weapon system. A thorough understanding by the operator and the commander of the selected weapon's functions and effects, coupled with contextual information (such as awareness of the situation on the ground, what other objects are in the target area, etc.), contribute to the assessment of whether a weapon is appropriate for a particular attack.[2]

Accordingly, Part III explores the breadth of what it means to be 'informed' of one's AWS. As established in Sect. 2.4.1, Awareness is a multidimensional concept that goes beyond mere technical knowledge of the system: it also covers knowledge of the operational environment and how this environment exerts influence upon the system. This dynamic was reflected in the MHC Framework by the four sub-facets of Awareness: that pertaining to the system (System Awareness), the environment (Contextual Awareness), the interaction between them (Interaction Awareness), and iterative assessment (Assessment Awareness). It is now time to expand our understanding of these concepts in a comprehensive manner. Figure 3.1 highlights in orange the components of the Framework that will be addressed in this chapter and those to follow.

The main issue explored in this part, as indicated in Sect. 1.5.2, is: *How does Deployer analyse the performance and risk of AWS in light of the unique properties of modern AI?* To address this matter, this part looks at two related questions. The first is explorative: *What aspects of modern AI introduce novel aspects for Deployer to consider prior to weapon selection and activation, which necessitate a shift in analytical methodology vis-à-vis legacy systems?* Some older paradigms transpose

[1] Billings 1996.

[2] UNIDIR 2014, p. 5.

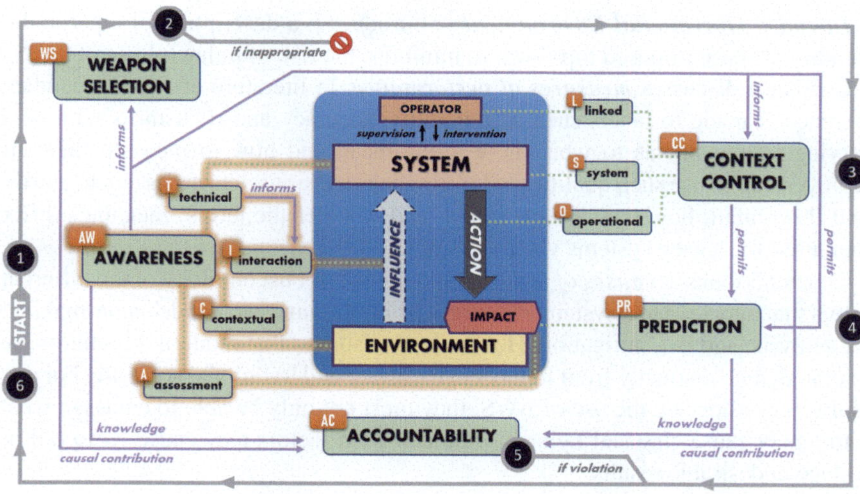

Fig. 3.1 MHC elements related to Awareness

relatively smoothly to AWS, while others may require entirely new methods of analysis. One key aim of this part is to highlight and explore both the similarities and differences.

Another aspect to consider is that several factors of Awareness are difficult for Deployer—who is acting at the operational or tactical level—to analyse or influence on their own. While Deployers ultimately remain responsible for weapon use,[3] it is inevitable that Deployers will need to rely on reviews, information and prior assurances that can only come from 'above', i.e. the Providing Entity.[4] The second question, then, seeks to *delineate the distribution of responsibilities related to Awareness between Deployer and the Providing Entity*. Clarity in this respect helps both Deployer and the Providing Entity understand what is expected of them, and in the latter case, provides an indication as to what preparatory steps must be taken during development, review, etc., to allow Deployers to use AWS correctly and informedly.

Four main themes are explored in Part III, which encompass the entirety of the system-environment-interaction triad.[5] First, the current chapter, introduces some ***fundamentals*** concerning modern AI, including what should be understood when one refers to 'artificial intelligence, the advantages and disadvantages of rule-based versus data-based approaches, and an AI's decision-making loop. It also considers the particularities of the context in which the AI will be used: the ***military environment***. This is a complex, dynamic and cluttered environment, which has consequences for what types of AI can be safely used within it. From this discussion, the concept of

[3] See Sect. 1.1.

[4] See Sect. 1.3.3. In many cases the Providing Entity will be the State, but one can also imagine insurgent-Deployers who receive their weapons, instructions, and rules of engagement from the organised armed group they are attached to.

[5] As found in the central box in Fig. 3.1. See also Sect. 2.3.

an ***Intended Operational Environment*** is introduced: a description of a particular operational space imposed top-down to minimise the risk of unlawful use of AWS.

Chapter 4 discusses ***measures of performance***. In literature on AWS, abundant reference is made to labels such as reliability, accuracy and robustness without a unifying framework as to what these terms mean and how to measure them. If Deployers are to use such qualities to inform their decisions, it is necessary to clarify what they entail, how they are measured, and whether the terms' meanings differ when used for legacy systems vis-à-vis AWS.

Chapter 5 looks at ***causes of failure***. Possessing a robust ontology of the different factors that may lead to a system's failure is an important aspect of decision-making, risk analysis, and risk mitigation. However, we also find that modern AI failures are generated quite distinctly from failures in hardware and traditional software. For any Deployer considering the use of AWS, they must not only be able to envisage what factors may cause classical failures,[6] but also what factors may cause AI to fail or produce undesirable results.

Finally, in Chap. 6, we embrace a very specific component of the *Influence* arrow in Fig. 3.1 in the form of ***adversarials***. Military operations almost invariably involve adversaries—external agents that actively attempt to reduce the effectiveness of our own systems. Countermeasures are as old as the art of war itself, but the use of AI has introduced new vulnerabilities that opponents can exploit. In the worst scenarios, adversarials can lead to aggravated harm to civilians because an AWS is brought to malfunction, confound legitimate from illegitimate targets, or even attack civilians purposely. In this chapter we explore different aspects of this problem. For a Deployer to release an AWS responsibly, it is necessary to foresee vulnerabilities, predict what adversarials the opponent will employ, how this might impact civilian safety, and how to reduce this risk.

3.2 Modern Artificial Intelligence: A Primer

Awareness of AWS requires, first and foremost, some basic understanding of its underlying technology: artificial intelligence. This section lays the groundwork for the coming substantive analyses by summarising the most important information concerning modern AI, thereby contributing toward the first component of Awareness: ***Technical Awareness***.[7]

---

[6] See Sect. 5.2.

[7] AW_T in Fig. 3.1.

To start, what is AI? How AI is defined or what it exactly constitutes is an unresolved issue,[8] but attempts have been made.[9] One of the most comprehensive and detailed definitions was proposed by the EU Commission High Level Expert Group (HLEG) in 2019. The HLEG defined AI as

> software (and possibly also hardware) systems designed by humans that, given a complex goal, act in the physical or digital dimension by perceiving their environment through data acquisition, interpreting the collected structured or unstructured data, reasoning on the knowledge, or processing the information, derived from this data and deciding the best action(s) to take to achieve the given goal. AI systems can either use symbolic rules or learn a numeric model, and they can also adapt their behaviour by analysing how the environment is affected by their previous actions.[10]

From this definition, we can identify two main components. The first sentence describes AI as a system that perceives its environment, processes this information and then makes decisions with a certain level of autonomy for the purpose of achieving a particular goal. This refers to the decision-making process unform to all goal-oriented agents (including humans),[11] and is discussed at length in Sect. 3.3. The second sentence mentions 'symbolic' or 'learned numeric' models, which is more technical. This refers to the two major strands of programming: symbolic AI and learning AI. Two approaches remain the most important categories of AI at the time of writing, each with their own advantages and weaknesses, and thus must be understood before proceeding further.

---

[8] Ministère des Armées 2019, p. 28. This is not for lack of trying: despite deliberate efforts from academia, industry actors and policymakers to reach a consensus, there is no universally accepted definition of AI. Bowne 2019, p. 75; AI Watch Joint Research Centre 2020, p. 7. Even within single fields (e.g. that of computer scientists or engineers) there is no one agreed understanding. Cummings 2018, p. 7.

[9] One useful and versatile definition was advanced by the US Defense Innovation Board: "an umbrella term that covers a variety of information processing techniques and technologies used to perform a goal-oriented task and the means to reason in the pursuit of that task". Defense Innovation Board 2019, p. 46. Many definitions include an element of approximating or simulating human thinking as a major component. For instance, the official French definition of AI reads "[c]hamp interdisciplinaire théorique et pratique qui a pour objet la compréhension de mécanismes de la cognition et de la réflexion, et leur imitation par un dispositif matériel et logiciel". Vocabulaire de l'intelligence artificielle. JORF n°0285 du 9 décembre 2018, texte n°58 (FRA). AI pioneer John McCarthy, to whom the invention of the term 'AI' is often attributed, defined AI as "the science and engineering of making intelligent machines, especially intelligent computer programs. It is related to the similar task of using computers to understand human intelligence, but AI does not have to confine itself to methods that are biologically observable". McCarthy 2007, p. 2.

[10] High-Level Expert Group On Artificial Intelligence 2019, p. 6.

[11] In military circles, it is often referred to as OODA. See Sect. 3.3.

3.2.1 Symbolic AI

Symbolic AI is sometimes also referred to as 'rule-based', 'old-fashioned' or 'handcrafted' and was the traditional way of building artificially intelligent systems,[12] characterised "by a high level of abstraction and a macroscopic view".[13] In this strand of AI, logic is key. Programmers work from known rules or knowledge and abstract them into language machines can understand, i.e. "making use of symbolic rules to represent and infer knowledge".[14] Because of the inductive nature of the endeavour, symbolic AI requires a great deal of prior knowledge by the designers, who often comprise a multidisciplinary team of scientists. As such, designing symbolic AI can be challenging when the pre-requisite knowledge is unquantifiable or indeterminate,[15] as may be the case with legal rules or legal principles. The human programmers are also entirely responsible for the resulting program, given that they both define and determine how the machine solves the problem.[16]

Symbolic AI are often quite challenging to program in more complex environments because of the 'handcrafted' nature, as programmers must manually transform complicated concepts into symbolic form.[17] Translating real-world percepts[18] into symbols is often not obvious. Actually "representing properties of dynamic, real-world environments", such as temporal information (changes in states over time), "is extremely hard".[19] On the other hand, because the resulting AI was crafted with deliberate, reasoned intent, it is easily understandable to fellow humans: these are machines which reason "according to rules and logic, making their inner workings transparent to anyone who care[s] to examine some code".[20]

3.2.2 Machine Learning

While symbolic AI are modelled after logic, machine learning (ML) is modelled after biology[21]: just as humans learn and develop naturally by accruing experiences, ML was developed based on the hypothesis that "intelligence would more easily emerge

[12] Wooldridge 2001, p. 16.

[13] Munakata 2008, p. 2.

[14] AI Watch Joint Research Centre 2020, p. 11.

[15] Boulanin 2016, p. 23.

[16] Ibid.

[17] Boulanin 2016, p. 23.

[18] See Sect. 3.3.2. A percept is any input an agent receives from the environment at any given instant, based on which it can construct a world model and make decisions. For example, how does one symbolically define a giraffe? Percepts were previously referenced in Sect. 2.3 as a form of Influence the Environment exerts upon the System; see Fig. 3.1.

[19] Wooldridge 2001, p. 21 (emphasis removed).

[20] Knight 2017.

[21] Munakata 2008, p. 2.

if machines took inspiration from biology, and learned by observing and experiencing".[22] ML is ubiquitous in modern times. It lies "at the core of many recent advances in science and technology"[23] and have been embraced as the dominant solutions for tasks such as computer vision, speech recognition, and NLP (natural language processing).[24] It has become so dominant and widespread vis-à-vis symbolic AI that the term 'ML' is sometimes conflated with the broader term 'AI'.[25]

ML is an incredibly powerful tool, enabling AI to resolve problems previously impossible for older strands, and has fundamentally changed how the global economy, business and strategic balancing landscape works.[26] DARPA, however, warned that ML is also a risk: "Today, machine learning (ML) is coming into its own, ready to serve mankind in a diverse array of applications .... However, if misapplied, misused or subverted, ML holds the potential for great harm—this is the double-edged sword of machine learning".[27]

ML develops in the absence of explicit instructions by the programmer.[28] In a nutshell, ML entails computers being told to teach themselves how to act.[29] When designing an ML model, the designer no longer is the 'programmer' in the strict sense, but takes up a coaching role.[30] In Molnar's view, this constitutes a "paradigm shift" from normal programming. No longer do instructions need to be explicitly provided to the computer; instead, the designer engages in 'indirect programming' by providing appropriate data and guiding the training process.[31] Instead of performing rule-based calculations, ML relies on datasets to generate its own algorithm that best maps input data to the desired output.[32] Through large quantities of training data, the model 'learns' from past activity, steadily improving its predictions and its problem-solving capability.[33] ML systems are data-driven agents—"a specific type of artificial intelligence, capable of perceiving an environment and acting upon it, based on the processing of massive amounts of digital data".[34]

ML performs its calculations primarily through learning from patterns of inference, by abstracting statistical relationships in data.[35] Any conclusions derived by ML remain hidden within its numeric model and any principles the model may extract

[22] Knight 2017.

[23] Ribeiro et al. 2016, p. 3.

[24] Engstrom et al. 2019, p. 1.

[25] UK House of Lords 2018, p. 16.

[26] Ministère des Armées 2019, p. 4; UNIDIR 2016, p. 7.

[27] DARPA 2019.

[28] Defense Innovation Board 2019, p. 46.

[29] Hofman 2020: "*In een notendop houdt dat in dat computers niet door mensen wordt verteld hoe ze moeten handelen, maar dat ze zichzelf leren hoe ze moeten handelen*".

[30] Kowert 2017, p. 183.

[31] Molnar 2019, p. 12.

[32] Molnar 2019, p. 10; Scharre 2016, p. 15.

[33] Fallon and Blaha 2018, p. 247.

[34] Hildebrandt 2016, p. 4.

[35] Boulanin 2016, p. 23.

are not written into explicit code.[36] Abaimov and Martellini summarise the process as follows:

> ML process computer systems adjust algorithms and statistical models to effectively perform a specific task, relying solely on patterns and inference. Abstract solution strategies are extracted from an extensive dataset, then they are supplemented, expanded and improved using data known and unknown to the system. Finally, the perfected solution strategies (models) are applied to specific problems.[37]

Literature generally distinguishes between different training styles, which nevertheless have in common that the programmer feeds large amounts of training data to the model, allowing it to produce a robust, generalisable formula.[38] Three styles, unsupervised, supervised and reinforcement training, are the most dominant.[39] *Unsupervised learning* amounts to 'clustering tasks', where the main goal is to use the ML model to identify patterns in the data but no specific outcome is sought.[40] In this approach, the data is supplied in raw, or 'unlabelled', form.[41] In *supervised learning*, the desired result of each potential input is known and the training process aims to 'teach' these correlations to the computer.[42] In this method, data is pre-labelled so the computer can determine the correct correlations between the desired input and output data.[43] In *reinforcement learning*, the trained agent is allowed to learn through iterative steps by interacting with the environment and assigning rewards or punishments based on the desirability of its previous action.[44] Little to no labelled data is required for this style of training; instead, progress is made through trial and error and by the computer attempting to maximise the net reward received through its interactions.[45] Russell and Norvig digestibly describe the method as follows: "Imagine playing a new game whose rules you don't know; after a hundred or so moves, your opponent announces, "You lose."'"[46]

---

[36] Deng 2015, p. 25.

[37] Abaimov and Martellini 2020, p. 144. The French Ministry of the Armed Forces also uses a very descriptive, comprehensive definition: "*famille d'algorithmes qui prend en entrée un corpus de données (ou un simulateur de données) annotées en fonction de la tâche à effectuer et qui produit en sortie un modèle capable de reproduire le comportement attendu sur le corpus initial et de généraliser ce comportement de manière pertinente sur de nouvelles données*". Ministère des Armées 2019, p. 4.

[38] UNIDIR 2016, p. 4; Knight 2019.

[39] High-Level Expert Group On Artificial Intelligence 2019, p. 3.

[40] Molnar 2019, p. 10; Katyal 2019, p. 69.

[41] Nilsson 1996, p. 1.

[42] Molnar 2019, p. 10; FRA, above n. 9.

[43] Fallon and Blaha 2018, p. 248; Defense Innovation Board 2019, p. 47. The actual task performed by the algorithm depends on the type of desired output. If the output is discrete (such as sex or combatant/non-combatant), the learning problem is classification; if the output is numerical (such as price or incidental civilian harm), the learning problem is regression. Russell and Norvig 2010, p. 696.

[44] Molnar 2019, p. 10; Defense Innovation Board 2019, p. 47.

[45] Fallon and Blaha 2018, p. 248; Leslie 2019, p. 34.

[46] Russell and Norvig 2010, p. 831.

Neural networks or neural nets are one tool of ML whereby the computer system is organised of multiple layers of nodes or 'neurons'.[47] Inputs are processed by the first layer of neurons, propagated through the middle layers, and link to the final layer which generates the model's output.[48] Some neural nets use a very high number of hidden layers stacked 'deeply', often referred to as deep learning.[49] Similarly to other ML techniques, but even more profoundly so due to the layer depth, the internal mechanisms of these processes are difficult to grasp beyond the first (input) and last (output) layer. These models "consume all the examples you might give them, forming their own webs of inference that can then be applied to pictures they've never seen before".[50] Deep neural nets are extremely powerful and have seen extensive successes, precisely due to the huge parametric space provided by layer depth.[51] They are generally described as the most accurate models,[52] delivering state-of-the-art performance in many domains, such as classification, speech, computer vision, and bioinformatics.[53] Some have emphasised that the performance of deep neural nets approach, match, or even exceed human-level performance on key benchmarks.[54] Nguyen et al. and Kuttichira et al. also note their flexibility, being able to work across different datasets with just slight tuning of the hyperparameters.[55]

3.2.2.1 Strengths

In addition to the raw performance metrics described above, there are several inherent advantages of ML compared to traditional AI, which explains their popularity. The first is that ML opens the door to *tasks which are too difficult to program manually*. To recall, symbolically representing complex aspects of the natural environment was one of the key challenges of symbolic AI. This task is difficult for programmers because it is not a very human thing to do: when recognising faces or driving, humans work

---

[47] Auerbach 2015; UK House of Lords 2018, p. 14.

[48] Defense Innovation Board 2019, p. 46. Knight provides a useful summary of the overall process: "A network's reasoning is embedded in the behavior of thousands of simulated neurons, arranged into dozens or even hundreds of intricately interconnected layers. The neurons in the first layer each receive an input, like the intensity of a pixel in an image, and then perform a calculation before outputting a new signal. These outputs are fed, in a complex web, to the neurons in the next layer, and so on, until an overall output is produced. Plus, there is a process known as back-propagation that tweaks the calculations of individual neurons in a way that lets the network learn to produce a desired output". Knight 2017. See also a useful simplified graphic representation of deep neural nets in UK House of Lords 2018, p. 15.

[49] Vocabulaire de l'intelligence artificielle, above n. 9; Nguyen et al. 2015, p. 1.

[50] Kuang 2017.

[51] Barredo Arrieta et al. 2020, p. 83.

[52] High-Level Expert Group On Artificial Intelligence 2019, p. 4.

[53] Fawzi et al. 2018, p. 1.

[54] Engstrom et al. 2019, p. 1.

[55] Nguyen et al. 2015, p. 1; Kuttichira et al. 2019, p. 4.

intuitively; they do not explicitly define every single relevant aspect of the inputs.[56] Many real-world objectives are difficult to encode as real-valued functions.[57] Bathaee draws a good analogy with 'knowing' how to ride a bicycle and how this is impossible to symbolically (theoretically) impart to a student. Instead, the student would be 'taught' by doing—machine learning.[58] Even seemingly banal tasks run into this issue:

> [I]f we need to classify emails as spam or not spam, we need a software program to do this. We could sit down, manually review a ton of email, and write if-statements to perform this task. People have tried. It turns out that this approach is slow, fragile, and not very effective. Instead, we can use machine learning techniques to solve this problem.[59]

Another challenge of manual programming relates to *indeterminacy*. If the intended operating environment is (partially) indeterminate, the number of possible scenarios to define rises exponentially. Not only is it impossible to anticipate all possible situations the agent might find itself on, it is also impossible to anticipate all possible changes in the environment itself.[60] It is for this reason that ML is dominant for tasks performed in more complex, unpredictable environments: they are more robust and can operate in situations which cannot be comprehensively described through symbolic behavioural rules.[61] Finally, some authors have pointed out the ability to learn as a benefit: describing the use of ML in autonomous cars, Thurnher remarks that "[t]he true breakthrough ... is the way in which they adapt and learn. These systems essentially are able to learn from their own mistakes".[62]

3.2.2.2 Issues

The unique way ML is designed also comes with crucial drawbacks. First, in the same way that humans are shaped by their formative environment, so too does data shape the resulting model. ML techniques rely on large, quality datasets to achieve the goal of creating a robust and generalisable model. In essence, the final ML model is nothing more than a function of the quality and quantity of the data fed to it. We shall refer to this generally as the problem of *data reliance*.

The problem of data reliance is multi-faceted. From the perspective of *quantity*, successful ML models require a large amount of data to program properly: generally, "[t]he more, the better".[63] It was this quantitative reliance that prevented ML to become a staple technique until relatively recently, when more datasets became

56 Boulanin 2016, p. 23.

57 Lipton 2016, p. 2.

58 Bathaee 2018, p. 902.

59 Brownlee 2020.

60 Russell and Norvig 2010, p. 693.

61 High-Level Expert Group On Artificial Intelligence 2019, p. 4; Abaimov and Martellini 2020, p. 144; Hofman 2020.

62 Thurnher 2012, p. 79.

63 Molnar 2019, p. 10.

available.[64] However, in some domains, including military tasks, such data may be less frequent, which generates concerns about whether programmers for such systems can amass sufficient data for training an ML model in that task.[65] In addition, not only must the quantity be high, the data must also be *qualitatively* sufficient. It is a common concern that the large amounts of available datasets distract from "questions about the quality, fidelity, and provenance" of the data itself.[66] This dependency on the quality of the underlying data can make ML models deceptively brittle if the problem is not properly pre-empted during its design process.[67]

Issues with the training data can impact the model's performance. Ultimately, the goal is to ensure that the trained model will *generalise*: that it performs well not only on the test instances, but also in practice.[68] This can only be achieved if the training data is a reasonable approximation of what will be met by the system 'in the wild'.[69] If the training data is unrepresentative, the system will be unable to generalise and fail to perform.[70] Relatedly, many writers have also raised concerns about training bias: if the training data is unrepresentative or inherently prejudiced, the resulting model will also be unrepresentative or discriminatory.[71] Finally, data reliance may also have adverse effects on adversarial resistance, creating additional weaknesses to attacks such as data poisoning and model inversions.[72] Alternatively, the trained model can exhibit *overfitting*. This occurs when the model is trained too much for accuracy, leading to excessive fidelity to the training set at the expense of generalisability.[73] Summarising, "*si les données d'apprentissage sont inexistantes, inaccessibles, en quantité insuffisante ou sans correspondance avec le cadre d'emploi souhaité, les résultats obtenus ne seront pas satisfaisants.*"[74]

Another issue concerns *opacity*. Because the machine learns 'intuitively' and does not (and often cannot) necessarily disclose how it reaches its conclusions from its learnt patterns of inference, many ML models essentially become black boxes and difficult to predict.[75] This is to be contrasted with rule-based AI, which has "one major virtue: it is always clear why the machine makes the choice that it does, because its

---

[64] Cukier 2018, p. 29; UK House of Lords 2018, p. 28.

[65] Defense Innovation Board 2019, p. 66; Abaimov and Martellini 2020, p. 146.

[66] Defense Innovation Board 2019, p. 16.

[67] Cummings 2018, p. 13.

[68] Bathaee 2018, p. 900.

[69] Gillespie 2014: "The most common problem in algorithm design is that the new data turns out not to match the training data in some consequential way. Sometimes new phenomena emerge that the training data simply did not include and could not have anticipated; just as often, something important was overlooked as irrelevant, or was scrubbed from the training data in preparation for the development of the algorithm."

[70] Katyal 2019, p. 70.

[71] UK House of Lords 2018, p. 41; Molnar 2019, p. 17.

[72] Defense Innovation Board 2019, p. 16.

[73] Nakkiran presents an effective graphical representation of this process. See Nakkiran 2019.

[74] Ministère des Armées 2019, p. 7.

[75] Boulanin 2016, p. 24.

designers set the rules".[76] Lack of predictability does not necessarily come uniquely from an AI's data-driven nature, but it is one of the dominant reasons. One may ask to what extent we truly can rely on opaque ML systems, knowing that they may be limited or vulnerable, but do not know in which way.[77]

These benefits and challenges greatly impact the risk assessment process when using AWS, and will be expanded upon in coming chapters.

3.3 The AI Decision-Making Process

A decision made by an AI is not a decision made in a vacuum. Any output must be preceded by an accompanying input. Then where does this input originate from in the context of an AWS? It is this broader decision-making process that we will discuss now. In this section, we zoom out from the software to the level of the AWS, or more generally, the ***agent***.

There are many conceptions of 'agent', so let us consider a few examples. Russell and Norvig define it as "anything that can be viewed as perceiving its environment through sensors and acting upon that environment through actuators".[78] Frank et al. present the following definition: "anything that can be viewed as perceiving its environment through sensors and acting upon that environment through effectors [and is] situated in some environment and capable of autonomous action".[79] According to Wooldridge, an AI agent is a "computer system that is situated in some environment, and that is capable of autonomous action in this environment in order to meet its design objectives". Tolk prefers a more descriptive approach and submits three main characteristics of intelligent software agents: (1) they are situated in, perceive, and act in their environment, (2) they can operate without the direct intervention of humans or others, and (3) they exhibit a degree of flexibility, i.e., they can act on their own knowledge and experiences, adapt to new circumstances, etc.[80]

While distinctly formulated, each of the definitions contain very similar components. First, there is a consistent chronological element of the agent taking in its surroundings ('perceiving'), contemplating, then acting upon the environment. Second, an agent is somewhat autonomous, in that it possesses the requisite sophistication to enact this decision-making process independently of outside assistance.[81] Finally, there is quite some emphasis on the surrounding environment itself: the agent is situated within this environment, from which it derives its perceptions, and exerts

[76] Deng 2015, p. 25.

[77] Hofman 2020.

[78] Russell and Norvig 2010, p. 34.

[79] Frank et al. 2001, sct 2.2.

[80] Tolk and Uhrmacher 2009, p. 77.

[81] Note the difference between 'autonomous' used in this sense, which designates the agent's capacity to independently complete its decision-making process, and autonomy in the delegative sense, which designates how much freedom the agent is granted to make decisions.

some influence on it based on its ultimate decision. Note that 'environment' here is not necessarily meant as a physical environment.[82] This differentiates *agents* from *robots*, with robots being a subset of the former. Robots are agents which necessarily live and effect changes in the 'real world'; i.e., there is an additional physical element to their being.[83] There is no requirement for the agent to completely transform its surrounding reality—partial influence suffices.[84]

Let us elaborate further on the first element, namely how an agent perceives, contemplates and acts.

3.3.1 Sensing, Deciding and Acting

How does an AI system achieve rationality?[85] At its core, not very differently from how humans do. While the exact descriptors may differ, almost all authors ultimately identify three fundamental steps in the decision-making process of any intelligent agent: *sensing* the environment, *deciding* a course of action, and *acting* upon it. The DoD found that "[a]t the most basic level, autonomy draws on three broad, multi-disciplinary technical fields: perception, cognition, and action". Cummings agrees that both human and artificial intelligence follows a "perception–cognition–action information processing loop".[86] Lyons and Havig speak of sensing, planning, and acting.[87] Boulanin found that autonomy "is always enabled by the integration of the same three fundamental capabilities: sense, decide and act".[88]

Some prefer a four-step framework. The EU HLEG found four components: perceiving, processing, deciding, and acting.[89] Parasuraman et al. and Theunissen endorse the approach of information acquisition, information analysis, decision selection, and action implementation.[90] We adopt Parasuraman et al.'s terminology in shortened form for the remainder of this book when referring to the four-step model: *acquisition*, *analysis*, *decision*, and *action* ('AADA').

There is not a fundamental difference between the three- and four-step approaches, and notably, the standard sense-decide-act loop remains present in the four-step model. The added value of the four-step model is the additional second step,

[82] An agent can, for example, act purely in a digital environment. AI cyberweapons would be one example of a weapon which is an agent, but not a robot.

[83] See e.g. the following definitions of *robot*: Russell and Norvig 2010, p. 971 ("physical agents that perform tasks by manipulating the physical world"); High-Level Expert Group On Artificial Intelligence 2019, p. 4 ("a physical machine that has to cope with the dynamics, the uncertainties and the complexity of the physical world").

[84] Wooldridge 2001, p. 5.

[85] High-Level Expert Group On Artificial Intelligence 2019, p. 3.

[86] Cummings 2018, p. 8.

[87] Lyons and Havig 2014, p. 182.

[88] Boulanin 2016, p. 11.

[89] High-Level Expert Group On Artificial Intelligence 2019, p. 1.

[90] Parasuraman et al. 2000, p. 287; Theunissen and Suarez 2015, p. 181.

'processing' or 'analysis' (which under the three-step model is subsumed under either sensing or deciding). Separating this 'analysis' into a separate step has the advantage of being more precise. Analysis refers to interpreting and transforming the percepts acquired during the acquisition step and synthesising that into an internally understandable format.[91] The four-step model for example yields this comprehensive narration of the intelligent agent's decision-making process:

> [What an AI system does is] perceiving the environment in which the system is immersed through some sensors, thus collecting and interpreting data, reasoning on what is perceived or processing the information derived from this data, deciding what the best action is, and then acting accordingly, through some actuators, thus possibly modifying the environment.[92]

Primarily in military works and manuals, one often finds a different model used to describe the decision-making process, the OODA loop. The acronym OODA refers to *observe*, *orient*, *decide*, and *act*.[93] This model, popularised by John Boyd in 1996, in essence explains the same process as discussed previously with a slight military twist. In the OODA loop, the agent *observes* its surroundings and gathers data, *orients* itself by interpreting the gathered information, weighs all potential courses of action and *decides* on one, and *acts* to execute its decision.[94] The value of Boyd's model lies in the additional insight he provided as to the adversarial component of decision-making.

Understanding this requires a short detour into the model's history. Boyd originally conceived the model to answer the question of why American F-18 fighter jets outperformed their Soviet MiG-5 counterparts. He found that the American jets were superior because they could both complete their OODA loop faster than the adversary, as well as disrupt their opponents from completing theirs (making them 'out of sync').[95] The model simplicity and effectiveness made it transcended its military roots: the OODA concept has become popular even in other competitive environments, such as business and sports.[96] This adversarial component is an important insight to consider, particularly when discussing the competitive aspect of AWS use: in Chap. 6, we return to discuss the contested military environment in greater detail.

Below, we discuss in some more detail specific steps of the AADA process.

3.3.2 Acquisition

In this step, the agent observes its surroundings, "using all his senses to take in the world around him … to absorb as much information about his environment as

[91] Marra and McNeil 2013, pp. 12–13.

[92] High-Level Expert Group On Artificial Intelligence 2019, p. 3.

[93] Boyd 1996. For more details, see Osinga 2005; Brown 2018.

[94] Boyd 1996.

[95] Marra and McNeil 2013, p. 10.

[96] Ibid.

possible".[97] A *percept* is any input the agent receives from the environment at any given instant.[98] For knowledge-based agents, outputs might not solely be based on the input at that moment, but also on previous experiences. For this, the agent might rely on a *percept sequence*, or "the complete history of everything the agent has ever perceived".[99] Percepts are gathered through sensors, sometimes colloquially referred to as the agent's 'senses'. *Sensors* are interfaces between the agent and outside world which measure some aspect of the environment.[100] Senses can be visual, auditory, olfactory, somatosensory and gustatory, based on balance or heat, etc.[101] For this, machines can use cameras, microphones, acoustic sensors, gyro sensors or other technology.[102] Some senses available to machines are inaccessible to humans, such as magnetic orientation, radio, infrared, GPS, wireless signals, or active sensing.[103] Finally, some sensors are linked to a human-machine interface: keyboards or touchscreens, for example, allow humans to interact with the machine in a way that their instructions can be translated into valid inputs by the agent.[104]

Artificial agents are inherently built to occupy a specific task environment.[105] It is thus not necessary to equip each agent with all possible sensory receptors, but it must be endowed with all those sensors which enable it to obtain all *necessary* inputs. Put another way, "we need to provide the AI system with sensors that are adequate to perceive the data present in the environment that are relevant to the goal given to the AI system by its human designer".[106] Finally, the acquisition phase has evident causal ramifications down the AADA ladder. Faulty, deficient, inaccurate, or incomplete observations will cause the received percepts to not properly reflect the surrounding environment, which may lead to inaccurate output. "As the saying goes, "garbage in, garbage out" … faulty information at the [acquisition] stage affects the rest of the process."[107]

---

[97] Marra and McNeil 2013, p. 12.

[98] Winikoff et al. 2001, p. 4.

[99] Russell and Norvig 2010, p. 34.

[100] Office of the Assistant Secretary of Defense for Research and Engineering 2015, p. 1; Russell and Norvig 2010, p. 928.

[101] High-Level Expert Group On Artificial Intelligence 2019, p. 2.

[102] Abaimov and Martellini 2020, p. 144.

[103] Russell and Norvig 2010, p. 928; Canada 2016. *Active sensing* refers to the agent actively emitting signals to measure its environment, such echolocation in bats. See Russell and Norvig 2010, p. 973.

[104] High-Level Expert Group On Artificial Intelligence 2019, p. 2.

[105] Simon 1996, p. 5.

[106] High-Level Expert Group On Artificial Intelligence 2019, p. 2.

[107] Marra and McNeil 2013, pp. 13–14.

3.3.3 Analysis

Sensors function as an interface between the agent and the outside world. They are merely observers. Thus, percepts by themselves do not mean anything—the cliché of machines seeing everything in zeroes and ones is true here.[108] To process these percepts, AI must *analyse*: in this stage, algorithms "turn those data into contextual understanding".[109] The EU HLEG report descriptively refers to this stage as *knowledge representation* (as opposed to *knowledge reasoning* for the Decide step).[110] By synthesising the observed information and converting it into knowledge internally understandable to the agent, it can "weave together many independent data points into a coherent portrait of the world".[111] This is particularly important if the system functions in a dynamic environment, which must be represented through a continually updating world model.[112]

The level of challenge for the analysis stage inherently depends on the envisaged task complexity. Structured input data (e.g. a relational database) requires less sophistication than unstructured data which does not have pre-defined organisation (e.g. an image or video feed).[113] A video feed contains an extremely high density of information, which the AI must learn to categorise and either interpret or ignore.[114] Cummings emphasises that task complexity also is a factor of the environmental complexity. For example, the world model that an unmanned aerial vehicle's AI must construct is less demanding than that of an autonomous car, owing to its operating environment. While the former operates in relatively open, uncluttered environments, the latter must interpret road signs, lanes, pedestrians and other traffic to create a robust world model.[115] This perceptual intelligence in more complex domains has been difficult to achieve until recently, and many agree that the solution to the challenges lies in ML and their ability to exhibit flexible, advanced situational understanding.[116] The DoD in 2015, for example, made optimistic comments of how it views the incorporation of higher-level perception as possible in the near future, including predicting intent or threat levels.[117]

[108] High-Level Expert Group On Artificial Intelligence 2019, p. 2.
[109] Office of the Assistant Secretary of Defense for Research and Engineering 2015, p. 1.
[110] High-Level Expert Group On Artificial Intelligence 2019, p. 3.
[111] Marra and McNeil 2013, pp. 12–13.
[112] Cummings 2018, p. 9.
[113] High-Level Expert Group On Artificial Intelligence 2019, p. 2.
[114] Russell and Norvig 2010, p. 929.
[115] Cummings 2018, p. 9.
[116] Boulanin 2016, pp. 23–24.
[117] Office of the Assistant Secretary of Defense for Research and Engineering 2015, p. 1.

3.3.4 Decision

The decision phase is when the agent translates its received and interpreted percepts into actions.[118] For a person, this occurs when "she weighs the potential courses of action based on the knowledge she has accumulated and decides how to act".[119] Boulanin uses the term *control system* to refer to this part of the agent's decision-making process (as it ultimately 'controls' the agent's actions). The EU HLEG refers to this step as 'knowledge reasoning', i.e., "making inferences through symbolic rules, planning and scheduling activities, searching through a large solution set, and optimizing among all possible solutions to a problem".[120] As indicated by this description, there is not necessarily a standard method to design a control system. Russell and Norvig describe many different approaches that can be taken, broadly to be divided into *reflex-based systems* (simple reflex and model-based reflex)[121] and *optimisation-based systems* (goal-based, utility-based, and learning-based).[122] The main difference between these categories lies in the fact that the latter is more flexible, resolving issues not through stringent if-then-else rules but by working towards a more general goal.[123]

Literature generally recommends certain approaches for certain envisaged task domains. For skill- and rule-based tasks, i.e. those which require simple sensory-motor actions, subroutines or set procedures, rule-based programs generally suffice because most elements can straightforwardly be represented mathematically.[124] The more general or unstructured the task, the stronger the push for optimisation-based systems, which provide the agent flexibility in balancing alternatives to determine the optimal route toward the overall goal.[125] Optimisation-based systems are also advantageous in cases where not every scenario is foreseeable or programmable during the design stage.[126] In practice, many complex analyses involve factors unknown ahead of time.[127] Returning to environmental complexity influencing the agent program, Russell and Norvig emphasise that uncertainty and dynamicity are one of the primary drivers for installing optimisation-based systems, such as value functions.[128] Tolk agrees that flexibility is "one of the critical aspects for an agent to achieve its tasks in a dynamic environment".[129] As most task domains envisaged for AWS are real

[118] Russell and Norvig 2010, p. 34.

[119] Marra and McNeil 2013, p. 10 (emphasis removed).

[120] High-Level Expert Group On Artificial Intelligence 2019, p. 3.

[121] See Russell and Norvig 2010, pp. 48–50.

[122] See Ibid., pp. 52–56.

[123] Ibid., p. 53.

[124] Cummings 2018, p. 11.

[125] Keeley 2015, p. 199.

[126] Boulanin 2016, p. 13.

[127] Office of the Assistant Secretary of Defense for Research and Engineering 2015, p. 2.

[128] Russell and Norvig 2010, p. 503. For how utility functions can provide an answer to environmental uncertainty, see Russell and Norvig 2010, pp. 615–625.

[129] Tolk 2015, p. 291.

battlefields, marked by "changing conditions, a threatening environment, and unpredictable consequences",[130] AWS control systems will have to account for this by mostly implementing optimisation-based approaches.

3.3.5 *Action*

An *action* or *output* is "something which an agent does".[131] It is the way "decisions made by the control systems are … exerted in the real world".[132] It is here where the reciprocal relationship of an agent with its surroundings is completed, through the exertion of influence on an environment from which it derived its inputs. The agent implements its decision through an *actuator*, which does not have to be physical: a digital output, a signal to another agent, or a line of text is also an output.[133] In physical agents, however, the actuator functions as "the control line that communicates a command to the *effector*",[134] which is a physical extension of the agent asserting force on the environment.[135] Just like humans are limited in what they can achieve by their physiology and biology, the range of tasks possible to an agent is limited by its technological design.[136] "If the program is going to recommend actions like *Walk*, the architecture had better have legs."[137] For AWS, its type and quantity of munitions also form part of its effectors. What effectors an AWS is equipped with thus greatly impacts its damage potential, flexibility, risk, etc.

3.4 The Military Environment

One thing that the discussion thus far has highlighted is the significant influence exerted by the environment on an AI's performance and decision-making. AI-systems that can be used relatively safely in one environment may be entirely unsuitable in others, and some contextual characteristics (e.g. the presence of hostile agents) may impose entirely new design demands on the system (e.g. resistance against adversarial action) before it can be reliably deployed. For Deployer, awareness of the operational environment is therefore just as crucial as technical knowledge of the system itself.

---

[130] Manekin 2017, p. 610.

[131] Winikoff et al. 2001, p. 4.

[132] Boulanin 2016, p. 13.

[133] High-Level Expert Group On Artificial Intelligence 2019, p. 3.

[134] Russell and Norvig 2010, p. 971 (emphasis added).

[135] Ibid.; Boulanin 2016, p. 13. There are different kinds of effector, such as a manipulator, mobile, and mobile manipulator, the details of which are not relevant. See Russell and Norvig 2010, pp. 971–972.

[136] Marra and McNeil 2013, p. 14.

[137] Russell and Norvig 2010, p. 46.

This section explores the importance of Contextual Awareness, what characterises the military environment in particular, and the implications this has on intelligence gathering.

3.4.1 Importance of Continuous Intelligence

Contextual Awareness, often also referred to as 'situational awareness' or 'situational understanding',[138] refers to the state of being informed of the environment in which a weapon system will perform actions. The utility of Contextual Awareness is summarised well in the 2019 NATO Manual:

> The role of intelligence is to contribute to a continuous and coordinated understanding of the operating environment, to support commanders by identifying conditions required to achieve objectives; avoiding undesired effects; and assessing the impact of adversary, friendly and neutral actors on the commanders' concept of operations. Intelligence is therefore an aid to provide situational awareness, develop understanding and is a critical tool for decision-making. Intelligence should drive operations by providing the user with timely and accurate products that supports their particular needs and is tailor-made to those requirements.[139]

Contextual Awareness is obtained through intelligence, surveillance and reconnaissance (ISR).[140] High-quality and complete ISR has always been an indispensable requirement for proper weapon use: "weapon precision is, at best, only as good as the information that supports it".[141] Because ISR is so crucial to proper decision-making, its collection is generally viewed as falling under the ambit of precautionary duties,[142] in the sense that commanders possess an active duty under IHL to gather timely and accurate ISR to the furthest extent feasible.[143] This general obligation persists irrespective of whether the weapon in question is conventional or AI-based.

Many sources, including the NATO Manual cited above, emphasise the importance of *continuity*. It is not sufficient that ISR is conducted once, for instance at the start of the targeting cycle, as the environment is continually in motion. Contextual Awareness is only effective for as long as the information upon which it is based remains relevant,[144] as unanticipated changes may entirely invalidate assumptions

---

[138] See Roorda 2015, p. 31; ICRC 2019.

[139] NATO 2019, para 1.50.

[140] For an extensive overview of ISR methods, see Kouba 2017, pp. 107–116. For a modern analysis, see Krupiy 2015.

[141] Waxman 2000, p. 60. Incidents such as the mistaken attack on the Chinese Embassy in Belgrade (1999) demonstrate that even great improvements in weapon sophistication and precision change little when Contextual Awareness is lacking. Waszink 2011, p. 20.

[142] Schmitt 2010, para 16.07.3; Durhin 2016, p. 189.

[143] Puckett 2004, p. 670. As Gillard submits, any unit planning attacks "must do everything feasible to have access to information and analysis on a range of factors that can affect incidental harm, and must make use of this information in their assessments". Gillard 2018, p. 47.

[144] Roff and Moyes 2016, p. 2.

and predictions upon which previous decisions were made.[145] In addition, one's *own* operations may have affected the environment, as demonstrated in Fig. 3.1 through the *Action* and *Impact* arrows. Contextual Awareness must thus be complemented with Assessment Awareness,[146] which entails updating our information and beliefs as soon as possible after each engagement.

3.4.2 Attributes of a Military Environment

Continuous ISR is necessary to counter the environment's ***dynamicity***, which is one aspect that distinguishes the military environment from other (civil) AI domains such as navigation, health care and goods and services: active battlefields are much more rapidly changing and evolving.[147] This factor has been accurately underlined by the DoD as an added challenge for AWS, as these dynamic and often unexpected changes offer considerably more opportunities for deployed systems to fail unforeseeably.[148] Environmental dynamicity must therefore be taken into consideration during Deployer's decision-making.

Many sources also emphasise the ***complex*** nature of military environments. They are relatively unstructured, and in contrast to civil domains, there is generally "no opportunity to structure the environment or map it to make the problem easier for the autonomous system".[149] Military environments involve many unknowns,[150] are 'open world', and frequently include multiple agents which may be uncooperative.[151] This complex, unstructured nature of battlefields is also one of the primary reasons why adaptive and data-driven AI will be particularly valuable in modern military systems (instead of rule-based ones).[152]

This complexity makes it quite difficult—in some views impossible—to provide 100% reliable statements on a system's performance, as edge cases and unforeseen performance-degrading elements always remain a possibility.[153] We will refer to this as the *infinite variance problem*,[154] and needs to be taken into consideration at all times. Second, some Context Controls are specifically designed to limit such variance, by imposing some structure to the environment or limiting the presence

[145] Roorda 2015, p. 160.
[146] See Sect. 2.4.6.
[147] Holland Michel 2020, p. 11.
[148] Defense Innovation Board 2019, p. 39.
[149] Defense Science Board 2016, p. 13.
[150] Danzig 2018, p. 7.
[151] Ministère des Armées 2019, pp. 4, 29.
[152] See Sect. 3.2.2.
[153] Scharre 2018, p. 83.
[154] See Sect. 4.3.

of other agents.[155] Nevertheless, these measures cannot compare to the consistency provided, for instance, by clear highway markings for autonomous cars.[156]

Finally, a military environment is ***adversarial***.[157] Beyond simply being uncooperative, agents will actively plan against the success of our systems. We comprehensively discuss this adversarial nature and all its ramifications in Chap. 6.

3.5 The 'Intended Operational Environment' (IOE)

Given what has been established so far, a problem arises. On the one hand, ML is crucial for AWS due to the unstructured and complex nature of (many) military environments. On the other, we are confronted with the *narrow AI limitation.* While some speculation about the viability of artificial general intelligence (AGI) exists,[158] it is generally viewed that (at least in the foreseeable future) most AI will remain 'narrow'.[159] One of the main characteristics of narrow AI is that it excels at performing tasks it was designed for, sometimes at superhuman levels, but often performs poorly outside of these bounds.[160] The narrow AI limitation entails that "even relatively sophisticated algorithms are subject to failure if they face situations outside of their intended design parameters".[161] Thus, ML is essential to navigate the military environment, but ML is simultaneously very vulnerable to variations and rapid changes that occur within it. What to do?

The solution proposed in this book is to establish an Intended Operational Environment (IOE). An IOE refers to the *operational context for which a particular system was designed, tested and validated.* Clearly defining an IOE for each AWS has the following benefits:

- ***Avoiding deployment beyond the system's limitations***. The IOE, as defined by the designer, constitutes the boundaries within which there are reasonable guarantees that the narrow AI functions as desired. Put another way, an IOE helps to "accurately characterize the bounds of a system's behavior—that is, when it will work and when it will not".[162]
- ***Avoiding out-of-distribution (OOD)***. Out-of-distribution is a prominent cause of modern AI failures and occurs when there is a disconnect between

---

[155] See also Sects. 2.4.3 and 8.7.

[156] Sulzbachner et al. 2015, p. 250.

[157] Boulanin et al. 2020, p. 16; Roff 2016, p. 6.

[158] See e.g. Tzimas 2021, pp. 40–44; Hidalgo et al. 2021, p. 143.

[159] Russell and Norvig 2010, p. 1020; UK Ministry of Defence 2011, para 623; Ministère des Armées 2019, p. 29. A large-scale survey also found broad scepticism about AGI ever materialising. See Müller and Bostrom 2016.

[160] UK House of Lords 2018, p. 15.

[161] Scharre 2011, p. 92.

[162] Flournoy et al. 2020, p. 8.

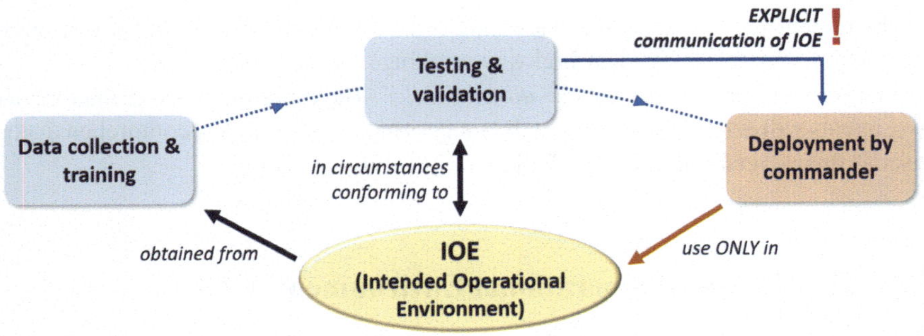

Fig. 3.2 Consistent IOE throughout lifecycle

the distribution of inputs received in the field and those for which the model was originally optimised.[163] We discuss this specific failure cause in Sect. 5.6.

- ***Performance metrics do not generalise***. Performance indicators for AI systems frequently come with the caveat that they only apply under "specified operating conditions".[164] To know whether these indicators can be relied upon, it is necessary to know the IOE they are based on. We return to this in Sect. 4.2.
- ***Legal reviews only cover intended use scenarios***. Pronouncements about the legality of weapons furnished by legal reviews are made on 'intended and anticipated use cases',[165] and do not guarantee that the weapon remains legal outside of this limitation. A weapon's IOE would reflect the assumptions made by the reviewers on aforementioned intended and anticipated use cases. Beyond this IOE, Deployer must be extremely weary as to whether the weapon can be legitimately used at all.

It is thus highly recommended that particularly for AWS, the IOE is made *concrete, clear and transparent* from the moment of design, applied during review, and clearly transmitted to operational commanders prior to use (see Fig. 3.2). Awareness of a weapon's IOE is a prerequisite to the ability to use it properly and legally.

By its very nature, ***an IOE is top-down***. It is a component of Awareness that the *Providing Entity must provide to Deployer*. Deployer is entitled to (1) demand an IOE for any AWS in their arsenal, and (2) is strongly encouraged to refuse use if an IOE was not made available. In later chapters, we shall return to specific cases where it is argued that Deployer is *legally* obliged to refuse use in the absence of an IOE.[166]

---

[163] Steinhardt 2015.

[164] Yoner 2001, p. 38.

[165] Sandoz et al. 1987, para 1466.

[166] For example, it is argued in Sect. 9.3.2 that knowingly using an AWS outside of its IOE should be considered as conducting an indiscriminate attack in the sense of Protocol Additional to the Geneva Conventions of 12 August 1949, and relating to the Protection of Victims of International Armed Conflicts, adopted 8 June 1977, entered into force 7 December 1978, 1125 UNTS 3 (API), Article 51(4)(b–c).

References

Abaimov S, Martellini M (2020) Artificial Intelligence in Autonomous Weapon Systems. In: Martellini M, Ralf T (eds) 21st Century Prometheus. Springer International Publishing, Cham, pp 141–177. DOI: https://doi.org/10.1007/978-3-030-28285-1_8

AI Watch Joint Research Centre (2020) Defining Artificial Intelligence: Towards an Operational Definition and Taxonomy of Artificial Intelligence. European Union, Luxembourg

Auerbach D (2015) Do Androids Dream of Electric Bananas?. Bitwise. https://slate.com/technology/2015/07/google-deepdream-its-dazzling-creepy-and-tells-us-a-lot-about-the-future-of-a-i.html. Accessed 29 April 2021

Barredo Arrieta A et al. (2020) Explainable Artificial Intelligence (XAI): Concepts, Taxonomies, Opportunities and Challenges toward Responsible AI. Information Fusion 58:82–115. DOI: https://doi.org/10.1016/j.inffus.2019.12.012

Bathaee Y (2018) The Artificial Intelligence Black Box and the Failure of Intent and Causation. Harvard Journal of Law and Technology 31:889–938

Billings C E (1996) Human-Centered Aviation Automation: Principles and Guidelines. NASA Technical Memorandum 110381

Boulanin V (2016) Mapping the Development of Autonomy in Weapon Systems: A Primer on Autonomy. Stockholm International Peace Research Institute, Stockholm

Boulanin V et al. (2020) Responsible Military Use of Artificial Intelligence: Can the European Union Lead the Way in Developing Best Practice. SIPRI, Stockholm

Bowne A S (2019) Innovation Acquisition Practices in the Age of AI. Army Lawyer 1:75–78

Boyd J R (1996) The Essence of Winning and Losing. Richards C, Spinney C (eds)

Brown I T (2018) A New Conception of War: John Boyd, the U.S. Marines, and Maneuver Warfare. Marine Corps University Press, Quantico

Brownlee J (2020) Difference Between Algorithm and Model in Machine Learning. https://machinelearningmastery.com/difference-between-algorithm-and-model-in-machine-learning. Accessed 7 November 2020

Canada (2016) Canadian Food For Thought Paper: Context, Complexity and LAWS. In: CCW Informal Meeting of Experts on Lethal Autonomous Weapon Systems. https://docs-library.unoda.org/Convention_on_Certain_Conventional_Weapons_-_Informal_Meeting_of_Experts_(2016)/2016_LAWS%2BMX_CountryPaper%2BCanada%2BFFTP2.pdf. Accessed 10 August 2023

Cukier K (2018) The Economic Implications of Artificial Intelligence. In: Cummings M L et al. (eds) Artificial Intelligence and International Affairs: Disruption Anticipated. Chatham House, London, pp 29–42

Cummings M L (2018) Artificial Intelligence and the Future of Warfare. In: Cummings M L et al. (eds) Artificial Intelligence and International Affairs: Disruption Anticipated. Chatham House, London, pp 7–18

Danzig R (2018) Technology Roulette: Managing Loss of Control as Many Militaries Pursue Technological Superiority. Center for a New American Security, Washington D.C.

DARPA (2019) Defending Against Adversarial Artificial Intelligence. Defense Advanced Research Projects Agency (DARPA). https://www.darpa.mil/news-events/2019-02-06. Accessed 25 October 2020

Defense Innovation Board (2019) AI Principles: Recommendations on the Ethical Use of Artificial Intelligence by the Department of Defense, Defense Innovation Board. US Department of Defense. https://media.defense.gov/2019/Oct/31/2002204458/-1/-1/0/DIB_AI_PRINCIPLES_PRIMARY_DOCUMENT.PDF. Accessed 2 August 2023

Defense Science Board (2016) Report of the Defense Science Board Summer Study on Autonomy. Secretary of Defense for Acquisition, Technology and Logistics

Deng B (2015) The Robot's Dilemma: Working out How to Build Ethical Robots Is One of the Thorniest Challenges in Artificial Intelligence. Nature 523:25–27

Durhin N (2016) Protecting Civilians in Urban Areas: A Military Perspective on the Application of International Humanitarian Law. International Review of the Red Cross 98(1):177–200
Engstrom L et al. (2019) A Rotation and a Translation Suffice: Fooling CNNs with Simple Transformations. In: International Conference on Machine Learning
Fallon C K, Blaha L M (2018) Improving Automation Transparency: Addressing Some of Machine Learning's Unique Challenges. In: Schmorrow D, Fidopiastis C (eds) Augmented Cognition: Intelligent Technologies. Springer, Cham, pp 245–254. DOI: https://doi.org/10.1007/978-3-319-91470-1_21
Fawzi A, Fawzi H, Fawzi O (2018) Adversarial Vulnerability for Any Classifier. http://arxiv.org/abs/1802.08686
Flournoy M A, Haines A, Chefitz G (2020) Building Trust through Testing: Adapting DOD's Test & Evaluation, Validation & Verification (TEVV) Enterprise for Machine Learning Systems, Including Deep Learning Systems. WestExec Advisors, Washington D.C.
Frank A U, Bittner S, Raubal M (2001) Spatial and Cognitive Simulation with Multi-Agent Systems. In: Montello D R (ed) Spatial Information Theory, Foundations of Geographic Information Science International Conference, COSIT 2001
Gillard E-C (2018) Proportionality in the Conduct of Hostilities: The Incidental Harm Side of the Assessment. The Royal Institute of International Affairs, Chatham House, London. https://www.chathamhouse.org/2018/12/proportionality-conduct-hostilities-incidental-harm-side-assessment. Accessed 2 August 2023
Gillespie T (2014) Algorithm [Draft] [#digitalkeywords]. Culture Digitally. https://culturedigitally.org/2014/06/algorithm-draft-digitalkeyword/. Accessed 13 November 2020
Hidalgo C A et al. (2021) How Humans Judge Machines. The MIT Press, Cambridge
High-Level Expert Group On Artificial Intelligence (2019) A Definition of AI: Main Capabilities and Disciplines. European Commission, Brussels
Hildebrandt M (2016) Law as Information in the Era of Data-Driven Agency. The Modern Law Review 79(1):1–30. DOI: https://doi.org/10.1111/1468-2230.12165
Hofman L (2020) De Nieuwste Wapenwedloop Gaat Niet Om Bommen, Maar Om Algoritmes (En Hoe Die Te Foppen). De Correspondent, 19 August 2020. https://decorrespondent.nl/11511/de-nieuwste-wapenwedloop-gaat-niet-om-bommen-maar-om-algoritmes-en-hoe-die-te-foppen/80252bb0-a43e-06da-0cf6-5468281fcfef. Accessed 2 August 2023
Holland Michel A (2020) The Black Box, Unlocked: Predictability and Understandability in Military AI. UNIDIR, Geneva. https://unidir.org/sites/default/files/2020-09/BlackBoxUnlocked.pdf. Accessed 2 August 2023
ICRC (2019) 'Statement of the International Committee of the Red Cross (ICRC) under Agenda Item 5(B)'. Convention on Certain Conventional Weapons (CCW), Group of Governmental Experts on Lethal Autonomous Weapons Systems (Geneva, 25–29 March 2019)
Katyal S (2019) Private Accountability in the Age of Artificial Intelligence. U.C.L.A. Law Review 66:54–141
Keeley T (2015) Auditable Policies for Autonomous Systems (Decisional Forensics). In: Williams A P, Scharre P D (eds) Autonomous Systems: Issues for Defence Policymakers. NATO, The Hague, pp 196–225
Knight W (2017) The Dark Secret at the Heart of AI. Technology Review. www.technologyreview.com/2017/04/11/5113/the-dark-secret-at-the-heart-of-ai. Accessed 2 July 2020
Knight W (2019) Military Artificial Intelligence Can Be Easily and Dangerously Fooled. MIT Technology Review. www.technologyreview.com/2019/10/21/132277/military-artificial-intelligence-can-be-easily-and-dangerously-fooled. Accessed 25 December 2020
Kouba M D (ed) (2017) Operational Law Handbook. 17th ed. International and Operational Law Department, The Judge Advocate General's Legal Center and School, Charlottesville
Kowert W (2017) The Foreseeability of Human-Artificial Intelligence Interactions. Texas Law Review 96:181–204

Krupiy T (2015) A Case against Relying Solely on Intelligence, Surveillance and Reconnaissance Technology to Identify Proposed Targets. Journal of Conflict and Security Law 20(3):415–449. DOI: https://doi.org/10.1093/jcsl/krv009

Kuang C (2017) Can A.I. Be Taught to Explain Itself?. The New York Times. 21 November 2017. www.nytimes.com/2017/11/21/magazine/can-ai-be-taught-to-explain-itself.html. Accessed 6 November 2020

Kuttichira D P et al. (2019) Explaining Black-Box Models Using Interpretable Surrogates. In: Nayak A C, Sharma A (eds) PRICAI 2019: Trends in Artificial Intelligence - 16th Pacific Rim International Conference on Artificial Intelligence. Springer, Cham, pp 3–15. DOI: https://doi.org/10.1007/978-3-030-29908-8_1

Leslie D (2019) Understanding Artificial Intelligence Ethics and Safety: A Guide for the Responsible Design and Implementation of AI Systems in the Public Sector. The Alan Turing Institute, London

Lipton Z C (2016) The Mythos of Model Interpretability. http://arxiv.org/abs/1606.03490

Lyons J B, Havig P R (2014) Transparency in a Human-Machine Context: Approaches for Fostering Shared Awareness/Intent. In: Shumaker R, Lackey S (eds) Virtual, Augmented and Mixed Reality: Designing and Developing Augmented and Virtual Environments, 6th International Conference, VAMR 2014, Lecture No. Springer, Cham, pp 181–190. DOI: https://doi.org/10.1007/978-3-319-07458-0_18

Manekin D (2017) The Limits of Socialization and the Underproduction of Military Violence. Journal of Peace Research 54(5):606–619. DOI: https://doi.org/10.1177/0022343317713558

Marra W, McNeil S (2013) Understanding "The Loop": Regulating the Next Generation of War Machines. Harvard Journal of Law and Public Policy 36(3):1–62

McCarthy J (2007) What Is Artificial Intelligence?. https://www-formal.stanford.edu/jmc/whatisai.pdf. Accessed 3 August 2020

Ministère des Armées (2019) L'intelligence Artificielle Au Service de La Défense. Ministère des Armées, Paris

Molnar C (2019) Interpretable Machine Learning: A Guide for Making Black Box Models Explainable. Lean Publishing

Müller V C, Bostrom N (2016) Future Progress in Artificial Intelligence: A Survey of Expert Opinion. In: Müller V C (ed) Fundamental Issues of Artificial Intelligence. Springer, Cham, pp 553–571

Munakata T (2008) Fundamentals of the New Artificial Intelligence. Springer-Verlag, London

Nakkiran P (2019) A Discussion of "Adversarial Examples Are Not Bugs, They Are Features": Adversarial Examples Are Just Bugs, Too. Distill 4(8). DOI: https://doi.org/10.23915/distill.00019.5

NATO (2019) Allied Joint Doctrine for the Conduct Of Operations. NATO Standard, AJP-3, Edition C Version 1, February 2019

Nguyen A, Yosinski J, Clune J (2015) Deep Neural Networks Are Easily Fooled: High Confidence Predictions for Unrecognizable Images. Computer Vision and Pattern Recognition (CVPR'15). IEEE. http://arxiv.org/abs/1412.1897

Nilsson N J (1996) Introduction to Machine Learning: An Early Draft of a Proposed Textbook. Stanford University, Stanford

Office of the Assistant Secretary of Defense for Research and Engineering (2015) Technical Assessment: Autonomy. US Department of Defense, Washington, D.C

Osinga F (2005) Science, Strategy and War: The Strategic Theory of John Boyd. Doctoral Thesis, University of Leiden

Parasuraman R, Sheridan T B, Wickens C (2000) A Model for Types and Levels of Human Interaction with Automation. IEEE Transactions on Systems, Man, and Cybernetics 30(3):286–297

Puckett C B (2004) In This Era of Smart Weapons, Is a State under an International Legal Obligation to Use Precision-Guided Technology in Armed Conflict. Emory International Law Review 18:645–724

Ribeiro M T, Singh S, Guestrin C (2016) Why Should I Trust You?: Explaining the Predictions of Any Classifier. In: Proceedings of the 22nd ACM SIGKDD International Conference on Knowledge Discovery and Data Mining

Roff H M (2016) Meaningful Human Control or Appropriate Human Judgment? The Necessary Limits on Autonomous Weapons. Briefing Paper for the Delegates at the Review Conference on the Convention on Certain Conventional Weapons, Geneva, 12–16 December 2016

Roff H M, Moyes R (2016) Meaningful Human Control, Artificial Intelligence and Autonomous Weapons. Briefing Paper for the Delegates at the Convention on Certain Conventional Weapons Informal Meeting of Experts on Lethal Autonomous Weapons Systems

Roorda M (2015) NATO's Targeting Process: Ensuring Human Control Over (and Lawful Use of) 'Autonomous' Weapons. In: Williams A P, Scharre P D (eds) Autonomous Systems: Issues for Defence Policymakers. NATO, The Hague, pp 152–168

Russell S J, Norvig P (2010) Artificial Intelligence: A Modern Approach. 3rd edn. Pearson, New Jersey

Sandoz Y, Swinarski C, Zimmerman B (1987) Commentary on the Additional Protocols of 8 June 1977 to the Geneva Conventions of 12 August 1949. Martinus Nijhoff, Geneva

Scharre P D (2011) Why Unmanned. Joint Force Quarterly 61:89–93. https://ndupress.ndu.edu/portals/68/Documents/jfq/jfq-61.pdf. Accessed 4 August 2023

Scharre P D (2016) Autonomous Weapons and Operational Risk. Center for a New American Security, Washington, D.C

Scharre P D (2018) Army of None: Autonomous Weapons and the Future of War. WW Norton & Co, New York

Schmitt M N (2010) Targeting in Operational Law. In: Gill T D, Fleck D (eds) The Handbook of the International Law of Military Operations. Oxford University Press, Oxford, pp 245–275

Simon H A (1996) The Sciences of the Artificial. 3rd edn. The MIT Press, Cambridge

Steinhardt J (2015) Long-Term and Short-Term Challenges to Ensuring the Safety of AI Systems. Wordpress https://jsteinhardt.wordpress.com/2015/06/24/long-term-and-short-term-challenges-to-ensuring-the-safety-of-ai-systems. Accessed 2 February 2021

Sulzbachner C, Zinner C, Kadiofsky T (2015) Passive Optical Sensor Systems For Navigation in an Unstructured, Non-Cooperating Environment. In: Williams A P, Scharre P D (eds) Autonomous Systems: Issues for Defence Policymakers. NATO, The Hague, pp 249–262

Theunissen E, Suarez B (2015) Choosing the Level of Autonomy: Options and Constraints. In: Williams A P, Scharre P D (eds) Autonomous Systems: Issues for Defence Policymakers. NATO, The Hague, pp 169–195

Thurnher J S (2012) No One at the Controls: Legal Implications of Fully Autonomous Targeting. Joint Force Quarterly 67:77–84

Tolk A (2015) Merging Two Worlds: Agent-Based Simulation Methods for Autonomous Systems. In: Williams A P, Scharre P D (eds) Autonomous Systems: Issues for Defence Policymakers. NATO, The Hague, pp 291–317

Tolk A, Uhrmacher A M (2009) Agents: Agenthood, Agent Architectures, and Agent Taxonomies. In: Yilmaz L, Oren T (eds) Agent-Directed Simulation and Systems Engineering. Wiley-VCH Verlag GmbH & Co KGaA, Weinheim, pp 73–109. DOI: https://doi.org/10.1002/9783527627783.ch3

Tzimas T (2021) Legal and Ethical Challenges of Artificial Intelligence from an International Law Perspective. vol 46. Springer, Cham. DOI: https://doi.org/10.1007/978-3-030-78585-7

UK House of Lords (2018) Select Committee on Artificial Intelligence, Report of Session 2017–19, AI in the UK: Ready, Willing, and Able?. HL Paper 100, 16 April 2018

UK Ministry of Defence (2011) The UK Approach to Unmanned Aircraft Systems. Joint Doctrine Note 2/11

UNIDIR (2014) The Weaponization of Increasingly Autonomous Technologies: Considering How Meaningful Human Control Might Move the Discussion Forward. UNIDIR Resources, No 2

UNIDIR (2016) Safety, Unintentional Risk and Accidents in the Weaponization of Increasingly Autonomous Technologies. UNIDIR Resources No 5

Waszink C (2011) Protection of Civilians under International Humanitarian Law: Trends and Challenges. Norwegian Peacebuilding Resource Centre Report, August 2011
Waxman M (2000) International Law and the Politics of Urban Air Operations. RAND Corporation, Santa Monica
Winikoff M, Padgham L, Harland J (2001) Simplifying the Development of Intelligent Agents. AI 2001: Advances in Artificial Intelligence, 10–14 December 2001
Wooldridge M (2001) Intelligent Agents: The Key Concepts. In: Mařík V et al. (eds) Multi-Agent Systems and Applications II (2001) 9th ECCAI-ACAI/EASSS 2001, AEMAS 2001, HoloMAS 2001 Selected Revised Papers
Yoner N (2001) Major Weapon Systems Acquisition and Life Cycle Cost Estimation: A Case Study. Master Thesis, US Naval Postgraduate School

Chapter 4
Measures of Performance

Contents

Abstract Literature on autonomous weapon systems (AWS) make frequent reference to measures of performance (MoP) like accuracy, reliability or robustness, often to make normative statements (e.g. regarding the prohibition on indiscriminate weapons). How users of AWS are expected to interpret and use such MoPs, however, is rarely addressed. This is problematic as many indicators, such as accuracy, are measured very differently for AI systems compared to conventional weapons. This chapter explores in depth four MoPs specific to AI—accuracy, robustness, reliability and understandability—that are crucial to consider when making legal decisions concerning the deployment of AWS. For accuracy, a warning is issued to not take the metric at face value, but instead to decompose the metric into Recall and Specificity, representing an AWS's military utility and ability to discriminate respectively. The importance of understandability from a legal and practical perspective is also highlighted, and juxtaposed to modern AI models which often feature a degree of opacity. For MoPs in general, the chapter concludes that this is an element of Technical Awareness that is largely out of a field commander's hands: instead, responsibility lies with the Providing Entity to engage in careful and effective development and testing to ensure legal and operational benchmarks are upheld. At the same time, end-users of AWS retain important supporting roles, e.g. by providing diligent reports after use to improve robustness and reliabillity predictions of systems.

J. Kwik, *Lawfully Using Autonomous Weapon Technologies*,
https://doi.org/10.1007/978-94-6265-631-4_4

Keywords Autonomous weapon system · Artificial intelligence · Machine learning · Accuracy · Recall · Specificity · Confusion matrix · Indiscriminate weapon · Robustness · Reliability · Explainable AI · Understandability · Opacity · Explainability

4.1 Introduction

In literature and discussions about AWS, liberal use is made of terms such as accuracy, reliability, robustness and transparency, frequently in conjunction with a normative statement. The one may endorse AWS because it would lead to 'more accuracy' or 'better precision',[1] while the other may reject it because the technology is 'not reliable enough' or 'not explainable'.[2] Unfortunately, authors often fail to specify what is meant by these terms and how they would be measured. This limits their practical relevance as they remain nebulous concepts that cannot be applied in engineering terms, nor used as references in normative benchmarks.[3]

This limitation has not gone unnoticed. A 2020 report urged the US DoD to develop a concrete framework and "establish a process for translating the testing framework into testable and verifiable requirements".[4] In this chapter, we take up this recommendation by considering the different Measures of Performance (MoP)[5] in literature: we identify which are of particular relevance for AWS and subsequently discuss these in detail. The aim is to develop a better understanding of the vital MoPs which Deployers should use during capability analysis to analyse the quality of their AWS. In other words, in this chapter, we will be taking a deep dive into one important component of Technical Awareness.[6]

Additionally, in Sect. 4.5, we also address a related parameter, *understandability*. Understandability acts as a *negation* of Awareness, whereby particular characteristics of the system may make it impossible for Deployer to attain the necessary information to make a reasoned decision.

---

[1] E.g. Heyns 2013, para 53; Ney 2019; Geiß and Lahmann 2017, p. 372.

[2] E.g. ICRC 2018, para 21; Crootof 2015, pp. 1873–74; UK House of Lords 2018, p. 38.

[3] Comparable sentiments have been voiced at a national level. See e.g. Eerste Kamer der Staten-Generaal, 'Grip Op Algoritmische Besluitvorming Bij de Overheid: De Rol van de Eerste Kamer, Motie van Het Lid Veldhoen C.S., Voorgesteld 21 Maart 2023, Eerste Kamer' (2023) 2022–2023, CXLVII, F (NLD); US Air Force Office of the Chief Scientist 2015, p. 23.

[4] Flournoy et al. 2020, p. 22.

[5] This term was borrowed from works such as: Doshi-Velez and Kim 2017, p. 1; Leslie 2019, p. 30. There are alternative terms used in literature, such as 'desideratum'; e.g. Hancox-Li 2020, p. 640. 'Measure of performance' is used as an umbrella term to refer to (semi-)quantitative representations of desiderata such as accuracy, reliability, robustness, explainability, etc. For one taxonomy of MoPs in systems, see Glinz 2007, p. 23.

[6] See the facet AW_T in Fig. 3.1.

4.2 Accuracy

Accuracy is a ubiquitous MoP that has been used to describe munitions' ability to strike targets,[7] to demonstrate the superiority of new technology,[8] to argue for the exclusion of some weapons in specific environments (e.g. wide-area weapons in urban contexts),[9] and even as a criterion to label weapons as indiscriminate.[10] However, an AI system is not 'accurate' in the same way a mortar is, and it is "likely that the accuracy and reliability of most autonomous systems will not be able to be measured in the usual ways".[11] Proper Awareness from the part of Deployers, therefore, requires some cognisance on how to assess AI-based accuracy metrics.

4.2.1 Confusion Matrix and Accuracy Metrics

For conventional weapons, accuracy is often operationalised as the degree to which a weapon can strike an intended aimpoint. Schmitt defines accuracy as "a weapon's capacity to strike the precise point at which it is aimed"[12] and Driels as "a quantitative measure of the capability of a weapon system to place ordnance on its intended target".[13] Alternatively, some construe accuracy as the avoidance of dispersion or collateral damage.[14] Measuring a weapon's accuracy and communicating this information to a commander has historically been relatively unproblematic.[15] Factors influencing the accuracy of weapons have generally also been clear.[16]

This is not necessarily the case for systems incorporating AI. Not only does the term 'accuracy' represent a fundamentally distinct concept when uttered by AI designers, but it also is measured differently. Accuracy in AI terms is almost always

---

[7] Article 36 and PAX 2016, p. 14.

[8] Herbach 2012, p. 13.

[9] Durhin 2016.

[10] E.g. SCUD missiles and cluster munitions. See UK Ministry of Defence 2004, The Joint Service Manual of the Law of Armed Conflict. UK Ministry of Defence, London, Joint Service Publication 383 (UK Law of Armed Conflict Manual), sct 6.4.1; Wiebe 2000, pp. 104–09. In *Gotovina*, the ICTY found that the artillery used for the shelling of Knin constituted an indiscriminate attack because they were 'too inaccurate' to be used against a populated area. ICTY (TC), *Prosecutor v. Ante Gotovina et al.*, Judgment, 15 April 2011, IT-06-90-T, para 1897.

[11] Grut 2013, p. 19.

[12] Schmitt 2005, p. 446.

[13] Driels 2013, p. 127.

[14] Brehm 2014, p. 24.

[15] Schuller 2017, p. 390.

[16] The influence of large blast/fragmentation effects, delivery inaccuracies, multiple firings, range to the target, and environmental effects have been extensively studied and are easily graspable by field commanders. See e.g. *Prosecutor v. Ante Gotovina et al.*, above n. 10, para 1165; Article 36 and PAX 2016.

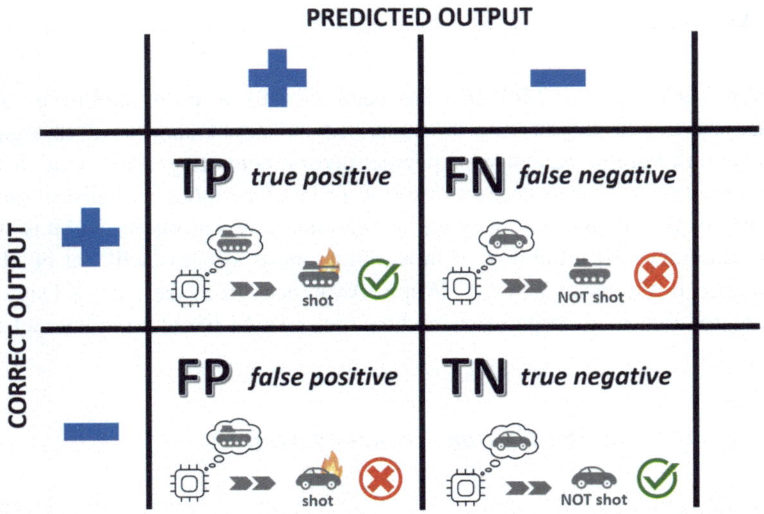

Fig. 4.1 Confusion matrix for AWS

associated with the frequency with which it generates a correct output.[17] An EU Expert Group defined accuracy as "a measure of how large the percentage of correct answers is"[18] while Marguilies et al. used "percentage of errors compared with accurate results".[19] Notably, given sufficient opportunity to test input and output instances, accuracy measurements can always be provided even without any knowledge of the model itself,[20] as accuracy is concerned only with outcomes, not with the model's inner processes.[21] Even in situations where understandability is 0,[22] accuracy can always be measured.[23]

AI accuracy is usually expressed in terms of a ***confusion matrix***. A confusion matrix categorises a system's performance based on *produced* outputs and *correct* outputs. The simplest confusion matrix is a binary configuration (Fig. 4.1). In this table, rows represent the correct output and columns the produced output (often called 'predicted output').[24]

---

[17] Leslie 2019, p. 30.

[18] High-Level Expert Group On Artificial Intelligence 2019, p. 4.

[19] Margulies 2017, p. 416.

[20] Cf. zero-understandability situations such as those described in Sect. 4.5.

[21] Venkatasubramanian 2019.

[22] For understandability, see Sect. 4.5.

[23] UK House of Lords 2018, p. 37.

[24] In practice, matrixes can feature multiple categories, in which case one no longer speaks of a 'positive' or 'negative' class. To produce such matrixes, the model is run on a large set of test inputs, after which the model's outputs are recorded and compared with the true labels. All instances are then tallied. An example of a tallied 10-dimensional matrix can be seen in Markham 2018.

In binary matrixes, it is standard to treat a class as a 'positive' class.[25] Target classification functions for AWS can likely be represented in a binary matrix, since IHL's view on the status of persons and objects is also binary: an entity is either lawful to target or it is not.[26] Indeed, IHL even adopts a so-called 'negative' definition to lawfully targetable entities, where anything not falling in the positive class (combatants, military objects, direct participants in hostilities) is automatically considered non-military (and immune to attack).[27]

In this light, it is intuitive to treat lawful targets as the 'positive' class and all other entities as the 'negative' class. An AWS works well if it accurately engages entities that are valid objectives (true positives) and avoids attacking those which are protected (true negatives). But mistakes can be made. Take an automated antitank system. As indicated by the bottom-left and top-right cells in Fig. 4.1, it can either incorrectly let an enemy tank approach unharmed (false negative) or incorrectly shoot an civilian vehicle (false positive).[28]

The distinction between false negatives and false positives is important since they represent distinct kinds of unwanted behaviour. Many separate metrics are used in the industry to aid in performance evaluation.[29] Table 4.1 displays the four most common metrics and how they are calculated.

Accuracy is established through running the model on test sets, and is analysed and optimised during development.[30] It is thus a ***component of Awareness that the Providing Entity must provide to Deployer***. The latter is entitled to rely on this information to make decisions and trust that it correctly reflects the system's performance.[31]

4.2.2 Be Wary of Accuracy

While Deployer is entitled to receive all information regarding accuracy from the Providing Entity, they are *not* entitled to rely on it blindly. One danger is that Deployers who are not properly trained on MoPs for AI do not properly appreciate that if read uncritically, accuracy statistics can be misleading.

---

[25] Sokolova et al. 2006, p. 1016.

[26] See Protocol Additional to the Geneva Conventions of 12 August 1949, and relating to the Protection of Victims of International Armed Conflicts, adopted 8 June 1977, entered into force 7 December 1978, 1125 UNTS 3 (API), Article 50, 52(2).

[27] Israel High Court of Justice, *Public Committee against Torture in Israel v. Israel* (Judgment) HCJ 769/02, 46 ILM 375 (11 December 2005), para 26; Melzer 2009, p. 21; Blum 2017, p. 27.

[28] They are alternatively called Type II and Type I errors respectively. See Sharma 2019.

[29] These include F-score, lift, ROC area, precision/recall break-even point, squared error, and Youden's Index, discriminant power and cross-entropy. E.g. Caruana and Niculescu-Mizil 2006; Sokolova et al. 2006, p. 1018.

[30] Venkatasubramanian 2019.

[31] Following the same rationale as why Deployer is entitled to demand, and rely on, an Intended Operational Environment (IOE) issued by the Providing Entity. See Sect. 3.5.

Table 4.1 Common accuracy metrics and their method of calculation

Metric	Explanation
Accuracy $\frac{TP+TN}{TP+TN+FP+FN}$	The most common metric and the one usually referred to when 'accuracy' is mentioned. It represents the proportion of correct outputs from all outputs. For instance, Accuracy = 0.8 can be read as 'you can rely on this model 80% of the time'.[32]
Recall $\frac{TP}{TP+FN}$	*When it encounters a positive instance, will it recognise it?* Also called *Sensitivity*. Recall = 0.8 would tell Deployer that for every 10 soldiers the system encounters, it will successfully recognise 8 of them.
Specificity $\frac{TN}{TN+FP}$	*When it encounters a negative instance, will it recognise it?* Equivalent to Recall, but for the negative class. Specificity = 0.8 would tell Deployer that for every 10 non-combatants the system encounters, it will successfully recognise 8 as such and not engage them.
Precision $\frac{TP}{TP+FP}$	*When it predicts yes, how often is it correct?*[33] Precision is the only standard metric that uses the produced output (column) as the denominator instead of the correct output (row).[34] This metric assesses the predictive power of the model.[35] Precision = 0.8 would tell Deployer that for every 10 times the system thinks someone is a combatant, it is correct 8 times.

To illustrate, take a hypothetical antipersonnel system: its intended function is to engage all persons of the positive class (e.g. soldiers) and leaves unharmed all persons of the negative class (e.g. civilians, soldiers *hors de combat*[36]). Prior to activation, Deployer consults the user manual and finds that the system's Accuracy[37] rate was tested to be 0.9. While this may seem impressive, it may not be, depending on the actual data distribution. Say that in an urban environment, there is a ratio of ten civilians for each enemy soldier. In that case, the system could obtain Accuracy = 0.91 simply by never engaging, i.e., always assuming persons it encounters are civilians.[38]

In the example above, the system is functionally equivalent to deploying a comatose soldier. Note that while militarily useless to Deployer (and likely harmful to force safety), it does not raise IHL concerns, as it has zero probability of inflicting harm on civilians. But consider the inverse example where the data distribution is

32 Afonja 2017.

33 Sharma 2019.

34 Markham 2018.

35 Sokolova et al. 2006, p. 1017.

36 A higher variation in negative class entities and the complexity with which each is identified increases the risk of false positives, i.e., of the system incorrectly identifying the entity as belonging to the positive class (and shooting). For this reason, it is argued in Sect. 8.5.1 that anti-object systems pose fewer issues under IHL than anti-person systems.

37 Capitalised, 'Accuracy' is meant to refer to the proportion of correct outputs from all outputs, i.e. (Tp+Tn)/(Tp+Tn+Fp+Fn). The umbrella term 'accuracy' which also includes metrics such as recall and specificity is not capitalised. See Table 4.1.

38 In this situation, it would be helpful to consult Null Error, the 'lazy model rate'. This measures how often the system would be wrong if it simply always defaulted to the majority class, which in this case also happens to be 0.999. Markham 2014.

Matrix (1)

	+	-
+	81	0
-	9	10

Acc.	0.91
Recall	1
Spec.	0.526

Matrix (2)

	+	-
+	81	9
-	0	10

Acc.	0.91
Recall	0.9
Spec.	1

Matrix (3)

	+	-
+	20	9
-	0	71

Acc.	0.91
Recall	0.69
Spec.	1

Matrix (4)

	+	-
+	20	0
-	9	71

Acc.	0.91
Recall	1
Spec.	0.88

Fig. 4.2 Four sample matrixes each yielding Accuracy = 0.91

reversed (e.g. a ratio of ten soldiers for each civilian). To obtain Accuracy = 0.91, the system can simply engage 100% of the time, as the majority class with a proportion of 10:1 is that of valid combatants. Indeed, despite it boasting a '0.9+ accuracy rate', the commander would have deployed an indiscriminate weapon in the truest sense of the word![39] This is the first important conclusion concerning accuracy: it is always recommended to consider the actual data distribution and consider if this could result in misleading accuracy scores.[40]

The second limitation of Accuracy is that it cannot help Deployers distinguish *what types* of errors the system makes. Consider once again the Accuracy = 0.91 system. Any of the matrixes in Fig. 4.2 would produce the same score:

However, the implications would vary drastically. System (1) boasts a Recall of 1, meaning it identifies enemy combatants without fail. However, its Specificity is very poor: almost 50% when it encounters a civilian, it incorrectly shoots them. There is little doubt this system would constitute an indiscriminate weapon under IHL.[41] In contrast, Systems (2) and (3) have perfect Specificity scores. These would be ideal weapons from an IHL perspective, as they never incorrectly engage an illegitimate target, but their usefulness for Deployer varies despite an identical Accuracy = 0.91 score. System (2) only misses 1 in 10 combatants it encounters, but System (3) does much worse, making mistakes almost one-third of the time. It is thus questionable if System (3) is worth using militarily,[42] despite its perfect performance in terms of sparing civilians.

As a simplification—and assuming the positive (+) class denotes legitimate targets—Recall therefore can be viewed as representing the system's military utility,

[39] This is substantiated legally in Sect. 9.3.1. See also Sect. 13.5.1, where we use this example in the context of criminal liability.

[40] Null Error, as mentioned previously, is a good tool to analyse this. Another useful metric is Lift, which measures how much *better* the system is vis-à-vis random chance. Lift provides an objective way to demonstrate, for example, why an Accuracy = 0.7 system could be superior to an Accuracy = 0.999 system and that the former should be deployed instead.

[41] See Sect. 9.3.1.

[42] The desirability of using AWS from a military perspective is discussed in Chap. 10.

while its Specificity reflects its discriminatory ability.[43] Balancing Recall and Specificity is a crucial consideration. For example, System (4) is militarily perfect: it never misses a valid target (Recall = 1). Its Specificity of 0.88 is however questionable.[44] Is it permissible to use a system that mistakenly shoots a civilian one-in-ten times, or must Deployer consider this a weapon that is "incapable of distinguishing between civilian and military targets"?[45]

In this regard, we can see that even if provided with all relevant information concerning a system's accuracy parameters, Deployer must still analyse how these metrics would translate in the actual operational environment. No top-down guidance can be given in this respect since the conclusions are so case-dependent. As such, we must ***appeal to Deployer to exercise due diligence*** and make reasonable decisions given the available information and circumstances. Deployer may not blindly trust crude accuracy metrics alone. Attributing this responsibility to Deployer, however, does indirectly imply the ***duty of the Providing Entity to empower its Deployers*** to be able to make the requisite analyses: this matter of accuracy metrics should thus be a mandatory training component for all commanders who are likely to wield AWS in future operations.

4.3 Robustness

Accuracy metrics such as Recall and Specificity are usually derived from running the model on test sets. While ideally, both training and test datasets should reflect actual inputs that the system would encounter during operations,[46] it is in practice impossible to capture all complexities of the real-world environment in a finite set of training and test instances.[47] This is another consequence of 'infinite variance'[48] in the real world. As such, accuracy metrics will only indicate the system's performance on a test set which is *presumed* to faithfully represent actual operations. It many cases, accuracy metrics will provide a relatively good approximation of the system's behaviour in the field, but studies have also shown that models can be quite fragile

---

[43] We return to this finding in more specifically legal terms in Sect. 9.3.

[44] This is despite the fact that a score of 0.88, in a vacuum, may already seem impressive to uninitiated observers.

[45] ICJ, *Legality of the Threat or Use of Nuclear Weapons*, Advisory Opinion, 8 July 1996, ICJ Rep 226, para 78. For the response to this question, see Sect. 9.3.1.

[46] European Commission 2020, p. 8.

[47] Freitas 2014, p. 2.

[48] See Sect. 3.4.1.

in the face of input perturbations,[49] even simple ones such as rotation and noise.[50] To address this, another MoP is frequently invoked, *robustness*.[51]

As with most MoPs, there is no universal conception of robustness in AI. Robustness is frequently referred to as the ability to maintain performance 'in the field'. Doshi-Velez et al. use it in terms of "whether algorithms reach certain levels of performance in the face of parameter or input variation",[52] while Holland Michel defines it as the "ability to perform as desired when receiving inputs for which it was not designed or tested".[53] Geirhos et al., while not explicitly defining it, used robustness to represent a model's accuracy in unknown conditions.[54] Another common way of operationalising robustness is as the ability to *generalise*: a robust model is able to draw on more generalised patterns learnt during training and continue performing well in the field, even if the input has never been encountered before.[55] Having considered these definitions, we will define robustness as the *ability of a model to maintain its performance level outside of laboratory instances*.[56]

In literature, the word 'robustness' is often associated primarily with adversarial action,[57] i.e., as a system's ability to withstand deliberate perturbations or input manipulations by adversaries.[58] Some sources have criticised this narrow-sighted focus, as AI are also frequently flummoxed by naturally-occurring perturbations—e.g. bad lighting, raindrops over the camera lens, or unusual accents.[59] As such, some definitions of robustness are broader to accommodate this factor. The DoD defines it as the ability to function "reliably and accurately under harsh conditions",[60] while Abaimov & Martellini refer to a model's "reliability while acting in complex, uncertain and adversarial environments".[61]

These last two definitions illustrate well that robustness can better be conceptualised as the ability to maintain performance in two different contexts (which are not

---

[49] See also Sect. 5.5.

[50] Geirhos et al. 2018; Engstrom et al. 2019.

[51] In classical systems engineering, 'robustness' refers to the physical durability of parts. See e.g. Camm 1993, p. 24. Other definitions incorporate a factor of consistent performance in the face of frequent external changes or the ability to incur and recover from disruption. See Tobin 2010, pp. 13–16. Some of these elements are retained in the AI concept of robustness, but with notable differences.

[52] Doshi-Velez and Kim 2017, p. 2.

[53] Holland Michel 2021, p. iv.

[54] Geirhos et al. 2018.

[55] Hendrycks et al. 2020b, p. 1.

[56] Robustness is sometimes also used in the sense of 'stability'. For example, a robust explanation is defined by Hancox-Li as one "that can be generated in multiple [at least partially] independent ways" [sic]. Hancox-Li 2020, pp. 641–42. This is not the conception of robustness used in this book.

[57] See Chap. 6.

[58] Hendrycks and Dietterich 2019, p. 2.

[59] Lohn 2020, p. 7.

[60] Defense Innovation Board 2019, p. 31.

[61] Abaimov and Martellini 2020, p. 146.

mutually exclusive): (1) in natural, possibly harsh and complex, conditions; (2) in the face of deliberate adversarial attempts. We shall call the first ***natural robustness*** and the second ***adversarial resistance***.[62] It is important to distinguish the two as Deployer might not always need high adversarial resistance if they do not foresee a large probability of adversarial action against the system.[63] In these cases, concentrating on natural robustness is more important. This is particularly the case if resistance would come at the *cost* of natural performance: some studies have shown that too much emphasis on making a system 'unattackable' can harm its standard accuracy.[64] It is obviously not desirable, for instance, to design a car which is capable of resisting even the most carefully doctored pixel attacks, but crashes when it unexpectedly encounters a worn-out or toppled stop sign.[65]

In the remainder of this section, we will only briefly comment on the value of natural robustness. The second category of robustness, adversarial resistance, will be discussed in the context of adversarial attacks proper in Chap. 6.

In terms of AI robustness, a majority of scholarship has been devoted to adversarial resistance, but natural input perturbations have recently gained increased attention. Several works have focused on techniques to improve natural robustness. Engstrom et al. argue that it is equally important to design systems that are "robust to simple, naturally-occurring transformations of their input".[66] It has been shown that these seemingly trivial alterations can reduce AI performance in the field.[67] This can take the form of snow, fog, blur or low-lighting noise,[68] the absence of an expected input,[69] or interactions with other (maybe even friendly) agents.[70] In this respect, Amodei et al.[71] and Hendrycks et al.[72] published extensive overviews on the different approaches found in literature to improve generalisation and reduce out-of-distribution errors.[73]

The advantage of focusing on improving natural robustness has been recorded in literature and reports. The French Ministry of the Armed Forces has specifically referenced the fact that AI "*restent encore peu robustes à des environnements inconnus, difficilement généralisables*" and that this should be taken into consideration when

[62] A third variant is sometimes mentioned, 'resilience', used by some sources to refer to a system's ability to rebound and maintain performance. E.g. Defense Science Board 2016, p. 92. It is occasionally used in the context of AWS. See e.g. US Air Force Office of the Chief Scientist 2015, p. 1; Luckcuck et al. 2020, p. 9.

[63] To make this determination, Deployer can employ the strategies discussed in Sect. 6.5.

[64] Tsipras et al. 2019; Ilyas et al. 2019, p. 10.

[65] Gilmer et al. 2018, p. 13.

[66] Engstrom et al. 2019, p. 1.

[67] The specific types of transformations that can cause such failures are discussed in greater detail in Sect. 5.5.

[68] Hendrycks et al. 2020a, p. 7.

[69] Gilmer et al. 2018, p. 13.

[70] Defense Innovation Board 2019, p. 37.

[71] Amodei et al. 2016.

[72] Hendrycks et al. 2020a.

[73] See also Section 5.6.

adopting and deploying AWS.[74] Hendrycks et al. draw a comparison with 'human robustness', which generalises very well with novel and perturbed inputs, and argue that approximating this human performance level to some extent, particularly for AI deployed in safety-critical applications, is essential.[75] Finally, Geirhos et al. draw a link with prediction and trust: having high natural robustness provides the user with more confidence when deploying the system for a task "that goes beyond a well-confined setting where one knows the exact test distribution".[76] Beyond only accuracy, Deployers should therefore also consider their systems' robustness to obtain a more rounded picture of the systems' overall reliability.

Robustness requires testing and fine-tuning at the developmental level, and it is thus mainly ***the Providing Entity's duty*** to assure that AWS are sufficiently robust before they are made available to Deployers.[77] One challenge lies in how the Providing Entity should communicate a system's robustness to Deployer: unlike accuracy, robustness is difficult to quantify due to the infinite variance problem,[78] since it is impossible to account for all possible deviations and variations in actual input distributions.[79] While there have been many proposals to evaluate robustness, no consensus has yet been reached on how to properly measure and represent it.[80] In practice, robustness can likely only be communicated in more qualitative terms, e.g. 'System A is more robust than B' or 'System C is quite robust'.[81] In many cases, however, this should be sufficient to allow Deployer to make an informed choice as to whether or not to use a particular AWS, particularly if Deployer also limits its use to the prescribed Intended Operational Environment.[82]

[74] Ministère des Armées 2019, p. 4.

[75] Hendrycks and Dietterich 2019, p. 1.

[76] Geirhos et al. 2018, p. 2.

[77] Many policy documents emphasise that weapons development must ensure that AWS are sufficiently robust before they may be greenlit for use. E.g. Defense Innovation Board 2019, p. 31; Ministère des Armées 2019, p. 29.

[78] See Sect. 3.4.2.

[79] Steinhardt 2015.

[80] See Hendrycks et al. 2020b.

[81] A different way robustness can be indicated is through OOD detection (for OOD, see Sect. 5.6). OOD detection is an anomaly detection method which allows a system to 'realise' when the input data it receives is beyond its original distribution (and would likely lead to failures), thereby preventing the execution of the task. Lohn 2020, p. 6. Emmott et al. have conducted a literature review of the different methods of OOD detection. Emmott et al. 2015, p. AD:1.

[82] See Sect. 3.5.

4.4 Reliability

Like accuracy and robustness, reliability is another MoP that is highly present in writings about AWS. Reliability has been framed as an incentive for more automation,[83] as a necessary component of meaningful control,[84] as a requirement for being able to lawfully deploy weapons,[85] as the basis of arguments for and against AI in weapon systems,[86] and as a crucial element for a commander's risk evaluation process.[87] However, like with other MoPs, sources only occasionally define this term, and many employ it colloquially.

Many sources include an element of *consistency* when referring to reliability. Leslie defines reliability as "the dependability with which it operationally conforms to its intended functionality".[88] In 2018, the ICRC framed reliability as "how consistently the system will function as intended, i.e. without failures or unintended effects",[89] and one year later, even more explicitly as "the quality of being trustworthy or performing consistently well".[90] Many also associate reliability with failures, or more specifically, the extent to which *failures can be avoided.* Article 36 defines a reliable system as one that "is not prone to failure" and Holland Michel views reliability as "the extent to which a system does or does not fail".[91]

Both these elements strike at the heart of how reliability is operationalised in a technical sense. In both classical engineering and AI, reliability essentially represents a *lack of failures over a period of time.* Let us view several definitions from literature to this effect:

> [T]he probability for failure-free operation of a program for a specified time under a specified set of operating conditions.[92]

> [T]he probability of failure-free software operation for a specified period of time in a specified environment.[93]

> [I]ts probability to perform its function within a defined period with certain restrictions under certain conditions[94]

---

83 Parasuraman et al. 2000, p. 286.
84 Article 36 2016, p. 4; UNIDIR 2014, p. 3.
85 van den Boogaard and Roorda 2021, p. 428.
86 Thurnher 2018, p. 100.
87 Mayer 2015, pp. 69–70.
88 Leslie 2019, p. 31.
89 ICRC 2018, para 42.
90 ICRC 2019a, p. 2.
91 Holland Michel 2020, p. 5.
92 Wohlin et al. 2001, p. 25.
93 Kumar and Singh 2012, p. 194.
94 Afsharnia 2017, p. 101.

> [T]he the probability that a system or product will perform in a satisfactory manner for a given period of time when used under specified operating conditions.[95]

From this small selection, it is quite noticeable how prudently these sources nuance their descriptions. In particular, two qualifications are consistently raised (in addition to the basic concept of failure-free operation over time). The first is that they always specify that reliability can only measure performance in *specified operating conditions*. This reinforces the previous recommendation in Sect. 3.5 that Deployers should always ensure whether operational circumstances match the system's Intended Operational Environment, as otherwise, metrics no longer represent the likely performance of the system in the field.

Reliability predictions are calculated based on large amounts of usage data collected from three main sources: testing, historic evidence and reporting.

- *Historic evidence* acts as a form of generalisation: if sufficiently similar systems have been used, one can reasonably deduce that the new system will fail at approximately the same rates and times as the old ones.[96] Militaries frequently publish established reliability standards and failure rates for matériel (sub)components based on previous experiences.[97] However, this is more difficult in cases where the technology has no precedent, as is likely the case for new AWS.
- *Testing* typically occurs before the product is released, during the final stages of development,[98] but here we stumble upon the same issues as discussed previously for accuracy: because it is impossible to cater for every real-life variation in input data, testing can only *approximate* performance in the field.
- Finally, *reporting* occurs when failure data is obtained post-release of the system, often directly from users when they encounter problems.[99] It is also sometimes referred to as 'usage-based testing'.[100] While this guarantees that the failures are indeed caused by inputs found in the real-world environment, it may be problematic in the military domain as this would entail that, for the early periods while data is being collected, weapons systems are being employed based only on measures derived from test instances.

Irrespective of the method used, there thus really is no true solution to the infinite variance problem,[101] and it would seem unreasonable to conclude that systems may never be deployed unless data is obtained from usage-based testing (which also begs the question of how usage-based data can then ever be collected in the first place). The best solution at this point, then, would seem to be that testing should be conducted with test environments that mimic actual operational circumstances to the furthest extent possible, and that mechanisms and policies be adopted which

---

[95] Blanchard and Blyler 2016, p. 144.

[96] Afsharnia 2017, p. 111.

[97] Ibid.

[98] IEEE Standards Association 2016, pp. 110–45.

[99] Jalote et al. 2004, p. 2.

[100] Wohlin et al. 2001, sct VI.

[101] See Sect. 3.4.2.

enable reporting of the results of AWS use in the field by Deployers, so predictive models can be continually improved. This can be enhanced with the implementation of automated reporting,[102] i.e., the systems are designed to automatically collect all relevant data which led to the failure and to transmit this to the user or developer. This method is generally preferred in literature as it provides more complete and consistent data.[103]

Historic evidence and reporting ties into the importance of Assessment Awareness and updating one's assumptions about a system's performance based on prior experience.[104] Deployers can contribute toward this process by providing Impact reports, e.g. battle damage assessments. Overall, however, reliability remains an MoP that must be ***communicated top-down to Deployers***—initially based on testing, and subsequently updated based on usage. The Providing Entity must develop policies, internal culture and mechanisms that aid in producing accurate and up-to-date reliability predictions for their AWS. Deployers must be able to trust that systems in their possessions are sufficiently reliable in general, and utilise these predictions to assess approximately how many times a given AWS will fail in the field, e.g. for the purposes of determining whether the system is sufficiently capable of distinguishing.[105]

4.5 Understandability

Contemporary AI models are often *opaque*:[106] this refers to the condition where users are able to access the input and output information of any given decision, but where the internal processes by which the decision was reached are partially or entirely obscured (this type of model is also often called a 'black box').[107] *Understandability* is used in this book as a negation of *opacity*,[108] and describes the state of a human user being

[102] Jalote et al. 2004, p. 6.

[103] Wohlin et al. 2001, sct III.C.

[104] See Sect. 2.4.6.

[105] See Sect. 9.3.

[106] See also Sect. 3.2.2.

[107] This is described *inter alia* as "a system that does not reveal its internal mechanisms" (Molnar 2019, p. 13), as "a system for which we know the inputs and outputs but can't see the process by which it turns the former into the latter" (Holland Michel 2020, p. iii) or simply systems whose "functioning cannot be explained" (ICRC 2019a, p. 3). In this book, we treat 'opaque model' and 'black box' as synonyms.

[108] There are multiple terms used in the context of opacity which are not standardised. Studies have shown that widely used terms such as 'explainability' and 'interpretability' have no universal definition and that depending on each author, each term "could mean different things". Kuttichira et al. 2019, p. 2. See also Karim et al. 2018, p. 1. The preference for 'understandability' is admittedly unorthodox: many authors prefer to use 'interpretability' or 'explainability' to describe the general state of 'not being opaque'. See e.g. Lipton 2016, p. 4; Biran and Cotton 2017, sct 1. However, it does have some precedent in literature; in particular, Holland Michel also adopts this position. See Holland Michel 2020, p. 1. We select understandability as the negation of opacity for its relative descriptiveness.

able to understand why an AI model makes its decision(s). While understandability does not describe a system's performance in the strict sense, it is raised in this chapter since it remains an important parameter that Deployer must consider during system analysis, and one which has direct and tangible effects on Deployer's ability to employ it lawfully.[109]

4.5.1 Opaque AWS and Solutions to Opacity

Opacity is a property relatively unique to modern AI systems.[110] Many machine learning models are "opaque constructs that are intrinsically hard to interpret".[111] Frequent comparisons are made with rule-based systems and old expert systems,[112] which have "one major virtue: it is always clear why the machine makes the choice that it does, because its designers set the rules".[113] In contrast, data-driven models derive their own (invisible) principles and heuristics from training data which are not formally represented in code, and thus cannot be analysed or audited[114] due to their high complexity and dimensionality.[115] Some authors frame opacity as a cost for higher performance.[116] By moving away from logic-based systems, we unlocked very powerful models; however, "[a]lthough these more opaque models are more effective, they are less explainable".[117]

A lack of understandability can also be caused by enabling *evolution and optimisation*. Allowing a system to learn while in-operation allows it to continually improve. It is one possible solution to counter drift[118] and adversarials,[119] but introduces uncertainty as to what exactly the system will learn and whether this is desirable.[120] With

---

[109] See Sect. 8.6.

[110] Freitas 2014, p. 1; Rudin 2018, p. 1; ICRC 2019b, p. 10; Horizon 2020 Commission Expert Group to advise on specific ethical issues raised by driverless mobility (E03659) 2020, p. 49.

[111] Vogelsang and Borg 2019, p. 1.

[112] Yampolskiy 2019, pp. 1–2; Haugh et al. 2018, p. 3–3.

[113] Deng 2015, p. 25.

[114] DARPA 2016, p. 5; Vogelsang and Borg 2019, p. 3.

[115] With regard to *complexity*, modern data-driven models are generally constructed from thousands if not millions of parameters, neurons, and layers. These neurons and layers are interconnected, creating a complex web of relationships, influences and backpropagation that make it impossible to understand which factors were ultimately responsible for leading a system toward one decision over another. Defense Innovation Board 2019, p. 70; Steinhardt 2015. *Dimensionality* refers to the fact that humans have a very limited capacity to visualise relations beyond the third dimension, while machines do so with ease. See e.g. Bathaee 2018, p. 905.

[116] Arya et al. 2019, p. 1; High-Level Expert Group On Artificial Intelligence 2019, p. 5.

[117] DARPA 2016, p. 5.

[118] See Sect. 5.6.

[119] See Sect. 6.4.

[120] Boulanin 2016, p. 24. See also European Commission 2020, p. 9; Roy 2018, p. 85; Holland Michel 2020, p. 7.

regard to military systems, some commentators have also raised the possibility that the system is technically understandable, but that its actual users (i.e. Deployers) are *not given access to this information.*[121] This is possible if the system was not developed in-house but rather purchased off-the-shelf or donated by other parties.[122]

In any event, it is thus likely that for AWS, some degree of opacity will be inevitable, as is the case with many systems in the civil domain. In response to the growing demand for more accountability and transparency in an era of algorithmic decisions, researchers began searching for solutions.[123] The general field of study commonly referred to as eXplainable AI (XAI) aims to "make AI systems results more understandable to humans".[124] DARPA's launch of a XAI funding programme in 2017[125] demonstrates how important understandability is considered for military systems.

A full exploration of techniques to reduce opacity would be well beyond the scope of this book.[126] Instead, it is more pertinent for our purposes to emphasise that developing and making available such XAI solutions is entirely out of Deployer's hands. There are two general ways models can be made more understandable: inherent and post-hoc solutions. Inherent solutions strive to develop "models that feature some degree of transparency, thereby interpretable to an extent by themselves",[127] i.e., the model is *designed* to be transparent. Post-hoc solutions leave the base model as-is, but attaches a XAI solution that provides an approximation or explanation of what the base model is doing.[128] We can see that neither type of XAI can be prepared ad-hoc, certainly not on the battlefield. The XAI solution must already be present. As such, ***the main responsibility for improving AWS' understandability lies with***

---

[121] Hofman 2020; Rudin 2018, p. 7.

[122] This problem has occurred many times even in cases where the client was a government agency. In the COMPAS case, producer Northpointe refused to disclose the parameters used to calculate risk scores, making it impossible for aggrieved defendants to challenge the decisions (or demonstrate that the results were racially biased). See Angwin et al. 2016. See also Sect. 5.8.

[123] Despite its relative youth, XAI has gained incredible traction as a research domain, with hundreds of papers and articles having been published on the subject. Yampolskiy 2019, p. 2.

[124] Adadi and Berrada 2018, p. 52139.

[125] Abdul et al. 2018, p. 2.

[126] There are several important contributions readily accessible which catalogue and summarise the many experiments on XAI in literature. See Guidotti et al. 2018; Adadi and Berrada 2018; Leslie 2019; Chakraborty et al. 2017; Barredo Arrieta et al. 2020.

[127] Barredo Arrieta et al. 2020, p. 108. There are several specific works theorising formal criteria that make a model inherently interpretable. See Leslie 2019, p. 42; Lipton 2016, pp. 4–5; Chakraborty et al. 2017, p. 1; Barredo Arrieta et al. 2020, p. 87.

[128] This process is described in different ways in literature: as 'reverse engineering' or 'reconstructing' the base model's behaviour (Guidotti et al. 2018, p. 11), as a 'proxy explainer' over the base black box (Abdul et al. 2018, p. 5), as a 'surrogate approximation' (Samek and Müller 2019, p. 12), or as "communicating understandable information about how an already developed model produces its predictions for any given input" (Barredo Arrieta et al. 2020, p. 92). The common theme is that the post-hoc XAI is only an approximation. It may nevertheless be very effective, providing all the necessary information that a user may need to sign-off on a product, predict behaviour and to deduce causes of failures, but by definition does not represent the base model one-to-one.

the Providing Entity. Deployer's action space is limited to doing everything in their power to study the model's decision-making process with the XAI solutions that are made available to them.

4.5.2 *Utility of Understandability*

Unlike other MoPs discussed in this chapter, understandability does not directly reduce risk of failures or improve reliability.[129] Then why is so much emphasis placed on understandability, both in military and civil systems? As implementing understandability potentially requires increased development time, resources and effort,[130] it might be tempting to consider understandability as a superfluous, or at least secondary, property to focus on. This is incorrect. As Kuttichira et al. note, "[f]or any model to be effective, both accuracy and explainability are important. If the decisions made by the model cannot be understood, the model might not be deployed."[131] This sentiment also is present in the military domain: DARPA noted that "the effectiveness of these systems will be limited by the machine's inability to explain its thoughts and actions to human users".[132] It is therefore useful to briefly outline why understandability is an important MoP for systems in general, and AWS in particular.[133]

First, understandability is important to impart *a priori* confidence in a system, that MoPs alone cannot provide. Metrics can only provide a general picture of the system's performance through averages and abstractions, and cannot guarantee *specific* behaviour: no formal proof of this can be provided.[134] What is also needed, then, is a way for decision-makers to evaluate a system's overall behavioural pattern before deploying it 'in the wild'.[135] Ribeiro et al.'s famous husky classifier demonstrates the value of understandability for sign-offs extremely well. This classifier boasted a high accuracy rating but incorrectly distinguished huskies from wolves based on the presence of snow in the background. But how did Ribeiro's team come to realise this? This mistaken proxy came to light when a XAI solution was applied to the opaque model, which provided an 'explanation' in the form of highlighting the areas of the input which the classifier relied upon the most to make its prediction

[129] Indeed, an *inverse* relation is often observed where increasing understandability instead comes at the cost of higher performance. Hansen and Rieger 2019, p. 42; Yampolskiy 2019, p. 3.

[130] Adadi and Berrada 2018, p. 52143.

[131] Kuttichira et al. 2019, p. 1.

[132] Gunning 2016, p. 2.

[133] This section summarises an extended argument provided in Kwik and Van Engers 2021.

[134] UNIDIR 2016, p. 8. It is impossible to test all possible inputs, and it is impossible to provide Deployers with a complete list of scenarios in which the system will fail. Doshi-Velez and Kim 2017, p. 3.

[135] Ribeiro et al. 2016, p. 1.

(a) Husky classified as wolf (b) Explanation

Fig. 4.3 XAI explanation for a husky/wolf classifier[137]

(see Fig. 4.3). The value of this experiment is best expressed by Ribeiro et al. themselves: "this experiment demonstrates the utility of explaining individual predictions for getting insights into classifiers knowing when not to trust them and why."[136]

Beyond providing Deployer with confidence of a system's quality, proof ex ante will also be necessary for adoption and review purposes. Before an AWS is fielded for production, one hopes it has "gone through an acceptable safety review", including reasonable guarantees that it is able to abide by IHL requirements.[138] This becomes much harder if the systems' decisions are incomprehensible.[139] In this respect, some have drawn specific links with the Article 36 review obligation. Properly reviewing whether a weapon's employment would be in violation of IHL requires a form of ex ante prediction of its behaviour.[140]

Understandability also helps Deployer with error mitigation more generally. The first step in error mitigation is identifying that a risk of failure exists. Authors frequently reference the importance of a *robust mental model* for this purpose. Mueller et al. define this—somewhat poetically—as "a constellation of well-developed knowledge about a system".[141] A good mental model helps Deployer predict and mentally simulate the system's functioning in a specific situation.[142]

Error mitigation can come in two forms: identifying potential errors and addressing them before deployment (preventive) and identifying and addressing failures which have already occurred (reactive). Both these efforts require understandability, particularly in light of the often invisible, unintuitive and unexpected

[136] Ibid., p. 9.

[137] Reproduced from Ibid.

[138] Keeley 2015, p. 214.

[139] Yampolskiy 2019, p. 9.

[140] ICRC 2016, sct 4; Goussac 2019.

[141] Mueller et al. 2019, p. 86.

[142] Ibid.

causes of failures of ML models.[143] If a model is opaque, it is often simply not possible to triangulate the exact reason for a failure, which also makes addressing the issue difficult.[144] "Knowing why the system is exhibiting undesired behavior is the first step toward fixing it."[145] Understandability, therefore, is vital for predicting and explaining failures.[146] Essentially, "XAI systems should enable the user to know whether, when, and why to trust and rely upon the XAI system and know whether, when, or why to mistrust the XAI and either not rely upon it, or rely on it with caution".[147]

Finally, understandability is also frequently cited as necessary for facilitating accountability. The basic concern is that with opaque models, decision-makers are rendered *factually unable* to know what decisions it will make and why, and post-hoc auditors or investigators are equally *unable to know* what led to a particular AI decision, making the determination of causation or the assignment of blame very difficult.[148] With regard to causality, opacity makes it difficult to isolate specific reasons for why an AI made a problematic decision.[149] Even with models where some insight is possible as to individual parameters, it is hard to decisively prove that a particular weight (even if it can be proven to be high) had *in fact* contributed toward the ultimate decision, and to what extent.[150]

In addition, some modes of legal responsibility (such as criminal liability[151]) require a certain degree of intent to be established. Opacity, however, offers potential loopholes. The idea of *Awareness → Accountability* in the MHC Framework[152] is that by enforcing Awareness, we can ensure that Deployer has attained the necessary epistemic threshold to be held responsible for any resultant behaviour of their AWS.[153] If a Deployer *willingly* remains ignorant while this information is available, one could hold that they *should have known* based on a reasonable commander standard.[154] However, what if no reasonable commander could have known this, due to the system's opacity? It could easily be argued that "if even the creator of the AI cannot foresee its effects, a reasonable person cannot either".[155]

---

143 Gilpin et al. 2018, p. 1. See more generally Chap. 5.

144 Yampolskiy 2019, p. 9.

145 Haugh et al. 2018, p. 3-2.

146 Yampolskiy 2019, p. 2.

147 Hoffman et al. 2018, p. 19.

148 Miller 2019, p. 8.

149 Knight 2017.

150 Bathaee 2018, p. 926. The unfortunate result may have been due to a clear Deployer mistake, a designer error, an intervening party (which may also be an adversary deliberately trying to influence the system), or an entirely unforeseeable third variable, but it is difficult to say for sure.

151 See Part V.

152 See Sect. 2.5.3.

153 Defense Innovation Board 2019, p. 28.

154 Gillard 2018, p. 16. As we discuss in Sect. 13.4.2, however, this does not necessarily mean that criminal liability will follow.

155 Bathaee 2018, p. 924.

From this short overview, we can see that opacity potentially introduces multiple problems that can affect Deployer's ability to implement IHL. It also raises difficult questions when trade-offs are involved, such as whether it is worth sacrificing an AWS's accuracy for more understandability and vice versa.[156] These are matters we shall return to in Sect. 8.6. In addition, we shall address the ramifications of opacity for criminal liability in Sect. 12.4.

4.6 Recommendations

MoPs are crucial components Deployer needs to make informed decisions concerning the use of AWS. Nevertheless, all MoPs discussed in this chapter rely on large amounts of data or testing to obtain, and must be generated well in advance of any operation in which the system in question is to be deployed. As such, ***the main responsibility for enabling Deployer's Awareness with respect to MoPs lies with the Providing Entity***. This duty rests on a few pillars:

- *Production of quality information.* MoPs must be made available in the first place and be derived from proper testing and analysis in environments that closely match the system's Intended Operational Environment.
- *Incorporating understandability.* Too much opacity prevents even the most good-faith Deployer from exercising the necessary due diligence vis-à-vis their system, because its decision-making can be *factually* unknowable.
- *Communication.* This information must be communicated to all Deployers in an effective, workable and complete manner.[157]
- *Technical empowerment*. The Providing Entity must provide the necessary formation to Deployers which enables them to read and utilise AI-specific MoPs to make legal decisions.

Nevertheless, we also found that in some respects, Deployer must exercise their own due diligence. This was the case for the minutiae related to accuracy metrics: only Deployer is in a position to make case-specific judgments related to particular operational conditions.

One conclusion that could be drawn overall is that even if very solid and well-substantiated MoPs are provided, Deployers should not solely rely on them in their decision-making. Instead, Deployers should also regard the particular circumstances of operation and consider casuistically if these could aggravate the risk of deployment. The DoD warns about this, stating that MoPs only capture averages and not

[156] See Kwik and Van Engers 2023.

[157] The information must be presented in a format that is easily applied in the field to make legal decisions. MoPs must be as comprehensive as possible while remaining workable: for instance, only an accuracy rating or only the statement "The system is reliable" are likely insufficient, but too much detailed testing data can be overwhelming. The Providing Entity must find the ideal way to communicate such data to Deployer.

"the probability of failure of a single software function".[158] This is echoed by many authors.[159] For the moment, we can conclude that there is a need for more information beyond generalised performance rates. This should come in the form of Deployers being aware of common faults that can lead to their AWS failing. This is the focus of the next chapter.

References

Abaimov S, Martellini M (2020) Artificial Intelligence in Autonomous Weapon Systems. In: Martellini M, Ralf T (eds) 21st Century Prometheus. Springer International Publishing, Cham, pp 141–177. https://doi.org/10.1007/978-3-030-28285-1_8

Abdul A et al. (2018) Trends and Trajectories for Explainable, Accountable and Intelligible Systems. In: Proceedings of the 2018 CHI Conference on Human Factors in Computing Systems. ACM, New York, pp 1–18. https://doi.org/10.1145/3173574.3174156

Adadi A, Berrada M (2018) Peeking Inside the Black-Box: A Survey on Explainable Artificial Intelligence (XAI). IEEE Access 6:52138–62160. https://doi.org/10.1109/ACCESS.2018.2870052

Afonja T (2017) Accuracy Paradox. Towards Data Science. https://towardsdatascience.com/accuracy-paradox-897a69e2dd9b. Accessed 15 October 2021

Afsharnia F (2017) Failure Rate Analysis. In: Ali A (ed) Failure Analysis and Prevention. InTech, pp 99–115

Amodei D et al. (2016) Concrete Problems in AI Safety. http://arxiv.org/abs/1606.06565

Angwin J et al. (2016) Machine Bias. ProPublica. https://www.propublica.org/article/machine-bias-risk-assessments-in-criminal-sentencing. Accessed 25 November 2020

Article 36 (2016) Key Elements of Meaningful Human Control, Background Paper to Comments Prepared by Richard Moyes, Managing Partner, Article 36. In: Convention on Certain Conventional Weapons (CCW) Meeting of Experts on Lethal Autonomous Weapons Systems (LAWS), Geneva, 11–15 April 2016

Article 36, PAX (2016) Areas of Harm – Understanding Explosive Weapons with Wide Area Effects. Article 36/PAX

Arya V et al. (2019) One Explanation Does Not Fit All: A Toolkit and Taxonomy of AI Explainability Techniques. http://arxiv.org/abs/1909.03012

Barredo Arrieta A et al. (2020) Explainable Artificial Intelligence (XAI): Concepts, Taxonomies, Opportunities and Challenges toward Responsible AI. Information Fusion 58:82–115. https://doi.org/10.1016/j.inffus.2019.12.012

Bathaee Y (2018) The Artificial Intelligence Black Box and the Failure of Intent and Causation. Harvard Journal of Law and Technology 31:889–938

Biran O, Cotton C (2017) Explanation and Justification in Machine Learning: A Survey. In: IJCAI 2017 Workshop on Explainable Artificial Intelligence (XAI). Pp 8–13

Blanchard B S, Blyler J E (2016) System Engineering Management. 5th edn. John Wiley & Sons, Inc

Blum G (2017) The Dispensable Lives of Soldiers. In: Ohlin J D et al. (eds) Weighing Lives in War, vol 1. Oxford University Press, pp 17-57. https://doi.org/10.1093/oso/9780198796176.003.0002

Boulanin V (2016) Mapping the Development of Autonomy in Weapon Systems: A Primer on Autonomy. Stockholm International Peace Research Institute, Stockholm

[158] US Department of Defense 2012, p. 14.

[159] Pan 1999; Radio Technical Commission for Aeronautics 2011, p. 12; Lohn 2020, p. 3.

Brehm M (2014) Unacceptable Risk: Use of Explosive Weapons in Populated Areas through the Lens of Three Cases before the ICTY. Boer R, Slijper F (eds). PAX

Camm F (1993) The Development of the F-100-PW-220 and F-11O-GE-100 Engines: A Case Study of Risk Assessment and Risk Management. N-3618-AF, RAND Note Prepared for the US Air Force

Caruana R, Niculescu-Mizil A (2006) An Empirical Comparison of Supervised Learning Algorithms. In: Proceedings of the 23rd international conference on Machine learning - ICML '06. ACM Press. http://portal.acm.org/citation.cfm?d=1143844.1143865

Chakraborty S et al. (2017) Interpretability of Deep Learning Models: A Survey of Results. In: 2017 IEEE SmartWorld, Ubiquitous Intelligence & Computing, Advanced & Trusted Computed, Scalable Computing & Communications, Cloud & Big Data Computing, Internet of People and Smart City Innovation (SmartWorld/SCALCOM/UIC/ATC/CBDCom/IOP/SCI). IEEE, pp 1–6. https://doi.org/10.1109/UIC-ATC.2017.8397411

Crootof R (2015) The Killer Robots Are Here: Legal and Policy Implications. Cardozo Law Review 36:1837–1915

DARPA (2016) Broad Agency Announcement: Explainable Artificial Intelligence (XAI). DARPA-BAA-16-53. www.darpa.mil/attachments/DARPA-BAA-16-53.pdf. Accessed 14 November 2020

Defense Innovation Board (2019) AI Principles: Recommendations on the Ethical Use of Artificial Intelligence by the Department of Defense Defense Innovation Board. US Department of Defense. https://media.defense.gov/2019/Oct/31/2002204458/-1/-1/0/DIB_AI_PRINCIPLES_PRIMARY_DOCUMENT.PDF. Accessed 2 August 2023

Defense Science Board (2016) Report of the Defense Science Board Summer Study on Autonomy. Secretary of Defense for Acquisition, Technology and Logistics

Deng B (2015) The Robot's Dilemma: Working out How to Build Ethical Robots Is One of the Thorniest Challenges in Artificial Intelligence. Nature 523:25–27

Doshi-Velez F, Kim B (2017) Towards A Rigorous Science of Interpretable Machine Learning. http://arxiv.org/abs/1702.08608

Driels M R (2013) Weaponeering, Second Edition. 2nd edn. American Institute of Aeronautics and Astronautics, Inc, Washington D.C. https://doi.org/10.2514/4.869259

Durhin N (2016) Protecting Civilians in Urban Areas: A Military Perspective on the Application of International Humanitarian Law. International Review of the Red Cross 98(1):177–200

Emmott A et al. (2015) A Meta-Analysis of the Anomaly Detection Problem. http://arxiv.org/abs/1503.01158

Engstrom L et al. (2019) A Rotation and a Translation Suffice: Fooling CNNs with Simple Transformations. In: International Conference on Machine Learning

European Commission (2020) Report on the Safety and Liability Implications of Artificial Intelligence, the Internet of Things and Robotics. COM/2020/64 final

Flournoy M A, Haines A, Chefitz G (2020) Building Trust through Testing: Adapting DOD's Test & Evaluation, Validation & Verification (TEVV) Enterprise for Machine Learning Systems, Including Deep Learning Systems. WestExec Advisors, Washington D.C.

Freitas A A (2014) Comprehensible Classification Models. ACM SIGKDD Explorations Newsletter 15(1):1–10. https://doi.org/10.1145/2594473.2594475

Geirhos R et al. (2018) Generalisation in Humans and Deep Neural Networks. http://arxiv.org/abs/1808.08750

Geiß R, Lahmann H (2017) Autonomous Weapons Systems: A Paradigm Shift for the Law of Armed Conflict?. In: Ohlin J D (ed) Research Handbook on Remote Warfare. Edward Elgar, Cheltenham, pp 371–404

Gillard E-C (2018) Proportionality in the Conduct of Hostilities: The Incidental Harm Side of the Assessment. The Royal Institute of International Affairs, Chatham House, London. https://www.chathamhouse.org/2018/12/proportionality-conduct-hostilities-incidental-harm-side-assessment. Accessed 2 August 2023

Gilmer J et al. (2018) Motivating the Rules of the Game for Adversarial Example Research. http://arxiv.org/abs/1807.06732

Gilpin L H et al. (2018) Explaining Explanations: An Overview of Interpretability of Machine Learning. http://arxiv.org/abs/1806.00069

Glinz M (2007) On Non-Functional Requirements. In: 15th IEEE International Requirements Engineering Conference (RE 2007). IEEE, Delhi, pp 21–26. https://doi.org/10.1109/RE.2007.45

Goussac N (2019) Safety Net or Tangled Web: Legal Reviews of AI in Weapons and War-Fighting. Humanitarian Law & Policy. https://blogs.icrc.org/law-and-policy/2019/04/18/safety-net-tangled-web-legal-reviews-ai-weapons-war-fighting/. Accessed 26 May 2021

Grut C (2013) The Challenge of Autonomous Lethal Robotics to International Humanitarian Law. Journal of Conflict and Security Law 18(1):5–23. https://doi.org/10.1093/jcsl/krt002

Guidotti R et al. (2018) A Survey Of Methods For Explaining Black Box Models. http://arxiv.org/abs/1802.01933

Gunning D (2016) Explainable Artificial Intelligence (XAI), DARPA/I2O. Distribution Statement 'A'. https://sites.cc.gatech.edu/~alanwags/DLAI2016/(Gunning)%20IJCAI-16%20DLAI%20WS.pdf. Accessed 30 November 2021

Hancox-Li L (2020) Robustness in Machine Learning Explanations. In: Proceedings of the 2020 Conference on Fairness, Accountability, and Transparency. ACM, New York, pp 640–647. https://doi.org/10.1145/3351095.3372836

Hansen L K, Rieger L (2019) Interpretability in Intelligent Systems – A New Concept?. In: Samek W et al. (eds) Explainable AI: Interpreting, Explaining and Visualizing Deep Learning. Springer Nature Switzerland, pp 41—49

Haugh B A, Sparrow D A, Tate D M (2018) The Status of Test, Evaluation, Verification, and Validation (TEV&V) of Autonomous Systems. Institute for Defense Analyses, Alexandria

Hendrycks D et al. (2020a) The Many Faces of Robustness: A Critical Analysis of Out-of-Distribution Generalization. http://arxiv.org/abs/2006.16241

Hendrycks D et al. (2020b) Pretrained Transformers Improve Out-of-Distribution Robustness. http://arxiv.org/abs/2004.06100

Hendrycks D, Dietterich T G (2019) Benchmarking Neural Network Robustness to Common Corruptions and Surface Variations. http://arxiv.org/abs/1807.01697

Herbach J (2012) Into the Caves of Steel: Precaution, Cognition and Robotic Weapon Systems Under the International Law of Armed Conflict. 4 Amsterdam Law Forum 4(3):3-20

Heyns C (2013) Report of the Special Rapporteur on Extrajudicial, Summary or Arbitrary Executions, A/HRC/23/47

High-Level Expert Group On Artificial Intelligence (2019) A Definition of AI: Main Capabilities and Disciplines. European Commission, Brussels

Hoffman R R et al. (2018) Metrics for Explainable AI: Challenges and Prospects. http://arxiv.org/abs/1812.04608

Hofman L (2020) De Nieuwste Wapenwedloop Gaat Niet Om Bommen, Maar Om Algoritmes (En Hoe Die Te Foppen). De Correspondent, 19 August 2020. https://decorrespondent.nl/11511/de-nieuwste-wapenwedloop-gaat-niet-om-bommen-maar-om-algoritmes-en-hoe-die-te-foppen/80252bb0-a43e-06da-0cf6-5468281fcfef. Accessed 2 August 2023

Holland Michel A (2020) The Black Box, Unlocked: Predictability and Understandability in Military AI. UNIDIR, Geneva. https://unidir.org/sites/default/files/2020-09/BlackBoxUnlocked.pdf. Accessed 2 August 2023

Holland Michel A (2021) Known Unknowns: Data Issues and Military Autonomous Systems. UNIDIR, Geneva. https://unidir.org/publication/known-unknowns. Accessed 2 August 2023

Horizon 2020 Commission Expert Group to advise on specific ethical issues raised by driverless mobility (E03659) (2020) Ethics of Connected and Automated Vehicles: Recommendations on Road Safety, Privacy, Fairness, Explainability and Responsibility. Publication Office of the European Union, Luxembourg

ICRC (2016) Views of the ICRC on Autonomous Weapon Systems. Paper of the ICRC prepared for the Meeting of Experts on Lethal Autonomous Weapons Systems, held in Geneva from 11-16 April

ICRC (2018) Ethics and Autonomous Weapon Systems: An Ethical Basis for Human Control?. Group of Governmental Experts of the High Contracting Parties to the Convention on Prohibitions or Restrictions on the Use of Certain Conventional Weapons Which May Be Deemed to Be Excessively Injurious or to Have Indiscriminate Effects, CCW/GGE1/2018/WP

ICRC (2019a) 'Statement of the International Committee of the Red Cross (ICRC) under Agenda Item 5(B)'. Convention on Certain Conventional Weapons (CCW), Group of Governmental Experts on Lethal Autonomous Weapons Systems (Geneva, 25-29 March 2019)

ICRC (2019b) Artificial Intelligence and Machine Learning in Armed Conflict: A Human-Centred Approach. ICRC, Geneva

IEEE Standards Association (2016) IEEE 1633-2016, IEEE Recommended Practice on Software Reliability. IEEE. https://standards.ieee.org/standard/1633-2016.html. Accessed 11 October 2021

Ilyas A et al. (2019) Adversarial Examples Are Not Bugs, They Are Features. http://arxiv.org/abs/1905.02175

Jalote P et al. (2004) Measuring Reliability of Software Products. Institute of Electrical and Electronics Engineers, Inc. MSR-TR-2004-145. https://www.microsoft.com/en-us/research/publication/measuring-reliability-of-software-products/. Accessed 11 October 2021

Karim A et al. (2018) Machine Learning Interpretability: A Science Rather than a Tool. http://arxiv.org/abs/1807.06722

Keeley T (2015) Auditable Policies for Autonomous Systems (Decisional Forensics). In: Williams A P, Scharre P D (eds) Autonomous Systems: Issues for Defence Policymakers. NATO, The Hague, pp 196–225

Knight W (2017) The Dark Secret at the Heart of AI. Technology Review. www.technologyreview.com/2017/04/11/5113/the-dark-secret-at-the-heart-of-ai. Accessed 2 July 2020

Kumar P, Singh Y (2012) An Empirical Study of Software Reliability Prediction Using Machine Learning Techniques. International Journal of System Assurance Engineering and Management 3(3):194-208. https://doi.org/10.1007/s13198-012-0123-8

Kuttichira D P et al. (2019) Explaining Black-Box Models Using Interpretable Surrogates. In: Nayak A C, Sharma A (eds) PRICAI 2019: Trends in Artificial Intelligence - 16th Pacific Rim International Conference on Artificial Intelligence. Springer, Cham, pp 3–15. https://doi.org/10.1007/978-3-030-29908-8_1

Kwik J, Van Engers T (2021) Algorithmic Fog of War: When Lack of Transparency Violates the Law of Armed Conflict. Journal of Future Robot Life 2(1–2):43–66. https://www.medra.org/servlet/aliasResolver?alias=iospress&doi=10.3233/FRL-200019. Accessed 4 August 2023

Kwik J, Van Engers T (2023) Performance or Explainability? A Law of Armed Conflict Perspective. In: Kornilakis A et al. (eds) Artificial Intelligence and Normative Challenges: International and Comparative Legal Perspectives. Springer Nature Switzerland AG

Leslie D (2019) Understanding Artificial Intelligence Ethics and Safety: A Guide for the Responsible Design and Implementation of AI Systems in the Public Sector. The Alan Turing Institute, London

Lipton Z C (2016) The Mythos of Model Interpretability. http://arxiv.org/abs/1606.03490

Lohn A J (2020) Estimating the Brittleness of AI: Safety Integrity Levels and the Need for Testing Out-Of-Distribution Performance. http://arxiv.org/abs/2009.00802

Luckcuck M et al. (2020) Formal Specification and Verification of Autonomous Robotic Systems. ACM Computing Surveys 52(5):1–41. https://doi.org/10.1145/3342355

Margulies P (2017) Making Autonomous Weapons Accountable: Command Responsibility for Computer-Guided Lethal Force in Armed Conflicts. In: Ohlin J D (ed) Research Handbook on Remote Warfare. Edward Elgar, Cheltenham, pp 405-442. https://doi.org/10.4337/9781784716998.00024

Markham K (2014) Simple Guide to Confusion Matrix Terminology. Data School. https://www.dataschool.io/simple-guide-to-confusion-matrix-terminology/. Accessed 15 October 2021

Markham K (2018) Making Sense of the Confusion Matrix. https://www.youtube.com/watch?v=8Oog7TXHvFY. Accessed 15 October 2021

Mayer C (2015) Developing Autonomous Systems in an Ethical Manner. In: Williams A P, Scharre P D (eds) Autonomous Systems: Issues for Defence Policymakers. NATO, The Hague, pp 65–82

Melzer N (2009) Interpretive Guidance on the Notion of Direct Participation in Hostilities. ICRC, Geneva

Miller T (2019) Explanation in Artificial Intelligence: Insights from the Social Sciences. Artificial Intelligence 267:1–38

Ministère des Armées (2019) L'intelligence Artificielle Au Service de La Défense. Ministère des Armées, Paris

Molnar C (2019) Interpretable Machine Learning: A Guide for Making Black Box Models Explainable. Lean Publishing

Mueller S T et al. (2019) Explanation in Human-AI Systems: A Literature Meta-Review Synopsis of Key Ideas and Publications and Bibliography for Explainable AI. DARPA XAI Program, Arlington

Ney Jr. P C (2019) General Counsel, U.S. Department of Defense. Lawfare, Keynote Address at the Israel Defense Forces 3rd International Conference on the Law of Armed Conflict, in Quinta Jurecic, Defense Department General Counsel Remarks at IDF Conference (28 May 2019)

Pan J (1999) Software Reliability. Carnegie Mellon University. https://users.ece.cmu.edu/~koopman/des_s99/sw_reliability. Accessed 12 January 2021

Parasuraman R, Sheridan T B, Wickens C (2000) A Model for Types and Levels of Human Interaction with Automation. IEEE Transactions on Systems, Man, and Cybernetics 30(3):286–297

Radio Technical Commission for Aeronautics (2011) RTCA DO-178C Software Considerations in Airborne Systems and Equipment Certification. Radio Technical Commission for Aeronautics

Ribeiro M T, Singh S, Guestrin C (2016) Why Should I Trust You?: Explaining the Predictions of Any Classifier. In: Proceedings of the 22nd ACM SIGKDD International Conference on Knowledge Discovery and Data Mining

Roy A (2018) National Strategy for Artificial Intelligence #AIFORALL. National Institution for Transforming India Aayog, New Delhi

Rudin C (2018) Stop Explaining Black Box Machine Learning Models for High Stakes Decisions and Use Interpretable Models Instead. http://arxiv.org/abs/1811.10154

Samek W, Müller K-R (2019) Towards Explainable Artificial Intelligence. In: Samek W et al. (eds) Explainable AI: Interpreting, Explaining and Visualizing Deep Learning. Springer Nature Switzerland, Cham, pp 5–22

Schmitt M N (2005) Precision Attack and International Humanitarian Law. International Review of the Red Cross 87(859):445–466

Schuller A L (2017) At the Crossroads of Control: The Intersection of Artificial Intelligence in Autonomous Weapon Systems with International Humanitarian Law. Harvard National Security Journal 8:379

Sharma P (2019) Decoding the Confusion Matrix. Towards Data Science. https://towardsdatascience.com/decoding-the-confusion-matrix-bb4801decbb. Accessed 15 October 2021

Sokolova M, Japkowicz N, Szpakowicz S (2006) Beyond Accuracy, F-Score and ROC: A Family of Discriminant Measures for Performance Evaluation. In: Sattar A, Kang B-h (eds) AI 2006: Advances in Artificial Intelligence. AI 2006. Lecture Notes in Computer Science vol 4304. Australasi, Springer, Berlin. https://doi.org/10.1007/11941439_114

Steinhardt J (2015) Long-Term and Short-Term Challenges to Ensuring the Safety of AI Systems. Wordpress https://jsteinhardt.wordpress.com/2015/06/24/long-term-and-short-term-challenges-to-ensuring-the-safety-of-ai-systems. Accessed 2 February 2021

Thurnher J S (2018) Feasible Precautions in Attack and Autonomous Weapons. In: von Heinegg W H, Frau R, Singer T (eds) Dehumanization of Warfare. Springer International Publishing, Cham, pp 99–117. https://doi.org/10.1007/978-3-319-67266-3_6

Tobin B P (2010) Supply Chain Resilience: Assessing USAF Weapon System Life Cycle. Master Thesis, Wright-Patterson Air Force Base, Ohio
Tsipras D et al. (2019) Robustness May Be at Odds with Accuracy. http://arxiv.org/abs/1805.12152
UK House of Lords (2018) Select Committee on Artificial Intelligence, Report of Session 2017-19, AI in the UK: Ready, Willing, and Able? HL Paper 100, 16 April 2018
UNIDIR (2014) The Weaponization of Increasingly Autonomous Technologies: Considering How Meaningful Human Control Might Move the Discussion Forward. UNIDIR Resources, No 2
UNIDIR (2016) Safety, Unintentional Risk and Accidents in the Weaponization of Increasingly Autonomous Technologies. UNIDIR Resources No 5
US Air Force Office of the Chief Scientist (2015) Autonomous Horizons: System Autonomy in the Air Force— A Path to the Future, Volume I: Human-Autonomy Teaming. AF/ST TR 15-01
US Department of Defense (2012) Department of Defense Standard Practice: System Safety. MIL-STD-882E
van den Boogaard J C, Roorda M P (2021) "Autonomous" Weapons and Human Control. In: Bartels R (eds) Military Operations and the Notion of Control Under International Law. TMC Asser Press, The Hague, pp 421–437. https://doi.org/10.1007/978-94-6265-395-5_20
Venkatasubramanian S (2019) Structural Disconnects between Algorithmic Decision-Making and the Law. Humanitarian Law & Policy. https://blogs.icrc.org/law-and-policy/2019/04/25/structural-disconnects-algorithmic-decision-making-law/. Accessed 26 May 2021
Vogelsang A, Borg M (2019) Requirements Engineering for Machine Learning: Perspectives from Data Scientists. http://arxiv.org/abs/1908.04674
Wiebe V (2000) Footprints of Death: Cluster Bombs as Indiscriminate Weapons under International Humanitarian Law. Michigan Journal of International Law 22(1):85–168
Wohlin C et al. (2001) Software Reliability. In: Meyers R A (ed) Encyclopedia of Physical Science and Technology, 3rd ed. Academic Press, pp 25–39
Yampolskiy R V (2019) Unexplainability and Incomprehensibility of Artificial Intelligence. http://arxiv.org/abs/1907.03869

Chapter 5
Causes of Failure

Contents

Abstract An important part of being able to deploy systems safely, is understanding when it is *not* safe to do so. To know when using a system is unsafe, one must understand why systems fail. To this end, this chapter presents a typology of different reasons that may lead autonomous weapon systems (AWS) to fail in the field: being cognisant of these factors enables AWS-users to predict whether there is increased risk of their systems failing after deployment. The chapter starts with distinguishing classical failures (human error and mechanical problems) from causes which are uniquely applicable to AI-systems. The chapter then discusses different possible causes of AI failure in sequence: training data issues, input data issues, out-of-distribution, proxy mistakes and bias. From this analysis, it is found that commanders play a particularly important role in predicting and addressing two causes of failure, input data issues and drift, as these arise from the particular context in which the system will be deployed. In contrast, commanders must be sensitive and knowledgeable about other causes of failure, but these are primarily for the Providing Entity to address. Finally, the chapter also discusses the concept of system failures, which holds that in some conditions, a convergence of circumstance occurs which produces a failure, but which cannot be predicted or prevented by definition. It is argued that both for prevention and post-hoc adjudication, system failure theory must be retained to avoid scapegoating.

J. Kwik, *Lawfully Using Autonomous Weapon Technologies*,
https://doi.org/10.1007/978-94-6265-631-4_5

Keywords Autonomous weapon system · Artificial intelligence · Component failure · System failure · Out-of-distribution · Bias · Drift · Human error · Reliability · Proxy error · Normal accident theory · Forced error · Training data

5.1 Introduction

An important part of being able to deploy systems safely, is understanding when it is *not* safe to do so. To know when using a system is unsafe, one must understand why systems fail. Developing an ontology of different factors that can lead to failures is integral in any safety-critical domain,[1] but for military systems in particular, the importance of this endeavour was emphasised strongly by the DoD:

> Creating a robust ontology of potential failures is important not only for designers and developers of AI systems, but also for users. Thus, understanding the type, scope, number, and scale of harm for potential failure modalities is increasingly important.[2]

Scharre argued that being cognisant of causes of failure enables Prediction:[3] when "failures can be anticipated in advance, human operators can account for these limitations. When failures are unanticipated, however, the result can be autonomous systems that slip out of control".[4] This preventive function was also raised by Holland Michel, who argued that risk evaluation and risk avoidance are possible if and only if the system's vulnerabilities and fault modes are known.[5] This in mind, in this chapter, we explore in greater detail the different reasons systems fail—and how AI systems fail *differently*—to provide this ontology and awareness to prospective Deployers.

At its most fundamental level, failures can be caused by component failures or system failures. *Component failures* involve one or more of the system's components (parts, units, subsystems) failing, which ultimately leads to the system ceasing to perform its intended function.[6] Component failures constitute the majority of causes of failure,[7] and we will focus our attention primarily on these causes. Specifically, we explore causes of *AI failures*, which are more counterintuitive and more poorly-described than mechanical failures.[8] Such AI failures can be contrasted with classical component failures such as human errors or mechanical failures, which are discussed as a point of comparison in Sect. 5.2.

System failures refer to situations where the cause of the failure is not reduceable to a component(s). Instead, the failure is a product of a multitude of (often latent)

---

[1] E.g. the medical sector. See Kohn et al. 2000, p. 28.

[2] Defense Innovation Board 2019, p. 39.

[3] This is a facet in the MHC Framework; see Sect. 2.4.4.

[4] Scharre 2016, p. 8.

[5] Holland Michel 2021.

[6] Perrow 1984, p. 70.

[7] Ibid., p. 71.

[8] Gilmer et al. 2018, p. 6.

faults which, only in combination, reacted in unexpected and non-linear ways.[9] How system failures are relevant to AWS discussions is briefly explored in Section 5.9. The main point to retain from system failure theory is that no system can be perfect, and that failures may occur due to the unfortunate convergence of factors that cannot be reduced to one single cause. This will remain true for AWS.[10]

As an additional caveat, we will not be considering *intentional* causes of failure in this discussion. One primary assumption made throughout this book is that AWS-users are law-abiding and do not wish to deliberately violate the law.[11] Technically, deliberate failures are also not as interesting as the cause is clear: a human intended for that system to fail, making causation and responsibility straightforward (even though this may be different in evidentiary terms). We explore the question of when failures can be construed as deliberate in *criminal* terms in Chap. 13.[12] Finally, depending on one's viewpoint, adversarials (anti-AI countermeasures) may be considered as the 'intentional' causing of failures by opponents: these will be discussed in Chap. 6 instead, as their mechanism of causing failures is distinct.

5.2 Classical Component Failures

As indicated above, a *component failure* describes a failure caused by faults occurring in parts, units and/or subsystems, and which can be linked to the failure through an anticipated sequence.[13] For traditional mechanical systems, there are generally two main components that 'fail': the human user, or the machine itself. These are important to cover briefly, since AWS retain a physical dimension[14] and sometimes a human element[15]: each component can fail independent of the AI.

---

[9] Scharre 2018, p. 151.

[10] See also Sect. 5.9. Legally, this means that perfect systems cannot be demanded by IHL. See Sect. 9.3.1.

[11] See Sect. 1.4.

[12] Perhaps more interesting is the question posed by some authors on the possibility of the AI *itself* purposely causing failures. This is sometimes called 'malevolent AI'. While an interesting proposition, it has been considered as a property only artificial general intelligence (AGI) is likely to be able to exhibit, making it fall outside of the ambit of this analysis. For more on this concept, see Yampolskiy 2015; Yampolskiy and Spellchecker 2016.

[13] Perrow 1984, p. 70.

[14] Recall that in Sect. 1.2, we limited our discussion of 'AWS' to physical weapon systems with an AI component.

[15] Depending on whether Deployer chooses to assign an Operator or not; see Sects. 1.3.2 and Section 8.7.1.

5.2.1 Human Error

Human error refers to situations where the system's failure can ultimately be traced back to a human's action or omission. Many an accident, disastrous or otherwise, has been attributed to human error. It is often said that "the greatest risk doesn't reside in the machinery, but rather in the humans operating them".[16] Human error has been identified as the greatest contributor to accidents (at 60–80%) across industries.[17] Humans can do so many things incorrectly in the operation or supervision of a system. A study on autopilot-related accidents identified at least five ways operators can make mistakes: they can incorrectly respond to decisions made by automated systems, make errors in setting up the system itself, act wrongly in response to false alarms, not act in the presence of justified alarms, and fail to properly monitor the system (due to e.g. lack of attention or being preoccupied elsewhere).[18] A more recent report related to software lists "omission or misinterpretation of user requirements in a software specification, incorrect translation, or omission of a requirement in the design specification" as examples of human error that could lead to failure.[19]

Indeed, the fact that humans make so many mistakes is frequently given as an argument for *more* automation, i.e., to remove the human element in order to reduce the overall number of failures (by removing human error as a fault). In the context of AWS, this comes in the form of claims that more delegation to AI would improve overall performance.[20] Theunissen, for instance, argued that increasing a system's autonomy would prevent all of the human error modes described in the autopilot study above from occurring.[21] This is not to say that increasing a system's autonomy does not come with downsides, but purely from the perspective of reducing overall failures, removing a component which is quite fragile and frequently induces faults makes theoretical sense.

One should be careful, however, in attributing failures to human error: it is sometimes reductionist as an explanation. An important concept to retain in this respect is forced errors. ***Forced errors*** refer to situations where a human does make an error (which may even directly cause the ultimate failure) but where this error itself was the inevitable result of priors in the overall system. Jennings illustrates this quite well: "Conditions such as fatigue, stress or complacency may lead to a mishap, but they are not specific actions by an operator, they are preconditions that set the stage for an accident".[22] Extremely long hours on duty, language barriers, 'macho' work cultures, and other factors frequently 'force' the human to make the error.[23] Realising when human errors were forced is important, as not doing so essentially amounts

[16] Sforza 2016, p. 512.

[17] Kohn et al. 2000, p. 53.

[18] Wiener and Curry 1980, pp. 5–9.

[19] IEEE Standards Association 2016, p. 15.

[20] See also Sect. 10.2.

[21] Theunissen and Suarez 2015, p. 184.

[22] Jennings 2008, p. 44.

[23] Perrow 1984.

to misdiagnosing the failure. The human blamed for the accident may be removed, be held legally accountable and perhaps criminally tried, but their replacement will be inserted into the unchanged work structure and eventually also be brought to commit the same forced error.[24] In such cases, adopting a system failure approach[25] is preferable.[26]

5.2.2 *Mechanical Faults Leading to AI Failure*

Malfunctions to mechanical parts of AWS will not be fundamentally different from those of other conventional weapons, and as such were not discussed further in this book.[27] One exception to be highlighted is that in some cases, mechanical issues can *lead to* AI failures: in this case, "AI fails because the hardware is incapable of robust performance across environments".[28] The mechanical failure of sensors (due to wear and tear, physical damage) one common way this might occur,[29] e.g. autopilots failing because external sensors have become frozen. Banerjee & Chanda expand this and note that the malfunction of any mechanical part involved in the AI's operation can potentially cause an AI failure, including processors (GPU, CPU, cloud servers) and casing and wiring of the computational device(s) running the AI.[30] It is thus important to keep these factors in mind when considering an AI's reliability.

5.3 AI Failures: Introduction

AI failures are very distinct from mechanical causes, making them crucial to discuss in detail. This is particularly the case for machine learning (ML) models, as these have "counterintuitive or poorly described failure modes that do not follow historical patterns of human, or even software, failures",[31] which Deployers must have at least a basic understanding of. Yampolskiy points out that failures involving older software were "not a direct consequence of particulars of intelligence available in such systems. AI Failures, on the other hand, are directly related to the mistakes produced by the intelligence such systems are designed to exhibit".[32] Comiter finds that older software problems generally amounted to programming mistakes (i.e.,

[24] Larouzée and Guarnieri 2014, pp. 6–7.

[25] See Sect. 5.9.

[26] Reason 2000, p. 768.

[27] This in fact is common practice in works focusing on AI. E.g. Bostrom 2011, p. 22.

[28] Banerjee and Chanda 2020, p. 3.

[29] Holland Michel 2021, p. 6; Rogers 2000, p. 171.

[30] Banerjee and Chanda 2020, p. 3.

[31] Gilmer et al. 2018, p. 6.

[32] Yampolskiy and Spellchecker 2016, p. 4.

human error); modern AI failures, on the other hand, do not stem from bugs, but are "inherent in the heart of the AI algorithms".[33] Flournoy et al. conclude from this that ML in particular has "increased potential for failure modes relative to other systems",[34] because of these additional causes of failure.

For older software, problems are frequently traced back to human error during design. This has certainly not disappeared for newer AI. Human mistakes are most pertinent when the software in question still uses rule-based AI or hybrid architectures that combine ML and symbolic techniques. Amongst others, mistakes in development can come in the form of bad overall system design,[35] inadequate, problematic, carelessly or incompetently written code,[36] and improperly designed utility functions.[37]

For data-based systems, in contrast, two main categories are usually distinguished based on *when* the cause emerges: during development (or 'learning' or 'training') and during operation (or 'performance').[38] Keeley words this somewhat differently, referring to internal causes ("something is broken or incorrect") and inputs ("faulty information was provided").[39] As with failures in general, many typologies in literature take a rather broad perspective and include environmental circumstances, interface (HMI), mechanical failures and adversarials as causes.[40] Some authors taken an even more macro view and include factors such as engineering design, inadequate quality control, and marketplace factors into consideration.[41]

For our purposes, we will be looking at five issues: training data issues; issues related to input data; out-of-distribution and drift; incorrect proxies; and bias. These were selected after a more general review of above-referenced sources on AI failure typologies, on the basis that they raise particular questions vis-à-vis Deployer's duties to implement IHL and reduce risk. They also fall into the 'counterintuitive' or 'poorly described' category, making it important for Deployers to properly understand them. It is generally found that training data issues and incorrect proxies are only within the ability of the Providing Entity to prevent, detect and fix,[42] while the other issues require more Deployer due diligence at the operational level.

Finally, before continuing, we should address a characteristic of AI which does not *cause* failure, but enables it to propagate faster once it occurs: ***state duplication***.[43]

---

[33] Comiter 2019, p. 4.

[34] Flournoy et al. 2020, p. 4.

[35] Russell et al. 2015, p. 108.

[36] Pan 1999; Scherer 2016, p. 366.

[37] Russell and Norvig 2010, p. 1037.

[38] Yampolskiy and Spellchecker 2016, p. 4; Haugh et al. 2018, pp. 2–3.

[39] Keeley 2015, p. 204.

[40] See and compare: Scherer 2016, p. 366; Meier 2017, p. 456; ICRC 2018, para 45; Bostrom 2011, pp. 22–24.

[41] Sahu and Srivastava 2020, p. 34.

[42] Deployer can in most cases only respond to failures caused by these factors by retiring the system.

[43] Many authors note that state duplication is decidedly unique to AI. State duplication here refers to the possibility of creating identical copies of any specific AI state and implanting them into different

Essentially, as AWS are produced, they may be outfitted with AI which have been duplicated based on an original trained model. While this ensures that the entire fleet preserves the same level of performance (based on which legal reviewers have greenlit the weapon), it also duplicates any hidden or latent problems. As such, these potential faults will apply to the entire force using the same base AI. A DoD report likened it to monoculture: a single disease or pest can destroy the entire harvest.[44]

The ramifications of state duplication must be taken into consideration by Deployers during risk assessment. Deployers must differentiate between AI systems and human-operated systems.[45] Humans are idiosyncratic: put in the same position, they will always act slightly differently, creating a type of buffer against widespread failures. Duplicated AI, on the other hand, would tend to respond to the same situation in the same way.[46] If this happens to lead to failure, it will cause systemic failures across the fleet.[47] State duplication is not necessarily a net negative—it also means that fixing one issue resolves the issue for all similar systems—but it does impact AWS' reliability at a group level.[48] If multiple AWS are released simultaneously which utilise the same base AI, Deployers should take this into consideration.

5.4 Training Data Issues

Learning-based AI is extremely data-reliant, and ML for many applications have become viable only relatively recently as large—often freely obtainable—datasets have become available.[49] In terms of data, the bottom line is quite simple: "The more, the better".[50] A European Commission report refers to this as *data dependency*: data is an essential prerequisite for producing systems which act and perform as intended.[51] All this is reflected in a popular axiom of computer scientists: "intelligence is in the data, not the algorithm".[52]

It is thus unsurprising that data also constitutes a primary cause of *failures*. Indeed, because data is so determinant, Russell and Norvig argue that for data-driven AI, it

---

agent bodies. It allows, for example, the training of a single AI before installing the program into mass-produced weapon systems, creating an army of identical agents which can be copied infinitely, rapidly, and cheaply. Molnar 2019, p. 10. The Defense Science Board sees this as not necessarily positive, fearing that this ease of duplication can make it easy for rival military powers or armed groups to have access to highly effective AWS with AI programs developed and trained abroad. Defense Innovation Board 2019, p. 14.

[44] Office of the Assistant Secretary of Defense for Research and Engineering 2015, p. 4.

[45] Scharre 2016, p. 23.

[46] Keeley 2015, p. 201.

[47] Lohn 2020, p. 2.

[48] See Sect. 4.4.

[49] Cukier 2018, p. 29.

[50] Molnar 2019, p. 10.

[51] European Commission 2020, p. 8.

[52] Haugh et al. 2018, pp. 2–3.

has become more important to worry about the data being used instead of the exact algorithm to apply.[53] The DoD has warned of many vulnerabilities linked to data inadequacies, and that these should be addressed before matériel relying on them are fielded.[54] In particular, we should consider circumstances which lead to the inability (or unwillingness) to collect sufficient data and validate its quality. As we will see below, frequent recourse to 'shortcuts' occurs in order to facilitate the data collection and training process, but these may well have undesired impacts to the product's quality or render the product vulnerable to adversarials. In short, "knowing where and how the data was gathered can be critical, along with understanding who made those choices and what their motivations were."[55]

What are the desired properties of data? As mentioned before, both quantity and quality matter. Some specific properties, however, have been highlighted in literature and official reports.[56] In terms of *quantity*, it is emphasised that data must be complete and of a sufficient scale: sometimes, "access to huge volumes of data" is necessary.[57] In terms of *quality*, the data must be accurate, relevant, from a trustworthy source, and quite importantly, it should properly reflect the Intended Operational Environment for which the system is developed.[58] Reneging on this last point leads to more frequent out-of-distribution problems, as discussed in Section 5.6, and reduces robustness, as mentioned in Sect. 4.3.

What circumstances, would prevent developers from properly obtaining data which fits these desiderata? Several factors could either prevent this or make it unattractive. First, despite the large volume of datasets already available, the ML community still experiences a chronic "insatiable need for data" that remains unfulfilled.[59] In some cases, this is due to data monopoly. Key industry players (such as Google, Amazon, Apple, Facebook and Microsoft) have access to massive and varied datasets, but are not keen on sharing. For smaller institutions—even military organisations—it can be quite difficult to obtain access to the same quantity of data.[60]

For military AI applications, which require rather particular types of data (e.g. images or videos of enemy personnel or matériel with a realistic military backdrop), this problem is compounded. This problem has been highlighted both by commentators and military institutions. Abaimov & Martellini have expressed concern about the "lack of high-quality (or any at all) training datasets",[61] as have the ICRC which

---

[53] Russell and Norvig 2010, p. 27.

[54] Defense Innovation Board 2019, p. 16.

[55] Weller 2019, p. 24.

[56] See Holland Michel 2021, p. 1; Ministère des Armées 2019, p. 7; Defense Innovation Board 2019, p. 16; European Commission 2020, p. 8.

[57] Boulanin 2016, p. 22.

[58] See Sect. 3.5.

[59] Vogelsang and Borg 2019, p. 5.

[60] UK House of Lords 2018, p. 45.

[61] Abaimov and Martellini 2020, p. 146.

pointed out that "high-quality, representative data for specific tasks is scarce" for military applications.[62] In a recent report, it was confirmed that even the US DoD "lacks sufficient available data that mimics the conflict condition in which these systems may operate in the future" and recommended the Department to pursue a coordinated strategy for data collection, cleaning, curation and cross-agency sharing.[63] The French Ministry of the Armed Forces also committed itself to invest further into data 'specific to the military domain'.[64]

This ties into another potential risk factor, namely that shortcuts may be taken to overcome this insatiable thirst. Many open-source datasets are made available on the internet, which presents an enticing and easy way to obtain enormous volumes of data. Many contemporary data collection practices constitute a 'dragnet', in the sense that "everything that can be collected is collected".[65] From a survey, it was found that frequently, organisations falsely assume that available datasets are trustworthy and have already been secured. In actuality, there is no guarantee that this data is accurate or safe. The data may be mislabelled, erroneous, or tampered with. Even if the data is not deliberately manipulated, such data must still be tested for its quality, fidelity, and provenance.[66] Otherwise, the data can become a primary cause of eventual failures: garbage-in/garbage-out.[67]

Training data issues are not actionable by Deployers beyond retiring the problematic system from use. Prevention should be carried out at the development level, by adopting good practices and policy regarding data collection and validation. Militaries should demand stringent standards from their contractors in this respect.

5.5 Input Data Issues

These failures are caused by properties associated with the input data received from the environment;[68] they are as such primarily associated with the deployment phase.[69] Numerous studies have demonstrated how AI performance drops as the inputs received are degraded in various ways.[70] The reason why this qualifies as a cause of failure is rather intuitive: AI-based agents rely on the input data they collect to understand, interpret, and respond[71] to cues from the operational environment. Even if the system is not fully autonomous, commands received from operators or

62 ICRC 2019, p. 11.

63 Flournoy et al. 2020, p. 9.

64 Ministère des Armées 2019, p. 5.

65 Comiter 2019, p. 29.

66 Defense Innovation Board 2019, p. 16.

67 Vogelsang and Borg 2019, p. 5.

68 For how AI agents receive and process input data, see Sect. 3.3.

69 Yampolskiy 2020.

70 See Lohn 2020, p. 7; Geirhos et al. 2018; Hendrycks et al. 2020.

71 For a more complete discussion on this process, see Sect. 3.3.

supervisors also constitute input data that can be degraded.[72] Lohn views issues with input data as amounting to a degradation of the *information* conveyed through those inputs, which naturally results in mistakes and a worse overall performance.[73]

Holland Michel compiled an extensive exposé on the different types of problematic input data and the circumstances which give rise to them. With regard to the input data itself, he identified four ways data can be degraded:[74]

- *Incomplete data.* The information necessary for the AI to make a correct decision is absent. This can occur because the source of the information is compromised, the system cannot collect the information (e.g. because a sensor or antenna is damaged), or the pertinent information was deliberately removed.
- *Low-quality data.* This is data which contains "errors or ambiguities that result in suboptimal or inappropriate responses".[75] One can think of disruptive lighting, clutter, abundant noise and sensor obstruction as examples.
- *Incorrect data.* The information the system bases its decision on is simply untrue. This is normally caused by humans either mistakenly (e.g. spelling mistakes, wrong format, feeding faulty data) or deliberately (adversarials), but can occasionally also occur due to sensor faults (e.g. the sensor is badly calibrated or defective).
- *Discrepant data.* While Holland Michel classifies this also under input data, we discuss this below under out-of-distribution.[76]

With regard to *why* the data can be degraded in those ways, Holland Michel identifies four main causes: harsh conditions, complexity and variance, adversarial actions, and drift.[77] The first two are usually what first come to mind when speaking of causes of input data problems: one may think of dust, smoke, raindrops or mist (visual), signal interference (radio), street noise, crosstalk and harsh wind (audio),[78] and accents, professional lingo and homophones (language processing) as factors which can cause input data decay.[79] Degradations can occur due to harsh operating environments (e.g. bad weather) or complexity (e.g. a dynamic urban backdrop). With regard to complexity, Gilmer et al. note that even random movements of background objects may sometimes degrade input data quality.[80] In military environments which are often cluttered and complex,[81] Deployers should therefore consider whether the environment would generate risk of input data decay.

[72] Holland Michel 2021, p 3.
[73] Lohn 2020, p. 7.
[74] Holland Michel 2021, p. 4.
[75] Ibid.
[76] Section 5.6.
[77] Holland Michel 2021, p. 6.
[78] Hendrycks and Dietterich 2019, p. 2.
[79] Chen 2021.
[80] Gilmer et al. 2018, p. 13.
[81] Section 3.4.2.

As one can deduce, the more vulnerable a system is to input degradations (natural or adversarial), the less robust it is. Studies have been conducted to determine to what extent transformations, perturbations and disruptions to input data affect overall model performance, and how robustness against such degradations can be improved.[82] While the Providing Entity is responsible for ensuring that systems are *generally* robust *a priori* (as found in Sect. 4.3), ***Deployer is primarily responsible*** for analysing the characteristics of the operational context and determining if a system will be sufficiently robust in the presence of foreseeable causes of input data decay, as this cannot be done in abstracto.

As to Holland Michel's third and fourth causes, input data which was deliberately manipulated to induce failures are a special case called adversarial inputs, which we discuss in Chap. 6.3. With regard to drift, it is argued that this is not purely a matter of input degradation, but a hybrid problem that also relates to design and training. We discuss this next.

5.6 Out-of-Distribution and Drift

Out-of-distribution (OOD) is a quintessentially modern AI problem for which no true analogy can be found in prior human experience; it is therefore important for users to comprehend correctly. Out-of-distribution is tied to the narrow AI limitation, the Intended Operational Environment, and the infinite variance problem.[83] How OOD occurs is perhaps best explained through the following sketch:

> All of us occasionally find ourselves in situations that our previous experience has not adequately prepared us to deal with … Such situations are inherently difficult to handle and inevitably lead to some missteps. However, a key (and often rare) skill in dealing with such situations is to recognize our own ignorance, rather than simply assuming that the heuristics and intuitions we've developed for other situations will carry over perfectly.[84]

Recall that one common conception of 'robustness' is the ability to *generalise*.[85] With regard to humans, our robustness is truly excellent: indeed, even when trained on (or having experienced) a narrow set of situations only, humans are rapidly able to formulate generic rules and filter what aspects of new information to focalise on.[86] Current-day AI,[87] in contrast, falls back on heuristics it has developed during training,

---

82 See e.g. Geirhos et al. 2018, p. 4; Gilmer et al. 2018, p. 13; Hendrycks and Dietterich 2019, p. 2; Chen 2021.

83 See Sects. 3.2.2 and 3.5.

84 Amodei et al. 2016, p. 16.

85 See Sect. 4.3.

86 Geirhos et al. 2018, p. 2. Humans are able to ignore confetti, rotations, and even abstract changes in structure and style to correctly identify what they are seeing, even if they have never seen confetti or impressionist art before. Hendrycks and Dietterich 2019, p. 1.

87 Some researchers are considering whether the higher robustness of humans may be due to the brain's neutral architecture, which implies that once successfully replicated, AI will also be able to generalise more robustly as humans do. See Geirhos et al. 2018; Lohn 2020.

but which often are inapplicable to the new situation, which generates mistakes.[88] OOD, essentially refers to a disconnect between the data distributions which the system was trained for and those it receives:[89] the inputs are 'out-of-the-intended-distribution'.[90]

OOD has been identified as a major source of AI failures, and are frequently warned about. It is particularly emphasised that a high initial accuracy score does not provide any guarantees of how well the system will respond to OOD situations.[91] Any result is technically possible: the model may still make the correct decision even in OOD, but it may also "utterly fail".[92] One study by Daumé & Marcu showed a classifier with Accuracy = 0.92 which experienced a drop to 0.58 on an out-of-distribution dataset.[93] Compounding this, it has been noted that the AI's *confidence* in the correctness of its decision often remains the same, or even increases: they "may not only exhibit poor performance, but also wrongly assume that their performance is good".[94] It is for this reason that in some views, the concept of robustness includes the ability to recognise when such situations occur (OOD detection).[95]

Under what circumstances is OOD likely? This is an important question to consider if a user wishes to prevent its occurrence. A few situations have been identified in literature. First, there can simply be a ***disconnect a priori***, where the training and operational distribution never corresponded well in the first place.[96] This can be a mistake during design (the data collected badly represented the IOE[97]) or during use (Deployer used the system outside of the prescribed IOE, thereby failing to match the two data distributions, as warned of in Sect. 3.5). A different problem that can arise during production is ***overfitting***, where the model is overly specialised, often due to excessive retraining for accuracy.[98] In this case the entire real world can be

---

[88] This is an inevitable characteristic of narrow AI that we must work around. See Sect. 3.2.2.

[89] Lohn 2020, pp. 5–6.

[90] OOD is sometimes also referred to as 'datashift' to describe the situation where AI fails because "there are broad differences between the training data and the input data". Holland Michel 2020, p 7. Alternatively, authors speak of 'brittleness' (how AI "cannot generalize and can only consider the quantifiable variables identified early on in the design stages"), 'fragility' ("difficulty processing unfamiliar events and scenarios"), or 'catastrophic forgetting' ("the inability to easily transfer learning from one context to another"). See Cummings 2018, p. 12; Leslie 2019, p. 32; Hayward and Maas 2021, p. 5. All these terms essentially describe the same basic problem that underlies OOD.

[91] European Commission 2020, pp. 8–9.

[92] Comiter 2019, p. 14.

[93] Daume and Marcu 2006.

[94] Amodei et al. 2016, p. 16.

[95] See Sect. 4.3.

[96] Pan and Yang 2010, p. 1345.

[97] See Sect. 5.4. See also Sect. 3.5.

[98] Nakkiran 2019.

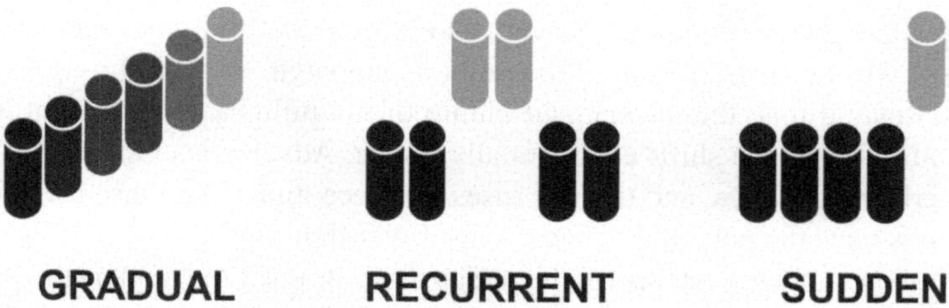

Fig. 5.1 Three patterns of data drift[102]

seen as out-of-distribution, as the model works solely for the specific data distribution it was trained on. Preventing this would be primarily the task of programmers and reviewers, and it would be quite damning if such a system even reached the operational stage in the first place.

A more insidious cause of OOD is ***drift***.[99] This refers to a situation where the training and operational distributions *initially* corresponded well (which would justify the system passing development and review), but 'drifted' apart over time. Drift can occur because most ML models operate on static weights, world models and rules derived from the training data; in other words, the heuristics 'crystalise' once development is complete.[100] However, at some point, the operational distribution may shift away from the (initially representative) training distribution, generating out-of-distribution over time.[101]

Drift may be foreseeable or unforeseeable. Figure 5.1 shows three variations of drift. Gradual and recurrent drift are relatively predictable in advance. Examples of gradual drift would be inflation or a progressively smaller proportion of combatants-versus-civilians as defenders are pushed out of a city they occupied. For recurrent drift, one can think of price shocks during holidays or increased enemy activity during summers vis-à-vis winters. While these patterns may be more difficult to discern in practice than in theory, they are at least somewhat consistent. Once understood, related out-of-distribution failures can be foreseen and prevented (e.g. by not using an AWS during wintertime or requesting updates or retraining to account for gradual shifts). In this regard, sudden shifts (e.g. demand spikes caused by a natural disaster, a pandemic) are the most problematic as they occur abruptly. This makes it difficult to plan for and prevent. If the sudden change occurs when a system is in operation, Deployer might only realise this took place after an incident has already occurred.

Drift occurs more often and more rapidly in dynamic situations,[103] and we have established this as a primary characteristic of the military environment.[104] As war

---

[99] Literature sometimes makes a more detailed distinction between concept drift and data drift, but the underlying reason for any errors induced remain the same. See Shendre 2020; Das 2021.

[100] Leslie 2019, p. 32.

[101] Nelson et al. 2014, p. 1.

[102] Adapted from Das 2021.

[103] Huang et al. 2011, p. 51.

[104] Section 3.4.2.

physically alters the environment, we can also foresee that (but not predict which) sudden drift will occur frequently throughout a campaign, or even throughout one operation. Beyond this, the *adversarial* nature of the military environment makes the probability of sudden shifts exponentially higher. Adversaries will adapt, adjust tactics, overhaul strategies, and try new ruses and deceptions. All these behavioural modifications have the potential to cause out-of-distribution.[105]

As mentioned above, systems can be updated or retrained to counter distribution shifts. Das provides a summary overview of best practices in the industry to respond to drift.[106] This can be done preventively (if a shift will occur, which in some cases can be determined with predictive models) or reactively (if a shift is observed).[107] If Deployer foresees the possibility that a shift has occurred which their AWS might not be able to accommodate, they should refrain from using that AWS during Weapon Selection[108] until it has been recalibrated.

One final potential solution to counter drift is to enable ***online learning***,[109] which negates the premise that the system's training distribution is static. Online learning gives the system the freedom to collect information during active operation, thereby allowing it to continually update its world model, rules and heuristics.[110] In theory, this allows it to 'chase' the operational environment's shifting distribution in real time by adapting its internal distribution accordingly, preventing OOD.[111]

As our discussion shows, out-of-distribution is a multifaceted issue that concerns both the development and use phases. ***The Providing Entity must ensure no problem exists a priori, but Deployer must stay vigilant during employment*** and identify developments that could induce drift. If so, Deployer must take appropriate mitigating measures, such as proactively requesting updates and (temporarily) retiring systems if necessary.

5.7 Proxy Mistakes

Proxy mistakes are linked to other causes of failure we have previously addressed, and authors often do not regard it as a 'separate' cause.[112] Proxy mistakes are caused by the system having learnt to use an incorrect proxy to arrive at conclusions, instead of a characteristic(s) which should be determinant. Yampolskiy describes the problem

---

[105] Holland Michel 2021, p. 9.

[106] Das 2021.

[107] Shendre 2020.

[108] See Sect. 2.4.2.

[109] Online learning was previously mentioned as a form of Context Control Deployer can implement. See Sect. 2.4.3.

[110] Nelson et al. 2014, p. 1.

[111] Das 2021.

[112] See and compare: Freitas 2014, p. 2; Yampolskiy and Spellchecker 2016, p. 4; Weller 2019, p. 27.

as follows: "The system can fail to learn what its human designers want it to learn and instead learn a different, but correlated function."[113] Amodei et al. outline different ways AI can learn incorrect proxies. These include problems with the training data,[114] design oversights (e.g. not properly penalising undesired effects in the reward function; ignoring reward hacking), and in some situations, convenience from the designer (proxies are knowingly used because they are simpler).[115] ***These are mostly problems only designers and reviewers can address***, even though Deployers must still be cognisant of the issue.

Many examples of proxy mistakes have been noted in literature, and they can be insidious in the sense that their accuracy statistics can seem quite promising: humans often do not immediately realise that the learnt functions are undesirable or fragile. A seminal example is the study of Ribeiro et al. mentioned previously,[116] whereby the classifier learnt to distinguish wolves and huskies not by the subject, but rather by the presence of absence of snow in the background.[117] More closely related to the military domain, a model learnt to identify friendly from enemy tanks based not on the vehicles' markings or shapes, but depending on whether the sky was overcast.[118]

As a pertinent hypothetical by Thorne, consider an AWS that destroys a clearly marked medical unit.[119] Medical units under IHL are allowed to arm themselves for their own defence, as long as they do not perform acts harmful to the enemy.[120] However, this AWS had erroneously learnt that weapon-bearing is the criterion based on which personnel can be targeted, leading to the accident. The association '*weapon = valid target*' is the mistaken proxy in this example. This scenario demonstrates well the importance of considering exceptions and details in legal rules, as well as the dangers of overly simplistic proxy formulas. Interestingly, this incident could have occurred also with purely rule-based systems if the programmers had simply defined '*bearing arms = valid target*' for convenience. This problem is thus not exclusive to ML systems.

The insidious nature of these examples comes from the fact that these systems often test highly on accuracy,[121] making the incorrect proxy problem not immediately obvious. Reviewers and users may not automatically realise that the system is making distinctions on illegitimate grounds if the overall accuracy seems acceptable at an

---

[113] Yampolskiy and Spellchecker 2016, p. 4.

[114] See Sect. 5.4.

[115] Amodei et al. 2016.

[116] See Sect. 4.5.2.

[117] Ribeiro et al. 2016.

[118] Guidotti et al. 2018, p. 4.

[119] Thorne 2020, p. 25.

[120] Geneva Convention for the Amelioration of the Condition of the Wounded and Sick in Armed Forces in the Field, adopted 12 August 1949, entered into force 21 October 1950, 75 UNTS 31 (Geneva Convention I), Article 21.

[121] Freitas 2014, p. 2.

initial glance. The system in Thorne's example may function with a seemingly high degree of accuracy for a lengthy period of time, raising no alarms from the part of Deployer even after several targeting cycles—until it encounters an armed medical unit.

5.8 Bias

This term refers to systematic bias in an AI's outputs derived from bias/prejudice in the training set (which the AI has internalised).[122] One well-studied example is the COMPAS case, an algorithm trained to determine risk of recidivism.[123] Bias is a rather peculiar cause of AI failure in that it is extremely prolific in civil AI literature, but does not *necessarily* create issues for military AI. To be clear, when discussing bias here, we are referring to bias that causes 'unfair' or discriminatory results. 'Bias' is used in two ways in literature: to describe situations where (1) the training set *inaccurately* reflects the IOE, or (2) the training set *accurately reflects unfair aspects* of the IOE.[124] In this section, we specifically refer to bias in the second sense. We have already discussed bias in the first sense above as part of the recommendation that training sets should be accurate and representative of the IOE.[125] This type of bias must be avoided in any AI application, including the military domain, to avoid failures. However, it is less clear to what extent bias in the second sense would be problematic from an IHL perspective.

In civil domains, there is a significant ethical incentive to avoid bias, based on fairness, non-discrimination and equitability.[126] In the COMPAS case, for instance, we expect courts to rule in equitable and non-discriminatory ways: bias in this domain would unquestionably constitute a failure condition in itself (one may even argue, *even if* the discriminatory result is technically accurate).[127] Similarly, we would find it inherently problematic if online ads for high-paying jobs are served disproportionately to men.[128] From an IHL perspective, however, this is more nuanced.

---

122 Defense Innovation Board 2019, p. 46.

123 After having been actively used by US courts for years, COMPAS was eventually determined to not only possess questionable predictive power (only 10% above chance level) but also to be biased against black defendants by labelling them as 'risky' on average twice as often as white defendants. See Lansing 2012; Angwin et al. 2016. The 137 questions judges answered as inputs did not include the defendant's race, so where did this bias come from? The answer is that the racial bias was ingrained prior to this, in the training sets used to develop the system. One could therefore see bias as a sub-type of training data issues. Many other such examples have been noted in websites, credit bureaus, and large companies such as Amazon. See Guidotti et al. 2018, p 4.

124 UK House of Lords 2018, p. 41.

125 Sections 3.5 and 5.4.

126 Leslie 2019.

127 Adadi and Berrada 2018, p. 52144.

128 Miller and Hosanagar 2019.

One can think, for instance, of a classifier which identifies enemy combatants of ethnic group X more reliably than those from ethnic group Y. Does this bias lead to a violation of IHL? As intuitively questionable (or even unethical) such a model may sound, the answer is: not necessarily. As long as the classifier's performance on Group Y is good (i.e., above the threshold for being a discriminate weapon[129]), IHL does not prohibit the system from being systematically *better* at identifying combatants from Group X. IHL is unconcerned with this bias as it involves false negatives in Group Y: it simply means that more Group Y combatants go unnoticed and are not shot.

In contrast, bias in the opposite direction could be more problematic. Assume now that a model is biased into believing that members of Group Y are predisposed to being terrorists due to historic or ethnic prejudice in the training set and, therefore, disproportionally labels them as valid targets and kills them. This type of bias would violate IHL and must be addressed. The reason is that the *distinction is not made on legitimate grounds.* IHL only allows distinguishing between legitimate and illegitimate targets based on their combatant status or hostile actions, not based on ethnic generalisations (or any other labels such as age, gender, race, etc.).[130]

Whether bias is a failure cause for AWS is, therefore, rather casuistic: it depends on the type of bias and the failure condition set by the evaluator. It is certainly possible that fairness or a comparable criterion can be included as a guiding principle of military operations. This position was taken, for instance, by Brazil which deemed "unacceptable discriminatory bias" as a reason to reject an AWS during review.[131] In such cases, bias constitutes a failure cause by virtue of the set failure condition. Absent this, for IHL, bias causing false negatives is less problematic than bias causing false positives. It also depends on what exactly the bias entails. If a system is 'biased' toward predicting that persons wearing a rebel army's uniform are more likely to be valid targets, we would not even call this bias in a derogatory sense; it would just form part of the system's intended functionality (this is referred to as operationally justified bias).[132]

5.9 System Failures

System failures refer to situations where the cause of the failure is not reduceable to a component(s). Instead, the failure is a product of a multitude of (often latent) faults which, only in combination, reacted in unexpected and non-linear ways to produce the ultimate result.[133] The concept of system failures is based on *normal accident*

---

[129] See Sect. 9.3 for when this would be the case.

[130] Moyes 2019, p. 7.

[131] Brazil 2019.

[132] UK House of Lords 2018, p. 41.

[133] Scharre 2018, p. 151.

theory proposed by Perrow in the 1980s.[134] In his seminal work, he argued that certain characteristics will make a system *inevitably* experience a failure: it is unavoidable, no matter how many countermeasures and safety precautions are taken.[135] The rather peculiar choice of naming them 'normal' accidents captures perfectly Perrow's idea that such accidents are rare, but inevitable: "It is normal for us to die, but we only do it once."[136]

Perrow's normal accident theory has since become mainstream in safety engineering and is applied in a wide variety of industries, including the military domain.[137] It has also been expanded by many authors, who developed their own models to explain how system failures occur. One dominant theory is the Swiss Cheese model advanced by James Reason in the 1990s, which frames system failures as an unlikely and unfortunate convergence of faults.[138] In this model, the 'holes' in the many layers of cheese represent small (latent) faults throughout the entire system's operation (this includes design decisions, policy decisions, small errors during use, small coincidences). By themselves, these holes pose no threat to the system's functioning: a molecule passing through one hole will be repelled by the next layer. However, at one point, a molecule will pierce every hole and cause a failure.[139] The Swiss Cheese concept has been used to produce in-depth models to explain system failures.[140]

There is little doubt that normal accident theory is applicable for military systems in general and AWS in particular. In Perrow's view, normal accident theory applies to systems which are interactively complex and tightly coupled. *Interactive complexity* refers to the existence of components which interact in unanticipated, incomprehensible and non-linear ways.[141] Nuclear plants were given as an example: here, there are "branching paths, feedback loops, jumps from one linear sequence to another because of proximity and certain other features".[142] *Coupling* refers to the lack of slack or buffer.[143] In tightly coupled systems, one shock propagates quickly and to many other components.[144] Both characteristics have been associated with the military domain.[145] When Scharre describes AWS as "complex systems that rely on seamless interaction between multiple types of tightly coupled sensors, algorithms,

---

[134] Normal accident theory postulates that accidents are "inevitable in certain systems. Although they may be rare, accidents are "normal" in complex, high technology industries". Kohn et al. 2000, p. 57.

[135] Perrow 1984.

[136] Ibid., p. 5.

[137] See e.g. Jennings 2008; Flournoy et al. 2020, p. 9.

[138] Reason 2000, p. 769.

[139] See Ibid.

[140] E.g. Lee 2011.

[141] Perrow 1984, p. 70.

[142] Ibid., p. 75.

[143] Kohn et al. 2000, p. 59.

[144] Perrow 1984, pp. 90–92.

[145] Ibid., p. 97.

actuators and human factors",[146] for instance, it immediately evokes the impression of an interactively complex and tightly coupled system. The following description from a DoD report suggests the same:

> The accuracy and precision of ML/DL systems is typically a composite effect that arises from a combination of the behaviors of different components, such as the training data, the learning program, and even the learning framework. These components are then embedded in larger systems, so interactions with the physical, computational, and human components of the system will ultimately affect system performance.[147]

The Swiss Cheese model was also used in a HFACS (Human Factors Analysis and Classification System) developed by the DoD in 2008.[148] Here, we encounter the first advantage of acknowledging normal accident theory for weapon systems: it facilitates *analysis and prevention* during Assessment procedures.[149] While the theory postulates that normal accidents cannot be prevented, an inquiry into the different 'holes' allows them to be closed so they cannot contribute to accidents during subsequent uses of the system. The HFACS model does this by looking holistically at various organisational, supervisory, circumstantial, and human factors in a comprehensive taxonomy.[150] While we do not know if that particular fault will ever form part of a 'convergence of holes' again, addressing the issue improves the system's overall integrity.

As to the second advantage of acknowledging normal accident theory for AWS, it makes us aware of the importance of acknowledging latent factors. One characteristic of high-reliability organisations such as civil aviation and nuclear plants (which have a disproportionately low accident rate) is that they are willing to adopt a 'system approach' and address latent factors.[151] In this regard, Kohn et al. warn against "simplifying the causes of an accident, highlighting a single element as the cause and overlooking multiple contributing factors".[152] In most organisations, there is a tendency to blame accidents on one or a few of the most prominently visible causes. Often blame is quickly placed on a human, and this is a convenient way to seemingly resolve the accident and assigning (legal) responsibility.

For AWS, Deployers are likely to be prime targets of this practice whenever an incident occurs. We are reminded, however, that this is often not the whole picture. Humans commit forced errors,[153] and sometimes, it was a convergence of prior faults which forced this error. This blaming approach is reductionist and extremely poor as a preventive measure. Larouzée and Guarnieri liken this to swatting mosquitoes

---

[146] Scharre 2018, p. 151.

[147] Flournoy et al. 2020, p. 9.

[148] Jennings 2008.

[149] See Sect. 2.4.6.

[150] See Jennings 2008, pp. 46–49.

[151] Reason 2000, p. 770.

[152] Kohn et al. 2000, p. 53.

[153] See Sect. 5.2.1.

one by one as they come, but this solves nothing: "*un autre moustique viendra aussi certainement qu'un autre opérateur commettra une erreur dans le même contexte*".[154]

There are two important conclusions we can draw from this discussion. First, we must remain open to the possibility that a Deployer's mistake involving an AWS (which led to harm) could have been a forced error and/or part of a system failure. This may have implications for assigning legal responsibility, as we discuss in Sect. 13.6.2, but it is also crucial for Assessment, particularly prevention. Correctly diagnosing the incident as a product of a system failure and systematically addressing the many faults (including organisational ones) which contributed to the failure—instead of convenient blaming—is the proper way to effectuate the duty to "prevent the commission, or the repetition, of acts contrary to [IHL]".[155] Second, when making normative judgments about acceptable levels of reliability for military systems, we (and the law) must accept that perfect performance is impossible, if only because a system failure can occur at any time—a failure which was completely unforeseeable and unpreventable by Deployers.

5.10 Recommendations

For Deployer, understanding causes of AI failure is complementary to understanding a system's measures of performance. Both are required to make informed decisions: measures of performance represent a global awareness of the system's qualities, while the variables discussed in this chapter enable Deployer to casuistically determine when—despite promising performance measurements in abstracto—they should nevertheless refrain from using a given system, because factors are present within the operational environment that could foreseeably cause an elevated rate of failures.

In particular, we identified two AI-specific risk factors that Deployers should be specifically sensitive to: input data issues and drift.[156] As in Sect. 4.6, the corollary to this conclusion is that the Providing Entity is required to provide the necessary training to Deployers to enable them to understand, identify and mitigate the conditions that could lead to these failures manifesting. Additionally, the Providing Entity is responsible for ensuring that factors such as training data issues, incorrect proxies and (potentially) bias are minimised, since these are causes of failure that Deployer cannot address or identify at the operational stage. Finally, failures are inevitable:

---

[154] Larouzée and Guarnieri 2014, p. 7.

[155] Pictet 1952, p. 367.

[156] This would be in addition to classical failure causes such as mechanical error or human error. See Sect. 5.2.

even the best system can still experience 'normal accidents'.[157] The ultimate aim of this chapter is thus not to eliminate failures outright, but rather to empower Deployer (and the Providing Entity) to mitigate them to acceptable levels.[158]

References

Abaimov S, Martellini M (2020) Artificial Intelligence in Autonomous Weapon Systems. In: Martellini M, Ralf T (eds) 21st Century Prometheus. Springer International Publishing, Cham, pp 141–177. https://doi.org/10.1007/978-3-030-28285-1_8

Adadi A, Berrada M (2018) Peeking Inside the Black-Box: A Survey on Explainable Artificial Intelligence (XAI). IEEE Access 6:52138–62160. https://doi.org/10.1109/ACCESS.2018.2870052

Amodei D et al. (2016) Concrete Problems in AI Safety. http://arxiv.org/abs/1606.06565

Angwin J et al. (2016) Machine Bias. ProPublica. https://www.propublica.org/article/machine-bias-risk-assessments-in-criminal-sentencing. Accessed 25 November 2020

Banerjee D N, Chanda S S (2020) AI Failures: A Review of Underlying Issues. http://arxiv.org/abs/2008.04073

Bostrom N (2011) Information Hazards: A Typology of Potential Harms from Knowledge. Review of Contemporary Philosophy 10:44–79. http://www.nickbostrom.com/information-hazards.pdf. Accessed 04 August 2023

Boulanin V (2016) Mapping the Development of Autonomy in Weapon Systems: A Primer on Autonomy. Stockholm International Peace Research Institute, Stockholm

Brazil (2019) Statement by Brazil. 2019 Group of Governmental Experts on Lethal Autonomous Weapons Systems (LAWS), 25–29 March 2019, Item 5a

Chen H (2021) Does Word Error Rate Matter?. SmartAction. https://www.smartaction.ai/blog/does-word-error-rate-matter/. Accessed 5 November 2021

Comiter M (2019) Attacking Artificial Intelligence: AI's Security Vulnerability and What Policymakers Can Do About It. Belfer Center for Science and International Affairs, Cambridge

Cukier K (2018) The Economic Implications of Artificial Intelligence. In: Cummings M L et al. (eds) Artificial Intelligence and International Affairs: Disruption Anticipated. Chatham House, London, pp 29–42

Cummings M L (2018) Artificial Intelligence and the Future of Warfare. In: Cummings M L et al. (eds) Artificial Intelligence and International Affairs: Disruption Anticipated. Chatham House, London, pp 7–18

Das S (2021) Best Practices for Dealing with Concept Drift. Neptune.ai. https://neptune.ai/blog/concept-drift-best-practices. Accessed 30 October 2021

Daume H, Marcu D (2006) Domain Adaptation for Statistical Classifiers. Journal of Artificial Intelligence Research 26:101–126. http://arxiv.org/abs/1109.6341

Defense Innovation Board (2019) AI Principles: Recommendations on the Ethical Use of Artificial Intelligence by the Department of Defense Defense Innovation Board. US Department of Defense. https://media.defense.gov/2019/Oct/31/2002204458/-1/-1/0/DIB_AI_PRINCIPLES_PRIMARY_DOCUMENT.PDF. Accessed 2 August 2023

European Commission (2020) Report on the Safety and Liability Implications of Artificial Intelligence, the Internet of Things and Robotics. COM/2020/64 final

Flournoy M A, Haines A, Chefitz G (2020) Building Trust through Testing: Adapting DOD's Test & Evaluation, Validation & Verification (TEVV) Enterprise for Machine Learning Systems, Including Deep Learning Systems. WestExec Advisors, Washington D.C.

---

[157] See Sect. 5.9.

[158] US Department of Defense 2023, p. 22.

Freitas A A (2014) Comprehensible Classification Models. ACM SIGKDD Explorations Newsletter 15(1):1–10. https://doi.org/10.1145/2594473.2594475

Geirhos R et al. (2018) Generalisation in Humans and Deep Neural Networks. http://arxiv.org/abs/1808.08750

Gilmer J et al. (2018) Motivating the Rules of the Game for Adversarial Example Research. http://arxiv.org/abs/1807.06732

Guidotti R et al. (2018) A Survey Of Methods For Explaining Black Box Models. http://arxiv.org/abs/1802.01933

Haugh B A, Sparrow D A, Tate D M (2018) The Status of Test, Evaluation, Verification, and Validation (TEV&V) of Autonomous Systems. Institute for Defense Analyses, Alexandria

Hayward K J, Maas M M (2021) Artificial Intelligence and Crime: A Primer for Criminologists. Crime, Media, Culture: An International Journal 17(2):209–233. https://doi.org/10.1177/1741659020917434

Hendrycks D et al. (2020) The Many Faces of Robustness: A Critical Analysis of Out-of-Distribution Generalization. http://arxiv.org/abs/2006.16241

Hendrycks D, Dietterich T G (2019) Benchmarking Neural Network Robustness to Common Corruptions and Surface Variations. http://arxiv.org/abs/1807.01697

Holland Michel A (2020) The Black Box, Unlocked: Predictability and Understandability in Military AI. UNIDIR, Geneva. https://unidir.org/sites/default/files/2020-09/BlackBoxUnlocked.pdf. Accessed 2 August 2023

Holland Michel A (2021) Known Unknowns: Data Issues and Military Autonomous Systems. UNIDIR, Geneva. https://unidir.org/publication/known-unknowns. Accessed 2 August 2023

Huang L et al. (2011) Adversarial Machine Learning. In: Proceedings of the 4th ACM workshop on Security and artificial intelligence. ACM, New York, pp 43–58. https://doi.org/10.1145/2046684.2046692

ICRC (2018) Ethics and Autonomous Weapon Systems: An Ethical Basis for Human Control?. Group of Governmental Experts of the High Contracting Parties to the Convention on Prohibitions or Restrictions on the Use of Certain Conventional Weapons Which May Be Deemed to Be Excessively Injurious or to Have Indiscriminate Effects, CCW/GGE1/2018/WP

ICRC (2019) Artificial Intelligence and Machine Learning in Armed Conflict: A Human-Centred Approach. ICRC, Geneva

IEEE Standards Association (2016) IEEE 1633-2016, IEEE Recommended Practice on Software Reliability. IEEE. https://standards.ieee.org/standard/1633-2016.html. Accessed 11 October 2021

Jennings J (2008) Human Factors Analysis & Classification Applying the Department of Defense System During Combat Operations In Iraq. Professional Safety 53(06)

Keeley T (2015) Auditable Policies for Autonomous Systems (Decisional Forensics). In: Williams A P, Scharre P D (eds) Autonomous Systems: Issues for Defence Policymakers. NATO, The Hague, pp 196–225

Kohn L T, Corrigan J M, Donaldson M S (2000) To Err Is Human: Building a Safer Health System. National Academies Press, Washington D.C. https://doi.org/10.17226/9728

Lansing S (2012) New York State COMPAS-Probation Risk and Need Assessment Study: Examining the Recidivism Scale's Effectiveness and Predictive Accuracy. Report to New York Office of Justice Research and Performance. https://www.criminaljustice.ny.gov/crimnet/ojsa/opca/compas_probation_report_2012.pdf. Accessed 25 November 2020

Larouzée J, Guarnieri F (2014) Huit Idées Reçues Sur Le(s) Modèle(s) de l'erreur Humaine de James Reason. Revue d'électricité et d'électronique 5:83–90

Lee R (2011) Integrated Safety Management Systems – Lessons from the Aviation Industry. In: Australian University Safety Association Conference, July 2011

Leslie D (2019) Understanding Artificial Intelligence Ethics and Safety: A Guide for the Responsible Design and Implementation of AI Systems in the Public Sector. The Alan Turing Institute, London

Lohn A J (2020) Estimating the Brittleness of AI: Safety Integrity Levels and the Need for Testing Out-Of-Distribution Performance. http://arxiv.org/abs/2009.00802

Meier M W (2017) The Strategic Implications of Lethal Autonomous Weapons. In: Ohlin J D (ed) Research Handbook on Remote Warfare. Edward Elgar, Cheltenham, pp 443–478. https://doi.org/10.4337/9781784716998.00025

Miller A P, Hosanagar K (2019) How Targeted Ads and Dynamic Pricing Can Perpetuate Bias. Harvard Business Review. https://hbr.org/2019/11/how-targeted-ads-and-dynamic-pricing-can-perpetuate-bias. Accessed 24 December 2022

Ministère des Armées (2019) L'intelligence Artificielle Au Service de La Défense. Ministère des Armées, Paris

Molnar C (2019) Interpretable Machine Learning: A Guide for Making Black Box Models Explainable. Lean Publishing

Moyes R (2019) Target Profiles: An Initial Consideration of "Target Profiles" as a Basis for Rule-Making in the Context of Discussions on Autonomy in Weapons Systems. Article 36, Article 36 Discussion Paper

Nakkiran P (2019) A Discussion of "Adversarial Examples Are Not Bugs, They Are Features": Adversarial Examples Are Just Bugs, Too. Distill 4(8). https://doi.org/10.23915/distill.00019.5

Nelson K, Corbin G, Blowers M (2014) Evaluating Data Distribution and Drift Vulnerabilities of Machine Learning Algorithms in Secure and Adversarial Environments. In: Blowers M, Williams J (eds) Proceedings Volume 9119, Machine Intelligence and Bio-inspired Computation: Theory and Applications VIII. P 911904. https://doi.org/10.1117/12.2053045

Office of the Assistant Secretary of Defense for Research and Engineering (2015) Technical Assessment: Autonomy. US Department of Defense, Washington, D.C.

Pan J (1999) Software Reliability. Carnegie Mellon University. https://users.ece.cmu.edu/~koopman/des_s99/sw_reliability. Accessed 12 January 2021

Pan S J, Yang Q (2010) A Survey on Transfer Learning. IEEE Transactions on Knowledge and Data Engineering 22(10):1345–1359. https://doi.org/10.1109/TKDE.2009.191

Perrow C (1984) Normal Accidents: Living With High-Risk Technologies. Basic Books, New York

Pictet J (1952) Commentary, I Geneva Convention. ICRC, Geneva. https://ihl-databases.icrc.org/en/ihl-treaties/gci-1949. Accessed 20 August 2023

Reason J (2000) Human Error: Models and Management. BMJ 320(7237):768–770. https://doi.org/10.1136/bmj.320.7237.768

Ribeiro M T, Singh S, Guestrin C (2016) Why Should I Trust You?: Explaining the Predictions of Any Classifier. In: Proceedings of the 22nd ACM SIGKDD International Conference on Knowledge Discovery and Data Mining

Rogers A P V (2000) Zero-Casuality Warfare. International Review of the Red Cross 837:165–181

Russell S J, Norvig P (2010) Artificial Intelligence: A Modern Approach. 3rd edn. Pearson, New Jersey

Russell S, Dewey D, Tegmark M (2015) Research Priorities for Robust and Beneficial Artificial Intelligence. Future of Life Institute. https://futureoflife.org/ai-open-letter/. Accessed 2 February 2021

Sahu K, Srivastava R K (2020) Needs and Importance of Reliability Prediction: An Industrial Perspective. Information Sciences Letters 9(1):33–37

Scharre P D (2016) Autonomous Weapons and Operational Risk. Center for a New American Security, Washington, D.C

Scharre P D (2018) Army of None: Autonomous Weapons and the Future of War. Ww Norton & Co, New York

Scherer M U (2016) Regulating Artificial Intelligence Systems: Risks, Challenges, Competencies, and Strategies. Harvard Journal of Law & Technology 29(2):353–400

Sforza P M (2016) Manned Spacecraft Design Principles. Butterworth-Heinemann, Elsevier. https://doi.org/10.1016/C2012-0-00344-4

Shendre S (2020) Model Drift in Machine Learning How and When Should Machine Learning Models Be Retrained. Towards Data Science. https://towardsdatascience.com/model-drift-in-machine-learning-models-8f7e7413b563. Accessed 30 October 2021

Theunissen E, Suarez B (2015) Choosing the Level of Autonomy: Options and Constraints. In: Williams A P, Scharre P D (eds) Autonomous Systems: Issues for Defence Policymakers. NATO, The Hague, pp 169–195

Thorne J G (2020) Warriors and War Algorithms: Leveraging Artificial Intelligence to Enable Ethical Targeting. Technical Report, 14-05-2020. https://apps.dtic.mil/sti/citations/AD1104171. Accessed 3 July 2021

UK House of Lords (2018) Select Committee on Artificial Intelligence, Report of Session 2017-19, AI in the UK: Ready, Willing, and Able?. HL Paper 100, 16 April 2018

US Department of Defense (2023) Autonomy in Weapon Systems. US DoD Directive 3000.09

Vogelsang A, Borg M (2019) Requirements Engineering for Machine Learning: Perspectives from Data Scientists. http://arxiv.org/abs/1908.04674

Weller A (2019) Transparency: Motivations and Challenges. http://arxiv.org/abs/1708.01870

Wiener E L, Curry R E (1980) Flight-Deck Automation: Promises and Problems. NASA Technical Memorandum 81206

Yampolskiy R V (2015) Taxonomy of Pathways to Dangerous Artificial Intelligence. In: Workshops at the Thirtieth AAAI Conference on Artificial Intelligence

Yampolskiy R V (2020) AI Will Fail, Like Everything Else, Eventually. Mind Matters. https://mindmatters.ai/2020/07/ai-will-fail-like-everything-else-eventually/. Accessed 31 October 2021

Yampolskiy R V, Spellchecker M S (2016) Artificial Intelligence Safety and Cybersecurity: A Timeline of AI Failures. http://arxiv.org/abs/1610.07997

Chapter 6
Adversarials: Anti-AI Countermeasures

Contents

Abstract A battlefield is an adversarial space, and opponents will prepare countermeasures against autonomous weapon systems (AWS). Unlike countermeasures against older systems, AI have unique vulnerabilities that can be exploited in novel ways, which must be understood by any AWS-user to prevent opponents from compromising the system's reliability, force and civilian safety, and mission success. This chapter features an in-depth exploration of adversarials—anti-AI countermeasures. The chapter first distinguishes adversarials from 'traditional' countermeasures, such as integrity attacks and jamming, by identifying the property unique to modern AI that adversarials exploit: data reliance. From this, three main types of adversarials are analysed. *Adversarial inputs* manipulate data the AWS uses to make decisions (e.g. through visual patches or perturbed ratio waves) in order to induce a particular behaviour, e.g. friendly-firing or shooting civilians. *Poisoning* compromises the AWS in its design phase, by manipulating the training data or model prior to development. Finally, *backdoors* are found to be a combination of the two above, and allow very sophisticated manipulation. From this analysis, it is found that much of the responsibility to collect relevant information and take the necessary precautions to mitigate risk from adversarials lies with the end-user, since it requires the construction of

J. Kwik, *Lawfully Using Autonomous Weapon Technologies*,
https://doi.org/10.1007/978-94-6265-631-4_6

a threat model unique to each adversary. To assist in this endeavour, the chapter concludes by providing a guide to conduct security analysis based on the opponent's goals, incentives, knowledge and power, which should inform commanders in the field about the risk of adversarials and possible counterplay.

Keywords Autonomous weapon system · Artificial intelligence · Countermeasure · Attack · Hacking · Adversarial · Input attack · Poisoning · Backdoor · Model replacement · Hacking · Jamming · Threat model

6.1 Introduction

> Every revolutionary, offensive technology is eventually met with a defensive counter.[1]
>
> Everything has a countermeasure.[2]

In Chap. 5, we have explored the different causes of failure in modern AI. One recalls that data-reliance is inextricably linked with many failure causes, such as training data issues and out-of-distribution, especially if 'shortcuts' are taken when this data is collected and processed. In addition, we encountered situations where input data is perturbed as another major cause of failure. In Sect. 3.4.2, the military environment was described as particularly *adversarial*. In wars, enemies will want to take advantage of vulnerabilities to reduce the effectiveness of our systems, and perhaps even turn them against us. Related to this, in Section 4.3, *adversarial resistance* was mentioned as a description of how robust a system is against attempts by the enemy to exploit these vulnerabilities.

In this chapter, we integrate much of the information discussed thus far to address the complex matter of adversarials against AWS: anti-AI countermeasures. Understanding adversarials forms an integral part of a Deployer's duty under Interaction Awareness.[3] Adversarials are interactive in the truest sense, covering both the *Action* and *Influence* arrows in the MHC Framework.[4] Adversarials arise only from the combination of an agent acting in an environment and the environment 'fighting back'. To properly predict and account for this interaction, Deployer must not only understand the system but also their opponent: they must obtain Awareness of the factors that make their system vulnerable to enemy exploitation, how opponents can do this, what the likely consequences are of such an attack, how this impacts their own legal obligations under IHL, and how to enact measures to minimise this risk. This is the task we will undertake in this chapter.

The concept of countermeasures is evidently as old as warfare itself: "the history of weapons is above all dominated by the contest between projectile and

---

[1] Puckett 2004, p. 715.

[2] Scharre 2018, p. 55.

[3] See Sect. 2.4.1.

[4] See Fig. 3.1.

armour, between mortar fire and fortification".[5] As the technological sophistication of the attacker develops, so too do their enemies' sophistication in defence.[6] While AWS-specific adversarials have received minimal exposure thus far, they are an inevitability: as AWS use develops, counter-AWS techniques will become part of normal warfare.[7] It is therefore important to discuss this matter, and its legal ramifications, early.

Historically, countermeasures have come not only in physical form, but also as information warfare, ruses and deception.[8] AWS-specific countermeasures may take either form. For the former, we can speak of 'old-fashioned' countermeasures applied to new technology.[9] In this chapter, we are more concerned with adversarials in the form of *information* which compromises the AWS's proper functioning.[10]

We first discuss ***adversarials by vulnerability***, i.e., what AI-specific weaknesses opponents exploit when conducting adversarials. To properly analyse a system's vulnerability against adversarials and how to mitigate against them, it is important to discuss the different types of adversarials a Deployer can expect to encounter. While authors frequently note that AWS can be vulnerable to 'hacking', 'spoofing' and 'appropriation',[11] this is not specific enough for our purposes. One effective way to understand and systematise adversarials is by analysing them on the basis of the AI vulnerability they exploit. In Chap. 5, we outlined several factors such as data-reliance and input data perturbations which may cause AI to fail. Rather expectedly, enemies also like to exploit these vulnerabilities to their own advantage. Most of these vulnerabilities are unique to AI and unavoidable. Comiter explains: "AI attacks exist because there are fundamental limitations in the underlying AI algorithms that adversaries can exploit in order to make the system fail … They are just shortcomings of the current state-of-the-art methods".[12]

Our duty, then, is to catalogue the novel ways AWS will be attacked. Kumar et al., in a survey on counter-responses to adversarials, provided an extended list of common adversarial techniques, with poisoning, model stealing, model inversion and backdoors being the adversarials respondents were most concerned about.[13] Comiter broadly divides adversarials into 'input attacks' and 'poisoning'.[14] Having

[5] Sandoz et al. 1987, para 1412.

[6] Scharre 2018, p. 40.

[7] Comiter 2019, p. 50.

[8] Vego 2002, p. 60.

[9] One can think of several ways AWS can be countered through classical means: firing a missile to destroy it before it has a chance to attack, throwing a paint bomb to blind its sensors, the use of camouflage, sabotaging its mechanical components, or simply overwhelming it with superior numbers. Kline 2018.

[10] While the dominant form of transmitting such information is digital, it does not necessarily have to be: in Sect. 6.3, we encounter a type of adversarial that uses physical objects as a vector to impart manipulative information to the target system.

[11] Scharre 2011, p. 92; Heyns 2013, para 98; Scharre 2016, p. 14.

[12] Comiter 2019, p. 12.

[13] Kumar et al. 2020, p. 2.

[14] Comiter 2019, pp. 7–10.

reviewed the literature, these two types of adversarials do seem the most prevalent and consequential. We will thus adopt Comiter's approach and discuss these two adversarials in greater detail.

Subsequent to this discussion, we focus on constructing an ***enemy profile*** as a part of security analysis. This methodology helps Deployers determine the risk to their AWS on the basis of their opponent's characteristics. This information can then be used to inform legal decisions; considerations we return to in Part IV.

6.2 Digital But Non-AI Specific Countermeasures

Before commencing with adversarial inputs and poisoning, which are novel and specific to AI systems, it may also be useful to briefly cover 'conventional' ways to attack an AWS which have been used effectively against other legacy systems. We will not address obvious physical countermeasures such as knocking off a system's camera, but we should briefly comment on integrity attacks and jamming.

Integrity attacks are not specific to AI systems, but they are relatively new in that they have formed a core part of warfare since the introduction of computers and software. *Integrity* is a "measure that demonstrates the authenticity of data as having not been altered from origination or otherwise corrupted by malicious or accidental means".[15] Integrity is also a Measure of Performance,[16] whose goal is to "prevent attackers from reaching system assets".[17]

From these definitions, we can surmise what the goal of an integrity attack would be: to breach an enemy system's defences for various goals, such as injecting viruses, trojans and malware or manipulating the system's digital assets.[18] There are several motives for doing so. The most benign is digital reconnaissance: the adversary is simply doing some 'preparatory prodding' to obtain information on the system, extract data or identify weaknesses.[19] Of course, digital reconnaissance can be a precursor to more dangerous attacks that can lead to remote access, overriding control, or entire models being replaced by the adversary.[20] In literature, these types of actions are often referred to broadly as 'cyber interference', 'cyberattacks' or 'hacking'.[21]

It should also be noted that integrity attacks may precede other attacks. Some adversarials require a breach of integrity first before they can be effectuated. For instance, an adversary may want to effect a model replacement,[22] but for this, they

---

[15] Nelson et al. 2014, p. 4.

[16] See Sect. 4.1.

[17] Barreno et al. 2010, p. 125.

[18] Yampolskiy 2015; Wilson 2020, p. 156.

[19] Barreno et al. 2010, p. 145.

[20] Comiter 2019, p. 32; Schmitt and Thurnher 2013, p. 242.

[21] Pytlak 2018, p. 4; Boothby 2018, p. 153; ICRC 2019, p. 11.

[22] See Sect. 6.4.

first need to access the target system using a cyberattack.[23] One important counter against (certain) adversarials, therefore, is for Deployers to increase security against integrity attacks in general.[24] Interestingly, this is not as evident as it should be: in particular, organisations that purchase AI software frequently do not realise that models are highly sensitive assets and thus fail to assign high levels of protection to them.[25] This leaves them vulnerable to integrity attacks, opening a breadth of new options for an adversary to compromise the system.

Another adversarial that is not AI-exclusive, but which has been mentioned as a strategy that is likely to be used against AWS, is jamming.[26] ***Jamming*** refers to disrupting the comms link between an Operator and a deployed system, with the goal of e.g. interfering with target coordinates, providing faulty GPS information, and disrupting communications.[27] This can be done through simple denial (through electromagnetic pulses or denial-of-service) or active spoofing.[28] Note that this type of adversarial is only effective against an AWS which has Linked Control active;[29] an effective counter-response would therefore be to deliberately cut the comms link.

Finally, Deployers should be cognisant that *any* connection, even if the system is dormant, is a potential vulnerability. Adversarials can be delivered more easily if the system is linked with the internet, internal networks or other systems.[30]

6.3 Adversarial Input

In 2018, Athalye et al. managed to trick an image classifier to almost consistently predict that it was seeing a rifle when it was in actuality shown a 3D-printed turtle from various angles.[31] It is a classic experiment which continues to be cited today to illustrate the concept of adversarial inputs,[32] perhaps due to the disturbing implications it evokes. One immediately can envisage an AWS being fooled by such a 'turtle' and killing civilians because it had misclassified a handbag for a rifle. It is indicative of how unintuitive and imperceptible AI-specific adversarials can be.

---

23 Comiter 2019, p. 32.

24 Some other adversarials, such as adversarial inputs, are not preceded by an integrity attack. Increasing a system's security will thus not help against this type of adversarial.

25 Comiter 2019, p. 26.

26 UNIDIR 2016, p. 11.

27 Wilson 2020, p. 137.

28 Ibid., pp. 157–60.

29 See Sect. 8.7.1

30 Ibid., pp. 158-61.

31 Athalye et al. 2018.

32 Knight 2019.

6.3.1 Concept

Adversarial inputs are manipulations to a target system's inputs, constructed to produce faulty behaviour which is beneficial to the adversary. While a majority of adversarial inputs in literature are visual, any input data (e.g. sound, digitalised information) can technically be doctored to induce a failure.[33] They are alternatively called input attacks ("patterns of changes to a target that will fool the AI system into making a mistake"),[34] spoofing attacks ("[d]eliberately feeding a machine false data to manipulate its behavior"),[35] OOD inputs ("a specific context for encountering OOD inputs (an intentional attack) and a confined set of techniques for creating them") or evasion attacks.[36]

Adversarial inputs are frequently warned about in literature on both civil AI applications and AWS. They have been used effectively in relatively benign circumstances, such as to evade email filters,[37] but have the potential to do much more. Observers warn that adversarial inputs can be used to induce accidents in autonomous cars by making them speed up when seeing a STOP sign,[38] to disorient and render ineffective drone swarms,[39] and in large-scale terrorist attacks against modern smart cities.[40] In weapons systems, there have been concerns that they can be used to render enemy soldiers or matériel 'invisible' to AWS (or simply render these systems less effective in general),[41] and more concerningly, that they can result in friendly or even civilian casualties.[42]

One particularly concerning aspect is that the failures caused by such inputs frequently make no logical sense for human observers.[43] The perturbations to the input data need not be significant, or even noticeable: to humans, there is nothing wrong with Althalye et al.'s turtle.[44] The creation of adversarial inputs is a rapidly expanding scientific field: the inputs become increasingly complex and less noticeable.[45] Experiments have shown successful adversarial inputs in the form of simple stickers pasted on objects,[46] patterns printed on T-shirts,[47] imperceptible patterns

---

33 Gilpin et al. 2018, p. 1.

34 Comiter 2019, p. 8.

35 Scharre 2018, p. 182.

36 Biggio et al. 2013; Goldblum et al. 2020, p. 13.

37 Biggio et al. 2013, p. 388.

38 Goodfellow et al. 2017.

39 Pauwels and Deton 2020, p. 118.

40 Comiter 2019, p. 3.

41 Hofman 2020; Ministère des Armées 2019, p. 7; Krupiy 2015, p. 33.

42 Defense Science Board 2016, p. 14.

43 Scharre 2016, p. 17; Fawzi et al. 2018, p. 1.

44 See the image at Athalye et al. 2018, p. 1.

45 Draper 2020.

46 Eykholt et al. 2018.

47 Xu et al. 2019.

shown on television screens,[48] and inserted phrases and paraphrased questions.[49] If the input data is digital, adversarial inputs can be even more subtle. Szegedy et al. showed how image classifiers could be made to malfunction with an average distortion of merely 0.006508,[50] and work is being done on algorithms that search for the smallest RGB corruptions which can cause an incorrect output.[51] In some cases, 'pixel attacks' are possible, where the only manipulation consists of a single or a few pixels.[52]

Many theories have been posited to explain why adversarial inputs are possible, and so effective, at inducing errors in AI. No definitive answer has yet been reached,[53] and it is beyond the scope of this book to address each hypothesis in detail. Nonetheless, it is relatively clear that the efficacy of adversarial inputs has close ties with the infinite variance problem of ML.[54] Ultimately, adversarial inputs can be viewed as a subset of non-naturally occurring (edge) inputs which are found and used by the adversary[55]: they exploit the fact that models never have a 100% accuracy rate.[56] As with (natural) OOD problems mentioned in Section 5.6, adversarial inputs frequently also make the AI *more* confident of its incorrect decision, sometimes reaching 99% confidence.[57] Under normal operation, these specific inputs may never be encountered, making the system's standard accuracy and robustness high. This is the reason why natural robustness does not equal resistance to adversarial inputs: even a model that naturally generalises very well to real-world inputs can still be fooled badly by simple transformations.[58] This was the motivation for distinguishing natural robustness from adversarial resistance in Sect. 4.3 as separate Measures of Performance.

6.3.2 Counters

Adversarial inputs are quite problematic from Deployer's point of view: they are both difficult to detect and difficult to prevent. They attack inherent weaknesses of modern AI, and it can never be completely excluded that an adversary finds an adversarial input to exploit.[59] There are a few silver linings for Deployer in this

48 Knight 2019.

49 See Hendrycks et al. 2020, p. 5.

50 Szegedy et al. 2014, p. 6.

51 Hendrycks and Dietterich 2019, p. 2.

52 Leslie 2019, p. 32.

53 See e.g. for an overview of hypotheses: Ilyas et al. 2019; Gilmer et al. 2018a.

54 See Sect. 3.4.2

55 Scharre 2018, p. 184.

56 Gilmer et al. 2018a, p. 2.

57 Scharre 2018, p. 181; Amodei et al. 2016, p. 16.

58 Szegedy et al. 2014, p. 10.

59 Hayward and Maas 2021, p. 5.

position, however. First, on the technical side, much work is being done to improve resistance against adversarial inputs.[60] New approaches are being found to identify which perturbations constitute threats and to train models to be more robust against them in general.[61] Deployers would not necessarily have to concern themselves as much with the development and implementation of these measures, and this should be made the responsibility of designers and reviewers. Deployers only need to be aware of the measures that have been taken (and which have not) when determining whether a particular weapon is viable for the operation in question.

Two things need to be established in relation to this. First, resistance against adversarial inputs can never be 100%.[62] This is a natural corollary of the infinite variance problem[63]: obtaining 100% resistance would require "models to produce good outputs *for every possible input*",[64] which is impossible. Rather, there is likely an 'optimal resistance level' that designers can strive for, which would represent the highest degree of resistance that is technically possible depending on the specific model. The fact that resistance cannot be 100% also agrees well with the conclusion drawn in Sect. 4.4, where it was argued that no weapon can be completely reliable; no legal standard can thus ever be established where this would be required from Deployers.[65]

Second, some have posited the existence of an ***opportunity cost*** between natural robustness and adversarial resistance.[66] While in the standard perspective natural robustness and resistance are usually treated as independent measures of performance that can be optimised separately,[67] some authors have demonstrated that too much training to improve resistance can come at the cost of generalisation, i.e., natural robustness.[68] This should therefore be considered carefully during development: how much standard accuracy and natural robustness should be sacrificed to improve resistance against adversaries? It should always be remembered that at some point, accuracy and natural robustness may fall so low as to make the system's ability to perform certain actions (e.g. distinguishing between legitimate and illegitimate targets, limiting collateral damage) drop below what is acceptable under IHL. In that case, standard metrics should be prioritised above resistance.[69]

---

[60] Fawzi et al. 2018, p. 1.

[61] Tsipras et al. 2019, p. 1.

[62] Gilmer et al. 2018a, p. 2.

[63] See Sect. 3.4.2.

[64] Goodfellow et al. 2017 (emphasis in original).

[65] See also Sect. 9.3.1.

[66] These were the two types of robustness discussed in Sect. 4.3, against natural perturbations and deliberate perturbations, respectively.

[67] Ilyas et al. 2019, p. 1.

[68] Tsipras et al. 2019; Gilmer and Hendrycks 2019.

[69] See also Sect. 6.5.

As Deployer's second silver lining, there is still much they can do to combat adversarial inputs in the form of security analysis. This does not involve manipulating the system's parameters—something Deployer is not likely able to do at the operational stage—but rather an assessment of the *adversary*, a task entirely in the domain of a military commander.

6.3.3 Prerequisites: What Do Opponents Need?

The first step to security analysis is to understand what one's opponents need in order to effectuate an adversarial. With regard to adversarial inputs, one major advantage of the adversary is that it requires no access to the target system at all. The adversary needs access neither the actual system nor its training data; it only needs to find a way to ***feed an input to the target system***.[70] Even the most highly-secured system that no hacker can possibly breach[71] can theoretically still be victimised by an adversarial input in the form of a sound pattern played from a speaker or a visual pattern pasted on a nondescript wall. The more means the adversary has to feed an input to the system, therefore, the larger the risk.

This has some practical implications for Deployers: they should consider the risk of adversarial inputs as *greater in operational situations where Defenders have (partial) control over the environment*. Control over the environment gives adversaries exponentially more access to 'vectors': objects (physical or digital) through which an adversarial pattern can be sent to the system.[72] This means that Deployers should be more wary of adversarial inputs when sending AWS to rebel-controlled cities than when defending a friendly area against attack.

Nevertheless, not any random soundbite or sticker will make an AWS malfunction. This is one limitation of adversarial inputs from the adversary's perspective: random guessing is not feasible. The adversarial input must be carefully constructed around the target system, which requires ***knowledge of the target model***. There are two ways an adversary can find a suitable adversarial input.

An advantageous situation for the adversary is if they can enact a ***white box attack***, where they have knowledge of the target system's internals.[73] This makes crafting an adversarial input relatively easy (e.g. using generative adversarial networks).[74] Deployer should carefully consider the likelihood that an enemy could have obtained

---

70 Comiter 2019, p. 17.

71 In the sense that it is (theoretically) immune to integrity attacks and hacking; see Sect. 6.2.

72 Ibid., p. 20.

73 A white box attack can be executed when "an attacker has full knowledge of the model internals and training data". Gilmer et al. 2018b, p. 4. As Comiter explains, an "input attack is relatively easy to craft if the attacker has access to the AI model being attacked. Armed with this, the attacker can automatically craft attacks using simple textbook optimization methods". Comiter 2019, p. 25.

74 Hayward and Maas 2021, p. 5.

such information. Integrity attacks[75] can be likely precursors to white box attacks, but information on the target model can be gained in other ways. If the AWS was *purchased from a third party*, for instance, the adversary need only purchase the same weapon in order to access the system's internals. Deployers should thus carefully consider the possibility that this has occurred. Additionally, Deployers should also be very careful during Assessment[76] to account for the *fate of any lost system*. Was it destroyed or captured? If captured, this could threaten other identical[77] systems in the fleet because their internals are now 'knowable' to the adversary. The same conclusion applies in cases where identical systems were looted by the opponent.[78] In any of these situations, Deployer should analyse the possibility of the opponent crafting a white box attack and, if this risk is deemed significant, Deployer could request identical systems to be (temporarily) withdrawn.

Here, understandability[79] can be turned against its owner, by instead helping the *opponent* construct adversarial inputs more easily.[80] Because understandability is indispensable for so many military and legal considerations,[81] it is not justifiable to sacrifice understandability just to deny opponents additional information in an adversarial context. Nevertheless, Deployers should take this factor into consideration when analysing how likely it is that opponents have developed adversarial inputs for specific systems (or how rapidly they can do so).

If the adversary cannot access the target system's internals, they must employ a ***black box attack***.[82] In this situation they are only privy to a system's input and output data.[83] In low-consequence situations such as spam filters, adversaries have more freedom to 'probe' the system for responses, but for AWS, this is more difficult. Weapons systems will likely be better secured, making digital probes difficult, and physical probes (e.g. approaching an AWS and testing its responses to different inputs) will be very dangerous. We can thus state that for AWS, the *number of queries possible*,[84] or the number of attempts an adversary is allowed for recording input-output pairs, is relatively low. Unfortunately, strands of *model-agnostic adversarials* are being developed to circumvent this limitation. These are techniques which, as the name implies, can be effective against many different models, even if the adversary

---

[75] See Sect. 6.2.

[76] See Sect. 2.4.6.

[77] Assuming state duplication as discussed in Sect. 5.3 applies.

[78] See Pamp et al. 2018, p. 433.

[79] See Sect. 4.5

[80] Barredo Arrieta et al. 2020, p. 101.

[81] As argued in Sect. 4.5.2. See also Kwik and Van Engers 2021; Kwik and van Engers 2023.

[82] A black box situation is one where to the adversary, "system details are unknown … [but] the attacker may interrogate it by asking it to label inputs". Gilmer et al. 2018b, p. 4.

[83] Hutson 2018.

[84] Gilmer et al. 2018b, p. 4.

has limited information about them.[85] There is no true response to this type of adversarial from Deployer's perspective, and Deployer will have to rely on developers to increase systems' general resistance to reduce this type of risk.

A pseudo-white box attack can take place when adversaries cannot access the target's internals, but have *access to the target's training data.* This could have been obtained through an integrity attack on Deployer's training set or perhaps simply from open-source databases (if the producer was careless enough to use these). With this training data, the adversary can create their own approximation of the target model and use it as a basis for crafting adversarial inputs.[86] While not as effective as a true white box attack, it is a potential threat to consider. Fortunately, the response to this issue should be evident and standard practice for all militaries: training sets should be secured just as carefully as the models themselves, and data collection shortcuts avoided if possible.[87]

6.4 Poisoning

6.4.1 Concept

Where adversarial inputs flummox a system in operation, poisoning compromises the system while in development. As a colloquial illustration of the concept, say a ground team is tasked with securing an enemy-held hotel. They have just forced the door and are entering the red-carpeted foyer. An adversarial input would be analogous to enemies hiding in the blind corners behind the door, relying on lighting and camouflage to avoid the soldiers from spotting them. Poisoning would be more insidious: the team enters the room, and the soldiers categorically fail to scan any of the corners before brazenly moving further in. They are then gunned down by the enemy. What happened? The soldiers had explicitly learnt during training to always rush immediately into the centre of red carpeted rooms. The enemy had covertly added that small detail into the soldiers' training programme without anyone's knowledge.

Of course, real soldiers would probably have asked their instructors why this oddly specific detail was added to the training material, but AI do not question in this way. Recall that for ML, the performance of the end product is determined entirely by the quality and quantity of the data used to train it.[88] This has evident implications for opponents: if they can compromise the data used for training AWS without the developers' knowledge, they can essentially co-author its final behaviour.[89] This is

[85] Draper 2020; Hayward and Maas 2021, p. 8.

[86] Comiter 2019, p. 26.

[87] Ibid. See Sect. 5.4.

[88] Poisoning is thus directly related to data-reliance. See Sect. 5.4.

[89] Shen et al. 2016, p. 510.

how poisoning functions: adversaries manipulate the training data covertly and in such a way so as to produce faulty behaviour from the system (once deployed) which is beneficial to them.[90]

Poisoning has been identified as a major threat to both civil and military AI applications. In Kumar et al.'s study, poisoning was ranked first by companies as the most concerning type of adversarial.[91] Reports to defence ministries also frequently warn of the risk of nefarious parties compromising data used for military systems.[92] Additionally, poisoning has had quite a cultural impact. Most infamously, the Microsoft chatbot Tay started using numerous racist slurs after only one day of users feeding it common right-wing phrases.[93]

With regard to the technical details of poisoning adversarials, a detailed analysis goes beyond the scope of this book,[94] but it can be useful to briefly discuss a specific technique called a ***backdoor***. A backdoor is a rather sophisticated adversarial that can be viewed as a multi-step attack requiring both poisoning and the delivery of an adversarial input. The poisoning process functions as a preparatory step to install a specific vulnerability, while the input is the 'trigger'.[95] The example of the team which suddenly disregarded all their training and stormed into the centre of a hostile hotel lobby was an analogy of this specific adversarial: because their irrational behaviour only manifested itself in red-carpeted rooms, their instructors never noticed that the soldiers' training was compromised until that fateful incident. This is one major strength of backdoors: executed well, they are impossible to detect by the user and allow the adversary to activate the desired behaviour at will.[96]

A backdoor is potentially very powerful as it allows the adversary full control over both the timing and exact nature of the malfunction. It also allows the adversary to select an input trigger that is most convenient to them.[97] With adversarial inputs, the adversary has to adapt to the target system: if the only effective pattern is a conspicuous banner, they have no choice than to use that pattern, but it will be quite noticeable by Deployers if the enemy suddenly hangs large, strange banners from bridges and apartment buildings. With backdoors, the model adapts to the adversary[98]: even tiny patterns (in the case of digital inputs: of only pixels) can be 'programmed in' as the trigger.[99] This makes it not only more difficult for Deployer to detect, but also more difficult to determine what the trigger was after the fact.

---

[90] See Barreno et al. 2010, p. 122; Wilson 2020, p. 148; Nelson et al. 2014, p. 2.

[91] Kumar et al. 2020, p. 2.

[92] Flournoy et al. 2020, p. 9; Ministère des Armées 2019, p. 7.

[93] Wakefield 2016.

[94] Goldblum et al. have constructed an effective taxonomy of different methods that can be used, such as label manipulation, *p*-tampering and generative models, and have included full references to studies which demonstrate how each is performed. See Goldblum et al. 2020.

[95] Ibid., p 2.

[96] Leslie 2019, p. 33.

[97] Gu et al. 2017, p. 2.

[98] Goldblum et al. 2020, p. 11.

[99] Gu et al. 2017, p. 6.

Because it requires both a successful poisoning process and the delivery of the trigger input, it also inherits the limitations of both. This also means that countermeasures against either adversarial are viable. Even if a model is poisoned with a backdoor, it will not trigger if the adversaries are denied the opportunity to deliver an adversarial input. In addition, adversaries have the difficult task to ensure that the backdoor does not reduce the model's standard performance.[100] If another (non-poisoned) model performs better than the poisoned model, developers will simply discard the backdoored model without even being cognisant of the fact that it had been compromised.

6.4.2 Threat Analysis

Poisoning is quite distinct from adversarial inputs in that it *fundamentally* compromises the base model.[101] In a way, the adversarial is thus permanently in force as long as the poisoned model remains in-use. This changes the way Deployers can respond to this adversarial, as they cannot prevent or avoid an opponent's action (as they can an adversarial input) that has already concluded in the past. In practice, counter-responses to poisoning rely strongly on designers and reviewers. We will thus depart briefly from Deployer as the main subject of our thesis, and instead address antecedent actors involved in production and policymaking.

By definition, poisoning requires some access to the system prior to deployment. The most obvious way to do this would be through an integrity attack.[102] Indeed, if security is particularly poor, adversaries can simply execute a ***model replacement***, where they replace a (properly) trained model with a compromised one.[103] In practice, one would hope that military systems are better protected, but there are indirect ways poisoning can be effectuated.

More subtle poisoning techniques generally rely on the use of *data shortcuts* by the developer.[104] High quantities data are required for training a well-functioning model. The data not only has to be of sufficient quality, but also needs to be properly labelled and IOE-accurate to prevent out-of-distribution after deployment.[105] Such data is hard to come by,[106] especially for military applications.[107] What is a developer to do in such a situation?

---

[100] Goldblum et al. 2020, p. 11.

[101] Comiter 2019, p. 28.

[102] See Sect. 6.2.

[103] Comiter 2019, p. 32.

[104] These were previously discussed in Sect. 5.4, and AWS developers were advised to steer clear of using such shortcuts.

[105] See Sects. 3.5 and 5.6.

[106] Vogelsang and Borg 2019, p. 5.

[107] Defense Innovation Board 2019, p. 66.

There is one way to prevent poisoning with a high level of certainty: the data should be *collected, processed and used to train models entirely in-house with stringent quality control mechanisms.* Unfortunately, this is extremely—and in the views of some, prohibitively—expensive,[108] particularly for smaller militaries or companies. To circumvent this problem, developers use various data shortcuts to facilitate data collection, labelling, training, etc.[109] However, by doing this, developers open themselves up to external influences.

The following are common data shortcuts[110] and how they can be exploited by adversaries to poison parts of the development process, leading to a compromised end product:

- *Data collection shortcuts.* To satisfy the immense need for data, it is frequently collected from convenient, but unreliable and unsafe, sources.[111] Using a *dragnet*, everything that can be collected is collected without much vigilance or quality assurance.[112] Producers sometimes also make use of large open-source datasets available on the internet. The data in these sets can come from any source, including adversaries who planted poisoned data in the hope that it is unwittingly 'harvested' by their opponent.[113]
- *Labelling shortcuts.* Once data is collected, it must be labelled to enable supervised learning, but if data reaches into the millions, this is extremely time-consuming and expensive. The process is therefore frequently outsourced, often to the private sector or even individual crowd workers.[114] It is not just civil AI applications that make use of this: the Pentagon has reportedly also made use of data obtained from gig economy workers for their drones.[115] Manipulating labels is a very common way to enact poisoning adversarials,[116] and militaries need to be conscientious of this fact.
- *Training shortcuts.* Training models on large datasets—which is desirable to increase performance—takes some time and can be very computationally intensive.[117] As such, developers rarely build their models from zero: one survey found that only 2 out of 28 respondents did so.[118] Most companies prefer to use available toolkits (e.g. Keras, PyTorch) to train their model or use 'ML as a service', where the actual training process is outsourced to the cloud.[119] Other options are

[108] Holland Michel 2021, p. 27.

[109] Comiter 2019, p. 48.

[110] For why these are often relied on by developers, see Sect. 5.4.

[111] Leslie 2019, p. 33.

[112] Comiter 2019, p. 29.

[113] Wilson 2020, p. 148. Exacerbating the situation, a survey revealed that many organisations naively assume that such data has already been validated and secured.

[114] Gershgorn 2021.

[115] Fang 2019.

[116] Nakkiran 2019.

[117] Shen et al. 2016, p. 505.

[118] Kumar et al. 2020, p. 2.

[119] Gu et al. 2017, p. 1.

collaborative learning, where the computational load is distributed to collaborators which individually complete a part of the training process,[120] or transfer learning, where an existing model is repurposed for a new task (thus saving on part of the computing process).[121]

Any of these shortcuts use potentially non-sterile components through which adversaries can intervene and effectuate a poisoning adversarial. These shortcuts "invite the outside world in"—a rather dangerous venture.[122] As mentioned above, the best way to avoid poisoning is to create datasets and train models entirely in-house, but if this is not feasible, militaries and contractors must be very cautious with how they collect and process data.

There is another way to 'invite the outside world in', even after deployment: *online learning*.[123] While online learning has its advantages, it introduces important vulnerabilities, and vulnerability to poisoning is one of them. If online learning is active, any input received during operation also functions as additional 'training' data, making simply interacting with the system a viable way to inject poisoned data.[124] There are many examples of this from civil applications, such as the Microsoft Tay case mentioned above, as well as many a spam filter that failed due to poisoned emails which mis-trained the models over time.[125]

Finally, it must be emphasised that poisoning is possible every time a system is being 'developed'—and this includes any updates and periodic re-training that may be scheduled.[126] It is thus incorrect to assume that systems are permanently safe from poisoning once they leave the development floor.

While Deployer cannot influence these factors much, it is nevertheless useful for them to understand what types of models are more susceptible to poisoning. They must continue to exercise caution: the possibility cannot be excluded that less-than-prudent measures were taken during development, and that Deployer was issued a poisoned model. At the very least, being aware of these facts allows Deployer to intervene more quickly if suspicions arise that an AWS in their possession was poisoned.

[120] See Shen et al. 2016, p. 517.

[121] Pan and Yang 2010.

[122] Goldblum et al. 2020, p. 1.

[123] To recall, this allows the model to continue developing its performance and associations in the field. See Sect. 5.6.

[124] Nelson et al. 2014, p. 4.

[125] Barreno et al. 2010, p. 127.

[126] Huang et al. 2011, p. 43.

6.5 Security Analysis, Threat Models and Counters

Thus far, we have primarily spoken of *how* opponents can effectuate adversarials and what weaknesses these exploit, in a predominantly technical sense. From Deployer's perspective, this is useful to understand, particularly for determining how to deny adversaries the opportunities they need to execute such adversarials. However, for Deployers, it is even more important to ask *why and what*. Why would these enemies want to execute an adversarial? What is their motive and goal? What result can be expected if they succeed? Would this risk be acceptable? These types of questions have formed the backbone of Part III. We will now apply it to adversarials through a process called security analysis.

Security analysis is a risk evaluation process applied specifically for adversarial threats. In order to accurately respond to adversarials, "it is critical to make a reasonable model of the attacker's information".[127] Most methods in literature focus on creating a threat model of the adversary. This is particularly important in the case of AI adversarials, as the opponent's specific activities are difficult (if not impossible) to discern. It is extremely hard, for instance, to construct an accurate theoretical model of how opponents generate an adversarial input: we cannot know what they are exactly doing, so it is difficult to prevent or predict specific adversarials.[128] An effective response, therefore, "requires a clear concept of an adversary",[129] lest one responds to illusory threats which are unrealistic or unlikely. This is particularly important if a resistance/natural robustness trade-off applies[130]: we definitely do not want to reduce standard performance to make the system more secure against a high-tech adversarial input, if we are fighting a low-sophistication guerrilla force.

Below, we discuss different aspects of security analysis which helps Deployer determine risk factors related to adversarials, starting with the construction of a threat model. Similar models have been used in military contexts, such as by the US Joint Chiefs of Staff.[131] A ***threat model*** is a "profile of attackers, describing motivation and capabilities".[132] From this definition, we can identify two main elements of a threat model: the opponent's *goal/incentives* and their *capability* to carry out the attack.[133] How 'capable' an adversary is, in turn, is a function of their *knowledge* and *power*.[134] We discuss these factors in turn. Finally, in Sect. 6.5.4 we also list supplementary assumptions of the adversary that may be useful for Deployer's analysis.

We do not discuss technical counter-responses to specific adversarials, as these are beyond the scope of this book, but much work is being done to make systems

[127] Ibid., p. 49.

[128] Goodfellow et al. 2017.

[129] Gilmer et al. 2018b, p. 3.

[130] This trade-off was mentioned in Sect. 6.3.2.

[131] See e.g. Chairman of the Joint Chiefs of Staff 2016, p. B-3 (under 'Accessibility' and 'Recognition').

[132] Barreno et al. 2010, p. 124.

[133] Gilmer et al. 2018b, p. 3; Huang et al. 2011, p. 49.

[134] Barreno et al. 2010, p. 125; Biggio et al. 2013, p. 389.

more resistant against adversarial inputs[135] and to detect and prevent poisoning.[136] In the military domain, some institutions such as DARPA have launched projects (e.g. GARD/Guaranteeing AI Robustness Against Deception) to study the appropriate counter-responses to various adversarials.[137]

6.5.1 Opponent's Goals and Incentives

Adversaries can use adversarials for many different goals, such as avoiding being targeted or detected, neutralising/capturing the system, searching for weaknesses, etc.[138] The DoD Defense Science Board found that generally, three motives can be distinguished: obtaining *information*, reducing *performance* (attacking the system's ability to "perform as designed and directed"), and *denial* (rendering the system unavailable to and denying any benefits it could have provided Deployer).[139] Evidently, the two latter motives are more immediately threatening,[140] although the first is also dangerous in terms of losing a comparative advantage in intelligence.[141]

Understanding the opponent's overall goal can help predict their strategy.[142] If their goal is to not be detected, they will focus on adversarials that induce false negatives, similar to the T-shirts of Xu et al. which make their wearers 'invisible' to public face-detection cameras.[143] If their aim is denial, a particularly nefarious group could instead poison a model to make it deliberately gun down as many civilians as possible (maximising false positives). Deployer will then be forced retire all identical systems from the front lines, giving the adversary an advantage. The motivation of the enemy, therefore, significantly alters Deployer's risk evaluation.

It can also be asked whether the adversary needs to produce a *specific* error, or whether *any* random error suffices.[144] This analysis is not only important for Deployer, but also for the adversary (at least assuming they are not deliberately trying to abuse IHL, like the nasty group described above). Random errors reduce the system's effectiveness at the population level[145]: they simply compromise the

---

[135] See e.g. Engstrom et al. 2019; Gilmer et al. 2018a; Gilpin et al. 2018; Tsipras et al. 2019.

[136] See e.g. Kumar et al. 2020; Goldblum et al. 2020; Shen et al. 2016.

[137] DARPA 2019.

[138] Huang et al. 2011, p. 43.

[139] Defense Science Board 2016, p. 27.

[140] Ibid., p. 28.

[141] Be it in terms of general military operations or specifically because it facilitates the crafting of adversarials such as white box attacks. See Bostrom 2011. See Sect. 6.3.3

[142] Barreno et al. 2010, pp. 125–26.

[143] Xu et al. 2019.

[144] Gilmer et al. 2018b, p. 3. See also Kwik 2024.

[145] Goldblum et al. 2020, p. 3.

system's performance overall.[146] This can still be an effective adversarial if performance drops to such a low level that Deployer can no longer justify its employment (because it is militarily ineffective or no longer allows IHL-compliant use).[147] This would de facto result in a form of denial, but ironically *relies* on Deployer knowing that their system was compromised: "If users detect the failure, they may lose confidence in the system and abandon it. If users do not detect the failure, then the risks can be even greater."[148] If Deployer does not realise that the adversarial has been effectuated, they will continue to use the system until harm is done, and this harm may involve civilians.[149]

In contrast, targeted errors are much more 'discriminate' in the sense that they are designed to produce a specific output.[150] In the case of backdoors,[151] these are maximally discriminate as they produce a specific output *only* in the presence of the trigger input. If this trigger input is crafted to be sufficiently unique (i.e., non-naturally occurring), the adversary has complete control over how and when the error manifests. For adversaries, sufficiently unique backdoors can thus be said to be the most discriminate adversarials. Random error poisoning is the least so, as they have no control over either the errors that occur nor the timing.

6.5.2 Knowledge

We have seen above that knowledge is a key factor determining how effectively adversarials can be effectuated.[152] Full knowledge allows for wanton white box attacks, while an adversary is much more limited if it can only prod for inputs and outputs.[153] More generally, Bostrom developed a framework of information hazards, outlining how enemy access to information amplifies various vulnerabilities.[154] For this reason, in adversarial literature, it is deemed crucial to always clarify the level of knowledge the opponent is *assumed* to have.[155] Deployers should adopt the same process and deduce, based on the circumstances and the opponent's characteristics, how much knowledge it is likely to possess.

---

146 Shen et al. 2016, p. 510.

147 Section 1.1.

148 Barreno et al. 2010, p. 122.

149 Adversaries are also bound to the law. Denial is not prohibited under IHL, but doing so by knowingly placing civilians at risk is. ICJ, *Legality of the Threat or Use of Nuclear Weapons*, Advisory Opinion, 8 July 1996, ICJ Rep 226, para 78.

150 Shen et al. 2016, p. 510.

151 See Sect. 6.4.1.

152 Section 6.3.3.

153 Gilmer et al. 2018b, p. 4.

154 Bostrom 2011.

155 See e.g. Barreno et al. 2010, p. 125; Nelson et al. 2014, p. 5.

Commentators note that it is particularly important to assess whether, and to what extent, the adversary has access to the following information:[156]

- The training dataset or part of it;
- The feature space (specific function) of the trained model;
- The type of the algorithm used and the form of its decision function;
- The finished model itself; or
- Input-output pairings.

If an adversary has knowledge of all of these factors, it can be assumed to have perfect knowledge; otherwise, it has limited knowledge.[157]

Some reasonable assumptions can be adopted with regard to the adversary's knowledge. First, *perfect knowledge* is relatively unlikely: "[i]n a true adversarial environment, the amount of information available to an adversary is often limited".[158] While it is the 'safest' assumption to take, it is not practically recommended, as it would unduly limit the use of effective systems which could mitigate risk to the civilian population.[159] Assumptions must be realistic: an overly pessimistic projection of an omnipotent adversary will make us doubt every system in our arsenal.[160]

In this regard, Huang et al. provide some general guidelines: it is generally wise to assume enemy knowledge of the algorithm (especially if common or open source), but it is rarer for opponents to have access to the feature space or dataset.[161] These baseline assumptions should naturally be refined based on actual security practices in the military organisation: how well does it guard its sensitive information? Is it sensitive of these dangers, and have appropriate policy measures been taken to secure models and data? At the other extreme, *perfect secrecy* should never be assumed. Deployers should always presume that some information is available or has been leaked to the opponent, even in the case of extreme secrecy and security measures. This is commonly known as Kerckhoff's Principle: the success of a system may never rely on unrealistic expectations of secrecy.[162] Finally, *iteration* is commonly modelled as beneficial for the adversary. For each repeated confrontation with the same opponent, enemy knowledge should be presumed to have increased every time.[163]

[156] Barreno et al. 2010, p. 125; Huang et al. 2011, pp. 49–50; Biggio et al. 2013, p. 389.

[157] Biggio et al. 2013, p. 389.

[158] Nelson et al. 2014, p. 5.

[159] See Sect. 9.6.

[160] Huang et al. 2011, p. 49.

[161] Ibid., pp. 49–50.

[162] Kerckhoffs 1883, p. 12; See Guillot 2013.

[163] Gilmer et al. 2018b, p. 8.

6.5.3 Power

In terms of threat analysis, this step involves gaining "an explicit and realistic consideration of the options available to the attacker".[164] Power reflects an adversary's action space: to what extent does it control factors that are necessary for executing adversarials? In this regard, Barreno et al. distinguish adversaries with exploratory versus causative power. *Exploratory enemies* observe and prod, hoping to find vulnerabilities for future adversarials, while *causative enemies* have the direct ability to compromise the target system.[165]

In the context of analysing risk of poisoning, Huang et al. provide different corruption paradigms that can be used to model the adversary's power, such as insertion (it can insert n amount of data) and alteration (it can alter existing data, limited to n).[166] Naturally, adversaries who can both insert and alter data are more powerful, and the larger the proportions of data (n) they can corrupt, the more freedom they have in crafting the adversarial, making risk higher.

The extent to which adversaries can be *covert* also reflects their power. We have touched upon this previously in the example of an adversary who could only deliver adversarial inputs through large, conspicuous banners.[167] This is a rather weak adversary, as their attempts are easily detected and foiled by simple observers. A more powerful adversary would have found a method to induce the same adversarial error through a more difficult-to-detect means, such as a nondescript advertisement pasted on a building. Gilmer et al. proposed a five-step spectrum of the adversary's action space in this context (Table 6.1).[168]

The ability to go higher in the covertness ladder is beneficial for the adversary. This is because flexibility gives power: if they cannot succeed using an indistinguishable manipulation, they can still try less-constrained adversarials.[169] The higher an adversary *can* go, the more powerful they are. Note however that who sets how high an adversary *must* go, is none other than Deployer. This is illustrated in the provided examples, which are deliberately constructed around the same scenario of a facial recognition-equipped checkpoint. We see that as we go further down the ladder, the adversarial attempts become increasingly brazen and crude. For the adversary, the actual technique used does not matter as long as it produces the desired result: their only interest is to pass the checkpoint. Restrictions set by the Deployer, however, place a floor on how low they can go.

In this example, Deployer uses human involvement as a risk treatment tool by limiting the adversary's action space. By posting an operator to remotely supervise the checkpoint, adversarial face-paint becomes non-feasible: even through a blurry monitor, the operator will notice something so conspicuous and intervene, making

---

[164] Ibid., p. 4.

[165] Barreno et al. 2010, p. 126.

[166] Huang et al. 2011, p. 49.

[167] See Sect. 6.3.3.

[168] Gilmer et al. 2018b.

[169] Ibid.

Table 6.1 Adversary action space based on demands of covertness

Level	Restriction	Example
Indistinguishable	Any manipulation must be completely undetectable	No real-life examples[170]
Content-preserving	Any manipulation possible as long as the core content is preserved	Using facial prosthetics to clear a *manned* checkpoint which uses facial recognition to identify whitelisted individuals
Non-suspicious	The manipulation must be inconspicuous	Using inconspicuous accessories to clear a *remotely-supervised* checkpoint which uses facial recognition to identify whitelisted individuals
Content-constrained	Any manipulation possible as long as the format is correct	Using adversarial face-paint to clear an *un*manned checkpoint which uses facial recognition to identify whitelisted individuals
Unconstrained	Any manipulation possible	Flashing a pattern printed on an A4 to clear an *un*manned checkpoint which uses facial recognition to identify whitelisted individuals

the adversarial fail. Small accessories, on the other hand, will likely not be seen as out of the ordinary, even if an operator is stationed on-site. Let us now say that Deployer instates an even more constrained autonomy level, e.g. 'AI suggests decision, human must approve'.[171] Adversarial accessories in this situation will also fail if the operator is instructed to always confirm if the person standing in front of them matches a photo the system has pulled from the database. Only very covert adversarials—e.g. prosthetics that fool both the system and the operator—have a chance of succeeding in such cases.

Here we see that adversarial capability (knowledge and power) is an *interactive* concept. Properly securing one's databases and models denies the enemy *knowledge*, making risks of adversarials lower. In the same vein, instating certain measures (such as many Context Controls[172]) can limit the opponent's *action space*, reducing their power.

Additionally, while Gilmer et al.'s model was primarily constructed with human observers in mind when determining how 'conspicuous' a manipulation is,[173] the model is quite effective in explaining how any counter-response which limits the adversary's action space reduces adversarial risk. It is not *restricted* to human involvement. In the above example, if Deployer had employed a secondary AI which detects unnatural markings, accessories, etc., and which blocks the face-recognition system's

[170] Ibid., p. 10.

[171] This corresponds to Level-5 in Sheradin's autonomy spectrum. See Parasuraman et al. 2000, p. 287.

[172] See Sect. 8.7.

[173] See Gilmer et al. 2018b, pp. 6–9.

decision until the subject removes these obstructions, a functionally identical restriction would be placed on the adversary's action space. Similarly, more security and better validation during development also restrains an adversary's action space with respect to how much data they can poison.[174]

6.5.4 Other Assumptions Related to Adversaries

A few other assumptions can be made during security analysis outside of the concepts discussed above. The first is what we shall call the ***efficient adversary***. It should be assumed that the adversary is more likely to choose the option with the lowest relative cost corresponding to the highest gain. While this may sound evident, literature often focuses on unrealistic adversarial scenarios while disregarding more efficient (and thus more realistic) alternatives.[175] Much attention, for instance, is devoted to adversarial stickers on stop signs (likely as a result of Eykholt et al.'s disconcerting study[176]) and making cars more robust against them. Gilmer et al., meanwhile, submit that car manufacturers should rather consider how effective simply knocking the sign over will be: this requires no technical preparation, little knowledge (in the sense of 'knowledge of the target system') and would have, in a way, a 100% success rate.[177] On a battlefield, the efficient adversary will prioritise this adversarial if it is comparably effective to a carefully constructed sticker.

This has some implications for Deployers. First, it means that counter-responses against low-sophistication adversarials are very important: ideally, they should be very strong so as to force the adversary into higher tiers of complexity in their action space. Deploying a system which is robust against sophisticated pixel attacks but whose camera is unsecured, giving enemies ample possibility to simply throw a Molotov cocktail at it and disable it, is absurd. Second, this gives additional credence to the conclusion that natural robustness should be prioritised over resistance if a trade-off applies,[178] as otherwise, efficient adversaries simply convert the system's (lack of) natural robustness into an adversarial. If a system is easily flummoxed by water droplets (but was naively deployed because the operation takes place in a desert and no rain has been forecast), enemies will simply use water bombs instead of adversarial patterns.

The second point to keep in mind is that for AI adversarials, a ***second mover advantage*** applies that favours the adversary. This is the inverse of most competitive situations or game theory scenarios, where it is generally regarded as a boon to act first and pre-empt the opponent.[179] In AI scenarios, it is disadvantageous to move first.

---

[174] Comiter 2019, p. 48.

[175] Gilmer et al. 2018b, p. 18.

[176] Eykholt et al. 2018.

[177] Gilmer et al. 2018b, p. 14.

[178] See Sect. 4.3.

[179] Kahneman 2016, p. 162.

The adversary does not craft an adversarial first, in response to which the Deployer builds a model which resists it. It is easy to respond to a *specific* adversarial,[180] but this is not the assigned task. Instead, the Deployer must "build one model that needs to be robust to all potential adversarial data distributions".[181] To allow an analogy, the Deployer must build a lock which is safe against any key, but the adversary succeeds if they can find *one* key which opens the lock. Even worse, in some situations (such as white box attacks), the adversary has a complete diagram of the tumbler positions. The second mover advantage is common knowledge in adversarial literature,[182] but it is important that Deployers also understand this in analysing their strategy.

6.6 Recommendations and Future Work

Countermeasures are unavoidable on the battlefield, and Deployer must, as a reasonable commander, expect them to be used against their AWS.[183] As adversarials are essentially enemy-induced failures, recommendations regarding adversarials will generally echo the conclusions drawn in Chap. 5, namely that much of the responsibility to collect relevant information and take the necessary precautions to mitigate risk to their systems and civilians ***lies with Deployer***.

No enemy will act the same, which makes empowering Deployer with both the technical awareness concerning adversarials, and the tools to make an enemy profile as discussed in this chapter, crucial. This is the task of the Providing Entity, but once equipped with this knowledge, it is up to Deployer to analyse both their own systems' vulnerabilities and the opponent's tendencies, tactics and action spaces to determine whether the risk is too great to use particular AWS. The Providing Entity, in this respect, must provide systems that are generally well-designed to resist adversarials, particularly by avoiding dangerous data shortcuts. The infinite variance problem will ensure, however, that at some point a sufficiently clever adversary will find a vulnerability and exploit it. It is up to Deployer to properly predict and react to such occurrences.

Finally, the question may arise: given that adversarials sometimes allow opponents to exert far-reaching influence over the target system's behaviour and performance, can it not be argued that a certain point, the *adversary* is primarily responsible for the AWS's actions? This would have significant legal implications, such as transferring obligations related to attack[184] from Deployer to said adversary. In addition, one may wonder whether some adversarials are illegal per se: for example, if an adversarial patch is intended to make the AWS classify enemy soldiers as 'ICRC personnel', thereby immunising them from attacks, does this not violate the prohibition against

[180] See e.g. Gilmer and Hendrycks 2019.

[181] Gilmer et al. 2018b, p. 5.

[182] Ibid.

[183] Boothby 2018, p. 154.

[184] See Chap. 9.

perfidy?[185] These matters are not trivial and were analysed in depth by the same author in *Is wearing these sunglasses an attack? Obligations under IHL related to anti-AI countermeasures.*[186]

References

Amodei D et al. (2016) Concrete Problems in AI Safety. http://arxiv.org/abs/1606.06565

Athalye A et al. (2018) Synthesizing Robust Adversarial Examples. In: 6th International Conference on Learning Representations (ICLR 2018). OpenReview.net, Vancouver. https://openreview.net/forum?id=BJDH5M-AW. Accessed 3 August 2023

Barredo Arrieta A et al. (2020) Explainable Artificial Intelligence (XAI): Concepts, Taxonomies, Opportunities and Challenges toward Responsible AI. Information Fusion 58:82–115. https://doi.org/10.1016/j.inffus.2019.12.012

Barreno M et al. (2010) The Security of Machine Learning. Machine Learning 81(2):121–148. https://doi.org/10.1007/s10994-010-5188-5

Biggio B et al. (2013) Evasion Attacks against Machine Learning at Test Time BT - Machine Learning and Knowledge Discovery in Databases. In: Blockeel H et al. (eds) Machine Learning and Knowledge Discovery in Databases: European Conference, ECML PKDD 2013 Prague, Czech Republic, September 23–27, 2013. Springer Berlin Heidelberg, Berlin, pp 387–402

Boothby W H (2018) Highly Automated and Autonomous Technologies. In: Boothby W H (ed) New Technologies and the Law in War and Peace. Cambridge University Press, Cambridge, pp 137–181. https://doi.org/10.1017/9781108609388.007

Bostrom N (2011) Information Hazards: A Typology of Potential Harms from Knowledge. Review of Contemporary Philosophy 10:44–79. http://www.nickbostrom.com/information-hazards.pdf. Accessed 04 August 2023

Chairman of the Joint Chiefs of Staff (2016) Joint Risk Analysis. CJCSM 310501

Comiter M (2019) Attacking Artificial Intelligence: AI's Security Vulnerability and What Policymakers Can Do About It. Belfer Center for Science and International Affairs, Cambridge

DARPA (2019) Defending Against Adversarial Artificial Intelligence. Defense Advanced Research Projects Agency (DARPA). https://www.darpa.mil/news-events/2019-02-06. Accessed 25 October 2020

Defense Innovation Board (2019) AI Principles: Recommendations on the Ethical Use of Artificial Intelligence by the Department of Defense Defense Innovation Board. US Department of Defense. https://media.defense.gov/2019/Oct/31/2002204458/-1/-1/0/DIB_AI_PRINCIPLES_PRIMARY_DOCUMENT.PDF. Accessed 2 August 2023

Defense Science Board (2016) Report of the Defense Science Board Summer Study on Autonomy. Secretary of Defense for Acquisition, Technology and Logistics

Draper B (2020) Guaranteeing AI Robustness Against Deception (GARD). DARPA. https://www.darpa.mil/program/guaranteeing-ai-robustness-against-deception. Accessed 25 October 2020

Engstrom L et al. (2019) A Rotation and a Translation Suffice: Fooling CNNs with Simple Transformations. In: International Conference on Machine Learning

Eykholt K et al. (2018) Robust Physical-World Attacks on Deep Learning Models. http://arxiv.org/abs/1707.08945

[185] See Protocol Additional to the Geneva Conventions of 12 August 1949, and relating to the Protection of Victims of International Armed Conflicts, adopted 8 June 1977, entered into force 7 December 1978, 1125 UNTS 3 (API), Article 37(1).

[186] See Kwik 2024.

Fang L (2019) Google Hired Gig Economy Workers to Improve Artificial Intelligence in Controversial Drone-Targeting Project. The Intercept. https://theintercept.com/2019/02/04/google-ai-project-maven-figure-eight/. Accessed 27 January 2021

Fawzi A, Fawzi H, Fawzi O (2018) Adversarial Vulnerability for Any Classifier. http://arxiv.org/abs/1802.08686

Flournoy M A, Haines A, Chefitz G (2020) Building Trust through Testing: Adapting DOD's Test & Evaluation, Validation & Verification (TEVV) Enterprise for Machine Learning Systems, Including Deep Learning Systems. WestExec Advisors, Washington D.C.

Gershgorn D (2021) The A.I. Industry Is Exploiting Gig Workers Around the World — Sometimes for Just $8 a Day' One Zero. https://onezero.medium.com/the-a-i-industry-is-exploiting-gig-workers-around-the-world-sometimes-for-just-8-a-day-288dcce9c047. Accessed 7 January 2022

Gilmer J et al. (2018a) Adversarial Spheres. http://arxiv.org/abs/1801.02774

Gilmer J et al. (2018b) Motivating the Rules of the Game for Adversarial Example Research. http://arxiv.org/abs/1807.06732

Gilmer J, Hendrycks D (2019) A Discussion of "Adversarial Examples Are Not Bugs, They Are Features": Adversarial Example Researchers Need to Expand What Is Meant by "Robustness". Distill 4(8). https://doi.org/10.23915/distill.00019.1

Gilpin L H et al. (2018) Explaining Explanations: An Overview of Interpretability of Machine Learning. http://arxiv.org/abs/1806.00069

Goldblum M et al. (2020) Dataset Security for Machine Learning: Data Poisoning, Backdoor Attacks, and Defenses. http://arxiv.org/abs/2012.10544

Goodfellow I et al. (2017) Attacking Machine Learning with Adversarial Examples. OpenAI. https://openai.com/blog/adversarial-example-research/. Accessed 12 November 2021

Gu T, Dolan-Gavitt B, Garg S (2017) BadNets: Identifying Vulnerabilities in the Machine Learning Model Supply Chain. http://arxiv.org/abs/1708.06733

Guillot P (2013) Auguste Kerckhoffs et La Cryptographie Militaire. BibNum. https://doi.org/10.4000/bibnum.555

Hayward K J, Maas M M (2021) Artificial Intelligence and Crime: A Primer for Criminologists. Crime, Media, Culture: An International Journal 17(2):209–233. https://doi.org/10.1177/1741659020917434

Hendrycks D et al. (2020) Pretrained Transformers Improve Out-of-Distribution Robustness. http://arxiv.org/abs/2004.06100

Hendrycks D, Dietterich T G (2019) Benchmarking Neural Network Robustness to Common Corruptions and Surface Variations. http://arxiv.org/abs/1807.01697

Heyns C (2013) Report of the Special Rapporteur on Extrajudicial, Summary or Arbitrary Executions, A/HRC/23/47

Hofman L (2020) De Nieuwste Wapenwedloop Gaat Niet Om Bommen, Maar Om Algoritmes (En Hoe Die Te Foppen). De Correspondent, 19 August 2020. https://decorrespondent.nl/11511/de-nieuwste-wapenwedloop-gaat-niet-om-bommen-maar-om-algoritmes-en-hoe-die-te-foppen/80252bb0-a43e-06da-0cf6-5468281fcfef. Accessed 2 August 2023

Holland Michel A (2021) Known Unknowns: Data Issues and Military Autonomous Systems. UNIDIR, Geneva. https://unidir.org/publication/known-unknowns. Accessed 2 August 2023

Huang L et al. (2011) Adversarial Machine Learning. In: Proceedings of the 4th ACM workshop on Security and artificial intelligence. ACM, New York, pp 43-58. https://doi.org/10.1145/2046684.2046692

Hutson M (2018) A Turtle—or a Rifle? Hackers Easily Fool AIs into Seeing the Wrong Thing. ScienceMag. www.sciencemag.org/news/2018/07/turtle-or-rifle-hackers-easily-fool-ais-seeing-wrong-thing. Accessed 8 August 2020

ICRC (2019) Artificial Intelligence and Machine Learning in Armed Conflict: A Human-Centred Approach. ICRC, Geneva

Ilyas A et al. (2019) Adversarial Examples Are Not Bugs, They Are Features. http://arxiv.org/abs/1905.02175

Kahneman D (2016) Système 1 / Système 2. Les Deux Vitesses de La Pensée. Clarinard R (tr). French Edi. Flammarion

Kerckhoffs A (1883) La Cryptographie Militaire. Journal des Sciences Militaires IX:5-38

Kline J (2018) Countertargeting: Offense Enabler and Defense Enhancer. US Naval Institute Blog. https://blog.usni.org/posts/2018/03/27/countertargeting-offense-enabler-and-defense-enhancer. Accessed 6 April 2020

Knight W (2019) Military Artificial Intelligence Can Be Easily and Dangerously Fooled. MIT Technology Review. www.technologyreview.com/2019/10/21/132277/military-artificial-intelligence-can-be-easily-and-dangerously-fooled. Accessed 25 December 2020

Krupiy T (2015) A Case against Relying Solely on Intelligence, Surveillance and Reconnaissance Technology to Identify Proposed Targets. Journal of Conflict and Security Law 20(3):415–449. https://doi.org/10.1093/jcsl/krv009

Kumar R S S et al. (2020) Adversarial Machine Learning — Industry Perspectives. http://arxiv.org/abs/2002.05646

Kwik J, Van Engers T (2021) Algorithmic Fog of War: When Lack of Transparency Violates the Law of Armed Conflict. Journal of Future Robot Life 2(1–2):43–66. https://www.medra.org/servlet/aliasResolver?alias=iospress&doi=10.3233/FRL-200019. Accessed 4 August 2023

Kwik J, Van Engers T (2023) Performance or Explainability? A Law of Armed Conflict Perspective. In: Kornilakis A et al. (eds) Artificial Intelligence and Normative Challenges: International and Comparative Legal Perspectives. Springer Nature Switzerland AG. https://doi.org/10.1007/978-3-031-41081-9_14

Kwik J (2024) Is wearing these sunglasses an attack? Obligations under IHL related to anti-AI countermeasures. International Review of the Red Cross. Published online: 1-28. https://doi.org/10.1017/S1816383124000067. Accessed 25 March 2024

Leslie D (2019) Understanding Artificial Intelligence Ethics and Safety: A Guide for the Responsible Design and Implementation of AI Systems in the Public Sector. The Alan Turing Institute, London

Ministère des Armées (2019) L'intelligence Artificielle Au Service de La Défense. Ministère des Armées, Paris

Nakkiran P (2019) A Discussion of "Adversarial Examples Are Not Bugs, They Are Features": Adversarial Examples Are Just Bugs, Too. Distill 4(8). https://doi.org/10.23915/distill.00019.5

Nelson K, Corbin G, Blowers M (2014) Evaluating Data Distribution and Drift Vulnerabilities of Machine Learning Algorithms in Secure and Adversarial Environments. In: Blowers M, Williams J (eds) Proceedings Volume 9119, Machine Intelligence and Bio-inspired Computation: Theory and Applications VIII. P 911904. https://doi.org/10.1117/12.2053045

Pamp O et al. (2018) The Build-up of Coercive Capacities. Journal of Peace Research 55(4):430–444. https://doi.org/10.1177/0022343317740417

Pan S J, Yang Q (2010) A Survey on Transfer Learning. IEEE Transactions on Knowledge and Data Engineering 22(10):1345–1359. https://doi.org/10.1109/TKDE.2009.191

Parasuraman R, Sheridan T B, Wickens C (2000) A Model for Types and Levels of Human Interaction with Automation. IEEE Transactions on Systems, Man, and Cybernetics 30(3):286–297

Pauwels E, Deton S W (2020) Hybrid Emerging Threats and Information Warfare: The Story of the Cyber-AI Deception Machine. In: Martellini M, Trapp R (eds) 21st Century Prometheus: Managing CBRN Safety and Security Affected by Cutting-Edge Technologies. Springer International Publishing, Cham, pp 107–124. https://doi.org/10.1007/978-3-030-28285-1_6

Puckett C B (2004) In This Era of Smart Weapons, Is a State under an International Legal Obligation to Use Precision-Guided Technology in Armed Conflict. Emory International Law Review 18:645–724

Pytlak A (2018) Lethal [Autonomous] Weapon. In: Civil society perspectives on the CCW Group of Governmental Experts on lethal autonomous weapon systems 9-13 April 2018, Volume 4. CCW Report, pp 1-6 https://reachingcriticalwill.org/images/documents/Disarmament-fora/ccw/2018/gge/reports/CCWR6.4.pdf. Accessed 29 June 2018

Sandoz Y, Swinarski C, Zimmerman B (1987) Commentary on the Additional Protocols of 8 June 1977 to the Geneva Conventions of 12 August 1949. Martinus Nijhoff, Geneva

Scharre P D (2011) Why Unmanned. Joint Force Quarterly 61:89-93. https://ndupress.ndu.edu/portals/68/Documents/jfq/jfq-61.pdf. Accessed 4 August 2023

Scharre P D (2016) Autonomous Weapons and Operational Risk. Center for a New American Security, Washington, D.C

Scharre P D (2018) Army of None: Autonomous Weapons and the Future of War. Ww Norton & Co, New York

Schmitt M N, Thurnher J S (2013) "Out of the Loop": Autonomous Weapon Systems and the Law of Armed Conflict. Harvard Law School National Security Journal 4:231–281

Shen S, Tople S, Saxena P (2016) Auror: Defending against Poisoning Attacks in Collaborative Deep Learning Systems. In: ACSAC '16: Proceedings of the 32nd Annual Conference on Computer Security Applications. ACM, New York. https://doi.org/10.1145/2991079.2991125

Szegedy C et al. (2014) Intriguing Properties of Neural Networks. http://arxiv.org/abs/1312.6199

Tsipras D et al. (2019) Robustness May Be at Odds with Accuracy. http://arxiv.org/abs/1805.12152

UNIDIR (2016) Safety, Unintentional Risk and Accidents in the Weaponization of Increasingly Autonomous Technologies. UNIDIR Resources No 5

Vego M N (2002) Operational Deception in the Information Age. Joint Forces Quarterly 2002:60–66

Vogelsang A, Borg M (2019) Requirements Engineering for Machine Learning: Perspectives from Data Scientists. http://arxiv.org/abs/1908.04674

Wakefield J (2016) Microsoft Chatbot Is Taught to Swear on Twitter. BBC News. https://www.bbc.com/news/technology-35890188. Accessed 2 August 2023

Wilson C (2020) Artificial Intelligence and Warfare. In: Martellini M, Trapp R (eds) 21st Century Prometheus. Springer International Publishing, Cham, pp 125–140. https://doi.org/10.1007/978-3-030-28285-1_7

Xu K et al. (2019) Adversarial T-Shirt! Evading Person Detectors in A Physical World. http://arxiv.org/abs/1910.11099

Yampolskiy R V (2015) Taxonomy of Pathways to Dangerous Artificial Intelligence. In: Workshops at the Thirtieth AAAI Conference on Artificial Intelligence

Part IV
AWS in the Legal-Operational Context

Chapter 7
Legal-Operational Analysis: Introduction

Contents

Abstract This chapter introduces Part IV, which is focused on legal-operational analysis of autonomous weapon systems (AWS). First, Part IV is situated within the framework introduced in Chap. 2 and the broader targeting process: at this point, it is assumed that the AWS-user has discharged all of their tasks indicated in Part III related to informing oneself of the system, the environment and interactive elements, and is about to perform targeting analysis and weaponeering. The chapter then explains the main questions that are explored in this part: "May I lawfully deploy this AWS?" and "How should I deploy this AWS?" look at the legal considerations, while "Why would I use this weapon?" looks at the military perspective. It is argued that both the legal and practical prongs must be satisfied before AWS will effectively be used in practice. To support the three chapters that follow, this chapter also provides some general notes concerning the methodology applied for the legal analyses, the specific targeting obligations that are analysed, and offers an overview of the structure of Part IV.

Keywords Autonomous weapon system · Artificial intelligence · Attack · Obligations in attack · Targeting · Distinction · Precautions · Proportionality · Warnings · Cancelling attacks · Customary IHL · Legal methodology · Teleological interpretation · Object and purpose

J. Kwik, *Lawfully Using Autonomous Weapon Technologies*,
https://doi.org/10.1007/978-94-6265-631-4_7

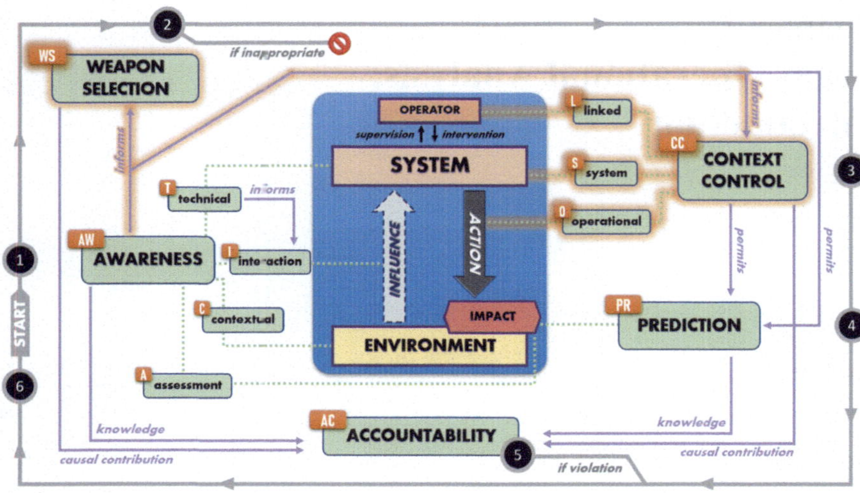

Fig. 7.1 Situation of Part IV within the MHC graph

7.1 Progression Within the MHC Framework

In Part III, we focused on the many aspects Deployer needs to inform themselves of when considering the use of AWS.[1] This information is crucial to answering substantive issues related to the system they are currently considering for use. In terms of the MHC Framework, we have now passed Step 1 (Awareness) and moved to Steps 2 and 3: *Weapon Selection* and *Context Control* (see Fig. 7.1).[2] This address *whether* and *how* AWS may be used, respectively.

---

[1] From this point onward, we adopt the assumption that Deployer has exercised all due diligence with respect to obtaining the necessary Awareness. I.e., they have studied the system to the best of their ability, have generally grasped its functionality and weaknesses, and have identified its performance indicators (*Technical Awareness*); have gathered sufficient intelligence as would be expected of a reasonable commander in their position (*Contextual Awareness*); and considered how the system would function in the operational environment and analysed possible enemy countermeasures (*Interaction Awareness*).

[2] One point to note is that while the outermost grey cycle implies a one-way progression from Weapon Selection to Context Control, Deployers can in practice alternate multiple times between Steps 2 and 3 until they are satisfied with the final choice of capabilities and controls. The reason for this is that Context Controls can impact the decision to approve a system or not. For a practical example, see Sect. 10.4.3. See also Table 14.1.

Legally, the obligation to consider the 'Whether and How' applies in all situations[3] and remains the responsibility of human commanders irrespective of how much autonomy is employed.[4] For our purposes, the two main legal questions Deployer faces are therefore: *May I lawfully deploy this AWS?* and *How should I deploy this AWS?*

In addition, a sometimes-overlooked matter related to AWS is practical, namely the question if using AWS over alternatives would be desirable in the first place. As such, the third question posed in this part is: *Why would I use this weapon?*

These matters are not always straightforward to resolve. While it is argued in this part that IHL *lex lata* is sufficiently broad and adaptable to effectively regulate the use of AWS technology,[5] many unique characteristics of AI systems demand a certain readjustment in terms of how we interpret and apply existing legal rules. For example, how does the law regard systems that statistically perform very well in terms of reliability and Specificity,[6] but are very opaque (leaving Deployer with minimal knowledge of how decisions are internally made)?[7] How generally may Deployer define the AWS's targets, before this becomes so broad so as to constitute an indiscriminate attack? How do contextual properties such as environmental dynamicity,[8] the presence of failure triggers in the operational environment[9] and enemy adversarial activity[10] influence Deployer's legal and military considerations? How should Deployer interpret the duties to warn and cancel when AWS are involved? The aim of the current part is to explore such questions in detail.

---

[3] Protocol Additional to the Geneva Conventions of 12 August 1949, and relating to the Protection of Victims of International Armed Conflicts, adopted 8 June 1977, entered into force 7 December 1978, 1125 UNTS 3 (API), Article 35(1); Hague Convention (IV) respecting the Laws and Customs of War on Land and its annex: Regulations concerning the Laws and Customs of War on Land, adopted 18 October 1907, entered into force 26 January 1910, International Peace Conference 1907, https://ihl-databases.icrc.org/en/ihl-treaties/hague-conv-iv-1907 (accessed 31 July 2023) (Hague Convention IV), Article 22; Program on HPCR at Harvard University 2013, HPCR Manual on International Law Applicable to Air and Missile Warfare. Cambridge University Press, Cambridge (HPCR Manual), para 4; McCormack and Mtharu 2006, para 11.

[4] Horowitz and Scharre 2015, p. 4.

[5] While not all agree, this is also the position adopted by the GGE in Geneva and several prominent commentators. See Moyes 2019, p. 12; ICRC 2014, p. 14; Thurnher 2014, p. 226.

[6] See Chap. 5 and Sect. 4.4.

[7] See Sect. 4.5.

[8] See Sect. 3.4.2.

[9] See Chap. 5.

[10] See Chap. 6.

7.2 Notes on Legal Methodology

As we have done throughout this book, we maintain commander-centric perspective by adopting the position of a hypothetical Deployer engaged in a targeting process, who is considering the use of (an) AWS to achieve a desired effect.[11] As this suggests a practical and operational setting, we focus mainly on legal tests related to targeting. More specifically, we explore the following rules[12] in depth and explore how they should be applied and interpreted in light of AWS technology:

- The prohibition on indiscriminate attacks, indiscriminate weapons and indiscriminate effects (Article 51(4));
- The duty to verify that objectives to be attacked are valid military targets (Article 57(2)(a)(i)) (the *verification rule*);
- The prohibition on launching attacks that would cause excessive incidental harm in relation to the anticipated military advantage (Article 57(2)(a)(iii)) (the *proportionality rule*);
- The duty to avoid, or in any event minimise, incidental harm to the furthest extent feasible (Article 57(2)(a)(ii)) (the *minimisation rule*);
- The duty to cancel or suspend attacks if new information reveals that an objective is not of a military character or that continuing the attack may breach the proportionality rule (Article 57(2)(b)); and
- The duty to provide warnings if an attack may affect the civilian population, except if circumstances do not permit (Article 57(2)(c)).

As these precautionary duties are broadly viewed as customary in nature,[13] the conclusions reached in this book also apply to non-API parties that use AWS.[14] In the case where disagreement exists between the API and customary norms, these will be highlighted.

For some rules, we also consider a slightly more normative angle. This secondary prong of the analysis is motivated by certain characteristics of AI technology that can be capitalised on to *improve* the protection of civilians, given the willingness to read existing rules through a more teleological lens. Note that it is never argued that

---

[11] US Department of the Army 2019, paras 1–76.

[12] The term 'rule' is used to refer to these obligations as it implies a more concrete legal test that commanders are expected to apply in a targeting context. This choice of terminology follows the example of several sources, e.g. UK Ministry of Defence 2004, The Joint Service Manual of the Law of Armed Conflict. UK Ministry of Defence, London, Joint Service Publication 383 (UK Law of Armed Conflict Manual), sct 5.33.2; Schmitt M N (ed) 2017, Tallinn Manual 2.0 on the International Law Applicable to Cyber Warfare. 2nd edn. Cambridge University Press, Cambridge (Tallinn Manual 2.0); ICTY (TC), *Prosecutor v. Stanislav Galić*, Judgment, 5 December 2003, IT-98-29-T, para 58; Schmitt and Schauss 2019; Ducheine and Gill 2018. 'Rule' is used in preference to 'principle' since the latter is often used in a broader sense, e.g. the 'principle of proportionality' encompassing both the proportionality rule and the minimisation rule. See Winter 2020, p. 244.

[13] Henckaerts and Doswald-Beck 2005, Rule 15; *Prosecutor v. Stanislav Galić*, above n. 12, para 58; Winter 2020, p. 245.

[14] Jensen 2021, p. 190.

existing law is *insufficient* to achieve this: in no instances do we argue for the adoption of new provisions.[15] The argument is quite the opposite: that evolved interpretations that ameliorate protections can already be derived from existing targeting provisions, if these are read based on the object and purpose of IHL: the protection of the civilian population. Very similar object and purpose interpretations have been utilised to expand protections related to other new technologies (such as cyber[16]), and a similar methodological process is applied to AWS in this part.

This exercise nevertheless remains normative and prospective, since IHL's targeting rules have never been applied to many types of AWS we discuss in this part. The aim is to show how these provisions *should* be interpreted when the technology is (one day) used. Because these conclusions are derived from black-letter law (i.e., API provisions), their applicability depends on a few factors:

- For Parties to API, they would apply as long as one accepts the teleological method of interpretation.[17] As such, they would remain valid interpretations under *lex lata* until explicitly contradicted in the future, e.g. by an international tribunal ruling on an AWS-related case that such a reading of the text is *not* allowed. As indicated above, one of the main objects and purposes of IHL is maximising the protection afforded to the civilian population, and the provisions are interpreted in this light.
- For non-API Parties to which only Customary IHL applies, these recommendations clearly fall into *de lege ferenda* territory since the technology's novelty excludes any finding of consistent practice. This nevertheless does not preclude States that use AWS from applying these interpretations if they find them convincing. If this practice becomes sufficiently widespread in the future, it may transition into an AWS-specific customary rule when accompanied by *opinio iuris*.[18]

[15] This is contrary to the positions of some States and commentators which "do not believe that existing law provides clear answers to all of the questions raised by technological developments in this area" and that new conventions or provisions are necessary for AWS technology. Moyes 2019, p. 12. See also Liivoja 2016, p. 1160.

[16] See e.g. Turns 2013; Schmitt 2011. In cyber, one main challenge was that a cyberattack in itself is not 'violent', despite 'violence' being required for an act to qualify as an attack under API, above n. 3, Article 49(1). By reading the provision through its purpose of protecting the civilian population, however, relative consensus was eventually reached that the violence criterion should be read as attaching to the act's *consequences*, instead of its violent nature. See Droege 2012, pp. 552–557. This approach was eventually adopted in the Tallinn Manual. Tallinn Manual 2.0, above n. 12, pp. 415–416.

[17] Which would be difficult to contradict since it is consistent with the general rule of treaty interpretation provided in the Vienna Convention. See Vienna Convention on the Law of Treaties, adopted 23 May 1969, entered into force 27 January 1980, 1155 UNTS 331, Article 31(1). See also Villiger 2009, p. 427.

[18] Statute of the International Court of Justice, adopted 26 June 1945, entered into force 24 October 1945, https://www.icj-cij.org/statute (accessed 31 July 2023) (ICJ Statute), Article 38(1)(b). See also ICJ, *North Sea Continental Shelf (Germany v Denmark)*, Merits, 20 February 1969, ICJ Rep 3, ICGJ 150, para 77.

As mentioned in Sect. 1.1, the discussion in this part assumes that IHL related to the conduct of hostilities applies, and also limits itself to analysing circumstances connected to it. It therefore makes no pronouncements on how Deployer would analyse the legality of AWS in other conditions (e.g. occupation) or under different legal regimes (e.g. human rights law). As established in Sect. 1.4, it also assumes that Deployer is a good faith actor committed to implementing IHL to the best of their ability.

Certain norms related to means and methods of warfare outside of those listed above, such as the prohibition on weapons that cause superfluous injury and unnecessary suffering,[19] may also lead Deployer to conclude that a particular AWS would be unlawful. These are not the focus of the current part: we limit ourselves to the five rules related to distinction and precautions listed above.

7.3 Structure

This part is divided into three substantive chapters. Chapter 8 first discusses *variables of complexity and facility*. We engage in a systematic examination of characteristics related to AWS that directly or indirectly make it more difficult for Deployer to use the system in a way compliant with IHL rules related to targeting. We also discuss Context Controls more specifically: these are measures that Deployer can implement to influence facility of use. This analysis leads to a comprehensive framework, which maps these variables to three overarching rationales of IHL: that of reducing (a) risk of collateral damage, (b) risk of false positives, and (c) risk of epistemic error.

Chapter 9 expands on the previous chapter by substantiating its conclusions through a comprehensive *legal analysis of IHL rules related to the conduct of hostilities*, particularly those found in API Articles 51 and 57. We discuss these rules both

[19] The superfluous injury and unnecessary suffering (‘*maux superflus*’) rule prohibits weapons “of a nature to cause superfluous injury or unnecessary suffering”. API, above n. 3, Article 35(2). See also Convention of 18 May 1977 on the Prohibition of Military or any Other Hostile Use of Environmental Modification Techniques, adopted 10 December 1976, entered into force 5 October 1978, 1108 UNTS 151 (ENMOD Convention), Article I(1). It is broadly regarded as constituting customary law. ICJ, *Legality of the Threat or Use of Nuclear Weapons*, Advisory Opinion, 8 July 1996, ICJ Rep 226, paras 78–79, 83; Henckaerts and Doswald-Beck 2005, p. Rule 70. This rule is not particularly interesting to discuss in light of our operational framing, since this rule is normally not associated with targeting but rather with weapon reviews. See ICRC 2006, p. 15; Boothby 2016, sct 19.5.3; Parks 2005, p. 129. It is irregular for such weapons to reach the targeting stage. The US Air Force Targeting Doctrine explicitly guarantees that all weapons made available to commanders are already cleared to not be in breach of the maux superflus rule. Curtis E. Lemay Center 2019, p. 90. The rule has minimal bearing on our discussion: AWS can certainly violate this rule if, for instance, they are designed to release blinding lasers or undetectable fragments (in violation of CCW-I and CCW-IV respectively), but this would be true even if the weapon had no AI installed. Whether the rule is breached is primarily a function of the weapon’s choice of munition (e.g. the type of bullet) rather than how the engagement decision was reached. Cherry and Johnson 2020, p. 11. Thus, this rule “ironically[] may be the least problematic LOAC principle” in terms of AWS controversies. Kastan 2013, p. 62.

in terms of how they would apply to AWS under their plain reading, and also propose teleological readings in light of novel possibilities provided by AI technology that provide greater protections to the civilian population.

Finally, Chap. 10 asks the practical question of when a commander *would* be interested in using AWS. We look here at the other side of the operational analysis, namely the AWS's military utility as a system (termed 'Benefit'). It is argued through a cost-benefit chart that Deployers would only use an AWS when its Benefit is commensurate with the Facility with which it can be used. We find that situations where AWS are truly indispensable are rare. Related to this, it is also argued that there is little academic or policy worth in discussing sensationalist AWS, since these are unlikely to be developed or used in the first place because they are either not useful enough or too legally cumbersome to employ.

References

Boothby W H (2016) Weapons and the Law of Armed Conflict. 2nd edn. Oxford University Press, Oxford

Cherry J, Johnson D (2020) Maintaining Command and Control (C2) of Lethal Autonomous Weapon Systems: Legal And Policy Considerations. Southwestern Journal of International Law 27:1–27

Curtis E. Lemay Center (2019) Air Force Doctrine Publication 3-60 – Targeting. Curtis E Lemay Center. www.doctrine.af.mil/Doctrine-Publications/AFDP-3-60-Targeting. Accessed 05 July 2021

Droege C (2012) Get off My Cloud: Cyber Warfare, International Humanitarian Law, and the Protection of Civilians. International Review of the Red Cross 94(886):533–578. DOI: https://doi.org/10.1017/S1816383113000246

Ducheine P, Gill T (2018) From Cyber Operations to Effects: Some Targeting Issues. Militair Rechtelijk Tijdschrift 111(3):37–41

Henckaerts J-M, Doswald-Beck L (eds) (2005) Customary International Humanitarian Law, Volume I – Rules. ICRC, Geneva

Horowitz M C, Scharre P (2015) Meaningful Human Control in Weapon Systems: A Primer. Center for a New American Security, Working Paper No 031315

ICRC (2006) A Guide to the Legal Review of New Weapons, Means and Methods of Warfare: Measures to Implement Article 36 of Additional Protocol I of 1977. ICRC, Geneva

ICRC (2014) Report of the ICRC Expert Meeting on "Autonomous Weapon Systems: Technical, Military, Legal and Humanitarian Aspects", 26–28 March 2014, Geneva

Jensen E T (2021) Autonomy and Precautions in the Law of Armed Conflict. In: Liivoja R, Väljataga A (eds) Autonomous Cyber Capabilities under International Law. NATO CCDCOE Publications, Tallinn, pp 181–205

Kastan B (2013) Autonomous Weapons Systems: A Coming Legal "Singularity"?. Journal of Law, Technology and Policy 2013(1):45–82

Liivoja R (2016) Technological Change and the Evolution of the Law of War. International Review of the Red Cross 97(900):1157–1177. DOI: https://doi.org/10.1017/S1816383116000424

McCormack T L H, Mtharu P B (2006) Expected Civilian Damage and the Proportionality Equation: To What Extent Should the Mid to Longer Term Consequences of Explosive Remnants of War Be Taken into Consideration in the Proportionality Assessment. In: Third Review Conference of the States Parties to the Convention on Prohibitions or Restrictions on the Use of Certain Conventional Weapons Which May be Deemed to be Excessively Injurious or to Have Indiscriminate Effects. United Nations Digital Library, Geneva

Moyes R (2019) Target Profiles: An Initial Consideration of "Target Profiles" as a Basis for Rule-Making in the Context of Discussions on Autonomy in Weapons Systems. Article 36, Article 36 Discussion Paper

Parks W H (2005) Conventional Weapons and Weapons Reviews. Yearbook of International Humanitarian Law 8:55–142

Schmitt M N (2011) Cyber Operations and the Jus in Bello: Key Issues. Israel Yearbook on Human Rights 41:113. https://digital-commons.usnwc.edu/cgi/viewcontent.cgi?referer=&httpsredir=1&article=1077&context=ils. Accessed 4 August 2023

Schmitt M N, Schauss M (2019) Uncertainty in the Law of Targeting: Towards a Cognitive Framework. Harvard National Security Journal 10:148–194

Thurnher J S (2014) Examining Autonomous Weapon Systems from a Law of Armed Conflict Perspective. In: Nasu H, McLaughlin R (eds) New Technologies and the Law of Armed Conflict. TMC Asser Press, The Hague, pp 213–228. DOI: https://doi.org/10.1007/978-90-6704-933-7_13

Turns D (2013) Cyber War and the Concept of "Attack" in International Humanitarian Law. In: Saxon D (ed) International Humanitarian Law and the Changing Technology of War. Brill-Nijhoff, Leiden, pp 207–227. DOI: https://doi.org/10.1163/9789004229495_011

US Department of the Army (2019) The Operations Process. ADP 5-0 (replacing ADP 5-0, dated 17 May 2012, and ADRP 5-0, dated 17 May 2012)

Villiger M E (2009) Commentary on the 1969 Vienna Convention on the Law of Treaties. Brill-Nijhoff, Leiden. DOI: https://doi.org/10.1163/ej.9789004168046.i-1058

Winter E (2020) The Compatibility of the Use of Autonomous Weapons with the Principle of Precaution in the Law of Armed Conflict. The Military Law and the Law of War Review 58(2):240–273. DOI: https://doi.org/10.4337/mllwr.2020.02.18

Chapter 8
Legally-Salient Variables for AWS

Contents

Abstract Why autonomous weapons (AWS) are problematic from a targeting perspective is controversial and inconsistent. This chapter argues that mono-dimensional approaches to this question are reductive: instead, variables such as level of autonomy, duration of search, etc., are only *a* factor that *may* influence whether an AWS can be used lawfully. It also hypotheses that some variables may compensate for each other, e.g. an AWS's inability to distinguish trams and tanks can be mitigated by limiting its search area to a space where trams are not present. From

J. Kwik, *Lawfully Using Autonomous Weapon Technologies*,
https://doi.org/10.1007/978-94-6265-631-4_8

these hypotheses, a robust typology of legally-salient variables is constructed related to the system's properties itself (e.g. performance, opacity), those of the operational environment (e.g. density of negative class entities), and operational parameters (e.g. spatial and temporal limitations, the types of target). Additionally, these variables are linked to Context Controls—actions AWS-users can take to mitigate risk of violating IHL—such as enabling dynamic munition selection or issuing specific instructions to the civilian population to avoid being incorrectly targeted. Finally, the hypothesis that variables can 'compensate' for each other is validated through the finding of three overarching Rationales that underpin targeting rules: the preference for minimising incidental harm, minimising false positives, and minimising the risk of epistemic error. It is also shown that in order for variables to compensate for each other, they must be linked to the same Rationales. The theories advanced in this chapter constitute the foundations for the legal analysis in Chap. 9 on interpreting targeting obligations.

Keywords Autonomous weapon system · Artificial intelligence · Targeting · Performance · Space and time · Collateral damage · Military objective · Valid target · Operational environment · Black box · Risk management · Human-machine interaction · Human control · Human-machine interface

8.1 Introduction

Why are autonomous underwater systems generally considered unproblematic,[1] while much concern is raised about systems meant for use in urban environments?[2] Why does the international community generally not dispute the lawfulness of the Harpy and fire-and-forget munitions,[3] when one commentator even describes the latter as "[going] after the first target it sees" like a "mad dog in a meat locker" once launched?[4] Why is the landmine, a quintessentially out-of-the-loop weapon[5] that is inherently incapable of hitting specific targets, not considered inherently unlawful?[6] Why have systems such as the Phalanx and Goalkeeper been used for many years with minimal controversy,[7] when they autonomously "search, detect, evaluat[e], track, engage, and kill"?[8] Why has the Kargu-22, that was "programmed to attack targets without requiring data connectivity between the operator and the munition"

[1] ICRC 2018, para 62.

[2] Cherry and Johnson 2020, p. 16.

[3] Van den Boogaard and Roorda 2021, p. 425.

[4] Scharre 2018, p. 41.

[5] Scharre and Horowitz 2015, p. 7.

[6] Lewis 2015, p. 1321.

[7] Adviesraad Internationale Vraagstukken and Commissie van Advies inzake Volkenrechtelijke Vraagstukken 2015, p. 13.

[8] Ekelhof 2018, p. 74.

and which was used to "hunt down" logistics convoys and retreating HAF troops in Libya in 2020,[9] not sparked universal outrage?

As this small selection of examples shows, in international discourse, controversy related to autonomy in weapon systems is not uniform, and sometimes (seemingly) inconsistent. There have been many attempts to develop explanatory theories that separate historically unproblematic weapons from those systems that have been deemed more controversial in the AWS polemics. These include distinguishing systems based on[10]:

(a) The role of the human controller (such as the popular in-, on- and out-of-the-loop typology)[11];
(b) Decision-making sophistication[12] (where 'automated' systems only carry out "preprogrammed rules" while 'autonomous' systems can "draw independent conclusions"[13]);
(c) Whether the autonomy lies in its 'critical functions' of selecting and attacking targets independently[14];
(d) Whether the system is 'defensive' versus 'offensive'[15];
(e) Whether the system is allowed to target humans or only inanimate objects[16]; and
(f) Whether the system is lethal or not[17] (hence the popular abbreviation 'LAWS'—*lethal* AWS).[18]

However, from our examples above, we see that none of these approaches can definitively aid us in determining when an AWS is legally problematic and when it is not. Several (d) offensive, (e, f) highly destructive and lethal weapons (b) exhibiting higher degrees of independence in (c) selecting and engaging targets, while (a) maintaining no communications link at all, have been used for years with no major legal issues.[19] Clearly, there are systems that would be highly difficult (if not impossible) to utilise correctly within the bounds of the law, but none of the above methodologies in isolation grasp the core essence of what would generate this challenge. A counterexample can seemingly always be found.

One main thesis advanced in this chapter is that a proper assessment of the difficulty with which a given system can be used in accordance with IHL can indeed not be made on the basis of isolated categorisations. Instead, the question must be

---

[9] United Nations 2021, para 63.
[10] This selection is illustrative and does not purport to list all approaches in literature.
[11] E.g. Noone and Noone 2015, p. 28; Abaimov and Martellini 2020, pp. 154–156.
[12] E.g. UK Ministry of Defence 2011, para 205; Wilson 2020, p. 127.
[13] Crootof 2015, p. 1864.
[14] E.g. Davison 2017, p. 5.
[15] E.g. Akerson 2013; Future of Life Institute 2015.
[16] E.g. Asaro 2012, p. 688; Moyes 2019, pp. 6–8. See Sartor and Omicini 2016, p. 72.
[17] E.g. Asaro 2012, p. 694.
[18] E.g. Group of Governmental Experts on Lethal Autonomous Weapons Systems 2019, Annex IV.
[19] Scharre made this observation already many years ago. Scharre 2014.

approached from a multidimensional perspective. There are two main rationales for this position. First, a mono-dimensional approach is reductive: all six characteristics mentioned above reference only *a* factor that *may* influence whether an AWS can be used lawfully. For similar reasons, a few authors[20] have over the years advocated for viewing typologies of AWS in concert (e.g. relationship-complexity-task[21]), to avoid oversimplifying the discussion.

Second, and often overlooked, are *interacting factors*. With munitions such as the Harpy, for example, their relatively high freedom is compensated by the type of objective sought, which has a very distinct military signature.[22] The theoretical difficulty of using the Samsung SGR-A1 lawfully (a lethal weapon that can target persons autonomously[23]) can be mitigated by the specific environment in which it used (a demilitarised zone). Antipersonnel landmines, the "most primitive autonomous … weapons" with no capability to distinguish at all,[24] can be used lawfully through a combination of limiting their active-time (installing a disarming timer) and exercising influence on the environment to ward off the negative class population (closing off the mined area to civilians).[25] Clearly, therefore, whether a particular system can be lawfully used depends on a great number of interrelated and mutually complementing variables. These are sometimes fixed, other times open to manipulation by Deployer.

This chapter explores *variables of complexity and facility*, which pursues the above prepositions in a more comprehensive way. A *variable* refers to a factor related to an AWS's technical characteristics, its functionality, or its operational environment. Propositions (a)–(f) above are also 'variables' within this understanding, but we shall not use any of them directly in our discussion. Instead, the variables selected for exploration in this chapter are more specifically chosen for their legal salience and practical workability. *Practical workability* refers to the fact that the variables proposed here are relatively objective and observable facts—facts that any Deployer can determine during capability analysis. *Legal salience* refers to the fact that the variables are directly or indirectly relevant for assessments under specific IHL provisions. This legal relevance bridges the gap between the operational and the legal, and allows Deployer to grasp why a particular factor is legally relevant to consider. To illustrate by negative example: whether a system is lethal, or offensive or defensive, are *non-legally salient* variables. Violence in the IHL sense is not limited to 'lethal'

[20] See e.g. Boulanin 2016; Sartor and Omicini 2016; Scharre 2018.

[21] Scharre 2015.

[22] Van den Boogaard and Roorda 2021, p. 425.

[23] Heyns 2013, para 45.

[24] Beard 2014, p. 630.

[25] Protocol on Prohibitions or Restrictions on the Use of Mines, Booby-Traps and Other Devices as amended on 3 May 1996 (Protocol II), to the Convention on Prohibitions or Restrictions on the Use of Certain Conventional Weapons Which May be Deemed to be Excessively Injurious or to Have Indiscriminate Effects, adopted 10 October 1980, entered into force 2 December 1983, amended 21 December 2001, 1342 UNTS 137 (CCW Protocol-II), Articles 3(8) and 6(3).

strikes but also extends to those which can cause injury, damage and some higher-order effects,[26] and IHL makes no distinction between 'offensive' and 'defensive' strikes.[27] While perhaps useful as an academic or diplomatic framing tool, they are of little use to field commanders.

In the current methodology, each variable is conceived on a spectrum that is tied to facility of use. This spectrum qualitatively expresses, *mutatis mutandis*, how difficult particular technical, environmental or interactive characteristics make it to lawfully use AWS. Consider 'environmental clutter'. On the spectrum, one can place underwater or aerial domains at 'easy', while urban environments would qualify as 'difficult'.[28] Assuming one wishes to faithfully apply all IHL obligations related to attack, one would expect that using AWS in the former situation would be easier than in the latter, all other things being equal.

Facility lies at the opposite end of *Complexity*.[29] For digestibility, we will often refer to a variable as 'increasing Facility' instead of 'decreasing Complexity'. Note that both Facility and Complexity are used descriptively instead of normatively: low Facility simply means more difficult—not impossible, illegal or undesirable. These latter pronouncements can only come after the variable is used for legal analysis and in conjunction with all other variables, as we see in the following chapters. For the current chapter, we remain content with simply enumerating the different variables, proposing sub-frameworks that enable us to place concrete situations on the Facility spectrum, and explaining their general relevance.

Throughout our discussion, we will also notice that the *reason* these variables are relevant can be explained by one of three overarching *Rationales*, which are linked directly to IHL's more general purposes and goals. These Rationales are enumerated, since they allow an integrated understanding of the relationship between the variables discussed in this chapter and the law.

As mentioned above, some variables are subject to manipulation or influence by Deployer. Deployer cannot transform an urban environment into an undersea one, but Deployer can restrict the AWS's area of operations, order evacuations, or issue warnings. In our MHC Framework, these manipulations were referred to as Context Controls,[30] and many have the ability to shift a particular variable's position on the spectrum. We will address more concretely with examples how Deployer can do this

[26] Cf. Schmitt (ed) 2017, Tallinn Manual 2.0 on the International Law Applicable to Cyber Warfare. 2nd edn. Cambridge University Press, Cambridge (Tallinn Manual 2.0), Rule 92. It is also often the case that non-lethal weapons can actually create worse humanitarian situations than lethal weapons. Schmitt 1998, p. 406.

[27] Henderson et al. 2017, p. 344. Cf. Protocol Additional to the Geneva Conventions of 12 August 1949, and relating to the Protection of Victims of International Armed Conflicts, adopted 8 June 1977, entered into force 7 December 1978, 1125 UNTS 3 (API), Article 49(1).

[28] Thurnher 2014, p. 221.

[29] 'Complexity' is used simply to mean challenging, interesting or complicated, and not 'irreducibly difficult to understand or predict' as the term is sometimes used in complexity studies. Cf. Bullock and Cliff 2004, p. 6 (referring to a complex system as one that is "difficult to understand, predict, control or explain due to the "entwined" nature of their multiple components").

[30] See Sect. 2.4.3.

when discussing each variable. This dynamic becomes relevant in Chap. 9, where we demonstrate that (*a priori*) unlawful-use-situations may be rendered lawful with the appropriate Context Controls, and in Chap. 10, when we discuss whether the operational opportunity costs related to these Context Controls justify choosing an AWS over other (legacy) alternatives.

8.2 Variables Related to System Performance

That the characteristics of the system itself strongly influence Deployer's ability to use it in accordance with the law is unsurprising. Most works on AWS include mentions of the system having to be sufficiently functional, reliable, consistent, secure, etc., to enable lawful use.[31] However, one common critique of such normative statements is that they remain relatively abstract: they do not provide concrete indicators as to what component (technical or otherwise) Deployer should focus on when making legal decisions.[32] In this section, we further advance our discussion of Measures of Performance (MoP) from Chap. 4 and determine more specific and measurable parameters that would impact Facility. While we start with MoPs more strictly, we subsequently move to other environmental variables which *interact* with the MoPs.

8.2.1 Measures of Performance Generally

One can generally state that a given system's MoPs as discussed in Chap. 4 are proportionally correlated with Facility. A hypothetical system with perfect accuracy, reliability, robustness and resistance would leave Deployer with few concerns of misclassifications, failures leading to civilian casualties, and harmful interference by the adversary. On the other end of the spectrum, a system with a measure approaching 0 in all of these parameters would be very hard to use. Note that we cannot go so far as to say 'impossible'[33]—extremely low complexity in other dimensions can compensate for deficiencies in this domain[34]—but lower MoPs make it exponentially less likely this system can be used lawfully.

A specific inquiry we can make at this stage is which of the four main AI accuracy metrics (Accuracy, Recall, Specificity and Precision[35]) are most relevant for IHL

---

[31] See e.g. ICRC 2016, p. 81; Corn 2016, p. 226; Henderson et al. 2017, p. 361; Boothby 2021, pp. 384–385.

[32] Kastan 2013, p. 47; UNIDIR 2014, p. 7; Schuller 2019, p. 108.

[33] An antipersonnel landmine, for example, essentially has a Specificity of zero but can still be used lawfully in certain conditions, such as when there are no civilians to misclassify. See Sect. 8.2.2.

[34] To remain with the landmine example, marking the mined territory with clear warnings to prevent civilians from mistakenly entering the area is a factor that can 'compensate' for the landmine's Specificity of zero. See Sect. 8.9.

[35] See Sect. 4.2.

Wp	Acc rate	Recall (false negative rate)		Specificity (false positive rate)	
		Rate	In absolute values	Rate	In absolute values
W_1	0.989	1	All 50 soldiers successfully shot	0.989	11 civilians mistakenly shot
W_2	0.989	0.8	Of 50 soldiers, 10 mistakenly left unharmed	0.999	1 civilian mistakenly shot
	Population: 1050 persons, of which 1000 civilians, 50 enemy soldiers				

Fig. 8.1 Two AWS with equal accuracy

analyses. Recall our prior discussion in Sect. 4.2.2 that Accuracy is a misleading metric since an AWS with equal Accuracy (in an AI sense) can boast very different ratios of false positives and false negatives.

Conceptually, both errors are problematic for Deployer.[36] An overly high false negative rate (low Recall) would be tactically jeopardous since the AWS would leave large proportions of valid targets unharmed. Alternatively, many false positives (low Specificity) would make the system very efficient at neutralising anything even suspected to be an enemy, but the high rate of misclassifications would lead to many civilian entities being damaged, injured or killed by mistake. It is thus necessary to conceptually separate the two metrics.

To illustrate, consider:

Scenario 1: Equal Accuracy. Deployer can choose between two AWS to use in a comingled environment as provided in Fig. 8.1.[37]

Both systems have an equal Accuracy score, but the predicted results vary wildly. Despite W_1 performing flawlessly in terms of identifying enemy soldiers, it raises legal concerns related to its capability to distinguish.

From this example we see that, at least for *legal* analyses, Specificity is clearly the more crucial of the two. Specificity describes how rarely an AWS positively mistakes a civilian entity for a military target. This is the essence of the distinction rule in IHL[38]: a weapon can 'distinguish' if it has the "capability to direct attacks solely at military objectives".[39] Thus, **Specificity can be considered as statistically representing an AWS's *capacity to distinguish*.** It is therefore this metric Deployer must focus on for many legal determinations.

[36] Kalmanovitz 2016, p. 155: "there are risks of tactical failure (not accomplishing missions and thus being a waste of time and resources) and the humanitarian risk of excessively harming protected persons and goods".

[37] Original confusion matrixes: W_1: Tp = 50, Tn = 989, Fp = 11, Fn = 0. W_2: Tp = 40, Tn = 999, Fp = 1, Fn = 10.

[38] API, above n. 27, Article 48; ICJ, *Legality of the Threat or Use of Nuclear Weapons*, Advisory Opinion, 8 July 1996, ICJ Rep 226, para 78.

[39] Fleck 2013, para 449.

In contrast, Recall is a variable that describes a system's military utility[40]; it is thus significant for operational analyses of whether one *would* use said system.[41] It is not immediately relevant for many legal analyses: IHL does not ask commanders to exercise constant care to spare persons in general; it specifically asks commanders to spare the "*civilian* population, civilians and civilian objects".[42] At its base, the law is agnostic as to how many soldiers or enemy barracks are (mistakenly) spared. Nonetheless, Recall can potentially be relevant for proportionality calculations: the less militarily effective a system, the less military advantage accrued from using it.[43]

Better metrics translate to higher Facility because it reduces ***risk of false positives***, which is one of the core values underpinning the principle of distinction in IHL. More Specificity makes a system easier to use lawfully in more situations, because the probability of civilian casualties due to mistakes is reduced. Let us refer to this **propensity of IHL to prefer fewer false positives** as ***Rationale-FP***.

8.2.2 Negative Class Frequency

8.2.2.1 Population Distribution Influence

In Scenario 1, it is perhaps surprising to see that despite a seemingly impressive Specificity rate of 0.989 (recall that Specificity represents a system's capacity to distinguish), W_1 is statistically likely to misclassify and kill eleven civilians. This calls into question whether W_1 is a weapon capable of distinguishing military from civilian targets, as required by API Article 51(4). The reason for this discrepancy is that Specificity as a rate *cannot be seen separately from the population distribution in which the system will operate.* To illustrate, consider Fig. 8.2.

Each box represents the distribution between lawful targets (shaded blue) and civilian entities (white) in a given environment, followed by the statistical prediction of how many misclassifications will occur when using system W_1 or W_2 against it. Comparing the left and centre scenarios, we see that despite using the same system (W_1), the centre scenario will produce ten times more mistakes than the left one. This clearly has legal implications: neutralising fifty objectives might justify the coin flip ($\mathbb{P} = 50\%$[44]) of a single misclassification, but not five victims on average. More interestingly, when comparing the left and right scenarios, we see that W_2, a system with a much weaker Specificity than W_1, actually produces the 'best' results in terms of risk to civilians, with nine objectives neutralised for the genuinely low risk ($\mathbb{P} = 20\%$) of one misclassification.

---

[40] See Sect. 4.2.2.

[41] See Chap. 10.

[42] API, above n. 27, Article 57(1) (emphasis added).

[43] See Sect. 9.5.

[44] $\mathbb{P}$ is used to denote *probability*.

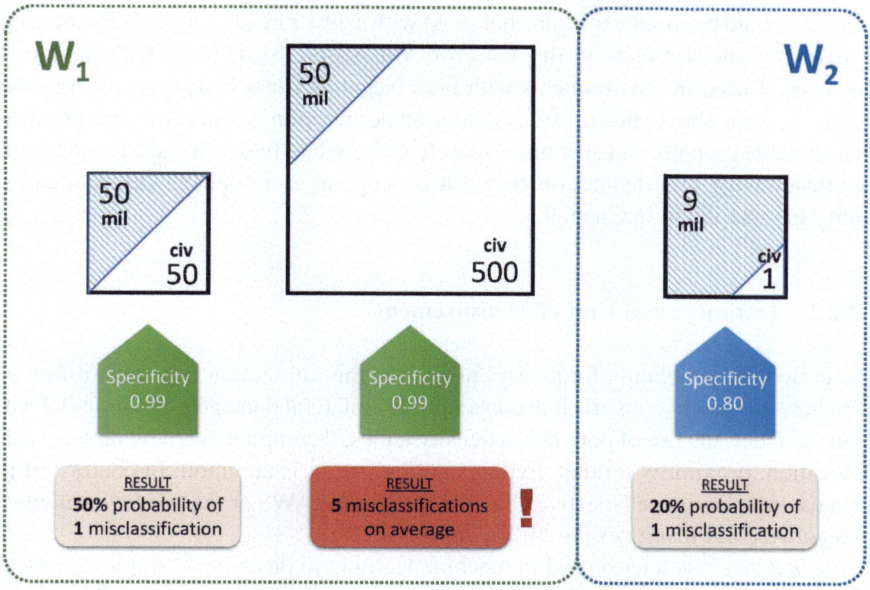

Fig. 8.2 Interaction between Specificity and population frequency

The variable that causes these discrepant results is ***Negative Class Frequency***. It is inversely correlated with Facility. The more civilian entities exist in a particular environment, the more complex using the weapon is, since *mutatis mutandis*, the probability of mistakes is higher. Differences in Negative Class Frequency are a major explanatory mechanism for many statements[45] claiming that AWS could be more easily used in "remote areas, such as underwater, deserts, or places like the Demilitarised Zone in Korea" but not in environments such as cities.[46]

Note that this variable applies for any weapon, and is applicable to the extremes. An antipersonnel mine essentially has a Specificity of zero: any person stepping on it will trigger the landmine.[47] However, if used in accordance with CCW Protocol-II which requires "fencing or other means, to ensure the effective exclusion of civilians from the area",[48] Negative Class Frequency *also* drops to zero, making the weapon no longer necessarily indiscriminate. In terms of Facility, the antipersonnel mine scores extremely poorly with regard to Specificity, but its user can compensate for this with an equally extreme measure in Negative Class Frequency (essentially forcing the 'easiest' environment imaginable, with zero civilians to misidentify).

We must be careful to separate a weapon's *conceptual* capability to distinguish and *concrete* results. As noted above, the former is represented by an AWS's Specificity

45 E.g. ICRC 2018, para 62; Thurnher 2018, p. 108; Cherry and Johnson 2020, p. 16.

46 Thurnher 2014, p. 221.

47 Schmitt 2010, p. 814.

48 CCW Protocol-II, above n. 25, Article 5(2)(a).

rating. It would be strange to argue that an AI with a 99% rate of accurately identifying civilians is indiscriminate in the sense of API Article 51(4)(b–c), for example.[49] However, if used in environments with high Negative Class Frequency such as the centre scenario above, this (*a priori* discriminate) weapon can nevertheless produce unacceptable casualties in absolute values (e.g. 5 civilian lives). We discuss the legal ramifications of this distinction between conceptual and concrete discriminatory ability in more detail in Chap. 9.

8.2.2.2 Instances as a Unit of Measurement

The notion of 'population frequency' as used in this subsection is notably different from how one might construe it in conventional collateral damage estimation (CDE). With the latter, the use of population density tables,[50] complemented by factors such as location, proximity to other civilian entities, etc.,[51] is common. In contrast, it is most useful to construe Negative Class Frequency for AWS as the *predicted number of negative class Instances the AWS will process.*

An *Instance*[52] is a term used in machine learning to describe a "single … observation from the domain",[53] for which the algorithm determines a particular output (see Fig. 8.3). An Instance is a useful unit of measurement for our purposes since it ignores non-processed persons or objects. To take a Patriot system as an example, each aerial object detected within its range of operations is one Instance: it is one observation the system makes, analyses, and classifies as a threat or benign.[54] To determine Negative Class Frequency related to a Patriot or similar systems, one would only consider tallying those civilian entities that can conceivably be mischaracterised as an aerial threat, such as civilian airliners or commercial drones (and not, for example, civilians swimming near the ship). Similarly, when using an antipersonnel AWS, Deployer will need to determine the likely number of protected class persons the system is likely to encounter, but may reasonably ignore the possibility of the system misclassifying a church for a soldier.

In Fig. 8.2, the numbers '50', '500' and '1' thus do not necessarily refer to the absolute number of civilians in the area of operations, but rather those entities the system is likely to encounter and process. To a city block of 6.000 people, for example, Deployer could be justified in assigning a Negative Class Frequency of 500 if a curfew is in place, depending on available intelligence.

---

[49] See Sect. 9.3.

[50] Thorne 2020, p. 47.

[51] NATO 2021, pp. 1–28.

[52] Capitalisation is used to distinguish the term from the colloquial use (e.g.: 'There are two instances where that is true').

[53] Brownlee 2013.

[54] See Hawley 2007, p. 1.

FEATURE

	v	w	x	y	z	class	
	0.69826	0.81528	0.34047	0.39366	0.43818	1	Train dataset
	0.93347	0.90607	0.91155	0.87103	0.67824	0	
	0.37667	0.90884	0.59954	0.53663	0.68801	1	
	0.40972	0.72356	0.97688	0.28099	0.18435	1	
	0.22628	0.58967	0.0807	0.70346	0.85218	0	
	0.51568	0.05481	0.89649	0.64251	0.91038	1	
	0.9784	0.17192	0.14121	0.93082	0.15868	1	
	0.04506	0.61865	0.7099	0.14718	0.14421	0	
INSTANCE	0.21964	0.36592	0.5691	0.47004	0.87466	1	
	0.25105	0.18687	0.99545	0.46306	0.5575	1	
	0.23257	0.92412	0.42776	0.38056	0.65267	0	
	0.80969	0.77158	0.39048	0.71352	0.45324	0	
	0.31395	0.85477	0.62251	0.42863	0.63161	0	
	0.30906	0.58164	0.9147	0.21074	0.07512	1	
	0.28275	0.57774	0.05766	0.14135	0.35752	1	
	0.39033	0.03989	0.96815	0.55242	0.95133	1	Test dataset
	0.95686	0.54748	0.76908	0.52146	0.37272	0	
	0.22539	0.74155	0.16859	0.62369	0.08199	0	
	0.64881	0.31876	0.97868	0.1087	0.76788	1	
	0.04272	0.60086	0.98966	0.00403	0.80139	0	

Fig. 8.3 Instances in machine learning[55]

Negative Class Frequency is a function of several factors. Traditional CDE elements such as population density, time of day, specific events, etc.,[56] remain applicable. However, as *each Instance* represents an opportunity for the AWS to make a mistake, other variables must also be taken in consideration, such as:

- *Active Time*. A single entity can be processed multiple times. The longer the AWS remains active, the more possible Instances per entity.[57]
- *Mobility*. Low mobility reduces frequency. A system guarding a checkpoint has little risk of 're-encountering' the same entity,[58] while this might be the case for a system patrolling an area.
- *Target Specificity*. Low target specificity[59] can exponentially increase Negative Class Frequency.[60]

---

[55] Adapted from Brownlee 2013.

[56] See Chairman of the Joint Chiefs of Staff 2012, p. D-1; NATO 2021, pp. 1–28.

[57] See also Sect. 8.3.1.

[58] Cf. ICRC 2016, p. 73.

[59] See Sect. 8.5.2.

[60] For example, a Patriot-like system only designed to intercept aerial threats will process fewer entities than a similar system that is also tasked to intercept surface and underwater threats at the same time. In the latter case, swimming civilians may very well be potential victims of misclassifications.

Like Specificity, low Negative Class Frequency increases Facility because it reduces ***risk of false positives (Rationale-FP)***. A system that is theoretically 'hard' to employ lawfully due to (relatively) poor Specificity could potentially be usable if there are very few Instances for it to make mistakes in, and an environment with zero negative class Instances (maximum Facility) can completely negate the problems tied to an inability of the weapon to distinguish, as we have seen with the landmine perimeter example.[61] The latter must be true for the entire duration of the system's expected use, however, which makes the temporal dimension a crucial one. We discuss this next.

8.3 Temporal and Spatial Variables

The temporal and spatial aspects of AWS use have received significant attention.[62] Restrictions in time and space are the most common proposals in literature to allow lawful AWS use.[63] In this section, we explore in more detail why the temporal and spatial dimensions are inversely correlated with Facility. They are also crucial for determining the scope of attack; see Sect. 9.2.

8.3.1 Temporal Variables

"Limiting the time in which a weapon system can operate"[64] is viewed as one of the main ways to maintain meaningful human control over AWS.[65] The temporal dimension is often represented in two ways in literature, which we shall refer to as *Delay* and *Active Time* respectively.

---

[61] Lewis 2015, pp. 1320–1321.

[62] See e.g. Article 36 2013, p. 2; Boothby 2018b, p. 44; ICRC 2019a, p. 4; UK 2020, para 17; Group of Governmental Experts on Lethal Autonomous Weapons Systems (GGE on LAWS) 2021, para 26.

[63] Very early in 2012 and 2013, Thurnher and Schmitt already mentioned that Deployers "should limit when and where LARs are employed to avoid potential proportionality issues" and that a geographical/temporal limiter could help commanders to avoid violating the indiscriminateness rule. Thurnher 2012, p. 83; Schmitt and Thurnher 2013, p. 250. Kalmanovitz, addressing scepticism about the ability to use AWS in conformity with the proportionality rule, noted that it would require "missions narrowly defined in time and space". Kalmanovitz 2016, p. 150. The human control debate also framed them this way. See Kwik 2022, pp. 12–13. Chengeta noted that "MHC should be defined in terms of the time frame and space over which the AWS is used. The greater time and space that a particular system covers, the more it is likely that a combatant or fighter has no MHC over it." Chengeta 2016, p. 885.

[64] UNIDIR 2014, p. 5.

[65] See also ICRC 2019a, p. 4; Roorda 2015, p. 162; Schmitt and Thurnher 2013, p. 250; Boothby 2018b, p. 44.

8.3.1.1 Delay

Delay has been described as the "time between the last decision made by a human and the execution of (lethal) force by the machine"[66] or "the time between the decision and the effect".[67] A slight modification is proposed for the purposes of our discussion, replacing *decision* with *observation.* Delay is thus the *timespan between the last observation and the execution of force.*

The longer the Delay, the more difficult for Deployer to use an AWS lawfully.[68] When Deployer makes the legal decision to use a certain AWS, they do so based on presumptions related to the environment gathered from intelligence[69] (e.g. the number and status of objectives, the presence of civilian entities) and those related to the broader military operation (e.g. military necessity). However, recall that one characteristic of the military environment is its dynamicity[70]: as a result, an increase in Delay comes with a higher probability of "prior assumptions not being valid and of unintended consequences occurring".[71] If sufficient change has indeed taken place in the period between the last observation and when force is applied, judgments concerning the military nature of the objective(s) and proportionality could be no longer relevant.[72]

Delay is a relevant variable for any attack that features a time-lapse between the moment of observation and decision-making and the actual use of force. With regard to the proportionality rule more generally, Oeter mentions that "time lag" between decision-making and the effective execution of an attack increases "epistemic uncertainty", and thereby risk of error.[73] IHL has some, but limited, tolerance for making decisions in conditions of epistemic uncertainty, and prefers as little uncertainty as possible.[74] This is a distinct Rationale: let us refer to ***risk of epistemic error*** as ***Rationale-EE***.

The 'last observation' (marking the start of when Delay is counted) does not necessarily need to be *Deployer*'s observation. A pilot executing a bombing order from their commander, who decides to divert their bomb away after noticing that the military barracks turns out to be a hospital,[75] has essentially dropped Delay to zero. Maintaining manual oversight (by an Operator) with AWS fulfils the same function.[76]

---

[66] Geiß and Lahmann 2017, p. 402.

[67] Roorda 2015, p. 162.

[68] ICRC 2019a, p. 4.

[69] See Sect. 3.4.1.

[70] Section 3.4.2.

[71] Moyes 2019, p. 9.

[72] Crootof 2015, p. 1878. See also Sect. 8.5.1.

[73] Oeter 2020, p. 350.

[74] See Sects. 8.6, 9.4.3 and 9.5.1.

[75] This is also called *shift cold*: "Deliberate action taken post-separation to cause a precision munition to miss its target". Office of the Chairman of the Joint Chiefs of Staff 2020, p. 170.

[76] See Linked Control under Sects. 2.4.3 and 8.7.1.

Long Delay can potentially be compensated by low dynamicity. Against a very static environment or against targets that are valid objectives by nature (e.g. a military HQ), Deployer may feel comfortable using a longer Delay under the reasonable belief that their assumptions will not change during the time lag. Against mobile individuals or military objects by purpose or use, in contrast, a long Delay will almost never be lawful.[77]

8.3.1.2 Active Time

Active Time can be seen as a system's "duration of autonomous operation".[78] It measures how long an AWS is allowed to make independent decisions. Active Time was a dimension used by Scharre (operationalised in his work as 'time to search') to draw a spectrum between sensor fused weapons, HARM missiles and Harpies, which in his view have a progressively climbing possible Active Time of "seconds", about 5 min, and 2.5 h, respectively.[79] Active Time does not necessarily overlap with "the timespan of the operation".[80] Deployer does not need to engage an AWS's autonomous functionality immediately after release, and the AWS may be part of a broader operation that started before, and continues after, its actual usage.[81]

There are several mechanisms explaining why low Active Time increases Facility. One main reason, as mentioned in Sect. 8.2.2, is that it proportionally reduces the number of Instances where the AWS can make mistakes (***Rationale-FP**, risk of false positives*). Clearly, where there is the possibility of false positives, "multiple iterations of that process increase the risk of unintended effects being produced".[82] Active Time is intricately linked with an increased probability of error in all domains.[83] The cause of the error can simply be statistical, or due to more specific factors as discussed in Chap. 5. For example, as the system remains active for longer timespans, the probability of mechanical degradation leading to input data problems,[84] or of the system encountering an out-of-distribution situation,[85] increases. As Holland Michel notes, a system

[77] See Sect. 8.5.1.

[78] ICRC 2019a, p. 4.

[79] Scharre 2018, pp. 47–52.

[80] Roorda 2015, p. 162.

[81] Program on Humanitarian Policy and Conflict Research at Harvard University 2010. Commentary on the HPCR Manual on International Law Applicable to Air and Missile Warfare, Harvard University, Harvard (HPCR Manual Commentary), p. 28.

[82] Moyes 2019, p. 10.

[83] In engineering, higher mission times are associated with more risk of failure following the formula $R(t) = e^{-\lambda t}$. IEEE Standards Association 2016, p. 80: "Reliability is the probability of success over some specified mission time. Once the failure rate is predicted, the reliability can be predicted by using $Reliability\ (mission\ time) = e^{(-mission\ time/MTBCFi)}$". See also Sforza 2016, p. 489.

[84] See Sects. 5.2.2 and 5.5.

[85] See Sect. 5.6.

> that only targets a small slice of airspace for a limited window of time is far less likely to encounter edge cases or run through a long series of unpredictable actions than an autonomous drone that can rove across thousands of square miles in search of targets.[86]

This quote also brings us to a second Rationale associated with Active Time. As a system remains active longer, assumptions may progressively become invalid (***Rationale-EE****, risk of epistemic error*). With respect to the degradation of awareness due to the passage of time, there is no practical difference between programming an AWS to activate in $t + 1$ h, and leaving an AWS active for one hour: in either situation, one hour has passed.

We see here that Rationale-EE also has a different dimension. Until this moment, we primarily associated epistemic error with the environment, but it can also refer to epistemic error with regard to the *system*. The "series of unpredictable actions" mentioned by Holland Michel can, for example, be brought about by the system experiencing drift induced by the passage of time (as discussed in Sect. 5.5),[87] meaning that it will *categorically* make more mistakes than Deployer had predicted. If Active Time is short, drift may still occur, but its consequences will be limited and Deployer will hopefully have noticed that more errors are occurring than expected.

Reducing Active Time has been frequently proposed for AWS.[88] Ekelhof suggested "limiting the time within which the weapon system is allowed to operate without direct human control" as a way to mitigate risk.[89] As an illustration how this has been applied historically, Hague Convention VIII provides time limitations on the active life of unanchored sea mines,[90] while CCW Protocol-II sets such limitations on remotely-delivered antipersonnel mines.[91]

8.3.1.3 Additional Notes on Delay and Active Time

A few additional notes may be useful for clarity. First, Delay and Active Time may overlap. Figure 8.4 shows a timeline of a hypothetical system's employment. After an *observation* followed by the positive decision to use a system (*deployment decision*), an initial time-lapse is possible before the system is actually launched (*preparations*), and more time may pass if the system needs to travel to the target location (*travel*

86 Holland Michel 2020, p. 7.

87 See particularly Fig. 5.1.

88 ICRC 2018, para 26; Davison 2017, p. 14; Roorda 2015, p. 162.

89 Ekelhof 2016, p. 56.

90 Hague Convention (VIII) Relative to the Laying of Automatic Submarine Contact Mines, adopted 18 October 1907, entered into force 26 January 1910, 36 UST 541 (Hague Convention VIII), Article 3.

91 CCW Protocol-II, above n. 25, Article 6.3.

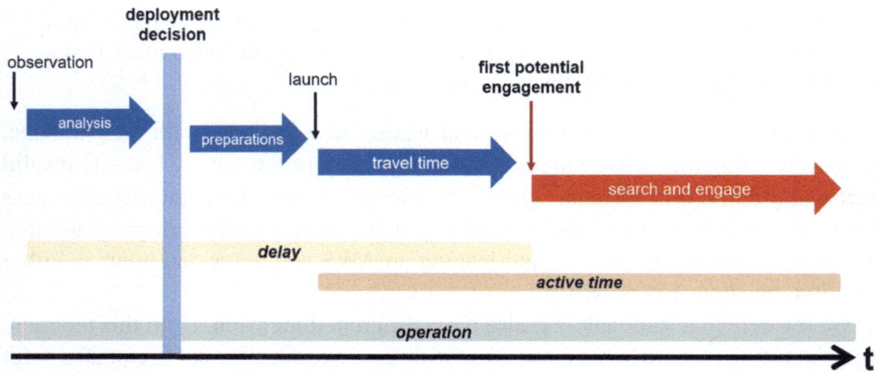

Fig. 8.4 Active time versus delay

time).[92] Once at its search location, *search and engage* commences, say for a tank platoon[93] that was previously identified in the area by Deployer.[94]

The timelapse between Deployer's initial observation and the moment force is applied would be *Delay*, while the period during which the system is programmed to operate autonomously would be *Active Time*. In the discussion that follows, Delay and Active Time are referred to together as 'Temporal variable',[95] but it is important to retain that it may be decomposed into two non-mutually exclusive concepts.

The figure also confirms the above remark that an operation is broader than either Delay or Active Time, since it also encompasses prior legal analyses and post-deployment activities (e.g. battle damage assessment).[96]

Second, this timeline better demonstrates why it was recommended to construe Delay as the period between the *last observation* and the *first potential autonomous use of force* by the AWS (instead of starting with the deployment decision, as is usually construed by authors):

- 'Last observation' would inject a crucial epistemic element which pervades the temporal element (Rationale-EE, risk of epistemic error). It is imaginable, for

[92] Whether these time-lapses do take place would depend on the system and exact circumstances of use. A Patriot system, for example, would likely already be on standby and can be activated immediately (making preparation time zero) and does not need to travel to its targets' location (making travel time zero). In contrast, a loitering munition would likely encounter some delay in both aspects.

[93] This example presumes that the tanks are sufficiently proximate in space so as to enable Deployer to group them into one objective. For the limited situations where this is possible, see Sects. 8.5.2 and 9.2.

[94] It is worth emphasising that identification and validation of targets may never be left to a system, and must be done by Deployer *prior* to ordering the system activated (i.e., before *deployment decision*). What the system does as described here is only searching for already-validated targets, not doing the legal validation 'for' Deployer. See also Sect. 1.1.

[95] E.g. Sect. 8.9.

[96] See Sect. 2.4.6.

example, that a human decides to order an AWS to strike a mobile target that was identified fifteen minutes ago. Even if the AWS is already on standby (e.g. loitering) at the location and immediately can commence search and engage upon receiving Deployer's command (meaning Delay = 0, if using the definitions from literature), the fifteen minutes since observation should be counted toward Delay. This recommendation is reflected in Fig. 8.4, where Delay is extended to the left of the *Deployment Decision* point.

- 'First potential autonomous use of force' caters for the likely scenario where an AWS encounters several civilian entities first, and only a few minutes later finally finds a valid target. Nevertheless, each of these encounters represents an Instance where force *could* have been used against civilians, which already triggers protections under IHL.[97] This recommendation is also reflected in Fig. 8.4, which notes 'first potential engagement' (instead of, for example, just 'engagement').

8.3.2 Environmental Dynamicity

The passage of time decreases epistemic certainty about both the environment and the AWS's fitness to operate within said environment. However, the *rate* at which this happens depends on how quickly the environment's properties shift, which can occur 'naturally' or due to opponent (or third party) action. In Sect. 3.4.2, this was referred to as an environment's ***dynamicity***. The more dynamic an environment, the less Facile using an AWS is,[98] for reasons of **Rationale-EE**.[99]

8.3.3 Spatial Dimension

The spatial variable has been operationalised in literature as an AWS's 'area of operation',[100] 'maximum range'[101] or 'search area'.[102] Like both Active Time and Delay, it is inversely proportional to Facility, for many similar reasons. As noted in Sect. 8.2.2, a smaller search range generally reduces the number of Instances the system can incorrectly process. Holland Michel's quote above[103] also astutely raised the spatial dimension in relation to out-of-distribution[104]: the more freedom an AWS

[97] API, above n. 27, Article 51(1); HPCR Manual Commentary, above n. 81, p. 27.

[98] See Leslie 2019, p. 32; Defense Innovation Board 2019, p. 39; ICRC 2018, para 43.

[99] In the lowest level of dynamicity, the environment can be "assumed to remain unchanged except by the performance of actions by the agent". Evidently in such situations, epistemic uncertainty is much reduced even with a higher temporal dimension. Wooldridge 2001, p. 7.

[100] Roorda 2015, p. 162.

[101] Schmitt and Thurnher 2013, p. 250.

[102] Van den Boogaard and Roorda 2021, p. 425.

[103] See Chap. 8, n. 86.

[104] See Sect. 5.6.

is given in space, the higher the probability that it will encounter an environmental makeup that it is not trained for, potentially leading to more errors (Rationale-FP) and Deployer's assumptions becoming invalid (Rationale-EE).

These rationales underpinning the spatial dimension explain some common positions in literature regarding AWS:

- First, it is frequently asserted[105] that technological pessimists should not write off AWS altogether since they can be "kept to areas where only military objectives are present [where] would be able to operate freely and without the need for detailed proportionality-based capabilities".[106] This ties into Rationale-FP: if the AWS is kept to an area where Negative Class Frequency is low or zero, their use could be rendered unproblematic because risk of false positives is low (even if one assumes poor metrics, like technological pessimists do).
- Second, it is often stated that limitations in space help predictability, which in turn allows Deployers to make the necessary legal decisions in advance,[107] which agrees with Rationale-EE.
- Finally, it explains why so-called 'defensive' systems are less controversial than offensive systems: the former are generally stationary, giving them the impression of being more 'under control'.[108] In reality, their stationary nature simply gives them less opportunities to encounter Instances (Rationale-FP), and makes them more epistemically stable to use (Rationale-EE).

8.4 Variables Related to Incidental Harm

Incidental harm or collateral damage[109] is the "incidental loss of civilian life, injury to civilians and damage to civilian objects or other protected objects or a combination thereof, caused by an attack on a lawful target".[110] The classic conception of incidental harm in an AWS context would be that of the system engaging in strikes

[105] E.g. Henderson et al. 2017, p. 351; Thurnher 2012, p. 83.

[106] Winter 2020, p. 257.

[107] Buchan and Tsagourias 2021, p. 331. Boothby argues for example: "Let us assume that the geographical areas where, and times during which, the autonomous or highly automated weapon system is permitted to operate are restricted such that the military value in attacking the targets the system is designed to engage will always comfortably exceed the incidental injury to civilians or damage to civilian objects that can be expected. In such circumstances, the proportionality evaluation that is made in advance of the sortie by human decision-makers may enable such an autonomous or highly automated sortie to be lawfully undertaken". Boothby 2018b, p. 44.

[108] Beard 2014, p. 679.

[109] We generally use 'incidental harm' to refer to all types of harm or damage (both to persons and objects) falling under this definition, although 'collateral damage' may also be used as a synonym. Cf. Gisel 2016, p. 32.

[110] Program on HPCR at Harvard University 2013, HPCR Manual on International Law Applicable to Air and Missile Warfare. Cambridge University Press, Cambridge (HPCR Manual), p. A.1.l.

on valid objectives, but which also cause harm to protected persons or objects, either in the immediate vicinity of the strike or through higher-order effects.[111]

One variable previously discussed, which is tightly correlated with incidental harm, is ***Negative Class Frequency***. By definition, variables discussed in this section only become relevant where Negative Class Frequency is *not* zero, since if it is, no incidental harm to protected entities can occur in principle. Indeed, a Negative Class Frequency of zero represents maximum Facility, and allows many legal tests such as proportionality and minimisation[112] to be skipped.[113]

Note that variables related to Rationale-EE (epistemic error) are *not* negated by zero Negative Class Frequency, since Deployer must also be certain that Negative Class Frequency will *stay* at zero.

8.4.1 Proximate Civilian Entities and Effectors

Many inputs used in current-day collateral damage estimation remain relevant for AWS use. These factors include weapon reliability and damage mechanism, target parameters (e.g. location, proximity to other protected entities, construction) and potential hazards.[114] The ***more proximate civilian entities***, the more risk overall of incidental harm being caused.

For AWS, Deployer must be careful to separately analyse the AWS itself (as a platform) and its weapons. In this regard, it may be useful to refer to the latter as *effectors*. Effectors are an AI system's "physical devices that assert physical force on the environment",[115] such as wheels or grippers.[116] In the case of AWS, its effectors are the actual munitions it uses to attack objectives, and they will vary depending on the AWS's intended type of target (counter-RAM, antitank, and antipersonnel AWS will use different types of munitions, with different damage mechanisms and different collateral potentials).

The reason that the system and its effectors must be analysed separately is that they represent two different sources of potential harm to civilians. The AWS, as established in prior sections, can cause civilian harm as a function of variables related to Rationale-FP (false positives). However, even a perfectly-functioning AI can cause unintended civilian casualties when the missile it (correctly) launches at a valid objective malfunctions and deviates, or when the missile correctly impacts the objective but also hits pedestrians in its proximity.

As mentioned, analysing the AWS's effectors and the risk of incidental harm they pose should be undertaken through procedures already in place for other strikes. For

[111] Gillard 2018, p. 35; Curtis E. Lemay Center 2019, p. 93.

[112] See Sects. 9.5 and 9.6.

[113] Infeld 1992, p. 120; Ducheine and Gill 2018, p. 6.

[114] See NATO 2021, pp. 1–28; Chairman of the Joint Chiefs of Staff 2012, p. D.

[115] Boulanin 2016, p. 13.

[116] Russell and Norvig 2010, p. 971.

example, if an AWS is used against an air defence installation in a populated area, Deployer will need to determine whether civilian entities in the target's vicinity will foreseeably be affected by the strike. In case multiple objectives will be engaged by the AWS,[117] Deployer will need to perform this evaluation for each objective. Secondary effects (e.g. secondary explosions, hazardous material escape) and risks of higher-order effects must also be considered.[118]

Heavier munitions, the number of protected entities near objectives, and other classical variables that increase the probability and extent of incidental harm decrease Facility, since Deployer might not be able to use the AWS if ***risk of incidental harm*** is too great.[119] Evidently, IHL prefers as little incidental harm to be caused as possible. This is the third and last distinct Rationale, which we will call ***Rationale-IH***.

It has been suggested that some AWS could come equipped with several types of munitions which it can select between quickly and dynamically depending on the situation,[120] in a way a human would not be able to.[121] An AWS with this functionality could for example use heavy munitions only against strongly-armoured tanks and select lighter rounds if it detects weaker plating, in an effort to keep the blast radius of each strike to a minimum.[122] This would be beneficial for Deployer, and marginally increase Facility.

8.4.2 Negative Class Detection

In Sect. 8.2.2, it was mentioned that the concept of Instances does not include entities that the AWS is unlikely to mistake for a valid target (e.g. persons, if the AWS is designed to search for tanks based on their size and heat signatures). This does not remove Deployer's obligation to consider the *collateral* risk to these entities. Depending on the circumstances, Deployer may need to take significant other efforts to ensure lawful use. This decreases Facility. Take for example:

---

117 See Sects. 8.5.2 and 9.4.2.

118 Schmitt et al. 2017, p. 303. See United Nations Office for the Coordination of Humanitarian Affairs 2017, p. 16; Gisel 2016, p. 45.

119 See Sect. 9.5.

120 Winter 2020, p. 266.

121 Because it would overburden them or, in any event, they would not be cognitively fast enough to determine during an engagement which munition to use. Kalshoven famously argued that the law cannot require soldiers to choose between more 'golf clubs' than they are realistically able to carry. Kalshoven 2007, p. 375.

122 Note that this is an advantage AWS have vis-à-vis human (infantry) soldiers only. Many manned or remote-controlled platforms such as tanks, fixed-wing and rotary-wing assets also come equipped with a range of 'golf clubs' they can dynamically choose between to reduce collateral risk depending on the situation. This AWS functionality can thus better be viewed as fixing a weakness of infantry soldiers, instead of providing a novel advantage.

Fig. 8.5 Danger of collateral damage

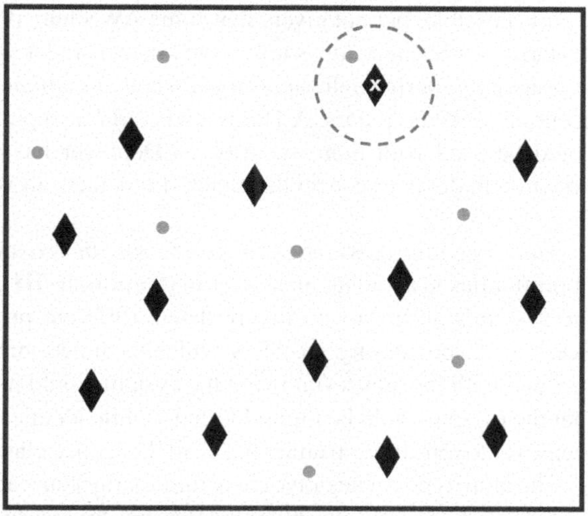

Scenario 2: Area-of-effect. Deployer plans to send an AWS to attack a group of tanks (◆) in an area with townsfolk (●) present.[123] The situation is as depicted in Fig. 8.5.

Following the recommendations from the previous subsection, Deployer dutifully analyses the range-of-effect of the AWS's munition (dashed circle), and finds that this is small enough to avoid all civilians except the person next to Tank-X. If this attack were carried out by a pilot, Deployer could order the pilot to refrain from engaging tanks such as Tank-X.[124] The pilot would destroy 12 tanks for zero incidental harm: a great result. An AWS that is purely trained to detect and engage tanks, however, cannot do this in its default state. It would simply (accurately) identify all 13 tanks and destroy them, but cause one civilian death in the process.[125] Depending on the circumstances, Deployer may find this incidental harm excessive, and be forced to avoid attacking entirely, order more expensive munitions equipped, etc.[126] We see here demonstrated that the *AWS's Facility is lower than that of the manned mission.* What is different between the pilot and AWS?

The difference is that the pilot is not only positively identifying a positive class (tanks), but also *positively identifying a different, negative class* (civilian persons). This allows the pilot to conclude that Tank-X is a valid objective, and also that incidental harm might be caused to the adjacent person. This requires a separate functionality which we shall call ***negative class detection***: the ability to recognise and identify protected entities that do not share the same signature as the entities the AWS is primarily designed to attack.

---

[123] Assume *arguendo* that the townsfolk are not mobile; e.g., they are being used by the adversary as shields.

[124] Indeed, the pilot would likely do this themselves even without Deployer's explicit command to do so.

[125] See Sect. 9.2 for when multi-Instance strikes can be considered as one attack in the legal sense.

[126] See Sect. 9.5.

It is possible, but not given, that some AWS may possess this extra functionality. A Harpy, for instance, does not: it only detects radar signals.[127] Deployer still needs to 'manually' perform the analysis of whether civilian entities will be affected by an accurate strike on radars. A Harpy that *could* also perform negative class detection could be used with more security, as Deployer has additional assurance that the system will delay or cancel the attack if it detects an *x*-number of civilian entities in the area-of-effect.

Thus, *negative class detection drastically increases Facility* because it increases opportunities to avoid incidental harm (**Rationale-IH**), and the more comprehensive the system's ability to positively detect different protected classes, the better. In Scenario 2, possessing an AWS with this functionality could allow Deployer to proceed with the attack (knowing the system would not attack Tank-X if it detected that the person would be injured/killed), while identical circumstances may have led Deployer to refrain from attacking at all if negative class detection were not available.

The more types of negative class entities a system can positively detect, the easier it is to use. For example, an antitank AWS that could also detect horse-drawn carriages, market stalls, etc., should these happen to be located in close proximity to the positive target, would be even more versatile and 'safe' to use than one which only can recognise civilian persons. As AI are also technically able to quickly integrate other forms of information that humans cannot (e.g. infrared, radio, uploaded infrastructure plans, etc.) that aid in accurately identifying negative class entities,[128] this is one way Rationale-IH may in fact one day push Deployers to prefer AWS over human-operated systems.[129]

Note that for negative class detection to be legally meaningful, the AWS needs to also be able to project the likely area-of-effect of its munitions, since it only needs to stall/cancel attacks for negative class entities that are likely to be affected by strikes.

For increased control over when a system with this functionality is allowed to proceed or not, Deployer may be able to set specific thresholds (e.g. 'Stall attack if 2+ persons likely affected by explosion').[130]

8.5 Variables Related to the Military Objectives

Characteristics of the intended objectives exert significant influence on how facile AWS are to use. This is particularly true when we consider the possibility of more independent, goal-oriented AI being developed and employed.[131] The importance

---

[127] Scharre 2014.

[128] Winter 2020, p. 267.

[129] Schmitt and Thurnher 2013, p. 262.

[130] See Sect. 8.7.3.

[131] See UNIDIR 2016, p. 8; Theunissen and Suarez 2015, p. 170; Defense Science Board 2016, p. 4.

of limiting the "type of target and task"[132] to enable lawful use of AWS has been mentioned several times in discussions.[133] In this section, we discuss two related variables: the *nature of the objective(s)* the AWS is designed to attack, and the *specificity with which Deployer defines* said objectives.

8.5.1 Type of Objective

IHL distinguishes two main categories of valid military objectives: persons and objects.[134] The former comprises "combatants and civilians directly participating in hostilities" (excluding those hors de combat),[135] while the latter is defined in API Article 52(2) as "those objects which by their nature, location, purpose or use make an effective contribution to military action and whose total or partial destruction, capture or neutralization, in the circumstances ruling at the time, offers a definite military advantage".[136] In theory, AWS can be designed to identify and attack any of these objectives. However, the facility with which Deployer could use such systems varies significantly. We can distinguish two general tiers of difficulty, on two axes. First, whether the objective is a person or object. Second, whether the objective is rendered lawful by virtue of durable or fluid characteristics.

Some military objectives are durable in the sense that their status as a valid target is relatively static and often recognisable by external, objective indicators. Highest in the Facility spectrum are *objects by nature*. These are "things used directly by armed forces" such as weapons, depots, barracks, HQs, etc.[137] They often possess uniquely military signatures (heat/radio/radar signatures, form, tonnage) that are difficult[138] to mistake for negative class entities.[139] Their Facility therefore derives from Rationale-FP: because there is little chance of signature overlap or similarity, the risk to civilian entities due to errors or misclassifications is relatively small.[140]

---

[132] UK 2020, para 17.

[133] E.g. Davison 2017, p. 14; Group of Governmental Experts on Lethal Autonomous Weapons Systems (GGE on LAWS) 2021, para 26.

[134] Holland 2004, p. 40. See also Australia 2006, Law of Armed Conflict. Defence Publishing Service, Canberra, Australian Defence Doctrine Publication 06.4 (Australian Law of Armed Conflict Manual), p. Glossary 5; Schmitt and Schauss 2019, p. 154.

[135] Fenrick 2005, p. 172.

[136] See also HPCR Manual, above n. 110, paras 22–27; Crawford 2017, pp. 58–59.

[137] Holland 2004, p. 40.

[138] This naturally depends on the situation. Iran Air 655 which was downed by the Vincennes's Aegis system in 1988 had a "course, speed, radar broadcast, and radio signal [that] all indicated that it was a commercial civilian flight", but was still mistaken for an Iranian fighter due to incorrect tuning of the Aegis to the operational environment. Grut 2013, pp. 14–15. See also US Department of Defense 1988.

[139] This is for example why the Harpy can be used with relatively little legal controversy. van den Boogaard and Roorda 2021, p. 425.

[140] Moyes conceptualised these as 'target profiles'. See generally Moyes 2019.

For many *objects by location*, their status as valid targets (particularly if entirely immobile, such as fortifications) are also somewhat durable, but these nonetheless present more challenges.[141] API Article 52(2) features a two-step test that requires an attack on objects to also impart a "definite military advantage".[142] Whether a particular location offers such an advantage is more fluid, and will depend on factors such as troop movement, broader operational goals, etc.[143]—i.e., "circumstances ruling at the time".[144]

This same complexity-by-circumstantiality applies to objects by purpose and use, but to an even greater extent.[145] *Use* renders an object a valid target on the basis of "its present function" in light of "circumstances prevailing",[146] which is highly contextual. This context cannot just be obtained through on-board sensors, but would require the system to be tied to an ISR network, and requires an AI that is trained to access and analyse the necessary information.[147] Finally, *objects by purpose* introduce a prospective element to the test: these are valid objectives by virtue of their "future intended use"[148] and "logical future possibilities".[149] Arguably, only a very advanced goal-oriented AI that is fully integrated into the ISR and operational planning networks could make such determinations.[150]

Turning now to *persons*, one factor that technically increases Facility vis-à-vis objects is that the two-step test does not exist: persons that carry military status can be targeted at any point and any time, and not just if doing so offers a definite military advantage.[151] There is no added complexity requiring the system to distinguish active and off-duty personnel, for example.[152]

---

141 Assuming Deployer intends to delegate to the AI the task of determining whether the object is a military objective by location, as otherwise, Deployer needs no AWS at all and simply needs to input the objective's coordinates into a GPS-guided munition.

142 Corn 2012, p. 448.

143 Holland 2004, p. 40.

144 API, above n. 27, Article 52(2). While this second step technically also applies to objects by nature (in the sense that attacking an abandoned munition depot thousands of kilometres away in the mountains technically does not generate a definite military advantage, for example), there is in any event little probability that Rationale-FP is breached for these objects even if the second step is not fulfilled.

145 Oeter considers nature and location to be 'static' characteristics, and purpose and use as 'dynamic' ones. Oeter 2020, pp. 345–350. Jensen, in contrast, groups location, purpose and use as "temporary" in character. Jensen 2003, p. 1156.

146 Australian Law of Armed Conflict Manual, above n. 134, para 5.29. See also Holland 2004, p. 41.

147 While this technology is not technically impossible, it will be much less common, at least in the near future. Sparrow 2016, p. 96.

148 Australian Law of Armed Conflict Manual, above n. 134, para 5.29 (emphasis added).

149 Holland 2004, p. 53.

150 We assume *arguendo* that this technology is possible at all. Cf. Tolk 2015, p. 292; Henderson et al. 2017, p. 341.

151 Blum 2017, p. 18.

152 Finkelstein 2017, p. 242.

Highest in the Facility spectrum are enemy personnel who wear regular uniforms or clearly defined markings to distinguish themselves as combatants.[153] Even in straightforward conditions against such opponents, however, a contextual exception remains in the form of combatants hors de combat.[154] In this regard, Scharre raises an interesting question regarding the ability to recognise intention, whereby an AWS must be able to recognise the "intention to surrender"[155] without being "too generous" in the face of malicious opponents seeking to abuse the gesture.[156] How to recognise genuine from perfidious signs of hors de combat clearly cannot be manually defined (human soldiers make the distinction intuitively). It is not unthinkable that this could be machine learnt,[157] but this clearly demonstrates an additional technological obstacle to what should be the 'easiest' type of persons to classify.

Recognising other persons is even more challenging.[158] DPH for example,[159] relevant in international but especially in non-international armed conflicts,[160] relies not on durable signatures such as external signs but careful nuances related to the person's conduct and behaviour.[161] It is notoriously complicated both technically and legally.[162] To allow for this functionality, the AI would need to reliably analyse "complex actions and goal-oriented activity".[163] Justly, literature has considered using AWS to identify and attack persons engaging in DPH as the most challenging.[164]

For both persons and objects, therefore, *durable* (objects by nature, members of standing armies) and *objective* (uniforms, insignia) signatures are higher in the Facility spectrum than *fluid* (objects by use or purpose, DPH) and *subjective or circumstantial* (behaviour, future usefulness) ones. The underlying reason for these trends is Rationale-FP: for the latter situations, there is more risk of error due to confusion and overlap with signatures of civilian entities. As Krupiy remarks,

---

[153] API, above n. 27, Article 44(3). Depending on the opponent's chosen markings, Deployer may also need to define the signature that distinguishes them as combatants.

[154] API, above n. 27, Article 41(1); NATO 2021, pp. 1–25.

[155] API, above n. 27, Article 41(2)(b).

[156] Scharre 2018, p. 260.

[157] This will require significant training data. How soldiers from different military cultures signal surrender may also vary.

[158] This is not meant to be an exhaustive exploration of the different ways persons can become lawful targets, and we only discuss a few examples in this section for illustrative purposes. See generally: Bothe et al. 2013, p. 342ff; Bundesministerium der Verteidigung 2013, Law of Armed Conflict Manual. Joint Service Regulation (ZDv) 15/2 (German Law of Armed Conflict Manual), paras 301–348; Parks 1990, pp. 116–146.

[159] API, above n. 27, Article 51(3).

[160] Szpak 2020, pp. 121–122.

[161] Schmitt and Schauss 2019, p. 155.

[162] See Melzer 2009; Schmitt 2010, pp. 831–837; Durhin 2016, p. 182. This even ignores other legal indeterminacies such as the time window within which a person is considered DPH, whether voluntary shields qualify as DPH, etc. Cf. Gillard 2018, p. 28; Ford 2019; HPCR Manual Commentary, above n. 81, p. 117ff.

[163] Boulanin 2016, p. 22.

[164] Asaro 2012, pp. 697–699; Margulies 2017, p. 408.

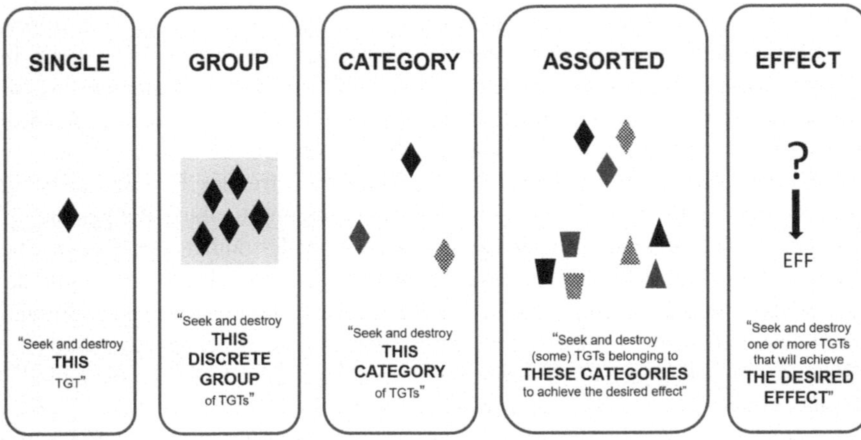

Fig. 8.6 Target specificity spectrum

> when a military objective has a distinct appearance or signature in comparison to civilian objects, technology is likely to enable attackers to accurately classify the object. The situation is different when civilian objects and military objectives share a common signature or have similar appearance.[165]

While persons are not subject to the two-step test of API Article 52(2), they are overall more difficult targets than objects because even the most straightforward situation (classifying regular combatants during international armed conflicts) requires some behaviour-based classification (the hors de combat exception). This also explains why antipersonnel AWS are much rarer (and in discourse, more controversial) than their antimatériel counterparts[166]: the former is simply a more difficult domain to lawfully apply autonomy in, due to legal rules in force.

8.5.2 Target Specificity

Target specificity refers to how granularly targets are conceived and defined by Deployer. We distinguish five levels from specific to general based on the scale in Fig. 8.6.

Single is a targeted strike. Deployer has a specific entity in mind to attack using the AWS. The entity has a unique identifier and is non-fungible. For example, Deployer orders targeted an "insurgent leader based on facial and voice recognition parameters".[167] For *Group*, Deployer's intended target is a discrete group of potential

---

[165] Krupiy 2015, p. 9.

[166] ICRC 2016, pp. 73–74; Scharre 2016a, p. 47.

[167] Toscano 2015, p. 237.

targets.[168] The unique identifier here attaches to the group, while the individual members can be interchangeable. There is a limit to how far a collection of entities qualifies as a group, hence the term 'discrete': this requires that the entities share some proximity in time in space,[169] for example, a "particular flight of enemy aircraft, a particular formation of enemy tanks, or a particular flotilla of enemy vessels".[170]

Category is less specific. Here, Deployer intends to target objectives that share a certain signature, but which are not necessarily proximate in time and space. For instance, Deployer may want to attack "a particular model of tank or aircraft" within a specific area.[171] Many systems currently in use fall into this tier. 'Defensive' systems such as C-RAM, ground-based sentries and air defence use signatures such as trajectory, form, size, etc. to determine whether entities fall within the designated threat profile.[172] The Tomahawk, in so far it was launched over-the-horizon against a presumed presence of Soviet ships (but not any particular one),[173] would also qualify. The distinguishing feature of this tier is the greater epistemic distance between Deployer and target(s). It is more impersonal. As Scharre remarks with regard to the Harpy, its user "does not know[] *which particular* radars are to be engaged, only that radars that meet the Harpy's programmed parameters will be".[174]

Assorted and *Effect* cover AWS with higher degrees of freedom and goal-orientation. In both situations, Deployer's main cognitive focus lies with the desired effect instead of the objectives themselves.[175] We briefly covered goal-oriented AWS in the previous section, but it may be useful to render the concept more concrete with a few examples. One famous autonomous goal-oriented attack[176] was Stuxnet, used in 2010 to attack an Iranian nuclear facility. The goal of the attack was to frustrate Iran's ability to enrich uranium by attacking the facility's centrifuges, but since the worm's authors could not access the facility's intranet themselves, the worm was designed to autonomously identify logic controllers linked to centrifuges, and made the latter spin too quickly and too long until they self-destructed.[177]

---

[168] This is used to define 'semiautonomous systems' under the DoD scheme. The full definition is "A weapon system that, once activated, is intended to only engage *individual targets or specific target groups that have been selected* by an operator", with Specific Target Group being defined as "A discrete group of potential targets, such as a particular flight of enemy aircraft, a particular formation of enemy tanks, or a particular flotilla of enemy vessels" (emphasis added). See US Department of Defense 2023, p. 23.

[169] See Sect. 9.2.1.

[170] Ibid.

[171] Ibid. Compared to Group, the difference lies in the fact that these entities are not part of a 'discrete group', as mentioned above.

[172] Ekelhof 2018, p. 74.

[173] See Markoff 2014.

[174] Scharre 2014.

[175] All targeting is effects-based, but the distinction here lies with how much (or indeed, little) attention is placed on the identity of the targets themselves. Cf. Curtis E. Lemay Center 2019, p. 3; US Department of the Army 2019, paras 1–76.

[176] Deeks 2021, p. 71.

[177] Buchan and Tsagourias 2021, pp. 322–323.

In the 2010 incident, the epistemic state of the worm's authors was Category: the authors knew Stuxnet would damage centrifuges, but not which specific units. However, there are many ways a nuclear facility can be made to stop: valves, safeties, scrams,[178] generators, etc. are all potential 'targets' that can achieve the same effect.[179] Given Stuxnet's sophistication and autonomous abilities,[180] one can easily envisage a worm being developed that can analyse different paths toward the ultimate goal of sabotaging a nuclear facility's functioning. Let us imagine an evolution of the 2010 worm, say *Stuxnet-2*, designed to do exactly this. What would Stuxnet-2's level of Target Specificity be? This depends on the authors' epistemic state.

For Stuxnet-2, there are two possible epistemic states the authors can have vis-à-vis the 'target'. First, the authors can be aware of the probability, but do not *know*, that Stuxnet-2 will ultimately destroy centrifuges. The centrifuges are *one* category of targets whose destruction could achieve the desired effect, *amongst others* that the authors also envisage (valves, scrams, etc.). This is *Assorted*: Deployer knows the AWS will select an entity(ies) from a closed list of categories to target,[181] but not which one(s).

In the second possible epistemic state, the list is not closed. Perhaps the authors *suspect* that centrifuges will be targeted, but do not consider what other objects might ultimately be chosen by the worm. In the most extreme situation, the authors might not even think about the centrifuges: they simply trust that the worm will find the proper object to target. This is *Effect*: Deployer is only aware of the effect to produce, not how the AWS will produce it.

As the emphasis on Deployer's mental state indicates, this variable is based on **Rationale-EE**, risk of epistemic error: as target specificity drops down the spectrum, Deployer epistemically grows more detached from the target. How exactly this makes lawful use increasingly challenging is explored in Sect. 9.4.

Note that target specificity does not prima facie imply anything about Rationale-IH and Rationale-FP. For example, even Single can be associated with a high risk of false positives (Rationale-FP) if Deployer uses non-unique characteristics to describe the insurgent leader (e.g. hair colour or ethnicity),[182] and high risk of incidental harm

---

[178] Scrams are emergency shutdown mechanisms that instantly terminate the fission reaction in nuclear facilities.

[179] Perrow 1984, p. 65; Scharre 2016a, pp. 25–28.

[180] Deeks describes Stuxnet as entailing "considerable autonomy: the cyber worm that the United States and Israel reportedly directed against Iran's nuclear centrifuges was 'an autonomous goal-oriented intelligent piece of software capable of spreading, communicating, targeting and self-updating'." Deeks 2021, p. 71.

[181] This closed list also comprising generators, scrams, etc., as noted above.

[182] Toscano's complete scenario reads as follows: "assume an X-47B aircraft is on mission to strike a targeted insurgent leader based on facial and voice recognition parameters. This scenario also assumes that the X-47B conducts a CDEM analysis inclusive of proportionality and the X-47B determines it can act autonomously. However, suppose the AWS errs by killing an innocent medical doctor, the twin brother of the targeted insurgent leader, who was visiting the area". Toscano 2015, pp. 237–238.

(Rationale-IH) if said leader currently hides in a densely-populated area. To contrast, Assorted/Effect could feature almost no risk of error or incidental harm if used against an exclusively-military environment with no dual-use interconnectivity (as was also the case with Stuxnet).[183] Lower target specificity nevertheless *generally* correlates with difficulties vis-à-vis Rationale-IH and Rationale-FP, because lower epistemic certainty makes it harder to gauge risk of incidental harm and false positives.

8.6 Opacity

A system's opacity significantly impacts the facility with which it can be employed, with fully understandable systems being the easiest to use and black boxes being the most difficult. Section 4.5.2 summarised reasons from general literature why understandability is considered an important parameter for AI systems. To rephrase these advantages in a more military-operational light, more understandability provides Deployer an improved capacity to:

- Generate a robust mental model of the system's behaviour and functioning;
- Comprehend what input factors the system uses to make decisions, and how these factors affect its decision-making;
- Predict a system's specific (instead of statistical) behaviour in light of operational variables and circumstances;
- Mitigate rate of failure by isolating the system from causes of such errors; and
- Take appropriate post-deployment action to avoid repetition of mistakes or unintended consequences.[184]

From these points alone, it is evident why from a legal perspective, the degree of understandability significantly impacts Deployer's ability to use a system in accordance with IHL rules.[185]

First, completely opaque systems prevent Deployer from exercising the due diligence required for analysing and selecting a weapon system. This includes reaching the reasonable satisfaction that the system performs sufficiently well (and will continue to perform well) in the prospective operational environment.

Second, understandability is paramount for prediction. Only by understanding the system and by having developed a robust mental model of the system's behaviour can Deployer foresee with a reasonable degree of certainty how it will behave. This is important to make reasoned projections of military advantage and incidental harm. A reasonable Deployer would likely also reject using a system where there is a (high) likelihood of failure-inducing factors being present in the environment. However,

---

183 Scharre 2018, p. 215.

184 We ignore the final benefit mentioned in that section—establishing responsibility—since this relates more to ex post accountability than operational decision-making. We discuss the ramifications of opacity with regard to responsibility (and particularly criminal liability) in Sect. 12.4.

185 For a more complete elaboration on these arguments, see Kwik and Van Engers 2021.

what these factors are cannot be known without an understanding of the model's behaviour, weaknesses, and causes of failure.

Third, the obligation to suppress and repress in IHL entails both the duty to enact preventive measures and to ensure legal responsibility for grave breaches. Both are frustrated if the systems are opaque, due to the factual 'inability to know' it imparts on the user and difficulties in determining causality. In practice, opacity might induce a military organisation to mis-blame, which does not serve IHL: the cause of the violation is not addressed, meaning that new violations can still occur in the future, and a person might potentially be held responsible for a violation they could not have foreseen or prevented.

These reasons clearly identify this variable as related to **Rationale-EE**: lower understandability increases the risk of Deployer (and indeed, post-hoc investigators) making epistemic errors with regard to a system's predicted behaviour, the entities that will be affected, expected incidental harm and anticipated military advantage. A pure black box is arguably impossible to use in accordance with IHL for these reasons, since its opacity would prevent meaningful legal analyses to be conducted in the first place.

High opacity makes AWS difficult to use lawfully due to these two rules in particular, which we discuss in greater depth in the following chapter:

- *Indiscriminate attack*: If Deployer cannot predict with a sufficiently high degree of certainty which entities will be attacked by the AWS because the logic with which it identifies objectives is obscured, Deployer is effectively launching an 'unaimed' attack, which is unlawful.[186]
- *Proportionality*: Deployer cannot conduct proportionality assessments as required by IHL if the system's opacity prevents Deployer from predicting to a reasonably accurate extent what incidental harm will be caused.[187]

8.7 Context Controls

Throughout this chapter, we have described and analysed the different variables as static givens: information that Deployer must consider, but cannot alter. In reality, Deployer can exercise various levels of influence over both their AWS and the environment, and impact Facility accordingly. In the MHC Framework, these are referred to as *Context Controls*.[188]

In this section, we briefly explore various Context Controls as they appear in literature, and associate them with the theories that were developed in this chapter. In particular, we draw connections with the Rationales (IH, FP and EE), since these allow us to understand why these measures would make AWS easier (or harder) to use lawfully.

[186] See Sect. 9.4.3.

[187] See Sect. 9.5.1.

[188] See Sect. 2.4.3.

8.7.1 In the MHC Framework

The MHC Framework features three general categories of Context Controls.[189] *System Controls* involve making changes to an AWS's internal settings and parameters, or programming specific commands or limitations. System Controls are a relatively new toolbox available to commanders. Compared to older systems[190] and even cyber,[191] AWS carry the potential to allow Deployers to make impactful programming adjustments in the field.[192] Depending on how expansive the human-machine interface is and how much freedom is accorded to Deployer to change specific settings,[193] Deployer could modify a significant number of parameters just before launch.

Operational Controls do not manipulate the system's settings themselves, but *how* the system is used and the *environment* it is used in. In literature, Operational Controls are mentioned frequently as precautionary measures commanders should consider, and are almost universally proposed in terms of restrictions in time and space.[194] We encountered the spatial and temporal variables before in this chapter, but we will also consider other Operational Controls that are less common, such as environmental manipulation.

Finally, *Linked Control* involves assigning a human[195] who supervises, vets or vetoes an AWS's decisions. In popular language, the term 'human-in-the-loop' or 'human-on-the-loop' is often used.[196] In more technical terms, Boothby described this as the *maintenance of a downlink and uplink*, whereby the downlink "conveys … data from on-board sensors to the operator who is monitoring the platform's activities" while the uplink "communicates *inter alia* instructions to the platform".[197] Compared to the other Context Controls discussed in this section, Linked Control is relatively straightforward since it corresponds with much of existing practice related

---

[189] See Fig. 7.1.

[190] While some kinetic weapons could also be modified in the field to a certain extent (e.g. by shortening or extending a bomb's fuse), commanders would in most cases not have much freedom to alter how a weapon system functions once it is in their possession, and would have to compensate for this rigidity through other precautionary techniques (such as altering their time of attack). See Thurnher 2018, p. 114; Quéguiner 2006, p. 800.

[191] The cyber domain introduced some flexibility, as the functioning of cyberweapons could more readily be adapted to a commander's preferences. A cyber capability could relatively easily be programmed to disable a dual-use system for a shorter timeframe than normal, for instance, by simply changing a value in the code. Schmitt and Schauss 2019, p. 181. Nevertheless, many cyber capabilities "tend to be purpose-built for particular operations" and the possibility to freely adapt their functioning may be limited. Väljataga and Liivoja 2021, p. 7.

[192] Roorda 2015, p. 162.

[193] See DARPA 2016, p. 6; Saariluoma 2015, pp. 232–240.

[194] See e.g. Article 36 2013, p. 2; Boothby 2018b, p. 44; ICRC 2019a, p. 4; UK 2020, para 17; Group of Governmental Experts on Lethal Autonomous Weapons Systems (GGE on LAWS) 2021, para 26.

[195] This person was designated as 'Operator' in Sect. 1.3.2.

[196] Human Rights Watch 2012, p. 2. These terms have been criticised for being too reductive, which is why they are not used in this book. Geiß 2015, p. 7.

[197] Boothby 2018a, p. 137.

to remote-controlled unmanned vehicles and robotics.[198] We will therefore not dedicate too much time describing the measure beyond emphasising the following two points:

1. The 'human' mentioned above can be Deployer themselves, or a subordinate (previously referred to as *Operator*[199]). The latter construction does not diminish Deployer's responsibility for the AWS's actions and any incidents that follow,[200] but does introduce a new natural person to the hierarchical chain who is responsible for their own actions. In cases of serious violations involving the AWS, liability would primarily fall on the Operator as they were directly in control[201] of the system; Deployer would only be criminally responsible if personal dereliction on their part can be determined.[202]
2. Linked Control is easy to implement incorrectly by making the human's role in the decision-making process biased, subordinate to the algorithm, or functionally non-existent. Because there are opportunity costs related to Linked Control, incorrectly implementing it is worse than not doing so at all. Section 8.8 provides additional guidelines that should be taken into consideration when Deployers opt to enable Linked Control.

What follows is an overview of Context Controls as proposed in literature. The list is illustrative, not exhaustive: the aim is to show the broad range of options Deployer might have available to improve their confidence that their AWS can be used in accordance with IHL.

Deployer's ability to implement Context Controls depends on design (whether an interface is made available to modify settings)[203] and operational conditions (e.g., an evacuation order requires some access to the civilian population). Deployer is expected to explore all Context Controls that may be available and make appropriate judgments on the consequences and (operational and legal) desirability of use, supported by our upcoming discussion in Chaps. 9 and 10.

8.7.2 Reducing False Positives

The following Context Controls can be employed to suppress the risk of AI mistakes leading to unintended death, injury or damage to civilian entities (**Rationale-FP**).

---

198 See generally Gross 2016, pp. 15–17; Defense Science Board 2012, pp. 15–20.

199 See Sect. 1.3.2.

200 Sandoz et al. 1987, para 3540.

201 In practice, this is not always guaranteed. See Sect. 8.7.6. We leave aside the question of whether this lack of de facto control, if proven, could provide some form of criminal defence for the Operator.

202 ICTY (TC), *Prosecutor v Zejnil Delalić, Zdravko Mucić, Hazim Delić, Esad Landžo ('Čelebići')*, Judgment, 16 November 1998, IT-96-21-T, para 334.

203 As Deployer generally cannot change a system's design on the battlefield, this responsibility falls on the Providing Entity. See Sect. 1.3.3.

8.7.2.1 Minimum Confidence Levels

While an AWS may make determinations of whether a particular entity is military or civilian, not all these determinations are made with the same degree of statistical certainty. One way to reduce false positives is to require a higher level of confidence before it may engage (e.g. > 80% instead of merely > 50%).[204] This solution is quite common in civil domains, where an AI's low base performance is sometimes compensated by setting high certainty thresholds. As Lohn remarks, commands such as *cede to operator if confidence < x%* "in effect allows systems with low [reliability] to be used because Controllability is high."[205] Note that Deployer has freedom in determining what the AWS's reaction should be if this certainty threshold is not reached. In Lohn's example, the AWS would send a signal to an Operator to take over for the system. However, this is not always possible, e.g. in comms-denied environments.[206] In such a case, Deployer must set a default output, which in most situations would simply be not to fire.

This Context Control can be partially effective, but Deployer and their staff should be cautious when determining its effectiveness to reduce errors. As noted in Sect. 5. 6, much like humans, AI can be very confident but exceptionally wrong at the same time. Setting a high threshold would reduce a certain set of false positives near the middle of the certainty spectrum, but would not prevent failures caused by datashift or OOD, which are often accompanied by high certainty. One solution is to install an OOD detection function, a relatively new technology that allows an AI to deduce if an input is OOD. It is specifically mentioned in literature as a risk treatment tool.[207] With this functionality, Deployer can request the AWS to fall back to a default output (e.g. 'do not engage', 'return to base') if OOD is detected.[208]

One comment made by Toscano related to this Context Control is that "[t]o the extent that an AWS could not identify or distinguish noncombatants on a particular mission, the AWS programming could have a preset default to count those persons as civilians".[209] This is a correct observation but worded too softly. When an AWS encounters entities it is not convinced of as being military, it *must* default to classifying those entities as civilian. IHL uses a 'negative' definition for civilians,[210] and everyone who is not a combatant is a civilian. IHL also provides that in case of doubt of whether an entity is of civilian nature, it must be considered thusly.[211] This should arguably not form part of Context Controls, but be a *required setting* for all AWS, i.e., as a matter of base design.

---

[204] Schuller 2019, pp. 114–115.

[205] Lohn 2020, p. 6.

[206] See Sect. 10.3.1.

[207] Lohn 2020, p. 6.

[208] See also Amodei et al. 2016, pp. 18–19.

[209] Toscano 2015, pp. 211–212.

[210] API, above n. 27, Article 50; Israel High Court of Justice, *Public Committee against Torture in Israel v. Israel* (Judgment) HCJ 769/02, 46 ILM 375 (11 December 2005), para 26.

[211] API, above n. 27, Article 50(1) (for persons); Article 52(3) (for objects).

8.7.2.2 Hard Failsafes

Following the same rationale as the auto-OOD detection functionality mentioned above, some specific failsafes or 'hard-wired responses'[212] can be introduced to further reduce the risk of incorrect outputs. One effective failsafe could be for Deployer to set conditions where the AWS is simply barred from making engagement decisions at all. Schuller proposed that such a rule could be triggered by a particular environmental profile. For an underwater AWS, he suggested "hard rules in place to stop the attack, for example if the enemy submarine was in a harbor or in close proximity to an unidentified vessel",[213] while for an aerial AWS, a restriction could be placed where it cannot vector its munition toward populated areas (this does not necessarily require the AWS to have sensors that are able to detect and identify these areas, since they can simply be defined beforehand by Deployer using GPS coordinates).[214]

For a more permanent failsafe, force quit conditions can be employed to automatically let the system abort its mission, suspend operations, or self-destruct.[215] Some of these conditions would for example be: damage or destruction to some sensors or subsystems (as damage to these components are likely to increase the risk of incorrect outputs), or no target being found in a specific area or after a specific time-frame.[216] For more safety, Deployer can also order the AWS to do this in the case of any abnormality, e.g. if it "confronts an event that fails to satisfy programmed restraint parameters, rules of engagement, or LOAC considerations such as distinction of protected persons".[217]

Another 'abnormality' that Deployer may consider as an abort condition is simply a change in its operational environment. Boothby suggests that

> a somewhat more basic autonomous technology might be programmed to detect whether there has been any material change in the circumstances pertaining in the area of search compared to that suggested by the pattern of life data that was fed into the mission control software in advance of the mission; in that event, the autonomous search for targets would, and should, be called off.[218]

Boothby humbly refers to this as a 'basic' precaution, but it is a very powerful control that Deployers would want to implement whenever the functionality is present. The reason this measure is so useful is identical to why almost all Operational Controls are implemented: it provides strong guarantees that assumptions made by Deployer during release remain valid at the moment the AWS makes engagement decisions (i.e., Rationale-EE).

---

[212] Kastan 2013, p. 59.

[213] Schuller 2019, p. 115.

[214] Schuller 2017, p. 391.

[215] For the legal context, see also Sect. 9.8.

[216] Boothby 2018a, pp. 150–151; Kastan 2013, p. 59.

[217] Toscano 2015, p. 212.

[218] Boothby 2018a, p. 151.

8.7.2.3 Shoot Last

Shoot last (sometimes also referred to as 'shoot second'[219]) is a popular proposal in AWS literature and sometimes adduced to demonstrate that AWS can be a superior choice to human soldiers in combat engagements. In its strictest sense, it involves requiring an AWS to engage an entity only when the enemy has attacked 'first'.[220] The reduction in risk from such a Context Control is obvious: it greatly reduces the likelihood of a misclassification, even in scenarios of irregular warfare where classifiers are expected to struggle the most,[221] by waiting for 'positive identification' of hostile intent by the enemy. It is an order that is unreasonable to demand of human soldiers but could very well be used effectively with AWS in many scenarios,[222] such as protecting a peacekeeping force or a friendly convoy in an occupied area where some enemy remnants may still reside.[223] Note that this Context Control is potentially crippling in offensive operations since opponents could very easily game the system by never using their weapons at all.

8.7.2.4 Anti-target Profiles

Signatures are usually defined for the positive class (i.e. the intended target(s)), but these signatures can also be defined negatively. Moyes in this respect introduced the concept of an 'anti-target profile' to "identify things that mean that force should not be applied in a particular situation".[224] Inputting these anti-target profiles to AWS would likely become common practice as a natural extension of restricted and no-strike lists: these are lists of entities the joint force accords specific protection to, and often include targets such as critical infrastructure, POW camps, and—indeed—sensitive objects such as dams.[225] Using such negative profiles, Deployer can greatly reduce risk of error simply by removing some possible incorrect outputs.

8.7.3 Reducing Risk of Incidental Harm

The following Context Controls can be made to suppress the risk of correct AI outputs causing incidental harm (**Rationale-IH**).

219 Scharre 2018, p. 328.
220 Sassòli 2014, p. 335.
221 Thurnher 2012, p. 80.
222 Kurosaki 2020, pp. 428–429.
223 Scharre 2018, p. 328.
224 Moyes 2019, p. 8.
225 NATO 2021, pp. 1–8, 1–9.

8.7.3.1 Setting Maximum Incidental Harm Limits

This type of Context Control involves Deployer setting an upper limit on how much incidental harm an AWS may cause per Instance[226] (i.e., each time it makes an engagement decision).[227] As an example, if the operational environment has a relatively low density of civilians (say a town whose civilian population has largely evacuated), Deployer may still be concerned that an occasional group of civilians may be gathered near a military target an AWS plans to engage. Using this Context Control, Deployer could determine that the AWS may not fire if more than one civilian is identified within a certain area around the target.[228] With this setting, if Deployer believes that around ten objectives are present, they also know that the absolute maximum number of civilian casualties from collateral damage will also be ten (and most likely be much lower).

As one can imagine, this type of Context Control provides a great degree of certainty concerning incidental harm, when the prediction range might otherwise be quite large. This added predictive accuracy can be beneficial for proportionality calculations.[229] Say Deployer assesses that the military advantage of the attack would not justify more than two civilian deaths. Without this Context Control, there is a reasonable chance (even though not a certainty) that this limit would be surpassed, and it might be illegal to deploy the weapon. With this measure, however, there is a negligible (practically zero) chance of this occurring.

The rationale underlying this Context Control is not new in any sense. In traditional military hierarchies, superior commanders also frequently set maximum acceptable civilian casualty numbers.[230] With this limit in force, subordinates may only approve an attack if the expected incidental harm is lower than the set maximum.[231] The reason superiors do this is to overcome the inherent uncertainty associated with delegating use of force decisions to component commanders, and concerns that proportionality benchmarks may be exceeded as a result.[232] Without intending to anthropomorphise, then, this is exactly analogous to how and why Deployers would impose maximum incidental harm values to their AWS: imposing a maximum threshold reduces uncertainty (Rationale-EE).

---

[226] See Sect. 8.2.1.

[227] Henderson et al. 2017, p. 352 (suggesting that a commander could "pre-determine the upper limit for civilian casualties and various types of property damage prior to authorising the AWS mission").

[228] Thurnher and Kalmanovitz have described a similar Context Control but framed slightly differently, as setting "threshold values" for what constitutes excessive incidental harm. Kalmanovitz 2016, p. 150. Thurnher argued that Deployer could "pre-determine what constitutes excessive collateral damage for a particular target". Thurnher 2014, p. 222. In essence, Deployer pre-sets how much incidental harm is acceptable for each engagement.

[229] Thurnher and Kalmanovitz presented these Context Controls as a response to scepticism that AWS could ever be used in compliance with the proportionality rule.

[230] See e.g. NATO 2021, pp. 1–29.

[231] Kastan 2013, p. 57.

[232] Corn 2015, p. 461.

A more extreme Context Control still would be to set a maximum incidental harm value of 0: i.e., an AWS may never engage if there is a possibility that a civilian will be affected by the blast radius. Boddens Hosang suggested a further failsafe involving the AWS shutting itself down automatically if any civilians are identified in the system's area of operations.[233] While setting a maximum incidental harm value of zero is certainly the optimal way to reduce risk caused by correct outputs, one must realise that this is likely to cripple the AWS's effectiveness in many situations where the enemy and civilians are spatially close. Whether Deployer must activate this setting is thus a question of feasibility.

8.7.3.2 Dynamic Munition Selection and Munition Bans

It is likely that some AWS will be large enough to be equipped with more than one type of arm or munition, and thus could be programmed to select the weapon best suited for the engagement situation. The notion of soldiers having to carry multiple weapons and having to choose the most 'discriminate one' in the middle of a firefight has been mocked as impracticable, with Kalshoven quipping that a soldier "simply cannot be equipped with a wide array of weapons for all kinds of situations, as the golf player is with his bag of golf clubs".[234] However, carrying golf clubs likely is within the realm of possibility for AWS, as they will be fast enough to make the calculations even in the heat of battle and not face problems of over-encumbrance. Indeed, this type of micro-weaponeering has been mentioned as one example of how AWS can improve the precautions available to a commander.[235] Thus for instance, an AWS may be commanded to use its missiles only against soldiers inside structures, while it must use its machine gun instead if the enemies are located in the open.

Schuller also suggested a negative variation to this Context Control, where Deployer instead *restricts* which munition an AWS may use under specific circumstances. In Schuller's hypothetical, Deployer releases an assassin AWS that is programmed to loiter if it cannot find the target terrorist leader immediately. Schuller argues therefore that as the AWS loiters for extended periods of time, "[w]e would have concerns … over collateral damage. We may instead require it to employ extremely-low-collateral-damage weapons such as a high velocity non-explosive bolt".[236]

8.7.3.3 AWS-Issued Warnings

The AWS could be programmed to issue a warning after identifying, but shortly before engaging, an objective, in order to enable proximate civilian entities to remove

[233] Boddens Hosang 2021, p. 405.
[234] Kalshoven 2007, p. 375.
[235] Winter 2020, p. 266. This is however not an advantage exclusive to AWS. See Sect. 10.3.
[236] Schuller 2017, p. 424.

themselves from the area. This is distinct from Deployer-issued warnings: we discuss some intricacies related to this proposal in Sect. 9.7.1.

8.7.4 Selecting Systems with Higher Levels of Understandability

While we argued previously that a system's degree of understandability is out of Deployer's control,[237] Deployer can still exert some influence at the operational level with regard to the choice of weapon. For example, Deployer may have an opaque system available that they only minimally understand, and a system whose behaviour they largely grasp because it was designed to be inherently transparent.[238] Choosing to employ the more understandable system is an effective way Deployer can suppress the probability of epistemic errors (Rationale-EE).[239]

8.7.5 Multifactorial Controls

These measures are particularly effective Context Controls since they address multiple Rationales at once.

8.7.5.1 Reducing the Temporal Variable

This flows naturally from our discussion in Sect. 8.3.1. Reducing the temporal timespan reduces the Instances the AWS has to process. This reduces both the risk of errors (Rationale-FP) and Deployer's epistemic distance vis-à-vis the conditions in which force is used (Rationale-EE).

---

[237] For a large part, understandability must be incorporated into a system in advance (e.g. through XAI solutions) and cannot be requested by Deployer ad hoc; Deployer can only work with the level of understandability they are given. See Sect. 4.5.1.

[238] Such dilemmas are very common in other task domains. See e.g. Williams 2017; Barredo Arrieta et al. 2020, p. 83. The problem has also been raised in the military domain. DARPA for example notes the tensions between "the learning performance (e.g., predictive accuracy) of the model to accomplish the target tasks and the effectiveness of the explanations in helping the user understand and manage the AI system". DARPA 2016, p. 12.

[239] Debate is still ongoing as to whether there is a 'bottom line' with regard to how opaque a system may be before it becomes unlawful under IHL. Our discussion in Sect. 4.5.2 certainly suggests this minimum requirement, although the exact boundary is more difficult to pinpoint. See also Kwik and Van Engers 2021. Some authors have proposed analysing the minimum amount of understandability required for weapon systems from a multidimensional perspective by taking into consideration the potential harm caused by epistemic mistakes, environmental conditions, etc. See e.g. Holland Michel 2020, p. 17.

8.7.5.2 Spatial Control: Playing to the System's Strengths

An AWS's reliability can be improved further by assigning it to an environment or context in which it excels, and by avoiding situations where it performs less well. This can be done through spatial control. Just as Deployer can restrict an AWS's Active Time,[240] so can Deployer restrict an AWS's range of movement. This variably is operationalised as its 'area of operation',[241] 'maximum range'[242] or 'search area',[243] but essentially involves Deployer limiting an AWS's interaction with the environment only to a spatial area where its performance would be optimal.

Spatial control is one way how AWS with zero Specificity can be used lawfully,[244] and how goal-oriented AWS can still be made to act predictably. For the former, an AWS with no distinction functionality at all can still be used discriminately by "by limiting an AWS's operating parameters to areas in which it has been assessed that any people present are lawful targets by virtue of either being combatants … or civilians taking a direct part in hostilities".[245]

Spatial control can be implemented in a number of ways. One is simply inputting a set of coordinates that the AWS can identify using GPS, and which it may not cross. This would be one method to respect the IOE restrictions.[246] If the Providing Entity defines an AWS's IOE as urban battlefields, for instance, Deployer can set coordinates corresponding to the city's urban area, thus preventing the risk of lower performance or OOD were the AWS to wander to surrounding farmland. Drawing inspiration from autonomous crop harvesters, Anderson also proposed geographical kill switches which automatically turn the harvester robot off if a predetermined perimeter is breached.[247] More generally, Deployers can opt to prohibit an AWS's access to locations that are likely to drop performance, e.g. overly cluttered, chaotic or adversarial-heavy areas.[248]

As an extrapolation, a general guideline can be adopted that a higher degree of spatial mobility increases risk of incidental harm, and that Deployer should therefore opt for a lower spatial setting if possible.[249] The Samsung SGR-A1, for instance, is a contemporary antipersonnel AWS that does not attract much criticism because of its static nature. Schuller argued that it would be much more controversial, and its compliance to IHL much more dubious, "if the system was modified such that it could roam the countryside, but was not granted more sophisticated sensor and/or

---

[240] See Sect. 8.3.1.

[241] Roorda 2015, p. 162.

[242] Schmitt and Thurnher 2013, p. 250.

[243] Van den Boogaard and Roorda 2021, p. 425.

[244] Winter 2020, p. 257.

[245] Henderson et al. 2017, p. 351.

[246] See Sects. 3.5 and 9.3.2.

[247] Anderson and Matsumura 2015, p. 142. The effectiveness of this Context Control must be weighed accordingly against its risks, e.g. of the disabled AWS being captured by enemies.

[248] Roorda 2015, p. 162; UNIDIR 2014, p. 5.

[249] See also Scharre 2018, pp. 47–48.

computational capabilities or limited by additional parameters".[250] Note however that this is not *necessarily* so in all cases. In the case of an anti-submarine AWS in an ocean sector far removed from civilian sea lanes, there is only a negligible difference in risk if set to roam a space of 1 km^3 versus 100 km^3, but a significant difference in their military viability (the former being practically useless).[251]

That time and space are significant multifactorial Context Controls explains why they are the most prominent measures recommended in literature to control AWS.[252]

8.7.5.3 Environmental Manipulation

Battlefields are complex and dynamic environments which change, both over time and abruptly.[253] Mutations in the environment can cause problems because, for instance:

- The frequency of instances increases (e.g. higher density of both civilians and military entities in the daytime compared to midnight, when the AWS was launched);
- Population distribution may change (e.g. a group of refugees arrives in the town);
- Environmental properties may change (e.g. snow may fall, in which the AWS is known to perform slightly worse).

Environmental manipulation[254] counters some of these negative effects by affecting the environment in the AWS's favour. This Context Control is only occasionally mentioned in the AWS debate. The ICRC advocated for enacting "physical controls over the environment"[255] and "manipulating operational parameters like the environment in which the weapon system is to operate"[256] to improve the likelihood of IHL-compliant use of AWS, while another scholar proposed "structuring [an AWS's] operational environment to keep out factors that may impact its performance".[257]

Environmental manipulations also provide additional benefit in that it makes the AWS's "operation more deterministic and predictable".[258] As Amoroso argues,

[250] Schuller 2017, note 81.

[251] This is a colloquial description of the AWS's Facility and Benefit respectively within the methodology of Chap. 10.

[252] Cf. Group of Governmental Experts on Lethal Autonomous Weapons Systems (GGE on LAWS) 2021, para 26; Moyes 2019, p. 9; Boothby 2018b, p. 44; Chengeta 2016, p. 885; Schmitt and Thurnher 2013, p. 250.

[253] Section 3.4.2.

[254] This is not to be confused with environmental *modification*.

[255] Davison 2017, p. 14.

[256] ICRC 2019a, p. 4.

[257] Amoroso 2020, p. 126.

[258] Buchan and Tsagourias 2021, p. 331.

> an effective way to prevent the machine from acting unpredictably is to structure its operational environment so as to keep out all those factors that are likely to put the machine's perceptual, cognitive and behavioural capabilities under stress, with the first factor among these being the presence of humans.[259]

Uncertainty increases as the "amount of time between the last decision made by a human and the execution of (lethal) force by the machine" also increases.[260] The longer this gap, the

> more chance there is of prior assumptions not being valid and of unintended consequences occurring. Controlling the space, duration and time of any such process are effectively mechanisms to allow humans to have adequate information about the context that these parameters enclose.[261]

Environmental manipulations, particularly those which help Deployer freeze the operational context in a specific state (preferably one that allows optimum performance of the AWS), can therefore potentially compensate for the added risk of longer active times.

In this respect, *movement restrictions* are one of the oldest ways commanders have done so. During targeting, one common measure to improve the likelihood that the effects of an attack remain within applicable legal or operational limits is "imposing measures that prevent changes to the current situation (e.g., establishing a perimeter)".[262] Practice related to landmines provides a strong example of how this reduces risk of incidental harm. As was also mentioned in the body of this book, antipersonnel landmines are a good analogue of a weapon with a Specificity of zero, i.e., any person it 'encounters' is engaged without reservation. A few of the required "[precautionary] measures to protect civilians" related to non-self-deactivating landmines include fencing, signs, warning and monitoring.[263] These measures all serve to impose movement restrictions on the negative class, i.e., civilians. Indeed, the CCW Protocol on landmines tells us they are meant to "ensure the effective exclusion of civilians from the area".[264] In civil domains, factories often segregate their human workers from industrial robots for a similar rationale.[265]

---

[259] Amoroso 2020, p. 126.

[260] Geiß and Lahmann 2017, p. 402.

[261] Moyes 2019, p. 9.

[262] Roorda 2015, p. 162.

[263] CCW Protocol-II, above n. 25, Article 10(b). As was also mentioned in Sect. 10.4, this is a good example of one Context Control compensating for the absence of another. This provision applies to landmines which cannot self-deactivate, i.e., these are technically weapons with a Specificity of 0 and an active time of ∞. They can nevertheless be used in accordance with IHL thanks to strict exclusionary measures. See van den Boogaard and Roorda 2021, p. 433 ("When in doubt of whether the use of a particular weapon will comply with IHL, additional measures may be taken to adjust the context, the functioning of a system, or a combination thereof. Such options depend on the capacity to shape the operating environment; and the capacity to formulate and implement rules by which the system will operate.").

[264] CCW Protocol-II, above n. 25, Article 5(2)(a).

[265] Amoroso 2020, p. 126.

The parallel for AWS, then, would be "an exclusion of those who are at risk of being mistakenly targeted from the area in which those processes are operating".[266] The UK also considered controlling "the environment to exclude civilians or civilian objects" as a way to allow IHL-compliant AWS use.[267] The UK's statement is too broad, however, and the first formulation is better attuned to AWS characteristics. Unlike landmines, it is not necessarily required that the combat environment be voided of civilians altogether (a demand that would likely be impossible to achieve[268]): it merely requires that *members of the negative class* (i.e., those we do not wish the AWS mistakenly engages) are excluded,[269] either entirely or to the maximum possible extent.

The restriction would probably also only need to be directed at the type of entity that is likely to be the victim of an incorrect output. For example, for an AWS designed to locate and destroy enemy tanks, Deployer may want to prohibit civilian vehicles from entering the area of operations—or, if Deployer is confident in their understanding of the AI, perhaps specifically vehicles of a size similar to the target tanks (since Deployer knows that the AWS relies on a heat signature in combination with a specific size profile to determine which entities to engage).[270] In contrast, excluding civilian persons may not have much impact on incidental harm since the likelihood is quite small that the AWS would misclassify a person as a tank. Similarly, when an AWS is used that defends an area against enemy aircraft, it makes sense that "risks can be mitigated by … closing certain areas of local airspace or terrain to civilian aircraft and vehicles", but not by closing the area to civilian cyclists.[271]

The availability of this type of Context Control is very context-dependent. In areas under friendly control or occupation, prohibiting civilians or certain vehicles from entering specified areas is easier than in contested or enemy-controlled areas.

8.7.5.4 Deployer-Issued Warnings

A special form of environmental manipulation, particularly for areas not under friendly control. These are discussed in depth in Sect. 9.7. Note these are distinct from the 'AWS-issued warnings' mentioned previously in Sect. 8.7.3.3. Unlike the latter, these warnings are issued by Deployer before the AWS attack commences (instead of automatically by the system once the attack is underway).

---

266 Moyes 2019, p. 10.

267 UK 2020, para 17.

268 Amoroso 2020, p. 126.

269 See Sect. 8.2.2.

270 This requires a high degree of understanding. See Sects. 4.5 and 8.6.

271 Boddens Hosang 2021, p. 405.

8.8 Linked Control: Do It Right

Irrespective of the legal and operational circumstances that leads Deployer to implement Linked Control,[272] it is important that *should* one choose to maintain it, it be *implemented correctly.* Because the Operator is actively involved in the AWS's operation and decision-making, an AWS with Linked Control enabled can functionally be viewed as a human-machine team.[273] There are dangers with this configuration. History has revealed[274] many human-machine interaction pitfalls which lead the humans in such teams to experience bias or degraded influence, and in the most extreme cases become little more than a rubber stamp.[275] It is important to avoid this, since maintaining Linked Control involves opportunity costs.[276] Applying Linked Control poorly is worse than not applying it at all, since important benefits are sacrificed for no additional de facto human control.

Proper implementation of Linked Control would need to include the following.

8.8.1 Proper Interface

As the Operator is spatially removed from the AWS's operational environment (not unlike a drone operator), the effectiveness of Linked Control depends on proper coordination between the system and its Operator. In this respect, the "human-machine interface is crucial to AWS' compliance with IHL".[277] The uplink is the Operator's only way to impact the system's actions and to perform risk treatment functions such as aborting, correcting or diverting the AWS, but the downlink is equally important. To make proper decisions in their function as a supervisor, the spatially-removed Operator must receive adequate information of the AWS's surroundings,[278] of the state of the system,[279] of compromising situations (e.g. adversarials),[280] and be able to interrogate the system for more information if necessary.[281] For both directions of communication, a proper interface is crucial: it needs to both "let users give commands to the artefacts and to inform them about the state of the artefact".[282]

[272] See Sect. 8.7.1.

[273] See Scharre 2018, p. 321; Parakilas and Bryce 2018.

[274] See UNIDIR 2016, pp. 14–15.

[275] Thorne 2020, p. 26.

[276] See *inter alia* the situations mentioned in Sect. 10.3.1.

[277] Margulies 2017, p. 432.

[278] Boothby 2018a, p. 137.

[279] iPRAW 2020, p. 1.

[280] Boothby 2021, p. 386.

[281] Roff and Moyes 2016, p. 2.

[282] Saariluoma 2015, p. 235.

Much has been studied in literature on effective uplink interface design that allows humans to pass commands quickly and accurately.[283] Downlink interface design, however, will be particularly crucial. Merely being informed that the AWS made the decision to engage a specific entity, for instance, is of little value. This communication needs to be accompanied by information that allows the Operator to verify whether the proposed decision is correct.[284] This may be raw sensory data (e.g. a camera feed) or some form of processed data which still allows the Operator to make their own judgments.

Saarilouma extensively discussed the ideal elements that an AWS interface should communicate to an Operator,[285] but the main design ideal is one that provides the necessary information for an Operator to make an *independent* decision[286] without overloading their cognitive ability to process it.[287] Extreme care must thus be taken at the design phase to avoid known pitfalls related to the supervision of AI systems, such as loss of system understanding or loss of situational awareness.[288] Without careful interface design consideration, the Operator will have insufficient information to make a reasoned decision, and Linked Control risks becoming a placebo.[289]

8.8.2 *Sufficient Delay*

Proper implementation of Linked Control requires slowing down the decision-making process to a human pace.[290] This applies to all aspects of the human-machine team. Information display, for instance, must remain at 'human speed'.[291] The Operator must also not be put under indirect pressure to make decisions at unreasonable tempos (e.g. because otherwise, friendly forces might die) and must have "sufficient time or alternative sources of information to make any meaningful counter-decision".[292] As one example from the civil domain, while contemporary autonomous vehicles still technically operate with Linked Control (drivers are still expected to remain on standby and intervene if they notice problems), the speed at which decisions are made on the road—often permitting only one or two seconds to react—often

[283] See e.g. Defense Science Board 2016, p. 15.

[284] iPRAW 2019, p. 2.

[285] See Saariluoma 2015, pp. 232–240.

[286] Anderson and Waxman 2013, p. 22; ICRC 2019b, p. 10.

[287] Lyons and Havig 2014, pp. 182–183; Fallon and Blaha 2018, p. 250.

[288] Parasuraman et al. 2000, p. 291; Cummings 2004, p. 2.

[289] Bryce and Parakilas 2018, p. 46.

[290] Asaro 2012, p. 695.

[291] ICRC 2019b, p. 7.

[292] Anderson and Waxman 2013, p. 22.

prevent them from meaningfully contributing: "Steering wheel or no, the driver is a *de facto* passenger along for the ride."[293] As with the interface requirement, insufficient decision time will render the human's role meaningless.[294]

8.8.3 Operator Requirements

Deployer must take care to appoint an Operator who has sufficient qualifications to perform their relevant tasks. Jain warns of the situation where an AWS is supervised by a soldier "who is unlikely to fully understand the complex working of the AWS or to have the final word on whether or not the action should be carried out".[295] If an Operator is assigned, Technical Awareness requirements[296] would also apply to the Operator. The Operator must have had the necessary formation and training that would allow them to properly interpret the AWS's actions and take meaningful action. This extends to protocol that applies when the Operator decides to intervene. The GGE emphasised the importance of States adopting "procedures for trained human operators to activate or deactivate functions in weapons systems".[297]

For many militaries, Operator training can simply be implemented as an extension of existing technical empowerment procedures (those for e.g. drone pilots and other overseers of autonomous systems). The DoD imposes certification requirements for any soldier involved in such technologies to ensure that they "have been trained in system capabilities, doctrine, and TTPs".[298] This should be a minimum requirement for any AWS Operator. Indeed, another DoD publication explicitly provides guidelines for training operators which will be involved in such human-machine teams.[299] If there is the possibility that Linked Control will be enabled, States should adopt similar training modules for not only Deployers, but also Operators.

8.8.4 Coordination Between Deployer and Operator

This requirement is rarely mentioned in literature yet of crucial importance for effective Linked Control use. One of the primary functions of Linked Control is that it allows the Operator to act as a dynamic stop if a systemic failure is observed, thus preventing further instances from being processed and more mistakes being made. In

[293] Scharre 2016b, p. 160.

[294] Geiß and Lahmann 2017, p. 378.

[295] Jain 2016, p. 314.

[296] See Sect. 2.4.1.

[297] Group of Governmental Experts on Lethal Autonomous Weapons Systems (GGE on LAWS) 2021, para 40.

[298] US Department of Defense 2012, Enclosure 4 para 8.a.(5).

[299] Defense Science Board 2012, p. 65.

this conceptualisation, the Operator thus does not *prevent mistakes* but *limits consequences*: "The human operator cannot necessarily prevent failure, but he or she can help ensure that if or when the system fails, the damage is limited."[300]

There is a nuance to this intervention, however, that sometimes goes unmentioned: not all of an AI's mistakes are necessarily *structural* failures that justify intervention. Deployer knows that a perfect system does not exist, but made the decision to use the system regardless.[301] As long as Deployer is a reasonable and good faith commander, this means that the decision to activate the system already took into consideration these statistical errors. To meaningfully reduce risk further through Linked Control, then, the Operator must be able to distinguish when a system structurally 'fails' vis-à-vis when the mistake was already pre-calculated by Deployer.

Say Deployer activates an AWS knowing that on average for a 10-min mission, two misclassifications may occur, and determined this was nevertheless a discriminate and proportional attack. If the Operator overzealously shuts off the system mid-operation after the first mistake, the Operator may be unwittingly jeopardising Deployer's mission when the system was functioning as intended. Five mistakes made in relatively quick succession, however, would reasonably indicate that something is indeed structurally wrong with the system (e.g. the enemy has unexpectedly compromised the system through poisoning), and an intervention would be justified. In this latter case, the added value of the Operator would be clear: by intervening at the correct time, they prevented a much higher death toll than what Deployer had reasonably predicted. It is thus *important for Deployer and the Operator to coordinate at the moment of release* as to what mistakes have been accounted for during the deployment decision and what Deployer's intent was when activating the system.

8.9 Synthesis: What Conditions Make AWS Use More Difficult?

We started this chapter with the question of why some systems with significant destructive potential, high degrees of autonomy, and/or *a priori* poor distinction abilities have been used for many decades without much legal controversy. To resolve this conundrum, we set out to discover what would make AWS difficult to employ lawfully on the basis of two assumptions: first, that complexity depends on a multidimensional, instead of linear, set of variables; and second, that these variables interact and can mutually compensate for difficulties in other dimensions. This yielded several variables which we analysed in detail, determining also what conditions within each variable would place a system on the 'easier' or 'harder' ends of the Facility spectrum. In addition, we identified three Rationales which tie the variables to concepts that underlie IHL targeting rules:

---

[300] Scharre 2016a, p. 11.

[301] See Sect. 9.3.1.

Table 8.1 List of identified variables

Variable		Linked to Rationale		
Name	Related to	-IH	-FP	-EE
Effector DMG potential	System	✗		
Negative class detection	System	✗		
Specificity rating	System		✗	
Opacity	System			✗
Temporal variable	Operation		✗	✗
Spatial reach	Operation		✗	✗
Target type	Operation		✗	✗
Target specificity	Operation			✗
Proximate CIV	Environment	✗		
Negative class frequency	Environment	✗	✗	
Environmental dynamicity	Environment			✗

- *Rationale-IH*: Characteristics that increase risk of incidental harm;
- *Rationale-FP*: Characteristics that increase risk of false positives;
- *Rationale-EE*: Characteristics that increase risk of epistemic error.[302]

In addition, we discussed Context Controls: a selection of proposals from literature to make AWS use more reliable or controllable. We also connected these to our prior theories, demonstrating that they would indeed make AWS easier to lawfully use by modifying variables toward the 'easy' end of the spectrum.

These findings thus far are visualised in Table 8.1 and Fig. 8.7.

Table 8.1 provides an overview of the different variables that were identified in this chapter and the Rationale(s) to which they are linked.

In this table, the variables are also sorted on the basis of whether they are properties related to the *system* itself, to *operational* parameters, or to the *environment*. Deployer has the most control over operation-related variables, since Deployer will often be in the position to alter them simply by changing mission details (e.g. the duration of the operation, what objectives are being targeted). In contrast, system-related variables and environment-related variables are less actionable by Deployer. The former are usually pre-determined by the Providing Entity, while the latter are factors that Deployer must often simply take as givens.[303]

Figure 8.7 integrates the information in Table 8.1 with the other findings of this chapter. It shows from left to right: the three main Rationales; the variables and how they connect to the Rationales; how to assess where a particular AWS falls on each variable's spectrum of Facility; and what Context Controls can be undertaken to modify the Facility of particular variables.

[302] To recall: where Deployer's presumptions upon which the deployment decision was based do not (or no longer) correspond with field conditions.

[303] Some Context Controls nevertheless allow Deployer to exercise some influence on these environmental variables, e.g. through environmental manipulations. See Sect. 8.7.5.3.

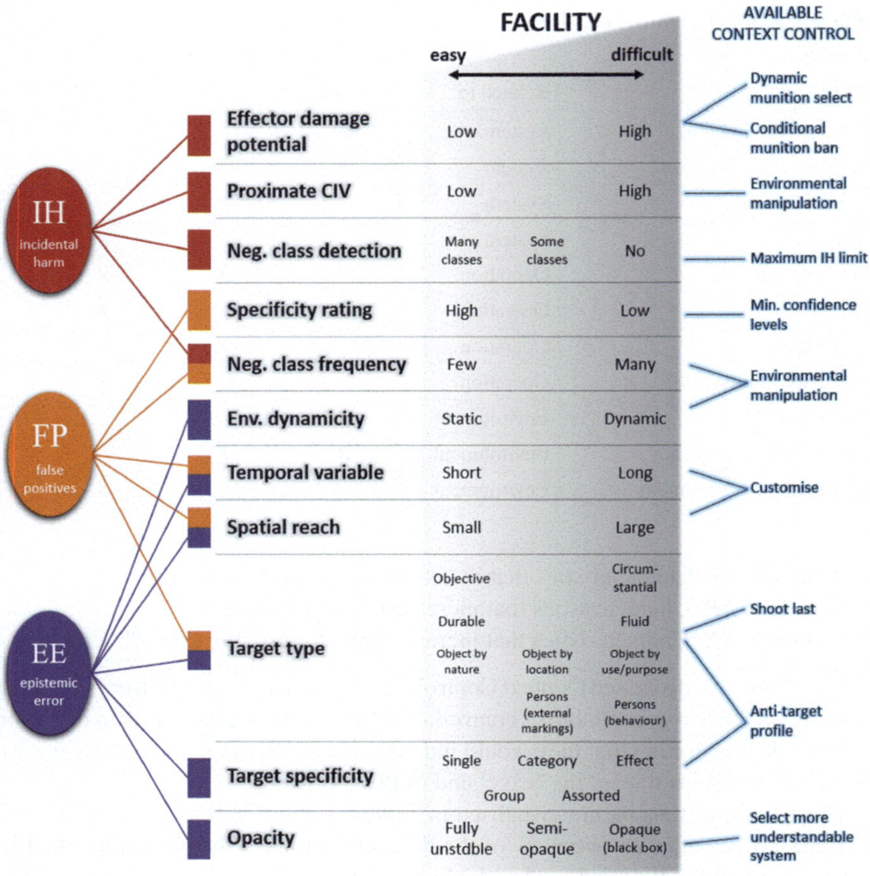

Fig. 8.7 Integrated graph of variables of complexity

This multidimensional approach provides a more nuanced method to analyse autonomy in weapon systems, since it allows us to see in which aspects a system is legally 'strong' (easy to use) and which aspects are potentially problematic.

The chart also allows us to determine whether complementary factors are applicable that can compensate for the problematic variable(s). Factors can be considered as *compensating for each other* if they are linked to the same Rationale.

Previously, we mentioned antipersonnel landmines as an example of a weapon that seemingly could be used lawfully despite its complete inability to distinguish civilian from military persons.[304] The graph above shows us why. We can see that Rationale-FP (false positives) is linked to five variables: Specificity, Negative Class Frequency, Temporal, Spatial and Target Type. When considering all these factors together, we can determine that the antipersonnel landmine:

---

[304] See Sect. 8.2.2.

Variable	Facility			Notes
Damage potential	■			Antipersonnel munitions, low risk of splash
Proximate CIV	■			No proximate civilian entities in DMZ
Neg. class detect.			■	Cannot detect other negative class entities
Specificity rate	■			Presumed high performance
Neg. class freq.	■			Almost zero in DMZ environment
Env. dynamicity	■			Static
Temporal			■	E.g. left on autonomous mode for 1 hour
Spatial	■			Immobile
Target type			■	Persons + behavioural recognition
Target specificity		■		Tier: Category
Opacity		■		Behaviour recognition presumes (part) ML

Fig. 8.8 Example Facility assessment of SGR-A1

- Scores *very poorly* in Specificity, Temporal and Target Type (it cannot make distinctions at all; it is armed for an extended time; and its targets are persons).
- Scores *very well* in Negative Class Frequency and Spatial (the mined area is clearly marked to ward off civilians; and the mine is entirely immobile).
- These in combination permit lawful use, since the two latter well-scoring categories 'compensate' for the landmine's weaknesses in the first three.

Identical analyses can be made with respect to any weapon, and with respect to any Rationale.

Let us now apply this methodology to a more comprehensive example, say the Samsung SGR-A1. This system can be analysed as shown in Fig. 8.8, assuming just a simple three-tier scoring system (easy-moderate-difficult) for convenience.

Using this methodology, we see that the primary variables of concern are Temporal (1 h, for illustrative purposes), Target Type (persons, behaviour-based), and the fact that there is no Negative Class Detection. Of moderate concern is Target Specificity (*Category*). However, we see that the SGR-A1 (as it is used in the DMZ) scores very well in all other variables.

In addition, we also see the compensating nature of variables at play. Take the *long temporal dimension.* In Fig. 8.7, we see that this variable is connected to both Rationale-FP and Rationale-EE. When we look at other variables linked to these Rationales, we see that for Rationale-FP, risk of false positives is mitigated by the low Negative Class Frequency and low proximity of civilian entities in the DMZ, while for Rationale-EE, the system's immobility and the static environment mitigate risk of epistemic error.[305]

---

[305] The same logic can be applied for other concerns. For example, the lack of negative class detection is not problematic if Proximate CIV is low, since there is no necessity for this functionality in the absence of other negative classes to distinguish. The same applies to the low damage potential (even if civilian entities were proximate, there is lower chance of collateral damage from an antipersonnel shot).

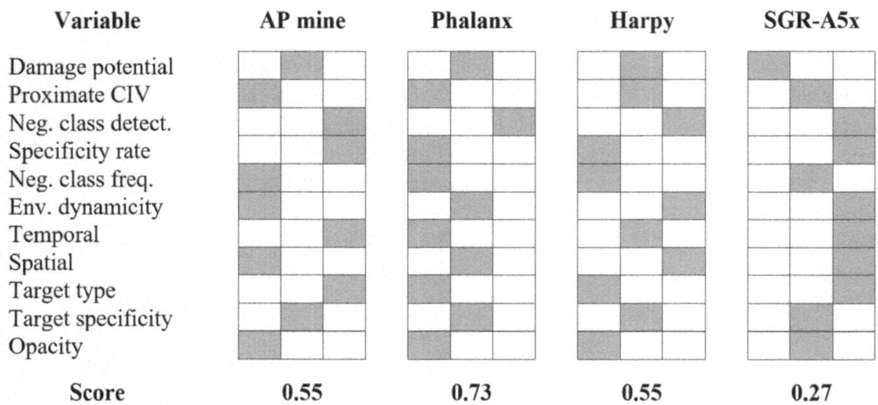

Fig. 8.9 Example Facility assessment of different weapons

Facility of use can be increased further with Context Controls. Some problem variables are not amenable to change by Deployer,[306] but Deployer can for example move Temporal left by increasing the frequency with which an Operator verifies if everything is still going well, thereby reducing Active Time.

Let us now apply this same methodology to systems mentioned in the opening of this chapter, to demonstrate why some are less controversial than others[307] (Fig. 8.9).

The first three weapons (antipersonnel mine,[308] Phalanx and Harpy) are examples of systems exhibiting characteristics that have been raised as counterpoints against AWS (e.g. lethality, autonomy, long Active Times), but which have been used lawfully. The Facility spectrums show why: their weaknesses are compensated in other areas, which *overall* makes lawful use possible. The fourth weapon, the SGR-A5x, is a fictional successor to the SGR-A1, described by Schuller as one that was:

> provided with broader physical capabilities [and] was modified such that it could roam the countryside, but was not granted more sophisticated sensor and/or computational capabilities or limited by additional parameters.[309]

A majority of the SGR-A5x's characteristics fall into the 'difficult' end of the spectrum, and few compensating variables are available. It is very hard to use this system lawfully[310] without modifying some variables using Context Controls, e.g. by sealing off the 'countryside'[311] from any civilian entities to improve Proximate CIV, Negative Class Frequency and Dynamicity.

---

306 For example, the lack of negative class detection can only be fixed during design, and Deployer cannot change the fact that persons are a difficult target type.

307 For elaborations per variable per weapon, see Appendix 1.

308 Assuming proper use pursuant to CCW Protocol-II, above n. 25, Articles 3(8) and 6(3).

309 Schuller 2017, note 81.

310 For a legal analysis of the various reasons why this is the case, see Chap. 9.

311 See Sect. 8.7.5.3.

Notably, all examples' Target Specificities fall into the Category-tier, showing that this level of specificity in targeting is not unusual. Additionally, none of the weapons have Negative Class Detection, a useful functionality that is only available with more advanced AI.[312]

It is also possible to qualitatively[313] determine a system's overall Facility as shown in the 'Score' row, which shows an aggregated average of each variable's assessment (1 for easiest, 0 for hardest). We see a marked drop in Facility with regard to the SGR-A5x, befitting its legally problematic nature. The Phalanx, arguably the least controversial of the four systems,[314] is appropriately also awarded the best score through this methodology.

In the coming chapters, additional context is provided in the legal and operational spheres that develops this methodology further, allowing practical application for targeting decisions beyond what has already been demonstrated in this chapter.

References

Abaimov S, Martellini M (2020) Artificial Intelligence in Autonomous Weapon Systems. In: Martellini M, Ralf T (eds) 21st Century Prometheus. Springer International Publishing, Cham, pp 141–177. DOI: https://doi.org/10.1007/978-3-030-28285-1_8

Adviesraad Internationale Vraagstukken and Commissie van Advies inzake Volkenrechtelijke Vraagstukken (2015) Autonome Wapensystemen: De Noodzaak van Betekenisvolle Menselijke Controle. AIV

Akerson D (2013) The Illegality of Offensive Lethal Autonomy. In: Saxon D (ed) International Humanitarian Law and the Changing Technology of War. Brill-Nijhoff, Leiden, pp 65–98. DOI: https://doi.org/10.1163/9789004229495_005

Amodei D et al. (2016) Concrete Problems in AI Safety. http://arxiv.org/abs/1606.06565

Amoroso D (2020) Autonomous Weapons Systems and International Law: A Study on Human-Machine Interactions in Ethically and Legally Sensitive Domains. Nomos Verlagsgesellschaft, Baden

Anderson J M, Matsumura J M (2015) Civilian Developments in Autonomous Vehicle Technology and Their Civilian and Military Policy Implications. In: Williams A P, Scharre P D (eds) Autonomous Systems: Issues for Defence Policymakers. NATO, The Hauge, pp 127–148

312 Henderson et al. 2017, p. 348.

313 The score is for illustrative and comparative purposes only. Developing such a scoring system in more objective and quantitative terms is possible, but in that case also needs to consider the following points:

- Whether more variables should be added.
- A clear and consistent methodology of how to measure each variable on the spectrum.
- A finer scale than simply {1, 0.5, 0} as used here.
- Whether some variables should be given greater aggregate weight than others
- How to account for and express compensating variables in the aggregate score.

With regard to the last point, it may be useful to consider providing separate aggregate scores for each of the three Rationales, since this would provide more clarity as to what Rationale is particularly deficient.

314 See Thurnher 2014, p. 216; UNIDIR 2014, p. 5.

Anderson K, Waxman M C (2013) Law and Ethics for Autonomous Weapon Systems: Why a Ban Won't Work and How the Laws of War Can. In: American University Washington College of Law Research Paper No. 2013-11. Stanford University, Stanford

Article 36 (2013) Structuring Debate on Autonomous Weapons Systems. In: Memorandum for delegates to the Convention on Certain Conventional Weapons (CCW), Geneva, 14–15 November 2013

Asaro P (2012) On Banning Autonomous Weapon Systems: Human Rights, Automation, and the Dehumanization of Lethal Decision-Making. International Review of the Red Cross 94(886):687–709

Barredo Arrieta A et al. (2020) Explainable Artificial Intelligence (XAI): Concepts, Taxonomies, Opportunities and Challenges toward Responsible AI. Information Fusion 58:82–115. DOI: https://doi.org/10.1016/j.inffus.2019.12.012

Beard J M (2014) Autonomous Weapons and Human Responsibilities. Georgetown Journal of International Law 45:617–681

Blum G (2017) The Dispensable Lives of Soldiers. In: Ohlin J D et al. (eds) Weighing Lives in War, vol 1. Oxford University Press, pp 17–57. DOI: https://doi.org/10.1093/oso/9780198796176.003.0002

Boddens Hosang J F R (2021) Control Through ROE in Military Operations: Autonomous Weapons and Cyber Operations as Reasons to Change the Classic ROE Concept?. In: Bartels R et al. (eds) Military Operations and the Notion of Control Under International Law. TMC Asser Press, The Hague, pp 393–420. DOI: https://doi.org/10.1007/978-94-6265-395-5_19

Boothby W H (2018a) Highly Automated and Autonomous Technologies. In: Boothby W H (ed) New Technologies and the Law in War and Peace. Cambridge University Press, Cambridge, pp 137–181. DOI: https://doi.org/10.1017/9781108609388.007

Boothby W H (2018b) Dehumanization: Is There a Legal Problem Under Article 36?. In: von Heinegg W H et al. (eds) Dehumanization of Warfare. Springer International Publishing, Cham, pp 21–52. DOI: https://doi.org/10.1007/978-3-319-67266-3_3

Boothby W H (2021) Control in Weapons Law. In: Bartels R et al. (eds) Military Operations and the Notion of Control Under International Law. TMC Asser Press, The Hague, pp 369–392. DOI: https://doi.org/10.1007/978-94-6265-395-5_18

Bothe M, Partsch K J, Solf W A (eds) (2013) New Rules for Victims of Armed Conflict: Commentary on the Two 1977 Protocols Additional to the Geneva Conventions of 1949. 2nd edn. Martinus Nijhoff, Leiden

Boulanin V (2016) Mapping the Development of Autonomy in Weapon Systems: A Primer on Autonomy. Stockholm International Peace Research Institute, Stockholm

Brownlee J (2013) Data, Learning and Modeling. Machine Learning Process. https://machinelearningmastery.com/data-learning-and-modeling/. Accessed 1 May 2023

Bryce H, Parakilas J (2018) Conclusions and Recommendations. In: Cummings M L et al. (eds) Artificial Intelligence and International Affairs: Disruption Anticipated. Chatham House, London, pp 43–46

Buchan R, Tsagourias N (2021) Autonomous Cyber Weapons and Command Responsibility. In: Liivoja R, Väljataga A (eds) Autonomous Cyber Capabilities under International Law. NATO CCDCOE Publications, Tallinn, pp 321–347

Bullock S, Cliff D (2004) Complexity and Emergent Behaviour in ICT Systems. HP Invent, HPL-2004-187, 27 October 2004. https://eprints.soton.ac.uk/261478/1/HPL-2004-187.pdf. Accessed 24 January 2024

Chairman of the Joint Chiefs of Staff (2012) Instruction – No Strike Policy and Collateral Damage Estimation. CJCSI 316001A

Chengeta T (2016) Defining the Emerging Notion of "Meaningful Human Control" in Autonomous Weapon Systems. International Law and Politics 49:833–890

Cherry J, Johnson D (2020) Maintaining Command and Control (C2) of Lethal Autonomous Weapon Systems: Legal And Policy Considerations. Southwestern Journal of International Law 27:1–27

Corn G S (2012) Targeting, Command Judgement, and a Proposed Quantum of Information Component: A Fourth Amendment Lesson in Contextual Reasonableness. Brooklyn Law Review 77(2):437–498

Corn G S (2015) War, Law, and the Oft Overlooked Value of Process as a Precautionary Measure. Pepperdine Law Review 42(3):419–466

Corn G S (2016) Autonomous Weapons Systems: Managing the Inevitability of "Taking the Man out of the Loop". In: Bhuta N et al. (eds) Autonomous Weapons Systems: Law, Ethics, Policy. Cambridge University Press, Cambridge, pp 209–242. DOI: https://doi.org/10.1017/CBO9781316597873

Crawford E (2017) The Principle of Distinction and Remote Warfare. In: Ohlin J D (ed) Research Handbook on Remote Warfare. Edward Elgar, Cheltenham, pp 50–78. DOI: https://doi.org/10.4337/9781784716998.00011

Crootof R (2015) The Killer Robots Are Here: Legal and Policy Implications. Cardozo Law Review 36:1837–1915

Cummings M L (2004) Automation Bias in Intelligent Time Critical Decision Support Systems. In: AIAA 1st Intelligent Systems Technical Conference. American Institute of Aeronautics and Astronautics. DOI: https://doi.org/10.2514/6.2004-6313

Curtis E. Lemay Center (2019) Air Force Doctrine Publication 3-60 – Targeting. Curtis E Lemay Center. www.doctrine.af.mil/Doctrine-Publications/AFDP-3-60-Targeting. Accessed 05 July 2021

DARPA (2016) Broad Agency Announcement: Explainable Artificial Intelligence (XAI). DARPA-BAA-16-53. www.darpa.mil/attachments/DARPA-BAA-16-53.pdf. Accessed 14 November 2020

Davison N (2017) A Legal Perspective: Autonomous Weapon Systems under International Humanitarian Law. In: UNODA Occasional Papers No. 30

Deeks A (2021) Will Cyber Autonomy Undercut Democratic Accountability?. In: Liivoja R, Väljataga A (eds) Autonomous Cyber Capabilities under International Law. NATO CCDCOE Publications, Tallinn, pp 67–105

Defense Innovation Board (2019) AI Principles: Recommendations on the Ethical Use of Artificial Intelligence by the Department of Defense Defense Innovation Board. US Department of Defense. https://media.defense.gov/2019/Oct/31/2002204458/-1/-1/0/DIB_AI_PRINCIPLES_PRIMARY_DOCUMENT.PDF. Accessed 2 August 2023

Defense Science Board (2012) The Role Of Autonomy in DoD Systems. US Department of Defense, Washington D.C.

Defense Science Board (2016) Report of the Defense Science Board Summer Study on Autonomy. Secretary of Defense for Acquisition, Technology and Logistics

Ducheine P, Gill T (2018) From Cyber Operations to Effects: Some Targeting Issues. Militair Rechtelijk Tijdschrift 111(3):37–41

Durhin N (2016) Protecting Civilians in Urban Areas: A Military Perspective on the Application of International Humanitarian Law. International Review of the Red Cross 98(1):177–200

Ekelhof M (2016) Human Control in the Targeting Process. In: Autonomous Weapon Systems: Implications of Increasing Autonomy in the Critical Functions of Weapons. ICRC, Versoix, pp 53–56

Ekelhof M (2018) Lifting the Fog of Targeting: "Autonomous Weapons" and Human Control through the Lens of Military Targeting. Naval War College Review 71(3):61–94

Fallon C K, Blaha L M (2018) Improving Automation Transparency: Addressing Some of Machine Learning's Unique Challenges. In: Schmorrow D, Fidopiastis C (eds) Augmented Cognition: Intelligent Technologies. Springer, Cham, pp 245–254. DOI: https://doi.org/10.1007/978-3-319-91470-1_21

Fenrick W J (2005) International Humanitarian Law and Combat Casualties. European Journal of Population/Revue européenne de Démographie 21(2–3):167–186. DOI: https://doi.org/10.1007/s10680-005-6421-y

Finkelstein C (2017) The Equality of Combatants in Asymmetric War. In: Ohlin J D, May L, Finkelstein C (eds) Weighing Lives in War, vol 1. Oxford University Press, pp 241–258. DOI: https://doi.org/10.1093/oso/9780198796176.003.0011

Fleck D (ed) (2013) The Handbook of International Humanitarian Law. 3rd edn. Oxford University Press, Oxford

Ford C M (2019) Personal Self-Defense and the Standing Rules of Engagement. In: Williams W S, Ford C M (eds) Complex Battlespaces: The Law of Armed Conflict and the Dynamics of Modern Warfare. Oxford University Press, Oxford, pp 109–124. DOI: https://doi.org/10.1093/oso/9780190915360.003.0004

Future of Life Institute (2015) Autonomous Weapons: An Open Letter from AI & Robotics Researchers. https://futureoflife.org/open-letter-autonomous-weapons. Accessed 3 August 2017

Geiß R (2015) The International-Law Dimension of Autonomous Weapons Systems. Friedrich Ebert Stiftung, Bonn. https://library.fes.de/pdf-files/id/ipa/11673.pdf. Accessed 2 August 2023

Geiß R, Lahmann H (2017) Autonomous Weapons Systems: A Paradigm Shift for the Law of Armed Conflict?. In: Ohlin J D (ed) Research Handbook on Remote Warfare. Edward Elgar, Cheltenham, pp 371–404

Gillard E-C (2018) Proportionality in the Conduct of Hostilities: The Incidental Harm Side of the Assessment. The Royal Institute of International Affairs, Chatham House, London. https://www.chathamhouse.org/2018/12/proportionality-conduct-hostilities-incidental-harm-side-assessment. Accessed 2 August 2023

Gisel L (2016) The Principle of Proportionality in the Rules Governing the Conduct of Hostilities under International Humanitarian Law. In: International Expert Meeting, 22–23 June 2016. ICRC. https://www.icrc.org/en/download/file/79184/4358_002_expert_meeting_report_web_1.pdf. Accessed 3 August 2023

Gross R (2016) The New Way of War: Is There A Duty to Use Drones?. Florida Law Review 67(1):1–72

Group of Governmental Experts on Lethal Autonomous Weapons Systems (GGE on LAWS) (2019) Report of the 2019 Session of the Group of Governmental Experts on Emerging Technologies in the Area of Lethal Autonomous Weapons Systems. UN Doc CCW/GGE1/2019/3, 25 September 2019

Group of Governmental Experts on Lethal Autonomous Weapons Systems (GGE on LAWS) (2021) Draft Report of the 2021 Session of the Group of Governmental Experts on Emerging Technologies in the Area of Lethal Autonomous Weapons Systems. CCW/GGE1/2021/CRP1

Grut C (2013) The Challenge of Autonomous Lethal Robotics to International Humanitarian Law. Journal of Conflict and Security Law 18(1):5–23. DOI: https://doi.org/10.1093/jcsl/krt002

Hawley J K (2007) Looking Back At 20 Years Of MANPRINT On Patriot: Observations And Lessons. Army Research Laboratory

Henderson I S, Keane P, Liddy J (2017) Remote and Autonomous Warfare Systems: Precautions in Attack and Individual Accountability. In: Ohlin J D (ed) Research Handbook on Remote Warfare. Edward Elgar, Cheltenham, pp 335–370. DOI: https://doi.org/10.4337/9781784716998.00022

Heyns C (2013) Report of the Special Rapporteur on Extrajudicial, Summary or Arbitrary Executions, A/HRC/23/47

Holland J (2004) Military Objective And Collateral Damage: Their Relationship And Dynamics. Yearbook of International Humanitarian Law 7:35–78. DOI: https://doi.org/10.1017/S1389135904000352

Holland Michel A (2020) The Black Box, Unlocked: Predictability and Understandability in Military AI. UNIDIR, Geneva. https://unidir.org/sites/default/files/2020-09/BlackBoxUnlocked.pdf. Accessed 2 August 2023

Human Rights Watch (2012) Losing Humanity: The Case against Killer Robots. Human Rights Watch

ICRC (2016) Background Paper Prepared by the International Committee of the Red Cross. In: ICRC (ed) Autonomous Weapon Systems: Implications of Increasing Autonomy in the Critical Functions of Weapons. ICRC, Versoix, pp 69–85

ICRC (2018) Ethics and Autonomous Weapon Systems: An Ethical Basis for Human Control?. Group of Governmental Experts of the High Contracting Parties to the Convention on Prohibitions or Restrictions on the Use of Certain Conventional Weapons Which May Be Deemed to Be Excessively Injurious or to Have Indiscriminate Effects, CCW/GGE1/2018/WP

ICRC (2019a) 'Statement of the International Committee of the Red Cross (ICRC) under Agenda Item 5(B)'. Convention on Certain Conventional Weapons (CCW), Group of Governmental Experts on Lethal Autonomous Weapons Systems (Geneva, 25–29 March 2019)

ICRC (2019b) Artificial Intelligence and Machine Learning in Armed Conflict: A Human-Centred Approach. ICRC, Geneva

IEEE Standards Association (2016) IEEE 1633-2016, IEEE Recommended Practice on Software Reliability. IEEE. https://standards.ieee.org/standard/1633-2016.html. Accessed 11 October 2021

Infeld D L (1992) Precision-Guided Munitions Demonstrated Their Pinpoint Accuracy in Desert Storm; but Is a Country Obligated to Use Precision Technology to Minimize Collateral Civilian Injury and Damage. George Washington Journal of International Law and Economics 26(1):109–142. https://heinonline.org/HOL/Page?handle=hein.journals/gwilr26&id=117&div=&collection=. Accessed 27 November 2021

iPRAW (2019) Statement by IPRAW during the CCW GGE on LAWS: Human Control. Delivered by Marcel Dickow, 29 March 2019

iPRAW (2020) Statement on Agenda 5c (Human Element). Statement by iPRAW during the CCW GGE on LAWS: National Weapon Reviews, 23 September 2019

Jain N (2016) Autonomous Weapons Systems: New Frameworks for Individual Responsibility. In: Bhuta N et al. (eds) Autonomous Weapons Systems: Law, Ethics, Policy. Cambridge University Press, Cambridge, pp 303–324. DOI: https://doi.org/10.1017/CBO9781316597873

Jensen E T (2003) Unexpected Consequences From Knock-On Effects: A Different Standard for Computer Network Operations?. American University International Law Review 18(5):1145–1188

Kalmanovitz P (2016) Judgment, Liability and the Risks of Riskless Warfare. In: Bhuta N et al. (eds) Autonomous Weapons Systems. Cambridge University Press, Cambridge, pp 145–163. DOI: https://doi.org/10.1017/CBO9781316597873.007

Kalshoven F (2007) The Soldier and His Golf Clubs. In: Reflections on the Law of War. Martinus Nijhoff Publishers, Leiden. DOI: https://doi.org/10.1163/ej.9789004158252.i-1118.66

Kastan B (2013) Autonomous Weapons Systems: A Coming Legal "Singularity"?. Journal of Law, Technology and Policy 2013(1):45–82

Krupiy T (2015) A Case against Relying Solely on Intelligence, Surveillance and Reconnaissance Technology to Identify Proposed Targets. Journal of Conflict and Security Law 20(3):415–449. DOI: https://doi.org/10.1093/jcsl/krv009

Kurosaki M (2020) Toward the Special Computer Law of Targeting. In: Kreß C, Lawless R (eds) Necessity and Proportionality in International Peace and Security Law. Oxford University Press, Oxford, pp 409–436. DOI: https://doi.org/10.1093/oso/9780197537374.001.0001/oso-9780197537374-chapter-14

Kwik J (2022) A Practicable Operationalisation of Meaningful Human Control. Laws 11(3):43

Kwik J, Van Engers T (2021) Algorithmic Fog of War: When Lack of Transparency Violates the Law of Armed Conflict. Journal of Future Robot Life 2(1–2):43–66. https://www.medra.org/servlet/aliasResolver?alias=iospress&doi=https://doi.org/10.3233/FRL-200019. Accessed 4 August 2023

Leslie D (2019) Understanding Artificial Intelligence Ethics and Safety: A Guide for the Responsible Design and Implementation of AI Systems in the Public Sector. The Alan Turing Institute, London

Lewis J (2015) The Case for Regulating Fully Autonomous Weapons. Yale Law Journal 124:1309–1325

Lohn A J (2020) Estimating the Brittleness of AI: Safety Integrity Levels and the Need for Testing Out-Of-Distribution Performance. http://arxiv.org/abs/2009.00802

Lyons J B, Havig P R (2014) Transparency in a Human-Machine Context: Approaches for Fostering Shared Awareness/Intent. In: Shumaker R, Lackey S (eds) Virtual, Augmented and Mixed Reality: Designing and Developing Augmented and Virtual Environments, 6th International Conference, VAMR 2014, Lecture No. Springer, Cham, pp 181–190. DOI: https://doi.org/10.1007/978-3-319-07458-0_18

Margulies P (2017) Making Autonomous Weapons Accountable: Command Responsibility for Computer-Guided Lethal Force in Armed Conflicts. In: Ohlin J D (ed) Research Handbook on Remote Warfare. Edward Elgar, Cheltenham, pp 405–442. DOI: https://doi.org/10.4337/9781784716998.00024

Markoff J (2014) Fearing Bombs That Can Pick Whom to Kill. New York Times. www.nytimes.com/2014/11/12/science/weapons-directed-by-robots-not-humans-raise-ethical-questions.html. Accessed 2 August 2023

Melzer N (2009) Interpretive Guidance on the Notion of Direct Participation in Hostilities. ICRC, Geneva

Moyes R (2019) Target Profiles: An Initial Consideration of "Target Profiles" as a Basis for Rule-Making in the Context of Discussions on Autonomy in Weapons Systems. Article 36, Article 36 Discussion Paper

NATO (2021) Allied Joint Doctrine for Joint Targeting. Edition B Version 1 (November 2021) AJP-39, NATO Standardization Office (NSO)

Noone G P, Noone D C (2015) The Debate Over Autonomous Weapons Systems. Case Western Reserve Journal of International Law 47(1):25–35

Oeter S (2020) Specifying the Proportionality Test and the Standard of Due Precaution: Problems of Prognostic Assessment in Determining the Meaning of "May Be Expected" and "Anticipated". In: Kreß C, Lawless R (eds) Necessity and Proportionality in International Peace and Security Law. Oxford University Press, Oxford, pp 343–366. DOI: https://doi.org/10.1093/oso/9780197537374.003.0012

Office of the Chairman of the Joint Chiefs of Staff (2020) DOD Dictionary of Military and Associated Terms, as Amended. The Joint Staff, Washington, D.C

Parakilas J, Bryce H (2018) Introduction: Artificial Intelligence and International Politics. In: Cummings M L et al. (eds) Artificial Intelligence and International Affairs: Disruption Anticipated. Chatham House, London, pp 1–6

Parasuraman R, Sheridan T B, Wickens C (2000) A Model for Types and Levels of Human Interaction with Automation. IEEE Transactions on Systems, Man, and Cybernetics 30(3):286–297

Parks W H (1990) Air War and the Law of War. Air Force Law Review 32(1):1–226

Perrow C (1984) Normal Accidents: Living With High-Risk Technologies. Basic Books, New York

Quéguiner J-F (2006) Precautions under the Law Governing the Conduct of Hostilities. International Review of the Red Cross 88(864):793–821

Roff H M, Moyes R (2016) Meaningful Human Control, Artificial Intelligence and Autonomous Weapons. Briefing Paper for the Delegates at the Convention on Certain Conventional Weapons Informal Meeting of Experts on Lethal Autonomous Weapons Systems

Roorda M (2015) NATO's Targeting Process: Ensuring Human Control Over (and Lawful Use of) 'Autonomous' Weapons. In: Williams A P, Scharre P D (eds) Autonomous Systems: Issues for Defence Policymakers. NATO, The Hague, pp 152–168

Russell S J, Norvig P (2010) Artificial Intelligence: A Modern Approach. 3rd edn. Pearson, New Jersey

Saariluoma P (2015) Four Challenges in Structuring Human-Autonomous Systems Interaction Design Processes. In: Williams A P, Scharre P D (eds) Autonomous Systems: Issues for Defence Policymakers. NATO, The Hague, pp 226–248

Sandoz Y, Swinarski C, Zimmerman B (1987) Commentary on the Additional Protocols of 8 June 1977 to the Geneva Conventions of 12 August 1949. Martinus Nijhoff, Geneva

Sartor G, Omicini A (2016) The Autonomy of Technological Systems and Responsibilities for Their Use. In: Bhuta N et al. (eds) Autonomous Weapons Systems. Cambridge University Press, Cambridge, pp 39–74. DOI: https://doi.org/10.1017/CBO9781316597873.003

Sassòli M (2014) Autonomous Weapons and International Humanitarian Law: Advantages, Open Technical Questions and Legal Issues to Be Clarified. International Law Studies 90:308–340
Scharre P D (2014) Autonomy, "Killer Robots," and Human Control in the Use of Force. Just Security. 9 July 2014. https://www.justsecurity.org/12708/autonomy-killer-robots-human-control-force-part/ and https://www.justsecurity.org/12712/autonomy-killer-robots-human-control-force-part-ii/. Accessed 10 June 2021
Scharre P D (2015) The Opportunity and Challenge of Autonomous Systems. In: Williams A P, Scharre P D (eds) Autonomous Systems: Issues for Defence Policymakers. NATO, The Hague, pp 3–26
Scharre P D (2016a) Autonomous Weapons and Operational Risk. Center for a New American Security, Washington, D.C
Scharre P D (2016b) Centaur Warfighting: The False Choice of Humans vs. Automation. Temple International & Comparative Law Journal 30(1):151–165
Scharre P D (2018) Army of None: Autonomous Weapons and the Future of War. Ww Norton & Co, New York
Scharre P D, Horowitz M C (2015) An Introduction to Autonomy in Weapon Systems. Center for a New American Security, Working Paper, Feb 2015
Schmitt M N (1998) Bellum Americanum: The U.S. View of Twenty-First Century War and Its Possible Implications for the Law of Armed Conflict. In: Schmitt M N, Green L C (eds) The Law of Armed Conflict: Into the Next Millennium. Naval War College, Newport, pp 389–428
Schmitt M N (2010) Military Necessity and Humanity in International Humanitarian Law: Preserving the Delicate Balance. Virginia Journal of International Law 50(4):795–839
Schmitt M N, Schauss M (2019) Uncertainty in the Law of Targeting: Towards a Cognitive Framework. Harvard National Security Journal 10:148–194
Schmitt M N, Thurnher J S (2013) "Out of the Loop": Autonomous Weapon Systems and the Law of Armed Conflict. Harvard Law School National Security Journal 4:231–281
Schmitt M N et al. (2017) Joint and Combined Targeting: Structure and Process. In: Ohlin J D, May L, Finkelstein C (eds) Weighing Lives in War, vol 1. Oxford University Press, pp 298–324. DOI: https://doi.org/10.1093/oso/9780198796176.003.0014
Schuller A L (2017) At the Crossroads of Control: The Intersection of Artificial Intelligence in Autonomous Weapon Systems with International Humanitarian Law. Harvard National Security Journal 8:379
Schuller A L (2019) Artificial Intelligence Effecting Human Decisions to Kill: The Challenge of Linking Numerically Quantifiable Goals to IHL Compliance. Journal of Law and Policy for the Information Society 15:105–122
Sforza P M (2016) Manned Spacecraft Design Principles. Butterworth-Heinemann, Elsevier. DOI: https://doi.org/10.1016/C2012-0-00344-4
Sparrow R (2016) Robots and Respect: Assessing the Case Against Autonomous Weapon Systems. Ethics & International Affairs 30(1):93–116
Szpak A (2020) Legality of Use and Challenges of New Technologies in Warfare – the Use of Autonomous Weapons in Contemporary or Future Wars. European Review 28(1):118–131. DOI: https://doi.org/10.1017/S1062798719000310
Theunissen E, Suarez B (2015) Choosing the Level of Autonomy: Options and Constraints. In: Williams A P, Scharre P D (eds) Autonomous Systems: Issues for Defence Policymakers. NATO, The Hague, pp 169–195
Thorne J G (2020) Warriors and War Algorithms: Leveraging Artificial Intelligence to Enable Ethical Targeting. Technical Report, 14-05-2020. https://apps.dtic.mil/sti/citations/AD1104171. Accessed 3 July 2021
Thurnher J S (2012) No One at the Controls: Legal Implications of Fully Autonomous Targeting. Joint Force Quarterly 67:77–84
Thurnher J S (2014) Examining Autonomous Weapon Systems from a Law of Armed Conflict Perspective. In: Nasu H, McLaughlin R (eds) New Technologies and the Law of Armed Conflict.

TMC Asser Press, The Hague, pp 213–228. DOI: https://doi.org/10.1007/978-90-6704-933-7_13

Thurnher J S (2018) Feasible Precautions in Attack and Autonomous Weapons. In: von Heinegg W H, Frau R, Singer T (eds) Dehumanization of Warfare. Springer International Publishing, Cham, pp 99–117. DOI: https://doi.org/10.1007/978-3-319-67266-3_6

Tolk A (2015) Merging Two Worlds: Agent-Based Simulation Methods for Autonomous Systems. In: Williams A P, Scharre P D (eds) Autonomous Systems: Issues for Defence Policymakers. NATO, The Hague, pp 291–317

Toscano C P (2015) "Friend of Humans": An Argument for Developing Autonomous Weapons Systems. Journal of National Security Law & Policy 8(1):189–246

UK (2020) Expert Paper: The Human Role in Autonomous Warfare, Group of Governmental Experts on Emerging Technologies in the Area of Lethal Autonomous Weapons System Geneva, 21–25 September 2020 and 2–6 November 2020, Agenda Item 5. CCW/GGE1/2020/WP6

UK Ministry of Defence (2011) The UK Approach to Unmanned Aircraft Systems. Joint Doctrine Note 2/11

UNIDIR (2014) The Weaponization of Increasingly Autonomous Technologies: Considering How Meaningful Human Control Might Move the Discussion Forward. UNIDIR Resources, No 2

UNIDIR (2016) Safety, Unintentional Risk and Accidents in the Weaponization of Increasingly Autonomous Technologies. UNIDIR Resources No 5

United Nations (2021) Panel of Experts Established pursuant to Security Council Resolution 1973. Letter dated 8 March 2021 from the Panel of Experts on Libya Established pursuant to Resolution 1973 (2011) addressed to the President of the Security Council. S_2021_229

United Nations Office for the Coordination of Humanitarian Affairs (2017) Reducing the Humanitarian Impact of the Use of Explosive Weapons in Populated Areas. https://www.unocha.org/sites/unocha/files/EWIPA Fact Sheet June 2017.pdf. Accessed 20 February 2020

US Department of Defense (1988) Investigation Report: Formal Investigation into the Circumstances Surrounding the Downing of Iran Air Flight 655 on 3 July 1988. AD-A203 557

US Department of Defense (2012) Autonomy in Weapon Systems. US DoD Directive 3000.09

US Department of Defense (2023) Autonomy in Weapon Systems. US DoD Directive 3000.09

US Department of the Army (2019) The Operations Process. ADP 5-0 (replacing ADP 5-0, dated 17 May 2012, and ADRP 5-0, dated 17 May 2012)

Väljataga A, Liivoja R (2021) Cyber Autonomy and International Law: An Introduction. In: Liivoja R, Väljataga A (eds) Autonomous Cyber Capabilities under International Law. NATO CCDCOE Publications, Tallinn, pp 1–11

van den Boogaard J C, Roorda M P (2021) "Autonomous" Weapons and Human Control. In: Bartels R (eds) Military Operations and the Notion of Control Under International Law. TMC Asser Press, The Hague, pp 421–437. DOI: https://doi.org/10.1007/978-94-6265-395-5_20

Williams R (2017) Lords Select Committee, Artificial Intelligence Committee, Written Evidence. AIC0206. http://data.parliament.uk/writtenevidence/committeeevidence.svc/evidencedocument/artificial-intelligence-committee/artificial-intelligence/written/70496.html#_ftn13. Accessed 7 May 2022

Wilson C (2020) Artificial Intelligence and Warfare. In: Martellini M, Trapp R (eds) 21st Century Prometheus. Springer International Publishing, Cham, pp 125–140. DOI: https://doi.org/10.1007/978-3-030-28285-1_7

Winter E (2020) The Compatibility of the Use of Autonomous Weapons with the Principle of Precaution in the Law of Armed Conflict. The Military Law and the Law of War Review 58(2):240–273. DOI: https://doi.org/10.4337/mllwr.2020.02.18
Wooldridge M (2001) Intelligent Agents: The Key Concepts. In: Mařík V et al. (eds) Multi-Agent Systems and Applications II (2001) 9th ECCAI-ACAI/EASSS 2001, AEMAS 2001, HoloMAS 2001 Selected Revised Papers

Chapter 9
AWS and Targeting

Contents

Abstract This chapter engages in a thorough examination of the five main targeting rules in IHL (indiscriminate attack, proportionality, minimising collateral damage, warnings, and delaying/cancelling) and how their application would be impacted by the unique properties of autonomous weapon systems (AWS). The chapter offers a dual approach: first, an analysis of how AWS-users should apply these obligations under a more strict interpretation of the law, and second, it considers a slightly more normative angle based on an object and purpose interpretation. This latter prong is motivated by certain characteristics of AI that can be capitalised on to *improve* the protection of civilians, given the willingness to read existing rules through a

J. Kwik, *Lawfully Using Autonomous Weapon Technologies*,
https://doi.org/10.1007/978-94-6265-631-4_9

more teleological lens. Several new and important concepts are presented related to AWS-attacks. The notion of Attack Scopes is introduced to limit how broadly AWS-attacks may be construed under IHL: this subsequently is used to demonstrate how proportionality and cancelling would be performed for AWS-attacks. Related to indiscriminate attack, it is argued that deploying an AWS in circumstances outside of its intended use-cases or without (human-performed) target validation should be considered an indiscriminate attack, even if the system itself is not indiscriminate. In addition, it is argued that all Context Controls discussed in Chap. 8 constitute forms of risk mitigation, that are obligatory under the precautionary rule. This chapter thereby offers an extensive and reasoned view on how commanders should navigate targeting rules when using a novel technology for which minimal guidance currently exists.

Keywords Autonomous weapon system · Artificial intelligence · Attack · Targeting · Proportionality · Precautions in attack · Indiscriminate attack · Indiscriminate weapon · Warning · Cancelling · Feasible precautions · Military advantage · Collateral damage · Target validation · Incidental harm · Black box · Uncertainty

9.1 Introduction

The previous chapter aimed to identify the circumstances that would make using AWS more or less difficult in light of applicable IHL rules. Discussion on targeting rules themselves, including the specific provisions listed in the introduction to this part,[1] was limited. In that respect, the analytical approach of Chap. 8 was more practical than (strictly) legal: it explained using the three Rationales why certain conditions make using AWS more cumbersome, without explicitly linking the discussion to particular provisions.[2]

Ultimately however, Deployers are responsible for implementing positive provisions instead of abstract rationales. It is therefore equally important to investigate some of these targeting obligations in greater detail, and discuss how AWS technology may influence how they should be read. As such, in the remainder of this chapter, we explore the rules related to distinction and precautions in greater detail.[3] As indicated in Sect. 7.2, each rule is analysed through the dual perspective of a conservative textual reading of the provision, followed by a more teleological interpretation in light of AI-unique properties of AWS.

---

[1] See Chap. 7.

[2] The Rationales were derived from applicable rules related to the conduct of hostilities, but have not categorically been linked with any particular provision.

[3] To recall, these were: Article 51(4) (indiscriminate weapons); Article 57(2)(a)(i) (verification); Article 57(2)(a)(ii) (minimisation); Article 57(2)(a)(iii) (proportionality); Article 57(2)(b) (cancelling or suspending); and Article 57(2)(c) (warnings). See Sect. 7.2.

The chapter proceeds as follows. First, Section 9.2 revisits a recurrent concept from Chap. 8: the *scope of attack*. This notion is analysed from a more strictly legal lens due to its importance: the interpretation of many rules discussed in this chapter depends on how Deployer construes the boundaries of their AWS attack. The *prohibition on indiscriminate warfare* is then addressed in Sects. 9.3 and 9.4, discussing indiscriminate means and unaimed attacks respectively. The chapter then explores how Deployer should interpret several precautions related to attack: *proportionality* (Sect. 9.5), *minimisation* (Sect. 9.6), *warning* (Sect. 9.7), and finally *cancelling* (Sect. 9.8).

9.2 The Scope of an AWS Attack

'Attack' is an important term of art in IHL[4] to which many protections such as distinction and precautions attach.[5] Difficulties in its interpretation are sometimes encountered as new technologies emerge, such as cyber.[6]

One aspect where AWS technology should not raise controversy regards *whether* its use would pass the attack threshold. As indicated by its API definition "acts of violence against the adversary",[7] the infliction of violence is an attack's *sine qua non.*[8] Given that AWS as discussed in this book are systems intended to inflict (physical) harm to military objectives, there is little reason to doubt that their use constitutes an attack.[9] As previously mentioned, whether an AWS's intended use is 'defensive' (e.g. C-RAM) or 'offensive' (e.g. search-and-destroy) is legally immaterial since the infliction of violence remains an attack "whether [committed] in offence or in defence".[10]

---

[4] Schmitt 2012, p. 284.

[5] Gisel et al. 2020, p. 312; Turns 2013, p. 227.

[6] See Sect. 7.2.

[7] Protocol Additional to the Geneva Conventions of 12 August 1949, and relating to the Protection of Victims of International Armed Conflicts, adopted 8 June 1977, entered into force 7 December 1978, 1125 UNTS 3 (API), Article 49(1). This definition has been reproduced in other legal instruments and jurisprudence. See Program on HPCR at Harvard University 2013, HPCR Manual on International Law Applicable to Air and Missile Warfare. Cambridge University Press, Cambridge (HPCR Manual), Rule 1(e); Schmitt M N (ed) 2017, Tallinn Manual 2.0 on the International Law Applicable to Cyber Warfare. 2nd edn. Cambridge University Press, Cambridge (Tallinn Manual 2.0), Rule 92; ICTY (TC), *Prosecutor v. Dragoljub Kunarac, Radomir Kovać and Zoran Vuković*, Judgment, 22 February 2001, IT-96-23-T & IT-96-23/1-T, para 415.

[8] Schmitt 2012, p. 290.

[9] While we do not currently discuss *intended* misuse of AWS (e.g. to target civilian entities), this would still constitute an attack despite the wording "against the adversary" in the API formulation. Program on Humanitarian Policy and Conflict Research at Harvard University 2010. Commentary on the HPCR Manual on International Law Applicable to Air and Missile Warfare, Harvard University, Harvard (HPCR Manual Commentary), p. 27. See Section 1.4.

[10] API, above n. 7, Article 49(1). See Sect. 8.1. This was also the reason why 'offensive' or 'defensive' was not selected as a variable in Chap. 8.

Instead, it is argued that the main challenge lies in properly interpreting the *scope* of what constitutes an attack when an AWS is involved. How broadly or narrowly we understand 'attack' has significant ramifications for how Deployer is expected to apply different rules. As such, in this section, we attempt to determine the proper way the scope of 'attack' should be defined.

First, let us clarify what is meant by 'scope'. An attack has been variably described as "the commission of acts of violence",[11] "combat action",[12] or "any military act of a violent nature".[13] As the last quote indicates, the bottom threshold is very low: even a single bomb or lone sniper shot can constitute an attack.[14] On other end of the spectrum, one draws a distinction between attacks and military operations. An attack is narrower than an operation[15]: the HPCR Manual notes that an operation "may consist of one or more attacks, or none at all".[16] Between these two extremes, however, there is less clarity on how we should construe an AWS attack. Consider:

> **Scenario 3: How many attacks?** At 1200 hours, Deployer activated an AWS to attack a tank platoon, during which the system released 7 shots at 5 tanks.[17] At 1500, Deployer sent the same AWS to attack 4 tanks guarding the city's four main arteries, during which the system released 5 shots.

How many attacks has Deployer engaged in today? This depends on what we consider the unit of measurement for 'attack':

- 'Each deployment decision' = 2 attacks
- 'Each tank' = 9 attacks
- 'Each released shot' = 12 attacks

This question is an important one since an attack can be viewed as the basic unit of reference for many legal obligations,[18] such as proportionality and the duty to cancel.[19] It also extends to certain proposals in the broader AWS debate, such as the notion of human control. Take the proposition that a "human should be in control of the system for each individual attack".[20] In itself, this statement is not particularly controversial, given that precautionary duties are addressed at "those who plan or decide upon an attack"[21] and most agree that systems cannot implement

---

[11] *Prosecutor v. Dragoljub Kunarac, Radomir Kovać and Zoran Vuković*, above n. 7, para 415.

[12] Sandoz et al. 1987, para 1880.

[13] HPCR Manual, above n.7, p. 28.

[14] Bothe et al. 2013, p. 329.

[15] Fleck 2013, para 442.

[16] HPCR Manual Commentary, above n. 9, p. 28.

[17] The additional shots were released because the AWS detected that the objective was still operational after the initial strike.

[18] Roff and Moyes 2016, p. 5.

[19] See Sects. 9.5 and 9.8.

[20] Chengeta 2016, p. 875.

[21] API, above n. 7, Article 57(2)(a).

IHL obligations 'for' Deployer.[22] However, this same statement can lead to entirely different requirements of human involvement depending on how one defines the scope of 'attack'. On one end of the spectrum, we find positions that construe 'attack' at the narrowest level (e.g. "the stage when the munition is fired"[23]), which essentially "precludes autonomous systems".[24] On the other, we find interpretations finding that an attack could also encompass the AWS's overall active period,[25] which would conceptually permit autonomy at the 'trigger-pulling' level.[26]

The current author perceives much of the disagreement in literature regarding the legality of 'autonomy' as derived from *imprecision* and *divergent interpretations* on the scope of attack.[27] The aim of this section, then, is to present the author's reasoned position on the proper way to conceptualise the scope of attack when using AWS.

Since scope is closely related to the extent to which entities may be grouped into one attack, it may be useful to revisit Fig. 8.4 on target specificity, reframed below in terms of Attack Scope. Each arrow represents different ways 'attack' can theoretically be conceived.[28]

In the remainder of this section, we address the following points. First, we explore the theoretical contours that limit how narrowly or broadly Attack Scope can be conceived. Second, having determined these contours, we provide more concrete factors that determine to what extent Deployer *may* aggregate multiple entities into one AWS attack.

9.2.1 Contours

Drawing the line too far to the 'left' or 'right' of the spectrum are both conceptually problematic. To see why, take the most restrictive option of seeing *each Instance* as a separate attack to which legal obligations attach. As noted above, many positions in the AWS polemics imply this proposition, but this is conceptually incorrect, inconsistent with practice and makes many related rules unworkable. Conceptually, API refers to "*acts* of violence"[29] and the API Commentary mentions "combat action" and "counter-*attacks*",[30] which implies that several individual strikes can constitute

[22] US Office of General Counsel of the Department of Defense 2015, Law of War Manual, Updated December 2016. US Department of Defense, Washington D.C. (US Law of War Manual), sct 6.5.9.3; Roorda 2015, p. 163; Cherry and Johnson 2020, pp. 17–19.

[23] Boothby 2021, p. 388.

[24] Jensen 2021, p. 191.

[25] E.g. Ekelhof 2019; van den Boogaard and Roorda 2021, pp. 425–430.

[26] I.e., each time a munition is released by the AI. See Jensen 2021, p. 192.

[27] See Roff and Moyes 2016, p. 5.

[28] For our discussion on Scenario 3, 'each released shot' would correspond to *Instance*, 'each tank' would correspond to *Single* (since one tank can be engaged with multiple shots), and 'each deployment decision' falls into *Group* for the 1200 sortie and *Category* for the 1500 sortie.

[29] API, above n. 7, Article 49(1) (emphasis added).

[30] Sandoz et al. 1987, para 1880 (emphasis added).

one attack.[31] The ICTY similarly referred to "the commission of *acts* of violence".[32] Bothe et al. confirm that an Instance-level-only interpretation was never the API drafters' intent.[33]

Additionally, the proposition is inconsistent with existing practice. An attack may involve the use of force against multiple objectives.[34] Many 'defensive' systems currently in-use,[35] such as C-RAM and active protection systems, would be impossible to operate if each shot were classified as a separate attack for which legal analyses must be conducted.[36] Commanders do not supervise when each landmine 'decides' to release force or not.[37] For rocket volleys fired at a concentration of tanks, one does not look at each individual munition and determine whether it was properly directed at a military objective, whether incidental harm is excessive, etc.[38]: instead, the volley as a whole is assessed.[39]

Finally, the proportionality rule, which requires that expected incidental harm may not be excessive to the anticipated military advantage, precludes an Instance-only interpretation. With respect to military advantage, a debate very reminiscent to our current discussion emerged in the past concerning the possibility of counting several strikes together for the purposes of determining an attack's military advantage.[40] Commentators asked if military advantage should be assessed on the basis of "a single strike or for a series of strikes",[41] "a single military objective, on the basis of a battle, a campaign or a war".[42] Consensus[43] was eventually reached that military

---

31 Bothe et al. 2013, p. 329.

32 *Prosecutor v. Dragoljub Kunarac, Radomir Kovać and Zoran Vuković*, above n. 7, para 415 (emphasis added).

33 Bothe et al. 2013, p. 329.

34 Roff and Moyes 2016, p. 5.

35 Many have been in-use for several decades. See Scharre and Horowitz 2015, Annex B; ICRC 2016a, sct 2.

36 Scharre 2014.

37 Cf. Moyes 2019, p. 4.

38 Assuming proper corrections are made after initial shots to ensure the volley is correctly directed at the intended targets. See Šustr et al. 2022, p. 80.

39 See also Sect. 9.5.2.

40 Blum 2011, p. 189.

41 Durhin 2016, p. 188.

42 Fenrick 2005, p. 177. Neuman asked: "what is the standard for measuring 'concrete and direct military advantage anticipated'? Should the military advantage be measured based on the specific tactical objective of a particular action ('case by case' basis), or should it be measured on a 'cumulative' basis, taking into account the contribution of the attack to the belligerent's overall strategic goals?". Neuman 2004, p. 96.

43 See US Law of War Manual, above n. 22, sct 5.6.7.3; UK Ministry of Defence 2004, The Joint Service Manual of the Law of Armed Conflict. UK Ministry of Defence, London, Joint Service Publication 383 (UK Law of Armed Conflict Manual), sct 5.33.5; Reservation of the French Republic to the Protocol Additional to the Geneva Conventions of 12 August 1949, and relating to the Protection of Victims of International Armed Conflicts reservation of 11 April 2001, https://ihl-databases.icrc.org/en/ihl-treaties/api-1977/state-parties/fr (accessed 31 July 2023) (French Reservation to API), para 10; Fleck 2013, para 445; Bothe et al. 2013, p. 366.

advantage should "relate to the attack considered as whole and not merely to isolated or particular parts of the attack",[44] indicating that an attack may indeed consist of multiple strikes on one or more entities.[45]

At the same time, defining 'attack' too broadly is similarly contrary to existing law, and also threatens many protections accorded by IHL. Take the notion that *each deployment decision* is an attack. Depending on how long the AWS is allowed to remain active, its freedom of movement, its target specificity, etc., this 'one attack' can theoretically span hours, many square kilometres, hundreds of entities, and thousands of Instances. Many protections granted by precautionary duties in attack would be compromised if this were amalgamated into one attack.[46] Conceptually, it would also render the proportionality rule moot. It is often noted that attack can in no event stretch to encompass strikes conducted during an entire military operation,[47] since this would justify almost endless levels of incidental harm on the basis that it permitted the belligerent to 'win the battle', or even the entire war.[48]

Given the above, Deployers must be able to conceive 'attack' broadly enough to allow some Instances to be processed in succession by the AWS without legal analysis being required for each, but not so broadly that it jeopardises Deployer's ability to implement obligations in attack. But how to determine the appropriate scope for *specific* AWS attacks? It is argued that this should be resolved pursuant to specific factors as follows.

9.2.2 Factors Influencing Scope

Two main factors determine the maximum extent to which Deployer may consider successive Instances within one AWS deployment as one attack. These are *proximity in time and space*.

Proximity in time and space are common indicators used in literature to delineate the limits of a particular attack. In the travaux for API, the ICRC noted that the term attack "is related to only one specific military operation, limited in space and time".[49] Dinstein similarly submits that "the temporal or geographic dimensions must be construed reasonably. They cannot be too remote or long-term".[50] The ICTY commission investigating NATO conduct in Kosovo also mentioned time and

[44] HPCR Manual, above n.7, para 1(w).

[45] Dinstein 2016, p. 108.

[46] Against this backdrop, the position that an AWS "cannot proceed from one attack to another, to another, without human legal judgment being applied" makes eminent sense. Article 36 2016, p. 3.

[47] HPCR Manual Commentary, above n. 9, p. 28; Fleck 2013, para 442.

[48] Gisel 2016, p. 13.

[49] Bothe et al. 2013, p. 329 at n2. An expert group convened by the ICRC in 2016 agreed that an attack "had to remain a finite operation with defined limits". Gisel 2016, p. 17.

[50] Dinstein 2016, p. 161.

space as contours for proportionality calculations.[51] With regard to spatial proximity specifically, recall also that API treats as an indiscriminate attack one which "treats as a single military objective a number of *clearly separated* and distinct military objectives".[52]

It is true that no fixed standard exists in terms of seconds or square kilometres as to how far one attack may stretch: the extent to which entities "should be geographically proximate to each other, and the duration over which a use of force may constitute an individual attack, are all open questions to some extent".[53] Abovementioned ICTY report also left the question open as an "unresolved" matter.[54] However, it is clear that too high a distance in time and space compromises Deployer's ability to properly implement their obligations in attack, particularly due to risk of epistemic error (Rationale-EE). Since Deployer

> needs to make legal judgements based on an anticipation of the interaction of a system with its operational context, there needs to be some bounding of that context in space and time in order for such judgements to be substantive. The wider the physical area, and the longer the duration of operation, the less detailed the information a commander will likely have regarding that area, and the less predictable that system's use will be.[55]

In light of this, we can make qualitative pronouncements on the boundaries in time and space with regard to an AWS attack. Given the high dynamicity of the operational environment,[56] the maximum permitted timeframe within which Instances may be grouped into one attack will be quite limited, and particularly so if many (mobile) collateral concerns are present. Spatially, objectives grouped together in close proximity can more easily be assessed on the basis on similar environmental presumptions. In contrast, objectives spaced further apart will inhabit distinct operational spaces that cannot be legally analysed as one attack.[57]

Let us apply these criteria to Scenario 3 posed at the start of this section to demonstrate. For the 1200 sortie, the tanks are co-located, and the AWS is presumably poised to engage all objectives in short succession. For this situation, it is argued that Deployer is entitled to analyse the sortie as a single Group-attack[58] as per Fig. 9.1. Deployer only needs to verify the tanks' military nature once before the engagement,

[51] ICTY, Final Report to the Prosecutor by the Committee Established to Review the NATO Bombing Campaign Against the Federal Republic of Yugoslavia, 2001, www.icty.org/en/press/final-report-prosecutor-committee-established-review-nato-bombing-campaign-against-federal (accessed 4 August 2023) (NATO Report), para 49.

[52] API, above n. 7, Article 51(5)(a) (emphasis added).

[53] Roff and Moyes 2016, p. 5.

[54] Nato Report, above n. 51, para 49.

[55] Moyes 2019, p. 9.

[56] Section 3.4.2.

[57] The spatial dimension also impacts the temporal dimension, assuming that the AWS may need to travel between locations. This adds to active time. See Sect. 8.3.1.

[58] Recall that for Group, the objectives must all belong to a Specific Target Group, which is the case for a tank platoon. See Sect. 8.5.2.

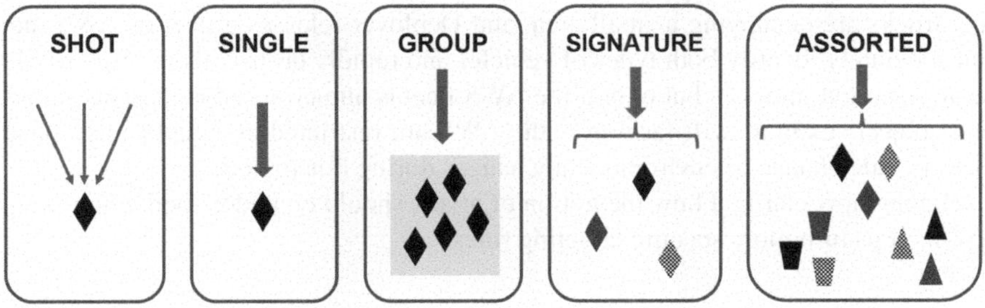

Fig. 9.1 Attack scope spectrum

may aggregate military advantage and incidental harm, etc.[59] This would be the same way an artillery volley against the same group of tanks would be characterised and assessed.

For the 1500 sortie, however, the tanks are geographically separated, presumably by a significant distance. In addition, due to the AWS's travel time between tanks, the delay between engagements will be quite large. Here Deployer cannot treat this as a single Group-scale attack: Deployer must consider each tank a separate Single-attack. This entails separate proportionality analyses, attempts at minimising risk of incidental harm, etc.[60] Crucially, Deployer must continually monitor the 'other' tanks while the AWS is occupied with the first, and cancel the strike(s) if circumstances change substantially (e.g. one tank rolls next to a busy stall).[61] This is the same assessment as when artillery would be used on the four tanks: they would constitute separate attacks and require distinct legal analyses.

We see here how significantly the scope of attack impacts Deployer's ability to allow an AWS to operate autonomously. There is thus no simple answer to whether autonomy 'is' or 'is not' allowed under IHL: it all is a question of whether such autonomy is used sufficiently narrowly in terms of Attack Scope.

The answer to the question posed at the start of this section is thus: Deployer engaged in five attacks today. One at 1200 hours, and four at 1500.

We have seen examples of Single- and Group-attacks. Can attacks also be of the other tiers? An *Instance*-attack is a special Single-attack, where the AWS is only poised to make *one* engagement decision, e.g. if the AWS is intended to crash into the objective. Are *Category*- and *Assorted*-attacks possible? While rare, theoretically yes if the spatial and temporal conditions remain satisfied. Say a mix of tanks and

---

[59] For example, if one building is predicted to be damaged because a tank is stationed in proximity to it, Deployer may find the military advantage from destroying five tanks sufficient to justify this collateral damage.

[60] To continue the previous example, if one building is predicted to be damaged because a tank is stationed in proximity to it, Deployer may no longer aggregate military advantage obtained from destroying four tanks to justify it. Deployer would need to weigh the military advantage of neutralising *one* tank against this collateral damage, which likely would not pass the proportionality test.

[61] API, above n. 7, Article 57(2)(b).

fuel trucks are occupying a small area, and Deployer releases a fleet of AWS that can accurately identify both types of vehicles and rapidly destroy them. This would be an Assorted-attack,[62] but only if the AWS fleet is numerous enough to neutralise most objectives in a swift fashion,[63] the AWS are restricted geographically,[64] and there is little chance of environmental changes during this period.

Having now clarified how the notion of attack should be understood when using AWS, let us turn more specific targeting rules.

9.3 Indiscriminate Means

API Article 51(4)(b-c) qualify attacks that employ a "means of combat which cannot be directed at a specific military objective" and those the "effects of which cannot be limited" as indiscriminate. Unlike subparagraph (a), which prohibits the indiscriminate use of *a priori* discriminate weapons,[65] subparagraphs (b-c)[66] cover weapons that are "by nature indiscriminate".[67] With respect our discussion, the question arises of how we can determine whether an AWS is inherently indiscriminate.

9.3.1 When is an AWS Inherently Indiscriminate?

One option to answer this question is to simply rely on qualitative descriptors, such as 'unable to be directed at military objectives',[68] 'blind',[69] 'strikes military and civilian entities without distinction',[70] or 'producing effects which are totally unforeseeable'.[71] Such descriptors have been used in the past to declare many systems

[62] Remember that Assorted is characterised by Deployer targeting entities from a *known and closed list* of possible objectives. See Sect. 8.5.2.

[63] If only a single AWS is sent, it is likely too 'slow' since it must engage each objective in succession, and other objectives will move away, foreseeably decreasing spatial proximity.

[64] See Sect. 8.7.5.

[65] Dinstein 2016, p. 72. See Sect. 9.4.

[66] We cover subparagraphs (b) and (c) together under this subsection since weapons that cannot be aimed at specific objectives and those whose effects cannot be controlled are usually considered as alternative forms of weapons that are inherently indiscriminate. Doswald-Beck 1997, p. 39; Crootof 2015, p. 1873.

[67] Henckaerts and Doswald-Beck 2005, Rule 71.

[68] Fleck 2013, para 449; Schmitt 2006, p. 140.

[69] Bothe et al. 2013, p. 346.

[70] Toscano 2015, p. 206.

[71] Doswald-Beck 1997, p. 41.

inherently indiscriminate,[72] and AWS that perform so poorly as to clearly be indiscriminate can also be identified as such on this basis.[73] A good-faith Deployer should in most instances be able to determine when an AWS in their possession would fall in this category, e.g. when it is demonstrably incapable of distinguishing civilian and military entities.[74]

Another interesting possibility is to tie this rule to measures of performance (MoP) of AI as discussed in Chap. 4. Many commentators have drawn the link between the indiscriminate means provision and MoPs such as reliability[75] and performance,[76] and have argued that AWS that cannot achieve certain minimum MoP standards may not be fielded pursuant to this rule.[77] Reference to more objective and measurable standards is not entirely foreign to Article 51(4)(b-c). The API Commentary describes indiscriminate weapons as those which because of their "*imprecision* … will indiscriminately affect the civilian population"[78] and the Australian Manual speaks of weapons that are too "inaccurate" to be directed at military objectives.[79] For legacy systems, poor measurements in accuracy, dispersion and circular error probable have been used to argue for why certain weapons are inherently indiscriminate.[80]

One recalls our previous finding that the Specificity metric represents an AI's capacity to distinguish in statistical terms.[81] A *sufficient level of Specificity* thus is required for an AWS to not breach the indiscriminate means rule.

Even having determined that Specificity is the key measurement, it is less settled what the specific standard would be for an AWS to be considered inherently indiscriminate. Evidently, IHL provisions provide no explicit guidance.[82] It is likely that in practice, specific quantitative standards will be adopted by States in decentralised fashion, for the purposes of design policy and review guidelines.[83] For operational purposes, it is likely more desirable for the adaptability of IHL for such standards

---

72 German V2 rockets, chemical and biological weapons, poison, and drifting armed contact mines are classic examples of inherently indiscriminate weapons under these definitions. See Henckaerts and Doswald-Beck 2005, pp. 249–50; Sandoz et al. 1987, paras 1958–59; US Department of the Navy 2017, sct 9.1.2.

73 Henderson et al. 2017, p. 361: "If a combatant employing a weapon system is aware that the weapon is so error prone as to be indiscriminate … then that combatant would be in breach of IHL."

74 Henckaerts and Doswald-Beck 2005, p. 247.

75 E.g. Boothby 2021, p. 385; ICRC 2016b, p. 81; Goussac 2019.

76 E.g. Schuller 2019, p. 108; Meier 2019, p. 309.

77 E.g. Corn 2016, p. 226; Sleesman and Huntley 2019, p. 34; Buchan and Tsagourias 2021, p. 339.

78 Sandoz et al. 1987, para 1410 (emphasis added).

79 Australia 2006, Law Of Armed Conflict. Defence Publishing Service, Canberra, Australian Defence Doctrine Publication 06.4 (Australian Law of Armed Conflict Manual), para 4.6.

80 See e.g. Wiebe 2000, pp. 110–11 (cluster munitions); ICTY (TC), *Prosecutor v. Milan Martić*, Judgment, 12 June 2007, IT-95-11-T, para 462 (M-87 Orkan); ICTY (TC), *Prosecutor v. Ante Gotovina et al.*, Judgment, 15 April 2011, IT-06-90-T, para 1897 (artillery).

81 See Sect. 8.2.1.

82 Goussac 2019.

83 Meier 2019, p. 309; Schuller 2019, p. 108.

to remain qualitative.[84] Nevertheless, we can provide some general pointers for Deployers as follows:

(1) The rule prohibits weapons that "cannot distinguish between military objectives and civilians".[85] Before greenlighting the use of a particular system, Deployer must be virtually certain that the system's false positive rate is low enough to describe it as 'capable of distinguishing'. When making this assessment, Deployer will find it helpful to translate metrics into more digestible descriptions. Instead of *Specificity=0.8*, Deployer should instead think *the AWS incorrectly shoots one-in-five civilians it encounters*, which any reasonable commander would describe as incapable of distinguishing (and thus is clearly unacceptable).
(2) A weapon can be indiscriminate by nature while not actually being predicted to cause many victims casuistically. Recall that in Fig. 8.2,[86] very low Negative Class Frequency led the system with Specificity=0.8 to cause only 1 misclassification 20% of the time. This does not change the fact that a Specificity=0.8 system is conceptually unable to properly distinguish military and civilian entities as we found previously, and remains illegal under Article 51(4)(b-c).
(3) Some authors have argued that AWS must be 100% reliable and accurate,[87] but this is an unworkable standard. Deployer must be permitted under Article 51(4)(b-c) to field systems that carry a low-but-acceptable rate of error,[88] since "it is impossible to guarantee that an autonomous machine will never fail".[89] This is the same standard we apply for legacy weapons[90] and targeting more generally.[91] One can be very demanding (e.g. Specificity=0.999), but one cannot demand perfection.

---

[84] Huffman 2012, p. 49: "For good reason, the law of war has never reduced the rules of indiscriminate fire and proportionality to mathematical formulas. The circumstances of combat and the factors affecting accuracy and data available to the commander at the time a targeting decision is made are infinitely variable. The law requires a commander to make a good faith judgment, oftentimes under extreme pressures of time and danger. When viewed in hindsight, such decisions warrant a healthy degree of deference."

[85] Henckaerts and Doswald-Beck 2005, p. 247.

[86] See Section 8.2.2.1.

[87] E.g. Sparrow 2015, p. 710.

[88] There is broad consensus on this matter. McDougall 2019, p. 75; Poitras 2018, p. 489; Corn 2016, p. 228; Heyns 2014, p. 47.

[89] Righetti 2016, p. 37. This is also an inevitable corollary of normal accident theory. See Sect. 5.9.

[90] Gross 2016, p. 57; Scharre 2016, p. 23; Boothby 2016, sct 6.1.2.

[91] Driels 2013, p. 135; Schmitt and Schauss 2019, p. 165.

9.3.2 IOE-Incompatibility Presumes the AWS is Indiscriminate

For AWS, it is additionally argued that the following (normative) guideline be adopted: *Deployer must treat an AWS as indiscriminate under Article 51(4)(b-c) when not used in accordance with its prescribed Intended Operational Environment (IOE).*

To summarise, in Sect. 3.5, the following arguments were made:

(a) An IOE must be defined and maintained throughout the AWS's entire lifecycle by the Providing Entity, and properly communicated to Deployer;
(b) Use of an AWS outside this IOE can lead to significant but unintuitive and unpredictable drops in reliability and performance.

We take care to note that the norm proposed above is not directly found in Article 51(4)(b-c), but can be derived from it. Read plainly, the provision only prohibits weapons that *are* indiscriminate (i.e., as a matter of fact). When Deployer uses an AWS outside of its IOE (say, using one designed and tested for clear weather during a storm), there is a *possibility*, but not a *guarantee*, that it will act indiscriminately. It is nevertheless argued that using an AWS in an IOE-incompatible way should automatically qualify as violating Article 51(4)(b-c).

If Deployer uses an AWS outside of its IOE, Deployer has no guarantees as to its legality;[92] and unlike with legacy systems, Deployer cannot extrapolate its performance from (seemingly) similar cases. An artillery officer might be able to predict to some extent what effect wind and rain might have on their shells' trajectories (even if the system has never been tested under such conditions), but Deployer cannot determine *ad hoc* what muted sunlight and windswept debris will do to their AWS. As established in Chap. 5, AWS failures are unintuitive to humans, and AI can fail structurally when subjected to unexpected and untested variables.[93]

In essence, Deployer is using a system they have *no information about* in terms of its ability to distinguish: it might be able to, or it might not. The reasoning for this recommended interpretation is thus that of Rationale-EE: Deployer epistemically cannot determine "with any reasonable assurance" whether the system can be used in accordance with Article 51(4)(b-c),[94] and as such, Deployer may not use it.[95] An IOE-incompatible system is *stochastically indiscriminate*, and reasonable commanders

---

[92] If the recommendations in Sect. 3.5 are followed, reviews will have cleared the AWS as lawful (i.e. not inherently indiscriminate). This review constitutes abovementioned positive confirmation of the AWS's discriminate nature, but it applies only in "normal or expected use" cases, i.e., the IOE test conditions. See Bothe et al. 2013, p. 231.

[93] Gilpin et al. 2018, p. 1.

[94] Bothe et al. 2013, p. 346.

[95] Davison argues that "a commander who knowingly decides to activate an autonomous weapon system whose performance and effects they cannot reasonably predict in a particular situation may be held criminally responsible for any serious violations of IHL that result, to the extent that their decision to deploy the weapon is deemed reckless under the circumstances". Davison 2017, p. 17. See also Cherry and Johnson 2020, p. 15; Henderson et al. 2017, pp. 364–65.

would not use a weapon on the battlefield unless they can *positively confirm* that it is discriminate.[96]

Evidently, the indiscriminate weapons rule in IHL has historically not prevented weapons from being employed outside of circumstances for which they were designed as long as commanders were sure their use would remain discriminate. However, in light of the nature of modern AI, the author argues the evolved interpretation proposed in this subsection fits into the overall rationale of the provision, and thus should form part of how the rule is applied whenever AWS are involved in the future.

9.4 'Unaimed' Use of AWS

9.4.1 An Absence of Targeting

Even if an AWS performs well enough not to be inherently indiscriminate as described in the previous section, it can still be used to conduct indiscriminate attacks. API Article 51(4)(a) lists attacks "not directed at a specific military objective" as indiscriminate. Unlike Article 51(4)(b-c), this provision refers to the use of lawful weapons in an indiscriminate fashion.[97]

One interesting question to pose, in light of the theoretical ability of (well-functioning) AWS to 'direct themselves' to only attack military objectives, is whether it is possible for Deployer to breach Article 51(4)(a) when their weapon is compliant with Article 51(4)(b-c). Take the following thought experiment:

> **Scenario 4: Futuristic**. In the year 2xxx, an AWS with perfect reliability and Specificity is invented (it never fails, and never mistakes a civilian entity for a target). Deployer sends this AWS to an enemy-held town to strike as many military objectives inside as possible in preparation for an infantry assault.

Clearly, this is the dream AWS from the perspective of Article 51(4)(b-c): it is the most discriminate weapon possible, better even than the best human.[98] However, it is argued that even in this fantastical situation, this perfectly discriminate weapon can be used indiscriminately, and that is exactly what Deployer did in above scenario. The reason is that Deployer made absolutely no attempt to even consider what entities would be targeted by their AWS in the town, let alone verify these objectives' military nature as required by Article57(2)(a)(i). Deployer simply trusted that their AWS would do the distinguishing, targeting, and validating for them. In so far as we reject the notion that machines are legal subjects that can implement IHL for Deployers,[99]

---

[96] Thurnher 2012, p. 83.

[97] Schmitt 2013, p. 10.

[98] Many would argue that the use of AWS over humans should be preferred in this situation, since it foreseeably would reduce harm to the civilian population. E.g. Jensen 2018; Nasu and McLaughlin 2014, p. 251.

[99] A notion we have maintained throughout this book. See Sect. 1.1.

this is an indiscriminate attack. As Ohlin submits, an indiscriminate attack is one which "represents the complete lack of "targeting" entirely".[100]

Article 51(4)(a)'s description mentions attacks "not directed at a specific military objective". This perfectly describes what Deployer engaged in: the AWS was not directed at any particular objective, but merely a vague agglomeration of objectives that are supposed to exist in the town.[101] The NIAC Manual's description of indiscriminate attacks, as those where "no attempt is made to identify specific military objectives",[102] is similarly reflective of what Deployer did (not do).

It is important to distinguish the result from the process: "merely failing to aim a weapon ... is unlawful regardless of the effects that weapon causes".[103] The AWS is "capable of being aimed at a lawful target, but the attacker does not do so".[104] As such, separately from whether the AWS is able (performance-wise) to distinguish military from civilian entities, and irrespective of how good the system is at doing this, Deployer is required under IHL to define, identify and analyse the objectives the AWS is intended to target. Failure to do so renders the attack indiscriminate (Article 51(4)(a)) and violates the duty to validate (Article 57(2)(a)(i)), regardless of the actual harm inflicted on civilians.[105]

Perfect systems as in Scenario 4 do not exist,[106] but it is likely that real-life Deployers may be lured into similar forms of complacency by imperfect, but seemingly extremely well-performing, systems.[107] When in possession of such systems, Deployers may feel they are launching discriminate attacks by default when they release the system against an area known to house military objectives that the system was designed to locate and engage. As has now been argued, this is incorrect: Deployer must still 'aim' the AWS at specific (groups or sets of) targets. This requires

---

[100] Ohlin 2013, p. 94.

[101] The USAF Manual gives this example which is partially analogous to what Deployer did: "Dropping munitions—guided or not—in a residential area without regard to whether there are combatants or military objectives in the area simply *because there may be adversary forces there* would be an indiscriminate attack". Curtis E. Lemay Center 2019, p. 90 (emphasis added).

[102] Schmitt et al. 2006, sct 2.1.1.3.3-4.

[103] Schmitt and Highfill 2018, p. 82.

[104] Schmitt and Thurnher 2013, p. 253.

[105] Note we must separate Article 51(4)(a) from Article 85(3)(b). The latter is a result-crime (requiring "death or serious injury to body or health") and requires mens rea ("knowledge that such attack will cause excessive loss of life, injury to civilians or damage to civilian objects"). For Scenario 4, Deployer would have engaged in an indiscriminate attack in the sense of Article 51(4)(a), but not be liable under Article 85(3)(b) (since no harm is caused).

[106] Parasuraman et al. 2000, p. 293.

[107] Scharre 2018, p. 149.

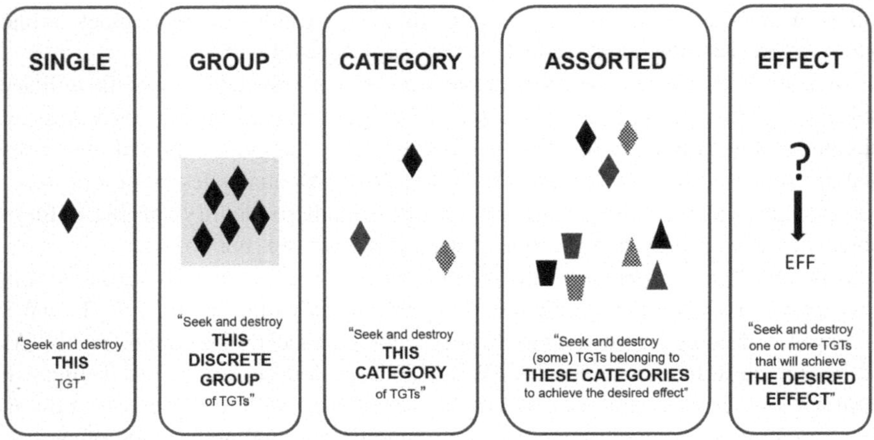

Fig. 9.2 Target specificity spectrum (reproduced)

pre-identification and pre-verification, *done by Deployer*.[108] The AWS's AI functionality merely provides Deployer with a reliable and efficient way to locate and engage these objectives, but it cannot do the targeting for them.

9.4.2 How Generally May Deployer Define the Objectives?

The API formulation requires attacks to be directed at "specific" objectives, but this does not necessarily mean that each entity must be treated as a separate objective. 'Objective' may be defined more broadly (e.g. 'a column of soldiers' or 'a group of tanks'),[109] but evidently cannot be stretched too far (as in Scenario 4). The question is therefore: under what conditions is Deployer considered to 'no longer be aiming' their AWS attack, rendering it indiscriminate? The target specificity spectrum of Fig. 9.2 is once again of use here.

It is clear that *Single and Group are specific enough* to be considered discriminate under Article 51(4)(a). In contrast, Effect clearly is not: Deployer is ignorant of the actual military objectives the AWS will strike. We can thus hold that *Effect-attacks are unlawful in principle*. For Category and Assorted, the situation is more complex. Deployer can still conduct 'aimed' attacks with these levels of target specificity, but under the following conditions:

[108] Quéguiner 2006, p. 797: "By requiring that those planning or deciding upon an attack do everything feasible to verify the nature of the objective, this provision aims to ensure that operations will target strictly military objectives and thus contributes to preserving the immunity of both civilian populations and objects. Therefore the duty to verify the nature of a target is a vital ramification of the principle of distinction."

[109] Many AWS in use are 'aimed' at such collective objectives. Scharre 2018, p. 52.

First, the military objectives that comprise these Categories or Assortments must be *separately identified and verified*. We found above that under specific conditions (proximity in time and space),[110] Category- and Assorted-attacks are possible. Deployer must nevertheless individually identify and verify the military nature of entities within these (assorted) categories for such attacks to be lawful.

Counting clearly separate entities as 'one' objective, unless they form a discrete Target Group,[111] is given as one type of indiscriminate attack under Article 51(5)(a).

Second, and related to the first, Deployer must *accurately predict* what entities their AWS will identify as military objectives based on its design, programming, etc. The more difficult the target type,[112] the more challenging this is. For example, if the AWS is supposed to find targets by nature (say military vehicles) within a 1 km^2 area, Deployer can scan positive class entities in the area (tanks, APCs, etc.) to fulfil the Article 51(5)(a) requirement. In contrast, if the AWS is supposed to find targets by purpose, the range of possible targets is immense, perhaps endless. Deployer would need to be intimately familiar with how the AWS determines if an entity is an objective by purpose, identify specific conditions on the ground that contribute toward these entities attaining this status, and validate each potential target as a valid objective.[113] If Deployer is not *positively convinced* they have identified all of the AWS's possible targets (i.e., the AWS might strike an entity Deployer did not foresee), then Deployer is once again engaging in an unaimed attack as argued in Sect. 9.4.1, by virtue of Rationale-EE (epistemic error).

Assigning Operators to monitor the AWS's operation effectively renders all attacks Instance-attacks, since a human would be performing a legal assessment[114] for every engagement. This is one way Deployer in Scenario 3 could lawfully order the 1500 sortie.

This subsection provides legal clarification for why in Sect. 8.9, lower target specificity and complex target types (such as objectives by purpose) were considered 'difficult' in the Facility spectrum. In practice, as we can see, these conditions may make it impossible to use AWS lawfully.

9.4.3 *Too High Opacity as an Unaimed Attack*

In this section so far, we have assumed that Deployer is *technically capable* of defining and validating the target objectives, but they did not take the effort to do so.

---

[110] Section 9.2.

[111] See Sect. 8.3.2.

[112] See Sect. 8.5.1.

[113] In addition, the intelligence upon which this assessment is based must be quite recent, as such circumstances change relatively rapidly. This aggravates the issue related to Rationale-EE. See also Sect. 8.3.1.

[114] At least, in the ideal circumstances. See Sect. 8.8.

However, there exists an exogenous factor that may *factually prevent* Deployer from doing this: opacity.[115]

As referenced in Sect. 8.6, predicting the system's likely actions in the field and which objectives will be attacked (and where and when) requires a *good mental model* of the AWS's internal logic. This mental model may be absent if the system is too opaque. As such, if Deployer uses a system that is opaque enough so as to prevent Deployer from making reasonably precise predictions as to what entities the system is likely to strike, *Deployer is engaging in an indiscriminate attack* in the sense of API Article 51(4)(a).

Analogously to our remarks concerning Scenario 4, this interdiction remains true even if the AWS is statistically proven to be (close to) perfect in terms of distinction. For example, even if Deployer had overwhelmingly convincing empiric proof of this AWS's reliability (for an extreme example, say the system has been tested and used over 10 years in a variety of environments, with almost zero mistakes), Deployer is still violating IHL if the system's opacity prevents them from predicting specific behaviour related to targets. This applies even if the AWS *in concreto* does not make any mistakes because its AI was so well-trained.[116] The problem lies in the fact that the attack was authorised without being properly directed at specific military objectives: that only military targets were struck is incidental in this regard. The *process*, not the *results* which happen to be discriminate, is determinative.[117]

As also was the case with the proposed interpretation concerning IOE-incompatibility in Sect. 9.3.2, Articles 51(4)(a) and 57(2)(a)(i) could not historically have been read to preclude the use of overly opaque systems, since no legacy weapon has been opaque to the extent that many ML-based AI are. However, it is argued that the underlying rationale of the prohibition on unaimed attacks and the duty to verify objectives provide a solid basis to derive a legal prohibition on excessively opaque systems from.

9.5 Calculating Proportionality

The proportionality rule found in API Article 57(2)(a)(iii) requires Deployers to ensure that attacks do not produce expected incidental harm that is excessive vis-à-vis the anticipated military advantage.[118] The proportionality rule is widely considered as the most problematic obligation to fulfil with regard to AWS[119] because both the

[115] See Sect. 4.5.

[116] While it is argued that using an opaque system is a violation of IHL on this basis, it would not constitute a war crime. The apparent lack of any harm to civilians would prevent this act from falling under Article 85(3), which contains result-crimes requiring actual 'death or serious injury to body or health' to have been caused. Bartels 2013, p. 300.

[117] Schmitt and Highfill 2018, p. 82.

[118] API, above n. 7, Article 57(2)(a)(iii).

[119] See Crootof 2015, pp. 1876–77; Kurosaki 2020, pp. 415–18; Henderson et al. 2017, p. 350.

evaluation of incidental harm and military advantage, and the subsequent weighing of the two variables, entails "qualitative rather than quantitative judgments" and requires "distinctly human judgment".[120]

That the proportionality test features an eminently subjective component,[121] possibly irreducible to quantification,[122] is relatively well-established in literature. However, discussants are incorrect when they portray the proportionality rule as an insurmountable obstacle that precludes lawful AWS use. The proportionality test is only a problem if we assume that the *system* is supposed to make these proportionality calculations internally,[123] but this is not the position taken in this analysis. What IHL demands is not that systems *perform*, but rather that they are used *in compliance with*, the proportionality rule.[124]

The way the proportionality obligation should be applied vis-à-vis AWS is very similar to how we applied Article 51(4)(a), above.[125] A system capable of conducting internal proportionality analyses would be a useful asset for Deployer,[126] but does not subsume Deployer's own duty as the person "plan[ing] or decid[ing] upon an attack"[127] to execute the proportionality test. Many commentators have followed this line of reasoning,[128] emphasising that when using AWS, the proportionality assessment should have "effectively been made in advance by the personnel who deployed the system based on the known capabilities of the AWS and the military situation",[129] i.e., prior to an AWS's activation and continually afterward if circumstances in the field change.[130] As with Article 51(4)(a), Deployer may not 'trust' their system to perform the proportionality test for them, even if it is hypothetically able to correctly perform proportionality-like analyses.

There are essentially three main steps that go into a proportionality assessment: estimating the anticipated military advantage from the attack; identifying and assessing expected incidental harm; and contrasting the two to determine whether incidental harm is excessive to military advantage.[131] Testing the proportionality of

---

[120] Heyns 2013, paras 72–73. See also Sect. 9.8.3.

[121] Jensen 2003, p. 1181; Henderson 2009, p. 222.

[122] Fenrick 2001, p. 499; Holland 2004, p. 46; Blank 2019, p. 331. Huffman notes that IHL "has never reduced the rules of indiscriminate fire and proportionality to mathematical formulas". Huffman 2012, p. 49.

[123] Which is unlikely in the near future, if ever. Boothby 2018, pp. 149–50. This comment is notwithstanding many important theoretical works from authors attempting to more precisely define concepts such as incidental harm, military advantage, what is 'excessive', and reasonableness so they could one day be subject to computation and analysis by AI. Cf. Arkin 2009; Toscano 2015, p. 211; Winter 2020, p. 264; Blank 2019, p. 332.

[124] Cherry and Johnson 2020, p. 17.

[125] See Sect. 9.4.1.

[126] We discuss proportionality analysis at the Instance-level (by the AWS) in Sect. 9.8.3.

[127] API, above n. 7, Article 57(2)(a).

[128] E.g. Schmitt and Thurnher 2013, p. 267; Crootof 2015, p. 1878; Kastan 2013, pp. 61–62.

[129] Henderson et al. 2017, p. 352.

[130] API, above n. 7, Article 57(2)(b).

[131] Blank 2019, p. 332.

an AWS attack does not in principle differ from that of a 'normal' attack, but there are some issues relatively unique to AWS to clarify. Two matters will be discussed here. First, what happens legally if, due to AI's inherently greater degree of indeterminacy, Deployer is unable to concretely assess the incidental harm and military advantage an AWS attack is expected to cause? Second, how do Attack Scopes affect proportionality assessments?

9.5.1 Uncertainty

The proportionality test features a strong prognostic component.[132] This is reflected in Article 57(2)(a)(iii) itself, which mentions 'anticipated' and 'expected'.[133] The real world is "necessarily embedded in probabilities".[134] Operations often occur under time-pressure[135] and the fog of war is ineluctable.[136] To accommodate this reality, IHL has some level of tolerance for decision-making in circumstances short of complete certainty.[137] Thus, the fact that AWS operate with some independence, and at some level of indeterminacy, does not necessarily preclude Deployer from making proportionality assessments for AWS attacks.

At the same time, IHL does not permit commanders to completely surrender to uncertainty. Particularly with regard to incidental harm, the law expects commanders to take reasonable efforts to "predict the harm that an attack may inflict on civilians".[138] Experts during an ICRC discussion agreed that this is an active obligation: "commanders have an obligation to proactively seek out and collect relevant and reasonably available information" that would allow them to obtain a relatively concrete measure of the incidental harm the attack is likely to produce.[139] That some technologies make this more challenging does not relieve commanders of this duty,[140] and failing to do this is a breach of the proportionality rule.[141] As Oeter submits,

[132] Oeter 2020, pp. 350–51.

[133] HPCR Manual Commentary, above n. 9, pp. 91–92.

[134] Dinstein 2016, p. 157.

[135] Oeter 2020, p. 354.

[136] Gisel 2016, p. 57.

[137] US Law of War Manual, above n. 22, para 5.3.2; Oeter 2020, p. 354.

[138] Haque 2017, p. 207. With many legacy systems, collateral damage prediction is done through established methodologies such as CDE.

[139] Gisel 2016, p. 48. As with all precautions, the extent to which this obligation persists depends on what can reasonably be expected from Deployer in the circumstances at the time.

[140] Schmitt, in the context of cyber, made a similar remark. "[W]hen caused by computer network attack such damage and injury, whether direct or indirect, are difficult to assess without knowing how the computer systems involved function and to which other systems they are linked. *Despite this obstacle*, planners and decision-makers have an *affirmative duty* to attempt to avoid collateral damage and incidental injury whenever feasible, a duty that necessarily implies an *effort to ascertain the damage or injury likely to result from an attack*." Schmitt 2002, p. 393 (emphasis added).

[141] Robinson and Nohle 2016, p. 140.

Deployer is already in violation of Article 57(2)(a)(iii) if they "simply acted careless in not seeking enough information to come to a reliable prognosis of expected incidental losses".[142]

Uncertainty becomes relevant with regard to AWS since depending on how they are used, it may become virtually impossible for Deployer to properly predict the incidental harm (and sometimes military advantage) that will result from an AWS attack. Variables[143] linked with Rationale-EE (epistemic error) produce this effect. For example:

- *Temporal*. As more time lapses, the higher the risk that civilian entities may move, civilian density changes, etc.[144] Proportionality calculations can be made 'in advance',[145] but on the condition that Deployer is reasonably certain that assumptions related to incidental harm and military advantage *hold* between the moment the deployment decision is made and the strike(s) is carried out by the AWS.
- *Target specificity*. If Deployer launches an Assorted-attack as in Scenario 4 without additional Context Controls,[146] Deployer cannot know which specific objectives will be struck, and at what location or which timing. This makes it practically impossible to predict the expected incidental harm. In contrast, if target specificity is higher (say, Group-level), Deployer can make relatively accurate predictions about incidental harm on the basis of what civilian entities are signalled in the discrete target group's vicinity.
- *Opacity* is a particularly problematic source of uncertainty.[147] An overly opaque system that introduces too much variability as to the probable entities hit, and when and under what circumstances they will be struck, effectively prevents Deployer from making proportionality assessments because incidental harm cannot be predicted to a sufficiently precise level.

Note that Deployer can use a system with high performance and 'aim' the AWS at predefined, validated objectives (satisfying Articles 51(4)(a-c) and 57(2)(a)(i)) but still violate Article 57(2)(a)(iii) because epistemic uncertainty is too great.[148]

---

142 Oeter 2020, p. 363.

143 See Fig. 8.7.

144 Crootof argues that when "there is a significant temporal span between deployment and potential engagements or where the weapon system is venturing into unknown territory, a commander could not reasonably take responsibility for conducting the proportionality requirement; too many of the conditions the weapon system might face would be unpredictable". Crootof 2015, p. 1878.

145 Schmitt and Thurnher 2013, p. 267.

146 The ability of the AWS to cancel strikes if too much incidental harm is predicted would be one Context Control that might make this attack possible. See Sect. 9.8.3.

147 See Sect. 8.6.

148 For example, Deployer wants to activate a very accurate aerial AWS that automatically shoots explosive rounds at (previously positively identified) enemy vehicles in a given area. The system is not inherently indiscriminate as it is very reliable (Article 51(4)(b-c)), and the objectives are clear and specific (Article 51(4)(a)). However, Deployer made no attempt to analyse the expected incidental harm since the vehicles are evasive (weaving in and out of busy streets) and Deployer

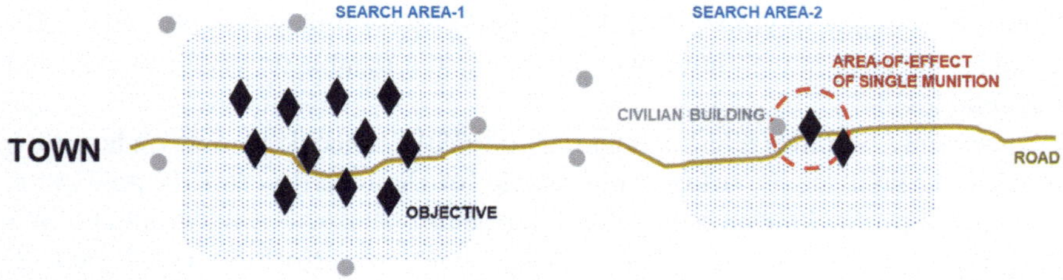

Fig. 9.3 Map of road to town

They are separate requirements that must cumulatively be fulfilled for an attack to be lawful.

9.5.2 Attack Scope

Attack Scope is a crucial notion in proportionality assessments, since both military advantage and incidental harm are compared on the basis of the 'attack as a whole' and not its isolated parts.[149] IHL permits several strikes to be counted jointly since military advantage is often not only derived from the tactical feat of destroying, capturing or neutralising individual objectives[150] but also from broader operational effects[151] that are not reduceable to its constituents.[152] In Section 9.2.1, we established the (maximum) contours of an AWS attack and what circumstances exceptionally allow broader conceptions (such as Category or Assorted). This in mind, Deployer can use the notion of Attack Scopes as an aide to analyse proportionality during more complicated multi-Instance situations as the following:

> **Scenario 5: Road to town.** Enemy armour has been positively identified on a road leading to a town as depicted in Fig. 9.3. Deployer considers sending AWS that very reliably can search and strike armour until they are neutralised, even when they take evasive action.

---

cannot predict if their AWS will encounter each vehicle while in a busy street or in a deserted alley. If Deployer still releases the AWS under these conditions, they failed in their duty to properly predict incidental harm and assess proportionality related to a planned attack.

[149] US Law of War Manual, above n. 22, sct 5.6.7.3; UK Law of Armed Conflict Manual, above n. 43, sct 5.33.5; HPCR Manual, above n.7, para 1(w).

[150] API, above n. 7, Article 52(2).

[151] While some argue that strategic effects are also countable, most restrict military advantage for proportionality tests to operational effects that directly relate to "defeating the enemy in the military realm". Gisel 2016, p. 16. See also HPCR Manual Commentary, above n. 9, p. 45; Fleck 2013, para 443. For contrary opinions, see e.g. Parks 1990, p. 176; Blum 2011, p. n131.

[152] Oeter 2020, p. 348.

There are no concerns regarding indiscriminate means or unaimed attacks.[153] On the other hand, it is relatively certain that the building in Area-2 will be affected, so Deployer must add this to the expected incidental harm. Is this attack proportional? That depends on how we characterise the scope of attack, of which there are two[154] options:

(a) *2 Group-attacks*, comprising Area-1 and Area-2 respectively. For Area-2, Deployer would damage 1 building just to destroy 2 tanks, which is probably excessive.
(b) *1 Category-attack*, with the length of the road as the AWS's search area. Deployer would damage 1 building to destroy 13 tanks. This is likely justifiable.

In these kinds of situations, Deployer will have to carefully consider which attack scope(s) would be applicable, since as we can see, it significantly affects what actions Deployer is permitted to take under the proportionality rule. In this scenario, whether Deployer can count this as a singular Category-attack will likely depend on the specific circumstances. The map features no scale, but if the distance between Area-1 and Area-2 is only 50 m, it would be easier to justify melding the objectives' military advantage and incidental harm than if the distance were 500 m. Similarly, if Deployer releases multiple platforms that attack the objectives simultaneously, it would be easier to classify as a unified attack than if a single platform first finishes with Area-2 before moving on to Area-1.[155] As established in Sect. 9.2.2, the temporal and spatial variables are once again key.

Deployers will be tempted to construe attack as broadly as possible because it carries important practical benefits. In the example above, if viewed as two Group-attacks, Deployer must delay or cancel the attack on Area-2, which may frustrate attempts to clear the road to the town.[156] Deployer must utilise the guidelines regarding Attack Scope in good faith and not to justify *a priori* disproportionate attacks.

In any event, properly considering Attack Scopes before launching an AWS attack is beneficial for Deployer. Particularly in cases where they are later called to account for any harm caused,[157] Deployer will be able to motivate how they chose the contours

[153] The system is "reliable", and the objectives are clearly identified and validated by Deployer, respectively.

[154] We disregard the alternative of characterising this as a collection of 13 Single attacks, since the tanks in Area-1 and Area-2 clearly constitute two Specific Target Groups. See Sect. 8.5.2.

[155] As also mentioned previously in Sect. 9.2.2, having multiple AWS reduces the overall time necessary to conclude the attack, reducing the temporal variable.

[156] If clearing the road is of *imperative* importance, then the attack on Area-2 would be justified even if construed as a Group-attack since military advantage would not only derive from the destroyed enemy matériel, but also from the contextual advantage (e.g., allowing beleaguered defenders in the town safe retreat). The point is to illustrate that in cases of marginal military advantage, broader attack scopes would allow the attack to proceed when deconstructing the operation into smaller attacks would not.

[157] Puckett 2004, p. 669.

of their attack(s) and explain for each attack why they did not deem the incidental harm to be excessive.[158]

9.6 Minimisation

The duty to minimise[159] is provided in API Article 57(2)(a)(ii) and is recognised as a customary rule.[160] It provides that if "there is a choice of weapons or methods of attack available, a commander should select those which are most likely to avoid, or at least minimize, incidental damage".[161] The obligation to select the "least damaging course of action compatible with military success" extends to both the weapon and method of employment.[162]

With regard to the former, this requires a comparison between weapons. With the introduction of AWS to a commander's arsenal, an entirely new range of weapons is entered into the equation. Deployer is thus required to compare AWS in their possession with other (legacy) systems, and determine which option would most reduce risk to civilians. Making such comparisons requires the ability to predict incidental harm. This adds an additional reason as to why a commander who activates AWS in circumstances that produce too much epistemic uncertainty (Rationale-EE) is in violation of targeting rules. It was previously argued that too much uncertainty may indirectly cause Deployer to violate the proportionality rule,[163] but this logic is also true for precautionary duties in general, including the minimisation rule. Once the likely incidental harm can be predicted, however, the minimisation rule at the weapon level is straightforward: Deployer must choose the option that has the best probability of reducing harm to civilians among all feasible alternatives.[164]

Two questions are outstanding. First, how is minimisation with AWS applied at the method level? Second, Deployer is only required to minimise in so far this is *feasible*, but how does this interact with some more specific characteristics of the

---

[158] "The commander's decisions on proportionality must be reasonable … the commander *must be able to explain* the expected military importance of the target and why the anticipated civilian collateral injury or damage is not expected to be excessive." US Law of War Manual, above n. 22, sct 5.10.2.2.

[159] The term 'minimisation' is employed in this book following the example of several scholars, although the term 'mitigation' is also sometimes used. For 'minimisation', see e.g. Schmitt 1999, p. 148; Thurnher 2018, p. 100. For 'mitigation', see e.g. Winter 2020, p. 265.

[160] Henckaerts and Doswald-Beck 2005, p. 57; Fleck 2013, para 448.1; Tallinn Manual 2.0, above n. 7, p. 480.

[161] Nato Report, above n. 51, para 21.

[162] Rogers 2000, p. 177. See also HPCR Manual Commentary, above n. 9, sct 32.(b).3; Schmitt 2010a, para 16.07.4.

[163] Section 9.5.1.

[164] Thurnher 2018, p. 100. See also Schmitt 2015; Herbach 2012, pp. 13–14; McLaughlin 2014, p. 235.

technology: their likely higher cost and lower availability, and force protection (one of their principal benefits)?

9.6.1 Context Controls as Obligatory Precautionary Measures

This section argues that at the method level, *any* Context Control such as those described in Sect. 8.7 is a form of minimisation. The corollary of this position is that as long as a Context Control is available and feasible,[165] Deployer must implement it as a precautionary measure.

A possible objection to this is that not all Context Control measures reduce the risk of *incidental* damage. One may recall that only Sect. 8.7.3 was titled 'Reducing risk of incidental harm' (i.e., relating to Rationale-IH). The other subsections gave examples of Context Controls which reduce false positives (Rationale-FP) and epistemic error (Rationale-EE).[166] The question is thus whether risk-reducing measures linked to Rationale-FP and Rationale-EE would *also* be obligatory under the minimisation rule, or *only* those linked to Rationale-IH.

A plausible argument could technically be made for the latter position. Many descriptions of the rule[167] refer to the obligation to "avoid or minimize *collateral* casualties or damage".[168] If read narrowly, this would mean that measures strictly linked to Rationale-FP (e.g. setting anti-target profiles[169] as an additional failsafe against false positives) or Rationale-EE (e.g. choosing a system that is more understandable[170]) are not mandatory. The position taken in this section is that this would be an overly narrow reading of the rule. To illustrate:

> **Scenario 6: Precautionary measures**. For an important operation, Deployer has System-A available. It is predicted to make a single misclassification 4% of the time. Only two civilians will be incidentally injured during this attack, which a reasonable commander would find non-excessive. [*Measure-1*] Deployer has System-B as an alternative, which is half as likely to make mistakes. [*Measure-2*] If Deployer delays the attack for one hour until night falls, civilian presence in the area will halve. Neither measure jeopardises mission success.

---

[165] For when such a measure would be feasible in the context of AWS, see Sect. 9.6.2.

[166] See Sects. 8.7.2 and 8.7.4 respectively.

[167] Even the API formulation cited above uses "incidental loss", which implies (just) collateral damage under a narrow interpretation.

[168] International Institute of Humanitarian Law 1994, San Remo Manual on International Law Applicable to Armed Conflicts at Sea. https://www.icrc.org/en/doc/resources/documents/article/other/57jmsu.htm (accessed 7 August 2023) (San Remo Manual), para 46(c) (emphasis added). For other examples where a narrower reference to just incidental harm is used, see e.g. HPCR Manual Commentary, above n. 9, sct 32.(b).3; Schmitt 1999, p. 148; Schmitt 2010a, para 16.07.

[169] See Sect. 8.7.2.4.

[170] See Sect. 8.7.4.

The 'basic' scenario (of attacking directly with System-A) is already discriminate and proportionate.[171] Based on the duty to minimise, however, Deployer would arguably be required to *both* select System-B (*Measure-1*) and delay the attack for one hour (*Measure-2*). Presumably, this aligns with most readers' intuition. Measure-1 essentially amounts to Deployer selecting the more reliable/accurate of the two means of warfare that are available,[172] and Measure-2 is a classic precaution found in most IHL textbooks.[173] However, note that two separate types of 'risk' are actually being reduced:

- By waiting until the civilian presence in the area halves, Deployer is likely to incidentally injure only one (or no) person instead of two. This corresponds with ***Rationale-IH***, reducing incidental harm.
- By selecting System-B, Deployer halves the risk of misidentification from 4% to 2% because of the latter's improved performance. Additionally, waiting until night halves Negative Class Frequency, dropping risk further to 1%.[174] This has nothing to do with incidental harm, but rather with suppressing false positives (***Rationale-FP***).

If one agrees that both Measure-1 and Measure-2 are obligatory under the minimisation rule, this demonstrates that the rule extends further than just reducing incidental harm. Instead, its underlying rationale is broader: it requires attackers to "reduce the *risk of harm* to civilians and civilian objects",[175] not *just* those arising from collateral effects in the narrow sense.[176]

The AP Commentary in that sense captures the spirit of the rule better than the actual wording of Article 57(2)(a)(ii). As the Commentary notes, "[t]his subparagraph deals with the choice of means and methods of attack to be used so as to

---

[171] If one of these conditions were not fulfilled, then it is of little use to discuss the minimisation rule since the attack would be unlawful in any event. See Wright 2012, p. 827; Haque 2017, p. 188. Note also that the minimisation rule's requirements are independent of those related to discrimination and proportionality. von Heinegg 2020, p. 327.

[172] As Bothe et al. note, the minimisation rule can be viewed an "injunction to promote the maximum feasible accuracy". Bothe et al. 2013, p. 406. Under this reasoning, it has been suggested that if feasible, commanders should select PGMs over dumb bombs, since the latter is more likely to miss. See e.g. Schmitt and Schauss 2019, p. 180; Quéguiner 2006, p. 803. More specifically with regard to AWS, it has for example been suggested that if "autonomous weapons became more precise and reliable than humans, the obligation to take "all feasible precautions" might *require* commanders to use them". Scharre 2018, p. 258 (emphasis in original).

[173] Sandoz et al. 1987, para 2200; Henckaerts and Doswald-Beck 2005, p. 58; US Law of War Manual, above n. 22, sct 5.11.3.

[174] See Sect. 8.2.2. We assume *arguendo* that no other external variable is liable to impact this prediction.

[175] US Law of War Manual, above n. 22, sct 5.11.6 (emphasis added).

[176] Thurnher describes precautions as obliging "combatants to operate with a view toward minimizing *harm* to civilian populations". Thurnher 2018, p. 100. Schmitt also describes the rule as requiring "that precautions be taken by the attacker to minimize *harm* to civilians and civilian objects". Schmitt and Highfill 2018, p. 82. Note that neither limits the harm to that of collateral effects only.

prevent loss or damage to the population."[177] As this loss or damage can occur as a result of collateral damage, false positives *or* epistemic errors, it stands to reason that Deployer is obligated to mitigate risk with respect to all three Rationales. From this, we can conclude that all AWS-specific Context Controls are also precautionary measures, and obligatory under Article 57(2)(a)(ii).

It is true that the Context Controls provided in Sect. 8.7 have never been mentioned as precautionary measures in textbooks, manuals, etc. This is unsurprising since they are unique to AI systems, and thus very new. However, their underlying logic of reducing risk to the civilian population is identical to 'classic' precautions. For example, "selecting munitions of appropriate size and type",[178] particularly if there are many proximate collateral concerns,[179] is frequently cited as an example of how commanders can mitigate risk to civilians. In Fig. 8.5, this corresponds with the variable *Damage Mechanism*, and one Context Control linked to that variable is *Conditional Munition Ban.* Thus, if this functionality is available with the chosen AWS and its use would not jeopardise mission success,[180] the minimisation rule would require Deployers to program conditions governing when their AWS is allowed to use which munition. The same logical process can be followed for all Context Controls.[181]

Deployers are thus encouraged to reference the Context Controls listed in Sect. 8.7, and consider them together with more traditional precautionary methods (e.g. attack timing,[182] choice of targets,[183] avoiding operations in populated areas[184]) to optimise risk-mitigation.

9.6.2 Feasibility and Military Considerations

The feasibility qualifier is an indispensable component that makes the minimisation rule workable in the field.[185] It permits Deployers to discard mitigating measures which would be 'unfeasible', i.e. those which are not "practicable or practically possible".[186] Whether a measure is feasible is contextual and left to the good-faith

[177] Sandoz et al. 1987, para 2200.

[178] US Law of War Manual, above n. 22, sct 5.11.6.

[179] Article 36 and PAX 2016, p. 27.

[180] Cf. Section 9.6.2.

[181] As Context Controls have been extensively discussed in Sect. 8.7, the reader may refer to this section for more details.

[182] UK Law of Armed Conflict Manual, above n. 43, sct 5.32.6; Thurnher 2018, p. 114.

[183] Schmitt et al. 2006, sct 2.1.2.b and d.

[184] Henckaerts and Doswald-Beck 2005, p. 58; Quéguiner 2006, p. 800.

[185] Ohlin 2013, pp. 122–23. In the case of API's drafting history, it was also necessary to make the rule acceptable to delegations.

[186] Tallinn Manual 2.0, above n. 7, p. 479.

commander.[187] AWS technology does not change most aspects regarding feasibility. For example, mission accomplishment can be invoked to justify why a particular mitigating option could not be used,[188] despite the higher protection it would provide to civilians.[189] Nevertheless, some elements related to other military considerations[190] are worth exploring briefly in more detail, since it is in many of these areas where AWS are purported to provide specific added value.

9.6.2.1 Iteration: Weapon Availability and Cost

A commander may decide that a measure is unfeasible due to iterative considerations, i.e., it may negatively impact future operations. With regard to legacy systems, munition availability is one common example, and commanders may economise on certain munitions if necessary.[191] This rationale extends to the weapon systems

---

[187] Sandoz et al. 1987, para 2198; HPCR Manual Commentary, above n. 9, sct 1.(q).3. For more specific lists of factors that Deployer can consider when making feasibility judgments, see e.g. US Law of War Manual, above n. 22, sct 5.2.3.2; Wright 2012, p. 827.

[188] US Law of War Manual, above n. 22, sct 5.2.3.2 (noting that circumstances which affect feasibility include "the effect of taking the precaution on mission accomplishment").

[189] As an example, abovementioned 'shoot last' setting is often referenced in literature as to why AWS could provide better protection to civilians compared to human soldiers. Sassòli raised it specifically in the context of minimisation: "an autonomous weapon could be a means to render certain precautions, which would not be available to a soldier, feasible". Sassòli 2014, p. 335. However, this option would not be feasible against enemy combatants who are known to exploit this command by deliberately withholding fire whenever they encounter the AWS. Thus, if the mission goal was to eliminate these combatants, Deployer is authorised to release the AWS without the setting enabled (even though this may increase risk of false positives).

[190] While this is not explicitly provided in the API formulation, most States have interpreted 'military considerations' as a valid factor for determining feasibility. Fenrick 2005, p. 177. Delegations had made this clear during the API conference, and many States have explicitly provided as such in their reservations upon signature. Sandoz et al. 1987, para 2198; Bothe et al. 2013, pp. 404–05. The second, third and fifth CCW Protocols similarly specify that States are only required to undertake "those precautions which are practicable or practically possible taking into account all circumstances ruling at the time, including humanitarian and military considerations". See Protocol on Prohibitions or Restrictions on the Use of Mines, Booby-Traps and Other Devices as amended on 3 May 1996 (Protocol II), to the Convention on Prohibitions or Restrictions on the Use of Certain Conventional Weapons Which May be Deemed to be Excessively Injurious or to Have Indiscriminate Effects, adopted 10 October 1980, entered into force 2 December 1983, amended 21 December 2001, 1342 UNTS 137 (CCW Protocol-II), Article 10; Protocol on Prohibitions or Restrictions on the Use of Incendiary Weapons (Protocol III), to the Convention on Prohibitions or Restrictions on the Use of Certain Conventional Weapons Which May be Deemed to be Excessively Injurious or to Have Indiscriminate Effects, adopted 10 October 1980, entered into force 2 December 1983, amended 21 December 2001, 1342 UNTS 137 (CCW Protocol-III), Article 5(1); Protocol on Explosive Remnants of War (Protocol V), to the Convention on Prohibitions or Restrictions on the Use of Certain Conventional Weapons Which May be Deemed to be Excessively Injurious or to Have Indiscriminate Effects, adopted 10 October 1980, entered into force 2 December 1983, amended 21 December 2001, 1342 UNTS 137 (CCW Protocol-V), Article 5(1).

[191] Sandoz et al. 1987, para 2200. Using PGMs is not feasible despite their higher precision if a commander knows they will be necessary to effectively prosecute an upcoming battle. In such

themselves. A commander is "entitled to take account of factors such as stocks of different weapons and likely future demands".[192]

AWS are likely to be more expensive than legacy systems, and this may make Deployers hesitant to deploy them in situations where there is a likelihood that they may be damaged or destroyed. Is Deployer allowed to withhold an AWS because its loss would be more costly in monetary terms, even though it offers more relative protection to civilians? Deployer is not. By itself, high cost cannot render an option 'unfeasible': only technical and operational elements may factor into feasibility determinations.[193]

However, cost may *indirectly* lead to an option being unfeasible for legitimate operational reasons. Higher cost will often correlate with lower availability.[194] As such, it is possible that due to their higher cost, Deployers will have fewer AWS available than legacy alternatives. It is thus probable that Deployers will justify the use of weapons that carry more risk to civilians (such as artillery) because of the perceived need to spare their AWS for important future engagements.[195] This is legitimate if done in good faith.

9.6.2.2 Force Protection

In military terms,[196] force protection is also an iterative benefit, since losses today lead to diminished capacity to inflict harm on the enemy tomorrow.[197] There is

---

conditions, the use of dumb bombs would be authorised, as long as they are not indiscriminate. Schmitt et al. 2006, sct 2.1.2.9. See also Australian Law of Armed Conflict Manual, above n. 79, para 4.48: "The existence of precision-guided weapons … in a military inventory does not mean that they must necessarily be used in preference to conventional weapons even though the latter may cause collateral damage. In many cases, conventional weapons may be used to bomb legitimate military targets without violating the LOAC requirements. It is a command decision as to which weapon to use. This decision will be guided by the basic principles of the LOAC".

[192] Nato Report, above n. 51, para 21.

[193] With regard to the expensive Reaper drones, Herbach stated that "what is relevant for the feasibility assessment is the Reaper's hovering ability rather than expense". Herbach 2012, p. 14. Similarly, Schmitt argued that there "is no basis in international humanitarian law for factoring expense into feasibility assessments. Once a belligerent purchases equipment and supplies it to its forces in the field, it must be used if it is available, makes good military sense and will minimize civilian impact." Schmitt 2005, p. 462.

[194] A study by Watts of US precision munition stockpiles confirmed that "the more expensive a given expendable munition is, the smaller the quantity actually procured is likely to be". Watts 2013, p. 20.

[195] The same dynamic has been observed with PGMs, where States often opt to use less precise munitions because of availability concerns. See Blum 2011, p. 193; Gross 2016, p. 48.

[196] I.e., disregarding domestic political backlash etc. from the loss of too many friendly troops. Sometimes, however, domestic backlash can directly threaten the war effort if it leads to a political impetus to abandon the State's involvement in the conflict. See Luban 2011, p. 44.

[197] Blum 2011, p. 199.

relative consensus in scholarship[198] and practice[199] that commanders may refrain from employing a mitigating measure for force protection. One particular challenge with regard to force protection is finding an appropriate balance between risk-to-force and risk-to-civilians. There is debate on how much risk a force may 'transfer' to the civilian population: IHL does not demand that an attacking force sacrifice all to diminish risk to civilians, but prioritising force protection above all else would be an opposite extreme.[200] With regard to AWS, similar concerns have been voiced[201] that Deployers could too easily justify the use of AWS on the basis that the manned alternative is 'unfeasible':

> there is a grave risk that states might rush to deploy an AWS that is less capable of complying with IHL, when compared to its human counterparts, simply to avoid risk to its own troops. In this situation, the lowering of risk to the attacking force would be accompanied by an increase of risk to the civilian population based on the possibility of errors committed by the system.[202]

Comparable debates have been waged in the past over similar situations. During the NATO campaign in Yugoslavia, NATO bombers opted to fly high in order to avoid air defence, but at the cost of accuracy.[203] This decision was criticised on the basis that "inadequate precautions were taken to avoid civilian casualties".[204] Similar controversies are likely to emerge once AWS become more prevalent, since their nature is so inherently linked with the advantage of preserving friendly forces. Unfortunately, this matter remains unsettled.[205] Through the proportionality rule, IHL can guarantee that AWS that perform excessively poorly may in any case not be deployed lawfully, but beyond this minimum requirement, disagreements will

---

[198] Tallinn Manual 2.0, above n. 7, p. 476. Schmitt and Schauss similarly opined that "the extent to which a possible precaution increases the risk to an attacking force is an appropriate military factor in determining whether it is feasible in the attendant circumstances". Schmitt and Schauss 2019, p. 186.

[199] The US Manual provides that "a commander may determine that a precaution would not be feasible because it would result in … an increased risk of harm to his or her forces", and the Australian Manual notes that when implementing precautions, "the attacker should naturally take into account likely friendly casualties". US Law of War Manual, above n. 22, sct 5.2.3.2; Australian Law of Armed Conflict Manual, above n. 79, para 2.9. Finally, the UK Manual lists "the risks to his own troops of the various options open to him" as a factor a commander must consider when choosing their weapons mix and attack method. UK Law of Armed Conflict Manual, above n. 43, sct 5.32.5.

[200] See Fenrick 1997, p. 546; Luban 2011, p. 6.

[201] Asaro 2012, p. 692.

[202] Ohlin 2017, p. 35.

[203] See e.g. Nato Report, above n. 51, paras 69–70.

[204] Human Rights Watch 2000. Note that, with some exceptions, critics did not assert that NATO was engaging in indiscriminate bombardments, but merely that they could have taken *more* care to reduce risk to civilians. See Nato Report, above n. 51, para 2; Voon 2001, p. 1099.

[205] Wright 2003, p. 139; Luban 2011, p. 43.

inevitably arise vis-à-vis to what extent Deployers must choose a manned option over an AWS to further reduce incidental harm, even if this entails risks to personnel.[206]

9.7 Warnings

The duty to issue warnings is listed in API Article 57(2)(c) and provides that "effective advance warning shall be given of attacks which may affect the civilian population, unless circumstances do not permit". It is generally considered Customary IHL in both international and non-international armed conflicts.[207]

Warnings were referenced in Sect. 8.7.5.4 as a special form of environmental manipulation useful for environments not under friendly control. If Deployer's control over civilian action and movement in the area is limited, measures such as blocking off an area to reduce Negative Class Frequency cannot be effectuated. In such conditions, warnings can serve as an alternative to mitigate risk.[208] A straightforward example is to issue a warning to civilians that an AWS will be used, with the hope that some will clear the area.[209] Warnings can also be used to reduce risk to the civilian population in other ways. For instance, instructions may be given to civilians of stances, gestures, types of clothing, etc., to avoid since these increase the chance of them being misidentified by the AWS. Alternatively, instructions may be given of a positive signal that guarantees they are recognised as non-combatants.[210]

In this section, we discuss some minutia regarding warnings. First, it is argued that one can actually distinguish two types of AWS-related warnings: Deployer-issued warnings which fall under Article 57(2)(c), and warning-*like* actions by the AWS that are better classed as falling under Article 57(2)(a)(ii). Then, we explore some more specific questions, such as when warnings may be omitted and what constitutes an 'effective' warning when AWS are involved.

---

[206] For different perspectives on this matter and what is an acceptable 'risk transfer ratio', see: Luban 2011, p. 42; Schmitt and Schauss 2019, p. 186; Haque 2012, pp. 86-87.

[207] Henckaerts and Doswald-Beck 2005, p. 62; HPCR Manual Commentary, above n. 9, p. 132.

[208] Roorda 2015, p. 162; Boddens Hosang 2021, p. 405.

[209] Once again, this is somewhat analogous to precautions associated with mines, where issuing clear warnings and placing clear markings around the perimeter of the mined area are ways to reduce risk to civilians, even if the force which placed the mines is no longer in control of the area. Moyes 2019, p. 10. See CCW Protocol-II, above n. 190, Article 5(2)(a).

[210] A similar technique is already being applied to the Samsung SGR-A1 in the Korean DMZ, which is capable of accepting surrender (which involves a person adopting a specific stance). Schuller 2017, note 81.

9.7.1 Deployer- versus AWS-Issued Warnings

Somewhat reminiscent of dynamic munition selection,[211] it has sometimes been suggested[212] that AWS could be programmed to issue a warning just before it engages an objective with the hope that this allows civilians to remove themselves from the proximate area.[213] For example, one commentator asked whether AWS should be

> outfitted with an array of different warning systems – potentially more than would be viable for human-operated systems to carry – to give them a wider palette to use in a similar way to that discussed above in the context of the panoply of weaponry they may carry.[214]

A few questions can be posed with respect to this proposal. First, are such AWS-issued warnings sufficient for Deployer to fulfil their duty to warn? Second, if not, would such AWS-issued warnings remain obligatory under IHL, and if yes, on the basis of what rule?

With regard to the first question, it is argued that such AWS-issued warnings are *not sufficient* to fulfil Deployer's obligation under Article 57(2)(c). The warning provision, while technically falling outside the 'those planning or deciding an attack'-chapeau of Article 57(2)(a),[215] nevertheless has historically been addressed at "[c]ommanders"[216] or the "officer in command".[217] Thus, this provision imposes upon *Deployer* the duty to provide a warning whenever an AWS attack is to be launched, and must be executed by Deployer even if the AWS is also equipped with a warning-like functionality. This argument is consistent with the overarching position adopted in this book that IHL obligations can never be fulfilled 'by' AWS.[218]

---

[211] See Sect. 8.7.3.2.

[212] See e.g. Thurnher 2018, pp. 111–12; Buchan and Tsagourias 2021, p. 339.

[213] One could see this as somewhat similar in purpose to the roof-knocking technique performed by the Israeli military. See United Nations 2015. Note that roof-knocking as practiced by the Israeli army is generally regarded as an ineffective precautionary measure since it is ambiguous and also provides insufficient opportunity for civilians to take effective action in response. See United Nations 2015, paras 236–39; Winter 2020, p. 272. If this functionality were to be implemented in AWS, these weaknesses must be resolved without making the system itself dysfunctional (e.g. by just allowing the enemy to clear the area or disable the system first).

[214] Winter 2020, p. 272.

[215] The API formulation gives no clarification as to who the primary addressee is. The HPCR Manual also provides no indication in this regard since passive voice is used ("effective advance warnings must be issued"). HPCR Manual, above n.7, Rule 37. The ICRC Customary Law study broadly refers to "[e]ach party to the conflict". Henckaerts and Doswald-Beck 2005, Rule 20.

[216] Instructions for the Government of Armies of the United States in the Field, adopted 24 April 1863, https://ihl-databases.icrc.org/en/ihl-treaties/liebercode-1863 (accessed 31 July 2023) (Lieber Code), Article 19.

[217] Hague Convention (IV) respecting the Laws and Customs of War on Land and its annex: Regulations concerning the Laws and Customs of War on Land, adopted 18 October 1907, entered into force 26 January 1910, International Peace Conference 1907, https://ihl-databases.icrc.org/en/ihl-treaties/hague-conv-iv-1907 (accessed 31 July 2023) (Hague Convention IV), Article 26. It has been interpreted the same way by commentators. Quéguiner 2006, p. 808; Corn 2015, p. 437.

[218] See Sect. 1.1.

However, this does not imply that such AWS-issued warnings are entirely optional. It is clear that they have the potential to mitigate some risk to civilians. It is thus argued that they should be viewed as precautionary measures that are obligatory under Article 57(2)(a)(ii), in the same way other AWS-specific Context Controls are.[219] Indeed, the Article 57(2)(c) obligation itself can be seen as a particular type of precautionary measure: the duty to warn historically has been "deduced from the principle of utmost minimization of collateral civilian casualties".[220]

Thus, if Deployer has AWS available with this functionality, and letting it issue such warnings prior to individual engagements (i.e., Instances) could lead to lower incidental harm[221] or false positives[222] and would not jeopardise the mission,[223] enabling this Context Control would be required under the minimisation rule. As noted above, this obligation is independent from *Deployer's* duty to warn under Article 57(2)(c). Where feasible and available, both must be done.

9.7.2 Feasibility

Feasibility limits under which conditions warnings must be issued, irrespective of whether this concerns a warning issued by Deployer or the AWS.

With regard to *Deployer-issued warnings*, Article 57(2)(c) has a qualifier in the form of the phrase 'unless circumstances do not permit'.[224] The most evident situation when this applies is when the attack's success is dependent on some element of surprise.[225] Whether success can be considered as conditional upon the element of surprise largely depends on the enemy's action space should they learn of the imminent attack. Mobile targets that can simply flee or be moved would certainly not permit the issuance of a warning, while it is more reasonable to expect warnings when the objective is completely immobile.[226] Whether the enemy can prepare a countermeasure is also determinative.[227] Although it has been suggested that a

---

[219] It was argued in Sect. 9.6.1 that all Context Controls are required precautionary measures in the sense of Article 57(2)(a)(ii). For this reason, AWS-issued warnings were already listed in Sect. 8.7.3.3 as a type of Context Control.

[220] Fleck 2013, para 456.

[221] E.g. by allowing proximate civilians to clear the area before the AWS releases its missile.

[222] E.g. by providing instructions on how to adopt gestures signalling they are non-combatants that the AWS is certain to understand.

[223] E.g. it is tasked with locating fixed targets that cannot be quickly moved.

[224] This qualifier is also present verbatim in other modern sources where the rule is mentioned. See e.g. HPCR Manual, above n.7, Rule 37; Henckaerts and Doswald-Beck 2005, Rule 20.

[225] Sandoz et al. 1987, para 2223. In Hague Convention IV, this situation is referred to as 'assault'. Hague Convention IV, above n. 217, Article 26.

[226] Schmitt 2010b, p. 827.

[227] For example, it is not reasonable to expect warnings for an air bombardment when this would only provide the enemy the time to prepare air defences. Quéguiner 2006, p. 806.

'goldilocks timing' could exist in certain situations (i.e., just enough time for civilians to evacuate, but not enough for the enemy to respond),[228] this is rarely workable in practice.

In the case of attacks using AWS, the mobility of targets will often *not* be sufficient for Deployer to declare that circumstances do not permit the issuance of a warning. One of the main advantages of AWS is precisely that they can dynamically track targets within their search area. Thus, even if a warning is issued and the target moves, the attack may not be compromised. In contrast, whether the warning allows the enemy to prepare an effective countermeasure will be of heightened importance. In the above example of the instruction to civilians to adopt a gesture that would guarantee their classification as a non-combatant, this would be highly compromising if it is known that the enemy would abuse the recognised stance to immunise themselves from attack (which is very likely), since this would render the AWS militarily ineffective.

When considering whether *AWS-issued warnings* should be enabled, Deployer may consider feasibility.[229] Winter remarks that it is possible that "by virtue of issuing a warning, a machine may give away its position and be destroyed and so there would be a potential financial and operational risk to the attacker of warnings"[230]—a good example of when activating such a setting would not be feasible.

9.7.3 The 'Effective' Requirement

As we often associate 'warnings' with pamphlets or broadcasts containing bombardment timings and locations, one may ask whether the example given in this section's introduction of instructions to adopt a 'non-combatant stance' would fall under the notion of 'warnings' as understood in Article 57(2)(c). It does: there is no fixed requirement in IHL as to what form a warning must take, nor its contents. IHL only requires the warning to be 'effective'.[231] An effective warning generally is concrete, credible, and timely enough for the civilian population to take appropriate action.[232]

While it is common to specifically designate which objectives will be subject to attack, it is not absolutely required. As the API Commentary notes, "[w]arnings may also have a general character. A belligerent could, for example, give notice by radio that he will attack certain types of installations or factories".[233] Such 'general hint warnings' provide a very attractive balance between effectiveness as a precautionary

[228] Rowe 2000, p. 154.

[229] Recall that AWS-issued warnings fall under the duty to minimise, and thus are subject to Article 57(2)(a)(ii)'s feasibility clause. See Sect. 9.6.2.

[230] Winter 2020, p. 272.

[231] Quéguiner 2006, pp. 808–09.

[232] HPCR Manual Commentary, above n. 9, p. 133; Durhin 2016, p. 192; Schmitt and Schauss 2019, p. 191.

[233] Sandoz et al. 1987, para 2225.

measure and not revealing to the enemy when a specific target will be attacked. By designating particular weapons or entities as objectives, civilians can independently determine which areas to avoid (i.e., those proximate to the designated objectives) irrespective of where they are located or are moved to by defenders.[234]

Such warnings conceptually allow Deployer to execute Category- or Assorted-attacks[235] while still fulfilling their obligation to warn. For example, by using general hint warnings (e.g. 'AWS will be used tomorrow to destroy radar installations in the city'), Deployer can satisfy their duty under Article 57(2)(c) by instructing civilians to clear areas near radar installations, while still leaving the enemy powerless to react (since Deployer provides no specific information that would enable defenders to determine when or where to move the installations to avoid detection by the AWS).[236]

9.8 The Duty to Cancel

The duty to cancel requires an attack to be cancelled or suspended if it becomes apparent that an objective is not a valid one, or the attack will cause excessive incidental harm.[237] How to interpret this rule for AWS technology has been subject to some diverging views, and has been described by prominent commentators as a "particularly tricky issue"[238] and "problematic".[239]

9.8.1 Attack- or Instance-Level Obligation?

One of the main questions in scholarship concerns whether the cancelling obligation applies at the Instance-level,[240] and whether the rule may oblige the activation of an

---

[234] Margulies 2012, p. 287.

[235] See Sect. 8.5.2.

[236] Once again, however, if the issuance of the warning would prompt the enemy to install air defence which effectively counters the aerial AWS Deployer plans to send, requiring a warning would become unreasonable. What type of warning is appropriate and whether a warning is to be issued at all is highly context-dependent.

[237] The full provision reads: "an attack shall be cancelled or suspended if it becomes apparent that the objective is not a military one or is subject to special protection or that the attack may be expected to cause incidental loss of civilian life, injury to civilians, damage to civilian objects, or a combination thereof, which would be excessive in relation to the concrete and direct military advantage anticipated". API, above n. 7, Article 57(2)(b).

[238] Sassòli 2014, p. 339.

[239] Henderson et al. 2017, p. 355.

[240] I.e., the possibility to cancel or interrupt each individual Instance must be guaranteed to fulfil this rule.

autonomous 'cancelling function'.[241] There is some reason to argue that either can be answered in the affirmative, subject to some conditions.

With regard to the subject to whom this rule is addressed, the duty to cancel is uniquely distinct from prior rules we discussed in this chapter. While all previous obligations are unequivocally addressed at 'those planning or deciding an *attack*',[242] the cancelling obligation applies "also and *primarily*[] to those executing them".[243] This is inherent in the rule's design and reflected in the wording of Article 57(2)(b).[244] A pilot flying to objectives listed by their commander, who observes that one of these objectives is a school instead of a military installation, is expected (and personally obligated) under IHL to abort the strike.[245] We can thus surmise that the duty to cancel indeed *applies at the Instance-level*, or in AWS terms, *each time the AI is making an engagement decision.*[246]

At the same time, the duty to cancel *also applies at the attack level.* Commanders who order an attack, but later discover that this decision was based on faulty intelligence, that circumstances on the ground have changed, etc., are required to have the attack aborted.[247] For convenience, let us refer to these two scales of cancelling as *attack-level cancelling* and *Instance-level cancelling* respectively.

9.8.2 Attack-Level Cancelling

Attack-level cancelling with AWS will in many cases remain unchanged vis-à-vis legacy systems, but some AI-specific factors which trigger the duty to cancel are useful to briefly discuss.

---

[241] Winter 2020, pp. 262–63.

[242] API, above n. 7, Article 57(2)(a). For the duty to warn, it does not fall under this chapeau but is still interpreted as addressed at the commander responsible for ordering the attack, as noted in Sect. 9.7.1.

[243] Sandoz et al. 1987, para 2220 (emphasis added).

[244] The provision is formulated in passive voice and thus suggests "that this norm applies to all soldiers at all levels, including those who only carry out attacks on targets selected by others". Haque 2017, p. 213.

[245] Quéguiner 2006, p. 803.

[246] The term 'attack' in API, above n. 7, Article 57(2)(b) is not meant to limit the obligation to the attack level only. As Bothe et al. recall, "[m]uch of the confusion [during the Conferences] was caused by a tendency to use the word "attacks" in its normal military usage as an offensive operation. Such an operation may indeed be difficult to halt, but any commander even at the lowest echelon can and must halt fire on a target that he has mistaken as a military objective when he realizes that his target consists of civilians or specially protected objects." Bothe et al. 2013, p. 408.

[247] Quéguiner 2006, p. 803. Note that in this case, the obligation is indeed directed at 'those who plan or decide' the attack—i.e., the commanders. As with previous rules, this does not refer to a specific rank but any person who has de facto "discretion in the way the attack is carried out". UK Law of Armed Conflict Manual, above n. 43, sct 5.32.9. See Sect. 1.3.1.

9.8.2.1 What Circumstances Must Bring Deployer to Cancel?

As a general rule, Deployer must cancel the system if doubt arises concerning the military nature of the objectives the AWS is 'aimed' at,[248] if changing circumstances lead Deployer to conclude that incidental harm will be excessive vis-à-vis the anticipated military advantage, or if Deployer foresees that circumstances will lead the system's performance to deteriorate enough to cast doubt on its ability to make the requisite distinctions.

The discovery of factors such as the following are particularly pertinent reasons to cancel an AWS attack:

- A previously unknown problem is discovered, such as poisoning;[249]
- Changes in the environment have taken place which compromise the system's performance (e.g. new entities that raise concerns of out-of-distribution have introduced themselves);[250]
- The enemy is employing or preparing to employ an adversarial that was unaccounted for when the attack was approved;[251]
- Sister models of the AWS have been reported to be involved in an incident where they did not perform as expected;[252]
- Planned Context Controls will be less effective than previously predicted (e.g. new civilian entities are discovered which fall within the target signatures planned for the operation, or planned movement restrictions can only be partially imposed since part of the operational area has fallen into enemy control).

The proposed interpretation in Sect. 9.3.2, that Deployer should by default reject the use of AWS if the target environment does not match the system's Intended Operational Environment, is particularly pertinent for the duty to cancel. The dynamic nature of military environments[253] renders it eminently possible that an environment which previously corresponded with the system's IOE (when Deployer made the attack decision) no longer does when the system is poised to engage objectives. If at any time the environment shifts into an IOE-incompatible state within this timespan, Deployer is obliged to cancel the attack.

---

248 See Sect. 9.4.

249 See Sect. 6.4.

250 See Sect. 5.6.

251 See Chap. 6.

252 See Sect. 9.2.2 OK. This assumes that Deployer exercised proper due diligence before launch and this is new information that emerged as the AWS attack was already underway. If this report were received earlier, Deployer should simply not have activated the AWS in the first place. Such reports from different component commanders introduce complications in terms of criminal liability: see Sect. 13.5.3.

253 See Sect. 3.4.2.

9.8.2.2 Until What Time Must the AWS Attack be Susceptible to Cancellation?

It is evident that between the moment that Deployer ordered the AWS attack and the system's activation, Deployer must ensure the attack can be interrupted. What is slightly more difficult to determine is up to what point *after activation* (i.e., after autonomous functionalities are engaged) Deployer must retain the possibility to interrupt the system. In some views, there is no cut-off point: Deployer must perpetually be able to intervene.[254] Because intervening requires a communication link with the system, this indirectly precludes leaving AWS to operate autonomously at all.[255]

The view taken in this book is that this extreme position ignores the fact that depending on the system and circumstances, Deployer may not have the possibility to cancel an AWS attack once it is underway. Many weapons have historically been used lawfully that also cannot be interrupted after the attack decision is made. As Henderson et al. note,

> If there were such a legal obligation, then 'fire and forget' weapons, such as GPS guided bombs, would be unlawful unless targets were kept under constant observation and there was an ability to guide-off the bomb or in some other way neutralise the attack.[256]

IHL in this regard is sufficiently conscientious of the limitations of practical warfare. The cyber domain is illustrative. Many cyberweapons feature a long delay between when the capability is activated or injected into an enemy network and when it actually takes effect. While in some cases (e.g. rootkits or logic bombs) annulling the attack afterward is possible, it often is not. As a result, the Tallinn Manual prefers remaining flexible, holding that the "practicality of suspending or cancelling a cyber attack is case-specific".[257]

A similar casuistic analysis will apply to AWS, and the evaluation may be informed by some factors discussed previously such as the temporal variable, Attack Scope and other details. For example, a Group-level attack[258] directed at a discrete tank platoon using an aerial AWS should remain cancellable until the moment the system

---

[254] For example, Sassòli believes the rule could require "that either the system itself through technical means, or the human beings using it, are able to acquire information indicating that the attack must be interrupted and either the machine or its human operators are able to react to such information". Sassòli 2014, p. 320. The ICRC wrote that "weapon systems must remain under human supervision, and must permit the user to, where feasible, cancel, suspend or modify attacks, up until the execution of the attack (or halting of the attack)". ICRC 2019, p. 1. Lewis argues that AWS users "may need to facilitate at least partial interaction by one or more humans with the system during the employment ... [in the form of] monitoring, suspension, or cancellation". Lewis 2021, p. 114.

[255] For the ability to intervene to be effective, the strict conditions provided in Sect. 8.8 must be maintained. One of these conditions is reducing the decision-making speed to human levels, which in practice negates many benefits of autonomous decision-making. Cf. Sect. 10.3.1. States and commentators have been aware of this implication, and as a result, finding consensus on this matter at a diplomatic level has been challenging. See Jensen 2021, pp. 181–88; Taylor 2021, p. 323.

[256] Henderson et al. 2017, p. 355.

[257] Tallinn Manual 2.0, above n. 7, p. 484.

[258] See Sect. 8.5.2.

reaches the platoon and prepares to use force, but Deployer would not be expected to scrutinise each potential shot against the tanks within a 20-second timespan. If the system is directed at multiple individual targets separated in time and space, on the other hand, Deployer must be able to cancel an attack on Target 2 while the AWS is busy with Target 1.[259] Practically is key. An AWS travelling at supersonic speeds clearly cannot be cancelled 'mid-flight', while the slow-moving aerial AWS above provides Deployer with ample opportunity to do so after take-off.[260]

9.8.3 Instance-Level Canceling

Instance-level cancelling refers to the granular level of potentially cancelling each individual shot or engagement. Instance-level cancelling can be done either by an Operator (if a communication link is maintained) and/or by the AWS itself (if this functionality is available). In the former case, the process would be practically identical to when this is done by aircraft or drone pilots.[261] Having an Operator as an additional safety has been mentioned by many commentators as a useful measure to reduce risk to the civilian population.[262] Thus, following the logic of the minimisation rule,[263] Deployer must assign an Operator as a way to minimise risk to civilians as long as this is feasible.

A more interesting prospect with regard to Instance-level cancelling is the possibility that this functionality could be fulfilled by a subsystem in the AWS itself.[264] As cancelling is required in response to the realisation (1) that an entity is not a valid

---

[259] This remark was also made previously in Sect. 9.2 when discussing Scenario 3. This agrees with our prior analysis in Sect. 9.2.2 that under situations involving temporal and spatial distance, each objective would qualify as a disparate attack that must be separately analysed, and thus also be individually susceptible to cancellation.

[260] Naturally, the technical *ability* of Deployer to interrupt this slow-moving AWS after launch is not something Deployer can influence at the operational level, since the functionality must be programmed in at the design stage. Deployer nevertheless can still veto using such a system if it cannot be interrupted once underway.

[261] Whenever Operator discovers that an entity is about to be engaged by the AWS that is not of a military character, or that this strike would cause disproportionate incidental harm, Operator is required by IHL to interrupt the strike. Note that the second prong of this obligation (disproportionate incidental harm) is not always straightforward and requires proper coordination between Operator and Deployer, as mentioned in Sect. 8.8.4. To make a proper assessment of whether a certain engagement would lead to excessive incidental harm (recall that proportionality is a relational test), Operator must be aware of what military advantage Deployer associated with the attack.

[262] Schuller 2019, p. 115; Buchan and Tsagourias 2021, p. 331.

[263] See Sect. 9.6.

[264] It may be noted that the wording 'cancel' is perhaps somewhat misleading in this context. An AWS does not 'cancel' a strike in the same way a human would. A human pilot is indeed 'cancelling' a strike in the sense that they had a prior notion of wanting to bomb a particular entity, but later reconsidered (for example, because the objective turned out to be a school). An AWS, in contrast, would simply decide not to strike the school because it identifies it as non-military; it did not have a prior 'want'. As both processes ultimately result in the same outcome (the school being protected

target or (2) that pursuing the strike would cause disproportionate incidental harm, let us consider the implementation of these two prongs by the AWS in turn.

9.8.3.1 Autonomous Cancelling in Response to Non-Military Nature

This functionality is mandatory for AWS and overlaps with the prohibition on indiscriminate means. A weapon that does not do this simply would fall in the category of 'Zero Specificity' systems that are inherently indiscriminate.[265] As Sassòli notes, if systems

> are able to distinguish in the first place, they should be equally able to sense changes in their situational context and to cancel an attack if the given information indicates it is unlawful. If they are not able to distinguish in the first place, it would be inconsistent with IHL to deploy them autonomously.[266]

9.8.3.2 Autonomous Cancelling in Response to Excessive Incidental Harm

Extreme scepticism is expressed in literature concerning this second prong of the cancelling obligation and "how well autonomous weapons might be able to satisfy this requirement".[267] The added difficulty arises from the fact that in order to make a decision to cancel based on proportionality, an AWS requires much more than just a well-performing classifier. To perform this particular function properly, an AWS *must be capable of Negative Class Detection*.[268]

Furthermore, actually performing an internal proportionality assessment is even more complex, since this requires operationalising both incidental harm and military advantage and the 'excessiveness' threshold, which are very context-dependent[269] and normally relies on the judgment of a reasonable commander.[270] As a result, of all functionalities, the ability of an AWS to conduct an internal proportionality evaluation has been regarded as the most difficult to program.[271] Although there are some more optimistic voices,[272] many commentators have (not unreasonably)

---

from attack), however, we can accept the figurative notion that a cancelling action is taking place in both situations for the purpose of discussions to follow.

[265] See Sects. 8.2.1 and 9.3.1.

[266] Sassòli 2014, p. 337.

[267] Winter 2020, pp. 281–82.

[268] See Sect. 8.4.2. As Scharre notes, it must be able to "scan the area around the target for civilians, estimate possible collateral damage, and then judge whether the attack should proceed". Scharre 2018, p. 256.

[269] Fenrick 2001, p. 499; Thorne 2020, p. 34.

[270] Parks 1990, p. 175; Tallinn Manual 2.0, above n. 7, p. 473.

[271] Heyns 2013, paras 72–73; Kurosaki 2020, pp. 412–18.

[272] See e.g. Arkin 2009; Toscano 2015, p. 211; Winter 2020, p. 259.

considered this particular function impossible to implement.[273] Given our inability to predict how technology will develop,[274] we shall make no pronouncements on this matter at the current time.[275]

Unlike cancelling in response to an objective's non-military nature, however, the inability of an AWS to cancel on the basis of proportionality does not make it unlawful per se. In fact, no weapon in history has been able to perform this test internally![276] In addition, even humans are often discouraged from cancelling individual strikes (which form part of a larger attack) on the basis of proportionality[277] except in situations of manifestly egregious and excessive harm.[278] Instead, subordinates are in most cases expected to "defer[] to their superiors, whose access to information, analysis, and legal counsel better positions them to make reliable proportionality judgments"[279] and "must assume that an appropriate assessment has been made by those who assigned the mission".[280]

Without anthropomorphising AWS, we can note that the role of AWS in many situations is functionally analogous to that of a 'subordinate'. Deployer in any event is not permitted activate the AWS without having made a proportionality assessment first, as explained in Section 9.5. Indeed, an AWS that cancels strikes because it paternalistically comes to the conclusion that 'excessive civilian casualties will fall', when these casualties have already been accounted for by Deployer's proportionality calculations, would be a troublesome and ineffective system.[281]

The ability to let the AWS cancel at the Instance-level is a useful risk-mitigation tool. For example, Deployer can order the AWS to not attack if a civilian is identified in the blast range of its munition's aimpoint, and if using this functionality is available and feasible, the minimisation rule requires Deployer to do so. However, whether to activate this functionality must be left to Deployer in light of specific circumstances.

---

[273] See e.g. UK Ministry of Defence 2011, para 508; Boulanin 2015, pp. 10–11; Sparrow 2015, p. 702.

[274] Safi 2019.

[275] In the absence of convincing evidence in either direction (i.e., that it is impossible or possible respectively), the correct response is to abstain from taking any strong positions until such evidence is presented. Schuller 2017, pp. 384–400.

[276] AWS may in fact be the first capable of doing so.

[277] "It is … unlikely and undesirable that a subordinate will question the legality of every order he is required to obey." van Sliedregt 2012, p. 304.

[278] US Law of War Manual, above n. 22, sct 5.10.2.4; Gillard 2018, p. 46.

[279] Haque 2017, p. 214.

[280] Bothe et al. 2013, p. 409. The US Manual explicitly draws a distinction between the right of subordinates to refuse an order based on the military nature of the objective (in which case there is a "duty of a subordinate to refrain from complying") and proportionality (in which case they "do not have an obligation to second-guess the judgments of their superiors"). US Law of War Manual, above n. 22, sct 5.10.2.4.

[281] To anthropomorphise one last time: the AWS "should be able to rely on his superior for this". van Sliedregt 2012, p. 304.

References

Arkin R C (2009) Governing Lethal Behavior in Autonomous Robots. CRC Press, Boca Raton
Article 36 (2016) Key Elements of Meaningful Human Control, Background Paper to Comments Prepared by Richard Moyes, Managing Partner, Article 36. In: Convention on Certain Conventional Weapons (CCW) Meeting of Experts on Lethal Autonomous Weapons Systems (LAWS), Geneva, 11–15 April 2016
Article 36, PAX (2016) Areas of Harm – Understanding Explosive Weapons with Wide Area Effects. Article 36/PAX
Asaro P (2012) On Banning Autonomous Weapon Systems: Human Rights, Automation, and the Dehumanization of Lethal Decision-Making. International Review of the Red Cross 94(886):687–709
Bartels R (2013) Dealing with the Principle of Proportionality in Armed Conflict in Retrospect: The Application of the Principle in International Criminal Trials. Israel Law Review 46(2):271–315. https://doi.org/10.1017/S0021223713000083
Blank L (2019) New Technologies and the Interplay between Certainty and Reasonableness. In: Williams W S, Ford C M (eds) Complex Battlespaces: The Law of Armed Conflict and the Dynamics of Modern Warfare. Oxford University Press, Oxford, pp 317-344. https://doi.org/10.1093/oso/9780190915360.003.0011
Blum G (2011) On a Differential Law of War. Harvard International Law Journal 52(1):164–218
Boddens Hosang J F R (2021) Control Through ROE in Military Operations: Autonomous Weapons and Cyber Operations as Reasons to Change the Classic ROE Concept?. In: Bartels R et al. (eds) Military Operations and the Notion of Control Under International Law. TMC Asser Press, The Hague, pp 393–420. https://doi.org/10.1007/978-94-6265-395-5_19
Boothby W H (2016) Weapons and the Law of Armed Conflict. 2nd edn. Oxford University Press, Oxford
Boothby W H (2018) Highly Automated and Autonomous Technologies. In: Boothby W H (ed) New Technologies and the Law in War and Peace. Cambridge University Press, Cambridge, pp 137–181. https://doi.org/10.1017/9781108609388.007
Boothby W H (2021) Control in Weapons Law. In: Bartels R et al. (eds) Military Operations and the Notion of Control Under International Law. TMC Asser Press, The Hague, pp 369–392. https://doi.org/10.1007/978-94-6265-395-5_18
Bothe M, Partsch K J, Solf W A (eds) (2013) New Rules for Victims of Armed Conflict: Commentary on the Two 1977 Protocols Additional to the Geneva Conventions of 1949. 2nd edn. Martinus Nijhoff, Leiden
Boulanin V (2015) Implementing Article 36 Weapon Reviews in Light of Increasing Autonomy in Weapon Systems. SIPRI Insights on Peace and Security 2015(1):1–27
Buchan R, Tsagourias N (2021) Autonomous Cyber Weapons and Command Responsibility. In: Liivoja R, Väljataga A (eds) Autonomous Cyber Capabilities under International Law. NATO CCDCOE Publications, Tallinn, pp 321–347
Chengeta T (2016) Defining the Emerging Notion of "Meaningful Human Control" in Autonomous Weapon Systems. International Law and Politics 49:833–890
Cherry J, Johnson D (2020) Maintaining Command and Control (C2) of Lethal Autonomous Weapon Systems: Legal And Policy Considerations. Southwestern Journal of International Law 27:1–27
Corn G S (2015) War, Law, and the Oft Overlooked Value of Process as a Precautionary Measure. Pepperdine Law Review 42(3):419–466
Corn G S (2016) Autonomous Weapons Systems: Managing the Inevitability of "Taking the Man out of the Loop". In: Bhuta N et al. (eds) Autonomous Weapons Systems: Law, Ethics, Policy. Cambridge University Press, Cambridge, pp 209–242. https://doi.org/10.1017/CBO9781316597873
Crootof R (2015) The Killer Robots Are Here: Legal and Policy Implications. Cardozo Law Review 36:1837–1915

Curtis E. Lemay Center (2019) Air Force Doctrine Publication 3-60 – Targeting. Curtis E Lemay Center. www.doctrine.af.mil/Doctrine-Publications/AFDP-3-60-Targeting. Accessed 05 July 2021
Davison N (2017) A Legal Perspective: Autonomous Weapon Systems under International Humanitarian Law. In: UNODA Occasional Papers No. 30
Dinstein Y (2016) The Conduct of Hostilities under the Law of International Armed Conflict. 3rd edn. Cambridge University Press, Cambridge
Doswald-Beck L (1997) International Humanitarian Law and the Advisory Opinion of the International Court of Justice on the Threat or Use of Nuclear Weapons. International Review of the Red Cross 316:35
Driels M R (2013) Weaponeering, Second Edition. 2nd edn. American Institute of Aeronautics and Astronautics, Inc, Washington D.C. https://doi.org/10.2514/4.869259
Durhin N (2016) Protecting Civilians in Urban Areas: A Military Perspective on the Application of International Humanitarian Law. International Review of the Red Cross 98(1):177–200
Ekelhof M (2019) Moving Beyond Semantics on Autonomous Weapons: Meaningful Human Control in Operation. Global Policy 10(3):343–348
Fenrick W J (1997) Attacking the Enemy Civilian as a Punishable Offense in Symposium: Justice in Cataclysm Criminal Trials in the Wake of Mass Violence. Duke Journal of Comparative & International Law 7(2):539–570
Fenrick W J (2001) Targeting and Proportionality during the NATO Bombing Campaign against Yugoslavia. European Journal of International Law 12(3):489–502
Fenrick W J (2005) International Humanitarian Law and Combat Casualties. European Journal of Population / Revue européenne de Démographie 21(2-3):167–186. https://doi.org/10.1007/s10680-005-6421-y
Fleck D (ed) (2013) The Handbook of International Humanitarian Law. 3rd edn. Oxford University Press, Oxford
Gillard E-C (2018) Proportionality in the Conduct of Hostilities: The Incidental Harm Side of the Assessment. The Royal Institute of International Affairs, Chatham House, London. https://www.chathamhouse.org/2018/12/proportionality-conduct-hostilities-incidental-harm-side-assessment. Accessed 2 August 2023
Gilpin L H et al. (2018) Explaining Explanations: An Overview of Interpretability of Machine Learning. http://arxiv.org/abs/1806.00069
Gisel L (2016) The Principle of Proportionality in the Rules Governing the Conduct of Hostilities under International Humanitarian Law. In: International Expert Meeting, 22-23 June 2016. ICRC. https://www.icrc.org/en/download/file/79184/4358_002_expert_meeting_report_web_1.pdf. Accessed 3 August 2023
Gisel L, Rodenhäuser T, Dörmann K (2020) Twenty Years on: International Humanitarian Law and the Protection of Civilians against the Effects of Cyber Operations during Armed Conflicts. International Review of the Red Cross 102(913):287–334. https://doi.org/10.1017/S1816383120000387
Goussac N (2019) Safety Net or Tangled Web: Legal Reviews of AI in Weapons and War-Fighting. Humanitarian Law & Policy. https://blogs.icrc.org/law-and-policy/2019/04/18/safety-net-tangled-web-legal-reviews-ai-weapons-war-fighting/. Accessed 26 May 2021
Gross R (2016) The New Way of War: Is There A Duty to Use Drones?. Florida Law Review 67(1):1–72
Haque A A (2012) Killing in the Fog of War. Southern California Law Review 86(1):63–116
Haque A A (2017) A Theory of Jus in Bello Proportionality. In: Ohlin J D, May L, Finkelstein C (eds) Weighing Lives in War, vol 1. Oxford University Press, pp 188–216. https://doi.org/10.1093/oso/9780198796176.003.0009
Henckaerts J-M, Doswald-Beck L (eds) (2005) Customary International Humanitarian Law, Volume I – Rules. ICRC, Geneva
Henderson I (2009) The Contemporary Law of Targeting: Military Objectives, Proportionality and Precautions in Attack under Additional Protocol I. Martinus Nijhoff Publishers

Henderson I S, Keane P, Liddy J (2017) Remote and Autonomous Warfare Systems: Precautions in Attack and Individual Accountability. In: Ohlin J D (ed) Research Handbook on Remote Warfare. Edward Elgar, Cheltenham, pp 335-370. https://doi.org/10.4337/9781784716998.00022

Herbach J (2012) Into the Caves of Steel: Precaution, Cognition and Robotic Weapon Systems Under the International Law of Armed Conflict. 4 Amsterdam Law Forum 4(3):3–20

Heyns C (2013) Report of the Special Rapporteur on Extrajudicial, Summary or Arbitrary Executions, A/HRC/23/47

Heyns C (2014) Increasingly Autonomous Weapon Systems: Accountability and Responsibility. Autonomous Weapon Systems: Technical, Military, Legal and Humanitarian Aspects Expert meeting, Geneva, Switzerland, 26–28 March 2014

Holland J (2004) Military Objective And Collateral Damage: Their Relationship And Dynamics. Yearbook of International Humanitarian Law 7:35–78. https://doi.org/10.1017/S1389135904000352

Huffman W B (2012) Margin of Error: Potential Pitfalls of the Ruling in The Prosecutor v. Ante Gotovina. Military Law Review 211:1–56. http://hdl.handle.net/10601/2104. Accessed 4 August 2023

Human Rights Watch (2000) Civilian Deaths in the NATO Air Campaign. Human Rights Watch. https://www.hrw.org/reports/natbm002.pdf. Accessed 20 April 2021

ICRC (2016a) Views of the ICRC on Autonomous Weapon Systems. Paper of the ICRC prepared for the Meeting of Experts on Lethal Autonomous Weapons Systems, held in Geneva from 11–16 April

ICRC (2016b) Background Paper Prepared by the International Committee of the Red Cross. In: ICRC (ed) Autonomous Weapon Systems: Implications of Increasing Autonomy in the Critical Functions of Weapons. ICRC, Versoix, pp 69–85

ICRC (2019) 'Statement of the International Committee of the Red Cross (ICRC) under Agenda Item 5(B)'. Convention on Certain Conventional Weapons (CCW), Group of Governmental Experts on Lethal Autonomous Weapons Systems (Geneva, 25–29 March 2019)

Jensen E T (2003) Unexpected Consequences From Knock-On Effects: A Different Standard for Computer Network Operations?. American University International Law Review 18(5):1145–1188

Jensen E T (2018) The Human Nature of International Humanitarian Law, Humanitarian Law & Policy. ICRC Blogs. https://blogs.icrc.org/law-and-policy/2018/08/23/human-nature-international-humanitarian-law/. Accessed 28 May 2021

Jensen E T (2021) Autonomy and Precautions in the Law of Armed Conflict. In: Liivoja R, Väljataga A (eds) Autonomous Cyber Capabilities under International Law. NATO CCDCOE Publications, Tallinn, pp 181–205

Kastan B (2013) Autonomous Weapons Systems: A Coming Legal "Singularity"?. Journal of Law, Technology and Policy 2013(1):45–82

Kurosaki M (2020) Toward the Special Computer Law of Targeting. In: Kreß C, Lawless R (eds) Necessity and Proportionality in International Peace and Security Law. Oxford University Press, Oxford, pp 409–436. https://doi.org/10.1093/oso/9780197537374.001.0001/oso-9780197537374-chapter-14

Lewis D A (2021) Preconditions for Applying International Law to Autonomous Cyber Capabilities. In: Liivoja R, Väljataga A (eds) Autonomous Cyber Capabilities under International Law. NATO CCDCOE Publications, Tallinn, pp 106–125

Luban D (2011) Risk Taking and Force Protection. Georgetown Public Law and Legal Theory Research Paper No 11-72. https://scholarship.law.georgetown.edu/facpub/654. Accessed 18 February 2022

Margulies P (2012) Valor's Vices: Against a State Duty to Risk Forces in Armed Conflict. Vermont Law Review 37:207–307. https://doi.org/10.1093/acprof:osobl/9780199941445.003.0005

McDougall C (2019) Autonomous Weapon Systems and Accountability: Putting the Cart before the Horse. Melbourne Journal of International Law 20(1):58–87

McLaughlin R (2014) Unmanned Naval Vehicles and the Law of Naval Warfare. In: Nasu H, McLaughlin R (eds) New Technologies and the Law of Armed Conflict. TMC Asser Press, The Hague, pp 229–246. https://doi.org/10.1007/978-90-6704-933-7_14

Meier M W (2019) Lethal Autonomous Weapons Systems. In: Williams W S, Ford C M (eds) Complex Battlespaces: The Law of Armed Conflict and the Dynamics of Modern Warfare. Oxford University Press, Oxford, pp 289–316

Moyes R (2019) Target Profiles: An Initial Consideration of "Target Profiles" as a Basis for Rule-Making in the Context of Discussions on Autonomy in Weapons Systems. Article 36, Article 36 Discussion Paper

Nasu H, McLaughlin R (2014) Conclusion: Challenges of New Technologies for the Law of Armed Conflict. In: Nasu H, McLaughlin R (eds) New Technologies and the Law of Armed Conflict. TMC Asser Press, The Hague, pp 247–254. https://doi.org/10.1007/978-90-6704-933-7_15

Neuman N (2004) Applying the Rule of Proportionality: Force Protection and Cumulative Assessment in International Law and Morality. Yearbook of International Humanitarian Law 7:79–112. https://doi.org/10.1017/S1389135904000790

Oeter S (2020) Specifying the Proportionality Test and the Standard of Due Precaution: Problems of Prognostic Assessment in Determining the Meaning of "May Be Expected" and "Anticipated". In: Kreß C, Lawless R (eds) Necessity and Proportionality in International Peace and Security Law. Oxford University Press, Oxford, pp 343–366. https://doi.org/10.1093/oso/9780197537374.003.0012

Ohlin J D (2013) Targeting and the Concept of Intent. Michigan Journal of International Law 35(1):79–130

Ohlin J D (2017) Remoteness and Reciprocal Risk. In: Ohlin J D (ed) Research Handbook on Remote Warfare. Edward Elgar, Cheltenham, pp 15–49. https://doi.org/10.4337/9781784716998.00010

Parasuraman R, Sheridan T B, Wickens C (2000) A Model for Types and Levels of Human Interaction with Automation. IEEE Transactions on Systems, Man, and Cybernetics 30(3):286–297

Parks W H (1990) Air War and the Law of War. Air Force Law Review 32(1):1–226

Poitras R (2018) Article 36 Weapons Reviews & Autonomous Weapons Systems: Supporting International Review Standard. The American University International Law Review 34(2):466–495

Puckett C B (2004) In This Era of Smart Weapons, Is a State under an International Legal Obligation to Use Precision-Guided Technology in Armed Conflict. Emory International Law Review 18:645–724

Quéguiner J-F (2006) Precautions under the Law Governing the Conduct of Hostilities. International Review of the Red Cross 88(864):793–821

Righetti L (2016) Emerging Technology and Future Autonomous Weapons. In: ICRC (ed) Autonomous Weapon Systems: Implications of Increasing Autonomy in the Critical Functions of Weapons. ICRC, Versoix, pp 36–39

Robinson I, Nohle E (2016) Proportionality and Precautions in Attack: The Reverberating Effects of Using Explosive Weapons in Populated Areas. International Review of the Red Cross 98(901):107–145. https://doi.org/10.1017/S1816383116000552

Roff H M, Moyes R (2016) Meaningful Human Control, Artificial Intelligence and Autonomous Weapons. Briefing Paper for the Delegates at the Convention on Certain Conventional Weapons Informal Meeting of Experts on Lethal Autonomous Weapons Systems

Rogers A P V (2000) Zero-Casuality Warfare. International Review of the Red Cross 837:165–181

Roorda M (2015) NATO's Targeting Process: Ensuring Human Control Over (and Lawful Use of) 'Autonomous' Weapons. In: Williams A P, Scharre P D (eds) Autonomous Systems: Issues for Defence Policymakers. NATO, The Hague, pp 152–168

Rowe P (2000) Kosovo 1999: The Air Campaign -- Have the Provisions of Additional Protocol I Withstood the Test?. International Review of the Red Cross 82(837):147–164

Safi M (2019) Are Drone Swarms the Future of Aerial Warfare?. The Guardian. 4 December 2019. www.theguardian.com/news/2019/dec/04/are-drone-swarms-the-future-of-aerial-warfare. Accessed 2 August 2023

Sandoz Y, Swinarski C, Zimmerman B (1987) Commentary on the Additional Protocols of 8 June 1977 to the Geneva Conventions of 12 August 1949. Martinus Nijhoff, Geneva

Sassòli M (2014) Autonomous Weapons and International Humanitarian Law: Advantages, Open Technical Questions and Legal Issues to Be Clarified. International Law Studies 90:308–340

Scharre P D (2014) Autonomy, "Killer Robots," and Human Control in the Use of Force. Just Security. 9 July 2014. https://www.justsecurity.org/12708/autonomy-killer-robots-human-control-force-part/ and https://www.justsecurity.org/12712/autonomy-killer-robots-human-control-force-part-ii/. Accessed 10 June 2021

Scharre P D (2016) Autonomous Weapons and Operational Risk. Center for a New American Security, Washington, D.C

Scharre P D (2018) Army of None: Autonomous Weapons and the Future of War. Ww Norton & Co, New York

Scharre P D, Horowitz M C (2015) An Introduction to Autonomy in Weapon Systems. Center for a New American Security, Working Paper, Feb 2015

Schmitt M N (1999) The Principle of Discrimination in 21st Century Warfare. Yale Human Rights and Development Law Journal 2(1):143–182

Schmitt M N (2002) Wired Warfare: Computer Network Attack and Jus in Bello. International Review of the Red Cross 84(846):365–399

Schmitt M N (2005) Precision Attack and International Humanitarian Law. International Review of the Red Cross 87(859):445–466

Schmitt M N (2006) War Technology and the Law of Armed Conflict. In: Helm A M (ed) International Law Studies Volume 82: The Law of War in the 21st Century: Weaponry and the Use of Force. Naval War College Newport, Rhode Island

Schmitt M N (2010a) Targeting in Operational Law. In: Gill T D, Fleck D (eds) The Handbook of the International Law of Military Operations. Oxford University Press, Oxford, pp 245–275

Schmitt M N (2010b) Military Necessity and Humanity in International Humanitarian Law: Preserving the Delicate Balance. Virginia Journal of International Law 50(4):795–839

Schmitt M N (2012) "Attack" as a Term of Art in International Law: The Cyber Operations Context. In: Czosseck C, Ottis R, Ziolkowski K (eds) 4th International Conference on Cyber Conflict. NATO CCD COE Publications, Tallinn

Schmitt M N (2013) Autonomous Weapon Systems and International Humanitarian Law: A Reply to the Critics. Harvard National Security Journal 2013:1-37. https://harvardnsj.org/wp-content/uploads/2013/02/Schmitt-Autonomous-Weapon-Systems-and-IHL-Final.pdf. Accessed 4 August 2023

Schmitt M N (2015) Regulating Autonomous Weapons Might Be Smarter Than Banning Them. Just Security. www.justsecurity.org/25333/regulating-autonomous-weapons-smarter-banning. Accessed 5 November 2017

Schmitt M N, Garraway C H B, Dinstein Y (2006) The Manual on the Law of Non-International Armed Conflict, With Commentary. International Institute of Humanitarian Law, San Remo

Schmitt M N, Highfill C (2018) Invisible Injuries: Concussive Effects and International Humanitarian Law. Harvard National Security Journal 9(1):72–99

Schmitt M N, Schauss M (2019) Uncertainty in the Law of Targeting: Towards a Cognitive Framework. Harvard National Security Journal 10:148–194

Schmitt M N, Thurnher J S (2013) "Out of the Loop": Autonomous Weapon Systems and the Law of Armed Conflict. Harvard Law School National Security Journal 4:231–281

Schuller A L (2017) At the Crossroads of Control: The Intersection of Artificial Intelligence in Autonomous Weapon Systems with International Humanitarian Law. Harvard National Security Journal 8:379

Schuller A L (2019) Artificial Intelligence Effecting Human Decisions to Kill: The Challenge of Linking Numerically Quantifiable Goals to IHL Compliance. Journal of Law and Policy for the Information Society 15:105–122

Sleesman R J, Huntley T C (2019) Lethal Autonomous Weapon Systems: An Overview. Army Lawyer 1:32–35

Sparrow R (2015) Twenty Seconds to Comply: Autonomous Weapon Systems and the Recognition of Surrender. International Law Studies 91:699-728 https://digital-commons.usnwc.edu/cgi/viewcontent.cgi?article=1413&context=ils. Accessed 4 August 2023

Šustr M et al. (2022) A Manual Method of Artillery Fires Correction Calculation. Military Operations Research 27(3):77. https://www.jstor.org/stable/27166357. Accessed 4 August 2023

Taylor I (2021) Who Is Responsible for Killer Robots? Autonomous Weapons, Group Agency, and the Military-Industrial Complex. Journal of Applied Philosophy 38(2):320–334. https://doi.org/10.1111/japp.12469

Thorne J G (2020) Warriors and War Algorithms: Leveraging Artificial Intelligence to Enable Ethical Targeting. Technical Report, 14-05-2020. https://apps.dtic.mil/sti/citations/AD1104171. Accessed 3 July 2021

Thurnher J S (2012) No One at the Controls: Legal Implications of Fully Autonomous Targeting. Joint Force Quarterly 67:77–84

Thurnher J S (2018) Feasible Precautions in Attack and Autonomous Weapons. In: von Heinegg W H, Frau R, Singer T (eds) Dehumanization of Warfare. Springer International Publishing, Cham, pp 99–117. https://doi.org/10.1007/978-3-319-67266-3_6

Toscano C P (2015) "Friend of Humans": An Argument for Developing Autonomous Weapons Systems. Journal of National Security Law & Policy 8(1):189–246

Turns D (2013) Cyber War and the Concept of "Attack" in International Humanitarian Law. In: Saxon D (ed) International Humanitarian Law and the Changing Technology of War. Brill-Nijhoff, Leiden, pp 207–227. https://doi.org/10.1163/9789004229495_011

UK Ministry of Defence (2011) The UK Approach to Unmanned Aircraft Systems. Joint Doctrine Note 2/11

United Nations (2015) Report of the Detailed Findings of the Independent Commission of Inquiry Established Pursuant to Human Rights Council Resolution S-21/1. A/HRC/29/CRP.4

US Department of the Navy (2017) The Commander's Handbook on the Law of Naval Operations. NWP 1-14M

van den Boogaard J C, Roorda M P (2021) "Autonomous" Weapons and Human Control. In: Bartels R (eds) Military Operations and the Notion of Control Under International Law. TMC Asser Press, The Hague, pp 421–437. https://doi.org/10.1007/978-94-6265-395-5_20

van Sliedregt E (2012) Individual Criminal Responsibility in International Law. Oxford University Press, New York

von Heinegg W H (2020) Considerations of Necessity under Article 57(2)(a)(ii), (c), and (3) and Proportionality under Article 51(5)(b) and Article 57(2)(b) of Additional Protocol I. In: Kreß C, Lawless R (eds) Necessity and Proportionality in International Peace and Security Law. Oxford University Press, Oxford, pp 325–342 https://doi.org/10.1093/oso/9780197537374.001.0001/oso-9780197537374-chapter-11

Voon T (2001) Pointing the Finger: Civilian Casualties of NATO Bombing in the Kosovo Conflict. American University International Law Review 16(4):1083–1113

Watts B (2013) The Evolution of Precision Strike. Center for Strategic and Budgetary Assessments, Washington, D.C

Wiebe V (2000) Footprints of Death: Cluster Bombs as Indiscriminate Weapons under International Humanitarian Law. Michigan Journal of International Law 22(1):85–168

Winter E (2020) The Compatibility of the Use of Autonomous Weapons with the Principle of Precaution in the Law of Armed Conflict. The Military Law and the Law of War Review 58(2):240–273. https://doi.org/10.4337/mllwr.2020.02.18

Wright J D (2012) "Excessive" Ambiguity: Analysing and Refining the Proportionality Standard. International Review of the Red Cross 94(886):819–854. https://doi.org/10.1017/S1816383113000143

Wright R G (2003) Combating Civilians Casualties: Rules and Balancing in the Developing Law of War. Wake Forest Law Review 38:129

Chapter 10
Desirability of Using AWS

Contents

Abstract Many advantages are ascribed in literature to autonomous weapons (AWS), but this must be balanced against two important points: first, that not all advantages are exclusive to AWS technology, and second, that any such advantages must be weighed against the difficulty attached to using a particular AWS in a given environment. To that end, this chapter argues that using AWS will in practice only be desirable in circumstances where the projected benefits outweigh the effort, time, resources and diligence that are required to use them lawfully and keep them under control. This chapter introduces two variables, Benefit and Facility, that can be used to rapidly analyse whether using AWS for particular missions is operationally justifiable. Benefit is assessed by first determining whether an AWS is *indispensably* necessary; if not indispensable, Benefit is assessed on a scale. Facility, representing how easily the system can be used lawfully, is derived from the analyses in Chaps. 8 and 9. The two variables are then placed on a two-axial diagram akin to other risk assessment methodologies common in military decision-making to determine the desirability of using particular AWS. It is demonstrated that only very specific conditions justify using AWS, given that they often provide only marginal comparative advantage to, and using them is often more cumbersome than, non-AWS alternatives. From this finding, it is recommended that the AWS debate should be directed more

J. Kwik, *Lawfully Using Autonomous Weapon Technologies*,
https://doi.org/10.1007/978-94-6265-631-4_10

toward these systems that are operationally desirable and realistically see a chance of being used, and away from fantastical Terminator-bots.

Keywords Autonomous weapon system · Artificial intelligence · Targeting · Risk assessment · OODA · Advantages of AWS · Speed · Force protection · Dull · Dirty · Dangerous · Bias · Communications-denied · Jamming · Unmanned system · Killer robot · Terminator

10.1 Introduction

One thing that has become evident from our discussion thus far is that using AWS is not always easy. Targeting rules in force may place exigent demands on Deployers in terms of precautionary measures. Such measures do not come for free: they require effort, time, resources and diligence that could be allocated elsewhere. The question thus arises: Why *would* Deployer choose to use AWS, over other (legacy) systems that might be available? The basic answer would be: because AWS provide an added value that cannot be obtained from alternatives.

However, *whether* this added value is present is not a matter that can be linearly resolved. It is a contextual and comparative question. It is *contextual*, since the added value of using AWS depends on many factors: its inherent utility, its usefulness in context, the measures that must be taken to ensure lawful use, etc. It is *comparative*, since a particular technology's added value also depends on what alternatives are available to achieve the same desired effect. If an AWS is the only system that can achieve a particular task, Deployer would be more inclined to expend effort and resources to ensure lawful use than when the same task could simply be performed by less complicated, more accessible, and less expensive systems or agents.

The aim of this chapter is to provide a cognitive framework that decision-makers can use to determine whether the benefit of using an AWS is worth the associated opportunity costs. For this, we need to juxtapose these two main factors: *Benefit* on one hand, and *Facility* on the other. Using a particular AWS would make no operational sense if the difficulties associated with using it outweigh the benefits.

Fortunately for our analysis, we have already discussed the 'Facility' axis quite extensively. Both preceding chapters were dedicated to exploring in great detail the different variables that would make using particular AWS more of less difficult under the law. This was represented through the Facility spectrums introduced in Chap. 8, and substantiated legally in Chap. 9. We thus already have a strong methodology for determining Facility. This chapter therefore starts by examining the other axis necessary for our evaluation: Benefit.

Section 10.2 first presents a short literature overview of the purported advantages of using AWS. Section 10.3 then reviews these advantages from a critical lens, before proposing an approach that Deployers can utilise to qualitatively assess the benefits of using AWS for particular operations. Subsequently, in Sect. 10.4 we demonstrate how the two axes can be directly compared to enable a reasoned and motivated evaluation as to whether using AWS would be desirable or not, followed by a few practical examples.

The analysis in this chapter demonstrates that circumstances where a reasonable commander would prefer AWS over alternatives are quite specific and less common than what is often implied in the popular debate. AWS would only be definitively desirable in situations where their advantages are significant, and the burdens related to lawfully using them are minimal. In many other circumstances, they likely pose more trouble to Deployer than they are worth.

10.2 Purported AWS Benefits

AI has been emphasised by world leaders, militaries and analysists as a highly desirable, advantageous, and potentially revolutionising technology, both in a military sense and for general applications.[1] AI has been characterised as the new revolution in military affairs,[2] and the most optimistic commentators have even viewed AI and autonomy in military systems as "inevitable",[3] "almost certain"[4] or a matter of 'when' instead of 'if'.[5] From a military perspective, however, technology is only developed and used when it provides tangible benefits vis-à-vis other alternatives and "a comparative advantage to the nation that owns it".[6] AI is often viewed as decisively providing such an advantage.[7] As two commentators opined, "military superpowers in the next century will have superior autonomous capabilities, or they will not be superpowers".[8] Instead of taking these assumptions at face value, however, it is worthwhile to consider them through a more critical lens.

In this section, we briefly but comprehensively explore the different advantages AWS would provide belligerents, as purported in literature. It is found that many of the popularly-cited benefits actually are not directly or uniquely derived from

[1] See e.g. Defense Science Board 2012, p. 1 (US); Associated Press, Reuters and Macdonald 2017 (Russia); Gao 2017 (China); Ministère des Armées 2019, p. 9 (France); Boulanin et al. 2020, p. 1 (EU). For statements by authors, see e.g. Russell and Norvig 2010, p. 1; Thurnher 2013; Bryce and Parakilas 2018, p. 44; Wilson 2020, p. 125.

[2] McAllister 2018, p. 252; Lamraski 2021, p. 9.

[3] Defense Science Board 2016, p. 92; Beard 2014, p. 620.

[4] Scharre 2018, p. 244.

[5] E.g. Herbach 2012, p. 15 ("seems to be a matter of 'when' robotic systems that are, to an extent, autonomous are rolled out widely within the military rather than 'if' this will happen"); Scherer 2016, p. 363 ("The complexity and scope of tasks that will be left in the hands of AI will undoubtedly continue to increase in the coming years"); Schuller 2017, p. 390 ("it is a safe assumption that autonomy will continue to increase in modern weapons"); Umbrello et al. 2020, p. 273 ("governments are not going to stop developing robotic devices such as LAWs for military purposes").

[6] Yoner 2001, p. 1.

[7] See e.g. Scharre 2018, p. 95; Hofman 2020.

[8] LaPointe and Levin 2016.

AWS technology itself, in the sense that the same advantage could not be attained through alternate means. On the other hand, we also identify some benefits which are uniquely obtainable through AI technology.

10.2.1 Advantages Not Unique to AI

Many advantages cited in support of AI in weapon systems are not AI-specific but rather are derived from the surrounding 'package' of technologies common to modern weapon systems, which may or may not involve AI. For example, force projection (extending the reach of the individual soldier, allowing them to see and strike further)[9] does not necessarily require AI: rather, it requires the effective functioning of an unmanned platform, which could be remote-controlled. Similarly, superior sensing abilities (which may outclass human sensory perception)[10] do not specifically entail an AWS, but rather are derived from the sophistication of the system's sensors.

Critics, too, can misattribute incentives. In the 2015 Future of Life Institute's letter in opposition to lethal autonomous weapons, the authors warn that these weapons "will become the Kalashnikovs of tomorrow" due to their ease of mass-production.[11] The authors overlook that ease of proliferation applies to any technology capable of being mass-produced.[12]

Another popular motivation for developing AWS relates to force protection. Thurnher remarked that autonomous weapons "offer tremendous promise in terms of protecting one's own forces from harm",[13] while the Dutch Advisory Council on International Affairs (AIV) argued that their usage could reduce losses to allied troops.[14] Relatedly, AWS have been cited as particularly attractive for the fulfilment of DDD (dull, dirty, dangerous) tasks.[15] However, remote-controlled platforms confer the same advantages! Indeed, many authors (correctly) ascribe this advantage to robotics instead of AI.[16]

---

[9] Arkin 2013, p. 1; Crootof 2015, p. 1866.

[10] Arkin 2010, p. 2; Marchant et al. 2011, p. 280.

[11] Future of Life Institute 2015.

[12] One characteristic unique to AI which may be touched upon here is state duplication, in the sense that once an AI is trained, it can be easily copied to thousands of individual units. However, whether this is a positive or negative aspect would depend on the qualities of the AI being copied, as copying a badly performing AI can hardly be viewed as an incentive. See Sect. 5.3.

[13] Thurnher 2014, p. 215.

[14] Adviesraad Internationale Vraagstukken and Commissie van Advies inzake Volkenrechtelijke Vraagstukken 2015, p. 11 ("*Inzet van autonome wapensystemen kan het aantal slachtoffers onder eigen troepen ... beperken*").

[15] Heyns 2013, para 51; Adviesraad Internationale Vraagstukken and Commissie van Advies inzake Volkenrechtelijke Vraagstukken 2015, p. 11; Defense Science Board 2012, p. 16.

[16] Lyons and Havig 2014, p. 181; Defense Science Board 2016, p. 11; Ministère des Armées 2019, p. 5.

As this short overview shows, many commonly-raised benefits of AWS are not *exclusive* to the technology. Note that this does not mean the claims are void: if Deployer can *only* choose between an AWS and sending a manned mission, for example, the force protection incentive becomes pertinent. The point to retain, rather, is that many of these advantages attach not to AWS technology itself, but rather to a related but non-exclusive characteristic (e.g. the ability to project force without putting humans at risk—which also can be achieved by remote-controlled systems). In isolation, these therefore do not provide Deployer with an intrinsic reason to prefer AWS technology over alternatives.

10.2.2 Advantages Related to Psychology and Physiology

AWS are often pushed for perceived advantages related to human psychology and physiology. We discuss this category separately, because determining whether they derive uniquely from AI or not is sometimes complicated.

Some cite the ability to be "operational 24/7"[17] or that they "don't get hungry, tired, bored, or sick"[18] as desirable advantages. This is only partially correct. It is true that infantry, drone operators or aircraft pilots are limited by their physiology as to the consecutive periods of time they can carry out missions. However, as some correctly point out, persistence is primarily an unmanned platform advantage.[19] Operators can be switched out while maintaining persistent stare[20] or persistent operations, circumventing physiological limitations. On the other hand, drone operators can still get bored and perform poorly, despite routine shift changes.

The removal of a soldier's self-preservation instinct is frequently quoted as an advantage,[21] with some noting that AI "need not be motivated by self-preservation"[22] and "do not need to protect themselves in cases of low certainty of target identification".[23] Once again, this is also the case with remote-controlled platforms, as some authors correctly point out.[24] This advantage is accrued by removing the soldier from the active battlefield, not from the use of AI specifically.

In contrast, some psychological effects persist even if the soldier is removed from the battlefield. For example, it has been demonstrated that drone pilots can experience similar post-combat stress responses as soldiers in the field, despite operating in

---

[17] Abaimov and Martellini 2020, p. 141.

[18] Sparrow 2016, p. 96.

[19] Waszink 2011, p. 16. The UK MOD even calls it "the unique selling point of an *unmanned* aircraft". UK Ministry of Defence 2011, para 314 (emphasis added).

[20] Persistent stare refers to "constant video surveillance that enables more time for decision making and more eyes on target". Drones are often used for this purpose. Arkin 2013, p. 1.

[21] Arkin 2010, p. 2; Heyns 2013, para 69.

[22] Crootof 2015, p. 1867.

[23] Marchant et al. 2011, p. 280.

[24] Stephens 2014, p. 764; Noone and Noone 2015, p. 30.

complete safety.[25] Arkin's suggestion that replacing human soldiers with AWS can reduce trauma, suicide rates and anxiety among friendly forces,[26] then, could be specifically attributed to the use of AI.

Another purported advantage concerns avoiding negative emotions.[27] Human soldiers have succumbed to anger, spite and prejudice,[28] and many war crimes are committed by combatants who seek to avenge comrades.[29] The fog of war can drive humans to panic.[30] Scenario fulfilment[31] is sometimes also cited as a cognitive bias that can be avoided through the use of AI.[32] In essence, it is argued that AI would never experience such negative emotions: "their judgment will not be clouded by emotions".[33] Whether AWS can truly provide Deployer with these purported benefits is quite context-dependent, and Deployer must analyse the situation carefully to determine this. Remote operators will likely experience less or no emotions such as panic or a desire for vengeance. On the other hand, operating a weapon remotely does not discount the possibility that decisions can be made on irrational, prejudicial or malicious grounds.[34] In this latter situation, using AWS could confer concrete comparative advantages,[35] assuming the system is indeed bias-free.[36]

---

[25] McCammon 2017.

[26] Arkin 2010, p. 7.

[27] The UK MOD summarised the position as follows: "A target is a series of ones and zeros, and once the decision is made, by whatever means, that the target is legitimate, then prosecution of that target is made mechanically. The robot does not care that the target is human or inanimate, terrorist or freedom fighter, savage or barbarian. A robot cannot be driven by anger to carry out illegal actions such as those at My Lai." UK Ministry of Defence 2011, para 521.

[28] Heyns 2013, para 54.

[29] Mayer 2015, p. 70.

[30] Schmitt 2015. As Walzer submits, "[f]ear and hysteria are always latent in combat, often real, and they press us toward fearful measures". Walzer 1997, p. 251.

[31] This effect refers to the tendency of humans to revert to pre-rehearsed chains of actions in stressful situations, exhibiting confirmation bias vis-à-vis new information that might contradict pre-set beliefs (by ignoring or distorting it to fit prior beliefs). Marchant et al. 2011, p. 280.

[32] Arkin 2010, p. 2; Venkatesh 2019, p. 126.

[33] Dinstein 2018, para 19. A 2018 study by the ICRC with Australian army cadets showed that stress, duress, fatigue and pressure – simulated by enforced sleep deprivation and food deprivation – lead to unethical and unlawful behaviour, so much so that the participants were shocked by their actions when shown the recordings afterward. See ICRC 2018b, p. 29.

[34] Russell and Norvig 2010, p. 1037.

[35] Note that the opposite position has also been raised, namely that machines' lack of emotions would be harmful because they cannot empathise or be moved into acts of compassion like humans can. See Human Rights Watch 2012, p. 38. While this may be true (at least with the current technology), compassion or empathy is not of any legal relevance under IHL (making it irrelevant in the broad scope of this study) and a counterincentive instead of an incentive (making it irrelevant in the context of this Subsection). See Sassòli 2014, p. 318.

[36] See Sect. 5.8.

10.2.3 Advantages Unique to AI

The previous subsections notwithstanding, "there are direct benefits from using AI that other systems cannot achieve".[37] Primarily, these comprise "faster execution of tasks, higher interoperability, lower error rates, and the increasing use of unmanned platforms, which decreases risk to life and improves operational access".[38]

Comparative performance is prominently raised. The ability to execute calculations incorporating exponentially more data and with greater consistency[39] allow AI to perform better in speed, precision and reliability compared to humans.[40] Many other advantages flow directly from this fundamental point:[41]

- *Shortened OODA*.[42] A higher processing speed would shorten the OODA loop, conferring an advantage vis-à-vis the 'slower' adversary.[43]
- *Split-second tasks*. AI is capable of acquiring, processing and executing decisions in a fraction of the time humans could.[44]
- *Data processing*. Some tasks[45] require the integration of an extremely high volume of data,[46] which only AI can perform.[47]

---

[37] Defense Innovation Board 2019, p. 14.

[38] Williams 2015, p. 37.

[39] Coleman 2014, p. 39; Geiß and Lahmann 2017, p. 372; Ministère des Armées 2019, p. 5; Hofman 2020.

[40] Heyns 2013, para 53; Scharre 2016, p. 151; Rosenberg and Markoff 2016; Defense Innovation Board 2019, p. 14.

[41] Relatedly, many argue that this increased performance would also improve overall compliance to IHL. E.g. US Office of General Counsel of the Department of Defense 2015, Law of War Manual, Updated December 2016. US Department of Defense, Washington D.C. (US Law of War Manual), sct 6.5.9.2 (it could "enhance the way law of war principles are implemented in military operations" by *inter alia* improving accuracy); Ministère des Armées 2019, p. 6 ("*contrairement à certaines idées reçues, l'IA recèle un potentiel qui, bien encadré et maîtrisé, conduit à une meilleure prise en compte par les armées françaises des principes fondamentaux du droit des conflits armés*"); Sassòli 2014, p. 310 ("my first feeling is not skepticism, but hope for better respect of IHL"); Kellenberger 2012, pp. 812–13 ("A robot could be programmed to behave more ethically and far more cautiously on the battlefield than a human being"); Thurnher 2014, p. 215 (they "may even be able to provide greater protections to civilians by delivering more precise and accurate strikes"); Boothby 2018b, pp. 50–51 ("Scientific and technical development of autonomous systems may, in the future, yield opportunities for improved compliance").

[42] OODA (Observe-Orient-Decide-Act) is a popular method to represent the cognitive decision-making process in military circles. It was first popularised by Boyd. See Boyd 1996. For how the OODA loop also generally reflects the decision-making process of AI agents, see Sect. 3.3.

[43] Marra and McNeil 2013, pp. 50–51; Wilson 2020, p. 126. See US Air Force 2009, p. 16.

[44] Heyns 2013, para 53; Defense Innovation Board 2019, p. 14.

[45] E.g. multimodal activities, multi-mission operations, simulation planning.

[46] Wallach and Allen 2009, p. 19; Defense Science Board 2016, p. 45; Ministère des Armées 2019, p. 5.

[47] The specific benefit of AI here is the ability to handle large amounts of information, to integrate information from multiple sources, and to analyse large datasets and use pattern recognition to

Removing the link requirement is another unique advantage. It is often argued[48] that AWS are "particularly attractive" for situations in which "remote control operation is not suited".[49] Such systems would "enable military operations in communications-degraded or -denied environments in which traditional systems may not be able to operate".[50]

Finally, *logistical and economic benefits* are sometimes mentioned. AWS would be less cost- and personnel-intensive than remote-controlled systems.[51] In addition, remote-controlled systems require Deployer to have access to trained operators, who might not always be available.[52]

10.3 How Useful is an AWS?

As the previous section has demonstrated, to what extent an AWS is useful to Deployer (and therefore whether this benefit outweighs the effort necessary to use it lawfully) is dependent on both the envisaged *task* and what *alternatives* are available for the same task. In this section, we develop a more streamlined method Deployers can use to determine how beneficial using particular an AWS would be, given an operational setting and a relatively short decision-making period. Two major indicators are proposed: *indispensability* and *comparative advantage.*

10.3.1 Indispensability

This indicator represents how absolutely necessary the advantages accrued from AI are for the accomplishment of the envisaged task. The nature of some tasks is such that no non-AI alternative is practically (or even theoretically) feasible without

derive conclusions. See respectively: Mayer 2015, p. 70; Crootof 2015, p. 1867; Parakilas and Bryce 2018, p. 2.

48 See Mayer 2015, p. 67.

49 SIPRI 2017, p. 133.

50 Sayler 2020.

51 Thurnher 2018, p. 105.

52 Schmitt explains that "it can take scores of people, from pilots and weapon systems operators to technicians and intelligence analysts, to operate a single tethered unmanned aircraft." Schmitt and Thurnher 2013, p. 237. In contrast, the only associated cost of an AWS would be maintenance, making them cost-effective. Coleman 2014, p. 39; Sparrow 2016, p. 96. With regard to preparatory costs, Crootof noted the lower cost of training one AI vis-à-vis one soldier, arguing that an AI can be trained "instantaneously". Crootof 2015, p. 1867. One counterargument that can be made is that training a commander to use AWS lawfully also requires time and resources. However, training Deployer is an investment that the military organisation must make *regardless* of whether an Operator is present or not. In that sense, the additional requirement to (also) have a trained Operator present is an additional logistical obstacle, although the extent to which this is the case will vary.

severely compromising the effectiveness with which the task is carried out. Drawing from our findings in the previous section, we can determine that AI is particularly indispensable when the task or mission demands advantages 'unique to AI'.[53] There are arguably only two main situations where this would be the case.

The first are tasks *requiring superhuman response times*. Some tasks are unamenable to human-speed decision-making, such as reacting in split-second time-frames (e.g. close-in defence systems)[54] and acting with high accuracy in situations where there is insufficient time to perform the required calculations (e.g. calculating interception trajectories).[55] In such situations, "the time of engagement would be too short for a human to respond".[56] This is likely the most imperative benefit of autonomy in weapon systems.

The second are missions where a *communications link cannot be maintained*.[57] There are a few situations where one can envisage this to be the case. First, the mission takes place in an environment that inherently precludes (regular) communications, such as undersea or underground operations,[58] or in closed environments (e.g. intranets).[59] Second, mission success depends on cutting communications, such as covert operations in enemy territory.[60] Third, enemy countermeasures may be a factor, such as when Deployer foresees that the adversary is likely to cut or jam communications.[61] Alternatively, opponents could be planning to hack, compromise or override the system as referenced in Sect. 6.2.[62] An AI capable of functioning autonomously would constitute an effective counter-response to these enemy tactics.

Indispensability could be measured on a spectrum depending on how effective the next-best solution would be. For instance, the next-best solution in a comms-denied environment would be sending a manned mission. This is risky but still technically possible for clearing an enemy-held industrial area, but out of the question if the area were radioactive.[63] Similarly, humans could perform vehicle active protection albeit

---

53 See Sect. 10.2.3.

54 Marra and McNeil 2013, pp. 46–47.

55 SIPRI 2017, p. 133; Hofman 2020.

56 Scharre and Horowitz 2015, p. 3.

57 "The military value of fully autonomous weapons for operations in communications-denied environments cannot be easily dismissed." Scharre 2016, p. 164. Frigoli similarly submits that "[h]unting mobile targets in communications-denied areas represents one the most relevant military utility" of AWS. Frigoli 2020, p. 42.

58 Defense Science Board 2016, p. 45; Canada 2016; Adviesraad Internationale Vraagstukken and Commissie van Advies inzake Volkenrechtelijke Vraagstukken 2015, p. 11; Anderson and Waxman 2013, p. 7.

59 Stuxnet, is so far as we view it as a cyber-AWS, is also an example where this was the case. The facility's intranet was cut from outside networks, making remote control impossible. See Buchan and Tsagourias 2021, pp. 322–23.

60 SIPRI 2017, p. 133.

61 Scharre 2018, p. 15.

62 Thurnher 2018, p. 106; Boothby 2018a 144.

63 Cf. Adviesraad Internationale Vraagstukken and Commissie van Advies inzake Volkenrechtelijke Vraagstukken 2015, p. 11.

at a much-decreased level of effectiveness,[64] but manually intercepting a missile salvo would be almost impossible.[65] In either example, Indispensability for the latter situations would thus be higher than the former.

10.3.2 Comparative Advantage

Even if AWS are not indispensable to a particular task, their use could be particularly attractive because they provide a significant comparative advantage vis-à-vis other alternatives. All other benefits discussed in Sect. 10.2 can factor into Deployer's consideration in this respect. Arguably, this variable can be subdivided into two major categories: relative performance advantage and relative logistical advantage.

Relative performance advantage refers to how AWS would function better than alternatives (either remote-controlled or manned options). This can manifest in for example:

- *Speed*, such as improved reaction times.[66] This would include OODA loop completion.[67]
- *Improved performance*, such as better measurements in "accuracy, precision, and reliability".[68]
- *Avoiding human pitfalls*, such as cognitive biases, emotions, etc.[69]

Relative logistical advantage refers to how using AWS would allow Deployer to accrue an operational and resource advantage vis-à-vis alternatives, such as:

- *Force protection*. As discussed in Sect. 9.6.2, this is one of the primary advantages of AWS, but note that *mutatis mutandis*,[70] the same benefit can be obtained from using remote-controlled systems.[71]
- *Resources (current and iterative)*. AWS may be more disposable or in higher availability. Deployer may lack trained Operators or legacy systems, or need them elsewhere for more important missions. Deployer may not be able to commit Operators to a long-term and relatively unimportant task (e.g. perimeter defence).[72]

---

[64] Cf. Eklund 2020, p. n5.

[65] See Defense Science Board 2016, p. 53.

[66] Kastan 2013, p. 52.

[67] Scharre 2018, p. 24. See Sect. 3.3.

[68] Scharre 2016, p. 156.

[69] Jensen 2018. See also Boothby 2018a, p. 159 ("decisions of robotic technologies will not be distorted by fear, anger, vengeance, amnesia, panic, tiredness or other peculiarly human fallibilities").

[70] I.e., assuming there are not indispensable factors at play, such as the mission taking place in a comms-denied environment.

[71] See Sect. 10.2.1.

[72] E.g. ICRC 2016, p. 73.

Deployer is entitled under IHL to use AWS over alternatives if such relative advantages are applicable. Improved performance will often correlate with fewer mistakes, which improves the protection of civilians (from both collateral damage and false positives).[73] With regard to logistical advantages such as force protection or iterative considerations, these are legitimate factors under feasibility that would permit Deployer to prefer the AWS option, if done in good faith.[74]

10.4 Synthesis

At this point in our discussion, we have both extensively discussed the benefits of using AWS (This Chapter) and the associated difficulties in doing so lawfully (Chaps. 8 and 9). Drawing from all of these considerations, this final section proposes an integrated methodology to allow Deployer to determine and motivate: *should* I use this AWS?

To provide a more concrete demonstration, let us compare these following (hypothetical[75]) systems:

Phalanx: Searches, recognises and automatically engages incoming threats such as missiles, aircraft, surface craft, and UAVs.[76] *Mission*: protect ship.

SGR-A6x: An improved version of the countryside-roving SGR system introduced in Sect. 8.9. This system is 50% better than humans in recognising combatants from civilians. Semi-opaque. *Mission*: secure a perimeter along the frontline.

Exterminator-2: All-purpose ground-based AWS designed for urban combat against regular personnel. Rapidly strikes combatants and military vehicles (tanks, APCs, etc.), automatically selecting the appropriate munition.[77] Almost perfect Specificity[78] thanks to sophisticated hybrid model. *Mission*: accompany infantry operation. *Optional Context Controls*: (a) no antivehicle strikes; (b) do not fire if *n*-number of civilians are in target's proximity.[79]

ATS-88 Goedendag: Aerial AWS capable of reliably distinguishing tanks and rapidly exploiting weak points in armour, but has trouble with trams. *Mission*: destroy tanks guarding road in Area-1 as in Scenario 5. Hit tanks can explode violently.

---

[73] Ohlin 2017, p. 35; ICRC 2018a, para 19; Mayer 2015, p. 67.

[74] See Sect. 9.6.2.

[75] All systems except the Phalanx are hypothetical and are inspired from real-world weapons or borrowed from hypothetical examples given in literature. The examples were chosen to illustrate how the proposed methodology works and to stimulate discussion (see Sect. 10.4.3).

[76] US Navy 2019.

[77] This refers to the Context Control 'dynamic munition selection'. See Sect. 8.7.3.2.

[78] I.e., it is extremely unlikely to mistake civilians for insurgents or persons engaging in DPH. This does not imply anything with regard to its Recall (i.e. how good it is at identifying DPH).

[79] This refers to the Context Control 'maximum incidental harm limit'. See Sect. 8.7.3.1.

IAI Pazuzu: Tiny loitering munition designed to locate and destroy radar/radio/electronic jammers. Small area-of-effect upon impact. *Mission*: destroy semi-mobile jamming assets currently in-use in town. Opponent has effective air defence against larger air assets.

SHL19-Lazerbot: Counterinsurgency system that shoots body-armour-cutting laser. For use "in close quarters as the first system to enter enemy held buildings".[80] Comparable accuracy as humans in distinguishing insurgents from civilians thanks to complex neural network, but can act more quickly.

10.4.1 Assessing Facility and Benefit

To assess ***Benefit***, Deployer can use the indicators proposed in Sect. 10.3 to assess how desirable the AWS is for the particular task. Deployer could use a scoring system or simply qualitative indicators (e.g. low-moderate-high).[81] For our purposes, we use a qualitative-descriptive grading system.[82]

For example, the SHL19-Lazerbot could be assessed as follows:

- *Indispensable?* No. Task can be achieved with the same efficacy using a remote-controlled system.
- *Relative advantage?* Ability to act more quickly than humans, at comparable levels of accuracy, offers only marginal advantage.
- *Benefit*: MARGINAL.

The Pazuzu, in contrast, could be assessed as follows:

- *Indispensable?* Yes. Remote-controlled impossible due to enemy jamming. Manned air assets unusable due to air defence.
- *Relative advantage?* No other alternatives available.
- *Benefit*: INDISPENSABLE.

Facility should be assessed as demonstrated in Sect. 8.9. For our purposes, we apply the scoring system previously discussed in that section.

---

80 This system is inspired by Schuller's Surrender Bot, described as follows: "Suppose … that a country developed a robot for deployment in urban combat called "Surrender Bot." It is equipped with a high-power laser that can cut through an enemy soldier's body armor. The country intends to deploy the robot in close quarters as the first system to enter enemy held buildings." The Surrender Bot is designed to inflict painful but non-lethal to drive the enemy to surrender, which Schuller uses to argue for a situation where the maux superflus rule would apply to AWS. This latter detail of the Surrender Bot was not included in our example since it would indeed make the system unlawful per se. See Schuller 2019, pp. 118–19.

81 The methodology would ideally be standardised by the military organization to which Deployer is attached.

82 The grades and associated scores used for this example are: INDISPENSIBLE (0.9); HIGH (0.7); MODERATE (0.6); LOW (0.4); MARGINAL (0.2). As this serves only as a demonstration, the scores chosen are arbitrary.

Table 10.1 Example desirability analysis

System	Benefit			Facility (0 = hard; 1 = easy)
	Indisp?	Rel. adv?	Assessment	
Phalanx	Yes		Indispensable	0.73
SGR-46x	No	Low	Low	0.32
Exterminator	No	Moderate	Moderate	0.27
Exterminator+CC				0.45
Goedendag	No	Low	Low	0.68
Pazuzu	Yes		Indispensable	0.45
Lazerbot	No	Marginal	Marginal	0.27

Following this methodology, the systems can be evaluated as follows in Table 10.1 (full justifications for each assessment are listed in Appendix 2).

10.4.2 Desirability: Comparing Facility and Benefit

Whether Deployer would use any of these systems is a function of whether their benefits outweigh the difficulties attached to their use. If a system offers only marginal extra benefit vis-à-vis the next best alternative (frequently this is a remote-controlled system), Deployer would likely only be willing to use the system if it presents minimal additional difficulties in terms of lawful use. In contrast, if the additional benefit is substantial (and particularly if the system is indispensable), Deployer may see the worth in using the system despite some associated risks.

This cost-benefit consideration is best captured on a Desirability chart (Fig. 10.1) mapping each system's position along the Facility and Benefit axes, with diagonal decision boundaries representing situations where Deployer would (a) in no circumstances, (b) with some serious consideration, or (c) relatively easily would agree to use the system. This two-axial method with diagonal decision zones is not foreign to militaries, since proportionality considerations (which also feature a cost-benefit analysis) are often conducted using similar graphs.[83] It should thus be relatively easy to incorporate the methodology introduced in this section to existing targeting policy.

Applying the evaluation in Sect. 10.4.1 to the chart, we can locate each system on the two axes as shown in Fig. 10.2.

[83] According to an expert panel hosted by the ICRC, frequently "collateral damage and military advantage are ranked on a scale of low, medium or high or using other more detailed categories, with the outcome that an attack expected to offer, for example, a low military advantage while causing high incidental harm would immediately be deemed excessive". Gisel 2016, p. 65. See e.g. the matrix proposed in Wright 2012, p. 852.

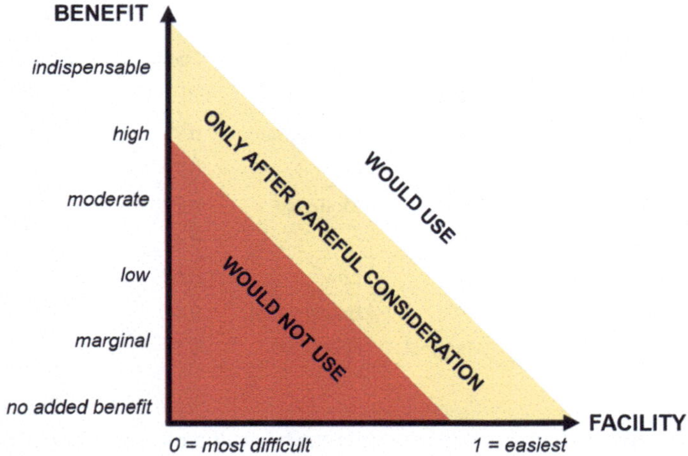

Fig. 10.1 Basic desirability chart

Fig. 10.2 Filled desirability chart

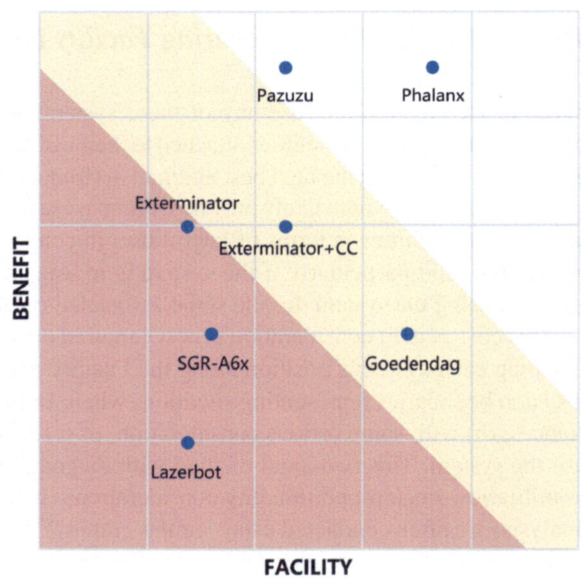

10.4.3 Discussion

Arraying the systems on the chart provides interesting insights into several topics discussed in this part. It also confirms some intuitions regarding what type of AWS Deployers would be interested in using, and which would simply be too unwieldy to even consider. It is important to emphasise this latter category, since systems a commander is unlikely to want to use would also be systems that are not worth developing or adopting in the first place.

Take the ***Lazerbot***, which is a somewhat stereotypical example of how AWS are sensationalised in the popular debate.[84] As its placement on the graph shows, this system is both very difficult to use and offers little advantage over human(-controlled) alternatives, if any. Militaries would think twice about investing in such systems, and Deployers would think twice before activating them. While commentators are right when they say such systems present problems for IHL compliance,[85] one wonders whether placing our academic focus on such systems is worthwhile if they stand little chance of ever being adopted.[86]

On the other end of the chart, the ***Phalanx***'s placement also conforms with the real-world observation that the system has seen (a) widespread use for decades (b) with little controversy.[87] The former is due to its high Benefit rating, while the latter is due to its high Facility. Both in combination make the Phalanx and similar systems[88] desirable and relatively non-cumbersome to use.

The ***SGR-A6x***'s placement teaches us that even a clear performance advantage (of 50%) vis-à-vis human-controlled systems is not always sufficient to make an AWS worth using. This conclusion disagrees with a somewhat common assertion in commentaries that AWS should be preferred over humans when they provide a clear improvement in performance.[89] The reason for this (for some, counterintuitive) conclusion is that, as found in Sect. 8.9, indicators such as the AI's 'reliability' or 'performance' (variables linked to Rationale-FP, false positives) represent only *part* of the factors that contribute toward Facility. Many contextual factors can make the system difficult to use, despite good results in terms of Rationale-FP. In this case, the SGR-A6x scores particularly poorly in variables related to Rationale-EE (epistemic

---

84 As noted above, the description advanced by Schuller is rather sensationalist (that of a robot designed to inflict as much pain as possible to force enemy combatants to surrender). Even though this was not Schuller's intent, it is quite reminiscent of the more alarmist way AWS have been represented in the popular debate. See Danzig 2018, p. 6.

85 This example was chosen since counterinsurgency situations are often given as examples to argue for why AWS would not be able to comply with IHL rules. E.g. Human Rights Watch 2012, pp. 30–32.

86 As Williams submits, in popular sources, sensationalist descriptors such as 'killer robots' and imagery reminiscent of the Terminator "are added to focus the attention of the public and policy makers on a particular issue", which is not constructive since these issues may not necessarily be the types of systems we *should* focus on. Williams 2015, p. 28.

87 Scharre and Horowitz 2015, p. 21.

88 See e.g. Ekelhof 2018, p. 74 (the Patriot) and ICRC 2016, p. 72 (the Iron Dome).

89 For example, it has been argued that "if an AWS could better distinguish between civilian and military aircraft, this would argue in favor of giving autonomous targeting protocols to an anti-aircraft missile system" Ohlin 2017, pp. 33–34 or that "[i]f autonomous weapons became more precise and reliable than humans, the obligation to take "all feasible precautions" might *require* commanders to use them" Scharre 2018, p. 258 (emphasis added). While these commentators take the care to qualify their statements with conditionals, the basic idea that AWS should be prioritised when they perform better than humans remains.

error) due to its free-roaming nature, dynamic operational environment and difficult target type,[90] making the system fall in the red ('undesirable') zone.

In terms of Benefit, the ***Goedendag*** scores similarly to the SGR-A6x, but falls in the yellow zone. The Goedendag is much less likely to act unforeseeably (Rationale-EE) due to its much stricter operational parameters, and its weakness (having problems with trams) is negated due to trams being absent on the countryside road, making risk of false positives low (Rationale-FP). Deployer thus only needs to consider collateral damage to buildings (Rationale-IH), which is possible but unlikely in Area-1. Despite the Goedendag only offering a minor relative advantage,[91] this is thus a system Deployer *might* consider employing, depending on operational circumstances.

In contrast, the ***Pazuzu***'s mission is less constrained in space and time, and its operating environment more difficult (urban with semi-mobile targets). This is reflected in its placement much to the Goedendag's left in terms of Facility. The Pazuzu nevertheless falls in the white zone because its Benefit is so substantial: its autonomous properties are indispensable for the particular operational context. This is an example of an autonomous system Deployer would be interested in, despite associated difficulties in its use.

Two supplementary observations are necessary. First, the Pazuzu lies very close to the yellow-white boundary line, which indicates that Deployers would have relatively more reservations to using it compared to systems such as the Phalanx. Second, note the very particular conditions specified in the description which allowed the Pazuzu to attain 'Indispensable'-status: defenders needed to both jam communications *and* have air defence,[92] as otherwise, remote-controlled systems or manned air assets would serve as viable alternatives. That the example is contrived demonstrates that situations where AWS would be truly indispensable are quite rare in practice. While proponents often make valid arguments with regard to the potential benefits of AWS technology for efficiency or IHL compliance,[93] these claims must be framed by the fact that only in very specific situations (particularly where superhuman speed and precision is required) does the advantage amount to indispensability. In most situations, the added value will be more limited, as we saw with the Goedendag.

Finally, the ***Exterminator*** shows us how Context Controls can help Deployer shift the position of a system toward a different Desirability zone on the chart. Despite its almost perfect Specificity, the Exterminator in its 'default' state is quite unwieldy in terms of Facility: there is high likelihood of collateral damage (Rationale-IH), and risk

[90] See Appendix 2.

[91] The minor advantage is derived from its speed, its ability to autonomously attack the weakest points in armour, and that it provides Deployer the ability to allocate other assets elsewhere. See Appendix 2.

[92] These factors correspond to 'comms denied environment' and 'force protection' respectively in terms of benefits that only AI can provide. See Sect. 10.3.1.

[93] For examples of commentators who argue in favour of supporting AWS development for its apparent ability to improve compliance to IHL on the battlefield, see e.g. Jensen 2020, Winter 2020.

of epistemic error is high (Rationale-EE).[94] Combined with the only moderate Benefit it provides, Deployer would be unlikely to use it. With both Context Controls enabled, however, its use is less cumbersome and carries less risk, making *Exterminator+CC* fall into the yellow zone. The same principle can be applied to all Context Controls discussed in Sect. 8.7: properly implemented, they shift a system's placement to the right, making the system more attractive to use. This also demonstrates that designers have a vested interest in incorporating more Context Control options into the systems they are developing: they make the AWS more attractive since they provide Deployers with more opportunities to employ the system.

10.5 Closing Thoughts

The approach advanced in this chapter is one way the desirability of AWS can be assessed. It answers the crucial question of when a Deployer *would* use an AWS. The methodology proposed in this chapter is useful at both the operational and developmental levels. Operationally, Deployer must be able to access a cognitive framework that helps them decide and motivate when employing an AWS is the correct course of action. For developers and procurement officers, understanding what conditions would make commanders more or less interested in using AWS helps guide design: it is unwise to invest into developing or purchasing systems no one would be interested in using.

The second major finding of this chapter relates to the fact that generally speaking, a set of particular circumstances must be fulfilled before a reasonable commander would use an AWS over (legacy) alternatives. Situations of indispensable benefit present the most compelling condition where AWS would be preferred, but these are quite specific.[95] In contrast, many examples often cited in the popular debate (e.g. AWS for urban fighting) clearly fall outside this Indispensable category. When contrasted with the difficulties associated with using them lawfully, they are often more trouble than they are worth. For the academic and diplomatic spheres, the relative scarcity of AWS desirability is an important point to retain. We would do well to focalise our discussions on systems falling into the yellow or white zones. 'Killer robots'[96] such as the Lazerbot are useful as thought experiments to explore

---

[94] The former is mainly due to the operational environment and potential splash caused by antivehicle munitions, while the latter is due to its opacity and broad target specificity (Assorted-tier). For complete details, see Appendix 2.

[95] Recall that the Pazuzu example was deliberately contrived to simulate circumstances beyond C-RAM or similar situations where an 'Indispensable' label would be warranted.

[96] The use of this term (and other emotive terms) has been avoided throughout the book, but it seems appropriate here to describe the Lazerbot. The fact that this term only has become relevant at this point in the book demonstrates that despite the emphasis in the broader polemics on the inexorable arrival of the killer robots, actual applications of AI in weapon systems are much more banal. See also Danzig 2018, p. 6; Heyns 2013, para 95.

how the law would react to particular extremes, but Hollywoodian otherwise and unnecessarily alarmist at worst.[97]

No pretentions are made that the methodology proposed above is the only way desirability can be evaluated. As indicated previously, organisations are likely to develop their own guidelines to determine when an AWS is worth using. Whatever the method chosen, it is likely to remain based on a juxtaposition of its ease of use in legal terms (for us, Facility) and military utility (for us, Benefit). Ultimately, this also perfectly captures the basic friction in IHL between humanity and necessity,[98] which often does not have an unequivocal answer to problems and instead relies on the good faith of commanders to find the proper balance during operations.[99]

In the next and final part, we will depart from this presumption of goodwill and also consider situations where Deployer may be less inclined to follow the law to the best of their ability.

References

Abaimov S, Martellini M (2020) Artificial Intelligence in Autonomous Weapon Systems. In: Martellini M, Ralf T (eds) 21st Century Prometheus. Springer International Publishing, Cham, pp 141–177. DOI: https://doi.org/10.1007/978-3-030-28285-1_8

Adviesraad Internationale Vraagstukken and Commissie van Advies inzake Volkenrechtelijke Vraagstukken (2015) Autonome Wapensystemen: De Noodzaak van Betekenisvolle Menselijke Controle. AIV

Anderson K, Waxman M C (2013) Law and Ethics for Autonomous Weapon Systems: Why a Ban Won't Work and How the Laws of War Can. In: American University Washington College of Law Research Paper No. 2013-11. Stanford University, Stanford

Arkin R C (2010) The Case for Ethical Autonomy in Unmanned Systems. Journal of Military Ethics 9(4):332–341. DOI: https://doi.org/10.1080/15027570.2010.536402

Arkin R C (2013) Lethal Autonomous Systems and the Plight of the Non-Combatant. AISB Quarterly 137:1–9

Associated Press, Reuters, Macdonald C (2017) Vladimir Putin Warns Whoever Cracks Artificial Intelligence Will "Rule the World". Dailymail. https://www.dailymail.co.uk/sciencetech/article-4844322/Putin-Leader-artificial-intelligence-rule-world.html. Accessed 31 July 2023

[97] As Scharre observes, "I am continually struck by how much the Terminator films influence debate on autonomous weapons. In nine out of ten serious conversations on autonomous weapons I have had … someone invariably mentions the Terminator. … I wonder if James Cameron had not made the Terminator movies how debates on autonomous weapons would be different. If science fiction had not primed us with visions of killer robots set to extinguish humanity, would we fear autonomous lethal machines?" Scharre 2018, p. 264. Singer made a related comment, noting that the "theme of robots taking on the work we don't want to do but then ultimately assuming control is a staple of science fiction that continues today in *The Terminator* and *The Matrix*. Today roboticists invoke the descriptors "unmanned" or "remote-operated" to avoid Hollywood-fueled visions of machines that are plotting our demise". Singer 2010.

[98] Sandoz et al. 1987, para 1389.

[99] As Huffman notes, IHL accords "commanders reasonable latitude in the exercise of good faith judgment under the myriad circumstances and difficult conditions of combat. This results in legal standards that are often intentionally and patently imprecise." Huffman 2012, p. 17.

Beard J M (2014) Autonomous Weapons and Human Responsibilities. Georgetown Journal of International Law 45:617–681

Boothby W H (2018a) Highly Automated and Autonomous Technologies. In: Boothby W H (ed) New Technologies and the Law in War and Peace. Cambridge University Press, Cambridge, pp 137–181. DOI: https://doi.org/10.1017/9781108609388.007

Boothby W H (2018b) Dehumanization: Is There a Legal Problem Under Article 36?. In: von Heinegg W H et al. (eds) Dehumanization of Warfare. Springer International Publishing, Cham, pp 21–52. DOI: https://doi.org/10.1007/978-3-319-67266-3_3

Boulanin V et al. (2020) Responsible Military Use of Artificial Intelligence: Can the European Union Lead the Way in Developing Best Practice. SIPRI, Stockholm

Boyd J R (1996) The Essence of Winning and Losing. Richards C, Spinney C (eds)

Bryce H, Parakilas J (2018) Conclusions and Recommendations. In: Cummings M L et al. (eds) Artificial Intelligence and International Affairs: Disruption Anticipated. Chatham House, London, pp 43–46

Buchan R, Tsagourias N (2021) Autonomous Cyber Weapons and Command Responsibility. In: Liivoja R, Väljataga A (eds) Autonomous Cyber Capabilities under International Law. NATO CCDCOE Publications, Tallinn, pp 321–347

Canada (2016) Canadian Food For Thought Paper: Context, Complexity and LAWS. In: CCW Informal Meeting of Experts on Lethal Autonomous Weapon Systems. https://docs-library.unoda.org/Convention_on_Certain_Conventional_Weapons_-_Informal_Meeting_of_Experts_(2016)/2016_LAWS%2BMX_CountryPaper%2BCanada%2BFFTP2.pdf. Accessed 10 August 2023

Coleman S (2014) Ethical Challenges of New Military Technologies. In: Nasu H, McLaughlin R (eds) New Technologies and the Law of Armed Conflict. TMC Asser Press, The Hague, pp 29-41. DOI: https://doi.org/10.1007/978-90-6704-933-7_3

Crootof R (2015) The Killer Robots Are Here: Legal and Policy Implications. Cardozo Law Review 36:1837–1915

Danzig R (2018) Technology Roulette: Managing Loss of Control as Many Militaries Pursue Technological Superiority. Center for a New American Security, Washington D.C.

Defense Innovation Board (2019) AI Principles: Recommendations on the Ethical Use of Artificial Intelligence by the Department of Defense Defense Innovation Board. US Department of Defense. https://media.defense.gov/2019/Oct/31/2002204458/-1/-1/0/DIB_AI_PRINCIPLES_PRIMARY_DOCUMENT.PDF. Accessed 2 August 2023

Defense Science Board (2012) The Role Of Autonomy in DoD Systems. US Department of Defense, Washington D.C.

Defense Science Board (2016) Report of the Defense Science Board Summer Study on Autonomy. Secretary of Defense for Acquisition, Technology and Logistics

Dinstein Y (2018) Autonomous Weapons and International Humanitarian Law. In: von Heinegg W H, Frau R, Singer T (eds) Dehumanization of Warfare. Springer International Publishing, Cham, pp 15–20. DOI: https://doi.org/10.1007/978-3-319-67266-3_2

Ekelhof M (2018) Lifting the Fog of Targeting: "Autonomous Weapons" and Human Control through the Lens of Military Targeting. Naval War College Review 71(3):61–94

Eklund A M (2020) Meaningful Human Control of Autonomous Weapon Systems: Definitions and Key Elements in the Light of International Humanitarian Law and International Human Rights Law. Totalförsvarets forskningsinstitut, Stockholm

Frigoli M (2020) The Twenty-First Century: The Epoch of Advanced Missile Systems and Growing Vulnerabilities. In: Martellini M, Trapp R (eds) 21st Century Prometheus: Managing CBRN Safety and Security Affected by Cutting-Edge Technologies. Springer International Publishing, Cham, pp 21-47. DOI: https://doi.org/10.1007/978-3-030-28285-1_2

Future of Life Institute (2015) Autonomous Weapons: An Open Letter from AI & Robotics Researchers. https://futureoflife.org/open-letter-autonomous-weapons. Accessed 3 August 2017

Gao C (2017) China Vows to Become an Artificial Intelligence World Leader. The Diplomat. https://thediplomat.com/2017/07/china-vows-to-become-an-artificial-intelligence-world-leader. Accessed 25 October 2020

Geiß R, Lahmann H (2017) Autonomous Weapons Systems: A Paradigm Shift for the Law of Armed Conflict?. In: Ohlin J D (ed) Research Handbook on Remote Warfare. Edward Elgar, Cheltenham, pp 371–404

Gisel L (2016) The Principle of Proportionality in the Rules Governing the Conduct of Hostilities under International Humanitarian Law. In: International Expert Meeting, 22-23 June 2016. ICRC. https://www.icrc.org/en/download/file/79184/4358_002_expert_meeting_report_web_1.pdf. Accessed 3 August 2023

Herbach J (2012) Into the Caves of Steel: Precaution, Cognition and Robotic Weapon Systems Under the International Law of Armed Conflict. 4 Amsterdam Law Forum 4(3):3–20

Heyns C (2013) Report of the Special Rapporteur on Extrajudicial, Summary or Arbitrary Executions, A/HRC/23/47

Hofman L (2020) De Nieuwste Wapenwedloop Gaat Niet Om Bommen, Maar Om Algoritmes (En Hoe Die Te Foppen). De Correspondent, 19 August 2020. https://decorrespondent.nl/11511/de-nieuwste-wapenwedloop-gaat-niet-om-bommen-maar-om-algoritmes-en-hoe-die-te-foppen/80252bb0-a43e-06da-0cf6-5468281fcfef. Accessed 2 August 2023

Huffman W B (2012) Margin of Error: Potential Pitfalls of the Ruling in The Prosecutor v. Ante Gotovina. Military Law Review 211:1–56. http://hdl.handle.net/10601/2104. Accessed 4 August 2023

Human Rights Watch (2012) Losing Humanity: The Case against Killer Robots. Human Rights Watch

ICRC (2018b) The Roots of Restraint in War. ICRC

ICRC (2016) Background Paper Prepared by the International Committee of the Red Cross. In: ICRC (ed) Autonomous Weapon Systems: Implications of Increasing Autonomy in the Critical Functions of Weapons. ICRC, Versoix, pp 69–85

ICRC (2018a) Ethics and Autonomous Weapon Systems: An Ethical Basis for Human Control?. Group of Governmental Experts of the High Contracting Parties to the Convention on Prohibitions or Restrictions on the Use of Certain Conventional Weapons Which May Be Deemed to Be Excessively Injurious or to Have Indiscriminate Effects, CCW/GGE1/2018/WP

Jensen E T (2018) The Human Nature of International Humanitarian Law, Humanitarian Law & Policy. ICRC Blogs. https://blogs.icrc.org/law-and-policy/2018/08/23/human-nature-international-humanitarian-law/. Accessed 28 May 2021

Jensen E T (2020) The (Erroneous) Requirement for Human Judgment (and Error) in the Law of Armed Conflict. SSRN Electronic Journal 96:26-57. DOI: https://doi.org/10.2139/ssrn.3548314

Kastan B (2013) Autonomous Weapons Systems: A Coming Legal “Singularity”?. Journal of Law, Technology and Policy 2013(1):45–82

Kellenberger J (2012) International Humanitarian Law and New Weapon Technologies 34th Round Table on Current Issues of International Humanitarian Law, San Remo, 8–10 September 2011. International Review of the Red Cross 94(886):809-813. DOI: https://doi.org/10.1017/S1816383112000793

Lamraski A M (2021) Preliminary Remarks on Lethal Autonomous Weapon Systems from an IHL Perspective. Asia Pacific Journal of International Humanitarian Law 2:8–30

LaPointe C, Levin PL (2016) Automated War: How to Think About Intelligent Autonomous Systems in the Military. Foreign Affairs. https://www.foreignaffairs.com/world/automated-war. Accessed 31 July 2023

Lyons J B, Havig P R (2014) Transparency in a Human-Machine Context: Approaches for Fostering Shared Awareness/Intent. In: Shumaker R, Lackey S (eds) Virtual, Augmented and Mixed Reality: Designing and Developing Augmented and Virtual Environments, 6th International Conference, VAMR 2014, Lecture No. Springer, Cham, pp 181–190. DOI: https://doi.org/10.1007/978-3-319-07458-0_18

Marchant G E et al. (2011) International Governance of Autonomous Military Robots. The Columbia Science and Technology Law Review 12:272–315

Marra W, McNeil S (2013) Understanding "The Loop": Regulating the Next Generation of War Machines. Harvard Journal of Law and Public Policy 36(3):1–62

Mayer C (2015) Developing Autonomous Systems in an Ethical Manner. In: Williams A P, Scharre P D (eds) Autonomous Systems: Issues for Defence Policymakers. NATO, The Hague, pp 65–82

McAllister A (2018) Stranger than Science Fiction: The Rise of A.I. Interrogation in the Dawn of Autonomous Robots and the Need for an Additional Protocol to the U.N. Convention against Torture. Minnesota Law Review 101:2527–2573

McCammon S (2017) The Warfare May Be Remote But The Trauma Is Real. NPR, April 2017. www.npr.org/2017/04/24/525413427/for-drone-pilots-warfare-may-be-remote-but-the-trauma-is-real?t=1620950231413. Accessed 14 May 2021

Ministère des Armées (2019) L'intelligence Artificielle Au Service de La Défense. Ministère des Armées, Paris

US Navy (2019) MK 15 - Phalanx Close-In Weapons System (CIWS). America's Navy. https://www.navy.mil/resources/fact-files/display-factfiles/article/2167831/mk-15-phalanx-close-in-weapon-system-ciws/#:~:text=MK 15 Phalanx CIWS provides,have penetrated other fleet defenses. Accessed 21 December 2019

Noone G P, Noone D C (2015) The Debate Over Autonomous Weapons Systems. Case Western Reserve Journal of International Law 47(1):25–35

Ohlin J D (2017) Remoteness and Reciprocal Risk. In: Ohlin J D (ed) Research Handbook on Remote Warfare. Edward Elgar, Cheltenham, pp 15–49. DOI: https://doi.org/10.4337/9781784716998.00010

Parakilas J, Bryce H (2018) Introduction: Artificial Intelligence and International Politics. In: Cummings M L et al. (eds) Artificial Intelligence and International Affairs: Disruption Anticipated. Chatham House, London, pp 1–6

Rosenberg M, Markoff J (2016) At Heart of U.S. Strategy, Weapons That Can Think. New York Times. 26 October 2016, A1

Russell S J, Norvig P (2010) Artificial Intelligence: A Modern Approach. 3rd edn. Pearson, New Jersey

Sandoz Y, Swinarski C, Zimmerman B (1987) Commentary on the Additional Protocols of 8 June 1977 to the Geneva Conventions of 12 August 1949. Martinus Nijhoff, Geneva

Sassòli M (2014) Autonomous Weapons and International Humanitarian Law: Advantages, Open Technical Questions and Legal Issues to Be Clarified. International Law Studies 90:308–340

Sayler K M (2020) Defense Primer: U.S. Policy on Lethal Autonomous Weapon Systems. Congressional Report Service

Scharre P D, Horowitz M C (2015) An Introduction to Autonomy in Weapon Systems. Center for a New American Security, Working Paper, Feb 2015

Scharre P D (2016) Centaur Warfighting: The False Choice of Humans vs. Automation. Temple International & Comparative Law Journal 30(1):151–165

Scharre P D (2018) Army of None: Autonomous Weapons and the Future of War. Ww Norton & Co, New York

Scherer M U (2016) Regulating Artificial Intelligence Systems: Risks, Challenges, Competencies, and Strategies. Harvard Journal of Law & Technology 29(2):353–400

Schmitt M N (2015) Regulating Autonomous Weapons Might Be Smarter Than Banning Them. Just Security. www.justsecurity.org/25333/regulating-autonomous-weapons-smarter-banning. Accessed 5 November 2017

Schuller A L (2017) At the Crossroads of Control: The Intersection of Artificial Intelligence in Autonomous Weapon Systems with International Humanitarian Law. Harvard National Security Journal 8:379

Schuller A L (2019) Artificial Intelligence Effecting Human Decisions to Kill: The Challenge of Linking Numerically Quantifiable Goals to IHL Compliance. Journal of Law and Policy for the Information Society 15:105–122

Singer P W (2010) War of the Machines: A Dramatic Growth in the Military Use of Robots Brings Evolution in Their Conception. Scientific American. https://www.scientificamerican.com/article/war-of-the-machines/. Accessed 27 October 2022
SIPRI (2017) Literature Review for the Policy and Operations Evaluations Department of the Dutch Ministry of Foreign Affairs, Final Report. SIPRI, Solna
Sparrow R (2016) Robots and Respect: Assessing the Case Against Autonomous Weapon Systems. Ethics & International Affairs 30(1):93–116
Stephens D (2014) Behaviour in War: The Place of Law, Moral Inquiry and Self-Identity. International Review of the Red Cross 96(895-896):751-773. DOI: https://doi.org/10.1017/S1816383115000235
Thurnher J S (2013) The Law That Applies to Autonomous Weapon Systems. American Society of International Law 17(4)
Thurnher J S (2014) Examining Autonomous Weapon Systems from a Law of Armed Conflict Perspective. In: Nasu H, McLaughlin R (eds) New Technologies and the Law of Armed Conflict. TMC Asser Press, The Hague, pp 213–228. DOI: https://doi.org/10.1007/978-90-6704-933-7_13
Thurnher J S (2018) Feasible Precautions in Attack and Autonomous Weapons. In: von Heinegg W H, Frau R, Singer T (eds) Dehumanization of Warfare. Springer International Publishing, Cham, pp 99–117. DOI: https://doi.org/10.1007/978-3-319-67266-3_6
UK Ministry of Defence (2011) The UK Approach to Unmanned Aircraft Systems. Joint Doctrine Note 2/11
Umbrello S, Torres P, De Bellis A F (2020) The Future of War: Could Lethal Autonomous Weapons Make Conflict More Ethical?. AI & Society 35(1):273-282. DOI: https://doi.org/10.1007/s00146-019-00879-x
US Air Force (2009) Unmanned Aircraft Systems Flight Plan. 2009–2047
Venkatesh S (2019) Legality of Autonomous Weapons Systems and Their Implications on Existing International Humanitarian Law Principles Approach: New Haven School of International Legal Theory. Groningen Journal of International Law 7(1):124–131. DOI: https://doi.org/10.21827/5d5141e815f80
Wallach W, Allen C (2009) Moral Machines. Oxford University Press, New York. https://academic.oup.com/book/10768
Walzer M (1997) Just and Unjust Wars. 4th edn. Basic Books
Waszink C (2011) Protection of Civilians under International Humanitarian Law: Trends and Challenges. Norwegian Peacebuilding Resource Centre Report, August 2011
Williams A P (2015) Defining Autonomy in Systems: Challenges and Solutions. In: Williams A P, Scharre P D (eds) Autonomous Systems: Issues for Defence Policymakers. NATO, The Hague, pp 27–64
Wilson C (2020) Artificial Intelligence and Warfare. In: Martellini M, Trapp R (eds) 21st Century Prometheus. Springer International Publishing, Cham, pp 125–140. DOI: https://doi.org/10.1007/978-3-030-28285-1_7
Winter E (2020) The Compatibility of the Use of Autonomous Weapons with the Principle of Precaution in the Law of Armed Conflict. The Military Law and the Law of War Review 58(2):240–273. DOI: https://doi.org/10.4337/mllwr.2020.02.18
Wright J D (2012) "Excessive" Ambiguity: Analysing and Refining the Proportionality Standard. International Review of the Red Cross 94(886):819–854. DOI: https://doi.org/10.1017/S1816383113000143
Yoner N (2001) Major Weapon Systems Acquisition and Life Cycle Cost Estimation: A Case Study. Master Thesis, US Naval Postgraduate School

Part V
Criminal Liability

Chapter 11
Criminal Liability: Problem Setting

Contents

Abstract Responsibility for harm that might arise from the use of autonomous weapons (AWS) on the battlefield has been one of the most prominent topics of academic and policy debate. The perceived inability to assign criminal liability for crimes involving AWS raises concerns of accountability the and possibility encouraging misuse or reckless use. This chapter lies the groundwork for Part V, which is centred around criminal liability for AWS-related harm. It presents a short history of the 'responsibility gap' debate surrounding AWS before focusing on the criminal liability gap. An overview is presented of the different Candidates for liability as proposed in literature, which includes the commander activating the AWS but also persons prior in the weapon's lifecycle (producer, programmer, reviewer, etc.). It then provides a roadmap of this chapter and Chap. 12, highlighting the issues that will be discussed in more detail. Finally, some general notes are given concerning jurisdictional differences in criminal law concepts, such as those related to the different fault degrees. A methodological choice is made to not restrict the analysis to one particular jurisdiction, in order to allow a broader application of this book's findings. This however necessitates a shared internal vocabulary, which is offered in this chapter.

Keywords Autonomous weapon system · Artificial intelligence · Criminal liability · War crime · Responsibility gap · Mens rea · Prosecution · Accountability · International criminal law · Common law · Civil law

J. Kwik, *Lawfully Using Autonomous Weapon Technologies*,
https://doi.org/10.1007/978-94-6265-631-4_11

11.1 Introduction

In our discussions thus far in this book, we have adopted a fundamental assumption of goodwill.[1] We have presumed that actors involved were of the general predilection to uphold IHL norms, and that commanders facing the decision to deploy an AWS undertake to implement their precautionary duties to the best of their abilities. Our analysis in Part III was analytical, with the aim of informing Deployers of the technical and legal complexities entailed by AI technology, and of providing the needed background to enable reasoned deployment decisions. Similarly, Part IV adopted a realistic, yet still relatively demanding, stance, providing an overview of how a model reasonable commander would best implement precautionary duties—demands that may not always be easy or expedient to carry out. In short, our discussion has taken place at an idealised level.

In this final part, we will move away from this presumption and ask: But what if such ideal conditions are *not* upheld? The real world is rarely as accommodating. Inevitably, AWS will come into the possession of commanders who are not entirely devoted to IHL. These persons may take into consideration only a limited part of the factors discussed in Part III, and implement only a fraction of the legal and operational recommendations provided in Part IV. They may do so out of a lack of care, due to the fog of war, for military expediency, out of genuine inability, or deliberately. In cases where such defaults lead to harm to protected entities, IHL prescribes action to be taken to hold involved actors responsible, which in serious cases amounts to criminal prosecution—a duty commonly referred to as *repression*.[2]

The introduction of AI technology does not change this basic normative framework. However, AI potentially alters the conditions under which such criminal prosecution is possible, and not in a way which is necessarily congruent with the aims of criminal law and IHL. Criminal law establishes certain elements, such as mens rea[3] and causality, as a way to only punish those with blame and to shield those who could not have foreseen or prevented an unfortunate outcome.[4] In this way, criminal law aims to track our moral intuition on fairness and moral responsibility.[5]

As we will see in this part, AI gives rise to certain situations where the result of a plain application of criminal law may clash with our intuitions of blameworthiness. Situations may emerge where we intuitively would have little hesitation in attributing blameworthiness, but where criminal liability is barred because certain legal elements

---

[1] Section 1.4.

[2] Geneva Convention for the Amelioration of the Condition of the Wounded and Sick in Armed Forces in the Field, adopted 12 August 1949, entered into force 21 October 1950, 75 UNTS 31 (Geneva Convention I), Art. 49; Protocol Additional to the Geneva Conventions of 12 August 1949, and relating to the Protection of Victims of International Armed Conflicts, adopted 8 June 1977, entered into force 7 December 1978, 1125 UNTS 3 (API), Article 86(1).

[3] Due to the frequency with which concepts such as mens rea and other Latin terms (e.g. dolus eventualis, actus reus) are used, an editorial decision was made to not italicise these words. See Sect. 11.6.

[4] Weigend 2014, p. 490.

[5] Ibid., p. 493; Keiler 2019, p. 112.

remain unfulfilled. This is particularly tangible in situations where we suspect that some parties involved were unreasonably reckless or may have knowingly fostered the conditions which prevent the application of criminal law. Our discussion in this part will therefore move quite a distance away from our idealised beginnings, and will even entertain a component of cynicism: where actors may deliberately be incentivised to abuse the criminal law framework, because AI renders this so much more convenient than before.

11.2 The Responsibility Gap: From Broad to Narrow

Responsibility is a key theme for this final part. The idea that AI makes the attribution of responsibility more challenging is a theme that frequently surfaces in discussions on all AI domains, ranging from autonomous vehicles to loan approval.[6] These discussions also extend to all forms of responsibility, including moral responsibility,[7] civil liability[8] and State responsibility.[9] To maintain greater focus, we will address exclusively *challenges to criminal liability* in this part. This does not imply that any of the aforementioned forms of responsibility are less important: moral responsibility is often seen as necessary for criminal liability,[10] and many authors promoting tort liability and State responsibility for AWS-related harms stress that they should be applied complementarily to criminal liability.[11]

At the same time, these alternate forms of responsibility should not be depended upon as a *substitute* for criminal liability.[12] The importance of criminal liability for violations involving AWS has been raised very early in the debate timeline and at

[6] Amoroso 2020, p. 122.

[7] Bigman et al. 2019, p. 367. See e.g. Brey 2014, pp. 128–31 (whether artificial agents can have moral responsibility); Himmelreich 2019 (whether a user can have moral responsibility over AWS).

[8] See e.g. European Commission 2020, pp. 12–16 (EU perspective on civil liability for AI systems); Pagallo 2017, pp. 20–21 (civil liability and accountable AI); Dunlap 2016, pp. 73–75 (possibility of civil damages for harm caused by AWS).

[9] See in general Burke and Persi-Vicentic 2014. Attributing State responsibility for AWS-caused harms is in the view of many an evident route to ensuring accountability for AWS use. See e.g. Haataja 2021; Chengeta 2016b, pp. 47–49; Gaeta 2016, p. 45. While there should be no legal obstacle in attributing damages caused by AWS to the deploying State, this does not rule out that claimants may encounter *evidentiary* problems. Cf. Schmitt 2021, p. 128.

[10] See e.g. Liu 2016, pp. 336–40.

[11] Stürchler and Siegrist 2017; Chengeta 2016b, p. 3; Marauhn 2014, p. 4.

[12] Some authors have posited that civil damages or State responsibility suffice as an 'alternative to' criminal liability when the latter is not possible. See e.g. Stewart 2011, p. 291; Gaeta 2016, p. 45. For instance, Thurnher argued that "[w]hile the need to hold someone accountable might be "visceral," it is not definitively required by law. Instead, international law demands that states not absolve themselves of liability with respect to a grave breach of the laws of war." Thurnher 2012, p. 82.

virtually all levels, including by the UN,[13] the ICRC,[14] military organisations,[15] NGOs[16] and in diplomatic conferences.[17] This emphasis is for good reason. In addition to being prescribed in law for serious breaches of IHL, criminal liability for war crimes is regarded as vital, *inter alia*, for preventing impunity,[18] enabling the protections granted by IHL,[19] upholding IHL's authority and legitimacy,[20] fulfilling victims' rights,[21] and maintaining the law's deterrent function on the battlefield.[22] Irrespective of whether civil damages can be claimed and States can be condemned for an internationally wrongful act, therefore, the ability to hold a natural person criminally responsible for AWS-related harms remains crucial. It is this question which we will explore in the current and coming two chapters.

Certain assumptions will be adopted during these chapters to enhance focus and maintain thematic cohesion with other chapters of this book. First, from the triad[23] of international crimes, we will mainly be considering *war crimes*. While it is certainly conceivable that AWS can be used to commit genocide or crimes against humanity,[24] our discussion thus far has concentrated on the targeting process, making war crimes the most relevant category to explore. In particular, given the nature of AWS as weapons used to effectuate attacks, we will refer primarily to crimes related to the principles of distinction and proportionality[25]—i.e., acts such as targeting civilians,

---

[13] Heyns 2013, para 111.

[14] ICRC 2013.

[15] UK Ministry of Defence 2011, para 521.

[16] Human Rights Watch 2015.

[17] Simon-Michel 2014, para 30.

[18] In Bassiouni's view, "[i]mpunity for international crimes and for systematic and widespread violations of fundamental human rights is a betrayal of our human solidarity with the victims of conflicts to whom we owe a duty of justice, remembrance, and compensation." Bassiouni 2002, p. 422.

[19] Geiß and Lahmann 2017, p. 385.

[20] Beard 2014, p. 643; Chengeta 2016b, p. 49.

[21] Stewart 2011, p. 292.

[22] Lewis 2015, p. 1312; Guiora 2017, p. 398. On Iraq's systematic abuses of IHL during the 1991 Gulf War, Hayes Parks commented that "no amount of law, however well written, is likely to alter the behavior of a malefactor where the deterrent effect of certain prosecution is lacking". Parks 1997, p. 70. Empirically, however, the deterrent impact of IHL prosecutions on the behaviour of belligerents on the battlefield is often called into question. See Anderson and Waxman 2013, p. 17; Marauhn 2014, p. 1.

[23] Disregarding the crime of aggression, which is the least likely to involve an AWS anyway.

[24] McDougall 2019, p. 65. For instance, McAllister considered the legal implications of an AI 'torture bot'. McAllister 2018.

[25] Ohlin 2016, p. 23.

attacking protected objects, launching indiscriminate or disproportionate attacks, etc. As such, API Article 85(3)[26] and similar provisions will be of specific interest.[27]

11.3 Candidates for Liability

In this part, we will speak of *Candidates* to refer to natural persons whom we consider as potentially criminally responsible for AWS-related harm. 'Candidate' is used instead of 'accused', 'defendant' or 'perpetrator' to signify that the discussion takes place at a very preliminary level, i.e., directly after an incident has occurred and interest emerges in finding a natural person to criminally blame. At this stage, investigators and prosecutors may scan a list of potential actors involved in the weapon's lifecycle to determine whether prosecuting them is feasible; if this is legally or practically impossible, then they are disqualified as a Candidate. This type of methodology (searching by elimination) is prevalent in academic circles. One common method of arguing a responsibility gap is to "proceed[] by elimination, ruling out each plausible candidate who could be responsible until none is left. Each candidate is shown to fail to meet a necessary condition for … responsibility".[28] Thus, one way to view the responsibility gap is simply as 'the absence of Candidates'.

In keeping with the theme of this book of regarding Deployer as our central protagonist, we will also be viewing the question of criminal liability with Deployer as the primary Candidate. Thus, our main aim is not so much to definitively prove whether a responsibility gap does exist (in the sense of 'total absence of Candidates', which would also necessitate an exhaustive analysis of all actors prior to the deployment decision), but rather to discuss whether and under what conditions a gap exists with respect to Deployer. Can their mens rea be established? Under what conditions is it unfair to blame them for AWS-related harms? Do they have the means and incentives to *generate* a gap to escape liability? It is these types of questions we will be asking first and foremost.

Nevertheless, it is undeniable that certain conditions may dictate that other actors earlier in the weapon's lifecycle also share blame, or perhaps even be exclusively responsible. Throughout this book, we collectively referred to these actors using the label 'Providing Entity',[29] but the current part's emphasis on criminal liability

---

[26] This paragraph lists acts that are considered as grave breaches of API when committed wilfully and resulting in death or serious injury to body or health, such as making civilian entities the object of attack, launching disproportionate attacks, or launching attacks with the knowledge that this will unleash dangerous forces, amongst others.

[27] Cf. equivalent articles of more specific courts and tribunals such as Statute of the International Criminal Tribunal for the Former Yugoslavia, as established by Security Council Resolution 827/1993 and last amended by Security Council Resolution 1877/2009 (ICTY Statute), Article 2 and Rome Statute of the International Criminal Court, adopted 17 July 1998, entered into force 1 July 2002, 2187 UNTS 90 (Rome Statute), Article 8(2).

[28] Himmelreich 2019, p. 753.

[29] Section 1.3.3.

of natural persons necessitates a finer scale of analysis, at the level of the individual. As such, we will refer to any person who has had involvement in the AWS's earlier lifecycle prior to deployment as a *Broader Chain Candidate* (BCC).[30] BCC is an umbrella term and can encompass parties involved in production (e.g. programmers, designers, labellers, production management),[31] testing and validation staff,[32] political decision-makers,[33] procurement officials,[34] and ROE drafters,[35] where applicable.

BCCs have been raised as potential Candidates for criminal liability in a few situations. First, it is possible that a responsibility gap truly surfaces with respect to Deployer for reasons discussed in Chap. 13. In such a case, it is often suggested that the looming threat of impunity can be 'fixed' by turning our gaze toward BCCs.[36] Many also regard blind focus on Deployer as likely 'unfair', particularly if closing the responsibility gap requires controversial measures such as imposing a strict liability regime.[37] Holland Michel, for instance, submits that

> assigning total individual responsibility to human operators for all harms would likely lead, in certain instances, to misattribution of culpability. In reality, the responsibility for harms that operators or their immediate superiors could not have prevented may lie further up the chain of command.[38]

It is also possible that Deployers and BCCs share the blame, or may even be part of a joint criminal enterprise[39] to effectuate the violation.[40] In such cases, it is evident that BCCs would also fall within the pool of Candidates. Entirely omitting BCCs from our analysis would therefore be short-sighted. We will thus adopt a middle ground.

---

[30] In literature, this group of candidates for criminal liability is referenced in different ways, such as "the wider system that produces and maintains the technology, and that produces information on the outcomes being sought and the context of use" (Article 36 2016, p. 4), the "entire sociotechnical system" (Johnson and Noorman 2014, p. 158) and the 'Military Industrial Complex' (Taylor 2021, p. 327).

[31] Jain 2016, p. 321.

[32] Kalmanovitz 2016, p. 157.

[33] Chengeta 2016b, p. 21.

[34] Corn 2016, p. 234.

[35] Horowitz and Scharre 2015, p. 14.

[36] "If front-line operators cannot be held responsible for the actions of autonomous weapons systems, it has been suggested that accountability could shift to the engineers, computer programmers, and designers who are responsible for creating the system in the first place". Grut 2013, p. 16. See also Jain 2016, p. 314; Taylor 2021, pp. 326–31.

[37] Kalmanovitz 2016, p. 157.

[38] Holland Michel 2021, p. 20.

[39] Joint Criminal Enterprise (JCE) is a group criminality doctrine developed by the ICTY to deal with a rather common characteristic of international crimes: a plurality of individuals working in support of a common plan. See ICTY (AC), *Prosecutor v Duško Tadić*, Judgment, 15 July 1999, ICTY-94-1-A, paras 185–229. Domestic systems will have their own doctrines to prosecute group criminality. For example, in the US system, conspiracy "renders criminal any agreement between two or more persons to commit a crime". Fletcher 1998, p. 191.

[40] Toscano 2015, p. 220; Israel 2019.

Whenever our discussion warrants expansion to BCCs, this will be indicated in the accompanying text. However, the primary target of our investigation into criminal liability remains Deployer—i.e., whether they would be criminally responsible for violations caused by an AWS they deployed. This choice is not merely a matter of methodology but also consistent with military practice and our MHC Framework.[41]

Finally, Operator[42] liability shall only be considered in passing. This is a purely methodological choice. In practice, Operators are likely to be the first Candidates that will be considered by investigators whenever they are involved[43] in an AWS-incident. The reason why Operators are afforded less attention in this part is because the presence of Operators reverts an AWS into a system with direct human influence over its decisions and operations. Such constructions are functionally comparable to that of current-day drone pilots, and methods of attributing criminal liability would be similar.[44] In this part, we instead concentrate on circumstances where an AWS is allowed to perform for some period of time without human interference.

11.4 The Responsibility Gap Problem

Turning now to the responsibility gap argument proper as it is presented within the context of the AWS polemics, let us start with the following quote by UN Rapporteur Heyns:

> The question of legal responsibility could be an overriding issue. If each of the possible candidates for responsibility identified above is ultimately inappropriate or impractical, a responsibility vacuum will emerge, granting impunity for all LAR use. If the nature of a weapon renders responsibility for its consequences impossible, its use should be considered unethical and unlawful as an abhorrent weapon.[45]

Dating back to 2007,[46] the responsibility gap is one of the oldest and most persistent challenges advanced with respect to military AI and is often listed as one of the top four popular arguments used by AWS opponents.[47] There is no fixed definition for the term 'responsibility gap',[48] but Taylor defined it in general terms as the situation

[41] See Sects. 1.1 and 2.3.

[42] See Section 1.3.2.

[43] This implies that Deployer has chosen to assign one to supervise the AWS. See Linked Control in Sect. 8.7.1.

[44] This does not mean establishing criminal liability for AWS Operators would necessarily be without obstacles. In particular, situations where the Operator lacked de facto control (as expanded upon in Sect. 8.8) may raise some questions. For example, can an Operator who was working with a poor interface, and therefore lacked proper situational awareness, be considered as possessing the requisite mens rea? The author keeps these more granular discussions on the criminal liability of Operators for future work.

[45] Heyns 2013, para 80.

[46] See Sparrow 2007; Stewart 2011, pp. 289–91.

[47] See Anderson and Waxman 2013, pp. 14–18; Amoroso and Giodano 2019, p. 212.

[48] Himmelreich 2019, p. 734.

"where nobody is responsible for an outcome"[49]—entirely consistent with our colloquial concept of 'absence of Candidates'.[50] Naturally, this would seem problematic in cases where the 'outcome' in question amounts to apparently egregious IHL violations, such as a massive civilian casualty event. Unsurprisingly, the responsibility gap was quickly picked up by States,[51] commentators,[52] NGOs[53] and international organisations[54] as a popular topic of discussion, generating a rich academic debate.

The quote by Heyns is a prototypical example of how the responsibility gap argument is often formulated in the context of AWS. As one may observe, it is a prohibitionist argument that actually consists of two sub-arguments that claim, first, that the nature of AWS may render it impossible to attribute responsibility to any Candidate, and second, that this makes the technology unlawful. Let us call these two arguments in conjunction the *Responsibility Gap Problem*. As noted above, 'responsibility' is a general notion that encompasses different types of accountability;[55] however, many authors refer specifically to difficulties in establishing *criminal* responsibility when advancing the Responsibility Gap Problem.[56] Given the choice of this study to limit our discussion to criminal liability, let us pursue this leg of the argument. In this context, the Responsibility Gap Problem can be reformulated as follows:

P1. AWS possess characteristics which make the fair imposition of criminal liability to persons for harm caused by their use impossible.

P2. The inability to impose criminal liability to persons for harm caused by the use of an AWS makes them unlawful.

C. AWS are unlawful.

Premise 2 captures the prohibitionist component of the Responsibility Gap Problem. Various rationales are proposed to assert why an inability to assign criminal liability would impact a weapon's lawfulness. These include the assertion that impunity is inherently problematic or unlawful,[57] that a lack of criminal consequences would damage the law's ability to influence belligerent behaviour on the battlefield,[58] and that it would damage the right of victims to see justice done.[59]

From a purely IHL perspective, however, the link between a weapon's lawfulness and the (in)ability to assign criminal responsibility is less evident, and parties advancing the Responsibility Gap Problem often do not explain in legal terms the

[49] Taylor 2021, p. 321.

[50] See Sect. 11.3.

[51] Simon-Michel 2014, para 30.

[52] Thurnher 2012, p. 82; Schmitt and Thurnher 2013, p. 277; Toscano 2015, p. 220.

[53] Human Rights Watch 2015, p. 19; Gubrud 2016.

[54] ICRC 2014, p. 14; UNIDIR 2016, p. 16.

[55] See Sect. 11.2.

[56] E.g. Asaro 2012, p. 693; Crootof 2016, p. 1385; Jain 2021, p. 298.

[57] Bassiouni 2002, p. 422.

[58] Ratner et al. 2009, p. 3.

[59] Chengeta 2016b, p. 49.

mechanism which establishes this link.[60] Opinions are heavily divided on this aspect. The most reasonable argument in support of the assertion seems to be a reference to the duty in IHL to respect and ensure respect (which includes the duty to repress all serious breaches),[61] since a responsibility gap would interfere with the State's ability to implement this obligation.[62] In contrast, others have vehemently opposed the notion that a lack of criminal liability can be equated with factors such as superfluous injury and indiscriminateness (which unequivocally render weapons inherently illegal).[63] In Crootof's view, "[w]hether a weapon is per se unlawful is not, and has never been, based on whether an individual can be held accountable for violations following from its use".[64] Scharre also argued that "there is no principle in IHL that says there must be an individual to hold accountable for every death on the battlefield".[65]

For the purposes of the present discussion, it not necessary to resolve this academic dispute at the current time. Instead, we will grant the general notion that—for reasons that may not necessarily flow from IHL itself—the lack of criminal liability for AWS use is potentially problematic, and at the very least undesirable (a position that should not be overly controversial). This allows us to focus instead on Premise 1, which captures well this book's general theme of exploring the effects of AI-specific properties on the application of the law.[66] This focus on Premise 1 notwithstanding, we will return to partially refute Premise 2 in Sect. 13.6, where it is argued that the hard Responsibility Gap Problem position (i.e. *any* type of responsibility gap is problematic) is unsustainable, in light of a category of scenarios we call *judicious gaps*—situations where we, perhaps paradoxically, *want* criminal law to function in a way where impunity occurs, even for incidents which intuitively shock the conscience.

Turning now to Premise 1, the heart of the assertion contends that AI would possess certain characteristics that makes fulfilling traditional elements required for criminal liability, such as mens rea and causality, difficult or impossible. Implicit in this claim is that these characteristics are *novel*—i.e., they exist with respect to modern AI but

---

[60] Often, prohibitionists simply assert Premise 2 without substantiating why a lack of criminal responsibility would make the weapon illegal *in se*. Heyns's quote above is one example of this.

[61] ICRC 2013: "If responsibility cannot be determined *as required by international humanitarian law*, is it legal ... to deploy such systems?" (emphasis added).

[62] Chengeta draws an analogy with child soldiers, stating that their use is illegal in IHL "because they cannot be prosecuted for any infractions of the law", although he tellingly adds that the prohibition is also borne "out of the need to protect children". Chengeta 2016a, p. 873. The view of the current author is that the position of international criminal law with respect to the agency (and thus: criminal liability) of child soldiers is too inconsistent to draw a conclusion by analogy supporting Premise 2. Cf. Kwik 2020.

[63] Sandoz et al. 1987, para 1410; US Office of General Counsel of the Department of Defense 2015, Law of War Manual, Updated December 2016. US Department of Defense, Washington D.C. (US Law of War Manual), sct 6.6-7; Boothby 2018, pp. 19–21.

[64] Crootof 2015, p. 1881.

[65] Scharre 2018, pp. 262–63.

[66] See Sect. 1.2.

not with older weapon systems. This implication follows from the fact that otherwise, the Responsibility Gap Problem would fail as an argument against AWS technology *specifically* and would also lead to the prohibition of non-controversial weapons already in use, which is an absurd result.

11.5 A Roadmap for the Current Part

This in mind, in the discussion that follows we will delve deeply into the Responsibility Gap Problem and Premise 1 in particular, analysing:

(a) What are the necessary conditions for criminal liability?
(b) To what extent do AWS-specific properties make fulfilling these elements more difficult?
(c) Are there other related characteristics of AWS technology (e.g. organisational factors, their likely use in a military setting, human-machine interaction variables), that make the fulfilment of these elements difficult or impossible?

If we determine that Responsibility Gap Problem proponents are correct and some situations do exist where a responsibility gap emerges, it is necessary to ask some follow-up questions:

(d) In the case where gaps are established, is it within the logic and interest of criminal law and IHL to 'resolve' them (i.e., to find legal solutions to extend criminal liability to these cases)? and
(e) If yes, what would characterise an effective solution?

Due to the analytical depth this last question would demand, we can only address question (e) in general terms, i.e., by identifying the essential components a solution would need to entail to be effective. These thoughts serve as useful points of departure for future work.

Chapter 12 approaches the questions above in a more general fashion, by considering all elements necessary for criminal liability and systematically considering to what extent AI-specific characteristics render establishing these elements more difficult. From this discussion, it is found that the epistemic element related to mens rea has the most potential to cause problems. On this basis, we proceed in Chap. 13 with a more in-depth analysis of the different fault degrees of mens rea, moving through the entire spectrum of fault from the highest level of intention to situations where no cognition or volition is present.

Overall, then, we will have dissected the issue of criminal liability with respect to AWS thoroughly by identifying the *loci* of the problems (and also identifying where commentators mistakenly claim problems exist), critically examining whether these are also normative problems (i.e., whether there is an interest in 'filling these gaps'), and if yes, starting some initial constructive exploration on the best means to alleviate the issues.

11.6 Housekeeping: Terms and Jurisdictions

A significant portion of our analysis which follows revolves around mens rea and terms such as 'dolus eventualis'. Due to the frequency of use of these terms in some paragraphs, an editorial decision was made to not italicise these words, as the added formatting makes the text more difficult to read than needed.

Turning to a more substantive point concerning mens rea, an unfortunate reality is that the concept of mens rea and various fault degrees[67] are far from standardised and differ significantly per jurisdiction,[68] with the most significant split being that of continental versus common law systems. As this book is intended for a general audience, we will not limit ourselves to merely discussing mens rea as conceived in a specific jurisdiction.

Elaborating on the nuanced differences between each fault degree in different jurisdictions goes beyond the scope of this book and is arguably not necessary for the analysis.[69] A general understanding of what is commonly entailed by 'dolus directus', 'knowingly', 'recklessly', etc. suffices for the purposes of our discussion, and specific doctrinal elements will be expounded upon as they become relevant. For clarity and future reference, Fig. 11.1 summarises the different fault degrees and approximate equivalents between continental and common law systems, with the caveat that there will be individual differences in terminology and doctrinal nuances for each category.

A particular editorial choice is made to group dolus eventualis, recklessness and conscious negligence together into an umbrella category called *risk-taking*. This is notwithstanding that dolus eventualis and conscious negligence fall under dolus and culpa respectively in continental systems, and that recklessness is a separate intermediate category in common law systems.[70] The reason is practical and tied to our jurisdiction-agnostic approach. 'Risk-taking' is a descriptive indicator of all three fault degrees in the sense that they all encompass a mental state where D[71] is

---

[67] There is surprisingly little consensus on how to refer to the different levels of mens rea. Amongst others, 'type of fault', 'fault element', 'forms', 'categories of mens rea' and 'modes of intentional fault' are used. Cf. Blomsma and Roef 2019, pp. 179, 189; van Sliedregt 2012, pp. 41–42; ICC (PTC), *Prosecutor v. Jean-Pierre Bemba Gombo*, Decision pursuant to Article 61(7)(a) and (b) of the Rome Statute on the charges of the prosecutor against Jean-Pierre Bemba Gombo, 5 June 2009, ICC-01/05-01/08, para 357; Nersessian 2006, p. 83; Weigend 2014, p. 494. For consistency, the term 'fault degree' is used to refer to the different degrees of liability such as dolus directus, dolus eventualis, recklessness, and unconscious negligence.

[68] Ohlin 2013, p. 87.

[69] For such an extensive comparative perspective, see Fletcher 1998, pp. 112–22; van Sliedregt 2012; Blomsma and Roef 2019.

[70] . For more detailed discussion, see Sect. 13.4.

[71] The letter 'D', instead of 'P', is used to denote the perpetrator in some works, e.g. Nersessian 2006. 'D' is used in this text to avoid confusion with the concepts of Performance and Probability. 'D' is also coincidentally the initial letter of 'Deployer', our primary Candidate under discussion, which may help the digestibility of the text through association. Note however that D and Deployer are not necessarily the same, since Broader Chain Candidates can also be perpetrators. See Sect. 11.3.

Continental		**Common law**	**Internal term**
	Dolus directus	Purposely	Intention
Dolus	Dolus indirectus	Knowingly	
	Dolus eventualis		
-		Recklessly	Risk-taking
	Conscious neg.		
Culpa	Unconscious neg.	Negligently	Negligence
	Strict liability	Strict liability	Strict liability

Fig. 11.1 Fault degrees comparison[72]

aware of the existence of a risk (but has different attitudes toward it).[73] As we will see in Sect. 12.4, much of our discussion pivots around D's cognitive state, particularly when exploring situations where AI-specific properties reduce D's ability to perceive associated risks.[74] Given the finer doctrinal differences between dolus eventualis, recklessness and conscious negligence,[75] the decision was made to maintain a slightly higher level of abstraction and focus on their unifying risk-taking characteristic instead. From this more general discussion, jurists can then apply the conclusions *mutatis mutandis* to their jurisdiction and system of choice.

Unlike some other works on this subject,[76] we will not restrict ourselves to a specific forum (such as the ICC) but take a more general approach. As we will see below,[77] an overly narrow focus on a particular forum or jurisdiction can lead to somewhat misleading conclusions, as not all legal systems are equipped with the same legal tools and doctrines to deal with specific situations such as unreasonable risk-taking and wilful ignorance. Instead, the choice to adopt a more open-ended approach allows us to compare and integrate concepts from different criminal legal systems, enabling us to identify whether some AI-induced challenges are jurisdiction-specific or truly universal.[78] Nevertheless, international criminal jurisprudence, particularly that of the ICC and ICTY, will remain important reference points with regard to

[72] Adapted from van Sliedregt 2012; Blomsma and Roef 2019.

[73] Nersessian 2006, p. 86.

[74] See Sect. 12.4.2.

[75] For more detailed discussion on these differences, see Fletcher 2007, p. 317; Blomsma and Roef 2019, p. 190; Ohlin 2013, pp. 89, 105.

[76] E.g. McDougall 2019, p. 64; Jain 2021, p. 293.

[77] Section 13.4.2.

[78] In that sense, the current approach is more akin to that adopted by Keiler in his analysis on the concepts of actus reus and mens rea. See Keiler 2019, p. 107.

the interpretation of related concepts, such as what constitutes a 'wilful' attack against civilians. Granted, this approach carries the disadvantage that it cannot give jurisdiction-specific doctrinal solutions to problems; however, this should be well compensated by the more universally applicable guidelines that will be provided over the course of the analysis. How these recommendations are implemented in each domestic or international forum is ultimately for the specific courts to decide.

References

Amoroso D (2020) Autonomous Weapons Systems and International Law : A Study on Human-Machine Interactions in Ethically and Legally Sensitive Domains. Nomos Verlagsgesellschaft, Baden

Amoroso D, Giordano B (2019) Who Is to Blame for Autonomous Weapons Systems' Misngs?. In: Carpanelli E, Lazzerini N (eds) Use and Misuse of New Technologies. Springer International Publishing, Cham, pp 211–232. https://doi.org/10.1007/978-3-030-05648-3

Anderson K, Waxman M C (2013) Law and Ethics for Autonomous Weapon Systems: Why a Ban Won't Work and How the Laws of War Can. In: American University Washington College of Law Research Paper No. 2013-11. Stanford University, Stanford

Article 36 (2016) Key Elements of Meaningful Human Control, Background Paper to Comments Prepared by Richard Moyes, Managing Partner, Article 36. In: Convention on Certain Conventional Weapons (CCW) Meeting of Experts on Lethal Autonomous Weapons Systems (LAWS), Geneva, 11–15 April 2016

Asaro P (2012) On Banning Autonomous Weapon Systems: Human Rights, Automation, and the Dehumanization of Lethal Decision-Making. International Review of the Red Cross 94(886):687–709

Bassiouni M C (2002) Accountability for Violations of International Humanitarian Law and Other Serious Violations of Human Rights. In: Post-Conflict Justice. Brill-Nijhoff, Leiden, pp 3–54. https://doi.org/10.1163/9789004479579_005

Beard J M (2014) Autonomous Weapons and Human Responsibilities. Georgetown Journal of International Law 45:617–681

Bigman Y E et al. (2019) Holding Robots Responsible: The Elements of Machine Morality. Trends in Cognitive Sciences 23(5):365–368. https://doi.org/10.1016/j.tics.2019.02.008

Blomsma J H, Roef D (2019) Forms and Aspects of Mens Rea. In: Keiler J, Roef D (eds) Comparative concepts of criminal law, 3rd edn. Intersentia, United Kingdom, pp 177–206

Boothby W H (2018) Regulating New Weapon Technologies. In: Boothby W H (ed) New Technologies and the Law in War and Peace. Cambridge University Press, Cambridge, pp 16–42. https://doi.org/10.1017/9781108609388.00

Brey P (2014) From Moral Agents to Moral Factors: The Structural Ethics Approach. In: Kroes P, Verbeek P-P (eds) The Moral Status of Technical Artefacts. Springer Netherlands, pp 125–142. https://doi.org/10.1007/978-94-007-7914-3_8

Burke M, Persi-Vicentic L (2014) Remedies and Reparations. In: Casey-Maslen S (ed) Weapons under International Human Rights Law. Cambridge University Press, pp 542–590. https://doi.org/10.1017/CBO9781139227148.024

Chengeta T (2016a) Defining the Emerging Notion of "Meaningful Human Control" in Autonomous Weapon Systems. International Law and Politics 49:833–890

Chengeta T (2016b) Accountability Gap: Autonomous Weapon Systems and Modes of Responsibility in International Law. Denver Journal of International Law & Policy 45:1–50

Corn G S (2016) Autonomous Weapons Systems: Managing the Inevitability of "Taking the Man out of the Loop". In: Bhuta N et al. (eds) Autonomous Weapons Systems: Law, Ethics, Policy.

Cambridge University Press, Cambridge, pp 209-242. https://doi.org/10.1017/CBO9781316597873

Crootof R (2015) The Killer Robots Are Here: Legal and Policy Implications. Cardozo Law Review 36:1837–1915

Crootof R (2016) War Torts: Accountability for Autonomous Weapons. University of Pennsylvania Law Review 164:1347–1402

Dunlap C J J (2016) Accountability and Autonomous Weapons: Much Ado About Nothing. Temple International & Comparative Law Journal 30(1):63–76

European Commission (2020) Report on the Safety and Liability Implications of Artificial Intelligence, the Internet of Things and Robotics. COM/2020/64 final

Fletcher G P (1998) Basic Concepts of Criminal Law. Oxford University Press, New York

Fletcher G P (2007) The Grammar of Criminal Law. Volume One. Oxford University Press

Gaeta P (2016) Autonomous Weapon Systems and the Alleged Responsibility Gap. In: Autonomous Weapon Systems: Implications of Increasing Autonomy in the Critical Functions of Weapons. Expert meeting, Versoix, Switzerland, 15–16 March 2016. ICRC, Versoix, pp 44–45

Geiß R, Lahmann H (2017) Autonomous Weapons Systems: A Paradigm Shift for the Law of Armed Conflict?. In: Ohlin J D (ed) Research Handbook on Remote Warfare. Edward Elgar, Cheltenham, pp 371–404

Grut C (2013) The Challenge of Autonomous Lethal Robotics to International Humanitarian Law. Journal of Conflict and Security Law 18(1):5–23. https://doi.org/10.1093/jcsl/krt002

Gubrud M (2016) Why Should We Ban Autonomous Weapons? To Survive. IEEE Spectrum http://spectrum.ieee.org/automaton/robotics/military-robots/why-should-we-ban-autonomous-weapons-to-survive. Accessed 1 July 2017

Guiora A N (2017) Accountability and Decision Making in Autonomous Warfare: Who Is Responsible?. Utah Law Review 2017(2):393–422

Haataja S (2021) Autonomous Cyber Capabilities and Attribution in the Law of State Responsibility. In: Liivoja R, Väljataga A (eds) Autonomous Cyber Capabilities under International Law. NATO CCDCOE Publications, Tallinn, pp 260–290

Heyns C (2013) Report of the Special Rapporteur on Extrajudicial, Summary or Arbitrary Executions, A/HRC/23/47

Himmelreich J (2019) Responsibility for Killer Robots. Ethical Theory and Moral Practice 22(3):731–747. https://doi.org/10.1007/s10677-019-10007-9

Holland Michel A (2021) Known Unknowns: Data Issues and Military Autonomous Systems. UNIDIR, Geneva. https://unidir.org/publication/known-unknowns. Accessed 2 August 2023

Horowitz M C, Scharre P (2015) Meaningful Human Control in Weapon Systems: A Primer. Center for a New American Security, Working Paper No 031315

Human Rights Watch (2015) Mind the Gap: The Lack of Accountability for Killer Robots. Human Rights Watch

ICRC (2013) Autonomous Weapons: States Must Address Major Humanitarian, Ethical Challenges. https://reliefweb.int/report/world/autonomous-weapons-states-must-address-major-humanitarian-ethical-challenges. Accessed 18 October 2014

ICRC (2014) Report of the ICRC Expert Meeting on "Autonomous Weapon Systems: Technical, Military, Legal and Humanitarian Aspects", 26–28 March 2014, Geneva'

Israel (2019) Statement by Mr. Asaf Segev, Arms Control Department, Ministry of Foreign Affairs, Israel. Meeting of the Group of Governmental Experts on Emerging Technologies in the Area of Lethal Autonomous Weapons Systems, 26 March 2019

Jain A G (2021) Autonomous Cyber Capabilities and Individual Criminal Responsibility for War Crimes. In: Liivoja R, Väljataga A (eds) Autonomous Cyber Capabilities under International Law. NATO CCDCOE Publications, pp 291–320

Jain N (2016) Autonomous Weapons Systems: New Frameworks for Individual Responsibility. In: Bhuta N et al. (eds) Autonomous Weapons Systems: Law, Ethics, Policy. Cambridge University Press, Cambridge, pp 303–324. https://doi.org/10.1017/CBO9781316597873

Johnson D G, Noorman M (2014) Artefactual Agency and Artefactual Moral Agency. In: Kroes P and Verbeek P-P (eds) The Moral Status of Technical Artefacts. Springer Netherlands, Dordrecht, pp 143–158. https://doi.org/10.1007/978-94-007-7914-3_9

Kalmanovitz P (2016) Judgment, Liability and the Risks of Riskless Warfare. In: Bhuta N et al. (eds) Autonomous Weapons Systems. Cambridge University Press, Cambridge, pp 145–163. https://doi.org/10.1017/CBO9781316597873.007

Keiler J (2019) Actus Reus and Mens Rea: The Elements of Crime and the Framework of Criminal Liability. In: Keiler J, Roef D (eds) Comparative concepts of criminal law, 3rd edn. Intersentia, United Kingdom, pp 107–120

Kwik J (2020) The Road to Ongwen: Consolidating Contradictory Child Soldiering Narratives in International Criminal Law. Asia Pacific Journal of International Humanitarian Law 1(1):135–163

Lewis J (2015) The Case for Regulating Fully Autonomous Weapons. Yale Law Journal 124:1309–1325

Liu H-Y (2016) Refining Responsibility: Differentiating Two Types of Responsibility Issues Raised by Autonomous Weapons Systems. In: Bhuta N et al. (eds) Autonomous Weapons Systems. Cambridge University Press, Cambridge, pp 325–344. https://doi.org/10.1017/CBO9781316597873.014

Marauhn T (2014) An Analysis of the Potential Impact of Lethal Autonomous Weapons Systems on Responsibility and Accountability for Violations of International Law. In: Presentation on the occasion of the CCW expert meeting on lethal autonomous systems, Geneva, 13–16 May 2014. CCW, Geneva

McAllister A (2018) Stranger than Science Fiction: The Rise of A.I. Interrogation in the Dawn of Autonomous Robots and the Need for an Additional Protocol to the U.N. Convention against Torture. Minnesota Law Review 101:2527–2573

McDougall C (2019) Autonomous Weapon Systems and Accountability: Putting the Cart before the Horse. Melbourne Journal of International Law 20(1):58–87

Nersessian D L (2006) Whoops, I Committed Genocide! The Anomaly of Constructive Liability for Serious International Crimes. Fletcher Forum of World Affairs 30(2):81–106

Ohlin J D (2013) Targeting and the Concept of Intent. Michigan Journal of International Law 35(1):79–130

Ohlin J D (2016) The Combatant's Stance: Autonomous Weapons on the Battlefield. International Law Studies 92:1–30

Pagallo U (2017) From Automation to Autonomous Systems: A Legal Phenomenology with Problems of Accountability. In: Proceedings of the Twenty-Sixth International Joint Conference on Artificial Intelligence, {IJCAI-17}. pp 17–23. https://doi.org/10.24963/ijcai.2017/3

Parks H (1997) The Protection of Civilians from Air Warfare. In: Dinstein Y, Domb F (eds) Israel Yearbook on Human Rights, Volume 27. Brill-Nijhoff, Leiden, pp 65–112B. https://doi.org/10.1163/9789004423114_005

Ratner S R, Abrams J, Bischoff J (2009) Accountability for Human Rights Atrocities in International Law: Beyond the Nuremberg Legacy. 3rd edn. Oxford University Press, Oxford

Sandoz Y, Swinarski C, Zimmerman B (1987) Commentary on the Additional Protocols of 8 June 1977 to the Geneva Conventions of 12 August 1949. Martinus Nijhoff, Geneva

Scharre P D (2018) Army of None: Autonomous Weapons and the Future of War. Ww Norton & Co, New York

Schmitt M N (2021) Autonomous Cyber Capabilities and the International Law of Sovereignty and Intervention. In: Liivoja R, Väljataga A (eds) Autonomous Cyber Capabilities under International Law. NATO CCDCOE Publication, Tallinn, pp 126–151

Schmitt M N, Thurnher J S (2013) "Out of the Loop": Autonomous Weapon Systems and the Law of Armed Conflict. Harvard Law School National Security Journal 4:231–281

Simon-Michel J-H (2014) Report of the 2014 Informal Meeting of Experts on Lethal Autonomous Weapons Systems (LAWS). UN Office Geneva

Sparrow R (2007) Killer Robots. Journal of Applied Philosophy 24(1):62–77

Stewart D M (2011) New Technology and the Law of Armed Conflict. International Law Studies 87:271–298

Stürchler N, Siegrist M (2017) A "Compliance-Based" Approach to Autonomous Weapon Systems. EJIL Talk. www.ejiltalk.org/a-compliance-based-approach-to-autonomous-weapon-systems. Accessed 7 June 2021

Taylor I (2021) Who Is Responsible for Killer Robots? Autonomous Weapons, Group Agency, and the Military-Industrial Complex. Journal of Applied Philosophy 38(2):320–334. https://doi.org/10.1111/japp.12469

Thurnher J S (2012) No One at the Controls: Legal Implications of Fully Autonomous Targeting. Joint Force Quarterly 67:77–84

Toscano C P (2015) "Friend of Humans": An Argument for Developing Autonomous Weapons Systems. Journal of National Security Law & Policy 8(1):189–246

UK Ministry of Defence (2011) The UK Approach to Unmanned Aircraft Systems. Joint Doctrine Note 2/11

UNIDIR (2016) Safety, Unintentional Risk and Accidents in the Weaponization of Increasingly Autonomous Technologies. UNIDIR Resources No 5

van Sliedregt E (2012) Individual Criminal Responsibility in International Law. Oxford University Press, New York

Weigend T (2014) Subjective Elements of Criminal Liability. In: Dubber M D, Hörnle T, Weigend T (eds) The Oxford Handbook of Criminal Law. Oxford University Press, Oxford, pp 490–511. https://doi.org/10.1093/oxfordhb/9780199673599.013.0022

Chapter 12
Obstacles to Criminal Liability: A Systemic Analysis

Contents

Abstract The criminal responsibility gap with respect to autonomous weapons (AWS) asserts that one or more elements required for criminal liability cannot be established due to the the technology's unique properties. To explore the validity of this hypothesis, this chapter starts by providing an overview of the different elements required for ciminal liability. It finds that mens rea and actus reus are universally applicable, but that some theories also add control and causality as necessary elements. The chapter first examines the latter two, finding that the significant influence exerted by the commander during the deployment decision is sufficient to establish both causality and control. In contrast, this is less easy to determine with respect to persons earlier in the lifecycle (e.g. programmers), due to the Problem of Many Hands. The actus reus element is analysed next: it is argued here that for AWS, the human decision to activate the system under the chosen conditions should be considered as the actus reus, instead of the (autonomous) activities of the AWS in the field. Finally, with regard to mens rea, it is found that this element presents the most challenges: humans both at the operational or preparatory stages will often experience reduced perceivability due to the complexity of the AI models, their opacity, etc.—this epistemic problem makes establishing mens rea difficult if higher degrees of cognition

J. Kwik, *Lawfully Using Autonomous Weapon Technologies*,
https://doi.org/10.1007/978-94-6265-631-4_12

are required for prosecution. The chapter concludes by identifying mens rea as the element that is most under pressure by the unique properties of AI.

Keywords Autonomous weapon system · Artificial intelligence · Criminal liability · War crime · Responsibility gap · Mens rea · Actus reus · Many hands · Causality · Control · Epistemic problem · Cognition

12.1 Preliminary Notes

12.1.1 Explicit and Implicit Elements of Criminal Liability

To understand what AWS characteristics can potentially cause a responsibility gap, it is useful to first outline what criminal law requires to hold someone accountable.[1] Two elements are provided almost universally: actus reus and mens rea,[2] classically derived from the Cartesian dualistic notion of the guilty act[3] and guilty mind.[4] Whether in national or international criminal law and irrespective of the legal culture, *actus reus non facit reum nisi mens sit rea* applies: proof of both mens rea and actus reus is necessary for holding someone criminally responsible for an occurrence.[5]

Mens rea, in turn, is frequently divided into the two sub-elements of *cognition* and *volition*—knowing and wanting the offence to be realised.[6] Depending on the extent to which cognition and volition are present, the accused may be assigned different levels of blameworthiness, ranging from the highest degrees of intent up to mere

[1] Many authors discussing AI-induced responsibility gaps follow the same methodology, departing first from the elements they argue are necessary for criminal liability and working backwards from there, analysing which elements are *not* fulfilled with respect to the technology being discussed. See e.g. Hallevy 2012, pp. 201–07; Himmelreich 2019, p. 743.

[2] Pardo and Patterson 2013, p. 121; van Sliedregt 2012, p. 39; Freitas et al. 2014, p. 147.

[3] Note that a 'guilty act' in this context can also come in the form of an inaction. King et al. 2020, p. 95; Hallevy 2016, p. 177.

[4] Shapira-Ettinger 2007, p. 2579. The US Supreme Court once described a crime as the "concurrence of an evil-meaning mind with an evil-doing hand". US Supreme Court, *Morissette v. United States*, 342 U.S. 246 (1952), p. 251.

[5] Ormerod 2008, p. 42; Pradel 1995, p. 232; Keiler 2019, p. 107.

[6] *Wissen und Wollen* in German systems, and *willens en wetens* in Dutch systems. van Sliedregt 2012, p. 40. In France, intent "*consiste ... en la volonté de commettre un acte en ayant la conscience de violer la loi pénale*". Desportes and Gunehec 2000, p. 399. In *Bemba*, the ICC held that intent "requires the existence of a volitional as well as a cognitive element". ICC (PTC), *Prosecutor v. Jean-Pierre Bemba Gombo*, Decision pursuant to Article 61(7)(a) and (b) of the Rome Statute on the charges of the prosecutor against Jean-Pierre Bemba Gombo, 5 June 2009, ICC-01/05-01/08, para 357. For consistency, the terms 'cognition' and 'volition' will be used exclusively in the remainder of this book to refer to these concepts.

Fig. 12.1 Relationship between different types of responsibility[12]

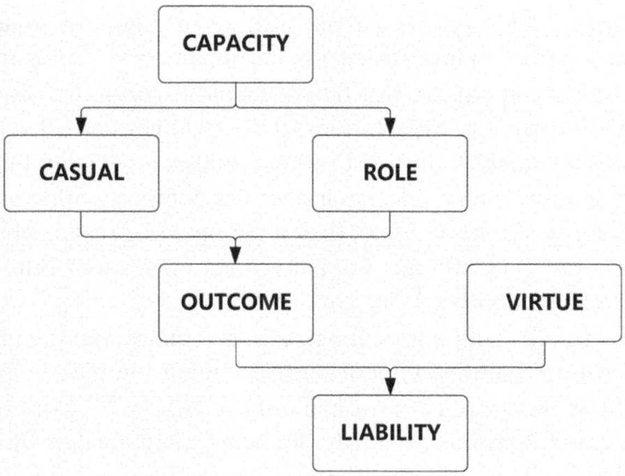

criminal negligence and, exceptionally, strict liability.[7] Depending on the jurisdiction and crime in question, however, not all fault degrees are always available: as we will see below,[8] this is a major procedural reason for why responsibility gaps manifest in practice.

Additionally, criminal law often requires *causality*, or that the harm be the result of the accused's action or inaction. For instance, the Model Penal Code holds that

Conduct is the cause of a result when:

(a) it is an antecedent but for which the result in question would not have occurred; and
(b) the relationship between the conduct and result satisfies any additional causal requirements imposed by the Code or by the law defining the offense[.][9]

One rationale for this requirement can be traced back to the philosophy of responsibility which holds that a person can only be morally responsible for an outcome if they both caused the outcome and, in doing so, violated an obligation or expectation which attaches to their role or function.[10] In Hart's terminology, outcome responsibility (i.e., what is generally referred to when one speaks of a person 'being responsible'[11]) is the convergence of causal and role responsibility. Without outcome responsibility, there can be no liability. Graphically, these relations can be represented through the diagram in Fig. 12.1.

For the purposes of our current discussion, this 'role' is quite crucial. Hart explains that role responsibility is derived from the fact that the person in question "occupies a distinctive place or office in a social organization, to which specific duties are

[7] Blomsma and Roef 2019, p. 179.

[8] Section 13.4.2.

[9] American Law Institute 1985, sct 2.03.(1). See also Turton and Kyd 2019; Cupido 2021.

[10] Hart and Honoré 1985.

[11] Vincent 2011, p. 17.

[12] Adapted from Ibid., p. 19.

attached to provide for the welfare of others or to advance in some specific way the aims or purposes of the organization".[13] As a military commander entrusted with the application of IHL,[14] Deployer occupies a very specific role which comes with particular expectations. IHL sets this standard at that of the reasonable military commander.[15] Thus, if Deployer makes a decision that causally results in a serious violation and this decision does not comport with what a reasonable commander in their position would do, they incur outcome responsibility.[16] Where this is proven in conjunction with mens rea, this outcome responsibility can then be transformed into criminal liability.[17]

Finally, although some disagree,[18] many commentators argue that there can be no criminal liability without *control*.[19] Such arguments "invoke that ... if *a* is responsible for *x* then *a* must have had control over *x*."[20] Control is not an official element a prosecutor must establish, but is arguably nestled within the rationale of mens rea. For instance, Blomsma argues that "*mens rea* denotes a sufficient degree of control and choice over actions. By requiring *mens rea*, it is safeguarded that the defendant is only held liable if he had capacity and opportunity to do otherwise".[21] In describing the concept of mens rea, Weigend also explains that "it is respect for a person's autonomy that excludes holding her responsible on the basis of an event she had no choice to avoid".[22] 'Doing otherwise' requires control.

At this point, we have established *actus reus*, *mens rea*, *causality* and *control* as four major subjects of interest. Not all analyses follow the same approach. Hallevy, for instance, only examined the criminal responsibility gap on the basis of whether mens rea and actus reus can be fulfilled.[23] Himmelreich is somewhat more extensive, distinguishing three elements: the epistemic condition, the control condition,

---

[13] Hart and Gardner 2008, p. 212.

[14] Sandoz et al. 1987, para 3550.

[15] Huffman 2012, p. 46.

[16] Corn 2012, p. 452. See e.g. ICTY (TC), *Prosecutor v. Stanislav Galić*, Judgment, 5 December 2003, IT-98-29-T, para 51.

[17] Corn 2012, p. 452. Note that by itself, a lack of reasonableness is in no way sufficient to establish criminal liability (except possibly for unconscious negligence). This is also due to the fact that the reasonableness standard in IHL is notoriously imprecise and does not provide objective standards for courts to apply in criminal cases. Sandoz et al. 1987, para 2187; Huffman 2012, p. 22.

[18] See Himmelreich 2019, pp. 739–40.

[19] Geiß and Lahmann 2017, p. 393; Taylor 2021, p. 323.

[20] Himmelreich 2019, p. 735. This assertion is implicit in any MHC argument that involves the Accountability facet: the idea that meaningful human control is required to ensure human accountability implies that control is a necessary condition thereof. See Sect. 2.4.5. Chengeta argued, for instance, that the "the only way to address the accountability challenges that are presented by AWS is to make sure that humans exercise 'Meaningful Human Control' over weapons". Chengeta 2016, p. 4.

[21] Blomsma and Roef 2019, p. 178.

[22] Weigend 2014, p. 490.

[23] Hallevy 2012, p. 207: "in order to impose criminal liability, the existence of *actus reus* and *mens rea* of the specific offense is adequate. No further capabilities are required for the imposition of criminal liability".

and blameworthiness.[24] The epistemic condition refers to a lack of awareness or foresight, and relates to the cognition component of mens rea.[25] The latter two elements correspond to our own concept of control and Deployer's reasonableness as derived from their role responsibility as a reasonable commander, respectively.

For completion, we will maintain our quadripartite approach in the following discussion. We depart from the assumption that an obstacle to establishing any of these conditions can be viewed as potentially causing a responsibility gap, but leave the question open as to whether causality or control are necessary conditions for criminal liability (if one believes they are not, the reader can simply disregard the conclusions in the corresponding sections).[26] Himmelreich's blameworthiness condition will not be considered as a separate criterion, but rather as a reference point for what constitutes reasonable conduct (pursuant to the 'reasonable military commander'-standard). Before we discuss these conditions in turn, however, it can be useful to briefly look at how these four elements would be established in a more perfect world, as a means of comparison.

12.1.2 Deployer Liability Within an Idealised MHC Framework

In Chap. 11, we have spoken of our discussions in previous parts having taken place at an idealised level. In an idealised state of IHL implementation, there is no responsibility gap: it is always possible to attribute responsibility to Deployer for harm caused by an AWS they released.[27] As established in Sect. 2.5.3, the scheme of facets and processes in the MHC Framework ensures this is the case. This is indicated by the highlighted process arrows leading toward Accountability (see Fig. 12.2).

In an ideal world, the *Knowledge* process arrows would cover the mens rea component, while the *Causal Contribution* arrows would cover the control and causality elements as follows:

Mens rea. The Knowledge process arrows connect Awareness and Prediction to Accountability. If Deployer has

- Mastery over the AWS's technical intricacies, has perfect intelligence on the operational environment, knows how the AWS reacts to stimuli, properly conducts analyses of previous engagements (*Awareness → Accountability*), and

[24] Himmelreich 2019, pp. 741–43. Note that Himmelreich is an ethicist and his views are not based on criminal law theory. Himmelreich nevertheless provides several interesting insights into the notion of responsibility, making his views worth citing. For example, see Sect. 12.2.1.

[25] See Sect. 12.4.1.

[26] That mens rea and actus reus are always necessary is generally not open to controversy. Ormerod 2008, p. 42.

[27] Kwik 2022, pp. 15–16.

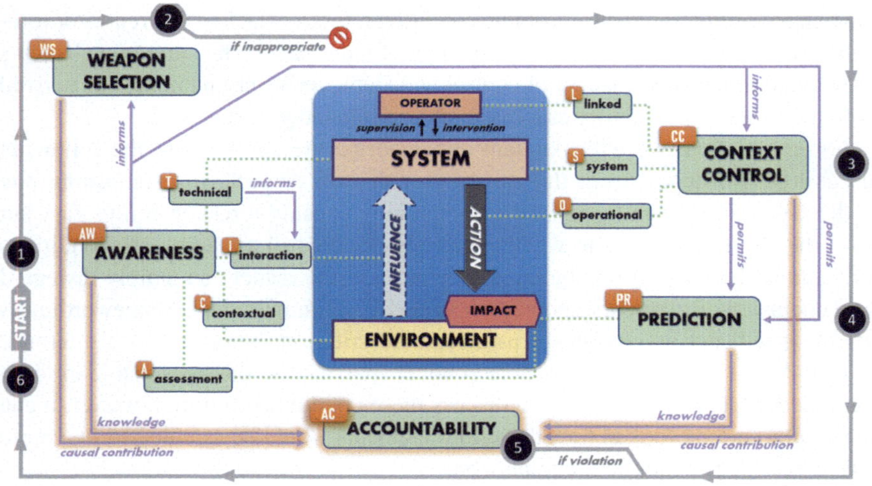

Fig. 12.2 MHC framework and processes leading to accountability

- Is able to anticipate how the AWS will act in the operational context (*Prediction → Accountability*),

then there is clearly clearly *cognition*. If Deployer nevertheless releases the system while knowing of the risk that it will cause a serious violation, mens rea can be inferred.[28]

Unfortunately, we cannot expect the real world to comport to this picture. There are many possible reasons why Awareness and Prediction will not be perfect. AWS are complex; military commanders are not AI experts and not all will have undergone the proper technical training;[29] intelligence will never be perfect;[30] the military organisation may not be diligent with after-action reports; and unexpected outputs and malfunctions can never be entirely eliminated, even with extensive testing.[31] There may even be adverse incentives to *not* implement these measures, if this would shield the commanders from criminal liability.[32] We will discuss these problems below in Sect. 13.5.3.

Causality and control. The Causal Contribution arrows connect the operational decision-making process discussed in Part IV to Accountability. The causal and

[28] Volition is often inferred if D acts despite awareness of (the risk of) an actus reus materialising, as volition is an "inner disposition of the actor" inaccessible to outside observers. Blomsma and Roef 2019, p. 187.

[29] Longobardo 2019, p. 78.

[30] Oeter 2020, p. 362.

[31] Matthias 2004, p. 182.

[32] The real possibility of commanders employing such bad-faith tactics is one reason why it was stated in Sect. 11.1 that this part uniquely also considers persons who do not necessarily operate in good faith. Cf. Sect. 1.4.

control components of Deployer's criminal liability would flow from the decisions taken during the Weapon Selection and Context Control stages. Put simply, it is argued that the *choice to select* the AWS in question and using it *in those circumstances* is sufficient to establish causality and control. To substantiate this particular assertion, it is useful to briefly discuss this point within the broader context of causality and control as a (potential) cause of an AWS responsibility gap.

12.2 Questions of Causality and Control

12.2.1 Whether and How as a Form of Conduct

The fact that AWS remove the direct chain of cause-and-effect between a human's decision and the resulting harm is deeply troubling for many commentators,[33] as causality requires a link between a human's conduct and the harmful outcome.[34] What, then, is the proximate human conduct when an AWS ultimately causes a violation? In the view of certain authors, there isn't one: it is the AI, after all, which makes and effectuates the ultimate decision. In this way, the AI can be viewed as an 'intervening variable' which itself cannot be held accountable.[35] Liu, for instance, posits that AI can disconnect causal and role responsibility: the AI is the causal reason for the outcome, but the role obligations are retained by Deployer.[36] This, in turn, severs the causal connection necessary for criminal liability.

However, there is no reason why we would have to define the *AI's output* as the 'conduct' for criminal law purposes. As discussed in Part IV, Deployer exerts extensive control over the *whether and how*: the deployment decision itself and under which circumstances they want the system to operate. In the MHC Framework, this is represented by the Weapon Selection and Context Control nodes. It is natural, then, to shift the locus of what we would deem the 'decision' (i.e., the point of reference for mens rea and causality) to this deployment decision,[37] in the same way how we would judge liability for an indiscriminate computer virus based on the commander's

---

[33] Asaro 2012, p. 693.

[34] American Law Institute 1985, sct 2.03.(1).

[35] Jain 2016, p. 306. One alternative would be to assign responsibility to the machine, a solution that is sometimes raised but which is rejected by almost all serious commentators. Gaeta 2016, p. 44; Jain 2016, p. 302; Toscano 2015, p. 235. We will thus not consider this proposition further in our analysis.

[36] Liu 2016, pp. 336–40.

[37] This rationale of 'moving the locus of responsibility forward' has extensive support in literature. The Dutch Advisory Council on International Affairs (AIV) found that the use of more autonomous technologies would simply have as a consequence that "*het zwaartepunt van de besluitvorming over het gebruik van geweld verschuift naar een eerder moment in het besluitvormingsproces*". Adviesraad Internationale Vraagstukken and Commissie van Advies inzake Volkenrechtelijke Vraagstukken 2015, p. 10. Other commentators came to the same conclusion. See Ekelhof 2016, p. 55; Thurnher 2014, p. 223.

intent and reasonableness at the time the program was released, instead of when the virus eventually 'decides' to shut down a hospital's power grid.

At this point, one may argue that the open-ended nature of modern AI would make this stance improper. After all, can we truly deem Deployer causally responsible for an outcome effectuated 'independently' by an AI, when all Deployer did was make the decision to release the system? The answer is yes. As mentioned above and explored in Part IV, the deployment decision is a substantial one: it entails creating the circumstances which led to the harmful outcome, as one could have chosen to deploy the system under different conditions or to not use the system at all.

Himmelreich refers to this as causal responsibility over a probabilistic outcome: if Killer K activates ('deploys') a torture machine which kills either Victim A or Victim B based on an incomprehensible algorithm, most would not hesitate in intuiting that *K is responsible for A's (or B's) death.*[38] As 'responsibility' is a fluid term, however,[39] we might be misled into interpreting this statement as 'K caused A's death'. Strictly speaking, K did not; the torture machine did. Rather, the correct explication of our intuition is 'K is responsible for *creating the conditions* which led to A's death'.[40] If K activated the machine with the requisite mens rea, then, K can be convicted for murder.[41]

This line of reasoning was similarly expressed before a US Senate hearing concerning Facebook in 2021, when Senator Blumenthal asked whistle-blower Frances Haugen whether Zuckerburg could escape responsibility because he ostensibly has no influence on how his algorithms operate. Haugen's reply was enlightening:

> *Blumenthal*: "Mark Zuckerburg is in fact the algorithm designer-in-chief, correct?"
>
> *Haugen*: "Mark has built an organisation that is very metrics-driven. It is intended to be flat; there is no unilateral responsibility. The metrics make the decision. Unfortunately that in itself is a decision."[42]

The fact that an AI system is deployed which may not act deterministically,[43] then, does not prevent us from establishing criminal liability based on Deployer's mindset and reasonableness at the moment of the deployment decision. Thus, *Weapon Selection → Accountability* and *Context Control → Accountability* hold: any action or inaction by Deployer when making a decision on *whether and how* to deploy an AWS will have caused the (conditions which led to the) outcome. The causality problem is thus not situated here.

---

[38] Himmelreich 2019, p. 742.

[39] Hart famously used 'responsible' six times in a single paragraph without any of the words carrying a similar meaning. See Hart 1968, p. 211.

[40] Himmelreich 2019, p. 742.

[41] This rationale of being responsible over a probabilistic outcome does not necessarily translate to mens rea. See Sect. 12.4.

[42] Haugen 2021.

[43] In the sense that it does not seem to do so for human decision-makers, since upon deployment we do not possess information of all the necessary inputs on which the algorithm bases its output.

12.2.2 Pinpointing Causes and the Problem of Many Hands

It is submitted that, instead of being a doctrinal barrier, the problem of causality predominantly entails evidentiary and procedural challenges. In particular, the obstacle will lie in pinpointing the true cause of an AWS failure. Chapter 5 extensively discussed the different reasons why an AI system can fail, and showed that these causes may be interlinked or buried beneath layers of subsystems.[44] For a prosecutor or investigative team, determining the root cause of a malfunction is likely to be quite difficult.[45] The causality problem will be particularly salient if one wishes to consider Broader Chain Candidates.[46] Say that objectively (as established by an omniscient observer), a failure was caused by a racist labeller who sneakily aimed to inject a bias into the AWS, and this system eventually targets a minority ethnic group. This is a paradigmatic BCC-only case where the commander is likely to have been entirely unaware of this bias, and where pursuing Deployer responsibility is likely to be impossible (and unwarranted). However, even if one would suspect that the incident was caused by malicious labelling,[47] identifying this labeller as the root cause of the failure—and even more problematically, proving this in court—will be very challenging.

It is on the other hand debatable whether this is a gap caused by AI technology, or rather by the nature of modern systems in general. Evidentiary difficulties in proving causality are not new, and are a common feature of cyberweapons, where identifying the perpetrator of cyber-inflicted harms is a notoriously difficult task.[48] Trusilo & Burri in fact argue that cyberweapons are much worse than AWS in this regard: where AWS at least have a physical component which can be captured, analysed or tracked, cyberweapons are disembodied and can potentially self-replicate.[49]

Additionally, modern systems with any degree of technological complexity are characterised by what is referred to as the *Problem of Many Hands*.[50] This refers to the situation where BCCs involved in the product's development and adoption chain are so extensive that "it is impossible or at least very difficult to hold someone reasonably responsible".[51] Many Hands make a causality assessment difficult for two main reasons. First, as already touched on above, isolating causes of failure becomes increasingly difficult as the number of hands increase: "the nature and complexity of these systems would make successfully attaching personal liability to any one programmer or engineer very difficult".[52] The prosecutor simply becomes

---

44 Beard 2014, p. 651.

45 Williams 2017.

46 See Sect. 11.3.

47 This example simplifies the problem by removing complexities related to mens rea, as the labeller clearly acted intentionally. See Sect. 12.4.

48 Jain 2021, pp. 291–98.

49 Trusilo and Burri 2021, pp. 61–62.

50 Giannini and Kwik 2023, pp. 58–59.

51 Van de Poel et al. 2012, p. 50.

52 Grut 2013, p. 16.

overwhelmed with options.[53] Second, a failure may be caused by consecutive faults. In the racist AWS example above, perhaps the injected bias would have been identified were it not for the producer cutting corners during quality assurance, and the reviewing authorities being placed under pressure to quickly greenlight the system to support the nation's failing war effort.[54] Under such conditions, identifying the 'cause' of the violation is difficult.

Once again, however, this is not a problem unique to AI. In fact, the Problem of Many Hands is applicable for "any sufficiently complex organisation".[55] When the problem was first coined by Thompson in 1980, it was meant to describe the general difficulties experienced in criminal law when the assumption of a lone, solitary figure making decisions is broken,[56] for instance with respect to public administrative bodies. Indeed, several doctrines in criminal law were developed specifically to address this inherent weakness, such as corporate liability (which blames the organisation as a whole), hierarchical models such as command responsibility (which assigns blame for the misconduct of a group to the person in a position of command) and collective responsibility (such as JCE doctrine),[57] demonstrating that it is a problem not exclusive to AWS. The nature of AI does, however, have the capacity to aggravate the problem. In 1996, Nissenbaum found Thompson's theory to be particularly applicable to software development, which is characterised by multiple

---

[53] King et al. 2020, p. 103.

[54] When discussing the Problem of Many Hands, Nissenbaum gives the cancer treatment machine Therac-25 as an example of such a 'consecutive error' scenario. After the machine overdosed six patients with radiation in the 1980s, subsequent investigation found, amongst others, that software errors, inadequate testing and quality assurance, exaggerated claims about its reliability and a bad interface had 'caused' the accident. Nissenbaum 1996, p. 30. Amoroso also gave the following example more specific to AWS technology, which is worth quoting in full:

> Let us consider … an autonomous UAV model which is programmed to distinguish between military and civilian buildings. Evidence collected in the UAV testing phase suggests that the system fails to identify as civilian objects buildings presenting certain perceptual features in 0,05 % of cases. These results, however, are inaccurate, as they do not take into account a number of environmental conditions that would raise the failure rate to 5 % … Inadequate testing by the manufacturer(s) is partly due to the need to accelerate the launch of the UAV on the market and beat potential competitors to the punch. When delivering the purchased system to the battlefield unit, the procurement officer omits to mention the failure rate, solely recommending the greatest caution in the use of the aircraft against targets in the proximity of civilian objects. Basing her or his judgment on a liberal interpretation of this directive, a military commander deploys the aircraft over a sparsely populated area. As a consequence of this chain of events, the UAV targets and bombs a small school, causing several civilian victims.

Amoroso 2020, p. 129.

[55] Taylor 2021, p. 324.

[56] Thompson 1980, p. 905.

[57] Bovens 1998; Amoroso and Giodano 2019, p. 216. This is consistent with the fact that collective accountability models such as JCE are commonly cited as methods to establish criminal liability for AWS designers and executive decision-makers—both BCCs. See Chengeta 2016, pp. 21–22; Amoroso 2020, p. 137.

development teams, multi-layered subsystems, hardware-software interactions, and the fact that the producing organisations, themselves, are also Many Hands entities.[58]

It was mentioned above that the Problem of Many Hands is particularly relevant when one wishes to pursue BCC liability. In contrast, Deployer arguably *is* the "solitary figure, single-handedly gathering information and implementing decisions" Thompson mentions.[59] While AWS may involve Many Hands throughout its lifecycle, the concept of the deployment decision in conjunction with a commander's duty under IHL to implement Awareness, Weapon Selection and Context Control re-funnel the sprawling network of causes and actors back toward a single person who makes the ultimate and final decision. We can thus conclude that the Many Hands problem is largely a procedural and evidentiary problem for BCC liability, but that the bottlenecking effect of the deployment decision serves to reduce its effects later in the lifecycle.

This 'bottlenecking' provides a solution to concerns regarding causality and control, but it may seem excessively harsh on Deployer. One may object that it is not equitable to concentrate all this responsibility (and blame) on the single commander. However, note that more is needed to establish criminal liability. Even admitting to the conclusions reached in this subsection, we see in the coming analysis that criminal law already is quite proficient in filtering out equitable from non-equitable attributions of liability, particularly through the mens rea element.[60] The purpose of the current section's discussion is to purely look at the causality and control elements, and argue that the obstacles to Deployer liability do not reside here.

12.2.3 Issues of Control

With regard to the control condition, this element requires that a person had sufficient control over the result in order to fairly hold them accountable. From a Deployer-centric perspective, this is once again relatively unproblematic. A strong degree of control is evident in light of the MHC Framework which demonstrates how much influence a Deployer has over an AWS they are activating. The rationale which establishes the control condition as unproblematic is thus similar to the rationale which causally linked Weapon Selection and Context Control to Accountability.

For BCCs, like with causality, the control condition is more of a potential hinderance. Even if the malicious labeller aimed to inject a bias into the algorithm, it is debatable if they had enough control over when and how the final product is used—perhaps months or years after the training data was mislabelled—seeing as this is

[58] Amoroso and Giodano 2019, pp. 215–16. Nissenbaum argued that most software "are the products not of single programmers working in isolation but of groups or organisations, typically corporations … which frequently bring together teams of individuals with a diverse range of skills and varying degrees of expertise … Consequently, when a system malfunctions and gives rise to harm, the task of assigning responsibility … is exacerbated and obscured". Nissenbaum 1996, pp. 28–29.

[59] Thompson 1980, p. 905.

[60] This is particularly so through the mens rea condition, as we discuss extensively in Chap. 13.

ultimately determined by a distant commander's deployment decision. The larger the distance between the actor and the final act that led to the harm, the more difficult it is to argue that they exercised 'control' over the outcome.[61]

12.2.4 *Causality and Control: Findings*

Problems related to causality and control are primarily obstacles to BCC liability due to their relative temporal and spatial distance. With regard to causality, the challenge will likely be technical and evidentiary: accurately pinpointing the cause of an AWS failure earlier in the lifecycle will be difficult, and proving it in court even more so. With regard to control, a genuine argument can be made that BCCs often will not have sufficient control over the outcome because their contribution is so far removed from the action. There are, of course, exceptions, e.g. when a programmer inserts a line of code which inevitably causes the system to target specific ethnic groups.

With regard to Deployers, causality and control are relatively less problematic due to the bottlenecking effect of Weapon Selection and Context Control: during their deployment decision, commanders exercise a high degree of influence on the Whether and How, which act both as a strong form of control and as the action which ultimately causes the (conditions which lead to the) harmful result. Even in the case of the malicious labeller above, these findings still hold. One would intuitively balk at the idea of punishing the good-faith commander for deploying that system when they had no idea that the algorithm had been injected with a racial bias, but this is not because we reject the idea that they exercised control over the Whether and How. Instead, the main problem to Deployer liability in this case—and in many others—arises from the phrase 'they had no idea': the cognition element of mens rea. It is this element which pervades the responsibility gap, and it is this problem which we discuss extensively in Sect. 12.4 and Chap. 13.

12.3 Actus Reus

Actus reus is an element of criminal liability which goes underexplored in commentaries about AI, and is generally presumed to be an unproblematic element to establish. In many works, an unspoken assumption is made that the deployed system is committing the *actus reus* 'for' a natural person, e.g. a commander or programmer, leaving the discussion to focus on seemingly more difficult elements such as mens rea

[61] Gogarty and Hagger 2008, p. 123.

or causality.[62] In this sense, the AWS is equated to another person or entity through whom the perpetrator is executing the actus reus. The question of whether a machine can perform an actus reus is also rarely viewed as problematic. When discussing criminal liability for machines, for instance, one commentator argued that an actus reus "is easily attributed to [AWS]", since "[a]s long as an [AWS] controls a mechanical or other mechanism that moves its parts, any act might be considered as performed by the [AWS]."[63]

However, these optimistic appraisals can be called into question. First, the concept of actus reus in criminal law is often linked to the idea of voluntariness.[64] The Model Penal Code, as an example, provides that "[a] person is not guilty of an offense unless his liability is based on conduct that includes a voluntary act or the omission to perform an act of which he is physically capable",[65] whereby spasms, convulsions, unwanted bodily movements and acts performed under hypnosis are regarded as involuntary actions.[66] One question that arises, then, is whether a machine's action can be rightfully regarded as a 'voluntary' act or if it should be characterised instead as a type of mechanical 'spasm'.[67] A second matter, briefly touched upon before, is whether it is possible to reconcile the fact that the actus reus is performed by a machine while mens rea still attaches to a human. Some believe it is not.[68] McAllister argues that "[a]utonomous robots have a unique capacity to splinter a criminal act, where a human manifests the mens rea and the robot commits the actus reus", which "poses serious challenges to the current international frameworks for imputing liability".[69]

The position taken in this book with respect to these fears is that the point of departure of identifying the *system* as the entity committing the actus reus is, in itself, mistaken. In this respect, the actus reus should not be confused with a harmful outcome which triggers criminal liability, such as that set out in API Article 85(3) ("death or serious injury to body or health"). When a clearly inadequately trained

[62] For example, Väljataga & Liivoja argue that it "is not controversial that commanders can be held criminally liable if they use an autonomous capability to commit the actus reus of a crime with the requisite intent or knowledge, or if they control the will of another person who in turn satisfies the elements of a crime". Väljataga and Liivoja 2021, pp. 9–10.

[63] Hallevy 2012, p. 208.

[64] This should not be confused with the volition component of mens rea. See Saunders 1988, p. 445.

[65] American Law Institute 1985, sct 2.01.(1). In a way, the voluntary act requirement betrays the anthropocentric underpinnings of criminal law, which is also the source of many theoretical or semantic challenges that arise as non-human agents such as AI are introduced.

[66] Ibid., sct 2.01.(2). See also Pardo and Patterson 2013, pp. 123–24.

[67] King et al. 2020, p. 95. Commentators note that this is different with respect to 'acts' by legal persons, as these still amount to acts of humans but made in the organisation's name. Freitas et al. 2014, p. 152.

[68] King et al. commented that "if it is admitted that an AA [autonomous agent] can perform the actus reus, … greater AA autonomy increases the chance of the criminal act or omission being decoupled from the mental state". King et al. 2020, p. 95.

[69] McAllister 2018, p. 2572.

AWS[70] is used which subsequently causes significant and foreseeable civilian casualties due to successive misidentifications, the AWS is indeed the entity aiming and shooting at the unarmed townsfolk. However, this is not the actus reus upon which criminal liability will be based. An actus reus is the "'bad act' [which] sets out the objective thing that needs to materialise before criminal law can be invoked",[71] which in this case is the plainly illegal decision to release the AWS in such circumstances.[72]

That releasing a system does not instantly cause the harm to manifest is unproblematic. Ormerod's description of actus reus in this sense is instructive: actus reus is the requirement that the perpetrator "has caused a certain event or that responsibility is to be attributed to him for the *existence of a certain state of affairs*, which is forbidden by criminal law".[73] Once again, therefore, the Causal Contribution process arrows in the MHC Framework[74] adequately capture how actions taken during Weapon Selection and Context Control can lead to criminal liability. As long as we do not fall into the trap of imbuing our tools with more moral and legal personality than is warranted, we will also not be tempted to assume that it is they who are performing actus rei.

12.4 Mens Rea

In the racist labeller case, we found that 'the commander had no idea' was the reason why we instinctively rejected the idea of holding the good-faith commander liable for the civilian deaths. This is an example of a mens rea problem. The mens rea problem asserts that some AI-specific characteristics are such that they create insurmountable obstacles related to establishing the Candidate's mens rea, barring criminal liability. Gaeta opined that for AWS in particular, "*mens rea* will be hard to prove",[75] McDougall submitted that the "main controversy... relates to the satisfaction of the mental elements of each crime",[76] and Kurosaki argued that "unlike other weapons systems equipped with computers that are less independent, fully AWS could by

70 A blatant example (where mens rea is not called into question) is used here to illustrate the point related to actus reus. That in many situations the risk is not as manifest is discussed in Sect. 13.5.1.

71 Keiler 2019, p. 107.

72 Gaeta has a more nuaced view on the actus reus of crimes involving AWS. In her view, it is necessary to carefully examine each individual element of crime to consider whether the person activating an AI system can be considered as performing the actus reus. For example, the crime of targeting civilians requires for an attack be ordered: the actus reus of this element of crime evidently refers not to the weapon's 'trigger-pulling actions' (see Sect. 9.2), but to the commander ordering the AWS-attack to be launched (i.e., Deployer). This rationale, she argues, also "applies to military attacks conducted with any kind of conventional weapon", making the actual properties and autonomy of the weapon system carrying out the violence at the Instance-level immaterial. See Gaeta 2023, pp. 1041–45.

73 Ormerod 2008, p. 42 (emphasis added).

74 See Sect. 12.1.2.

75 Gaeta 2016, p. 44.

76 McDougall 2019, p. 66.

definition make decisions that humans did not intend".[77] Many other commentators have made similar statements.[78]

Some authors make a clearer reference to the two constituent elements of mens rea, cognition and volition. For example, Davison argued that Candidates "may not have the *knowledge* or *intent* required to be found liable, owing to the fact that the machine, once activated, can select and attack targets independently".[79] The mens rea problem is grounded in the fact that for criminal law, moral responsibility in the Hartian sense is usually insufficient for liability: in addition to having caused the outcome, the accused also needs to have had a specific, blameworthy state of mind.[80]

This section more generally explores the challenges related to mens rea which arise from AI-specific characteristics. In particular, it is argued that the main weight of the mens rea problem rests on what we shall call the *epistemic problem*. The epistemic problem is an umbrella term used to refer to the reduction or absence of awareness, foresight and predictive capacity from the part of the Candidate, caused by characteristics unique to AI. It therefore clearly pertains to cognition, or more specifically, the lack thereof. As we will explore below, causes of epistemic difficulties are numerous and they can even be contrived to induce a responsibility gap. From this analysis, we draw the general conclusion that the mens rea condition is indeed potentially the most challenging element to fulfil whenever AWS-related harm occurs. This provides a good bridge to Chap. 13, where we engage in a more detailed diagnostic as to the mens rea requirement to determine whether the problem is omnipresent or only notable for specific cognitive states.

12.4.1 The Epistemic Problem

The epistemic problem is described by Himmelreich as the contention that Candidates are "not responsible because they lack foresight ... foreseeability, awareness, and the like".[81] It is a concern that is raised more generally with respect to AI technologies which function with some degree of operational freedom. Hayward & Maas, when discussing the criminology of AI crimes, mention how "using AI as an 'independent' criminal intermediary poses serious questions for cornerstone legal standards such

[77] Kurosaki 2020, p. 432.

[78] E.g. Jain 2021, pp. 291–92 ("if the impugned conduct is effectuated by an algorithm or by a human relying on an algorithm, there is no human being with the *mens rea* required for the crime"); Asaro 2012, p. 693 (AWS "eliminate the possibility of establishing any individual criminal responsibility that requires moral agency and a determination of *mens rea*").

[79] Davison 2017, p. 17 (emphasis added). It is not always straightforward to determine whether a statement pertains to mens rea globally or one of its subcomponents. In this statement, for example, the word 'intent' clearly is intended as a reference to the volition component. In the previous statements, however, 'intent' refers to mens rea more generally.

[80] Ormerod 2008, p. 42.

[81] Himmelreich 2019, pp. 734–35.

as … the knowledge threshold, foreseeability and liability".[82] Hayward and Maas's statement is provocative due to the context in which it is uttered: as part of their exposé on ways that AI can be deliberately misused to commit crimes. In other words, they refer to situations where we intuitively would ascribe intent to the Candidate, but where the application of a mens rea test fails because cognition is missing—causing the culprit to escape liability. This scenario seems to perfectly reflect the Responsibility Gap Problem: An element necessary for criminal liability is difficult to satisfy due to an AI-specific characteristic (Premise 1), and the resultant inability to assign criminal liability is seemingly unacceptable (Premise 2).[83]

To better understand this assertion, let us first elaborate on why the level of foreseeability that is usually associated with AI systems conflicts with mens rea's cognition element. Reduced perceivability is often referred to as a 'lack of predictability' in commentaries.[84] Amoroso & Giordano refer to the "inherent unpredictability of autonomous machines" as one of the two major causes of responsibility gaps.[85] The root of the problem is perhaps best formulated by a Council of Europe report on AI crimes, which presents this as a dilemma: On the one side, "humans cannot be expected to foresee all possible outcomes of an employment of AI", and on the other, "criminal culpability … requires foreseeability of the risk of harm".[86] Let us briefly examine the two aspects of the dilemma in turn.

12.4.2 Reduced Perceivability Leading to Lower Cognition

That modern AI tends to induce reduced perceivability is a pervasive theme throughout this book: we have seen how reliability metrics can only represent average rates of performance, not an understanding of casuistic action;[87] we have seen how opacity makes the operation of AWS less understandable and that XAI was developed specifically to counter this issue;[88] we have seen how modern AWS must necessarily function dynamically to operate properly in an equally dynamic environment with dynamic opponents;[89] and even the entire MHC Framework was developed to limit how much uncertainty Deployer is faced with when activating an AWS.[90] Validating our prior findings, we often see these disadvantages also invoked in literature to

---

82 Hayward and Maas 2021, p. 9.

83 See Sect. 11.4.

84 See e.g. Dinstein 2018, para 22; Sparrow 2007, p. 70; Jain 2016, p. 307.

85 Amoroso and Giodano 2019, p. 213 (emphasis removed). The other, in their opinion, is the Many Hands Problem.

86 European Committee on Crime Problems (CDPC) 2020, p. 5.

87 See Chap. 4.

88 See Sect. 4.5.

89 See Sect. 3.4.2 and Chap. 6.

90 See Sect. 2.5.2.

support the assertion that the cognition element cannot be fulfilled. Amongst others, commentators highlight that:

- The *high technical complexity* of AI reduces the Candidate's ability to perceive how it functions or would act in specific situations, causing them to fail to foresee outcomes.[91]
- Similarly, *opacity* also can reduce the Candidate's ability to perceive how the system functions or would act in specific situations, causing them to fail to foresee outcomes.[92]
- *Unexpected interactions* can cause outcomes which Candidates would not be able to foresee.[93]
- *Online learning and evolution* result in reduced predictability.[94] The Candidate cannot predict how the system would evolve, and thereby cannot foresee the harmful outcome.[95]
- *Edge cases* and *system failures* are by definition unavoidable and unforeseeable the first time they occur,[96] making it impossible to establish cognition from the part of the Candidate.

In addition, reduced perceivability may manifest itself because of the characteristics of the *Candidate* instead of the system. Even if a system is completely transparent

---

[91] UK 2020, para 9 (an AWS might behave "in an unexpected way and, due to its complexity and unpredictability, those involved in its development or deployment neither intended nor foresaw the outcome"); Wallach and Allen 2013, p. 132 ("to expect operators to anticipate the actions of intelligent systems becomes more and more unreasonable as the systems and the environments in which they operate become more complex"). King et al. argue for instance that "the complexity of the [system's] programming makes it possible that the designer, developer, or deployer (i.e., a human agent) will neither know nor predict the AA's criminal act or omission", leading to "[t]he absence of a knowledge-based *mens rea*". King et al. 2020, p. 95.

[92] European Committee on Crime Problems (CDPC) 2020, p. 5; Williams 2017; Geiß and Lahmann 2017, pp. 392–93.

[93] This effect is often observed in trading algorithms, for example, where collusion can unexpectedly emerge as a result of interactions amongst bots. King et al. 2020, p. 99. The interacting elements can also be internal to one system, e.g. between two subsystems created by different developers. Taylor presents the following example at the code level: "Two computer programmers each write part of the code that directs the behaviour of an autonomous weapon. Each strives to ensure that their section of the code will not lead to nonliable individuals being targeted. Despite this, the two sections of code interact in unexpected ways, and the weapon targets a group of surrendering soldiers." Taylor 2021, p. 324.

[94] See Sect. 5.6.

[95] Matthias, who first coined the term 'responsibility gap', highlighted this characteristic of AI in particular to substantiate his argument. Matthias 2004. Taylor presents the following scenario as an example: "A group of computer programmers write the whole code that directs the behaviour of an autonomous weapon. They strive to ensure that the code will not lead to nonliable individuals being targeted. However, the weapon utilises machine-learning technologies that lead to a rewriting of its code in an attempt to improve outcomes based on past experience. The rewritten code directs the weapon to target a group of surrendering soldiers." This results in a gap in cognition because "they lack the epistemological precondition … that is, they may not have been able to predict that the machine they create would evolve in the way it does". Taylor 2021, p. 325.

[96] See Sects. 3.4.2, 5.3 and 5.9.

and entirely understandable for those with the requisite know-how, the Candidate in question may *lack the training or technical understanding* required to achieve this level of cognition.[97] This concern is common to all AI domains, and has also been raised with regard to autonomous vehicles.[98]

While a lack of technical understanding can lead to a lack of understanding for all weapon systems, one may nevertheless qualify it as a problem relatively unique to AWS simply because the behaviour of AI is so much less intuitively understandable than legacy systems (such as artillery). While one can reasonably attribute understanding of how an artillery piece functions by virtue of a person's general familiarity with the system and knowledge of basic ballistic trajectories,[99] it is less evident that such cognition exists with regard to an AI whose behaviour depends on a range of inputs and whose performance is expressed in unintuitive performance metrics.[100] In that sense, AWS can better be compared to cyberweapons, a technology which faces similar concerns of commanders not possessing the necessary technical understanding to foresee what direct and higher-order harms they may cause.[101]

For liability of Broader Chain Candidates, we have held thus far that the Problem of Many Hands primarily relates to evidentiary and procedural challenges, particularly with regards to the causality and control elements.[102] However, a Many Hands situation can also introduce an epistemic problem. The plurality of actors, of moving parts, of interactions, etc., can often make it very hard for a BCC to 'know' of the risk of a certain result manifesting.[103] Thus, with respect to two programmers whose work

---

[97] Indeed, this is precisely the reason why Heyns found that it "will be important to establish … whether military commanders will be in a position to understand the complex programming of LARs sufficiently well to warrant criminal liability". Heyns 2013, para 78.

[98] The Council of Europe remarked that "holding drivers automatically liable if they fail to comply with the instructions given by the AI system through … lack of technical knowledge could also be considered unfair", recommending obligatory training for AV drivers on this basis. European Committee on Crime Problems (CDPC) 2020, pp. 9, 14.

[99] To take one example, in *Martić*, one of the main defences attempted by the Accused essentially amounted to a lack-of-technical-understanding claim. Martić argued that while he gave the order to use the M-87 Orkan to attack Zagreb (which in the Prosecution's view amounted to an indiscriminate attack), he had no mens rea because he "did not have the appropriate military knowledge of the effects of the M-87 Orkan". The Appeals Chamber rejected this claim by inferring knowledge from Martić's "involvement in matters concerning the weaponry in the possession of the RSK, his statements in relation to the shelling itself and his position as President of the RSK". ICTY (AC), *Prosecutor v. Milan Martić*, Judgment, 8 October 2008, IT-95-11-A, para 256. One can ask if the Chamber would have come to the same conclusion if the system in question was instead a complex AWS.

[100] See Sect. 4.2.

[101] Schmitt M N (ed) 2017, Tallinn Manual 2.0 on the International Law Applicable to Cyber Warfare. 2nd edn. Cambridge University Press, Cambridge (Tallinn Manual 2.0), pp. 399–400.

[102] See Sect. 12.2.2.

[103] Nissenbaum 1996, pp. 28–30. Van de Poel et al. come to a comparable conclusion with respect to climate change lawsuits, which are Many Hands situations par excellence: "Since the ability to foresee undesirable consequences is usually seen as a condition for responsibility, this raises doubts whether it is reasonable to hold someone responsible for the accident that occurred". van de Poel et al. 2012, p. 50.

only produces an unreliable AI *in combination* (an interaction that is hard to foresee), it will be hard to assert any kind of cognition on their part. Taylor argues that "neither could have known this", and that therefore, imputing any kind of responsibility to them would be unjustified.[104]

We can thus agree that the first branch holds.

12.4.3 Mens Rea Requires Foreseeability

That mens rea requires foreseeability of the risk of harm is generally also true. Indeed, many view this is one of the core functions of mens rea: to filter out cases where the Candidate could not have foreseen the result, in which case punishing them would be a perverse and even counterproductive outcome.[105] Weigend expresses that

> Criminal punishment imposed on a person expresses blame for what the person did. In a rational system of law, it makes no sense to blame and punish a person for harmful occurrences that he had no possibility to prevent or that she was unable to foresee.[106]

Punishing in the absence of foreseeability also negates core penological functions of criminal law. "Punishment that is merely based on unfortunate outcomes is neither deserved nor useful."[107] If the result was not foreseen by the Candidate, it would be incorrect to reproach them for what occurred (retributivism), nor can punishment deter the Candidate or others from committing similar acts (deterrence) if all is simply a matter of luck.[108]

However, it is sometimes ignored in responsibility gap discussions that criminal law accepts different degrees of foreseeability. The extent to which cognition and volition needs to be fulfilled for mens rea is usually reflected through the various fault modes, and they do not always need to be satisfied to equal degrees. For instance, while viewed by some as a mental state which fully "encapsulates knowledge and willingness",[109] dolus directus is described by others as a fault degree where cognition is, in practice, of marginal importance: instead, the perpetrator's will (volition) is key.[110] As a common example, most courts would accept that D killed victim V purposely if D aims a rifle at extreme range with the intent of killing V, even though

[104] Taylor 2021, p. 324.

[105] Chengeta 2016, p. 19; Sartor and Omicini 2016, p. 64.

[106] Weigend 2014, p. 490.

[107] Blomsma and Roef 2019, p. 178.

[108] Ibid.

[109] Van Sliedregt 2012, p. 40.

[110] Weigend 2014, p. 495. For instance, the Model Penal Code conception of 'purposely' makes no mention of how cognisant a perpetrator must be of the (risk of the) outcome manifesting: it suffices that "it is his conscious object to engage in conduct of that nature or to cause such a result". American Law Institute 1985, sct 2.02.(2).(a).

D knows the risk of actually hitting V is miniscule.[111] Similarly, if it can be proven that Deployer's conscious objective when activating an AWS was to cause massive civilian casualties, it is less relevant that they were not precisely aware of the system's performance metrics or how the system makes its classifications.[112]

Even ignoring fault degrees such as negligence[113] and strict liability[114] which we do not consider in this analysis,[115] we can thus hold that while it is generally correct to hold that cognition is a vital component of securing criminal liability, it is not true for all fault degrees. As such, the extent to which difficulties in establishing a Candidate's cognition generate a responsibility gap also depends on the fault degree(s) under consideration and which fault degrees are available for the crime and forum in question. This is an important, frequently overlooked finding which we will develop in the following chapter.

12.5 Summation of Findings

This chapter utilised a methodical approach to analyse which of the four main elements of criminal liability pose the most difficulties for a hypothetical AWS release. It was found that the causality and control elements constitute challenges for establishing liability of Broader Chain Candidates due to factors such as temporal and spatial distance and the problem of Many Hands. On the other hand, with regard to Deployer (the main focus of this book), the 'bottlenecking' effect of the targeting process re-centres the causal chain back unto a single identifiable person. The actus

[111] Weigend 2014, p. 495. "[I]f it is proven that the actor's "conscious object" was to kill, and he succeeded, he is guilty of murder." Gegan 1990, p. 447.

[112] A similar conclusion can be reached with respect to the racist labeller, who had the conscious objective of inducing the system to target the desired ethnic group. At least from a mens rea perspective, the labeller will still act intentionally even though they may not 'know' specifically when the system will be activated down the line. See Sect. 13.2.

[113] As clarified in Sect. 11.6, when mentioned without a clarifier, this term is meant to capture the concept of unconscious negligence ('negligently'). It is also a fault mode which does not require cognition; in fact, it is explicitly constructed to punish "not what a person's state of mind was, but what it *should* have been". van Sliedregt 2012, p. 41.

[114] Strict liability does away with the mental element of a crime entirely: an actus reus alone suffices for conviction. Keiler 2019, p. 111; Nersessian 2006, p. 83.

[115] These are occasionally mentioned in AWS-related literature as potential solutions to the Responsibility Gap Problem. E.g. Jain 2016, p. 318; King et al. 2020, p. 95 (negligence); ICRC 2018, para 33 (strict liability). They are not analysed further in this discussion since it is highly unusual for legal systems to permit war crime prosecutions on the basis of negligence. Even for crimes in general, negligence is not widely accepted as a fault degree. See Hallevy 2012, p. 206; Keiler 2019, p. 113. Dunlap notes that US military law does provide criminal liability for simple negligence, although this certainly does not translate to all States. Dunlap 2016, p. n65. With regard to strict liability, a no-fault regime for prosecuting war crimes is in the views of many entirely unacceptable. Geiß and Lahmann 2017, p. 394; Kalmanovitz 2016, p. n36; Chengeta 2016, p. 24; Beard 2014, p. 644.

reus element is an issue which many commentators seem to ignore, but may theoretically present doctrinal problems. The position taken in this book is that the deployment decision (instead of the machine's 'trigger-pulling actions') should be viewed as the illegal act to which liability attaches, which resolves the issue.

Ultimately, the mens rea component presents the most potential challenges, owing to the epistemic problem and the reduced perceivability of modern AI systems. However, as also noted above, mens rea is not a monolithic concept. It is thus overly reductive to state that mens rea as a whole is threatened by AWS technology. Instead, the next chapter will perform a detailed and meticulous analysis of the mens rea requirement to diagnose exactly where the epicentre of challenges might lie.

References

Adviesraad Internationale Vraagstukken and Commissie van Advies inzake Volkenrechtelijke Vraagstukken (2015) Autonome Wapensystemen: De Noodzaak van Betekenisvolle Menselijke Controle. AIV

American Law Institute (1985) Model Penal Code: Complete Text of Model Penal Code as Adopted at the 1962 Annual Meeting of The American Law Institute at Washington, D.C. American Law Institute, Philadelphia

Amoroso D, Giordano B (2019) Who Is to Blame for Autonomous Weapons Systems' Misngs?. In: Carpanelli E, Lazzerini N (eds) Use and Misuse of New Technologies. Springer International Publishing, Cham, pp 211–232. DOI: https://doi.org/10.1007/978-3-030-05648-3

Amoroso D (2020) Autonomous Weapons Systems and International Law : A Study on Human-Machine Interactions in Ethically and Legally Sensitive Domains. Nomos Verlagsgesellschaft, Baden

Asaro P (2012) On Banning Autonomous Weapon Systems: Human Rights, Automation, and the Dehumanization of Lethal Decision-Making. International Review of the Red Cross 94(886):687–709

Beard J M (2014) Autonomous Weapons and Human Responsibilities. Georgetown Journal of International Law 45:617–681

Blomsma J H, Roef D (2019) Forms and Aspects of Mens Rea. In: Keiler J, Roef D (eds) Comparative concepts of criminal law, 3rd edn. Intersentia, United Kingdom, pp 177–206

Bovens M (1998) The Quest for Responsibility Accountability and Citizenship in Complex Organisations. Cambridge University Press, Cambridge

Chengeta T (2016) Accountability Gap: Autonomous Weapon Systems and Modes of Responsibility in International Law. Denver Journal of International Law & Policy 45:1–50

Corn G S (2012) Targeting, Command Judgement, and a Proposed Quantum of Information Component: A Fourth Amendment Lesson in Contextual Reasonableness. Brooklyn Law Review 77(2):437–498

Cupido M (2021) Causation in International Crimes Cases: (Re)Concenptualizing the Causal Linkage. Criminal Law Forum 32(1):1–50. DOI: https://doi.org/10.1007/s10609-020-09410-0

Davison N (2017) A Legal Perspective: Autonomous Weapon Systems under International Humanitarian Law. In: UNODA Occasional Papers No. 30

Desportes F, Gunehec F Le (2000) Le Nouveau Droit Pénal. 7th edn. Economica, Paris

Dinstein Y (2018) Autonomous Weapons and International Humanitarian Law. In: von Heinegg W H, Frau R, Singer T (eds) Dehumanization of Warfare. Springer International Publishing, Cham, pp 15–20. DOI: https://doi.org/10.1007/978-3-319-67266-3_2

Dunlap C J J (2016) Accountability and Autonomous Weapons: Much Ado About Nothing. Temple International & Comparative Law Journal 30(1):63–76

Ekelhof M (2016) Human Control in the Targeting Process. In: Autonomous Weapon Systems: Implications of Increasing Autonomy in the Critical Functions of Weapons. ICRC, Versoix, pp 53–56

European Committee on Crime Problems (CDPC) (2020) Feasibility Study on a Future Council of Europe Instrument on Artificial Intelligence and Criminal Law. CDPC(2020)3Rev

Freitas P M, Andrade F, Novais P (2014) Criminal Liability of Autonomous Agents: From the Unthinkable to the Plausible. In: Casanovas P et al. (eds) AI Approaches to the Complexity of Legal Systems. Springer, Berlin, pp 145–156.. DOI: https://doi.org/10.1007/978-3-662-45960-7_11

Gaeta P (2016) Autonomous Weapon Systems and the Alleged Responsibility Gap. In: Autonomous Weapon Systems: Implications of Increasing Autonomy in the Critical Functions of Weapons. Expert meeting, Versoix, Switzerland, 15–16 March 2016. ICRC, Versoix, pp 44–45

Gaeta P (2023) Who Acts When Autonomous Weapons Strike? The Act Requirement for Individual Criminal Responsibility and State Responsibility. Journal of International Criminal Justice 21(5):1033–1055. DOI: https://doi.org/10.1093/jicj/mqae001

Gegan B E (1990) More Cases of Depraved Mind Murder: The Problem of Mens Rea. St. John's Law Review 64(3):429–469

Geiß R, Lahmann H (2017) Autonomous Weapons Systems: A Paradigm Shift for the Law of Armed Conflict?. In: Ohlin J D (ed) Research Handbook on Remote Warfare. Edward Elgar, Cheltenham, pp 371–404

Giannini A, Kwik J (2023) Negligence Failures And Negligence Fixes. A Comparative Analysis Of Criminal Regulation Of AI And Autonomous Vehicles. Criminal Law Forum 34:43–85. DOI: https://doi.org/10.1007/s10609-023-09451-1

Gogarty B, Hagger M C (2008) The Laws of Man Over Vehicles Unmanned: The Legal Response to Robotic Revolution on Sea, Land and Air. Journal of Law, Information and Science 19:73–82

Grut C (2013) The Challenge of Autonomous Lethal Robotics to International Humanitarian Law. Journal of Conflict and Security Law 18(1):5–23. DOI: https://doi.org/10.1093/jcsl/krt002

Hallevy G (2012) Unmanned Vehicles—Subordination to Criminal Law Under the Modern Concept of Criminal Liability. Journal of Law, Information and Science 21(200):200–211

Hallevy G (2016) The Criminal Liability of Artificial Intelligence Entities—from Science Fiction to Legal Social Control. Akron Intellectual Property Journal 4:171–201

Hart H L A, Gardner J (2008) Punishment and Responsibility. 2nd edn. Oxford University Press, Clarendon. DOI: https://doi.org/10.1093/acprof:oso/9780199534777.001.0001

Hart H L A, Honoré T (1985) Causation in the Law. 2nd edn. Oxford University Press, Oxford. DOI: https://doi.org/10.1093/acprof:oso/9780198254744.001.0001

Hart H L A (1968) Punishment and Responsibility: Essays in the Philosophy of Law. Clarendon Press, Oxford

Haugen F (2021) Former Facebook Product Manager, Testimony before U.S. Congress. www.youtube.com/watch?v=ZRu93KLU868. Accessed 7 October 2021

Hayward K J, Maas M M (2021) Artificial Intelligence and Crime: A Primer for Criminologists. Crime, Media, Culture: An International Journal 17(2):209–233. DOI: https://doi.org/10.1177/1741659020917434

Heyns C (2013) Report of the Special Rapporteur on Extrajudicial, Summary or Arbitrary Executions, A/HRC/23/47

Himmelreich J (2019) Responsibility for Killer Robots. Ethical Theory and Moral Practice 22(3):731–747. DOI: https://doi.org/10.1007/s10677-019-10007-9

Huffman W B (2012) Margin of Error: Potential Pitfalls of the Ruling in The Prosecutor v. Ante Gotovina. Military Law Review 211:1–56. http://hdl.handle.net/10601/2104. Accessed 4 August 2023

ICRC (2018) Ethics and Autonomous Weapon Systems: An Ethical Basis for Human Control?. Group of Governmental Experts of the High Contracting Parties to the Convention on Prohibitions or Restrictions on the Use of Certain Conventional Weapons Which May Be Deemed to Be Excessively Injurious or to Have Indiscriminate Effects, CCW/GGE1/2018/WP

Jain N (2016) Autonomous Weapons Systems: New Frameworks for Individual Responsibility. In: Bhuta N et al. (eds) Autonomous Weapons Systems: Law, Ethics, Policy. Cambridge University Press, Cambridge, pp 303–324 DOI: https://doi.org/10.1017/CBO9781316597873

Jain A G (2021) Autonomous Cyber Capabilities and Individual Criminal Responsibility for War Crimes. In: Liivoja R, Väljataga A (eds) Autonomous Cyber Capabilities under International Law. NATO CCDCOE Publications, pp 291–320

Kalmanovitz P (2016) Judgment, Liability and the Risks of Riskless Warfare. In: Bhuta N et al. (eds) Autonomous Weapons Systems. Cambridge University Press, Cambridge, pp 145–163. DOI: https://doi.org/10.1017/CBO9781316597873.007

Keiler J (2019) Actus Reus and Mens Rea: The Elements of Crime and the Framework of Criminal Liability. In: Keiler J, Roef D (eds) Comparative concepts of criminal law, 3rd edn. Intersentia, United Kingdom, pp 107–120

King T C et al. (2020) Artificial Intelligence Crime: An Interdisciplinary Analysis of Foreseeable Threats and Solutions. Science and Engineering Ethics 26(1):89–120. DOI: https://doi.org/10.1007/s11948-018-00081-0

Kurosaki M (2020) Toward the Special Computer Law of Targeting. In: Kreß C, Lawless R (eds) Necessity and Proportionality in International Peace and Security Law. Oxford University Press, Oxford, pp 409–436. DOI: https://doi.org/10.1093/oso/9780197537374.001.0001/oso-9780197537374-chapter-14

Kwik J (2022) A Practicable Operationalisation of Meaningful Human Control. Laws 11(3):43. DOI: https://doi.org/10.3390/laws11030043

Liu H-Y (2016) Refining Responsibility: Differentiating Two Types of Responsibility Issues Raised by Autonomous Weapons Systems. In: Bhuta N et al. (eds) Autonomous Weapons Systems. Cambridge University Press, Cambridge, pp 325–344. DOI: https://doi.org/10.1017/CBO9781316597873.014

Longobardo M (2019) Training and Education of Armed Forces in the Age of High-Tech Hostilities. In: Carpanelli E, Lazzerini N (eds) Use and Misuse of New Technologies. Springer International Publishing, Cham, pp 73–91. DOI: https://doi.org/10.1007/978-3-030-05648-3

Matthias A (2004) The Responsibility Gap: Ascribing Responsibility for the Actions of Learning Automata. Ethics and Information Technology 6(3):175–183. DOI: https://doi.org/10.1007/s10676-004-3422-1

McAllister A (2018) Stranger than Science Fiction: The Rise of A.I. Interrogation in the Dawn of Autonomous Robots and the Need for an Additional Protocol to the U.N. Convention against Torture. Minnesota Law Review 101:2527–2573

McDougall C (2019) Autonomous Weapon Systems and Accountability: Putting the Cart before the Horse. Melbourne Journal of International Law 20(1):58–87

Nersessian D L (2006) Whoops, I Committed Genocide! The Anomaly of Constructive Liability for Serious International Crimes. Fletcher Forum of World Affairs 30(2):81–106

Nissenbaum H (1996) Accountability in a Computerized Society. Science and Engineering Ethics 2(1):25–42. DOI: https://doi.org/10.1007/BF02639315

Oeter S (2020) Specifying the Proportionality Test and the Standard of Due Precaution: Problems of Prognostic Assessment in Determining the Meaning of "May Be Expected" and "Anticipated". In: Kreß C, Lawless R (eds) Necessity and Proportionality in International Peace and Security Law. Oxford University Press, Oxford, pp 343–366. DOI: https://doi.org/10.1093/oso/9780197537374.003.0012

Ormerod D (2008) Smith & Hogan's Criminal Law. 12th edn. Oxford University Press, Oxford

Pardo M S, Patterson D (2013) Minds, Brains, and Law. Oxford University Press, Oxford. DOI: https://doi.org/10.1093/acprof:oso/9780199812134.001.0001/acprof-9780199812134

van de Poel I et al. (2012) The Problem of Many Hands: Climate Change as an Example. Science and Engineering Ethics 18(1):49–67. DOI: https://doi.org/10.1007/s11948-011-9276-0

Pradel J (1995) Droit Pénal Comparé. Dalloz

Sandoz Y, Swinarski C, Zimmerman B (1987) Commentary on the Additional Protocols of 8 June 1977 to the Geneva Conventions of 12 August 1949. Martinus Nijhoff, Geneva

Sartor G, Omicini A (2016) The Autonomy of Technological Systems and Responsibilities for Their Use. In: Bhuta N et al. (eds) Autonomous Weapons Systems. Cambridge University Press, Cambridge, pp 39–74. DOI: https://doi.org/10.1017/CBO9781316597873.003
Saunders K W (1988) Voluntary Acts and the Criminal Law: Justifying Culpability Based on the Existence of Volition. University Of Pittsburgh Law Review 49:443–476
Shapira-Ettinger K (2007) The Conundrum of Mental States: Substantive Rules and Evidence Combined. Cardozo Law Review 28:2577–2596
van Sliedregt E (2012) Individual Criminal Responsibility in International Law. Oxford University Press, New York
Sparrow R (2007) Killer Robots. Journal of Applied Philosophy 24(1):62–77
Taylor I (2021) Who Is Responsible for Killer Robots? Autonomous Weapons, Group Agency, and the Military-Industrial Complex. Journal of Applied Philosophy 38(2):320–334. DOI: https://doi.org/10.1111/japp.12469
Thompson D F (1980) Moral Responsibility and Public Officials: The Problem of Many Hands. American Political Science Review 74(4):905–916
Thurnher J S (2014) Examining Autonomous Weapon Systems from a Law of Armed Conflict Perspective. In: Nasu H, McLaughlin R (eds) New Technologies and the Law of Armed Conflict. TMC Asser Press, The Hague, pp 213–228. DOI: https://doi.org/10.1007/978-90-6704-933-7_13
Toscano C P (2015) "Friend of Humans": An Argument for Developing Autonomous Weapons Systems. Journal of National Security Law & Policy 8(1):189–246
Trusilo D, Burri T (2021) Ethical Artificial Intelligence: An Approach to Evaluating Disembodied Autonomous Systems. In: Liivoja R, Väljataga A (eds) Autonomous Cyber Capabilities under International Law. NATO CCDCOE Publications, Tallinn, pp 51–66
Turton G, Kyd S (2019) Causing Controversy: Interpreting the Requirements of Causation in Criminal Law and Tort Law. Northern Ireland Legal Quarterly 70(4):425–444. DOI: https://doi.org/10.53386/nilq.v70i4.242
UK (2020) Expert Paper: The Human Role in Autonomous Warfare, Group of Governmental Experts on Emerging Technologies in the Area of Lethal Autonomous Weapons System Geneva, 21–25 September 2020 and 2–6 November 2020, Agenda Item 5. CCW/GGE1/2020/WP6
Väljataga A, Liivoja R (2021) Cyber Autonomy and International Law: An Introduction. In: Liivoja R, Väljataga A (eds) Autonomous Cyber Capabilities under International Law. NATO CCDCOE Publications, Tallinn, pp 1–11
Vincent N A (2011) A Structured Taxonomy of Responsibility Concepts. In: Vincent N A, van de Poel I, van den Hoven J (eds) Moral Responsibility: Beyond Free Will and Determinism, vol 27. Springer Netherlands, Dordrecht, pp 15–35. DOI: https://doi.org/10.1007/978-94-007-1878-4
Wallach W, Allen C (2013) Framing Robot Arms Control. Ethics and Information Technology 15(2):125–135. DOI: https://doi.org/10.1007/s10676-012-9303-0
Weigend T (2014) Subjective Elements of Criminal Liability. In: Dubber M D, Hörnle T, Weigend T (eds) The Oxford Handbook of Criminal Law. Oxford University Press, Oxford, pp 490–511. DOI: https://doi.org/10.1093/oxfordhb/9780199673599.013.0022
Williams R (2017) Lords Select Committee, Artificial Intelligence Committee, Written Evidence. AIC0206. http://data.parliament.uk/writtenevidence/committeeevidence.svc/evidencedocument/artificial-intelligence-committee/artificial-intelligence/written/70496.html#_ftn13. Accessed 7 May 2022

Chapter 13
Across the Spectrum of Intent

Contents

Abstract This chapter examines in detail the complete spectrum of fault degrees available in criminal law, from the highest levels of intent to no-fault regimes, to determine whether the challenges in establishing mens rea as found in Chap. 12 are uniform to all fault degrees. It is found it is not uniform, and that three main categories can be identified. First, conditions where no gap exists in practice: in situations where an AWS-user acts purposely or knowingly, criminal liability can generally be ascribed, even with AWS. Second, conditions leading to judicious gaps are similarly unproblematic: these refer to mental states corresponding to no intent (negligence or strict liability) where it is argued that an inability to hold anyone criminally liable is the *intended* result according to criminal law theory. The true problem is identified to lie in the medium levels of intent related to risk-taking, and particularly so in situations where the properties of AI obscure the nature and extent of the risk involved with a deployment decision: these are referred to as *unknown* and *generic risk*. Finally, the chapter also highlights the insidious situation of *manufactured ignorance*: this occurs where commanders *could* have known more specifically about the risk attached to the use of particular AWS through iterative analysis of prior deployments, but do not undertake this effort for practical or operational reasons. It is argued that future

J. Kwik, *Lawfully Using Autonomous Weapon Technologies*,
https://doi.org/10.1007/978-94-6265-631-4_13

discussions should focus on unknown risk, generic risk and manufactured ignorance, and on finding solutions in criminal law to remedy these gaps.

Keywords Autonomous weapon system · Artificial intelligence · Criminal liability · War crime · Responsibility gap · Mens rea · Intent · Risk-taking · Negligence · Opaque recklessness · Generic risk · Epistemic problem · Manufactured ignorance · Wilful blindness

13.1 Introduction

As established in the previous chapter, mens rea is potentially the most comprehensive challenge to criminal liability. At the same time, the form and extent of the cognition required for mens rea are not uniform, and reductions in perceivability can vary widely based on the factors in play.[1] AWS are not uniformly unpredictable, and not all fault degrees require 100% predictability. Both are dynamic variables that change casuistically. It is thus argued that blanket findings asserting a total inability to establish mens rea whenever AWS are involved are overly pessimistic.[2] Instead, we can identify very specific instances where issues may arise.

A more constructive approach, then, is to identify under which circumstances the epistemic problem has a higher likelihood of manifesting. This is the aim of the current section. To maintain structure, we will anchor ourselves in the fault degrees as outlined in Sect. 11.6. The range of fault degrees is a useful initial reference point because it naturally (and in the view of many, by design[3]) features a sliding-scale of increasingly lower epistemic demands. Under the common law scale for

---

[1] The system's complexity, XAI, online learning and the Candidate's technical background, amongst others, all impact the extent to which cognition is present.

[2] Some examples of such statements include:

- "The crux of the issue is that, by definition, AI robots will be unpredictable. … The main dilemma, perhaps, will relate to the application of international criminal law." Dinstein 2018, para 22.

- "[One major aspect] is salient for responsibility – the epistemic uncertainty that is built into the system design and that is in fact crucial to its successful functioning. If the conduct of an AWS is unpredictable by design, on what basis can a human agent be held responsible for this unintended and unanticipated action if it results in tremendous harm?" Jain 2016, p. 307.

- "[T]he unpredictability of[] an autonomous weapon system could make it difficult to find individuals … liable for serious violations of IHL. They may not have the knowledge or intent required for such a finding, owing to the fact that the machine can select and attack targets independently." ICRC 2016, pp. 81–82.

[3] See Weigend 2014, p. 493; Keiler 2019, p. 112.

example, 'knowingly' requires virtual certainty,[4] but 'recklessly' admits risk-taking as an epistemic state, i.e., awareness of only the *probability* of an outcome. As such, systematically going 'down the spectrum' allows us to stagger our discussion in terms of *how certain* our Candidate is of the AWS causing a violation, and what conditions would lead to such an epistemic state.

From this analysis, we find that the main challenge lies at the level of *intermediate and generic risk* and *situations of manufactured ignorance*. We also find that some concerns related to the epistemic problem are actually not endemic to the technology itself, but rather jurisdictional restrictions related to available fault degrees for targeting crimes. Once again, these findings refine our understanding of Premise 1 and how we can act to resolve the emergent issues. This nuanced perspective, with clear delineations indicating where the epistemic problem is a factor for concern, is also much more desirable from an academic and policymaking point of view. For academic discussions relying on the Responsibility Gap Problem, it refines Premise 1 by explaining specifically why and under what conditions the cognition requirement of mens rea fails, making the overall argument more robust and convincing. For policymaking, the clearly identified conditions allow for more structured and directed countermeasures to resolve the points of concern.

13.2 Dolus Directus: Desiring a Result

Dolus directus or 'purposely' involves a direct desire to bring about a certain result. Direct intent is understood relatively identically throughout the world's legal systems, including in international criminal law.[5] It is "intention in its purest legal and linguistic sense. It is 'acting in order' or 'deciding or seeking to bring about'".[6] As such, the volitive element (the "actor's will") is dominant.[7] Of course, AWS can potentially be used in this way. It is far from inconceivable that AWS can be deployed with the intention of committing a war crime, and many commentators have warned of this real possibility.[8] Soberingly, if not an indictment of the historic constant that is "[h]uman wickedness in warfare",[9] this is not at all a product of AWS technology. Deliberate misuse of military assets occurs with any weapon system,[10] and indeed,

---

[4] Ohlin 2013, p. 98.

[5] See e.g. van Sliedregt 2012, p. 40 (Germany, France); American Law Institute 1985, sct 2.02.(2).(a) (US); ICC (PTC), *Prosecutor v. Jean-Pierre Bemba Gombo*, Decision pursuant to Article 61(7)(a) and (b) of the Rome Statute on the charges of the prosecutor against Jean-Pierre Bemba Gombo, 5 June 2009, ICC-01/05-01/08, para 358 (international criminal law).

[6] Blomsma and Roef 2019, p. 180.

[7] Weigend 2014, p. 494.

[8] McFarland and McCormack 2014, p. 375; Amoroso 2020, pp. 131–32.

[9] Amoroso and Giodano 2019, p. 217.

[10] Meier 2019, p. 298.

with any technological development. "While the intent behind the research [into AI] is usually good, any developed technology could be used for good or evil purposes."[11]

As mentioned previously,[12] reduced perceivability actually does not prevent a Candidate from being held criminally liable if it is clear that they directly desire to bring about the outcome. Even if the Candidate is not exactly aware of the statistical probability that the AWS will target civilians, or is aware that there is only a low chance of this occurring, dolus directus can still apply, and society still maintains that this actor is worthy of the highest blame.[13]

It is not difficult to conceive of how actors involved with AWS can purposely commit war crimes using them.[14] Amongst others, Deployers can purposely make Context Control decisions with the aim of effectuating a war crime,[15] purposely deploy an AWS where they knew there was an incompatibility with the Intended Operational Environment (IOE) to provoke the violation,[16] or purposely not intervene with the intent of allowing a crime to occur.[17]

Note that in agreement with our above observation that cognition plays a lesser role in dolus directus cases, it is not necessary that Deployer knows with a high level of certainty that any of their actions *will* cause the civilians' deaths. Deployer's purposeful desire to bring about this result suffices. Even if Deployer knows that a desired error will statistically only manifest 10% of the time, this would not change our assessment that Deployer acted purposely.

---

[11] Yampolskiy and Spellchecker 2016, p. 2.

[12] Section 12.4.3.

[13] Speaking of the crime of murder more generally, Gegan explains: "[A]ll commentators start out with the intentional killing as the paradigm of the greatest culpability. Why? ... an intent to kill demonstrates the grossest form of indifference to human life. Where there is an intent to kill, the law is not concerned with the degree of risk *ex ante*. ... if it is proven that the actor's "conscious object" was to kill, and he succeeded, he is guilty of murder. Only in the case of an unintended killing does the law concern itself with the degree of risk *ex ante*." Gegan 1990, p. 447.

[14] For theoretical summaries of how AI can be used to commit crimes, see Hayward and Maas 2021; Yampolskiy 2015.

[15] For instance, they can rig the internal settings of antipersonnel system to make it execute civilians or deliberately order farmers moved into an AWS's operational space, knowing the system is not outfitted with the functionality to distinguish civilian from military persons. Cf. Sect. 13.3. See also Amoroso 2020, p. 132.

[16] It was argued that using an AWS outside of its Intended Operational Environment should be automatically considered as an indiscriminate attack under IHL in Sect. 9.3.2. For instance, an AWS can be "given a task beyond its capability so that it was destined to perpetrate a grave breach", such as using it in an area where civilians are present. Henderson et al. 2017, p. 364. See also ICRC 2016, p. 82. Note that here, blame attaches to the *positive* decision to deploy the system in combination with the *absence* of Context Control, whereas the first point concerns *active* Context Control measures to contrive the war crime's realisation.

[17] For instance, if Deployer knew a system was designed to also target civilians, and intentionally did not try to stop the action, they acted purposely. See Nasu and McLaughlin 2014, pp. 250–51. Failure to intervene is also one of the most likely ways an Operator would commit a crime purposely using AWS. See Sect. 11.3.

Broader Chain Candidates can also purposely commit war crimes using AWS. The racist labeller, for instance, would act with dolus directus, as would any person who intentionally programs a system to act contrary to IHL.[18]

As such, the reduced perceivability of AI does not produce an inability to prosecute actors where dolus directus is present. This is ***therefore a no-gap situation***, and many commentators rightly agree. "Criminal culpability [for AWS] is self-evident in the case of intent."[19] Quite simply, if "the person who launched the weapon intended to kill civilians, it would be a war crime",[20] and the same applies to BCCs: the "individual responsibility of a programmer who programmed, or a commander who ordered, an AWS to behave unlawfully is uncontentious".[21] The human ability to desire ('will') the manifestation of an atrocity is in no way impacted by a lack of technical understanding nor the system's autonomy, complexity, or opacity.

13.3 Dolus Indirectus: Certain Risk

With dolus indirectus or 'knowingly', the cognitive element takes priority, as it involves a "subjective, practical certainty that a particular result will occur in the ordinary course of events, but *without any positive desire to bring it about*".[22] This fault degree allows legal systems to ascribe intent to an actor who, without desiring it, knows a particular outcome will result from their action, and takes the action anyway.[23] With regard to the volitional element, this is often inferred from D's awareness of overwhelming risk. If D activates a system with the aim of expediently

[18] Another example would be the following: "[U]pon request by the military, a team of software developers program a class of AWS so that they will target civilian objects along with military objectives with a ratio of 1:15. This is intended to sap the enemy troops' morale. One of these AWS is subsequently employed to this end, resulting in the bombing of a hospital." Amoroso 2020, p. 133. This case also demonstrates how, depending on the actors involved, blame can be shared between BCCs of different levels and influence: here, both the military officers placing the order and the developers will be held liable. Amoroso and Giodano 2019, p. 218. Beard suggests that the officers would be regarded as principals while the developers would act as accessories or aiders or abettors to the crime, similarly to how the producers of Zyklon-B were prosecuted in 1946. Beard 2014, p. 649. Cf. British Military Court, *United Kingdom v. Bruno Tesch and Two Others*, 1 to 8 March 1946, I Law Reports of Trials of War Criminals 93, Hamburg. That mens rea can be established for BCCs in this case does not take away from the fact that prosecutors will likely still experience difficulties with the causality and control requirements, as argued in Sect. 12.2.

[19] Stürchler and Siegrist 2017.

[20] Scharre 2018, p. 261.

[21] Liu 2016, p. 329.

[22] Nersessian 2006, p. 83 (emphasis added).

[23] The Model Penal Code defines a 'knowing actor' as one who "is aware that it is practically certain that his conduct will cause such a result". American Law Institute 1985, sct 2.02.(2).(b). The ICC held that dolus indirectus "does not require that the suspect has the actual intent or will to bring about the material elements of the crime, but that he or she is aware that those elements will be the almost inevitable outcome of his acts or omissions". *Prosecutor v. Jean-Pierre Bemba Gombo*, above n. 5, para 358.

routing an enemy battalion stationed in a town, and this system (inevitably) also shoots down panicking townsfolk because it was not equipped with the functionality to recognise civilians, the Defence will not succeed by claiming that Deployer 'did not *want* to kill them':

> [A]n actor who does an act that he knows is very likely to cause a result is legally presumed to have "willed" this result, because the law does not accept the self-contradiction that lies in his assertion that he foresaw the result of his conduct but did not wish it to come about.[24]

Through all the ways Deployers can commit war crimes purposely using an AWS, they can also do so knowingly: only the subjective mental state changes. For instance:

- Deployer can choose to maximise Recall and sacrifice all Specificity,[25] knowing this will make the system shoot all enemy soldiers without fail but with the knowledge that it will also engage any civilian person it crosses.
- Deployer launches an IOE-incompatible system with the goal of relieving a unit caught in an ambush within a town, while being aware of warnings from the weapon developer that the classifier becomes indiscriminate in urban settings.[26]
- Deployer is aware that a system was developed with a racist bias but nevertheless continues to use it because it is so militarily efficient, even though Deployer knows that the operational area's population is predominantly of that ethnic group.

In none of these scenarios, Deployer aimed to kill the civilians, and all examples fulfil the Test of Failure:[27] Deployer is not disappointed if the civilians miraculously do survive, but is indifferent if they do perish. Dolus indirectus is also possible with respect to Broader Chain Candidates: take for example the reviewer who greenlights the distribution of an AWS they know is highly faulty, because the system is urgently needed to bolster a failing front line.[28]

It is submitted that for military systems, dolus indirectus scenarios will be more common than dolus directus scenarios. While the deliberate misuse of AI technology is very common in civil contexts such as trading, phishing, fraud and cyberterrorism,[29] it is argued that commanders and BCCs who wish to *deliberately* commit war crimes will be in the minority. Instead, the more likely scenarios will be those like the above: officers, developers, procurement officers, etc., who simply want to accomplish a tactical, strategic, political or economic goal, find that AWS provide an efficient way of achieving these aims, and accept that this entails IHL-noncompliance.

---

[24] Weigend 2014, p. 496.

[25] As discussed in Sects. 13.4.2.2 and 8.2.1, high Recall maximises the chances of striking valid targets even though this may also entail false negatives, while high Specificity minimises the chances of non-valid entities being targeted even though this may cause valid targets to escape unharmed.

[26] See Sect. 9.3.2.

[27] The Test of Failure is a tool sometimes used in criminal legal theory to distinguish dolus directus from indirectus. The test essentially asks: *If the envisaged result does not materialse, does the actor consider their plan to have failed?* See Blomsma and Roef 2019, p. 181.

[28] Again, this assessment with regard to the possibility to establish the reviewer's mens rea says nothing about how a prosecutor would prove causality and control. See Sect. 12.2.

[29] King et al. 2020, p. 90; De Arman 2019, p. 992.

The absence of direct intent to commit a war crime nevertheless does not prevent criminal liability from being attached. Dolus indirectus is present in many[30] legal systems as a form of intention, on par with dolus directus. Utter callousness and indifference can be just as reprehensible as actively desiring an outcome.[31] The "advertent taking of an obvious and overwhelming risk of a certain result" can be "considered to be just as deplorable as if it had been his or her primary purpose to bring about the result",[32] and in many systems, both the purposeful actor and the knowing actor are regarded as "just as culpable".[33] Such scenarios therefore ***also amount to a no-gap situation***.

13.4 Known Risk-Taking

Dolus eventualis, recklessness and conscious negligence all cover a mental state which is variably described as "advertent risk-taking", "conscious risk-taking",[34] "risk acceptance"[35] and 'disregard of a (unjustifiable) risk'.[36] It is sometimes also called constructive liability.[37] As noted in Sect. 11.6, we generally refer to the mental state associated with these fault degrees as 'risk-taking'. The common law term 'recklessness' intuitively describes that it involves risk-taking ventures: "a person is deemed reckless because he knowingly took the risk that his conduct would produce prohibited results".[38]

Like dolus indirectus, the cognitive element is dominant with respect to risk-taking, since the perpetrator does not have the outcome as their main aim. Instead, they foresee that their conduct might lead to this outcome, and accept this possibility. Criminal law nonetheless has an interest in punishing such behaviour. With risk-taking,

> the offender's aims are incongruent with the injury that actually results. Nevertheless, he is deemed to have sufficiently passed a moral threshold of wrongdoing to justify holding him liable for the irreversible consequences of his conduct.[39]

At this juncture, it is interesting to highlight the concept of probability ($\mathbb{P}$) since this ties strongly both with the statistical nature of AI-related performance measurements (which represent the *probability* of systems erring)[40] and the legal notion of

---

[30] But not all. France, for instance, does not recognise dolus indirectus. van Sliedregt 2012, p. 41.

[31] Weigend 2014, pp. 496–97.

[32] Bohlander 2008, p. 62.

[33] Blomsma and Roef 2019, pp. 181–82.

[34] Weigend 2014, p. 499.

[35] Amoroso and Giodano 2019, p. 222.

[36] Ohlin 2013, p. 88.

[37] Nersessian 2006, p. 88.

[38] Sherrin 2014, p. 720.

[39] Nersessian 2006, p. 86.

[40] See Chap. 4. The notion of $\mathbb{P}$ was used previously in Sect. 8.2.2.

D being aware of a *probability* of risk. As such, we will take some time to dissect the idea in greater detail, and consider what impact the greater transparency provided by quantitative probability indicators (such as accuracy and reliability metrics) may have.

13.4.1 Quantitative Risk and AI: Knowing Too Much?

A risk-taker acts at a lower epistemic state than those who act with intention.[41] Luban respectively distinguishes the two as "awareness of high probability" vis-à-vis "knowledge",[42] and Sherrin as 'uncertainty' versus 'certainty'.[43] Fletcher, speaking from a common law background, notes that a "major conceptual divide runs between the culpability of risk-taking (negligent, reckless, and even knowing risk-taking) and the culpability of intentions. The former is manifested exclusively in *running a particular objective risk*."[44]

It might seem odd, then, that throughout the previous subsection, we have sometimes referred to dolus indirectus as the acceptance of (an overwhelming) risk. This was not an error. While dolus indirectus technically is concerned with 'certainty' as to an outcome manifesting,[45] framing it as a 'risk' of an outcome manifesting is arguably more faithful to the idea that persons can never be *certain* of a future occurrence: they can only believe its likelihood to a maximal degree of certainty.[46] In this light, one could frame dolus indirectus as a form of risk-taking, albeit one where the probability ($\mathbb{P}$) of the risk is so overwhelmingly high that it becomes practically certain.[47] The separator between dolus indirectus and risk-taking can then also be construed as such: "The dividing line that runs between intent and risk-taking *is the degree of risk* that a certain consequence materializes."[48]

What is less clear is where, in terms of $\mathbb{P}$, the boundary exactly lies.[49] "[P]erhaps it is ninety percent certainty, ninety-five percent certainty, etc."?[50] In practice, our inability to represent this threshold numerically has been unproblematic. Generally,

---

[41] 'Intent' here is used as outlined in Sect. 11.6 to refer to the two highest fault degrees (dolus directus and indirectus).

[42] Luban 1999, p. 961.

[43] Sherrin 2014, pp. 720–21.

[44] Fletcher 1998, p. 120 (emphasis added).

[45] Sliedregt states for example that "[a]t this level, knowledge must amount to 'being certain'". van Sliedregt 2012, p. 41.

[46] Weigend 2014, p. 497.

[47] Note that dolus directus is not a type of risk-taking, since the concept of risk is subordinate to the concept of will.

[48] Van Sliedregt 2012, p. 42 (emphasis added).

[49] This matter has been debated by scholars for a long time. Luban 1999, p. 961.

[50] Sarch 2014, p. 1034.

drawing bright-lines in percentile points is an academic exercise only, as cognition is an internal mental state that can never accessed by outside observers. They are "inherently indeterminate concepts and the boundary between them is semantic and constructed rather than natural and immutable".[51] It is impossible to know, for instance, whether D was '95% confident' that a gunshot to the chest would kill a person, or only '90% confident' that a virus they created would successfully overload a nuclear power plant in enemy territory. Outside observers can only make a relative judgment of mens rea based on assumptions of "what the defendant must have known rather than what they did know".[52]

Increased transparency brought by AI can, however, change this dynamic. Say Deployer learns, based on a performance indicator, that releasing a system under the current conditions would involve $\mathbb{P} = 95\%$ of the system targeting a protected cultural site. Now, D's epistemic state is no longer internal: outside observers, including prosecutors and arbiters, *know* that D knew the risk to be 95%. As one can see, the importance of delineating the boundary between dolus indirectus and risk-taking potentially increases as such situations become more common.

The bottom boundary also becomes important. Say D chooses to use System S_{SP90} which has Specificity = 0.9 (i.e., it misidentifies civilians as combatants 10% of the time).[53] Is D 'accepting the 10% risk' of the system attacking civilians, and therefore wilfully[54] attacking them? Some would say yes through a broad interpretation of what constitutes risk-taking,[55] but others could also dispute this by pointing at the fact that risk-taking generally does not consider knowledge of low or 'empirically unlikely' risks as sufficient.[56] Once again, however, what would constitute 'low risk' is up for debate. As Henderson et al. remark, this

> would lead to difficult questions about what rate of error should cause an AWS to be regarded as unlawfully indiscriminate for its use to be regarded as causing the wilful death of civilians through recklessness.[57]

Sometimes, knowing too much can be just as burdensome.

We will not expand on this idea much further in this book, as this is a complex debate worthy of a separate analysis entirely. For the moment, we can nevertheless say some important things on this matter. One main point to retain is that the availability

---

[51] Jain 2021, p. 311.

[52] Ibid., pp. 311–12.

[53] See Sect. 13.4.2.2.

[54] We discuss whether 'wilful attack' constitutes dolus indirectus or eventualis below. See Sect. 13.4.2.

[55] Henderson et al. 2017, p. 363.

[56] "Chances that are empirically not likely to occur are not relevant for *dolus eventualis*". Blomsma and Roef 2019, p. 183. See also ICC (TC), *Prosecutor v. Thomas Lubanga Dyilo*, Judgment, 14 March 2012, ICC-01/04-01/06, para 1012; ICTY (AC), *Prosecutor v. Tihomir Blaškic*, Judgment, 29 July 2004, IT-95-14-A, para 41.

[57] Henderson et al. 2017, p. 363. As this was written as a chapter in a military-operational handbook, the use of 'wilful' here by the authors presumably is not meant to carry a specific meaning in criminal law terms (in the sense of intention).

of performance metrics can make the risks attached to AWS *more* transparent than with many legacy systems. These quantitative scores can also generate a shared epistemic reality between the decision-maker and auditors and judges, whereby *ex post* observers no longer need to infer what risk the decision-maker was aware of: they *know* what the decision-maker was aware of. This can create uncomfortable situations reminiscent to trolley problems where the definitive knowledge that an action will result with $x\%$ risk (and accepting it) seemingly makes the action more blameworthy than proceeding in relative ignorance of the exact probability.[58]

Second, the approach of not drawing definitive bright-lines between intention, risk-taking and (unconscious) negligence is likely to be the best approach for criminal law moving forward, despite the rise of more quantitative indicators of cognition. The reason for this position is that throughout the current subsection, we have spoken only of *unjustified* risk-taking.[59] This idea of reasonability is more pronounced in common law than continental approaches. For example, dolus eventualis requires awareness of an $x\%$ amount of risk (cognitive component) and acceptance of this risk (volitive component),[60] embracing our 'probability theory' more narrowly.[61] As a result, low risk-actions (in an empiric sense) are more likely to be rejected as dolus eventualis for the reason that, as noted above, adjudicators can only infer volition from other observable circumstances. In Germany, for instance, low $\mathbb{P}$ is often seen as

> an evidential indication that the actor did not accept the consequences occurring … The less likely a result was to occur, the more likely a court will … decide that the defendant did not accept this possibility.[62]

Similarly, Weigend remarks that because it is externally impossible to determine D's 'acceptance' of the risk, courts tend to infer the volitive element from $\mathbb{P}$. If $\mathbb{P}$ is high, the court is likely to accept dolus eventualis. If not, D is often regarded as having acted without intent, leaving open only negligence charges.[63] One critique of this approach is that it disregards baseline statistics. In the Netherlands, for example, a 1% chance of HIV transmission through intercourse was regarded as insufficient for dolus eventualis,[64] even though in medical terms, even a 0.5% chance of transmission is considered high.[65]

This is different in common law. Recklessness requires two elements to be fulfilled: (1) D's awareness of the risk and (2) that the risk be *objectively unreasonable*.[66] The Model Penal Code for instance provides that the

[58] Malle et al. 2015, sct 5.2.

[59] Cf. Sect. 13.6.

[60] Blomsma and Roef 2019, pp. 183–88.

[61] Ohlin 2013, p. 106.

[62] Blomsma and Roef 2019, p. 186.

[63] Weigend 2014, p. 501.

[64] Hoge Raad der Nederlanden, HR 18 januari 2005, NJ 2005, 154, ECLI:NL:HR:2005:AR1860.

[65] Blomsma and Roef 2019, p. 184.

[66] Nersessian 2006, p. 83; Sherrin 2014, pp. 720–21. It is not necessary for D to appreciate its unreasonability.

> risk must be of such a nature and degree that, considering the nature and purpose of the actor's conduct and the circumstances known to him, its disregard involves a *gross deviation from the standard of conduct* that a law-abiding person would observe in the actor's situation.[67]

Clearly, this 'standard of conduct' echoes Hart's concept of role responsibility[68] and agrees nicely with IHL's concept of the reasonable military commander.[69] IHL's reasonability standard being notoriously qualitative,[70] this in itself necessitates the conclusion that thresholds in percentage points of $\mathbb{P}$ are unsustainable: instead, courts will have to casuistically adjudicate whether the conduct falls within the realm of recklessness.[71] Thus, there is possibility that our continental S_{SP90} user would be acquitted of dolus eventualis because 10% is low in absolute terms, while common law prosecutors could make an argument that D acted recklessly because a reasonable commander would not have taken this 10% risk of harming civilians. Arguably, the latter is a more nuanced result.

These findings agree well with the risk management formula commonly used in engineering, $R = f(\mathbb{P}, C)$.[72] This expresses that *risk* is a function of *probability* and *possible harm*, whereby a higher probability of an occurrence might nonetheless be acceptable (i.e., reasonable) because the consequences are less serious, and vice versa. To determine if a risk is reasonable, recklessness also considers the *extent* of the harm in addition to the *probability* of it manifesting. Generally, "the more grievous the harm risked, the less likelihood one needs to believe it has of materializing" for it to count as reckless behaviour.[73] Thus, our S_{SP90} user might be regarded as acting reasonably if there is a 10% chance of damaging a civilian building, but recklessly if this happens to be a nuclear power plant.

There is therefore the possibility that in continental systems, D will try to argue that because $\mathbb{P}$ was objectively (and demonstrably, through adducing system logs) intermediate-to-low, they did not possess the requisite intent for dolus eventualis, even though we intuitively would consider the act rash and worthy of blame, e.g. because the consequences were so significant. (In contrast, common law prosecutors

---

[67] American Law Institute 1985, sct 2.02.(2).(c) (emphasis added).

[68] See Sect. 12.1.1.

[69] The question is "whether a reasonable man having such foresight would have proceeded with his conduct notwithstanding the risk". Blomsma and Roef 2019, p. 193.

[70] Corn 2012, pp. 451–52.

[71] This, however, also necessitates caution from the part of courts, as IHL's reasonability standard – originally conceived for military operations – has been criticised for being too imprecise as a criminal liability benchmark, potentially violating the principle of legality. See Sandoz et al. 1987, para 2187; Huffman 2012, p. 22. One solution advanced by Corn is that courts must use the reasonability standard judiciously, giving commanders any benefit of the doubt as to why they could have believed their conduct to be reasonable. "Proof beyond a reasonable doubt requires the prosecutor to exclude every fair and rational hypothesis except that of guilt." Corn 2012, p. 458.

[72] Where R is risk, $\mathbb{P}$ is probability of failure, and C is the cost associated with this failure. See Perrow 1984, p. 344; Chairman of the Joint Chiefs of Staff 2016, p. B-4; Parasuraman et al. 2000, p. 292.

[73] Sarch 2014, p. 1082. Weigend and Blomsma & Roef both cite this characteristic of recklessness as the express reason why fixed percentage points in terms of $\mathbb{P}$ cannot be assigned. Weigend 2014, p. 449; Blomsma and Roef 2019, p. 193.

can more easily adapt to unjustifiable-but-low-$\mathbb{P}$ risk-taking by inserting the $R = f(\mathbb{P}, C)$ formula into the equation, and characterising the act as unreasonable.) Whether the Deployer before the continental tribunal would succeed with this line of argumentation, however, is more dubious. Judges applying dolus eventualis would undoubtedly already take into consideration Deployer's (elevated) role responsibility and derive from circumstantial observations whether D truly believed everything would 'go alright'[74] or did know and reconciled themselves with the risk (however objectively small).[75]

In summary, the higher transparency with regard to risk and $\mathbb{P}$ introduced by AI technologies introduces interesting considerations for risk-taking fault degrees. In the past, jurists were content with only approximating the probability of risk D was aware of, and only could infer this from D's actions and external circumstances. With $\mathbb{P}$ becoming objective, there is a chance that increased impetus will manifest for establishing bright-lines in terms of $\mathbb{P}$ for thresholds between dolus indirectus, risk-taking and negligence. This section argued that in light of the $R = f(\mathbb{P}, C)$ formula, this is unwise: the threshold is variable and also depends on the possible harm and D's background and function. For Deployer, this role standard is elevated: they are expected to act as a reasonable military commander.[76] What seemed to be a possible gap (low-but-unreasonable $\mathbb{P}$ in continental systems) is in practice less likely to be one: judges will be trained to take the abovementioned factors into consideration.

We can thus hold at this point that purely doctrinally, 'standard' practices of risk-taking with AWS should not produce gaps. Then why do so many commentators foresee difficulties in holding AWS-users liable?

13.4.2 Gravitation Toward Risk-Taking, Mitigations, and Small Gaps

Just as it was argued above that dolus indirectus will be more common than dolus directus,[77] it is argued that risk-taking will be more common than dolus indirectus. In fact, it is submitted that the gap in frequency will be massive, and that the overwhelming majority of AWS cases will involve risk-taking at most. Let us call this *gravitation toward risk-taking*. Instances where Deployers purposely or knowingly use AWS to violate IHL will be the exception rather than the rule.[78] Bo is of the

[74] In which case D would only be liable for conscious negligence. See Sect. 13.4.2.

[75] For instance, the judge can find that D acted with manifest indifference to the risk, which is sufficient in many conceptions of dolus eventualis. As the ICTY also noted, "if the killing is committed with "manifest indifference to the value of human life", *even conduct of minimal risk* can qualify as intentional homicide". ICTY (TC), *Prosecutor v. Milomir Stakić*, Judgment, 31 July 2003, IT-97-24-T, para 587 (emphasis added).

[76] See Sect. 12.1.1.

[77] See Sect. 13.3.

[78] Amoroso 2020, p. 138.

similar opinion that most AWS operators "will not have intended to attack civilians, but [have] 'only' taken the risk of such occurrence".[79] While some wars such as the Yugoslavia conflicts do feature systematic targeting violations, these are the unusual cases.[80] The same applies for Broader Chain Candidates, whereby to rise above the level of risk-taking, they would have to deliberately design or permit systems they intend or know to be IHL-noncompliant. There is little indication of such malice in the military-industrial complex—quite the opposite is true.[81] Nothing suggests that developers and military organisations would intentionally and systematically create IHL-noncompliant AWS.[82]

Instead, it is argued that misuse will come from acquiescing to risks under operational pressure, a lack of care, or indifference. Commentators agree.[83] Gaeta argues that "[i]n most cases there will be no direct intent to use the autonomous weapon system to commit a war crime, but only an "acceptance of the risk" that the machine may take the wrong targeting decision".[84] Ohlin submits that "the most likely scenario is that the military commander was reckless in his deployment of the AWS, in the sense that he was aware of the risk that the AWS would violate a core prohibition in IHL, but the military commander decided to deploy the system anyway".[85] Väljataga and Liivoja also find that the "mental state of operators with respect to harm caused by autonomous systems is more likely to be negligence, recklessness or *dolus eventualis*".[86]

13.4.2.1 Jurisdictional Barriers

Given that risk-taking will be the most common type of mental state relevant to AWS use, and that risk-taking fault degrees exist in criminal law to capture most of these situations,[87] it is strange to note the ubiquity of the Responsibility Gap

---

[79] Bo 2021, p. 278.

[80] "Such misuse is not … a common scenario for most types of military engagements." Beard 2014, p. 662.

[81] Most States have confirmed in no uncertain terms their commitment to respect IHL with regard to their (prospective) AWS. Group. of Governmental Experts on Lethal Autonomous Weapons Systems (GGE on LAWS) 2019, Annex IV. E.g. US Office of General Counsel of the Department of Defense 2015, Law of War Manual, Updated December 2016. US Department of Defense, Washington D.C. (US Law of War Manual), sct 6.5.9.2 (US); Zhang 2016, p. 40 (China); Biontino 2017 (Germany); UK 2020, para 6 (UK).

[82] Toscano 2015, p. 207

[83] Beard 2014, p. 658; Amoroso and Giodano 2019, p. 223

[84] Gaeta 2016, p. 44

[85] Ohlin 2016, p. 26

[86] Väljataga and Liivoja 2021, p. 9. The mixing of risk-taking and negligence here by the authors is less important than the underlying argument that for AWS, the applicable fault degree will in any event likely lie 'below' intention.

[87] The mental state corresponding with conscious negligence (in continental forums) may be an exception to this, as discussed below.

Problem in the overall debate. If intentional and risky use of AWS can both be accommodated, where does the gap lie? The answer is rather surprising, and has to do with how Responsibility Gap Problem discussions are framed by many authors. For a prototypical example, consider the following quotes by Jain:

> The soldier who deploys or relies on [AWS] with reason short of certainty to doubt the IHL compatibility of the ensuing actions exposes a gap in the criminal enforcement of IHL.[88]
>
> The responsibility gap is concerned with the impossibility of intent to commit a war crime in the soldier who has reason short of certainty to believe that their deployment of or reliance on [AWS] might lead to an attack against civilian targets.[89]

Clearly, Jain is describing risk-taking (indicated by the phrase 'short of certainty'). As long as the risk is not very low or justifiable,[90] such actions can be covered by risk-taking fault degrees. Then why does she insist there is a gap? The answer is nestled in this following statement: "[this soldier] is difficult to accommodate within the mental element *required by the Rome Statute*".[91] Indeed, the Rome Statute's Article 30 is often interpreted both by commentators[92] and the ICC itself[93] as only admitting dolus directus and indirectus.[94] The reason for the gap Jain identified thus becomes clear: it arises out of the fact that the ICC does not accept risk-taking as a mental state for liability. Many other authors also limit their discussion to the ICC,[95] which leads to the same conclusion that there is a lacuna with respect to risk-taking endeavours using AWS, but taking these conclusions as representative of the idea that AWS technology as a whole generates a gap is clearly misleading. The ICC is not the only forum to try war crimes and will likely play a minimal role in prosecuting AWS-related harms compared to domestic courts, where the limitation to only dolus directus and indirectus is less likely to exist.[96]

---

[88] Jain 2021, p. 302.

[89] Ibid., p. 312.

[90] See Sect. 13.6.

[91] Ibid., p. 300 (emphasis added).

[92] Schabas 2017, pp. 221–23; van Sliedregt 2012, p. 47; Ohlin 2013, p. 102; McDougall 2019, p. 66.

[93] *Prosecutor v. Jean-Pierre Bemba Gombo*, above n. 5, para 360; ICC (TC), *Prosecutor v. Germain Katanga*, Judgment Pursuant to Article 74 of the Statute, 07 March 2014, ICC-01/04-01/07-3436-tENG, para 775.

[94] Note that there is also the needed controversy in this respect. See Bo 2021, pp. 284–95; Werle and Jessberger 2005, p. 52; Dörmann 2003, p. 43. Some judgments of the ICC have contradicted this position explicitly, allowing dolus eventualis. ICC (PTC), *Prosecutor v. Thomas Lubanga Dyilo*, Decision on the Confirmation of Charges, 29 January 2007, ICC-01/04-01/06, para 352; *Prosecutor v. Thomas Lubanga Dyilo*, above n. 56, para 1012.

[95] See e.g. Buchan and Tsagourias 2021; Ohlin 2016; Amoroso and Giodano 2019.

[96] One conceptual question that can be posed is whether war crimes prosecuted under risk-taking can justifiably be considered as international crimes on the same level of graveness as those prosecuted under intention. This touches upon complex questions related to labelling. See e.g. Nersessian 2006, p. 96. Ohlin has raised these concerns with respect to AWS: "is it really appropriate to convict this military commander for the exact same crime as the war criminal who *intentionally* targets civilians or intentionally executes a fallen soldier who is *hors de combat* or a prisoner of war? Surely, the war criminal who commits these intentional crimes (whether by his own hands or indirectly through the

How do we know that domestic enforcement will likely not encounter the same problems as asserted by abovementioned authors? While this may certainly vary by jurisdiction, risk-taking generally is a readily accepted fault mode in domestic forums.[97] "In many, if not most, domestic systems, a mens rea below *dolus directus* or intention warrants full criminal responsibility of the offender. Common standards are recklessness and *dolus eventualis.*"[98] Second, as indicated above,[99] AWS-related harms will likely result in charges based on (domestic implementations of) API Article 85.[100] This article's *mens rea* standard is 'wilfully', which is widely considered to encompass "intention or recklessness, [but] not simple negligence".[101] At most, we can say that a gap emerges *where risk-taking is not allowed as a fault degree for targeting crimes*, but this is not an indictment of the technology itself.[102]

13.4.2.2 Egregious Risk-Taking

Another mitigating variable in favour of the conclusion that the gap is narrower than expected relates to what we shall term *egregious risk-taking*. The idea here is that within the higher echelons of ℙ, courts may categorise acceptance of a substantial risk as a form of dolus indirectus, even though it technically does not reach the level of 'practical certainty'.[103] A person who launches a system that has a 90% probability of misclassifying civilians knows of the very high likelihood that the attack will be indiscriminate.[104] Reading dolus indirectus strictly, a 10% chance of this *not* occurring might be large enough to argue that there was no 'practical certainty'.

---

deployment of an AWS) is much more culpable than the commander who has recklessly deployed an AWS that fails to abide by the restrictions imposed by IHL. As it stands now, there is no convincing way to codify these distinctions". Ohlin 2016, p. 27. We will leave this normative discussion here as this is an outstanding issue that applies to all international crimes.

[97] Nersessian 2006, p. 86; Sherrin 2014, p. 732.

[98] Werle and Jessberger 2005, p. 51. For international tribunals, see e.g. ICTY (TC), *Prosecutor v. Tihomir Blaškic*, Judgment, 3 March 2000, IT-95-14-T, para 152.

[99] Sect. 11.2.

[100] In contrast, States that directly implement or translate the Rome Statute for criminalising war crimes would maintain the ICC's limitation to only dolus directus and indirectus. See e.g. Wet internationale misdrijven. BWBR0015252 (1 januari 2020) (NLD).

[101] ICTY, Final Report to the Prosecutor by the Committee Established to Review the NATO Bombing Campaign Against the Federal Republic of Yugoslavia, 2001, www.icty.org/en/press/final-report-prosecutor-committee-established-review-nato-bombing-campaign-against-federal (accessed 4 August 2023) (NATO Report), para 28. See Sandoz et al. 1987, para 3474; ICTY (TC), *Prosecutor v. Stanislav Galić*, Judgment, 5 December 2003, IT-98-29-T, para 54; ICTY (TC), *Prosecutor v. Momčilo Perišić*, Judgment, 6 September 2011, IT-04-81-T, para 100.

[102] There will also be the practical realities of domestic war crime prosecutions to consider, since these frequently include a political element. States that are generally not keen on enforcing IHL compliance would also not be inclined to prosecute reckless Deployers. This is a critique on such States' commitment to IHL enforcement, and not necessarily on the technology.

[103] Luban 1999, p. 961.

[104] In the sense that this is an attack that uses "a method or means of combat which cannot be directed at a specific military objective" as prohibited by Protocol Additional to the Geneva Conventions

However, courts may be prepared to accept this as dolus indirectus through inference. AI metrics only make $\mathbb{P}$ public knowledge in empirical terms: how this was *perceived* by D is another matter entirely, and remains locked to outside observers—once again making inference indispensable.[105] For instance, would a person truly observe a prognosis of *90% chance that civilians will mistakenly be shot*, and think 'Sure, but there is a 1-in-10 chance that this attack *will* be discriminate, so let's do it'? A prosecutor may argue that at that point, any normal person would depart from the assumption that the attack *will* be indiscriminate (making it a case of dolus indirectus), and the court may be inclined to agree.[106] Thus, even in legal systems that do not accept risk-taking fault degrees, instances of egregious risk-taking using AWS may nevertheless, in practice, be prosecuted under dolus indirectus. This limits the responsibility gap further.

13.4.2.3 The Overly Optimistic Deployer

There is one exception to this finding that no true gaps exist with regard to risk-taking, and that concerns the mental state corresponding to *conscious negligence*. This describes the situation where D "is conscious of the risk, but trusts in a good outcome. He does not take it for granted, but thinks everything will be all right".[107] This mental state was grouped under 'risk-taking' in Sect. 11.6 for descriptive purposes, but is classed under culpa (not dolus) in continental systems. As an example related to AWS, one can think of a good faith (perhaps overly naïve) Deployer who knows the system is untested in snowy conditions, but 'trusts' that this will not impact the system's performance.

In common law, this person could be liable under recklessness if the risk is unreasonable, but the absence of volition would prevent continental judges from going beyond conscious negligence.[108] Because war crimes are generally not tried under

---

of 12 August 1949, and relating to the Protection of Victims of International Armed Conflicts, adopted 8 June 1977, entered into force 7 December 1978, 1125 UNTS 3 (API), Article 51(4)(b). This action would be prosecuted under subparagraph (a) or (b) of Article 85.3, depending on the exact circumstances.

105 "[I]t is hard to determine—and even harder to prove—what went on in the defendant's mind at the time the offense was committed. But whether or not the law explicitly says so, proof of intention can often be inferred from the objective facts … so that on the whole proving intention does not create insurmountable problems." Weigend 2014, p. 508.

106 Luban calls this "converting the word "knowledge" into a legal term of art". Luban 1999, p. 961. Jain also argued that "the probative practice of inferring intent from conduct and circumstances allows for the assimilation of egregious cases of recklessness or *dolus eventualis* into the category of intent, notwithstanding the conceptual impossibility of intent". Jain 2021, p. 311.

107 Blomsma and Roef 2019, p. 196.

108 The logic would be similar to that described in Hoge Raad der Nederlanden, *Porche-arrest*, HR 15 oktober 1996, NJ 1997, 199, ECLI:NL:HR:1996:ZD0139, para 5.5.

negligence,[109] one could technically call the inability to hold overly optimistic[110] Deployers liable in continental systems a gap, albeit a minor one.[111] Even if we do, however (i.e., answering Question (c) in Sect. 11.5 in the affirmative), the question that follows is whether we would necessarily *want* to extend criminal liability to this good-faith but unduly optimistic person. We return to this matter in Sect. 13.6.

13.5 Unknown and Generic Risk-Taking

In the previous section's title, one may notice that the word 'known' was added before 'risk-taking', but that this inclusion was not explained or motivated in the text. The word 'known' refers to the heightened transparency provided by AI metrics, and most of our discussion in the previous section revolved around the legal ramifications of having $\mathbb{P}$ so readily available. But AI technology can simultaneously—and somewhat paradoxically—also create an effect in the opposite direction, *obscuring* what risk D is exactly taking. As we will see, this is a much larger threat to the application of risk-taking fault degrees that goes relatively unappreciated.

Let us first start with some baseline assumptions. We shall presume a mental state whereby D knows unequivocally that their action is risky, i.e., $0 < \mathbb{P} < 1$. Assuming knowledge of the existence of risk should be uncontroversial with respect to activities such as weapons release, and indeed military operations in general.[112] With regard to what crime D risks committing, for simplicity, let us just limit ourselves to API Article 85(3)(a), (b), and (4)(d), i.e. making civilians the object of an attack, launching a disproportionate attack, and attacking undefended specially protected monuments, respectively.[113] The former two crimes are tied to the "death or serious injury to body or health" of civilians and the latter to the "extensive destruction" of the object, and the connection between AWS failures (e.g. misclassifications) and said harm is easy to make. Thus, D is always aware of the risk of weapon imperfections that may result in harm to protected persons or objects (as is any weapons deployer). When such

---

[109] As noted in Sect. 13.4.2.1, 'wilfully' in API, above n. 104, Article 85 explicitly excludes negligence. McDougall also notes more generally that "[i]nternational criminal law has also not generally recognised negligence as being sufficient to establish criminal guilt for the majority of international crimes". McDougall 2019, p. 67.

[110] "[U]nwarranted optimism" is often used to describe a consciously negligent person's mindset. Weigend 2014, p. 509.

[111] One possible mitigation, to the extent that this is deemed desirable, is that conscious negligence is often tried as dolus eventualis or unconscious negligence instead as it occupies a rather awkward space in continental systems. Weigend 2014, p. 509. See also Blomsma and Roef 2019, pp. 196–97. It is thus possible that for AWS-cases, the same shift to dolus eventualis or unconscious negligence will also occur in practice.

[112] NATO 2019, para D.5

[113] Under the Rome Statute, equivalent crimes can be found in Article 8(2)(b)(i-iv) and (ix).

harm does manifest,[114] however, D's criminal liability under risk-taking fault degrees depends on the risk they foresaw when they made the deployment order. If this risk is sufficiently high or unreasonable, they can be liable, as discussed above.[115] So far, so good.

Some aspects of AWS and how they will be used in the field, however, can potentially obscure the risk related to its deployment *objectively*[116]—i.e., making it so D factually does not know enough about the risk of deployment to fulfil the cognition element. It is argued this comes in two forms: *unknown risk* and *generic risk*. In addition, unknown and generic risk can be contrived by deliberately avoiding precautionary measures that would provide information to alleviate it. We shall call this *manufactured ignorance*. This section's main argument is that criminal law (in conjunction with IHL) is relatively badly equipped to deal with these situations. We shall now discuss them in turn.

13.5.1 Unknown Risk

Unknown risk refers to risks which are factually present within a given deployment decision, but which are very difficult if not impossible to detect, at least initially (before they manifest for the first time).

In Chap. 5, we have spoken about the many factors that can cause failures, and which are often unintuitive, unperceivable and undetectable, even after rigorous testing. Take for example biases that cause the AWS's accuracy to drop substantially in the presence of a population with a specific skin pigment, or undetected edge cases which cause the AWS to make successive misclassifications because a specific type of building happens to be prevalent in current battlefield. Objectively speaking, the risk produced by these triggers can be substantial, say a 50% chance of the AWS causing hundreds of civilian casualties or bombing a historic monument. 50% is a coin flip, and under any conception of risk-taking, D should be liable for wilfully making civilians the target of attack or attacking a protected object. However, in this situation, cognition was factually lacking because D could not have known about the fact that their AWS was so unreliable until it was too late.

Factors discussed in Sect. 12.4.2, such as complexity, opacity and lack of technical training may also lead to unknown risk manifesting. Take for instance the leader of a small battalion of insurgents who just received a 'very accurate' AWS from foreign donors but has no prior training with the system, or the commander who receives an opaque AWS with only a '*Proven! 99% accuracy rate*' note. Say that

[114] These crimes are result-crimes, meaning criminal liability is only triggered when such harm indeed does occur. Bartels 2013, p. 300.

[115] We disregard the volitive element required for dolus eventualis, and focus on the cognitive requirement to streamline the discussion.

[116] This should be contrasted with the situation where D *did* know the risk at the time of commission, but it is hard for external observers such as judges to determine ex post what D's mental state was at the time.

we, as omniscient observers, know that this AI (mistakenly, through an incorrect proxy[117]) learnt to identity combatants by the form of military helmets. Armed with this information, we would also know that sending this system into an area where villagers have taken a liking to wearing old helmets left behind after the prior civil war would likely result in a large number of misclassifications. Both our commanders above, however, cannot know this, and no matter how rash we may perhaps find it to use a weapon we have no training in or whose decision-making mechanism we do not understand, cognition is lacking in a criminal law sense.

Unknown risk is the true face of the epistemic problem raised in Sect. 12.4.1, and is a problem not even the availability of risk-taking fault degrees can resolve, at least by itself. Unknown risk must be addressed in cooperation with military best practice to address the root causes of the ignorance, such as making the system less complex, adding more XAI, and providing more technical training. The problem of (lack of) incentives to realise this we discuss in Sect. 13.5.3. There may also be situations where the risk is so unknowable that we might find the intervention of criminal law to be inappropriate, despite the enormous harm caused: this circumstance we discuss in Sect. 13.6.

13.5.2 Generic Risk

Say now that instead of receiving 'very accurate' systems, our two commanders are in the following situation:

- Our insurgent leader receives some antimateriel AWS, hastily smuggled across the border to the village they are defending, with no information at all other than the promise that it will help them alleviate an encirclement of their position by government armour. They look the system up online and find several articles mentioning misclassification incidents of buildings, although none have taken place in a rural setting. They decide not to waste more time, and deploy the system.
- Our commander receives some antimateriel AWS touted as being highly reliable. However, they read in the manual that the system is 'untested in snowy conditions', and it just happens to be snowing that day. Pressed to capture the village before it is reinforced, the commander releases the system.

In both situations, the system malfunctions and destroys a specially protected monolith in the village's centre, which provokes international outrage. Have they knowingly engaged in risk-taking in the mens rea sense?

It is probably fair to criticise these persons for acting brazenly. Faced with a similar situation, a decently prudent officer would probably have erred on the side of caution and refrained from using the systems. Clearly, all information available indicated that releasing the systems could end badly. It is arguably in the interest of IHL to

[117] See Sect. 4.5.2.

deter this type of brash risk-taking, particularly reckless IOE-incompatible weapon releases as demonstrated by our second commander.[118] However, their conception of risk was limited to just this general feeling of 'something could go wrong'. Neither envisaged that their AWS would target a stationary monument, and certainly did not foresee that the monolith would be destroyed.

The problem is that here, the commanders are operating under what Kalmanovitz terms 'Level-2 Uncertainty', or "uncertainty about the probabilistic range of action".[119] In other words, they are unsure even of the exact probability of risk—and to what or whom—entailed by the deployment decision; they only recognise that releasing the weapon constitutes 'risky business'. We shall call this *generic risk*. Generic risk is to be contrasted with Level-1 Uncertainty, where a $\mathbb{P}$-value is available to D (this corresponds to 'known risks' in the previous section, which Kalmanovitz agrees is unproblematic from a criminal law perspective).[120]

The extent to which generic risk is a problem depends on "how concrete or exacting the defendant's conception of the risk needs to be" in the criminal legal system under consideration.[121] Does prosecuting the commanders require foresight of (the risk of) *exact* harm ('I might destroy the monolith'); a *category* of harm ('I might destroy a protected object'); or simply a *general notion* that a harmful occurrence might result ('This system seems iffy')? Arguably, this incident can only be prosecuted if the third and most general type of epistemic state is admitted, since in both cases the commanders lacked awareness even of the possibility that their anti-armour AWS might target monuments at all.[122]

The problem that emerges with generic risk is that legal conceptions of risk-taking which cover this last epistemic state ("simply be[ing] aware that there is a substantial and unjustifiable risk of a 'dangerous' occurrence"[123]) are quite rare: most legal systems require a link between D's cognition and the harmful outcome with at least some specificity. The result is that instances of generic risk can potentially result in a gap. Ferzan argued as much by giving an example of a carefree driver who, while speeding through a red light, causes a pedestrian to be killed.[124] Like our commanders above, any normal driver would recognise that speeding through a red light is 'risky business'. Ferzan argues that nevertheless, charging the driver with reckless killing

---

[118] It was argued that weapon releases in conditions not corresponding to the Intended Operational Environment would be contrary to IHL in Sect. 9.3.2. However, criminal liability requires more than just IHL noncompliance.

[119] Kalmanovitz 2016, p. 156.

[120] Ibid.

[121] Jain 2016, p. 317.

[122] Analysing this mental state at face value, it would correspond most with (unconscious) negligence, since the only statement that can be made with respect to D's awareness is that they *should* have been aware of the risk. The potential problem arises when we make the normative judgment that this type of lax behaviour *should* fall within the criminal law sphere of risk-taking, which for the examples cited above, is not an unreasonable position to adopt.

[123] Jain 2016, p. 317.

[124] Ferzan 2001, p. 597. Ferzan refers to what we have called generic risk as 'opaque recklessness'. We will not use this term to avoid confusion with the term 'opaque' in AI terms.

will be difficult because the specific thought '*I might kill someone by running this light*' required for recklessness likely never crossed D's mind.[125]

Aggravating the situation is that the level of generality induced by AI is far worse than that experienced by a driver running a red light. With Farzan's example, an argument could be advanced that a normal person would have considered the possibility of a pedestrian crossing the road, raising the level of uncertainty from Level-2 to Level-1.[126] Making a similar argument with respect to the monolith attack is quite difficult. This is a key point: the dynamic and open-ended nature of AI will make generic risk a far more common occurrence than with legacy systems. Some authors have made comments to this effect.[127] Bartels perhaps presents the best summary of the problem of generic risk: "Even though the attacker would normally know that a weapon system could fail and miss a target, he would not necessarily have known that the system would fail in this particular instance."[128] That AWS-users will be faced with Level-2 Uncertainty is almost inevitable. It is inherent in the complexities of AI and how dynamically they operate.

To illustrate why this is an AI-intrinsic problem that applies less to legacy systems, let us compare the cognitive states of two commanders. Commander-A is equipped with a rocket system and Commander-B with an AWS, and each hopes to disable enemy tanks within a city. Both were given performance indicators in the form of Circular Error Probable (CEP) and accuracy metrics respectively, and must decide whether or not to use their weapons in light of factual operational conditions. Assume also *arguendo* that intelligence is complete and accurate, meaning that both commanders have perfect information. The subsequent decision-making process will be quite comparable. The commanders will consider the probability of failures, what effect this will have on the civilian population, and decide whether this risk is reasonable.

[125] As Ferzan elaborates, "for you to have been reckless here, you must have consciously disregarded the substantial and unjustifiable risk that you could kill someone as a result of your actions. But you did not engage in this mental calculation. While you knew that there was some inherent danger in running the red light, you certainly never thought, "well, I might kill someone but I am going to run that light anyway"". Ibid., p. 598.

[126] And even this may be difficult. A famous judgment by the Dutch Supreme Court indicates that such situations would be evaluated as conscious negligence at most. The *Porche* case concerned a drunk driver who made multiple attempts to overtake a car on a 2-lane road. After hesitating on three attempts, the driver finally persisted on the fourth try and crashed violently into a car in the opposing lane, killing all its passengers. The Appellate Court ruled that the driver possessed conditional intent to kill the victims, but this was reversed by the Supreme Court, which found that the driver's prior behaviour indicated his earnest (but misplaced) belief that the fourth attempt would be successful. In the Court's words, the driver had "*meermalen—kennelijk om een botsing te vermijden—een ingezette inhaalmanoeuvre ... afgebroken vooraleer de in de bewezenverklaring bedoelde fatale inhaalmanoeuvre uit te voeren, hetgeen er op wijst dat althans in de voorstelling en naar de verwachting van de verdachte laatstbedoelde manoeuvre niet tot een botsing zou leiden*". *Porche-arrest*, above n. 108, para 5.5.

[127] Chengeta posits that a commander "may not anticipate all the actions of the robot. As a result of that unpredictability, it is difficult if not impossible to establish a guilty mind". Chengeta 2016b, p. 24. See also e.g. Stewart 2011, p. 290; Davison 2017, p. 17; McDougall 2019, p. 68.

[128] Bartels 2013, p. 280.

Say now that both are quite hot-headed individuals. They order the deployment of the weapons, but something goes wrong.

- Commander-A's salvo deviates wildly, and hits a market on the edge of the projected CEP range, causing massive civilian casualties. According to the CEP table, a hit in this area had a 20% chance of occurring.
- Commander-B's AWS temporarily glitches because of a reflection of sunlight off of a church's stained-glass windows and fires a missile against a market, causing massive civilian casualties. Later analysis suggests this failure forms part of the 20% inaccuracy statistic noted in AWS's manual.

In both scenarios, the commanders 'knew' of the 20% risk of something going wrong in terms of general statistics. However, their ability to foresee *what is entailed* by such a failure rate was very different. An artillery commander has a very limited set of possibilities to consider as to what could result from the failure rate manifesting. Invariably, the rocket will land *somewhere*. Thus, if the area surrounding the target location is predominantly civilian housing, they 'know' they are taking a 20% risk of hitting said civilian concentrations.

In contrast, what will happen when an AWS fails is less clear, even if we know that it is unreliable 20% of the time. Commander-B is aware of *a* risk, but not any risk in particular. The system might attack a personnel carrier, a bus, a horse-drawn cart, a building, friendly forces—or do nothing at all. Note that the attacked target was a market—something that in our human eyes, looks nothing like a tank.[129] Thus, even if Commander-B correctly took into consideration the risk to civilian vehicles, it is unlikely they could have anticipated this particular counterintuitive misclassification. In other words, the seemingly identical $\mathbb{P}$-statistic produced different levels of uncertainty in practice. It was enough to inform Commander-A of the 20% risk that civilian objects would be hit, but only informed Commander-B that 20% of the time, *something* would not go as planned.

13.5.3 Iteration and Manufactured Ignorance

When discussing unknown risk, we ended by stating that the unknown can be made known, at least partially,[130] through measures to address the root causes of the reduced perceivability of AI (such as XAI or more training). Another way the unknown can become known is through *iteration*.

Say that after an incident where our previous antipersonnel AWS gunned down farmers who were tending their fields while wearing old civil war helmets, it becomes known that the system identifies enemy combatants by the shape of their headwear.

---

[129] This example also demonstrates that unknown risk (of the stained-glass edge case) and generic risk (of the 20% probability of something going wrong) may coincide in certain situations.

[130] Some risk can never be known until it manifests, even with all the testing in the world. Scharre 2018, p. 83; McDougall 2019, p. 75.

The next time this commander contemplates using this system, the risk is no longer unknown: if the commander continues using this system in a similar village setting the following day, the argument could be made that they are wilfully attacking civilians,[131] because they know of the high likelihood that the system will misclassify them.

Similarly, iteration can render generic risk no longer generic. If after the market incident, an after-action analysis indicates that the system glitched temporarily because of the reflection from a stained-glass window, this particular edge case no longer forms part of the vague 20% statistic—it becomes a *specific* risk that has a particular cause and consequence. Thus, if two days later, this commander is aiming to capture another town famous for its medieval chapels and releases the same system, they have the requisite cognition for criminal liability: the prior incident put them on notice of the known risk of their AWS failing. This seems, therefore, to be a silver lining to our conclusions regarding unknown and generic risk. Even if a gap does manifest, it can only do so *once*.

13.5.3.1 Iteration in a Non-Idealistic Reality

This, however, assumes many ideal conditions that are not guaranteed in practice. Primarily, it assumes faithful implementation of Assessment Awareness[132] by commanders involved in AWS deployments. It requires that after AWS-related incidents (and indeed, to achieve best practice,[133] after each deployment), an investigation and technical analysis is conducted of the system's performance, near-misses, and failures and what caused these failures. This would reveal that the helmet-proxy was the cause of the farmer incident, and stained-glass was the cause of the market incident.

However, such due diligence is certainly not guaranteed. Commanders may be pressed for time and prefer to defer the analysis until after the current operation ends; have difficulties finding technical staff; or cannot access all necessary data (e.g. the exact inputs received by the AWS at the moment of failure) to perform the analysis because the area is not under friendly control. In the period of delay between the incident and when the analysis is carried out, the risk remains unknown or generic, even though it is *technically* knowable.

One could argue that after the first incident, it is blameworthy to continue using the system, and that a prudent commander would have retried the system until this

[131] It was held in *Galić* that "indiscriminate attacks, that is to say, attacks which strike civilians or civilian objects and military objectives without distinction, may qualify as direct attacks against civilians". *Prosecutor v. Stanislav Galić*, above n. 101, para 57. Whether this argument could lead to criminal conviction in this iterative example is up for debate.

[132] See Sect. 2.4.6.

[133] "The commander is responsible for ensuring the force takes into account the requirement to capture lessons learned during all stages of an operation and that an appropriate mechanism has been established from the beginning." NATO 2019, para E.5.

analysis is performed, just to be safe.[134] While one could assert this from an IHL perspective, omitting an analysis certainly does not translate into legal proof of cognition of a specific risk. In addition, the accused could reasonably advance the counterargument that they genuinely assumed the incident to be a one-time accident instead of a structural error (such as a mistaken proxy). As we will see in Sect. 13.6, criminal enforcement of IHL *must* cater to genuine accidents to remain legitimate, so we cannot eliminate the possibility of defendants using this argument. "Mistakes or faulty weaponry can result in outcomes that IHL aims to prevent, but these outcomes do not necessarily constitute violations of IHL as they were not intended by the attacker."[135]

There are more logistical problems with the idealistic picture of perfect Assessment Awareness. Say identical models of the same AWS are used by different battalions spread across a theatre, and Commander-A takes note of the stained-glass edge case after an incident occurs. The week after, Commander-A wisely refuses using this system in a chapel-rich region. However, this same day that Commander-A correctly avoids this risk (a risk that is now known and specific), a similar incident occurs 50 km further north in a town attacked by Commander-B using a sister system, triggered by the same edge case. Theoretically, one can criticise the military organisation's suboptimal implementation of Assessment Awareness: ideally speaking, Commander-A should have immediately communicated their findings to all colleagues who are using the same model AWS, 'spreading' the cognition of risk around.[136] In reality, however, Commander-A has not done so, and Commander-B therefore did not possess the necessary cognition of the risk. Many more such constructions can be envisaged, where the risk is technically specific and knowable, but in practice is not.

Note that from an IHL and operational perspective, the obligations incumbent upon militaries using AWS are clear and uncontroversial: performing measures to obtain the necessary Assessment Awareness *is* required.[137] "In IHL, [after-action] review is part of a State's duty to exhibit 'constant care' in reducing needless harm to civilians."[138] The US Manual also files "After-Action Assessments and Investigations" under its obligations to implement feasible precautions in planning and conducting attacks.[139] However, defaulting on this obligation is not a grave breach,

---

[134] Buchan and Tsagourias 2021, p. 340.

[135] Bartels 2013, p. 280. Indeed, international criminal law is known to place an even higher bar before criminal liability can be established for crimes such as disproportionate attacks, which under the Rome Statute require the expected harm to be "clearly excessive" vis-à-vis the anticipated advantage. Rome Statute of the International Criminal Court, adopted 17 July 1998, entered into force 1 July 2002, 2187 UNTS 90 (Rome Statute), Article 2(b)(iv). As Rogers notes, this higher standard was intended to limit liability to "cases where the excessiveness of incidental damage was obvious, not in cases that involved errors of judgement by commanders in the field". Rogers 2000, p. 180. See also Sect. 13.6.

[136] Margulies 2012, p. 304.

[137] Henderson et al. 2017, p. 369.

[138] Margulies 2021, p. 177.

[139] US Law of War Manual, above n. 81, sct 5.11.1.3.

and this transgression cannot be legally transformed into criminal liability for war crimes such as attacking civilians. The problem is the multi-step nature of the process. Failing to properly implement Assessment Awareness 'only' causes lowered cognition, and this lowered cognition 'only' acts as a barrier to foreseeing the risk of subsequent harms. Lowered cognition itself is not a grave breach.

13.5.3.2 Contrived Ignorance

Finally, we arrive at possibly the most insidious prospect. If Candidates are aware that they currently are operating within a state of unknown or generic risk and that this creates obstacles to prosecution if harm does occur, they may prefer to maintain this status quo rather than take steps to improve their cognition. Even if lack of cognition can be remedied by diligently implementing Assessment Awareness (sharing data of previous engagements, improving technical training programmes, incorporating more XAI, etc), there is no direct incentive to encourage this and every incentive not to. Thus, it may be the case that militaries or commanders prefer to avoid or minimise abovementioned cognition-improving measures to:

- Reduce the possibility of criminal prosecution;
- Allow deniability of the accused's awareness of risk, if prosecution does occur;
- Avoid operational inconveniences, such as

  Commanders, in good faith, retiring an entire fleet of AWS because they heard of an edge case by a colleague, or
  Commanders, in good faith, avoiding the use of a highly effective AWS that could have won the military a battle because they are cognisant of a risk (which they could have been ignorant of until the battle was won), or
  Commanders being unable to use an AWS in a crucial battle because an incident is being analysed by technicians.

Ignorance can be convenient.

Note again that these are all obligations falling under precautionary duties in IHL. Substantive IHL is not the issue. However, because criminal law provides no incentives to take these measures, it becomes attractive to remain blissfully ignorant. This contrived ignorance cannot engender criminal liability for the harm that is 'caused' (in a colloquial sense of the word) by it,[140] meaning people will not be deterred from (and in fact may be rewarded by) doing it.[141] Evidently, this is a highly

[140] Deliberately staying ignorant as a tactic to avoid criminal liability is of course not unique to AWS, and criminal law has developed doctrines such as wilful blindness to address them. See Luban 1999, p. 959.

[141] This does not imply that IHL is strictly reliant on criminal prosecution to uphold its rules. Many have pointed out that criminal liability is only a subsidiary way to increase IHL compliance. E.g. Marauhn 2014 1; Anderson and Waxman 2013, p. 17. However, it cannot be denied that it weakens the protection afforded by IHL if prospective perpetrators *know* that remaining ignorant is the best way to reduce the risk of future prosecution.

perverse result which clashes with IHL's idea that constant care must be exerted to reduce risk to civilians,[142] but unlike other problematic practises that similarly clash with IHL's core principle,[143] manufactured ignorance is not punishable as a grave breach. This is thus a genuine concern and one which ideally must be addressed when discussing possible remedies.

13.6 Judicious Gaps

In our discussion of manufactured ignorance, we mentioned that criminal law 'must cater' to genuine accidents to remain legitimate. Take for instance the stained-glass incident one more time. We had some reservations with this commander's conduct because they seemed reckless in releasing a system with a 20% failure rate (in that initial discussion) or because they declined to investigate the incident, which led to a repeat event (in our discussion about iteration). Say now that the system only had a 0.5% failure rate—low enough to say that our commander was reasonable in their decision-making[144]—and it was indeed the very first time that the edge case manifested. But this edge case had catastrophic consequences: 200 marketgoers were killed. Should they be held liable for causing this massive civilian casualty event?

13.6.1 Criminal Law Acting as Intended

Undoubtedly, the market incident will provoke widespread media attention and international outrage.[145] There will be cries for the commander to be criminally prosecuted. When we apply a criminal liability analysis to this event, however, we will certainly find a gap. The failure trigger was very unusual, and the output entirely unforeseeable (recall that the system in question was an antitank AWS, but the glitch caused it to shoot a market). Under no circumstance can it be argued that the commander had the necessary cognition, and they will go free despite the 200 deaths. Is this justified? The answer is yes. This is a *genuine accident*, and despite the likely public moral recoil at the apparent injustice, it *must* go unpunished.[146] It has been emphasised in this book that perfect systems with 0% failure rates do not

[142] UN General Assembly 1970, para 3.

[143] E.g. complete disregard for civilian life by launching indiscriminate weapons.

[144] Let us assume in any event that this decision was in conformity with indicators provided in Sect. 9.3.1 concerning when an AWS can be considered as capable of distinguishing.

[145] The intensity of the condemnation will increase further because of the inherent controversy related to AI technologies and the perceived sophistication of the AWS-wielding belligerent, who may be characterised as 'terrorising' or 'bullying' the poor marketgoers. See Schmitt 2007, pp. 468–69; Blum 2011, p. 175.

[146] Note that the marketgoers' families and survivors will not go entirely without a remedy. The fact that this is a 'genuine accident' does not preclude them from claiming reparations from the

exist, and that IHL cannot impose such a no-failure condition on belligerents.[147] If it does, IHL will lose any credibility and will be discarded,[148] making the situation on the battlefield worse overall.

The same is true for the criminal law enforcement of IHL. Imposing criminal liability for an unforeseeable and unavoidable event such as this would be "fundamentally unfair".[149] Criminal law principles do not only exist to safeguard victims' rights, but also those of the accused.[150] Thus far, we have only spoken of elements such as cognition as hinderances to holding (sometimes obviously blameworthy) persons responsible. However, many cases such as this will also exist, where the requirements of mens rea block criminal law from overreaching and creating scapegoats in the face of high public pressure. We shall call these *judicious gaps*: circumstances where a responsibility gap does exist in the sense that 'no Candidate is available', but where this is the correct outcome. As Liu argues, "the fight against impunity for the development and deployment of AWS must be tempered with limitations to prevent the law from perpetrating injustice".[151] Upholding judicious gaps is the way to do this.

One may disagree with the characterisation of this situation as a 'gap': surely, that such accidents are not punished is a basic function of criminal law, not a lacuna. However, the inability to prosecute genuine accidents involving AWS is frequently sketched as problematic, and many commentators have made such statements.[152] As an illustration, consider the following quote:

> The application of the law, however, is particularly challenging if all involved human beings deployed the autonomous weapons system under the assumption that it works perfectly well and *without acting negligently or with the intention of harming protected persons*. Rather, the scenario at issue is one in which the unpredictability inherent in any autonomous weapons systems materializes in unlawful damage on the battlefield, that is, where an *otherwise perfectly functioning robot unexpectedly kills a human being*.[153]

The text summarises well how a gap materialises in such a situation, but errs in its framing. The application of the law is not 'challenged' in such situations. The fact that no one can be held criminally responsible where there is no intent, recklessness or

State involved in that operation. The point is that a *criminal* remedy will be unavailable to them, and that this is the 'correct' result.

[147] See Sect. 9.3.1.

[148] Fenrick 2005, p. 168.

[149] Weigend 2014, p. 490.

[150] Sartor and Omicini 2016, p. 64.

[151] Liu 2016, p. 342.

[152] See e.g. Sartor and Omicini 2016, p. 69 (sketching as problematic the responsibility gap that emerges from "a military system that is usually highly precise in computing missile trajectories may under exceptional environmental conditions fail to work appropriately, causing unjustified harm to civilians); Chengeta 2016a, p. 875 (arguing how there is a gap where "a combatant with no intentions to commit any crime deploys an AWS to kill legitimate targets but the system—because it has decision-making powers exercisable without the intervention of a human—makes an unlawful choice").

[153] Geiß and Lahmann 2017, p. 392 (emphasis added).

negligence and where the incident was entirely unexpected *is* the correct application of the law. The intensity of harm does not change this.

> AWS, like any other system, will at times not otherwise operate as intended. Unfortunately, this may result in civilian casualties. Provided such casualties are unintentional, then there is no reason to suppose that commanders will be held criminally liable for the unintended actions of the AWS.[154]

Several other commentators agree.[155] Jain submitted, almost matter-of-factly, that the "soldier who has no reason to doubt the prospective IHL-compliance of [AWS] but is implicated in a breach of IHL is not culpable and need not concern us further".[156] Crootof stated simply that "[a]bsent … willful human action, no one can—*or should*—be held criminally liable".[157]

Thus, we are speaking of a gap, but it is a judicious one, for any other result would be unfair vis-à-vis the accused. Any framing of the inability to prosecute such AWS-related incidents as being problematic, or even as a reason to ban the technology, is thus highly misleading. Any discussion on the Responsibility Gap Problem must include the word 'fair' in Premise 1, for without it, it is unsustainable as an argument. Alternatively, one can see judicious gaps as a refutation for Premise 2: not all instances of impunity are problematic, and therefore, impunity cannot be used as a prohibitory argument against a particular technology.

13.6.2 What Makes a Gap Judicious?

A few additional notes must be made with respect to judicious gaps. First, what types of failures do we consider as 'justly' resulting in a judicious gap? There are two: genuine accidents and acceptable risk. There is no definition of what constitutes a

[154] Henderson et al. 2017, p. 369.

[155] McDougall 2019, p. 75; Taylor 2021, p. 322.

[156] Jain 2021, p. 299.

[157] Crootof 2016, p. 1375.

'genuine accident',[158] particularly in terms of criminal liability as we discuss it here, but we might make do with some characteristics. A genuine accident is one:

- In which, notwithstanding all feasible precautions employed, a failure occurs;[159]
- Where $\mathbb{P}$ of failure was extremely low;[160]
- Where there was no foreseeability of the outcome, despite due diligence[161] or extensive technical training of persons involved;[162] or
- Involving a system failure.[163]

In addition, situations of *reasonable risk-taking* should evidently also result in a lack of prosecution. The proportionality rule in IHL admits by design that weapon inaccuracies can occur and that this is acceptable, as long as the anticipated civilian harm is not excessively disproportional to the military gain.[164] Thus, if a commander properly calculates how much incidental harm will likely be accrued throughout the AWS's attack[165] and finds this proportional vis-à-vis the anticipated military advantage, they are acting within *reasonable risk*. They are not wilfully attacking civilians, nor engaging in a disproportionate attack, despite acting with full conscience of the

---

[158] For a good narrative example of a genuine accident, consider the following scenario by Liu:

> [C]onsider an individual fulfilling the role of a programmer, manufacturer or commander of an AWS. The individual is clearly responsible for fulfilling the expectations and obligations that attach to his/her function in relation to the AWS, but this equally becomes the full extent of his/her responsibility. When he/she has fulfilled these obligations, he/she is deemed to have acted responsibly. For example, a programmer has discharged his/her role responsibility if he/she has taken sufficient care to ensure that his/her algorithms function according to the requirements. A manufacturer has fulfilled his/her duties where the AWS has been built according to the design specifications. A commander who has taken the necessary steps in deploying the system has satisfied the obligations of his/her position. Where an AWS nevertheless goes wrong, the individual in each instance would have discharged his/her role obligation.

Liu 2016, p. 337.

[159] Toscano 2015, p. 237. See also Kalmanovitz 2016, p. n36; Dunlap 2016, p. 71.

[160] Sartor and Omicini give an example of "a military system that is usually highly precise in computing missile trajectories may under exceptional environmental conditions fail to work appropriately, causing unjustified harm to civilians". Here they argue that "nobody is at fault, nobody is blameworthy—and, thus, nobody, it seems, should be criminally liable". Sartor and Omicini 2016, p. 69.

[161] Geiß and Lahmann 2017, p. 393.

[162] Jain 2016, p. 319; Dunlap 2016, p. 69.

[163] McLaughlin 2014, p. 236. See Sect. 5.9.

[164] Holland 2004, p. 50.

[165] For an analysis as to what extent an operation involving an AWS can be grouped into a single attack in IHL terms for the purposes of proportionality calculations, see Sect. 9.2.

risks that this deployment will pose to the civilian population.[166] This type of calculated risk-taking is entirely within the boundary of standard operations sanctioned by IHL,[167] and AWS technology makes no difference in this matter.

Secondly, note that we have been very careful to note that all scenarios spoken about above concern *first occurrences*. No matter how unlikely, unexpected or unforeseeable a failure is, it is only unexpected the first time it occurs. Repeated accidents no longer remain genuine, since their causes could have been identified and remedied after the first occurrence. Thus with iteration, a genuine accident can transform into a situation of manufactured ignorance, which according to our prior analysis *is* a problematic gap.

There are some outstanding questions. In Sect. 13.4.2, we discussed the overly optimistic Deployer who, while appreciating a risk exists, trusts everything will go OK. We concluded at that time that in continental systems, this mental state would fall under conscious negligence, i.e., outside of dolus. Assuming war crimes cannot be prosecuted on the basis of negligence,[168] this would thus be a 'gap', and unlike the situations discussed above of genuine accidents or miniscule risk, one may see some blameworthiness (or at least undesirable behaviour) in these persons' actions. The question is whether we view this behaviour as falling under the *criminal* sphere. This question is left open at this time as a point of reflection: if yes, then we are dealing with another (albeit limited) gap.[169]

13.7 Conclusion: Across the Spectrum

This final section is both retrospective and prospective. First, we review the findings of previous sections and emphasise where, across the spectrum of intent, the true problems vis-à-vis the Responsibility Gap Problem for AWS lie. This part address Questions (a)–(c) as listed in Sect. 11.5. Subsequently, having identified where the main gaps lie, we summarise our findings regarding the *desirability* of bringing these mental states into the criminal law sphere, responding to Question (d). Finally, having narrowed down the issue to only those gaps that are genuinely problematic or which provide perverse incentives, some preliminary recommendations are issued for future

[166] Cf. API, above n. 104, Arts. 85(3)(a), (b).

[167] For a full analysis, see Ohlin 2013.

[168] As noted in Sect. 13.4.2.1.

[169] The current author has doubts whether we should, and feels that the many alternative forms of responsibility listed in Sect. 11.2 may suffice in addressing the consciously negligent Deployer, particularly in combination with more constructive efforts like encouraging the Providing Entity to develop a military culture that is more risk-sensitive. For example, the US DoD has a quite stringent risk mitigation culture, demanding that "[p]otential risk mitigation(s) shall be identified, and the expected risk reduction(s) of the alternative(s) shall be estimated and documented". US Department of Defense 2012, p. 12. Such good practices go a long way in preventing this type of overly optimistic behaviour of Deployers.

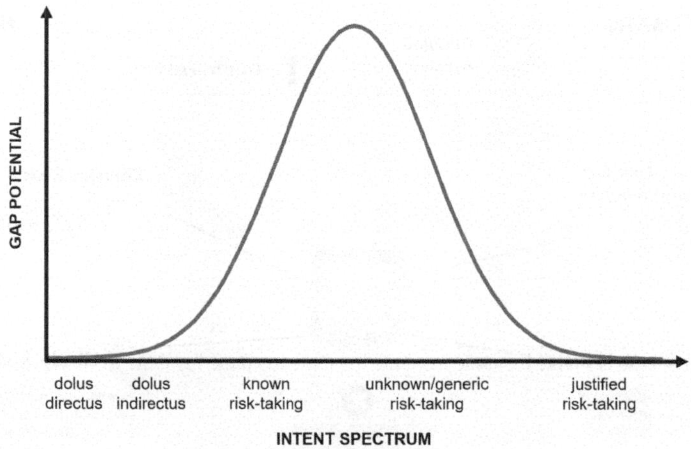

Fig. 13.1: Bell-curve of difficulty across the spectrum

research, particularly by noting the properties a solution would need to possess to be effective, thereby responding to Question (e).

If we take the level of intent as a proverbial x-axis and the challenges introduced by AWS technology as a y-axis, we can imagine a type of bell-curve emerging as illustrated in Fig. 13.1.

At the higher levels of intent (dolus directus, dolus indirectus), there is no problem: such mental states are not impacted by AI technology, and almost all legal systems allow these fault degrees when prosecuting war crimes. Moving right, to known risk-taking, we also find that there are minimal conceptual problems, and even that enhanced transparency can facilitate ex post analysis of a Candidate's epistemic state. Concerns about gaps in this regard concern mostly jurisdictional limitations, particularly if legal systems such as the ICC are used as a point of reference, since these do not recognise risk-taking as a fault degree. A minor potential gap was found here with regard to the overly optimistic Deployer in continental systems, whose mental state most likely corresponds to conscious negligence. The question was left open, however, whether (continental) criminal law should bring this type of person into the dolus-sphere, or whether the 'current' result is the most equitable one.

Moving further right, we encounter the main crux of the challenges: unknown risk, generic risk, and manufactured ignorance. Many legal systems have no or limited answers to these mental states, and the result is that actors with such mental states may escape criminal liability, despite being intuitively blameworthy from an IHL perspective.

Finally, at the far right, while a 'gap' technically does exist (in the sense that persons involved in such accidents cannot be found to possess the requisite mens rea for prosecution), these are situations where criminal law's lack of involvement is *desirable.* A state of 'impunity' will result in the presence of genuine accidents,

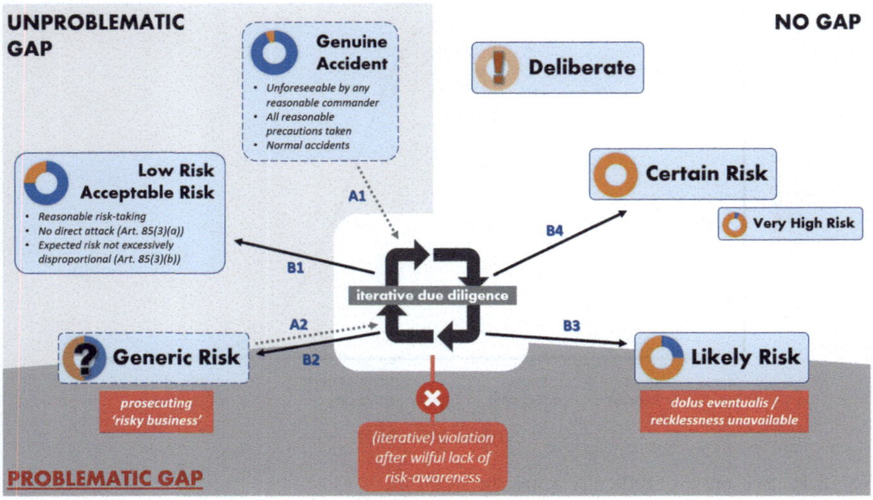

Fig. 13.2 No-gaps, problematic gaps, and judicious gaps

system failures and reasoned risk-taking, but this is a judicious result. Criminal law works as intended here by *enforcing* a gap, preventing scapegoating.

Viewed in another way, and inserting a more temporal dimension, we can also represent our findings as illustrated in Fig. 13.2.

This graphic better captures the role of Assessment Awareness and the problems that emerge if not properly executed. We can distinguish a sector called 'No Gap' in the top-right, representing situations where establishing mens rea should not pose problems. The sector 'Unproblematic Gap' in the top-left contains situations where a gap is desirable to protect the accused from scapegoating.

The true challenges are located in the bottom sector, 'Problematic Gap' (i.e., there will be gaps, and they are not desirable). *Likely Risk* is placed in a grey zone between No Gap and Problematic Gap because this epistemic state is mainly problematic if the jurisdiction does not allow risk-taking for war crimes ('*dolus eventualis/recklessness unavailable*'). *Generic Risk* also has a jurisdictional component: it becomes a significant problem if the legal system requires a more precise link between D's epistemic awareness of risk and the outcome, which occurs in the majority of criminal law systems ('*prosecuting 'risky business'*'). It is placed in a grey area between Problematic and Unproblematic Gaps, however, since generic risks may also be very unlikely risks, in which case they may also fall under low-risk situations or genuine accidents.

The true problem that emerges relates to *iterative situations involving generic risk and genuine accidents.* In an ideal system, such events are immediately subjected to Assessment (arrows ***A1*** and ***A2***). From this Assessment process ('*iterative due diligence*'), commanders may find that the incident:

- [**B1**: Assessment → *Low/Acceptable Risk*] Was a truly rare occurrence and which is unlikely to repeat, or which still falls within acceptable risk in terms of proportionality ();[170]
- [**B2**: *Assessment* → *Generic Risk*] Cannot yet be explained, but that the commander is henceforth put on notice that such a failure can possibly manifest again, making repeat use of the system riskier than before the incident occurred;
- [**B3**: Assessment → *Likely Risk*] Is likely to repeat again, meaning that the commander will act recklessly if they do re-release the system;
- [**B4**: *Assessment* → *Certain Risk*] Is certain to repeat again, meaning that the commander will act knowingly if they do re-release the system.

As we can see, from the lens of an *ideal* system, one occurrence will be the maximum. After an incident manifests, the commander will have the necessary cognitive state for prosecution if they do act rashly and continue using the system (*Likely* or *Certain Risk*), and might refrain from using the system if the risk is present but as of yet indeterminate (*Generic Risk*), just to be safe. Unfortunately, continued use in the presence of generic risk itself is not always easy to prosecute, and failure to effectuate the entire Assessment Awareness process cannot be linked to any harm that is eventually 'caused' by the lack of cognition it precipitates. It is this gap that the international community should be most concerned about, and take active efforts to close.

Finally, let us consider some constructive recommendations for future research. At this point, we have identified the (few, but still concerning) circumstances where Premise 1 of the Responsibility Gap Problem holds: there are certain conditions, primarily brought about by AWS technology, that cause Candidates whom we would find desirable to punish to possibly escape criminal liability. Primarily, we found that this concerns the following:

- Known risk-taking (*note*: primarily jurisdictional limitation);
- Generic risk-taking;
- Manufactured ignorance (through failure to ensure Assessment Awareness, instate proper technical training, install cognition-improving features such as XAI, etc.).

This list should inform future studies and discussions regarding what problems must mainly be focused on in the search for an effective response to Responsibility Gap Problem-related concerns. Having diagnosed the problem, we can proceed in a more systematic and methodical way to find legal means to resolve its symptoms. An ideal measure in response to these concerns is one which would provide the necessary legal tools to address all issues at once. It is unlikely such a singularly effective solution exists, but a solution that succeeds in addressing a majority of them would already be quite valuable. The author hopes to return to this issue in a later work.

---

170 With regard to the higher standard for prosecuting disproportionate attacks, see also this chapter n135.

References

American Law Institute (1985) Model Penal Code: Complete Text of Model Penal Code as Adopted at the 1962 Annual Meeting of The American Law Institute at Washington, D.C. American Law Institute, Philadelphia

Amoroso D, Giordano B (2019) Who Is to Blame for Autonomous Weapons Systems' Misngs?. In: Carpanelli E, Lazzerini N (eds) Use and Misuse of New Technologies. Springer International Publishing, Cham, pp 211–232. DOI: https://doi.org/10.1007/978-3-030-05648-3

Amoroso D (2020) Autonomous Weapons Systems and International Law : A Study on Human-Machine Interactions in Ethically and Legally Sensitive Domains. Nomos Verlagsgesellschaft, Baden

Anderson K, Waxman M C (2013) Law and Ethics for Autonomous Weapon Systems: Why a Ban Won't Work and How the Laws of War Can. In: American University Washington College of Law Research Paper No. 2013-11. Stanford University, Stanford

Bartels R (2013) Dealing with the Principle of Proportionality in Armed Conflict in Retrospect: The Application of the Principle in International Criminal Trials. Israel Law Review 46(2):271–315. DOI: https://doi.org/10.1017/S0021223713000083

Beard J M (2014) Autonomous Weapons and Human Responsibilities. Georgetown Journal of International Law 45:617–681

Biontino M (2017) General Statement by H.E. Ambassador Michael Biontino, Permanent Representative of Germany to the Conference on Disarmament and Ambassador for Global Disarmament Affairs. First Meeting of the Group of Governmental Experts on Lethal Autonomous Weapons Systems, Geneva, 13 to 17 November 2017

Blomsma J H, Roef D (2019) Forms and Aspects of Mens Rea. In: Keiler J, Roef D (eds) Comparative concepts of criminal law, 3rd edn. Intersentia, United Kingdom, pp 177–206

Blum G (2011) On a Differential Law of War. Harvard International Law Journal 52(1):164–218

Bo M (2021) Autonomous Weapons and the Responsibility Gap in Light of the Mens Rea of the War Crime of Attacking Civilians in the ICC Statute. Journal of International Criminal Justice 19(2):275–299. DOI: https://doi.org/10.1093/jicj/mqab005

Bohlander M (2008) Principles of German Criminal Law. Bloomsbury Publishing, London

Buchan R, Tsagourias N (2021) Autonomous Cyber Weapons and Command Responsibility. In: Liivoja R, Väljataga A (eds) Autonomous Cyber Capabilities under International Law. NATO CCDCOE Publications, Tallinn, pp 321–347

Chairman of the Joint Chiefs of Staff (2016) Joint Risk Analysis. CJCSM 310501

Chengeta T (2016a) Defining the Emerging Notion of "Meaningful Human Control" in Autonomous Weapon Systems. International Law and Politics 49:833–890

Chengeta T (2016b) Accountability Gap: Autonomous Weapon Systems and Modes of Responsibility in International Law. Denver Journal of International Law & Policy 45:1–50

Corn G S (2012) Targeting, Command Judgement, and a Proposed Quantum of Information Component: A Fourth Amendment Lesson in Contextual Reasonableness. Brooklyn Law Review 77(2):437–498

Crootof R (2016) War Torts: Accountability for Autonomous Weapons. University of Pennsylvania Law Review 164:1347–1402

Davison N (2017) A Legal Perspective: Autonomous Weapon Systems under International Humanitarian Law. In: UNODA Occasional Papers No. 30

De Arman A (2019) The Wild, Wild West: A Case Study of Self-Driving Vehicle Testing in Arizona. Arizona Law Review 61(4):983–1012

Dinstein Y (2018) Autonomous Weapons and International Humanitarian Law. In: von Heinegg W H, Frau R, Singer T (eds) Dehumanization of Warfare. Springer International Publishing, Cham, pp 15–20

Dörmann K (2003) Elements of War Crimes under the Rome Statute of the International Criminal Court: Sources and Commentary. Cambridge University Press, Cambridge

Dunlap C J J (2016) Accountability and Autonomous Weapons: Much Ado About Nothing. Temple International & Comparative Law Journal 30(1):63–76

Fenrick W J (2005) International Humanitarian Law and Combat Casualties. European Journal of Population / Revue européenne de Démographie 21(2-3):167–186. DOI: https://doi.org/10.1007/s10680-005-6421-y

Ferzan K K (2001) Opaque Recklessness. Journal of Criminal Law and Criminology 91(3):597–652

Fletcher G P (1998) Basic Concepts of Criminal Law. Oxford University Press, New York

Gaeta P (2016) Autonomous Weapon Systems and the Alleged Responsibility Gap. In: Autonomous Weapon Systems: Implications of Increasing Autonomy in the Critical Functions of Weapons. Expert meeting, Versoix, Switzerland, 15–16 March 2016. ICRC, Versoix, pp 44–45

Gegan B E (1990) More Cases of Depraved Mind Murder: The Problem of Mens Rea. St. John's Law Review 64(3):429–469

Geiß R, Lahmann H (2017) Autonomous Weapons Systems: A Paradigm Shift for the Law of Armed Conflict?. In: Ohlin J D (ed) Research Handbook on Remote Warfare. Edward Elgar, Cheltenham, pp 371–404

Group of Governmental Experts on Lethal Autonomous Weapons Systems (GGE on LAWS) (2019) Report of the 2019 Session of the Group of Governmental Experts on Emerging Technologies in the Area of Lethal Autonomous Weapons Systems. UN Doc CCW/GGE1/2019/3, 25 September 2019

Hayward K J, Maas M M (2021) Artificial Intelligence and Crime: A Primer for Criminologists. Crime, Media, Culture: An International Journal 17(2):209–233. DOI: https://doi.org/10.1177/1741659020917434

Henderson I S, Keane P, Liddy J (2017) Remote and Autonomous Warfare Systems: Precautions in Attack and Individual Accountability. In: Ohlin J D (ed) Research Handbook on Remote Warfare. Edward Elgar, Cheltenham, pp 335–370. DOI: https://doi.org/10.4337/9781784716998.00022

Holland J (2004) Military Objective And Collateral Damage: Their Relationship And Dynamics. Yearbook of International Humanitarian Law 7:35–78. DOI: https://doi.org/10.1017/S1389135904000352

Huffman W B (2012) Margin of Error: Potential Pitfalls of the Ruling in The Prosecutor v. Ante Gotovina. Military Law Review 211:1–56. http://hdl.handle.net/10601/2104. Accessed 4 August 2023

ICRC (2016) Background Paper Prepared by the International Committee of the Red Cross. In: ICRC (ed) Autonomous Weapon Systems: Implications of Increasing Autonomy in the Critical Functions of Weapons. ICRC, Versoix, pp 69–85

Jain N (2016) Autonomous Weapons Systems: New Frameworks for Individual Responsibility. In: Bhuta N et al. (eds) Autonomous Weapons Systems: Law, Ethics, Policy. Cambridge University Press, Cambridge, pp 303–324. DOI: https://doi.org/10.1017/CBO9781316597873

Jain A G (2021) Autonomous Cyber Capabilities and Individual Criminal Responsibility for War Crimes. In: Liivoja R, Väljataga A (eds) Autonomous Cyber Capabilities under International Law. NATO CCDCOE Publications, pp 291–320

Kalmanovitz P (2016) Judgment, Liability and the Risks of Riskless Warfare. In: Bhuta N et al. (eds) Autonomous Weapons Systems. Cambridge University Press, Cambridge, pp 145–163. DOI: https://doi.org/10.1017/CBO9781316597873.007

Keiler J (2019) Actus Reus and Mens Rea: The Elements of Crime and the Framework of Criminal Liability. In: Keiler J, Roef D (eds) Comparative concepts of criminal law, 3rd edn. Intersentia, United Kingdom, pp 107–120

King T C et al. (2020) Artificial Intelligence Crime: An Interdisciplinary Analysis of Foreseeable Threats and Solutions. Science and Engineering Ethics 26(1):89–120. DOI: https://doi.org/10.1007/s11948-018-00081-0

Liu H-Y (2016) Refining Responsibility: Differentiating Two Types of Responsibility Issues Raised by Autonomous Weapons Systems. In: Bhuta N et al. (eds) Autonomous Weapons Systems. Cambridge University Press, Cambridge, pp 325–344. DOI: https://doi.org/10.1017/CBO9781316597873.014

Luban D (1999) Contrived Ignorance. Georgetown Law Journal 87:957–980
Malle B F et al. (2015) Sacrifice One For the Good of Many?. In: Proceedings of the Tenth Annual ACM/IEEE International Conference on Human-Robot Interaction. ACM, New York, pp 117–124. DOI: https://doi.org/10.1145/2696454.2696458
Marauhn T (2014) An Analysis of the Potential Impact of Lethal Autonomous Weapons Systems on Responsibility and Accountability for Violations of International Law. In: Presentation on the occasion of the CCW expert meeting on lethal autonomous systems, Geneva, 13–16 May 2014. CCW, Geneva
Margulies P (2012) Valor's Vices: Against a State Duty to Risk Forces in Armed Conflict. Vermont Law Review 37:207–307. DOI: https://doi.org/10.1093/acprof:osobl/9780199941445.003.0005
Margulies P (2021) A Moment in Time: Autonomous Cyber Capabilities, Proportionality and Precautions. In: Liivoja R, Väljataga A (eds) Autonomous Cyber Capabilities under International Law. NATO CCDCOE Publications, Tallinn, pp 152–180
McDougall C (2019) Autonomous Weapon Systems and Accountability: Putting the Cart before the Horse. Melbourne Journal of International Law 20(1):58–87
McFarland T, McCormack T (2014) Mind the Gap: Can Developers of Autonomous Weapons Systems Be Liable for War Crimes?. International Law Studies 90:361–385
McLaughlin R (2014) Unmanned Naval Vehicles and the Law of Naval Warfare. In: Nasu H, McLaughlin R (eds) New Technologies and the Law of Armed Conflict. TMC Asser Press, The Hague, pp 229–246. DOI: https://doi.org/10.1007/978-90-6704-933-7_14
Meier M W (2019) Lethal Autonomous Weapons Systems. In: Williams W S, Ford C M (eds) Complex Battlespaces: The Law of Armed Conflict and the Dynamics of Modern Warfare. Oxford University Press, Oxford, pp 289–316
Nasu H, McLaughlin R (2014) Conclusion: Challenges of New Technologies for the Law of Armed Conflict. In: Nasu H, McLaughlin R (eds) New Technologies and the Law of Armed Conflict. TMC Asser Press, The Hague, pp 247–254. DOI: https://doi.org/10.1007/978-90-6704-933-7_15
NATO (2019) Allied Joint Doctrine for the Conduct Of Operations. NATO Standard, AJP-3, Edition C Version 1, February 2019
Nersessian D L (2006) Whoops, I Committed Genocide! The Anomaly of Constructive Liability for Serious International Crimes. Fletcher Forum of World Affairs 30(2):81–106
Ohlin J D (2013) Targeting and the Concept of Intent. Michigan Journal of International Law 35(1):79–130
Ohlin J D (2016) The Combatant's Stance: Autonomous Weapons on the Battlefield. International Law Studies 92:1–30
Parasuraman R, Sheridan T B, Wickens C (2000) A Model for Types and Levels of Human Interaction with Automation. IEEE Transactions on Systems, Man, and Cybernetics 30(3):286–297
Perrow C (1984) Normal Accidents: Living With High-Risk Technologies. Basic Books, New York
Rogers A P V (2000) Zero-Casuality Warfare. International Review of the Red Cross 837:165–181
Sandoz Y, Swinarski C, Zimmerman B (1987) Commentary on the Additional Protocols of 8 June 1977 to the Geneva Conventions of 12 August 1949. Martinus Nijhoff, Geneva
Sarch A F (2014) Willful Ignorance, Culpability, and the Criminal Law. St. John's Law Review 88:1023–1102
Sartor G, Omicini A (2016) The Autonomy of Technological Systems and Responsibilities for Their Use. In: Bhuta N et al. (eds) Autonomous Weapons Systems. Cambridge University Press, Cambridge, pp 39–74. DOI: https://doi.org/10.1017/CBO9781316597873.003
Schabas W A (2017) An Introduction to the International Criminal Court. 5th edn. Cambridge University Press, Cambridge. DOI: https://doi.org/10.1017/9781316459997
Scharre P D (2018) Army of None: Autonomous Weapons and the Future of War. Ww Norton & Co, New York
Schmitt M N (2007) 21st Century Conflict: Can the Law Survive?. Melbourne Journal of International Law 8:443–476

Sherrin C (2014) Blindness: A Confused and Unnecessary Basis for Criminal Liability?. University of British Columbia Law Review 47(2):709–741
Stewart D M (2011) New Technology and the Law of Armed Conflict. International Law Studies 87:271–298
Stürchler N, Siegrist M (2017) A "Compliance-Based" Approach to Autonomous Weapon Systems. EJIL Talk. www.ejiltalk.org/a-compliance-based-approach-to-autonomous-weapon-systems. Accessed 7 June 2021
Taylor I (2021) Who Is Responsible for Killer Robots? Autonomous Weapons, Group Agency, and the Military-Industrial Complex. Journal of Applied Philosophy 38(2):320–334. DOI: https://doi.org/10.1111/japp.12469
Toscano C P (2015) "Friend of Humans": An Argument for Developing Autonomous Weapons Systems. Journal of National Security Law & Policy 8(1):189–246
UK (2020) Expert Paper: The Human Role in Autonomous Warfare, Group of Governmental Experts on Emerging Technologies in the Area of Lethal Autonomous Weapons System Geneva, 21–25 September 2020 and 2–6 November 2020, Agenda Item 5. CCW/GGE1/2020/WP6
UN General Assembly (1970) Basic principles for the protection of civilian populations in armed conflicts. A/RES/2675
US Department of Defense (2012) Department of Defense Standard Practice: System Safety. MIL-STD-882E
Väljataga A, Liivoja R (2021) Cyber Autonomy and International Law: An Introduction. In: Liivoja R, Väljataga A (eds) Autonomous Cyber Capabilities under International Law. NATO CCDCOE Publications, Tallinn, pp 1–11
van Sliedregt E (2012) Individual Criminal Responsibility in International Law. Oxford University Press, New York
Weigend T (2014) Subjective Elements of Criminal Liability. In: Dubber M D, Hörnle T, Weigend T (eds) The Oxford Handbook of Criminal Law. Oxford University Press, Oxford, pp 490–511. DOI: https://doi.org/10.1093/oxfordhb/9780199673599.013.0022
Werle G, Jessberger F (2005) "Unless Otherwise Provided": Article 30 of the ICC Statute and the Mental Element of Crimes under International Criminal Law. Journal of International Criminal Justice 3(1):35–55. DOI: https://doi.org/10.1093/jicj/3.1.35
Yampolskiy R V, Spellchecker M S (2016) Artificial Intelligence Safety and Cybersecurity: A Timeline of AI Failures. http://arxiv.org/abs/1610.07997
Yampolskiy R V (2015) Taxonomy of Pathways to Dangerous Artificial Intelligence. In: Workshops at the Thirtieth AAAI Conference on Artificial Intelligence
Zhang X (2016) Legal Issues Concerning Autonomous Weapon Systems. In: Autonomous Weapon Systems: Implications of Increasing Autonomy in the Critical Functions of Weapons. ICRC, Versoix, pp 40–42

Part VI
Conclusions

Chapter 14
Integration and Closing

Contents

Abstract This chapter reviews the overarching conclusions, lessons and insights of this study. In doing so, it retains the book's emphasis on considering both academic and operational perspectives related to autonomous weapon systems (AWS) by presenting a twofold output. The first is theoretical: a recapitulation is provided of all major legal findings related to each chapter's main theme. Emphasis is placed on the most important concepts that were introduced in this book ,and which can be adopted in future academic works and discussions to advance our understanding of targeting law related to AWS. The second is practical and operational: in order to aid commanders, one of the main beneficiaries of this book, to use AWS responsibly and lawfully under realistic battlefield conditions, this chapter offers a practical flowchart that Deployers can employ as a cognitive framework to ensure no legally-relevant considerations or measures are forgotten during the decision-making process leading up AWS release. The chapter ends with reflections on the overall study, and by highlighting important matters that merit analysis and discussion in future work.

Keywords Autonomous weapon system · Artificial intelligence · Summary · Conclusion · Guide · Flowchart

J. Kwik, *Lawfully Using Autonomous Weapon Technologies*,
https://doi.org/10.1007/978-94-6265-631-4_14

14.1 Introduction

This study recontextualised three major topics of discussion related to AWS—how to control the technology, how IHL can be respected when it is used, and if criminal liability is possible in cases of harm—from the point-of-view of the operational commander, whom we have called *Deployer*. The influence of operational commanders on how weapons technologies are used is substantial, but at least in the near future, AWS users will face challenges. There is minimal existing guidance related to legal interpretation of targeting rules, how to conduct a targeting cycle, or what consistent methodology commanders should apply to ensure all necessary factors are taken into consideration before weapons release. The findings in this book provide much-needed clarity to many of these questions. This is beneficial for Deployers interested in upholding IHL norms in attack,[1] for the Providing Entity in terms of directing policymaking, and for academic discussion on the complex and often over-sensationalised topic of AWS.

In this final concluding chapter, we take a step back and consider the overarching conclusions, lessons and insights of this study. In keeping with this book's emphasis on considering both academic and operational perspectives related to AWS, this chapter also is broadly divided into, on the one side, theoretical reflections on the legal and technical dimensions related to the lawful use of AWS; and on the other, a set of guidelines which capture most of this study's findings from a more practical angle.

Section 14.2 commences with an overview of each preceding chapter. This section recapitulates the major legal findings related to each subject matter, thereby providing a concise summary of the most important arguments advanced in this book. Then, in Sect. 14.3, we use this theoretical foundation to construct a more practical flowchart that Deployers can employ as a cognitive framework to ensure no legally-relevant considerations or measures are forgotten during the decision-making process leading up AWS release. Section 14.4 closes with reflections on the limitations of this study, and recommendations as to where future research is particularly pertinent for the continued improvement of legal clarity and protection of civilians when AWS are involved.

---

[1] As noted in Sects. 1.1 and 1.4, Deployer does not need to 'believe' in the virtue of IHL to see the interest in ensuring that AWS attacks remain compliant to it.

14.2 Summary of Findings

14.2.1 Meaningful Human Control: A Novel Operationalisation

Part II discussed the results of an empiric study concerning how the concept of meaningful human control (MHC) has been conceived in discourse since 2013. MHC was found to be a point of unification between international actors and academic commentators, even at the highest diplomatic levels such as the GGE in Geneva. At the same time, the notion as currently conceptualised is argued to be too imprecise to act as more than a political talking point.

Chapter 2 presented a conciliatory framework borne from the deconstruction of dozens of MHC formulations to its fundamental components ('Facets'). These Facets were then arranged chronologically by studying causal mechanisms ('Processes'), which provided new insights into how Deployers can exercise meaningful control over AWS, even if these systems exercise some form of autonomous decision-making on their behalf.

In this respect, MHC was found to comprise the following major Facets:

- *Awareness*: Deployer must take care to study and understand the three central components that influence the behaviour of AWS in the field. These are (a) the intrinsic characteristics and parameters of the system, (b) the operational environment, and (c) contextual factors which exercise influence over the AWS's behaviour (such as enemy countermeasures).
- *Weapon Selection and Context Control*: Deployer must analyse the information obtained from the Awareness step in light of IHL rules related to the conduct of hostilities, and determine whether the use of the system in the envisaged context would be in conformity with basic targeting rules such as distinction, precautions and proportionality. Depending on this assessment, Deployers can also enact additional measures called Context Controls, which further reduce risk to the civilian population.
- *Prediction*: All previous measures provide Deployer with the ability to predict to a reasonable degree of precision how the AWS will act in the field, despite its (partially) autonomous nature.
- *Accountability*: Deployer's close involvement in all previous steps provides a means to attribute responsibility to them for the final result of the deployment decision. This entails both moral and legal responsibility, including criminal liability where applicable.

- *Assess and iterate*: As military operations are comprised of a succession of attacks,[2] Deployer is required to take the results of prior AWS attacks into consideration to determine whether previous assumptions remain correct, or whether their beliefs must be updated accordingly. The process then repeats.[3]

In addition, it was found that the Facets listed in the Framework generally agree well with the steps of a targeting cycle, both in terms of content and timing. In this way, the main contribution of this part is that the MHC Framework provides a systematic and chronological list of 'tasks' Deployer must perform throughout the targeting process to ensure control is retained throughout the AWS attack, from the preparatory phase up to post-deployment assessment. This is the 'consistent methodology' referred to in the introduction to this chapter.

Based on this observation that the Facets constitute a logical forward progression in the targeting process, the following parts in this book were structured accordingly. Part III focused on the element of *Awareness* by exploring different ways the novel characteristics of modern AI can perturb, limit or alter military commanders' assumptions related to weapon systems' performance, risk assessment and risk mitigation, and the effects of enemy activity. Part IV subsequently looked at the *Weapon Selection and Context Control* component, discussing how these novel elements of AI can influence how AWS should be analysed from both a legal and operational perspective. Finally, Part V looked at the *Accountability* component, in particular how (and if) *criminal liability* would be established for AWS-related harm.

14.2.2 Awareness: Knowing Your System

Part III focused on the different aspects of *Awareness*, placing particular attention on factors which differentiate AWS systems from legacy systems (i.e., those not incorporating modern AI technology[4]). Between Deployer on the one hand and the Providing Entity on the other, it was also explored which actor would be better placed to enact risk-mitigating measures for each identified component.

Chapter 3 provided an introduction to the basic strengths and weakness of modern AI, but also established the concept of the *Intended Operational Environment* (IOE). An IOE is a predefined description of the environment for which the system was designed and reviewed. Establishing an IOE is one of the most important tasks of the Providing Entity. The chapter established the elements the Providing Entity must establish and communicate to Deployer, while also arguing that the latter must be obligated to respect the provided IOE at all times. The rationale for this proposed norm

[2] Program on Humanitarian Policy and Conflict Research at Harvard University 2010. Commentary on the HPCR Manual on International Law Applicable to Air and Missile Warfare, Harvard University, Harvard (HPCR Manual Commentary), p. 28.

[3] See also the explanation provided in Sect. 14.3.1.

[4] See Sect. 1.2.

is that AI systems have the potential to fail systemically and unintuitively outside of specific pre-tested conditions, something that cannot be foreseen by Deployer.

Chapter 4 discussed *measures of performance* (MoPs). Legal literature and policy statements are saturated with references to descriptors such as robustness, accuracy and reliability, but it is often unclear how these measurements are assessed, and it is often ignored how evaluations may deviate from those of legacy systems. For Deployer to make meaningful legal assessments in the field, a clear understanding of these notions is important. This chapter analysed how such concepts can be applied in a military-operational context. Four main MoPs were discussed: Accuracy, reliability, robustness and understandability. One important finding was that an AWS's Accuracy itself should be decomposed into Recall and Specificity, the former of which represents the system's *military* utility while the latter represents its ability to *distinguish in IHL-relevant terms*: it is thus *Specificity* which was used in subsequent legal analyses, e.g. to determine whether the system is indiscriminate.

The second important point relates to opacity, a unique characteristic of (some) modern AI systems which prevents users from discerning with various degrees of difficulty how and why their system makes decisions. It was emphasised that Deployers must be (made) aware of this property and that they must make the necessary adjustments during legal assessment commensurate with how opaque the AWS in question is. Finally, it was determined that absent a few minor factors, Deployer has minimal ability to affect their systems' performance. This also highlights where the action space *is* located: at the level of development, review and adoption, which we attribute to the Providing Entity. Policymakers should thus ensure that appropriate quality standards are set at this level, and that these are supported by clear guidelines or laws.

Chapter 5 discussed *causes of failure*. While MoPs help Deployers with more global and statistical assessments of their AWS's actions, it is also necessary that Awareness is ensured with regard to more specific factors that can cause systems to fail. This Awareness allows Deployer to identify if these problem factors are present. The main challenge with regard to AWS is that many of these causes of failure are distinct from those of legacy weapons, and often unintuitive. Several failure modes unique to AI, and how these would impact legal analysis, were discussed: training data issues, input data issues, out-of-distribution (OOD), drift, proxy mistakes, and bias. The main conclusion of this chapter is that unlike with MoPs, Deployer, as a field actor, can and must play a significant role in mitigating risk. Deployer must do this by identifying and analysing the specific failure triggers present in the environment, and by proactively identifying and enacting measures to mitigate them—or by rejecting the AWS outright.[5] An important corollary of Deployer's elevated role in this respect is that they must be *empowered* to make the requisite analyses: the Providing Entity is thus urged to ensure that the requisite technical formation on AI-specific causes of failure is provided to Deployers, if not their technical advisers.

[5] This is the 'whether and how', which has been characterized in this book as 'the ultimate form of human control' that Deployer can exercise over weapon systems. See Sects. 2.4.2, 7.1 and 12.2.1.

Finally, Chap. 6 discussed a frequently-overlooked component of warfare: countermeasures. Against AWS, opponents may employ countermeasures that exploit unique vulnerabilities of AI technology, such as data reliance and unintuitive edge cases. We referred to these AI-specific countermeasures as *adversarials*, focusing on three in particular: adversarial inputs, poisoning, and backdoors. Adversarial inputs were identified as particularly dangerous for AWS, since the enemy can execute the adversarial without having to access the system itself. It is on Deployer to identify whether the system is vulnerable to this type of adversarial, in light of the enemy's current and past activities. In this respect, the chapter also examined security analysis theory and identified the main parameters based on which Deployer can determine the level of risk the opponent poses. With regard to poisoning attacks, on the other hand, Deployer is powerless since this largely relates to development: it is thus the Providing Entity's responsibility to adopt good practices relating to data and model safety to insulate their systems from poisoning attacks.

With regard to Awareness as a whole, the overarching conclusion that can be drawn is that neither the Providing Entity nor Deployer can address the issues identified in this part independently. Only through cooperation and coordination can AWS be used responsibly. Many aspects, such as a system's MoPs and vulnerabilities to poisoning, are beyond Deployer's capacity to influence and must be resolved at the developmental and review stages. At the same time, the Providing Entity needs informed, reasonable and good-faith Deployers at the operational level to consider casuistic and environmental factors, to prevent the use of (otherwise well-performing) AWS in situations with many failure triggers or enemies who are able to exploit vulnerabilities. For this, however, the Providing Entity must invest into proper technical empowerment of commanders. Only with the requisite training can Deployer make the requisite analyses described above.

More specifically, the distribution of responsibilities between Deployer and the Providing Entity are summarised in Table 14.1.

14.2.3 Legal and Operational Analysis: The 'May I' and 'Should I'

Part IV considered *if* and *under what conditions* Deployer, having taken into consideration all elements related to Awareness, can use AWS. These questions were posed through two different lenses: the legal and military-operational. A theoretical separation between these two perspectives was necessary since a weapon that could technically be usable *legally* may nevertheless be undesirable *operationally*. The first two subsequent chapters addressed the legal perspective, while the chapter that followed considered the operational question.

Chapter 8 started by highlighting an apparent inconsistency in literature and discourse concerning what makes AWS controversial, and discarded several popular distinctions (e.g. autonomy, lethality, critical functions). It was instead hypothesised

Table 14.1 List of tasks mainly attributable deployer or the providing entity

Top-down (Duty of providing entity)	Bottom-up (Duty of deployer)	Providing entity must train deployer on
Provide: IOE	*Monitor*: IOE—reject use if IOE is not provided	
		Using/reading MoPs to make predictions and decisions
Ensure: Accuracy *Provide*: Complete accuracy metrics (inc. Specificity and Recall)	*Use*: Accuracy to make legal decisions *Caution*: Be wary of accuracy	Being wary of accuracy
Ensure: Robustness		
Ensure: Reliability *Ensure*: Culture of reporting	*Ensure*: Reporting is carried out	
		AI failure modes (in general)
Avoid: Training data problems		
Avoid: Incorrect proxies		
Ensure: Mechanical robustness to reduce input data issues caused by sensor failings	*Stay sensitive to and monitor*: Environmental factors that can cause input data issues	Input data issues
Avoid: OOD by design *Communicate*: IOE	*Stay sensitive to and monitor*: Drift	OOD and factors that can cause drift
		AI-specific vulnerabilities that can be exploited by adversaries
Assume: Adversarials will be used by enemy	*Assume*: Adversarials will be used by enemy	
Ensure: General resistance against adversarials		
Avoid: Practices that lead to vulnerabilities (e.g. data shortcuts)		
	Carry out: Adversary analysis *Produce*: Threat model	Security analysis theory for AI-adversarials
	Stay sensitive to and monitor: Enemy behaviour and adaptation	
Consider: Opportunity cost between robustness and adversarial resistance	*Consider*: Opportunity cost between robustness and adversarial resistance	

that what renders a system legally problematic is a multidimensional matter, with the possibility of 'compensating' weaknesses in one area by strengthening control in others. A variety of variables were analysed in light of applicable rules and principles of IHL. These included variables related to internal properties of the system (e.g. metrics and opacity), properties of the operational environment (e.g. density of negative class entities) and choices related to how the system is employed (e.g. active time, spatial reach).

For each variable, an assessment was made as to what circumstances would make the use of an AWS more or less legally problematic. As many of these variables exist on a spectrum, a *spectrum of Facility* was conceived for each, along with the appropriate descriptors for easy assessment in the field.

A major finding of this chapter relates to the identification of three main *Rationales*umbrella-variables which directly link with fundamental aims of IHL. These are:

- *Rationale-IH*: Conditions which increase the risk of collateral damage.
- *Rationale-FP*: Conditions which increase the risk of false positives.
- *Rationale-EE*: Conditions which increase the risk of epistemic errors by Deployer.

Increased risk in any of these Rationales increases the difficulty with which an AWS can be deployed lawfully. In extreme cases, it becomes virtually impossible to do so in good faith. It was also found that some variables can influence multiple Rationales at the same time (e.g. *Target Type* influencing both Rationale-FP and Rationale-EE).

The concept of Rationales provides clarity as to the different aspects that influence an AWS's legality, and the complex interplay between them. It also highlights mechanisms that allow high Difficulty in one area to be compensated by Facility in another. For example, landmines' total inability to distinguish (poor score in Rationale-FP) can be compensated by reducing Negative Class Frequency to zero (very good score, also in Rationale-FP) by warding off civilians with a perimeter.

Finally, Context Controls were discussed. These are active precautionary measures Deployer can take to influence the Facility of particular variables.

Chapter 9 provided theoretical substantiation to the notion of Rationales and why they make the lawful use of systems 'easier', by analysing the main rules related to the conduct of hostilities in depth. This chapter analysed IHL through its plain reading, but also issued teleological interpretations in light of IHL's main aim of protecting the civilian population to the maximum extent.

The chapter first discussed how the *scope of an AWS attack* should be conceived, since this has significant implications for the application of other rules such as discrimination and proportionality. The challenge lies in finding the correct middle ground. It was argued that limiting attacks to 'Instances' (each time the AI makes a decision) is too narrow, but that Deployer may also not construe attacks too broadly. A middle ground is proposed, using criteria based on time and space.

Indiscriminate means and methods were explored next. It was argued that MoPs should never serve as quantitative benchmarks, as whether a system is discriminate also depends on specific conditions in the field. A normative recommendation was issued that *IOE-incompatibility should automatically qualify the AWS as indiscriminate*: Deployer has no positive proof that it is indiscriminate, but also cannot guarantee that it is *not*. The latter situation was argued to be sufficient for a reasonable Deployer to refuse its employment. It was also argued that the use of AWS would be indiscriminate if targets *are not* or *cannot* be defined sufficiently precisely. The former applies by will (i.e., Deployer construes the targets too generally), the latter by inability (e.g. due to opacity). In either case, the AWS may not be used.

Precautions were discussed next, starting with *proportionality*. It was argued first that Rationale-EE (risk of epistemic error) requires Deployers to *ensure the ability to predict* incidental harm and military advantage in the first place. Situations such as overly imprecise target specificity and too high opacity that prevent this analysis automatically breach the proportionality rule. The notion of attack scope was then used to demonstrate how Deployer can make proportionality assessments, even if some more granular engagement decisions are delegated to the system's AI.

For the *duty to minimise*, it was first argued that this obligation stretches further than merely mitigating the risk of collateral damage, but that instead, the rule requires Deployers to ensure *risk to the civilian population in general* is minimised. This is an important finding, since a narrow reading of the rule would only require Deployer to enact mitigating measures with respect to variables related to collateral damage (Rationale-IH). Instead, it was argued that *all* Context Controls, i.e. including those that reduce risk of false positives (Rationale-FP) and epistemic mistakes (Rationale-EE), would be mandatory under the minimisation rule if feasible.

With regard to *warnings*, a distinction was made between Deployer-issued warnings and those issued autonomously by the system. It was found that the obligation to warn is imposed on Deployer, and that Deployer cannot fulfil this obligation by 'delegating' this task to the AWS. However, it was also argued that the minimisation rule actually can be interpreted as requiring *warning-like measures* executed by the AWS itself, if this can further reduce risk to the civilian population (and does not jeopardise Deployer's operation).

For the *duty to cancel*, a distinction was drawn between cancelling at the attack-level and cancelling at the Instance-level. The former more traditionally attaches to Deployer and applies from the moment an observation is made up to the moment it is no longer realistic to expect Deployer to retain the possibility to intervene in an ongoing attack. The notion of attack scope is once again used as the guiding criterion to determine the cut-off point. With regard to the latter, retaining the possibility to cancel strikes at the Instance-level is recommended if done through an Operator, while some nuanced scepticism was expressed with respect to enabling an autonomous cancelling function by the AWS.

Finally, Chap. 10 contrasted the Facility with which an AWS can be used with its military utility. This chapter aimed to inject some realism into (sometimes fantastical) AWS that are evoked in the overall discourse, by arguing that only very specific AWS will be developed and used. These are systems whose difficulty-to-use is commensurate with the operational benefit they provide. Through a two-axial chart (Facility vs. Benefit), it was demonstrated that only specific types of AWS will likely draw the interest of future militaries and Deployers. These are systems with indispensable benefits and/or systems that are very high in the Facility scale. The chapter's main conclusion is that academics and policymakers would do well to move away from systems which a reasonable commander would clearly find overly cumbersome to use (such as 'terminator-bots'[6]), and constructive dialogue should instead centre on those systems which are identified as desirable to use.

Overall, Part IV presents a comprehensive exploration on AWS from a legal and practical perspective. It identifies those factors that make the use of AWS legally challenging, how this relates to broader values of IHL (Rationales), how Deployers should interpret existing IHL rules, and proposes teleological readings that flow from the basic purpose of IHL: protecting civilians. One main argument of this part is therefore that existing IHL is sufficiently adaptable to regulate AWS technology.

14.2.4 Criminal Liability: What If Something Goes Wrong?

Critics often reject AWS because their autonomous nature would ostensibly generate obstacles to holding persons responsible for resulting harms. One point emphasised in Part III was that weapon systems can never be perfect, while it was argued in Part IV that IHL also does not require them to be. This means that AWS will inevitably fail and cause harm to civilians or civilian objects, and this harm can be immense. At the same time, not all AWS users will be good-faith commanders (as prior parts did mainly presume): there is a possibility that Deployers can deliberately, recklessly or negligently misuse their systems.

The main matter explored in Part V is, first, whether the concern in literature is warranted, and second, where the main centre of gravity lies with regard to challenges to accountability. This part's methodological approach is comparable to a diagnosis: the aim was to pinpoint exactly where (if at all) the problem lies, and vis-à-vis what Candidate for liability. While this question can be examined vis-à-vis many different forms of responsibility, *criminal liability* was chosen for this study.

Chapter 12 started the diagnosis more broadly, by exploring the different elements required for criminal liability. With regard to the element of *causality*, the main concern raised in literature is that AWS removes the direct chain of cause-and-effect between a human's decision and the resulting harm. However, it was argued that Deployer's decision of Whether and How to use AWS as established in Part IV is nevertheless proximate enough to causally attribute the final result of an AWS attack to them. In contrast, the lack of proximity in time and space vis-à-vis Broader Chain Candidates (i.e. those involved with production/development/adoption) is acknowledged as being more difficult. With regard to actus reus, it was argued that commentators are mistaken when assuming that the machine is 'committing' the crime: instead, it is the *deployment decision* which should be considered as the unlawful act to which liability attaches. This solves the concern of whether liability is possible when the

[6] See Sect. 10.4.

actus reus is seemingly performed by a machine, while mens rea still attaches to a human.

Ultimately, *mens rea* was established as the main source of difficulty for establishing criminal liability. The main causes are the epistemic problem (Candidates, including Deployers, are less likely to be able to predict an AWS's exact behaviour) and reduced perceivability (characteristics such as opacity, unexpected interactions, edge cases and unintuitive failure causes inherently reduce humans' ability to foresee the result of a deployment). These are potentially problematic, since mens rea often requires foreseeability.

With mens rea being identified as the problem's epicentre, Chap. 13 narrowed the diagnostic analysis to the different degrees of fault. The entire spectrum of mens rea was analysed, starting from the highest form of deliberation (intention/dolus), followed by risk-taking (recklessness/dolus eventualis/conscious negligence), up to no-fault situations. From this analysis, a proverbial bell-curve was drawn symbolising where the main difficulty is located. It was found that the main challenge lies with a specific category of risk-taking called *unknown* and *generic risk*. Unknown risk refers to the situation where the actor knows risk exists, but this risk is very difficult if not impossible to detect due to inherent epistemic limitations related to AI. Generic risk, in contrast, refers to situations where the actor only knows something is likely to go wrong, but (also due to epistemic limitations) cannot determine with any level of precision what the harmful result would be: an epistemic state that in many legal systems is too imprecise for the cognitive component of mens rea. The chapter's main conclusion is that these cognitive states in particular present the highest likelihood of generating 'criminal liability gaps'. In addition, attention was drawn to the possibility of manufactured ignorance: situations where Deployers *could* have obtained the cognitive state necessary for mens rea, but maintain their state of epistemic uncertainty through omissions (e.g. not properly studying abnormalities reported during prior engagements). Future academic and policy arguments should focus on these problems in particular.

14.3 A Practical Guide for Deployers

In the spirit of this book's emphasis on supplementing academic analysis with more practical recommendations, this section reframes the conclusions of the previous section in a more applied format. Inspiration is drawn from procedural flowcharts as commonly seen in military publications, such as the US Army's targeting manual.[7]

Presenting this study's conclusions in this format has two benefits. First, the matters addressed in this book span a significant range of subjects across the entire AWS lifecycle. The format proposed below streamlines the conclusions in an uncluttered and organised way. Second, while no pretentions are made that this output can

[7] See US Joint Chiefs of Staff 2013, p. II–24.

be incorporated directly into policy, it may serve as an initial template or foundation from which Providing Entities can develop their own guidelines.

14.3.1 High-Level Flowchart

This first flowchart, Fig. 14.1, summarises all components discussed in this book in broader steps. It spans the full targeting cycle, and also any necessary measures that must be taken preceding and following an AWS attack.

The two swimlanes differentiate the duties of Deployer (at the operational/tactical level) and those of the Providing Entity, which prevents role confusion. The coloured containers reference the main themes of the three preceding parts (Awareness; Legal and operational analysis; Criminal liability).

The process STARTs at the level of the Providing Entity. For each AWS it distributes to Deployers, the Providing Entity draws from technical databases, reviews, policy, etc.[8] to provide *Technical Information* and a clear *IOE*. The Providing Entity must also ensure that sufficient *Technical Training* related to this system has been provided to Deployer.

Armed with this information, Deployer starts DEPLOYMENT ANALYSIS. The first step, as established in the MHC Framework,[9] is for Deployer to obtain the requisite Awareness pertaining to all aspects of the system and environment (*Technical, Environmental, and Interaction Analysis*). These permit exploration of more specific elements related to operations, such as analysing the AWS's performance statistically (*Measures of Performance*), with respect to particular failure triggers (*Causes of Failure*), and adversarial threats (*Adversarial Analysis*).

After completing this process, Deployer moves to the Weapon Selection and Context Control steps in the MHC Framework. Deployer asks first whether it is legally permissible to employ the AWS based on targeting rules (*Legally OK?*). Additionally, even if legally permissible, Deployer must still consider whether its use makes military sense (*Use desirable?*). If the response to either of these is NO, Deployer has the option to change some circumstances of use through Context Controls, in which case Deployer can re-evaluate whether use would be lawful under these new circumstances. If not, Deployer must REJECT USE. The questions of whether AWS under consideration are lawful and desirable are complex, and expanded upon in the detailed *Legal* and *Desirability Charts* discussed below.

If both the legal and desirability analyses output favourably, Deployer can DEPLOY the system. This must always be followed by ASSESS RESULT, during which Deployer determines if the AWS attack proceeded as predicted. If it did, Deployer can ITERATE by looping around to a new deployment decision. If not,

---

[8] Note that some earlier steps such as development, review and adoption fall outside this flowchart, and it is assumed that they have already been satisfactorily conducted in accordance with the law.

[9] See Sect. 2.4.1.

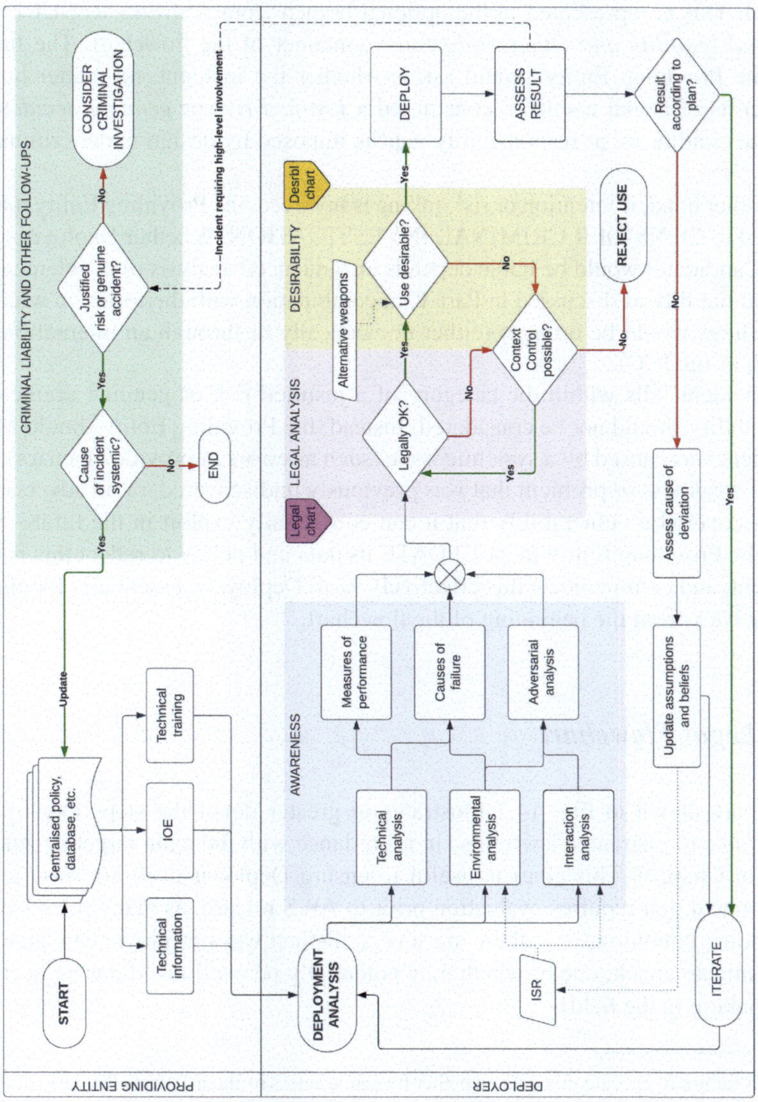

Fig. 14.1 High-level flowchart

Deployer must *assess the cause of the deviation* and *update their assumptions and beliefs*,[10] including by updating intelligence if needed,[11] before ITERATING.

In some situations, the RESULT is notable enough to warrant particular inspection at the level of the Providing Entity, e.g. if an unexpected result occurred (e.g. a new edge case or systemic vulnerability was discovered) or significant civilian harm was caused. This is represented in the optional branch from ASSESS RESULT to the *Criminal Liability and Other Follow-ups* container of the flowchart. The first question the Providing Entity should ask is whether the incident, no matter how grave in terms of actual results,[12] constituted a *justified risk* or *genuine accident*. Under these conditions, a 'responsibility gap' is imposed by design under criminal law.[13]

On the other hand, if intention or risk-taking is involved, the Providing Entity may see the need to CONSIDER CRIMINAL INVESTIGATION. Whether Deployer (or any other Candidate) would be liable depends on a nuanced analysis of the elements for criminal liability as discussed in Part V, in combination with the forum in which the proceedings would be brought (either domestically or through an international forum such as the ICC).

If the incident falls within the category of a justified risk or genuine accident, criminal liability should not be considered. Instead, the Providing Entity should ask if the incident was caused by a systemic issue (such as errors in provided metrics), a categorical weakness or problem that was previously undiscovered, or an adversary that has discovered a vulnerability that it can consistently exploit in the future. In this case, the Providing Entity must UPDATE its data and policy to reflect this new development, and communicate this effectively to all Deployers, essentially looping the process back from the beginning of the flowchart.

14.3.2 Legal Flowchart

The flowchart shown in Fig. 14.2 illustrates in greater detail the steps Deployer must undertake to guarantee lawful use in accordance with the main targeting rules discussed in Chap. 9. This chart is useful to ensure Deployer does not miss any legal component that requires evaluation prior to AWS release, as many rules have multiple failure conditions (e.g. there are several distinct ways Deployer can launch an indiscriminate attack, one of which may potentially be overlooked during hectic decision-making in the field).

---

[10] Deployer's failure to execute this duty (whether by carelessness or intent) forms the basis of the 'manufactured ignorance' Responsibility Gap as discussed in Sect. 13.5.3.

[11] As discussed in Sect. 13.5.3, best practices would also involve Deployer updating the intelligence available to other commanders active in the theatre who use sister models of the same AWS.

[12] It was noted in Sect. 13.6 that the Providing Entity must always judge such incidents purely on the merits and the actual fault of involved parties, and not on the basis of the actual magnitude of the harm or of (international) public pressure.

[13] As argued in Sect. 13.6.

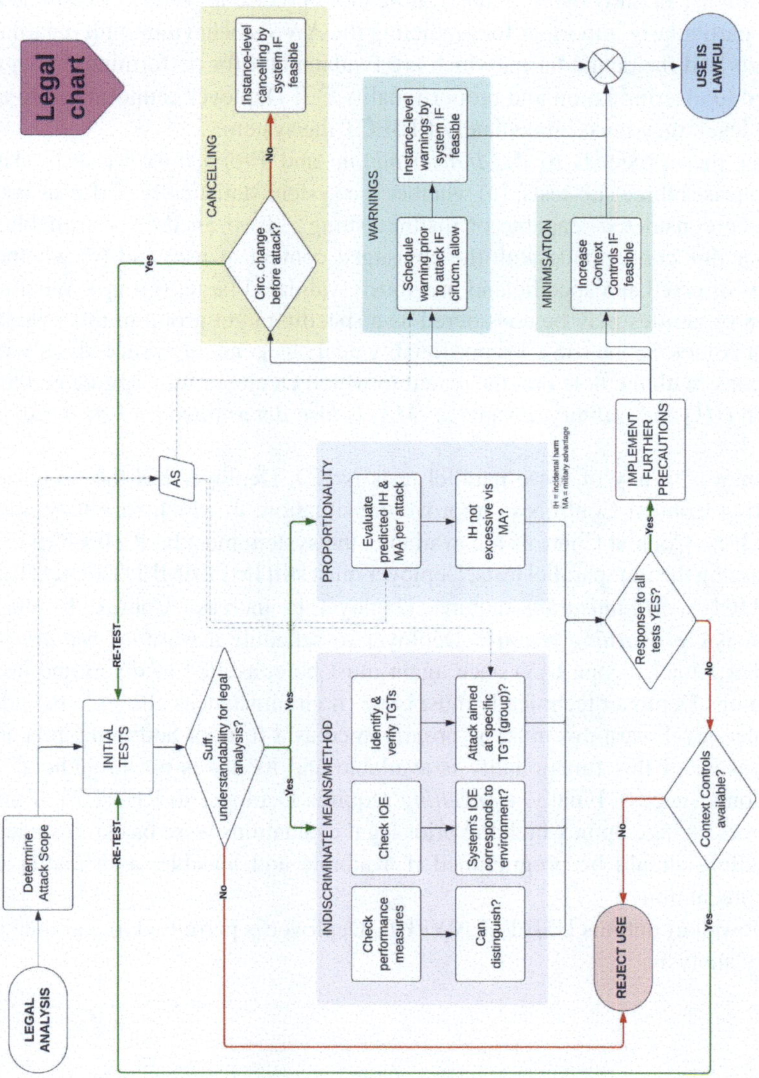

Fig. 14.2 Legal flowchart

Because the notion of Attack Scope is so central to many legal analyses,[14] Deployer is required to determine this first before any other tests are performed. The chosen Attack Scope then forms the basis of other evaluations, as indicated by the data shape 'AS'.

From this, it is recommended that Deployer first assess whether the system's *understandability* permits them to make sufficiently precise legal determinations at all. This is particularly important for predicting the AWS's behaviour with regard to likely targets and incidental harm, which are fundamental for performing the legal tests related to discrimination and proportionality.[15] If Deployer cannot do so to an acceptable level, they must immediately REJECT the system.

Deployer then proceeds to the *Indiscriminate* and *Proportionality* tests. The former comprises three sub-tests: (a) whether the system statistically performs well enough to be considered 'capable of distinguishing'; (b) if an IOE is available[16] and whether this corresponds with the envisaged context of use; and (c) whether the attack is directed at a specific and previously-validated target (group). Whether a collection of entities may be considered as a specific target group in this context depends on Attack Scope (*AS*). Proportionality analysis generally proceeds as with other weapons, with the note that the extent to which Deployer may aggregate incidental harm (*IH*) and military advantage (*MA*) is also determined by Attack Scope (*AS*).

If the answer to any of these parallel tests is NO, Deployer has the option of implementing Context Controls to improve the situation, in which case they must RE-TEST. If no Context Controls are available, the system must be REJECTED.

After passing the four parallel tests, Deployer must still IMPLEMENT FURTHER PRECAUTIONS. *Minimisation* requires Deployer to increase Context Controls further if feasible. *Warning* requires Deployer to schedule a warning *per attack*, meaning that Attack Scope (*AS*) once again must be consulted to determine how many warnings Deployer technically must issue (if circumstances allow).[17] In addition, Instance-level warnings must be programmed as a form of additional precautionary measure, if this functionality is available and its use is not prejudicial to the operation's success. Finally, *Cancelling* requires Deployer to RE-TEST if any circumstances change upon which the prior legal evaluations were based. Instance-level cancelling should be programmed if available and feasible, as a matter of additional precautions.

If this flowchart outputs USE IS LAWFUL, Deployer is permitted to continue to Desirability analysis.

[14] This is also the reason why the notion of Attack Scope was discussed first in Chapter 9.

[15] See Sects. 4.5 and 9.5.1.

[16] It was argued in Sect. 3.5 that Deployer should categorically reject an AWS if the Providing Entity fails to provide them with a clear IOE.

[17] See the example provided in Scenario 3 in Sect. 9.2.

14.3.3 Desirability Flowchart

Figure 14.3 shows the Desirability Analysis portion in greater detail. Evaluating Desirability is relatively simpler than legality, but still requires Deployer to consider multiple inputs related to the mission, intelligence (ISR) and the system, making this flowchart helpful.

The *Facility* container primarily reflects the discussion of Chap. 8 by summing up the various elements Deployer needs to consider to determine how facile a system is to use. The variables all meld into the three Rationales (IH—incidental harm; FP—false positives; and EE—epistemic error) because they are interlinked and mutually compensating.

The *Benefit* container summarises the discussion of Sect. 10.3 and involves Deployer determining first whether an AWS is 'indispensable', and if not, how beneficial the AWS is compared to other systems in Deployer's possession.

Benefit and Facility are then juxtaposed to determine Desirability in COMPARE ON CHART. As indicated in Sect. 10.4, the final decision of whether or not a system is Desirable is a qualitative one and left to the reasonable commander as guided by the two-axial decision-making chart. Chapter 10 provided one example of how Facility, Benefit and the decision-making boundaries can be qualitatively evaluated, but this procedure is ultimately for the Providing Entity to standardise.

As noted in Sect. 8.7, Deployer can use Context Controls to improve the Facility with which an AWS can be used. A new Context Control, however, changes the circumstances in which an AWS is used. This obliges Deployer to REPEAT LEGAL ANALYSIS, instead of the AWS being usable immediately. Deployer must return to the Legal Chart and repeat the process before Desirability can be re-assessed.

14.4 Reflections and Future Work

In this final section, some closing reflections are made concerning this work's contribution to the overall academic and policy debate, its limitations, and where future research is particularly necessary to develop the ideas introduced in this book further.

This work set out to analyse a contentious and often sensationalised issue—AI and autonomy in weapon systems—from a more sober lens. The topic was approached without preconceived notions of whether AWS technology is moral, legal or ethical. Instead, the matter was analysed strictly on the basis of legal-operational considerations: to what extent the technology can be used in compliance with applicable rules related to the conduct of hostilities on the one hand, and on the other, what practical measures can be taken by its users (both Deployer and the Providing Entity) to ensure sufficient control is maintained over these systems so military goals on the battlefield can be reliably achieved.

This dualist approach is preserved throughout the book. Part II first establishes the overall elements that would allow users to sustain control even if their systems

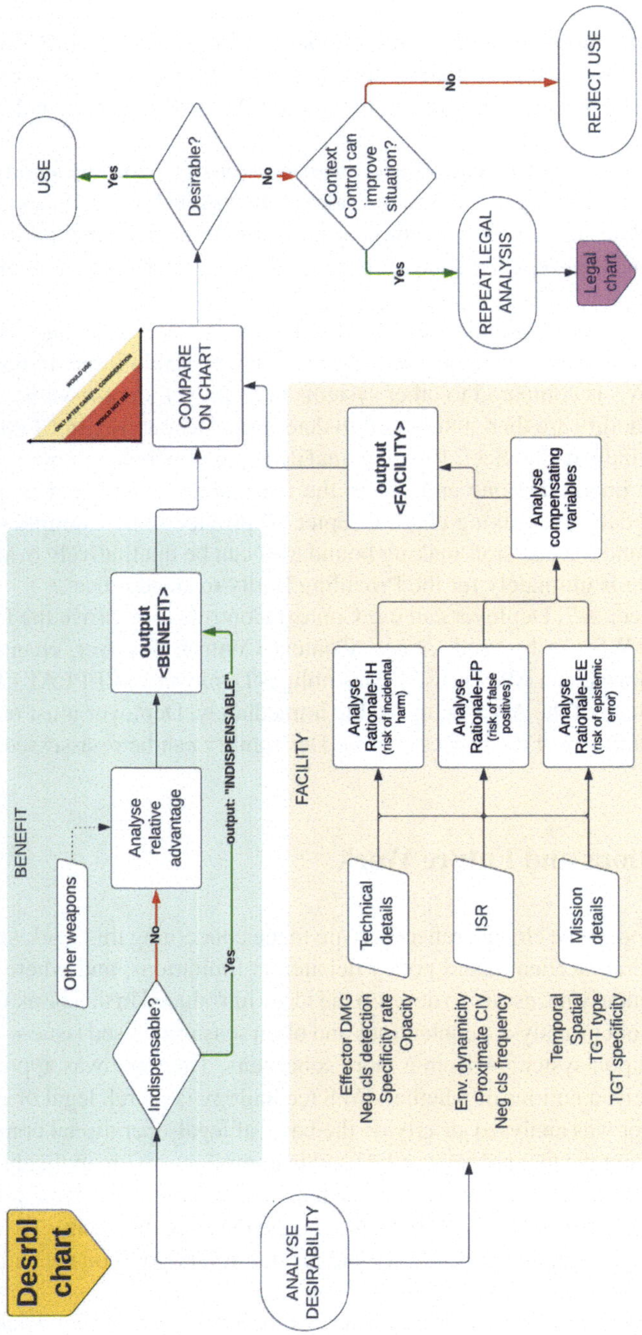

Fig. 14.3 Desirability flowchart

exhibit some degree of autonomous decision-making. Part III then demonstrates how control can be retained *cognitively and intellectually*, by enumerating matters Deployers must be knowledgeable of and must take active care to inquire about. Part IV subsequently argues how control can be asserted *legally and operationally* by enumerating how Deployers can analyse the desirability of their system, both in terms of how easily it can be used in accordance with targeting rules and how beneficial it is militarily. Finally, Part V shows one way how control can be asserted even *when things go wrong*: with the exception of a few circumstances identified in the analysis, autonomous decision-making does not compromise the ability of criminal law to hold the blameworthy liable, while also ensuring that those acting in reasonable areas of risk are not scapegoated.

The relatively narrow focus of this book on practical decision-making allowed this study to construct a comprehensive and detailed accounting of how AWS should be used by commanders in the field. Inevitably, the choice to prioritise one perspective—in our case, that of Deployer—comes with sacrifices as to the level of depth that can be devoted to other perspectives. The most significant casualty is undoubtedly the pre-deployment phase, i.e., development, review and adoption. While this aspect of the AWS lifecycle was not entirely ignored with the inclusion of discussion on the duties of the Providing Entity, particularly in Part III, truly in-depth analyses of (no less important) matters such as programming standards, the review obligation, and the responsibility of Broader Chain Candidates for liability could not be effectuated in this book. Fortunately, these topics have been extensively discussed in literature.[18] This study's focus on the operational level should be viewed as complementary, instead of taking away from, these other works.

The MHC Framework in Chap. 2 primarily served as a theoretical backbone for the rest of this study. Nevertheless, given the popularity of MHC in diplomatic discourse and its role as a "point of coalescence"[19] between international actors, the framework as proposed in this book has the potential to further guide discussions and even the formulation of soft or hard laws, e.g. in forums such as the GGE.[20] One of the main contentions of this study is that current rules of IHL provide sufficient protections against misuse of AWS technology, but this does not detract from the possibility that its findings can be used to inspire future legal drafting. The main conclusions in this book were crafted with care to be as concrete as possible, which should facilitate

[18] See *inter alia*:

- Reviewing AWS: Chengeta 2016; Farrant and Ford 2017; Boulanin 2015.
- Recommendations for test, evaluation, verification and validation (TEV&V) of AWS: Haugh et al. 2018.
- Recommendations for TEV&V of AI systems: Lohn 2020.
- Extensive technical literature study on technical verification methods for robotic systems: Luckcuck et al. 2020.

[19] Roff and Moyes 2016, p. 1.

[20] In fact, the current author had the opportunity to present this MHC Framework before the delegates at the GGE on LAWS in Geneva, 8 March 2023.

adaptation into hard rules, soft laws[21] or guidelines[22] if this is deemed desirable and diplomatically feasible.

Space limitations made omissions regarding some substantive, but no less important, matters in each part unavoidable. The problem of *opacity* and its implications for the lawful use of AWS deserves much greater attention and analysis than what was possible in this book. The different types of XAI solutions, the extent to which humans can be considered to 'understand' an AI system, the trade-off between understandability and performance, and how all of this impacts both a Deployer's ability to lawfully employ an AWS (particularly in light of concerns related to Rationale-EE, epistemic error) and the possibility to assign criminal liability are all questions that demand much closer consideration. The author has addressed a few of these matters in related works,[23] but hopes to expand these theories further in the future.

The problem of *adversarials* raised in Chap. 6 also is ripe for further legal analysis, particularly in light of the interplay between precautions in attack and precautions in defence. For example, is there a point at which the control of an enemy over the result of an adversarial becomes so significant that they should be considered the 'attacking' party?[24] How should concepts such as perfidy, ruses and human shielding be interpreted when AWS are used on one side and cyberattacks are used on the other to deceive the target systems? More clarity would only improve protection to civilians by making it less ambiguous which party holds the primary precautionary obligation to mitigate civilian harm.

Part V primarily offered a diagnostic of where the main problems related to criminal liability lie, but this can be expanded significantly in two directions. First, keeping with criminal liability, successfully identifying the main issue as pertaining to generic and unknown risk is only the first step. Future research should concentrate on these problems in particular. A more targeted discussion is encouraged on how these potential lacunae can be addressed, perhaps through recourse to particular doctrines.[25] Second, the same diagnostic methodology can be applied to other forms of legal responsibility, such as civil or State responsibility. Claims of responsibility gaps are equally made with respect to these fields, and a similar interrogation can be conducted to determine whether these alarms are justified or not.

Finally, the most significant normative restriction of this study is that it limited itself to examining rules related to the conduct of hostilities. This focus came naturally with the study's concentration on operational decision-making, but AWS can be analysed through a variety of normative frames. Within IHL itself one can think of the use of AWS during occupations or counterinsurgency situations, and outside of IHL one can think of examining AWS from the perspective of human rights law,

---

[21] One can think of a manual specific to AWS following the example of the Tallinn Manual.

[22] Academic publications of influential authors may also be of great importance to the development of IHL in this field.

[23] See Kwik and Van Engers 2021, 2023.

[24] See Kwik 2024.

[25] Options such as command responsibility and Joint Criminal Enterprise have been offered in literature, and are worth exploring further.

ethics or disarmament. Each of these points-of-view are important to consider, and complete the picture of how the international community should respond to AWS technology.

The current author hopes this book has provided a meaningful contribution to one of these perspectives: the use of AWS through the eyes of the operational commander.

References

Boulanin V (2015) Implementing Article 36 Weapon Reviews in Light of Increasing Autonomy in Weapon Systems. SIPRI Insights on Peace and Security 2015(1):1–27

Chengeta T (2016) Are Autonomous Weapon Systems the Subject of Article 36 of Additional Protocol I to the Geneva Conventions?. U.C. Davis Journal of International Law & Policy 23:65–99

Farrant J, Ford C M (2017) Autonomous Weapons and Weapon Reviews: The UK Second International Weapons Review Forum. International Law Studies 93:389–422

Haugh B A, Sparrow D A, Tate D M (2018) The Status of Test, Evaluation, Verification, and Validation (TEV&V) of Autonomous Systems. Institute for Defense Analyses, Alexandria

Kwik J, Van Engers T (2021) Algorithmic Fog of War: When Lack of Transparency Violates the Law of Armed Conflict. Journal of Future Robot Life 2(1-2):43–66. https://www.medra.org/servlet/aliasResolver?alias=iospress&doi=https://doi.org/10.3233/FRL-200019. Accessed 4 August 2023

Kwik J, Van Engers T (2023) Performance or Explainability? A Law of Armed Conflict Perspective. In: Kornilakis A et al. (eds) Artificial Intelligence and Normative Challenges: International and Comparative Legal Perspectives. Springer Nature Switzerland AG

Kwik J (2024) Is wearing these sunglasses an attack? Obligations under IHL related to anti-AI countermeasures. International Review of the Red Cross. Published online: 1–28. https://doi.org/10.1017/S1816383124000067. Accessed 25 March 2024

Lohn A J (2020) Estimating the Brittleness of AI: Safety Integrity Levels and the Need for Testing Out-Of-Distribution Performance. http://arxiv.org/abs/2009.00802

Luckcuck M et al. (2020) Formal Specification and Verification of Autonomous Robotic Systems. ACM Computing Surveys 52(5):1–41. https://doi.org/10.1145/3342355

Roff H M, Moyes R (2016) Meaningful Human Control, Artificial Intelligence and Autonomous Weapons. Briefing Paper for the Delegates at the Convention on Certain Conventional Weapons Informal Meeting of Experts on Lethal Autonomous Weapons Systems

US Joint Chiefs of Staff (2013) Joint Targeting. Joint Publication 3–60

Appendix

Appendix 1: Explanations for Fig. 8.9

Antipersonnel mine

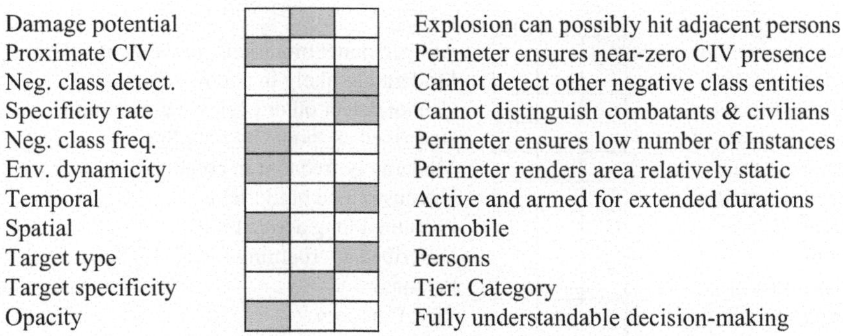

Phalanx

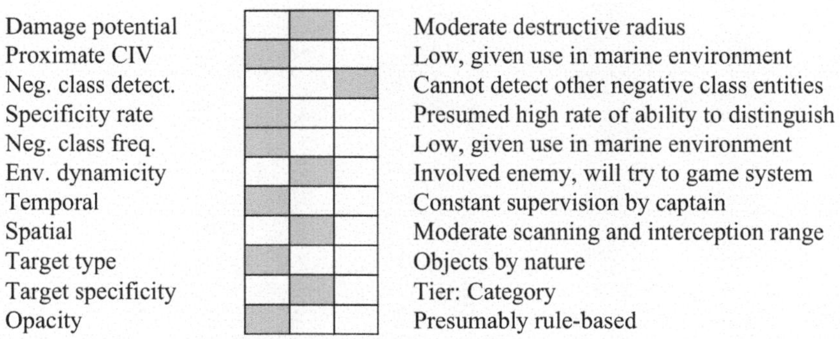

J. Kwik, *Lawfully Using Autonomous Weapon Technologies*,
https://doi.org/10.1007/978-94-6265-631-4

Harpy

Damage potential		■		Moderate destructive radius
Proximate CIV		■		Possible, depending on radar location
Neg. class detect.			■	Cannot detect other negative class entities
Specificity rate	■			Very accurate distinction capabilities
Neg. class freq.	■			Few civilian radars with similar signature
Env. dynamicity			■	Unconstrained battlefield, enemy adaptive
Temporal		■		Moderately high delay
Spatial			■	Large search range
Target type	■			Objects by nature
Target specificity		■		Tier: Category
Opacity	■			Fully understandable decision-making

SGR-A5x

Damage potential	■			Antipersonnel munitions, low risk of splash
Proximate CIV		■		Moderately likely in countryside
Neg. class detect.			■	Cannot detect other negative class entities
Specificity rate			■	Described as 'poor' by Schuller
Neg. class freq.		■		Moderately frequent in countryside
Env. dynamicity			■	Unconstrained battlefield
Temporal			■	Presumed long active time
Spatial			■	Described as 'roaming freely' by Schuller
Target type			■	Persons
Target specificity		■		Tier: Category
Opacity		■		Behaviour recognition presumes (part) ML

Appendix 2: Explanations for assessment of example systems

Phalanx: Searches, recognises and automatically engages incoming threats such as missiles, aircraft, surface craft, and UAVs. *Mission*: protect ship.

FACILITY				
Damage potential		■		Moderate destructive radius
Proximate CIV	■			Low, given use in marine environment
Neg. class detect.			■	Cannot detect other negative class entities
Specificity rate	■			Presumed high rate of ability to distinguish
Neg. class freq.	■			Low, given use in marine environment
Env. dynamicity		■		Involved enemy, will try to game system
Temporal	■			Constant supervision by captain
Spatial		■		Moderate scanning and interception range
Target type	■			Objects by nature
Target specificity		■		Tier: Category
Opacity	■			Transparent decision-making
Score		**0.73**		

BENEFIT		
Indispensable?	YES	Speed & accuracy required for calculations surpasses human capabilities.
Rel. advantage?	N/A	No other alternatives available.
Score	**INDSP**	

SGR-A6x: An improved version of the countryside-roving system introduced in Chap. 8, Sect. 8.9. This system is 50% better than humans in recognising combatants from civilians. Semi-opaque. *Mission*: secure a perimeter along the frontline.

FACILITY				
Damage potential	■			Antipersonnel munitions, low risk of splash
Proximate CIV		■		Moderately likely in countryside
Neg. class detect.			■	Cannot detect other negative class entities
Specificity rate	■			Presumably good if better than even humans
Neg. class freq.			■	Moderately frequent in countryside
Env. dynamicity			■	Unconstrained battlefield
Temporal			■	Presumed long active time
Spatial			■	Roams freely along perimeter
Target type			■	Persons
Target specificity		■		Tier: Category
Opacity		■		Semi-opaque
Score		**0.32**		

BENEFIT		
Indispensable?	NO	Task can be achieved with the same efficacy with an on-the-loop system that warns an Operator when a potential target is identified.
Rel. advantage?	LOW	50% better distinction than humans. Can theoretically help avoid human cognitive biases, but these are not particularly pertinent for this task.
Score	**LOW**	

Exterminator-2: All-purpose ground-based AWS designed for urban combat against regular personnel. Rapidly strikes combatants and military vehicles (tanks, APCs, etc.), automatically selecting the appropriate munition. Almost perfect Specificity thanks to sophisticated hybrid model. *Mission*: accompany infantry operation. *Optional Context Controls*: (a) no antivehicle strikes; (b) do not fire if *n*-number of civilians are in target's proximity.

FACILITY (without Context Control)

Damage potential		■		Anti-vehicle munitions likely include splash
Proximate CIV			■	Very high in urban environments
Neg. class detect.			■	Can positively recognise civilians, but not enabled
Specificity rate	■			Almost perfect specificity
Neg. class freq.			■	Very high in urban environments
Env. dynamicity			■	Unconstrained battlefield
Temporal			■	Presumed long active time
Spatial		■		Follows infantry advance
Target type		■		Regular personnel (distinguishable visually)
Target specificity			■	Tier: Assorted
Opacity		■		Semi-opaque (hybrid model)
Score		**0.27**		

FACILITY (with Context Control)

Damage potential	■			Antipersonnel munitions only
Proximate CIV			■	Very high in urban environments
Neg. class detect.	■			Can positively recognise civilians and enabled
Specificity rate	■			Almost perfect specificity
Neg. class freq.			■	Very high in urban environments
Env. dynamicity			■	Unconstrained battlefield
Temporal			■	Presumed long active time
Spatial		■		Follows infantry advance
Target type		■		Regular personnel (distinguishable visually)
Target specificity		■		Tier: Category
Opacity		■		Semi-opaque (hybrid model)
Score		**0.45**		

BENEFIT

Indispensable?	NO	Task can be achieved with the same efficacy with a remote-controlled system, perhaps with AI support.
Rel. advantage?	MED	(a) Almost perfect Specificity, (b) speed and (c) ability to instantly determine if more than *n*-number of civilians will be hit are all valuable in combat engagements.
Score	**MED**	

ATS-88 Goedendag: Aerial AWS capable of reliably distinguishing tanks and rapidly exploiting weak points in armour, but has trouble with trams. *Mission*: destroy tanks guarding road in Area-1 as in Scenario 5 (Chap. 9, Sect. 9.5.2). Hit tanks can explode violently.

FACILITY	1	2	3	
Damage potential		■		Antitank munitions + tanks can explode on hit
Proximate CIV		■		Occasional buildings, no persons
Neg. class detect.			■	Cannot detect other negative class entities
Specificity rate	■			High. Tram weakness irrelevant
Neg. class freq.		■		Perhaps other civilian vehicles on the road
Env. dynamicity		■		Outside of town; semi-dynamic
Temporal		■		Relatively short, must fly to destination
Spatial	■			Limited to Area-1
Target type	■			Objects by nature
Target specificity	■			Tier: Group
Opacity	■			Intimate knowledge (even tram weakness known)
Score		**0.68**		

BENEFIT		
Indispensable?	NO	Task can be achieved with the same efficacy with a remote-controlled system.
Rel. advantage?	LOW	Speed, ability to autonomously attack weakest points in armour, and ability to allocate other assets elsewhere offers some comparative advantage.
Score	**LOW**	

IAI Pazuzu: Tiny loitering munition designed to accurately locate and destroy radar/radio/electronic jammers. Small area-of-effect upon impact. *Mission*: destroy semi-mobile jamming assets currently in-use in town. Opponent has effective air defence against larger air assets.

FACILITY	1	2	3	
Damage potential		■		'Small area-of-effect upon impact'
Proximate CIV			■	Urban environment
Neg. class detect.			■	Cannot detect other negative class entities
Specificity rate	■			Presumably high
Neg. class freq.		■		Possibly other signal-emitting civilian objects
Env. dynamicity			■	Urban environment; targets semi-mobile
Temporal			■	Travel + search time can span many minutes
Spatial		■		Limited to district
Target type	■			Objects by nature
Target specificity		■		Tier: Category
Opacity	■			Identification based on emitted signals
Score		**0.45**		

BENEFIT		
Indispensable?	YES	Remote-controlled impossible due to enemy jamming. Manned air assets unusable due to air defence.
Rel. advantage?	N/A	No other alternatives available.
Score	**INDSP**	

SHL19-Lazerbot: Counterinsurgency system that shoots body-armour-cutting laser. For use "in close quarters as the first system to enter enemy held buildings". Comparable accuracy as humans in distinguishing insurgents from civilians thanks to complex DNN, but can act more quickly.

FACILITY				
Damage potential	■			No risk of ricochet, fragmentation, etc.
Proximate CIV			■	Urban environment
Neg. class detect.			■	Cannot detect other negative class entities
Specificity rate		■		As good as humans
Neg. class freq.			■	Likely many civilians in same buildings
Env. dynamicity			■	Urban environment
Temporal		■		Relatively short as likely followed by infantry
Spatial		■		Limited to building or even room
Target type			■	Persons by behaviour
Target specificity		■		Tier: Category
Opacity			■	DNN = opaque
Score		**0.27**		

BENEFIT		
Indispensable?	NO	Task can be achieved with the same efficacy with a remote-controlled system.
Rel. advantage?	MRG	Ability to act more quickly than humans at similar levels of accuracy offers only marginal advantage.
Score	**MRG**	

Index

J. Kwik, *Lawfully Using Autonomous Weapon Technologies*,
https://doi.org/10.1007/978-94-6265-631-4

SPRINGER NATURE

GPSR Compliance

The European Union's (EU) General Product Safety Regulation (GPSR) is a set of rules that requires consumer products to be safe and our obligations to ensure this.

If you have any concerns about our products, you can contact us on ProductSafety@springernature.com

In case Publisher is established outside the EU, the EU authorized representative is:

Springer Nature Customer Service Center GmbH
Europaplatz 3
69115 Heidelberg, Germany